Theory of Computation

Theory of Computation

WALTER S. BRAINERD
Burroughs Corporation

LAWRENCE H. LANDWEBER
University of Wisconsin

A Wiley-Interscience Publication
JOHN WILEY & SONS
New York London Sydney Toronto

Library of Congress Cataloging in Publication Data

Brainerd, Walter S.
Theory of computation.

"A Wiley-Interscience publication."
Bibliography: p.
1. Sequential machine theory. 2. Recursive functions.
3. Programming languages (Electronic computers)
I. Landweber, Lawrence H., joint author. II. Title.

QA267.5.S4B68 519.4 73-12950
ISBN 0-471-09585-0

Printed in the United States of America

10 9 8 7 6 5 4 3 2 1

to
Betty and Jean

Preface

Much of the original work on the theory of computation was done by mathematicians interested in applying the theory to problems in the foundations of mathematics. With the advent of modern digital computers, the theory has taken on new importance because it provides insight about the problem-solving capabilities of real computers. Today the theory of computation is an integral part of most computer science curricula.

Our goal has been to give a mathematically rigorous presentation of this theory that will also appeal to the computer scientist. For example, whenever possible we attempt to relate the results obtained to programming languages which are used to express algorithms for digital computations. Indeed, because many of the important results have been motivated by questions about computers and programming languages, we feel that this is the proper approach for both mathematicians and computer scientists.

We have maintained the goal of providing the best possible methods of presenting the important basic results of the theory of computation. To accomplish this we have made changes in the traditional definitions and notation. It is worthwhile to note that when changes were made in definitions and proofs of theorems to make them more understandable to the computer scientist, there was almost always an improvement from the mathematical point of view. The following points indicate the most important ways in which we have deviated from the traditional approach:

1. Algorithms are expressed as programs in languages designed to facilitate the description of algorithms. Two types of languages, machine-independent languages (such as FORTRAN, ALGOL, and SNOBOL) and machine-dependent languages (such as assembly languages) are considered. As opposed to the traditional approach, we emphasize machine-independent languages. The language of the Turing machine is presented as a specific example of a machine-dependent language.

2. Computations process strings of symbols (words) rather than integers. This reflects more accurately the way digital computers process information and also avoids the technical problem of Gödel numbering. However, since strings of symbols are used to represent numbers, the important arith-

metic computations are included. Since both programs and inputs to programs are words, a universal program can be designed which operates on words which are another program and its inputs. In Chapter 5 we obtain such a universal program for a language which resembles the programming language SNOBOL.

3. The partial recursive functions are defined using exponentiation, which corresponds to FOR/DO/LOOP programming statements, and repetition, which corresponds to a WHILE programming statement, rather than the traditional primitive recursion and minimization. Exponentiation and repetition are simpler operations than primitive recursion and minimization. Also, the former more closely parallel common programming language statements than do the latter.

4. Functions may have multiple inputs and multiple outputs. This facilitates the description of functions computed by programs. To deal with such functions we use a simple operation on functions called combination ($\times$) which satisfies $(f \times g)(x,y) = (fx,gy)$. With this operation, only four initial functions (rather than the usual infinite set of initial functions) are needed to define the partial recursive functions.

We have designed the book as a text for either upper-level undergraduate or beginning graduate-level use. The main prerequisite is an ability to follow mathematical proofs. The book should also be useful as a reference for the more basic results in the theory of computation. However, we have not attempted to provide a complete reference work by including all significant research results, particularly those which have been obtained in recent years. An exception is the theory of computational complexity (Chapters 9 and 10). Complexity theory has been extensively studied in recent years because of its relevance to real computing problems. We have included basic results of the two branches of complexity theory which are most closely related to the material presented in earlier chapters. The selection of results considered basic and important today may well be quite different in a few years.

In our experience teaching this material at Columbia University and the University of Wisconsin, we have found that a careful treatment of the first seven chapters plus parts of the eighth chapter has taken one semester. More advanced students with a strong mathematics background should also be able to handle selected topics from later chapters in a single semester. Certain sections are starred indicating that they may be omitted without missing results needed later. Certain sections will be of interest primarily to students of mathematics and logic and may be omitted by those more interested in computing. These sections are: Sections 7.5 and 7.9 and Chapter 8. On the other hand, those interested primarily in mathematics should be able to cover Chapters 1, 2, and 4 quickly and could omit Sections 5.3, 7.7, and 7.8. An exercise marked Δ is one that is exceptionally difficult or tedious.

Chapter 11, written by George W. Petznick, provides an extensive treatment of the Λ-calculus and the combinatory calculus. It should be of interest both to mathematicians and computer scientists, the latter because of the relevance of these calculi to programming languages such as LISP, TRAC, and the applicative languages currently being studied by those interested in the semantics of programming languages.

We would like to acknowledge that much inspiration and knowledge have come from contact with J. Richard Büchi, Samuel Eilenburg, and Paul Young. We would like to thank Alan Borodin and Jerry Shelton for their careful reading of parts of the original manuscript. We would also like to thank Mrs. Beatrice Williams, Mrs. Betty Clutters, Mrs. Dale Malm, and Mrs. Pat Hanson for special assistance in typing and preparing the manuscript.

Claremont, California *Walter S. Brainerd*

Madison, Wisconsin *Lawrence H. Landweber*

Contents

CHAPTER 6

Recursively Enumerable Sets 135

CHAPTER 7

Formal Languages 159

CHAPTER 8

Reducibility 190

List of Symbols

size	size function	122
statement	statement function	122
label	label function	122
left	left function	122
right	right function	122
goto	goto function	122
next	next function	122
C	compute function	122
$\varphi_m, {}_s\varphi_m$	mth partial recursive function	124
$\mathcal{A}(m)$	mth LMA	124
T	T-predicate	124
K	Kleene index function	130
r.e.	recursively enumerable	137
$\bigvee_x$	there exists x	138
ι_A	restriction of identity function to A	138
D_m	the mth r.e. set	143
$\approx$	equivalent function indices	147
$\sim$	equivalent set indices	151
$\mathcal{F}_{\mathrm{P}}$	partial recursive functions	153
$\mathcal{F}_{\mathrm{R}}$	recursive functions	153
$\mathcal{F}_{\mathrm{PM}}$	primitive recursive functions	153
F_m	the mth finite set	156
$\square$	variable in a PPS	160
$\rightarrow$	rule in a PPS	160
$\Rightarrow$	directly derivable in a PPS	160
$\overset{*}{\Rightarrow}$	derivable in a PPS	160
$\lvert\mathcal{S}\rvert$	language generated by PPS $\mathcal{S}$	160
$\forall$	for all quantifier	184

CHAPTER 1

Introduction

Before beginning a formal discussion of the theory of computation, we consider some of the intuitive notions which have led to the development of this theory. Section 1.1 defines and discusses, on an intuitive level, the important concept of an effective procedure. Indeed, the definition and representation of effective procedures and processes are probably the central issues in this book. In Section 1.2 we outline the historical development of the theory and its relationship to the ideas discussed in Section 1.1.

The remainder of this chapter contains basic definitions and notation (Section 1.3, Sets, Relations, and Functions; Section 1.6, Some Special Functions; Section 1.7, Operations on Functions) and mathematical concepts of importance for the study of the theory of computation (Section 1.4, The Representation of Data; Section 1.5, Induction; Section 1.8, Cardinality). The former may be skimmed quickly and used for later reference. We have purposely included this material in Chapter 1 so as to facilitate the retrieval process. Section 1.4 contains an important discussion of our representation scheme for data and should be read carefully. The amount of time devoted to the remaining sections will depend on the reader's background.

1.1 Algorithms

This section informally explores what it means for a computation to be performed in a mechanical or effective manner. Common properties of systems for specifying effective procedures and algorithms are also discussed. Our goal is to present the reader with the intuitive ideas behind these concepts independent of any particular formalism. Various methods of formally defining effectiveness and effective procedures will be studied in later chapters.

An *effective procedure* is a finite, unambiguous description of a finite set of operations. The operations must be effective in the sense that there is a strictly mechanical procedure for completing them.† Also, the process of deciding the order in which to perform operations must be effective, though there are formalisms, such as Λ-calculus, which is discussed in Chapter 11, where the result obtained does not depend on the particular order of execution selected. An effective procedure may perform a task, compute a function, or just perform a sequence of unrelated operations. Computer programs are examples of effective procedures. To emphasize this fact we will use *program* as a synonym for effective procedure. Other examples of effective procedures are the instructions for completing an income tax form and the driving instructions for a sports car rally. A recipe in a cook book or a set of instructions for fixing a flat tire may or may not be an effective procedure depending on whether they are described in a precise, unambiguous fashion. Finiteness of description and effectiveness of operation are the most important characteristics of effective procedures.

An effective procedure which specifies a sequence of operations which always halts is called an *algorithm*. Computer programs which always halt for any input, that is, never go into an infinite loop, are algorithms. The point at which an algorithm will halt is not necessarily calculable in advance.

Effective procedures will be written as finite sets of sentences, called *statements*, of languages which are designed to expedite the representation of effective procedures. These *algorithmic* or *procedural* languages may either be carefully chosen unambiguous subsets of natural languages such as English or French, or artificial languages such as ALGOL, FORTRAN, or a Λ-calculus. The statements of the language will describe the operations which are to be executed. The form or format of effective procedures in a particular algorithmic language is specified by a set of rules, called *syntax rules*. All algorithmic languages have the following syntactic properties:

1. there is a finite set of symbols called the *alphabet* of the language
2. the number of statements in a program (effective procedure) is finite
3. there is a mechanical procedure for checking whether an arbitrary finite sequence of alphabet symbols is a statement and whether an arbitrary finite set of statements has the form of a program

Associated with each algorithmic language is a set of rules for determining the order in which the operations of a program will be executed, which opera-

† Of course what is effective, precise, or unambiguous to one may be totally obscure to another. Perhaps one might require that such an operation be executable by a machine though even then one may argue about the effectiveness of operations not yet implemented on a machine or even about what constitutes a machine. The intent of this discussion is to appeal to the reader's intuition and experience without attempting to precisely define the terms and concepts employed.

tion will be executed first, and when execution of operations is to cease.†
As an example, there is a FORTRAN rule which says that

```
GO TO 5
```

results in a transfer to the statement with label 5. In ALGOL,

```
FOR I = 1 STEP 2 UNTIL 20 DO
   BEGIN;
      ⋮
   END;
```

causes those statements occurring between BEGIN and END to be executed 10 times (barring transfers, etc.) with I having the successive values 1, 3, . . ., 19.

Various statements of a program may be interpreted as referencing and/or modifying data contained in a *storage* or *memory area* which is available to the program. A program might itself be stored in such a memory admitting the possibility of self-modifying programs, as is the case with programs in computer assembly or machine languages. At each instance of time the storage area will be finite, though with the capability of unbounded expansion. This expandability is analogous to the ability of computer programs to call for additional magnetic tape, though of course in the ideal case, where the extra tape is always available. The method of access to data in the storage area will depend on the interpretation of statements referencing the memory. The storage area might be accessed sequentially as with magnetic tape, randomly as with traditional computer core memories, or by a combination of sequential and random means as with computer disks and drums. Corresponding to most modern computer systems, the storage area might be divided into segments having different access methods. It is important to note that *all* storage devices, including those usually classified as "internal core" and "external bulk", are included in the notion of storage area discussed above.

There are many interesting problems which are not solvable by any effective procedure. For example, for any of the algorithmic languages considered in this discussion, there is no effective procedure in the language for deciding whether or not any two arbitrarily chosen effective procedures are equivalent—that they solve the same problem. Another question not admitting an effective solution is whether an effective procedure written in an algorithmic language is actually an algorithm, that is, will always halt. These negative results are true of all known algorithmic languages, a fact which, because of

† In some languages, such as a Λ-calculus, there may be a finite number of operations which can be performed at each execution step without changing the final value produced by the program. However, when a Λ-calculus is implemented, as in the form of a LISP interpreter, a specific order of execution is to be expected.

the scope and diversity of attempts to define such languages, has led to the widespread acceptance of the idea that no such intuitively effective procedures exist in any algorithmic language.

One implication of the nonexistence of an effective solution to the problem of deciding whether an effective procedure is an algorithm is that there is no effective procedure for deciding whether, for some input, an arbitrary FORTRAN program will go into an infinite loop. We shall pursue this discussion in greater depth in Chapter 2.

Problems which have an effective solution are said to be *decidable*, *effectively solvable*, or *computable*. All other problems, such as the halting problem for FORTRAN programs described above, are said to be *undecidable*, *not decidable*, or *noncomputable*. In Section 2.3 we shall prove that there are interesting undecidable problems. The distinction between algorithms and effective procedures will also be discussed.

1.2 History

Until 1931 the proposition that any well-posed mathematical problem could be solved, possibly by a demonstration of its falsity, was widely accepted. A leading proponent of this idea was the great mathematician David Hilbert [1901, 1926]. In his famous 1900 address, "Mathematical Problems", and in a 1925 address entitled "On the Infinite" he clearly stated his belief in the tractability of mathematical problems to human reason:

> As an example of the way in which fundamental questions can be treated I would like to choose the thesis that every mathematical problem can be solved. We are all convinced of that. After all, one of the things that attracts us most when we apply ourselves to a mathematical problem is precisely that within us we always hear the call: here is the problem, search for the solution; you can find it by pure thought, for in mathematics there is no *ignorabimus*.† ††

Hilbert, of course, recognized the possibility of negative solutions to problems:

> Occasionally it happens that we seek the solution under insufficient hypotheses or in an incorrect sense, and for these reasons do not succeed. The problem then arises: to show the impossibility of the solution under the given hypotheses or in the sense contemplated....every definite mathematical problem must necessarily be susceptible of an exact settlement either in the form of an actual answer to the question asked, or by the

† Latin for "it shall not be known".
†† Reprinted with permission of Springer-Verlag from *Mathematische Annalen*, vol. 95, p. 180.

proof of the impossibility of its solution and therewith the necessary failure of all attempts.†

The key to Hilbert's program for the solution of mathematical problems was to discover a mechanical (effective) procedure for checking the truth or correctness of mathematical propositions. The rules or methods of the procedure were to be finitistic and intuitively convincing. Hilbert called the problem of finding such a procedure to determine whether a formula of a system called the first-order predicate calculus is valid (true for all interpretations) the *entscheidungsproblem*. A variant of the entscheidungsproblem is the problem of deciding whether an arbitrary first-order proposition is true of arithmetic, that is, of the system $\langle N, +, \times \rangle$, the natural numbers under addition and multiplication.†† The latter would be of great importance providing a solution to such difficult open mathematical problems as "Fermat's last theorem"** and the "twin prime problem",‡ since both of these problems can be expressed as first-order propositions.

Unfortunately Hilbert's hopes for a mechanization of the theorem-proving process were not to be realized. In 1931 Gödel published his famous incompleteness theorem which, together with its corollaries, ruled out the existence of an effective procedure for deciding truth or falsity of first-order statements about $\langle N, +, \times \rangle$. The incompleteness theorem states that for any consistent‡‡ formal system (axioms plus rules of inference) whose axioms adequately define addition and multiplication of natural numbers, there are propositions which are true of $\langle N, +, \times \rangle$ but which are not provable within the system, that is, which are not derivable from the axioms using the rules of inference.

For the first time mathematicians had to consider the existence of propositions which could neither be proved nor disproved within a given formal

† Reprinted with permission of the American Mathematical Society from *Bulletin of the American Mathematical Society*, Copyright © 1900, Volume VIII, p. 444.

†† A first-order proposition is a formula of the predicate calculus in which quantification is applied only to individual variables. If individual variables are interpreted as ranging over the natural numbers N, k-ary predicate variables over subsets of N^k, and distinguished ternary predicates $A(x,y,z)$ and $M(x,y,z)$ are interpreted as addition ($A(x,y,z)$ means $(x+y=z)$) and multiplication ($M(x,y,z)$, means $(x \times y = z)$) respectively on N, then first-order propositions are statements about the system $\langle N, +, \times \rangle$.

** Fermat indicated, in the margin of a translation of Diophantine's *Arithmetica*, that it was true that for $n \geq 3$ there do not exist natural numbers $x,y,z > 0$ such that

$$x^n + y^n = z^n,$$

but that the margin was not big enough for the "truly remarkable" proof. A proof of this proposition has since eluded mathematicians.

‡ Do there exist infinitely many natural numbers p such that p and $p+2$ are prime?

‡‡ A formal system is (*simply*) *consistent* if for no formula A is it possible to derive both A and its negative $\neg A$ from the axioms of the system. Actually Gödel's proof assumed a stronger type of consistency. The proof for simple consistency was given by Rosser [1936].

system. Moreover, though the use of additional axioms might enlarge the class of provable propositions, the essential incompleteness of Gödel's theorem remained so long as the resulting system was adequate for describing the natural numbers, addition and multiplication.

In order to rigorously prove that the entscheidungsproblem for arithmetic was not decidable, it was necessary to precisely define what was meant by the term *effective procedure*. An important feature of Gödel's proof was his use of natural numbers (called Gödel numbers) to code symbols, formulas, and sequences of formulas. Statements about formulas could then be represented by functions $f:N^k \to N$ mapping k-tuples of natural numbers into natural numbers. For example,

$$f(x) = \begin{cases} 1 & \text{if } x \text{ is the Gödel number of a provable formula} \\ 0 & \text{otherwise} \end{cases}$$

Another example is

$$g(x,y,z) = \begin{cases} 1 & \text{if } x \text{ is the Gödel number of a FORTRAN program} \\ & \text{which on input } y \text{ halts after executing exactly } z \\ & \text{statements} \\ 0 & \text{otherwise} \end{cases}$$

Hence questions concerning the existence of effective procedures for deciding properties of formulas are reducible to consideration of the effective computability of the corresponding number theoretic functions. For example, $f(x)$ above is effectively computable iff there is an effective procedure for deciding whether an arbitrary formula is provable. Because of this correspondence between the effective computability of functions and the existence of effective procedures for solving problems, attempts to formalize the latter have generally involved formalizations of the former. To date there has been no reason to question the adequacy of this approach. In fact, quite the opposite is true. Though a great deal of effort has gone into attempts to formalize the general notion of effectiveness, no one has succeeded in specifying an effective procedure not representable by an effectively computable function.

In his incompleteness proof, Gödel [1934] used the class of primitive recursive functions, mapping k-tuples of natural numbers into natural numbers, which had been earlier defined by Dedekind [1888] and others. Gödel [1934] points out that "[Primitive] recursive functions have the important property that, for each given set of values of the arguments, the function can be computed by a finite procedure".† Furthermore, he states that the converse seems to be true if a larger class of functions, now called the recursive functions, defined by Herband and Gödel, is considered. That is, any

† Reprinted with permission of Raven Press from Martin Davis, editor, *The Undecidable*, 1965, p. 43.

function computable by a finite procedure can be specified by a recursive function definition. However, Gödel [1934] further states that "This cannot be proved, since the notion of finite computation is not defined, but it serves as a heuristic principle".† Though he was apparently the first to propose the identification of a particular formally defined class of functions with those which are effectively computable, Gödel did not attempt to justify this identification. In fact, he later stated that he had not been completely convinced of its correctness.

Church [1936b] employed two characterizations of effective computability, the λ-definable functions (see Chapter 11) of Church and Kleene, and the recursive functions of Herband and Gödel to prove that the entscheidungsproblem for arithmetic was not effectively solvable. In fact, the proof could have been presented in terms of either formalism alone because their equivalence, (f is λ-definable iff f is recursive) had been proved by Kleene [1936b]. The fact that two such different characterizations of effective computability were equivalent led Church [1936a] to suggest "that they constitute as general a characterization of this notion as is consistent with the usual intuitive understanding of it". This hypothesis, called *Church's thesis*, has not been contradicted. Church's thesis will be discussed in Chapter 2.

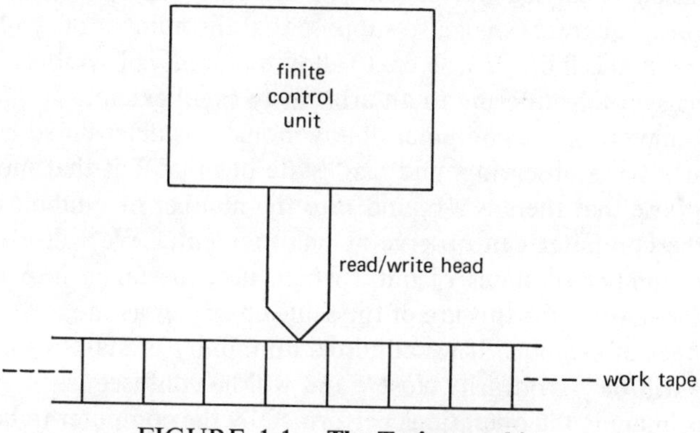

FIGURE 1-1. **The Turing machine.**

Independently of Church, Turing [1936] proposed a formalism for the representation of effective procedures. Turing's approach is particularly significant because for the first time it identified programs written for a simple "automatic computing machine" with intuitive notions of effectiveness. The Turing machine (Figure 1-1) has a single two-way infinite work tape, divided into squares each of which can contain a symbol from a finite alphabet. At each instance of time the tape read/write head scans a single square. Based on the contents of the square scanned, the instruction executed will select the

† *Ibid.*, p. 44.

next instruction and either change the symbol scanned or move the head one square right or left. A version of Turing's machine will be discussed in Chapter 4. One can then define how a machine program computes a function, or as in Turing's case, how a machine program generates a sequence. With regard to arguments for his hypothesis that every intuitively effective procedure can be implemented by a Turing machine program, Turing [1936] states:

> All arguments which can be given are bound to be, fundamentally, appeals to intuition, and for this reason rather unsatisfactory mathematically. The real question at issue is "What are the possible processes which can be carried out in computing a number?" The arguments I shall use are of three kinds: (a) A direct appeal to intuition. (b) A proof of the equivalence of two definitions (in case the new definition has a greater intuitive appeal). (c) Giving examples of large classes of numbers which are computable.†

Turing [1936] proceeds to explain his choice of formalism.

> Computing [by people] is normally done by writing certain symbols on paper. In elementary arithmetic the two-dimensional character of the paper is sometimes used. But such a use is always avoidable...I assume that the computation is carried out on one-dimensional paper, that is, on a tape divided into squares. I shall also suppose that the number of symbols which may be printed is finite. If we were to allow an infinity of symbols, then there would be symbols differing to an arbitrarily small extent....
>
> The behavior of the computer at any moment is determined by the symbols which he is observing, and his "state of mind" at that moment. We may suppose that there is a bound *B* to the number of symbols or squares which the computer can observe at one moment....We will also suppose that the number of states of mind which need be taken into account is finite. The reasons for this are of the same character as those which restrict the number of symbols. If we admitted an infinity of states of mind, some of them will be "arbitrarily close" and will be confused....
>
> Let us imagine the operations performed by the computer to be split into "simple operations" which are so elementary that it is not easy to imagine them further divided. Every such operation consists of some change of the physical system consisting of the computer and his tape. We know the state of the system if we know the sequence of symbols on the tape, which of these are observed by the computer (possibly with a special order), and the state of mind of the computer. We may suppose that in a simple operation not more than one symbol is altered. Any other changes can be split up into simple changes of this kind....We may therefore, without loss of

† Reprinted with permission of Clarendon Press from *Proceedings of the London Mathematical Society*, vol. 42, p. 235.

generality, assume that the squares whose symbols are changed are always "observed squares".

...The new observed squares must be immediately recognizable by the computer. I think it is reasonable to suppose that they can only be squares whose distance from the closest of the immediately previously scanned squares does not exceed a certain fixed amount.†

The similarity between Turing's automatic computing machines and modern computers which use magnetic tapes is striking. As an indication of Turing's intuition with regard to the meaning of effectiveness, one need only mention that any program for any real computer can be simulated by a Turing machine program. Moreover many of the characteristics of algorithms discussed in Section 1.1 were originally noted by Turing. The Turing machine has played an important role in the development of the theory of computation.

Since 1936 a great deal of effort has gone into attempts to characterize the effectively computable functions. Such seemingly unrelated models as the recursive functions of Gödel and Herband, the λ-definable functions of Church and Kleene, Turing's machine programs, the normal algorithms of Markov [1954], the canonical systems of Post [1943], the register machine programs of Shepherdson and Sturgis [1963], and the random access stored programs of Elgot and Robinson [1964] have all turned out to be equivalent. Each in turn has added to the credibility of Church's thesis so that today its correctness is generally accepted. Hence one may study computability from an intuitive viewpoint, confident that such intuitively effective procedures can be represented in terms of each of the formal characterizations mentioned above. The equivalence of several of these characterizations will be proved in Chapters 2–5, 7, and 11.

Given a precise definition of what is meant by an effective procedure and an effectively computable function, the question as to whether a problem is effectively solvable becomes meaningful. Studies in this area have shown that many important and intuitively appealing problems are in fact undecidable. For example, if programs in an algorithmic language such as FORTRAN are considered and if (a) an unlimited supply of tape is available, and (b) no external execution time limit is imposed, then the following problems are not effectively solvable, that is, there is no effective procedure that will always provide the correct answer.

1. given an arbitrary input free program, will it ever halt?
2. given two programs, do they compute the same function?
3. given an arbitrary program, will its fifth instruction ever be executed?

The undecidability of each of these assertions is proved in Chapter 6.

† *Ibid.*, pp. 235–236.

1.3 Sets, Relations, and Functions

This section should be skimmed rapidly and reviewed later if necessary. However, note carefully the definition of function given here. We assume familiarity with elementary set theory and the concepts of set membership $\in$, set union $\cup$, set intersection $\cap$, set complementation $^{-}$, the empty set $\varnothing$, the subset relation $\subseteq$, and the proper subset relation $\subset$.

If X and Y are sets, then $X \times Y$, the set of ordered pairs $\{(x,y) \mid x \in X, y \in Y\}$, is called the *Cartesian product* of X and Y. If X and Y are the same set, say $X = Y = W$, then $X \times Y$ may be written as W^2. Similarly ordered triples, 4-tuples, etc. of members of a set W may be constructed and there is a natural way of combining r-tuples and s-tuples to form $(r+s)$-tuples: $((x_1,\ldots,x_r), (y_1,\ldots,y_s)) = (x_1,\ldots,x_r,y_1,\ldots,y_s)$. Variable symbols such as x and y may stand for r-tuples (vectors) as well as individual quantities and we adopt the convention that $(x,y) \in W^{r+s}$ means that $x \in W^r$ and $y \in W^s$. There is a single 0-tuple $()$ constituting the set W^0, so that $()(x_1,\ldots,x_r) = (x_1,\ldots,x_r)() = (x_1,\ldots,x_r)$, and $W^0 \times W^r = W^r \times W^0 = W^r$. (If this seems a bit strange at first, think of the set R of real numbers, so that $R^3 = R \times R \times R$ is the set of points in three-dimensional space, R^2 is the plane, R is the real line, and R^0 is the single point at the origin.)

A *relation* $f{:}X \rightarrow Y$ from X to Y is any collection of ordered pairs $(x,y) \in X \times Y$, that is, any subset of $X \times Y$. Intuitively, a relation may be viewed as an unusual sort of computation, which, given input $x \in X$, may produce many $y \in Y$ or may not produce any output at all. Then $(x,y) \in f$ if on input x, one of the outputs produced by the computation f is y. The *domain* of f, written $\operatorname{dom} f$, is $\{x \mid (x,y) \in f, \text{ for some } y\}$, that is, the set of inputs which produce some output. If $x \in \operatorname{dom} f$, then f is *defined* at x, and we write $f(x)\downarrow$. If $x \notin \operatorname{dom} f$, then $f(x)$ is *undefined*, written $f(x)\uparrow$. The *range* of f, written $\operatorname{ran} f$, is $\{y \mid (x,y) \in f, \text{ for some } x\}$, that is, the set of outputs. If $A \subseteq X$, then $f(A) = \{y \mid (x,y) \in f, \text{ for some } x \in A\}$ is the set of outputs produced by inputs from A. Thus $f(\operatorname{dom} f) = \operatorname{ran} f$. The notations $f(x)$ and fx will be used in place of $f(\{x\})$, for $x \in X$. The *restriction* of f to A, denoted $f \mid A$, is the relation consisting of input/output pairs $(x,y) \in f$ such that $x \in A$. The *inverse* $f^{-1}{:}Y \rightarrow X$ of a relation $f{:}X \rightarrow Y$ is the set of pairs $\{(y,x) \mid (x,y) \in f\}$.

A relation $f{:}X \rightarrow Y$ is a *function* if $f(x)$ contains at most one element for each $x \in X$, that is, each input produces a unique output or no output at all. If, in addition, $\operatorname{dom} f = X$, so that each input produces exactly one output, f is called a *total* function.

A relation (or function) f is 1-1 if $f(x) = y$ and $f(x') = y$ imply $x = x'$, that is, two different inputs never produce the same output. A relation $f{:}X \rightarrow Y$ is *onto* if $\operatorname{ran} f = Y$. Thus a function f is 1-1 if its inverse f^{-1} is a function and is onto if f^{-1} is total. A 1-1 onto function is called a *bijection*.

A relation $f{:}X \to X$ is an *equivalence relation* on X if

1. $(x,x) \in f$ for all $x \in X$ (f is reflective)
2. $(x,y) \in f$ implies $(y,x) \in f$ (f is symmetric)
3. $(x,y) \in f$ and $(y,z) \in f$ imply $(x,z) \in f$ (f is transitive)

EXERCISES

1. Show that the inverse of a 1-1 relation is a function.

2. Show that the inverse of a bijection is also a bijection.

3. If $f{:}X \to Y$ is a function, show that $\{(x, x') \mid fx = fx'\}$ is an equivalence relation on X.

1.4 The Representation of Data

A programmer who is primarily interested in using the computer to solve mathematical problems naturally tends to think of the computer as a processor of *numbers*. The computer scientist who is more interested in how a computer actually performs numerical calculations may think of the computer as a processor of symbols (such as 0's and 1's) which *represent* numbers. A systems programmer primarily interested in compilers or a scholar of literature interested in analyzing eighteenth century English poetry is mainly concerned with manipulating symbols that have no numerical interpretation at all.

The distinction between numbers and their representations is also illustrated by considering a child who is learning elementary arithmetic. The student is learning properties of the numbers themselves, such as how to count with them and how adding them corresponds to forming the union of disjoint sets. The student must also learn to perform calculations, such as multiplying two six-digit numbers; these tasks involve the manipulation of representations of the numbers, usually using strings of the decimal digits 0, 1, ..., 9.

Throughout this book, we will primarily be interested in computations involving strings of symbols. In many cases, it will be important to be able to interpret each string of symbols as a representation of a member of $N = \{0,1,2,\ldots\}$, the set of *natural numbers*. These conventions will now be discussed.

An *alphabet* Σ is a nonempty finite set of symbols or letters. In many cases, it will be convenient to use symbols 1, 2, 3, ..., n for the n members of Σ and the *alphabet* $\{1,2,\ldots,n\}$ will be designated by Σ_n. In other cases, it may be convenient to use a, b, $+$, $/$, or other symbols as members of Σ.

A *word* in Σ is any finite string of symbols from Σ; for example, 2131 and 112 are words in Σ_3. The set of words in Σ will be denoted by W. The *length* of a word x is the number of symbols in x; for example, length(2131) is four and length(112) is three. There is one word of length zero, called the *null word*. The symbol 0 will be used to denote the null word. Two words may be *concatenated* by writing one after the other. Concatenation is denoted by · so that 2131 · 112 = 2131112. Note that

$$0 \cdot x = x \cdot 0 = x \qquad \text{for all } x \in W$$

and

$$x \cdot (y \cdot z) = (x \cdot y) \cdot z \qquad \text{for all } x, y, z \in W$$

Concatenation is commutative ($x \cdot y = y \cdot x$) iff Σ contains only one letter.

The word x is a *subword* of y, written $x \preccurlyeq y$, if there are words u and v such that $u \cdot x \cdot v = y$. For example, $212 \preccurlyeq 321243$, where $u = 3$ and $v = 43$; and $212 \preccurlyeq 2123$, where $u = 0$ and $v = 3$. Note that $0 \preccurlyeq x$ and $x \preccurlyeq x$ for all x in W. If $x \preccurlyeq y$ and $x \neq y$, then we write $x \prec y$.

The operation of concatenation can be repeated, giving "powers" of a word defined by

$$x^0 = 0 \qquad x^{k+1} = x^k \cdot x \qquad k \geq 0$$

Concatenation of sets and powers of sets can be defined by

$$A \cdot B = \{x \cdot y \mid x \in A, y \in B\}$$
$$A(0) = \{0\}$$
$$A(k+1) = A(k) \cdot A, \qquad k \geq 0$$

Note that $A(0)$ is not the empty set; it contains one element, the null word. If A contains a single element x, then $A \cdot B = \{x\} \cdot B$ may be written $x \cdot B$. For all $A, B, C \subseteq W$, the following hold.

$$A \cdot (B \cdot C) = (A \cdot B) \cdot C$$
$$0 \cdot A = A \cdot 0 = A$$
$$\varnothing \cdot A = A \cdot \varnothing = \varnothing \qquad \varnothing \text{ is the empty set}$$

Define $A^+ = \bigcup_{k=1}^{\infty} A(k)$ and $A^* = A(0) \cup A^+$.

To illustrate this definition, if $A = \{11,2\}$, then

$$A(0) = \{0\}$$
$$A(1) = \{11,2\}$$
$$A(2) = \{1111,112,211,22\}$$
$$\vdots$$

The set A^* consists of all words in which the symbol 1 occurs only in pairs.

Another example is the set $\{2\}^* \cdot (\{1\} \cdot \{2\}^* \cdot \{1\} \cdot \{2\}^*)^*$, usually written $2^*(12^*12^*)^*$, which consists of all words in Σ_2 containing an even number of 1's.

Note that $W = \Sigma^*$. The set $W_n = \Sigma_n^*$ can be nicely represented as a tree with the null word 0 at the root and words $x \cdot 1, x \cdot 2, \ldots, x \cdot n$ above each word x. Part of this infinite tree for the set W_3 is shown in Figure 1-2.

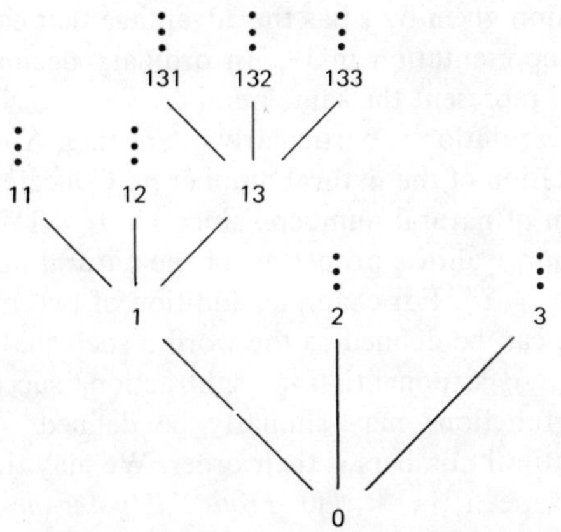

FIGURE 1-2. **Tree representation of Σ_3^*.**

Each word $x = \sigma_k \cdots \sigma_1\sigma_0$ in Σ_n may be interpreted as a natural number using the function

$$v(x) = v(\sigma_k \cdots \sigma_1\sigma_0) = \sum_{i=0}^{k} \sigma_i \times n^i = \sigma_k \times n^k + \cdots + \sigma_1 \times n + \sigma_0$$

For example, in W_4,

$$v(231) = 2 \times 4^2 + 3 \times 4 + 1 = 45$$

This definition and example illustrate some of the difficulties which arise when we attempt to distinguish between numbers and their representations. In $v(231)$, the digits are symbols in Σ_4 and 231 is a word in W_4. In $2 \times 4^2 + 3 \times 4 + 1$, each digit stands for a number, that is, a member of N. Finally, 45 also stands for a number; it is the usual decimal representation of the number forty-five.

In this book, we will be primarily interested in functions applied to words in some alphabet. Whenever a string of digits appearing in the text is supposed to represent a number, this should be clear from the context.

If $v(x) = m$, $x \in W_n$, then x is called the *n-adic representation* of the number m. This is not the usual representation of numbers in base n because digits 1 to n are used rather than 0 to $n - 1$. Table 1-1 shows the 2-adic representation of some of the natural numbers.

TABLE 1-1. 2-adic Representations of Natural Numbers.

x	0	1	2	11	12	21	22	111	112	121
$v(x)$	0	1	2	3	4	5	6	7	8	9

The representation given by v has the advantage that each natural number has exactly one representation in W_n. In ordinary decimal notation, 0460, 00460, and 460 all represent the same number.

The 1-adic representation is particularly interesting. A word of length m in Σ_1 is the representation of the natural number m. Concatenation in Σ_1 corresponds to addition of natural numbers, since $1^i \cdot 1^j = 1^{i+j}$.

The interpretation v allows properties of the natural numbers to be transferred to the set $W = \Sigma^*$. For example, addition of two members x and y of W, written $x + y$, can be defined as the word z such that $v(z) = v(x) + v(y)$. Multiplication $x \times y$, exponentiation, subtraction, successor $(x + 1)$, and other arithmetic functions may similarly be defined. Another important property of the natural numbers is their order. We may thus define $x < y$ for members of W to mean $v(x) < v(y)$. *From this point on, we assume that all statements about natural numbers also make sense when applied to members of* W. Further examples are: "x is even", "x is a prime", "x is more than twice as large as y", and "execute the statement x times".

If an alphabet contains symbols other than the digits 1, 2, ..., n, it is still useful to be able to interpret each word uniquely as a natural number. To do this, simply set up any correspondence between the n members of the alphabet and the alphabet $\{1,2,\ldots,n\}$. To illustrate this idea, suppose $\Sigma = \{1,2,a,b,*\}$. Treat a, b, and $*$ as if they were the digits 3, 4, and 5 respectively, so that $v(b * 2) = v(452) = 4 \times 5^2 + 5 \times 5 + 2 = 127$ in standard base 10 notation.

EXERCISES

1. Let $A, B, C \subseteq W$. Prove the following:

a. $A \cdot (B \cup C) = A \cdot B \cup A \cdot C$

b. $A \cdot (B \cap C)$ is not always equal to $A \cdot B \cap A \cdot C$

c. $(A^*)^* = A^*$

d. $A \subseteq B$ implies $A^* \subseteq B^*$

e. $A^* \cup B^* \subseteq (A \cup B)^*$

f. $X = A^* \cdot B$ satisfies the linear equation $X = A \cdot X \cup B$

g. if length$(x) = k$ and $x \in A^*$, then $x \in \bigcup_{i=0}^{k} A(i)$, that is, $x \in A(i)$ for some $i \leq k$

2. Calculate 212×11 in Σ_2.

3. Give a procedure for adding in Σ_2 that does not involve converting to natural numbers.

4. Give a procedure for deciding whether or not $x < y$ in Σ_3 without using the function v.

5. Explain how to multiply by 3 using 3-adic notation.

6. Prove that concatenation in Σ is commutative iff Σ contains one symbol.

7. Show that $W^* = W$, where $W = \Sigma^*$, Σ finite.

8. Give a procedure for directly converting a p-adic number into a q-adic number for $p, q > 0$. *Do not* convert to ordinary base 10 notation as an intermediate step!

1.5 Induction

Induction provides an important method for defining functions and proving theorems. The most common form of induction is usually stated for sets of natural numbers, but because of the 1-1 correspondence given by v, the same principle may be applied to sets of words.

INDUCTION PRINCIPLE I. Let $A \subseteq W$. If $0 \in A$ and if, for all x, $x \in A$ implies $x + 1 \in A$, then $A = W$.

A slightly different form of the induction principle is often useful in proofs.

INDUCTION PRINCIPLE II. Let $A \subseteq W$. If $0 \in A$ and for all $x > 0$, there is a $y < x$ such that $y \in A$ implies $x \in A$, then $A = W$.

There is a third form of the induction principle that is particularly applicable to sets of words.

INDUCTION PRINCIPLE III. Let $A \subseteq W$. If $0 \in A$ and if, for all $x \in W$ and all $\sigma \in \Sigma$, $x \in A$ implies $x \cdot \sigma \in A$, then $A = W$.

This form of induction may be viewed either as an example of an induction scheme based on the length of x or as the second form of induction with $x = y\sigma$. A slight variation of this induction principle is obtained by replacing "$x \in A$ implies $x\sigma \in A$" by "$x \in A$ implies $\sigma x \in A$".

It is possible to use the induction principles to define functions. As an example, the function $v: W_n \to N$ may be defined inductively by

$$v(0) = 0$$
$$v(x\sigma) = n \times v(x) + \sigma$$

where $\times$ and $+$ are multiplication and addition, respectively, on N.

If A is the set of words for which v is defined, then Induction Principle III asserts that v is defined for all $x \in W_n$. The first line of the definition tells us how to compute $v(0)$; then assuming that $v(x)$ can be computed, the second line tells us how to compute $v(x\sigma)$.

The inductive definition of v may actually be a little harder to understand than the one given in Section 1.4; however, if a function is defined by induction, then it is possible using that definition, to prove properties of the function by induction. More examples of inductive definitions will be given in the next section.

1.6 Some Special Functions

Most of the relations discussed in this book will be functions $f: W^r \to W^s$, where $W = \Sigma^*$ and Σ is a finite alphabet. The following list contains some of the functions which play a fundamental role.

1. $\iota: W \to W$, where $\iota(x) = x$, is the *identity* function
2. $\pi: W \to W^0$, where $\pi(x) = ()$, is the *projection* function
3. $\zeta: W^0 \to W$, where $\zeta() = 0$, is the *zero* function
4. $\varsigma: W \to W$, where $\varsigma(x) = x + 1$ is the *successor* function
5. $x \dot{-} y = \begin{cases} x - y & \text{if } x \geq y \\ 0 & \text{otherwise} \end{cases}$ is called *proper subtraction*
6. concatenation, a function from W^2 to W was defined in Section 1.4
7. $\rho: W \to W$, where $\rho(\sigma_1 \cdots \sigma_k) = \sigma_k \cdots \sigma_1$, is the *reversal function*; the function ρ may be defined inductively by

$$\rho(0) = 0$$
$$\rho(x\sigma) = \sigma \cdot \rho(x)$$

8. if $A \subseteq W^r$, then $\chi_A: W^r \to W$, defined by

$$\chi_A(x) = \begin{cases} 1 & \text{if} \quad x \in A \\ 0 & \text{if} \quad x \notin A \end{cases}$$ is called the *characteristic function* of A

It should be emphasized that each of the functions 1–8 is a mapping from words to words. Thus 0 denotes the null word (the n-adic representation of zero), not the number zero itself. To illustrate the use of inductive definitions in proofs, we now prove some simple properties of the functions ρ and ι using the induction principles discussed in Section 1.5.

The first theorem asserts that ρ could also be defined by a "left induction". The theorem is proved using Induction Principle III.

THEOREM 1.1. For all $x \in W$ and $\sigma \in \Sigma$, $\rho(\sigma \cdot x) = \rho(x) \cdot \sigma$

Proof. For $x = 0$, $\rho(\sigma \cdot 0) = \rho(0 \cdot \sigma) = \sigma \cdot \rho(0) = \sigma \cdot 0 = 0 \cdot \sigma = \rho(0) \cdot \sigma$. Thus the theorem is true for $x = 0$. We now show that $\rho(\sigma \cdot x\sigma') = \rho(x\sigma') \cdot \sigma$ using the induction hypothesis that $\rho(\sigma x) = \rho(x) \cdot \sigma$.

$$\begin{aligned} \rho(\sigma \cdot x\sigma') &= \rho(\sigma x \cdot \sigma') && \text{since } \cdot \text{ is associative} \\ &= \sigma' \cdot \rho(\sigma x) && \text{by the definition of } \rho \\ &= \sigma' \cdot \rho(x) \cdot \sigma && \text{by the induction hypothesis} \\ &= \rho(x\sigma') \cdot \sigma && \text{by the definition of } \rho \quad \blacksquare \end{aligned}$$

THEOREM 1.2. $\rho[\rho(x)] = x$, for all $x \in W$.

Proof. The proof is by induction on x; see Exercise 1. ∎

THEOREM 1.3. $\rho(x \cdot y) = \rho(y) \cdot \rho(x)$.

Proof. Let $A = \{y \mid \rho(x \cdot y) = \rho(y) \cdot \rho(x)$, for all $x \in W\}$. We prove by induction on y that $A = W$.

$$\rho(x \cdot 0) = \rho(x) = 0 \cdot \rho(x) = \rho(0) \cdot \rho(x)$$

Hence $0 \in A$. Assume $y \in A$ and show that $y\sigma \in A$ for all $\sigma \in \Sigma$.

$$\begin{aligned} \rho(x \cdot y\sigma) &= \rho(xy \cdot \sigma) = \sigma \cdot \rho(xy) \\ &= \sigma \cdot \rho(y) \cdot \rho(x) \text{ by the induction hypothesis} \\ &= \rho(y\sigma) \cdot \rho(x) \quad \blacksquare \end{aligned}$$

The successor function could also be defined as follows using Induction Principle III:

For $\sigma \in \Sigma_n$, $\sigma \neq n$, let σ' be the next digit larger than σ.

$$\varsigma(0) = 1$$

$$\varsigma(x\sigma) = \begin{cases} x \cdot \sigma' & \text{if } \sigma \neq n \\ \varsigma(x) \cdot 1 & \text{if } \sigma = n \end{cases}$$

To prove that this definition is equivalent to the one given previously, it is necessary to prove that

$$\nu(\varsigma x) = \nu(x) + 1$$

using the definition of $\varsigma(x)$ just given (see Exercise 6).

Addition in Σ can be defined inductively (using Induction Principle I) from successor in Σ as follows:

$$x + 0 = x$$

$$x + (y + 1) = \varsigma(x + y)$$

Similarly multiplication in Σ can be defined inductively (using Induction Principle I) from addition in Σ by

$$x \times 0 = 0$$

$$x \times (y + 1) = (x \times y) + x$$

The reader should keep in mind that the above define addition and multiplication, respectively, on words in Σ^* assuming that $\varsigma(x)$ is already defined for words in Σ^*. The actual mappings performed by ς, $+$, and $\times$ of course depend on the alphabet Σ. Functions like concatenation and reversal differ from successor, addition, and multiplication in that the former are less dependent on the alphabet. For example

$$\rho(1212) = 2121$$

in Σ_2 and in Σ_3. On the other hand $\varsigma(11212)$ equals 11221 in Σ_2 and 11213 in Σ_3. This results from the fact that successor, addition, and multiplication are usually thought of as being number theoretic functions. Hence, for different methods of representing numbers, we would expect to have different procedures for computing such functions. Reversal and concatenation on the other hand are primarily viewed as functions which manipulate strings of data; the definition not depending on the alphabet Σ.

EXERCISES

1. Prove by induction on x that $\rho\,[\rho(x)] = \iota(x) = x$.

2. Give an inductive definition of x^y from $\times$ and $+$.

3. Give an inductive definition of $f(x) = 1^{\mathrm{length}(x)}$.

4. $R_\sigma(x) = x \cdot \sigma$ and $L_\sigma(x) = \sigma \cdot x$ are the *right* and *left successor* functions, respectively. Prove by induction that $R_\sigma(x) = \rho(L_\sigma(\rho(x)))$.

5. Calculate $\varsigma^k(0)$ in Σ_3 for a few values of k.

6. Using the inductive definition of ς and ν, prove by induction that $\nu(\varsigma x) = \nu(x) + 1$, where $+$ means addition on N.

1.7 Operations on Functions

Relations and functions can be combined in several important ways.

If $f{:}X \to Y$ and $g{:}\,Y \to Z$, then the *composition* of f and g is $g \circ f{:}X \to Z$, the set of ordered pairs $\{(x,z) \mid (x,y) \in f$ and $(y,z) \in g$, for some $y \in Y\}$. If f and g are functions, then $(g \circ f)(x) = z$ if $y = f(x)$ and $z = g(y)$, that is, $z = g[f(x)]$. Thus $x \in \mathrm{dom}(g \circ f)$ if $x \in \mathrm{dom}\, f$ and $f(x) \in \mathrm{dom}\, g$.

A set of relations (or functions) is *closed* under some operation (such as composition) if the operation applied to members of the set always produces other members of the set. The composition of two functions is also a function, thus the set of functions is closed under composition. The set of total functions and the set of 1-1 functions are also closed under composition.

The operation of composition combines two functions in a *serial* manner as shown in Figure 1-3. It is also possible to combine functions in *parallel* as illustrated in Figure 1-4. The resulting function $f \times g$ will be called the *combination* of f and g. Formally, if $f{:}W^r \to W^s$ and $g{:}W^t \to W^u$, then $f \times g{:}W^{r+t} \to W^{s+u}$ is given by $(f \times g)(x,y) = (fx, gy)$. Note that $(x,y) \in \mathrm{dom}(f \times g)$ iff $x \in \mathrm{dom}\, f$ and $y \in \mathrm{dom}\, g$. Thus $\mathrm{dom}(f \times g) = \mathrm{dom}\, f \times \mathrm{dom}\, g$.

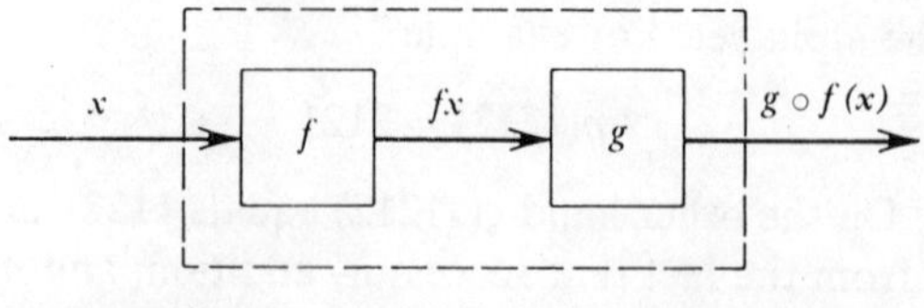

FIGURE 1-3. **Schematic representation of $g \circ f$.**

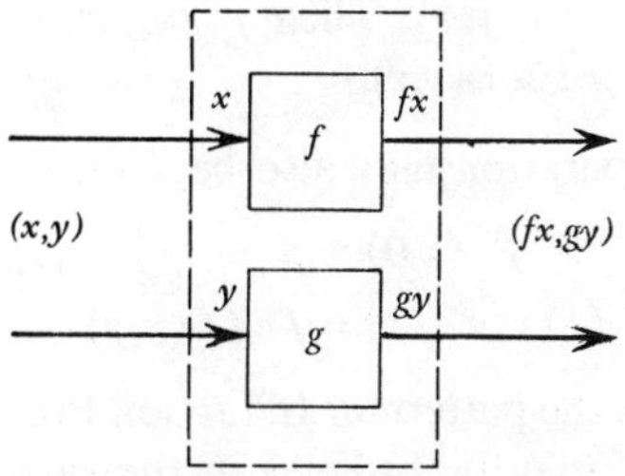

FIGURE 1-4. **Schematic representation of $f \times g$.**

If $f{:}W^r \to W^s$ and $g{:}W^r \to W^t$ are functions, define $\langle f,g\rangle{:}W^r \to W^{s+t}$ by $\langle f,g\rangle(x) = (fx,gx)$. The function $\langle f,g\rangle$ is computed by making a copy of the input x and then computing f and g in parallel as illustrated in Figure 1-5.

Example. $\langle \varsigma, \varsigma \circ \varsigma\rangle(x) = (x+1, x+2)$

Suppose $f{:}W^r \to W^r$ is a function, then a new function, the *exponentiation* of f, $f^{\#}{:}W^{r+1} \to W^r$ can be defined by

$$f^{\#}(x,y) = \overbrace{f \circ f \circ \cdots \circ f}^{y \text{ times}}(x)$$

Note that $f^{\#}(x,0) = x$, for all x.

To compute $f^{\#}(x,y)$, f is composed with itself y times and the result is applied to input x. In place of $f^{\#}(x,y)$, $f^y(x)$ will usually be written.

Note that $f^{\#}(x,y)$ is defined only if $f(x)$, $f \circ f(x)$, $f \circ f \circ f(x)$, ... are all defined, that is, $(x,y) \in \text{dom}(f^{\#})$ iff $f^k(x) \in \text{dom} f$, fc $\cdot\, 0 \le k < y$.

Example.

$$x + y = \varsigma^{\#}(x,y) = \varsigma^y(x)$$

Thus, addition of words in an arbitrary alphabet may be defined in terms of the successor function via the use of exponentiation.

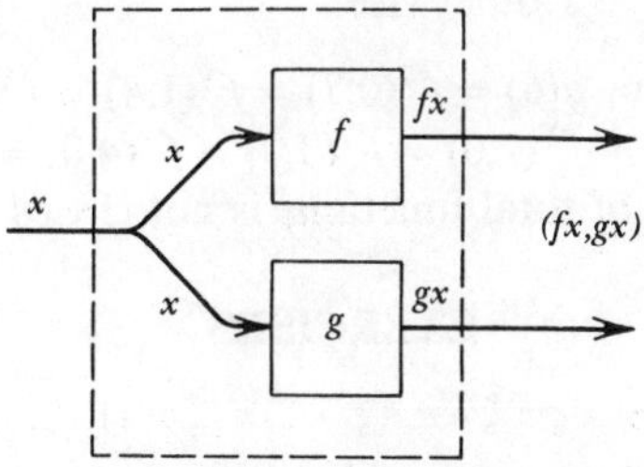

FIGURE 1-5. **Schematic representation of $\langle f,g\rangle$.**

Example. Let $f(x,y) = (x + y,y)$. Then $f^{\#}(0,y,z) = f^{z}(0,y) = (y \times z,y)$, so $y \times z = (\iota \times \pi) \circ f^{\#} \circ (\zeta \times \iota \times \iota)(y,z)$.

The exponentiation operation may also be defined inductively as follows

$$f^{\#}(x,0) = x$$
$$f^{\#}(x,y + 1) = f \circ f^{\#}(x,y)$$

This definition follows the pattern of Induction Principle I and uses the fact that the members of W may be ordered in the same way that the natural numbers are ordered.

The inductive definition of exponentiation provides a proof of the following trivial result.

THEOREM 1.4. $\varsigma^{x}(0) = x$

Proof. $\varsigma^{0}(0) = 0$ by the definition of exponentiation.

$$\begin{aligned} \varsigma^{x+1}(0) &= \varsigma \circ \varsigma^{x}(0) && \text{by definition of exponentiation} \\ &= \varsigma(x) && \text{by the induction hypothesis} \\ &= x + 1 \quad \blacksquare \end{aligned}$$

The operation of exponentiation specifies that f is to be composed with itself a certain indicated number of times. Another operation, repetition, specifies that a given function f be composed with itself until a certain criterion is met. Suppose $f{:}W^{r+1} \to W^{r+1}$. Let k be the smallest value such that $f^{k}(x,y) = (x',1)$ for some $x' \in W^{r}$. Then the value of the *repetition* of f, $f^{\nabla}{:}W^{r+1} \to W^{r}$ is defined to be x'. If there is no such k, then $f^{\nabla}(x,y)$ is undefined. In other words, f is repeatedly applied until the last argument is 1; the remaining values are then the output. Note that $f^{\nabla}(x,1) = x$, since $f^{0}(x,y) = (x,y)$.

Example. If $f(x,y) = (x + 1,\ y \dot{-} 3)$ then

$$g(y) = f^{\nabla}(0,y + 1) = \begin{cases} \dfrac{y}{3} & \text{if } y \text{ is a multiple of 3} \\ \uparrow & \text{otherwise} \end{cases}$$

To calculate g for $y = 6$, $g(6) = f^{\nabla}(0,7) = f^{\nabla}(1,4) = f^{\nabla}(2,1) = 2$. For $y = 4$, $g(4) = f^{\nabla}(0,5) = f^{\nabla}(1,2) = f^{\nabla}(2,0) = f^{\nabla}(3,0) = f^{\nabla}(4,0) = \cdots$, so $g(4)$ is undefined. Thus the set of total functions is not closed under repetition.

EXERCISES

1. Determine the value of $\langle \varsigma \circ \zeta \circ \pi,\ (\varsigma \times \iota) \circ (\zeta \times \iota)\rangle(2)$ in Σ_2.
2. Consider the following three sets of functions
   a. the set of all functions $f{:}W \to W$

b. the set of all total functions $f:W \to W$
c. the set of all 1-1 functions $f:W \to W$

Show that each set is closed under composition and combination. Which sets are closed under exponeniation? Repetition?

3. Let $f(x,y) = (x \times y, y)$. What is the value of $f^{\#}(1,3,4)$?

4. Let $f(x,y,z) = (x \dot{-} y,\ y,\ (((x+1) \dot{-} y) \dot{-} y) + 1)$. Let $g(x,y) = f^{\nabla}(x+y,y,0)$. What is the value of $g(x,y)$, for $y > 0$? What is the value of $g(x,0)$?

5. Give a function $f(x,y)$ which is not total, such that $g(x) = f^{\nabla}(x,y)$ is total.

6. Let $f:X \to Y$ be a total function. Prove that $f^{-1} \circ f$ is an equivalence relation on X.

1.8 Cardinality

Two sets A and B are said to have the same cardinality, written cd A = cd B, if there is a bijection $h:A \to B$. The cardinality of A is less than or equal to the cardinality of B, written cd $A \leq$ cd B if there is a 1-1 function $h:A \to B$ or equivalently a bijection $h:A \to C$, $C \subseteq B$. Also cd $A <$ cd B if cd $A \leq$ cd B and cd $A \neq$ cd B.

Example. If N is the set of natural numbers and $E \subseteq N$ is the set of even numbers, then cd E = cd N, because $h(x) = 2x$ is a bijection $h:N \to E$. Thus a set and one of its proper subsets may have the same cardinality. Indeed, this is a characteristic of all infinite sets.

The cardinality of a set is a measure of its size. For a finite set $A = \{a_1,\ldots,a_k\}$, cd A is k, the number of elements in A. The reader who is unfamiliar with these ideas will probably be surprised to discover that not all infinite (nonfinite) sets have the same cardinality. Of particular interest to us is the cardinality of the set of natural numbers. The notation $\aleph_0$ where $\aleph$ is the Hebrew letter "aleph" is commonly used to denote cd N. Hence a set has cardinality $\aleph_0$ if it can be put into 1-1 correspondence with the natural numbers. A set which is finite or has cardinality $\aleph_0$ is said to be *countable*. Note that a set A is countably infinite (countable and infinite) iff it can be written as a sequence $a_0, a_1, a_2, \ldots$; the required bijection is $h(a_i) = i \in N$. The sequence $a_0, a_1, \ldots$ is called an *enumeration* of A.

THEOREM 1.5. If A is finite, then cd $A < \aleph_0$. Also cd $\{a_1,\ldots,a_k\} <$ cd $\{b_1,\ldots,b_j\}$ if $k < j$.
Proof. Exercise 1. ▌

THEOREM 1.6. If cd $A \leq$ cd B and cd $B \leq$ cd A, then cd A = cd B.
Proof. Exercise 3. ▌

LEMMA 1.7. If a set $A \subseteq N$ is unbounded (for each x, there is a $y \in A$ such that $y > x$), then A is countably infinite.

Proof. Let a_0 be the smallest member of A. Such an a_0 exists because A is unbounded. Assume $a_0 < a_1 < \cdots < a_{n-1}$ are the n smallest members of A. Because A is unbounded,† there is a smallest $a_n > a_{n-1}$, $a_n \in A$. Continuing in this way we get a 1-1 correspondence between A and N so A is countable. ▮

THEOREM 1.8. If cd $A \leq \aleph_0$, then A is countable, that is, $\aleph_0$ is the smallest nonfinite cardinality.

Proof. Since cd $A \leq \aleph_0$ there is a 1-1 map $h: A \to N$. If $h(A)$ is unbounded, then cd $A = \aleph_0$ by Lemma 1.7. If $h(A) \subseteq \{0,\ldots,k-1\}$ for some k, then cd $A \leq k$. ▮

Example. The set $A = \{0,2,4,\ldots\}$ of even numbers is countable via the bijection $h: A \to N$, where $h(x) = x/2$.

Example. The set $A = \{(x,y) \mid x,y \in N\}$ is countable. To see this consider Figure 1-6. An enumeration of A is (0,0), (0,1), (1,0), (0,2), ….

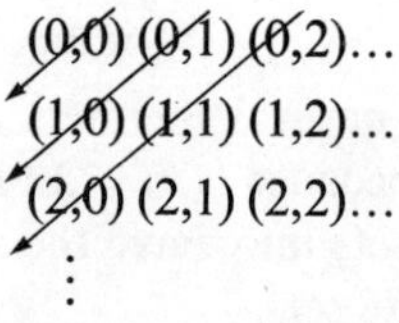

FIGURE 1-6. **Enumeration of** $\{(x,y) \mid x,y \in N\}$.

Example. There is a 1-1 correspondence between the set of positive rational numbers and a nonfinite subset of the set A of the previous example and so the set of rationals is countable by Theorem 1.8. The correspondence is given by $h(p/q) = (p,q)$.

Example. The set of words over a finite alphabet $\Sigma = \{a_1,\ldots,a_k\}$, that is, $W = \Sigma^*$ is countable where $h = v$, the bijection from Σ^* onto N defined in Section 1.4.

Example. The set of programs of any programming language is countable because for any language there is a finite Σ such that each program is in Σ^*. Since programs may be arbitrarily long, there are a nonfinite number of them. Hence by Theorem 1.8 and the previous example there are a countable number of programs.

A set A is said to be *uncountable* if cd $A > \aleph_0$. In 1874 Cantor invented a

† Also used is the fact that N is well-ordered by $\leq$, so that every nonempty subset of N has a smallest member.

new method, since called the *Cantor diagonal method*, to prove that there are uncountable sets. To illustrate this method let $A = \{f \mid f$ a total function, $f{:}N \to N\}$ (see Figure 1-7). Assume that A is countable, that is, that there is an enumeration $f_0, f_1, f_2, \ldots$ of A. Then define a new function $\bar{f}$ by

$$\bar{f}(x) = f_x(x) + 1 \qquad \text{for all } x$$

By construction $\bar{f} \notin \{f_i\} = A$. However $\bar{f}$ is total and $\bar{f}{:}N \to N$ which is a contradiction. Therefore A cannot be enumerated, that is, there is no 1-1 correspondence between A and N.

$$\begin{array}{llllll} f_0 & f_0(0) & f_0(1) & f_0(2) & f_0(3) & \cdots \\ f_1 & f_1(0) & f_1(1) & f_1(2) & f_1(3) & \cdots \\ f_2 & f_2(0) & f_2(1) & f_2(2) & f_2(3) & \cdots \\ f_3 & f_3(0) & f_3(1) & f_3(2) & f_3(3) & \cdots \\ & \vdots & & & & \end{array}$$

FIGURE 1-7. **The Cantor diagonal method.**

The function $\bar{f}$ is defined by consideration of the diagonal of Figure 1-7. For each x, $\bar{f}$ differs from f_x on input x. Hence $\bar{f}$ does not appear in the given enumeration and the set considered is uncountable since such an $\bar{f}$ exists for any chosen enumeration.

Another example of an uncountable set is the set $\{1,2\}^\omega$ of sequences of the form $a_0 a_1 a_2 \cdots$ where each $a_i \in \{1,2\}$. To prove this assume $\{1,2\}^\omega$ is countable and let $\alpha_0, \alpha_1, \alpha_2, \ldots$ be an enumeration of $\{1,2\}^\omega$ where

$$\alpha_i = a_{i0} a_{i1} a_{i2} \cdots \in \{1,2\}^\omega$$

Then define $\bar{\alpha} = \bar{a}_0 \bar{a}_1 \bar{a}_2 \cdots$ by

$$\bar{a}_j = 3 \mathbin{\dot{-}} a_{jj} = \begin{cases} 1 & \text{if } a_{jj} = 2 \\ 2 & \text{if } a_{jj} = 1 \end{cases}$$

Then $\bar{\alpha}$ differs from α_j at the jth place so the enumeration does not include $\bar{\alpha}$. Thus $\{1,2\}^\omega$ is not countable. Hence $\{1,2\}^*$, the set of finite words on $\{1,2\}$, is countable but $\{1,2\}^\omega$ is not countable.

A diagonal argument may be used to prove that there is no maximum cardinality. Let $P(S)$ be the set of all subsets of the set S, the *power set* of S. Our next theorem shows that cd $P(S) >$ cd (S) for any set S.

THEOREM 1.9. For any set S, cd $P(S) >$ cd S.

Proof. First note that cd $S \leq$ cd $P(S)$ via the 1-1 function $h{:}\ S \to P(S)$ given by $h(a) = \{a\}$. Suppose there is a bijection $g{:}S \to P(S)$. Let $S' \in P(S)$ be the set $\{a \in S \mid a \notin g(a)\}$. Then for no $b \in S$ is it the case that $g(b) = S'$ since such a b must satisfy $b \in S'$ iff $b \notin g(b) = S'$. Therefore g does not exist and cd $S \neq$ cd $P(S)$. ▮

The set S' of Theorem 1.9 is defined by "diagonalizing" over the set $\{g(a)\}$. For any $a \in S$, $S' \neq g(a)$ because $a \in S'$ iff $a \notin g(a)$.

Diagonal arguments are very important in the study of computability theory. In Section 2.3 we will consider a more sophisticated type of diagonalization.

EXERCISES

1. Prove Theorem 1.5.

2. If cd $A \leq$ cd B and cd $B \leq$ cd C, then cd $A \leq$ cd C.

3.[Δ] Prove that cd $A \leq$ cd B and cd $B \leq$ cd A imply that cd $A =$ cd B.

4. Prove that the following sets are countable.

a. $\{0,1,2,\ldots\} \cup \{-1,-2,-3,\ldots\}$
b. $\{(x,y,z) \mid x,y,z \in N\}$
c. $\bigcup_{n=1}^{\infty} \{(x_1,\ldots,x_n) \mid x_i \in N, 1 \leq i \leq n\}$
d. the set of all grammatically correct English sentences
e. the set of rational numbers
f. the set of rational numbers in the closed interval $[i, i+1]$, $i \in N$

5. Prove that the following sets are not countable.

a. $\{f \mid f\colon N \to \{0,1\}, f \text{ a total function}\}$
b. $\{f \mid f\colon N \to N\}$
c. $\{f \mid f\colon N \to N, f \text{ a bijection}\}$
d. the set of real numbers
e. the set of real numbers in any closed interval $[a, b]$, $a < b$, a, b real numbers

6. Prove that cd $P(N) =$ cd $\{f \mid f\colon N \to \{0,1\}, f \text{ total}\}$

7. Prove that the sets of Exercise 5 all have the same cardinality.

CHAPTER 2

An Algorithmic Language

Computer programming languages are algorithmic languages as described in Chapter 1. In this chapter we define a very simple programming language, called PL. In spite of its simplicity, many interesting features of the widely used programming languages can be implemented in PL. In fact, PL is computationally as powerful as any "real" programming language. By this we mean that any function $f: W^r \to W^s$ which can be computed by a computer program can also be computed by a PL program.

Many interesting problems are known to be algorithmically unsolvable. This chapter contains an informal proof that the halting problem for PL programs is unsolvable. That is, there is no effective procedure for deciding if an arbitrary PL program halts for an arbitrary input. The proof is informal because it makes use of a conjecture, called Church's thesis, to infer the existence of a certain PL program. Those familiar with programming techniques will have little difficulty understanding how such a program could be constructed. In Chapter 5, we give a more formal proof that the halting problem is undecidable.

2.1 The Language PL

In this section we define a simple algorithmic language, called PL for programming language. Examples illustrate its computing power, which will later be shown to be equivalent to that of the characterizations discussed in the previous chapter. This method of describing the effectively computable functions should be particularly appealing to those familiar with actual programming languages.

We use a slight modification of Backus–Naur form (BNF) notation to partially specify the syntactic features of PL. The BNF facilitates the definition and naming of subsets of Σ^* where Σ is a finite alphabet. Set names in BNF are of the form $\langle word \rangle$ where *word* is a member of $\{a,b,\ldots,z\}^+$. In the following let $\Sigma = \{A,B,C,D,+,1,2,3,4,5,6\}$. Then

$$\langle xyz \rangle = \text{A} \cup \text{BCD} \cup ++3\text{A} \cup 0$$

defines the set $\langle xyz \rangle$ whose members are the words A, BCD, ++3A, and 0. Names of sets can be used to define other sets. For example,

$$\langle a \rangle = \langle xyz \rangle \cup \langle xyz \rangle \langle xyz \rangle 2 + \langle b \rangle$$

defines a set whose members are either members of $\langle xyz \rangle$ or are formed by concatenating a member of $\langle xyz \rangle$ with a member of $\langle xyz \rangle$ (not necessarily the same member) with 2+ with a member of $\langle b \rangle$ (this definition and those following assume the associativity of concatenation).

Definitions can be recursive in the sense that a set name may be used in its own definition. The set $\langle ab \rangle$ defined by

$$\langle ab \rangle = \langle ab \rangle + 3 \cup 56$$

is equal to $56(+3)^* = \{56(+3)^n \mid n \geq 0\}$. In other words, a word in $\langle ab \rangle$ is either 56 or any word in $\langle ab \rangle$ followed by +3. Another example of a recursively defined set is

$$\langle e \rangle = \mathrm{A}\langle e \rangle \mathrm{B} \cup \mathrm{A}\langle e \rangle \mathrm{BB} \cup \mathrm{C} \cup 0$$

The set $\langle e \rangle$ contains all words of the form $\mathrm{A}^m\mathrm{CB}^n \cup \mathrm{A}^m\mathrm{B}^n$, with $0 \leq m$ and $m \leq n \leq 2m$. One must exercise care in using recursive definitions, to avoid defining the empty set as is the case with $\langle w \rangle$ given by

$$\langle w \rangle = \langle d \rangle \cup \langle w \rangle 4$$
$$\langle d \rangle = 53 \langle w \rangle$$

Before proceeding with a formal definition of PL, we present, without further explanation, a simple PL program which sets the variable V to Y + Z if W = 0 or X + Z if W ≠ 0.

Example.

```
       V ← 0;
       LOOP W;
           LOOP X;
               V ← V + 1;
           END;
           GOTO L;
       END;
       LOOP Y;
           V ← V + 1;
       END;
    L: LOOP Z;
           V ← V + 1;
       END;
```

The syntax of PL program names, both for variables and statement labels is given by

$$\langle \textit{letter} \rangle = \mathrm{A} \cup \mathrm{B} \cup \cdots \cup \mathrm{Z}$$

$$\langle \textit{digit} \rangle = 0 \cup 1 \cup \cdots \cup 9$$

$$\langle \textit{name} \rangle = \langle \textit{letter} \rangle \cup \langle \textit{name} \rangle \langle \textit{digit} \rangle \cup \langle \textit{name} \rangle \langle \textit{letter} \rangle$$

Hence any string of letters and digits beginning with a letter is a name. In the case of variables, the variable name will be used to denote both the variable and its value.

The remainder of the BNF specification for PL is given by:

$$\langle \textit{assignment} \rangle = \langle \textit{name} \rangle \leftarrow 0 \cup \langle \textit{name} \rangle \leftarrow \langle \textit{name} \rangle + 1 \cup \langle \textit{name} \rangle \leftarrow \langle \textit{name} \rangle$$

$$\langle \textit{instruction} \rangle = \langle \textit{assignment} \rangle \cup \mathrm{GOTO}\langle \textit{name} \rangle$$

$$\langle \textit{label instruction} \rangle = \langle \textit{name} \rangle{:}\langle \textit{instruction} \rangle; \cup \langle \textit{instruction} \rangle;$$

$$\langle \textit{loop} \rangle = \mathrm{LOOP}\langle \textit{name} \rangle; \cup \langle \textit{name} \rangle{:}\mathrm{LOOP}\langle \textit{name} \rangle;$$

$$\langle \textit{end} \rangle = \mathrm{END}; \cup \langle \textit{name} \rangle{:}\mathrm{END};$$

$$\langle \textit{program} \rangle = \langle \textit{label instruction} \rangle \cup \langle \textit{loop} \rangle \langle \textit{program} \rangle \langle \textit{end} \rangle \cup \langle \textit{program} \rangle \langle \textit{program} \rangle$$

A PL program is a word of syntactic type $\langle \textit{program} \rangle$, which may also be viewed as a sequence of *statements*, each ending with a semicolon. A statement is thus a word in $\langle \textit{label instruction} \rangle \cup \langle \textit{loop} \rangle \cup \langle \textit{end} \rangle$, but not all sequences of statements are programs, due to the fact that LOOP-END statements must occur properly paired. A program is a labeled instruction, or a LOOP statement followed by a program followed by an END statement, or the concatenation of two programs.

In order to understand the computation that is specified by a PL program, it is convenient to think of each occurrence of syntactic type $\langle \textit{name} \rangle$ within an instruction as a variable whose value is stored in a memory area using words in some fixed alphabet. In many cases, the particular alphabet used will not be relevant. Throughout this chapter and in most of Chapter 3, the reader will experience no difficulty by ignoring the representation and considering the values of all variables to be natural numbers.

At the beginning of each program, all variables have the value 0. There are two types of statements, assignment and sequencing. There are three assignment statements: set a variable to 0, set a variable to the value of a second variable, and set a variable to the value of another variable plus 1. The same variable may appear on the right and left sides of an assignment statement. The variable on the right side is modified only if it also appears on the left side. Examples of assignment statements are:

```
XW4 ← XW3;
ABC ← 0;
XR2 ← XR2 + 1;
```

PL statements are normally executed in the order in which they appear in the program. This order of execution may be modified by the sequencing statements.

The LOOP and END statements provide for the repetitive execution of groups of statements. As indicated in the syntax specifications each LOOP is paired with an associated END. The variable named in the LOOP statement is called the LOOP *variable*. The group of instructions following the LOOP, including its associated END, is called the *scope* of the LOOP. When a LOOP statement is encountered, the value of the LOOP variable specifies the number of times the group of statements in the scope of the LOOP is to be executed. This could be implemented by copying the value of the LOOP variable into a special register which is decremented by 1 each time the END statement is reached. When this register becomes 0, the statement following the scope is executed. Note that the above process does *not* change the value of the LOOP variable. The value of a variable may only be changed by the execution of an assignment statement. For example,

```
LOOP  X;
        X ← X + 1;
END;
```

results in the doubling of the value of the variable X.

There are no restrictions on uses of the LOOP variable within the scope of the LOOP and changing the value of the LOOP variable within the LOOP does not affect the number of times the scope is executed, since a special register is used for counting that number. Indeed any PL program may occur between a LOOP statement and its associated END statement, including another LOOP statement using the same variable.

Another example using LOOP statements to compute Z ← X × Y is given by

```
Z ← 0;
LOOP Y;
    LOOP  X;
            Z ← Z + 1;
    END;
END;
```

The GOTO statement transfers control to the statement whose label is referenced by the GOTO. In order to provide an interpretation for each syntactically correct program, we adopt the following conventions:

1. If there are two or more identical labels, a GOTO will transfer control to the first one in the program.
2. A transfer to a nonexistent label halts execution.
3. A transfer to a statement within the scope of a LOOP statement from outside the scope of the LOOP statement is made to the outermost LOOP statement whose scope includes the referenced statement but not the GOTO statement itself.

A program *halts* or *stops* after executing the last statement (if not a GOTO) or by executing a transfer to a nonexistent label.

Throughout the preceding discussion we implicitly assume the existence of a device which interprets and executes the statements of a PL program. A good model for such a device is a stored program digital computer with a random access memory. PL variable names may then be considered to name locations in the memory of the computer. The control section of the computer executes program statements in the proper order, modifying variable values when necessary. PL statements may also be stored in the computer's memory though the restriction that statement labels may only be referenced by GOTO statements means that the programs may not modify themselves. We assume the existence of an unlimited number of special registers for implementing LOOP statements. Note that many implementations of computer languages restrict the depth of nesting of loops to coincide with the availability of special hardware registers.

The full expressive power of PL is not exploited in the preceding simple examples. In particular the GOTO statement is not essential (see Exercise 3). In fact, it is probably the case that any computer program which solves a practical problem can be recoded in PL without the GOTO, which means that labels are also not necessary. This rather ambitious claim will be discussed in Chapter 10.

EXERCISES

1. For $x = \sigma_1\sigma_2 \cdots \sigma_k \in \Sigma^*$, $\rho(x)$, the reversal of x, equals $\sigma_k \cdots \sigma_2\sigma_1$. Give a BNF definition of $\{x \cdot \rho(x) \mid x \in \Sigma^*\}$. Informally explain why this is not possible for $\{x \cdot x \mid x \in \Sigma^*\}$.

2. Give a BNF definition for ⟨*arith-exp*⟩, the set of fully parenthesized arithmetic expressions which can be formed using variable names, the arithmetic operators $+$, $\times$, $/$, $-$ (unary and binary), and parentheses (and). Examples of members of ⟨*arith-exp*⟩ are Y, $((X + Y) \times Z)$, and $(((Z/Y4) + Y)/(A + B))$.

3. Show that there is a program which does not contain a GOTO statement which sets V to Y + Z if W = 0, or X + Z if W ≠ 0.

4. Give an algorithm for deciding whether an arbitrary BNF definition defines a nonempty set.

5.[Δ] Give an algorithm for deciding whether an arbitrary BNF definition defines an infinite set.

2.2 PL-Computable Functions

In this section we investigate the computational power of PL. The class of functions computed by PL programs is shown to include various common number theoretic functions. In addition, we indicate how other features of programming languages may be coded in terms of PL statements, thus providing evidence for our claim that PL is computationally as powerful as any real computer language.

The PL program $\mathcal{I}$ *computes the function* $f: W^r \to W^s$, if when started with $x_1, \ldots, x_r$ as the values of the variables X1, ..., Xr and with all other program variables initially 0

1. $\mathcal{I}$ halts with $y_1, \ldots, y_s$ as the values of the variables Y1, ..., Ys, respectively, if $(x_1,\ldots,x_r) \in \operatorname{dom} f$ and $f(x_1,\ldots,x_r) = (y_1,\ldots,y_s)$ or
2. $\mathcal{I}$ never halts if $f(x_1,\ldots,x_r)$ is undefined.

X1, ..., Xr and Y1, ..., Ys are called the *input variables* and *output variables*, respectively. If there is a $\mathcal{I}$ which computes f, then f is said to be *PL-computable.*

According to the definition given, each PL program computes a different function $f: W^r \to W^s$, for each r, $s \geq 0$. There is no requirement that the variables X1, ..., Xr and Y1, ..., Ys actually appear in the program, since there is the convention that each variable, except the input variables X1, ..., Xr, is initially 0.

Example. The PL program

$$\text{Y2} \leftarrow \text{X1};$$
$$\text{Y3} \leftarrow \text{Y3} + 1;$$
$$\text{Y4} \leftarrow \text{X2};$$

computes each function shown in Table 2-1.

We have adopted the point of view that input and output operations are not a part of the computation specified by a PL program. Of course, it would be easy to require that each PL program begin with a statement

INPUT X1, ..., Xr;

TABLE 2-1. Selected Functions Computed by a PL Program.

r	s	$f: W^r \to W^s$
0	0	$f() = ()$
1	2	$f(x_1) = (0,x_1)$
1	3	$f(x_1) = (0,x_1,1)$
1	4	$f(x_1) = (0,x_1,1,0)$
2	3	$f(x_1,x_2) = (0,x_1,1)$
2	4	$f(x_1,x_2) = (0,x_1 1,x_2)$
2	5	$f(x_1,x_2) = (0,x_1,1,x_2,0)$
4	7	$f(x_1,x_2,x_3,x_4) = (0,x_1,1,x_2,0,0,0)$

and end with a statement

OUTPUT Y1, ..., Ys;

but having no input/output statements in PL programs makes them more like other methods used in Chapters 4 and 5 to specify procedures.

If $\mathcal{T}$ computes $f: W^r \to W^s$, then $\mathcal{T}$ is *defined* on $x_1, \ldots, x_r$ if $(x_1,\ldots,x_r) \in \text{dom} f$, that is, $f(x_1,\ldots,x_r)$ is defined. Otherwise $\mathcal{T}$ is *undefined* on $(x_1,\ldots,x_r)$. If for a fixed r and s, a PL program $\mathcal{T}$ halts on all possible input values, then it computes a total function and $\mathcal{T}$ is an algorithm. All PL programs are effective procedures. Every PL-computable function is effectively computable in the intuitive sense of Section 1.1. We believe that this statement and its converse are true; however, because of its informal nature, it is impossible to give a mathematical proof of its correctness. We instead will try to provide motivation for this hypothesis by proving the equivalence, with respect to computational power, of several very different methods for describing the effectively computable functions. Further discussion along these lines may be found in Section 2.3.

Most computability theory texts study functions which take r-tuples of inputs into a single output. Throughout this book we shall consider functions whose outputs are s-tuples. We adopt this convention because computer programs may easily be and commonly are used to compute functions with more than one output. Hence, in this case a restriction to one variable is somewhat artificial and indeed complicates proofs of the equivalence of programming languages to other systems for specifying algorithms. Although one can code s-output functions as single-output functions, as will be seen in Sections 3.8 and 3.9, the present convention simplifies the notation and should be more appealing to those readers who are familiar with programming concepts.

THEOREM 2.1. The functions π, ι, ζ, and ς defined in Section 1.6 are PL-computable.

Proof. a. The function $\pi: W \to W^0$, where $\pi(x) = ()$, is computed by X1 ← 0;

b. The function $\varsigma: W \to W$, where $\varsigma(x) = x + 1$ is computed by Y1 ← X1 + 1;

The remaining parts, $\zeta() = 0$ and $\iota(x) = x$ are left as an exercise. ▮

It is convenient to be able to abbreviate a sequence of PL program statements that might be used often. To illustrate, the statements given previously which double the value of the variable X could be abbreviated

$$X \leftarrow 2 \times X;$$

and statements which multiply the values of X and Y and assign the result to Z could be abbreviated

$$Z \leftarrow X \times Y;$$

In general, once a function $f: W^r \to W^s$ has been shown to be PL-computable it is possible to construct a sequence of PL statements that will calculate the function f applied to the values of the variables $U_1, \ldots, U_r$, assign the calculated values of f to the variables $V_1, \ldots, V_s$, and then proceed to the next statement. This sequence of statements will be represented by

$$(V_1, \ldots, V_s) \leftarrow f(U_1, \ldots, U_r);$$

which should not be interpreted as an exact abbreviation of a program that computes f, as previously defined, but one which has been appropriately modified to use input/output variables $U_1, \ldots, U_r, V_1, \ldots, V_s$, not necessarily all distinct, and to give control to the next statement after the function has been calculated, unless f is undefined on $(U_1, \ldots, U_r)$, in which case control will never pass to the next program statement. Also assume that, except for $U_1, \ldots, U_r, V_1, \ldots, V_s$, the variables used do not appear elsewhere in the program.

Notice that if it is assumed that the variables X, Y, and Z are all distinct in the following example, then some of the programs would be made a little shorter.

Also note that the value of each variable on the right side of the abbreviating expression remains unchanged unless it is also the variable on the left side.

Examples.

a.
```
Z ← X + Y;
    V ← Y;
    LOOP X;
        V ← V + 1;
    END;
    Z ← V;
```

b. $Y \leftarrow X \dot{-} 1;$ where $X \dot{-} 1 = \begin{cases} X-1 & \text{if } X \geq 1 \\ 0 & \text{if } X = 0 \end{cases}$

```
Z ← 0;
LOOP X;
    V ← Z;
    Z ← Z + 1;
END;
Y ← V;
```

c. $Z \leftarrow X \dot{-} Y;$ where $X \dot{-} Y = \begin{cases} X - Y & \text{if } X \geq Y \\ 0 & \text{otherwise} \end{cases}$

```
V ← X;
LOOP Y;
    V ← V ∸ 1;
END;
Z ← V;
```

d. $X \leftarrow 3;$

```
X ← 0;
X ← X + 1;
X ← X + 1;
X ← X + 1;
```

e. $Y \leftarrow \neg X;$ where $\neg X = \begin{cases} 1 & \text{if } X = 0 \\ 0 & \text{if } X > 0 \end{cases}$

```
V ← 1;
LOOP X;
    V ← 0;
END;
Y ← V;
```

f. $Z \leftarrow X \leq Y;$ where $X \leq Y = \begin{cases} 1 & \text{if } X \leq Y \\ 0 & \text{if } X > Y \end{cases}$

```
Z ← X ∸ Y;
Z ← ¬Z;
```

g. $Z \leftarrow X \vee Y;$ where $X \vee Y = \begin{cases} 1 & \text{if } X > 0 \text{ or } Y > 0 \\ 0 & \text{if } X = 0 \text{ and } Y = 0 \end{cases}$

```
Z ← X + Y;
LOOP Z;
    Z ← 1;
END;
```

Recall that we are assuming that auxiliary variables, such as the variables V and Z in Example b, do not appear anywhere else in the program.

Similarly, other "arithmetic" operations such as × and /; other "relational" operations such as =, ≠, <, ≥, and >; and "logical" operations ∧ (and), and ⊃ (implies) can be computed without using the GOTO statement (see Exercises 2 and 3). Notice that we treat 0 as the logical value "false" and values greater than 0 as "true". The implementations of the IF and WHILE statements discussed later in this section provide further examples of this convention.

PL programs compute functions which map r-tuples of words in W into s-tuples of words in W, that is, functions $f: W^r \to W^s$ where $W = \Sigma^*$. The alphabet depends on the characteristics of the memory in which program variables are stored. Some functions, such as addition and multiplication, are computed by the same PL programs regardless of the alphabet chosen. Indeed this is true of all functions which are essentially numerical in nature. For this reason, languages such as PL are often said to be *machine* or *representation independent*. FORTRAN, ALGOL, and other so-called higher level computer languages are also of this type. Some functions require different PL programs for different alphabets. For example, $y = x_1 \cdot x_2$, the concatenation of x_1 and x_2, is not computed by the same PL program in Σ_2 and Σ_3 since concatenation equals $x_1 \times 2^{\text{length}(x_2)} + x_2$ in Σ_2 and $x_1 \times 3^{\text{length}(x_2)} + x_2$ in Σ_3.

The bijection $\nu: W \to N$, defined in Section 1.4, provides a 1-1 correspondence between functions on W and functions on N. That is, $\bar{f}: N \to N$ corresponds to $f: W \to W$ given by $f = \nu^{-1} \circ \bar{f} \circ \nu$. The statements above can be interpreted as meaning that for each $\bar{f}: N \to N$, there is a program which computes $\nu^{-1} \circ \bar{f} \circ \nu$, regardless of the alphabet Σ.

The next theorem deals with closure properties of the PL-computable functions. The operations of composition, combination, exponentiation, and repetition were defined in Section 1.7.

THEOREM 2.2. The composition, combination, exponentiation, and repetition of PL-computable functions are PL-computable.

Proof. a. Let $g: W^r \to W^s$ and $f: W^s \to W^t$ be PL-computable. The composition $f \circ g: W^r \to W^t$ is computed by

(Z1,...,Zs) ← g(X1,...,Xr);
(Y1,...,Yt) ← f(Z1,...,Zs);

b. Let $f: W^r \to W^s$ and $g: W^t \to W^u$ be PL-computable. The combination $(f \times g): W^{r+t} \to W^{s+u}$ is computed by

(Y1,...,Ys) ← f(X1,...,Xr);
(Y($s+1$),...,Y($s+u$)) ← g(X($r+1$),...,X($r+t$));

c. Let $f: W^r \to W^r$ be PL-computable. The exponentiation $f^{\#}: W^{r+1} \to W^r$ is computed by

```
LOOP X(r + 1);
(X1,...,Xr) ← f(X1,...,Xr);
END;
(Y1,...,Yr) ← (X1,...,Xr);
```

d. Repetition is left as an exercise. ▌

PL is not a very convenient programming language. The reason for defining PL to be such a simple language is to facilitate proofs of its equivalence to other formalisms for specifying algorithms; we will show, for example, that all PL-computable functions are partial recursive and computable by a Markov algorithm. To illustrate that the computational power of PL is not restricted, we will now show how some features usually found in programming languages can be implemented in PL. In all cases, these new statements and features should be regarded as abbreviations for the corresponding PL statements.

The Examples a–g illustrate how some fairly complicated computations may be made. It is certainly possible to abbreviate several computational steps by using an arbitrary expression on the right side of an assignment statement. For example

```
Z ← (X × Y) + (2 × Z);
```

is an abbreviation for

```
V1 ← X × Y;
V2 ← 2 × Z;
 Z ← V1 + V2;
```

and

```
CHECK ← (X > Y) ∧ (Z > 0);
```

is an abbreviation for

```
V1 ← (X > Y);
V2 ← 0;
V3 ← (Z > V2);
CHECK ← (V1 ∧ V3);
```

These expressions could also appear in place of a variable name in a LOOP statement, so that

```
LOOP (X + Y);
```

is an abbreviation for

```
Z ← (X + Y);
LOOP Z;
```

One of the main inconveniences of PL involves the artificial methods which must be used to conditionally branch, depending on the result of a test. If a programmer wishes to have control transferred to L1 if $X \leq Y$ and to L2 if $X > Y$, he must write

```
LOOP (X ≤ Y);
GOTO L1;
END;
GOTO L2;
```

A more useful method of conditional branching is provided by some kind of IF statement, such as

```
IF (X ≤ Y) THEN; GOTO L1; END;
           ELSE; GOTO L2; END;
```

Another example using an IF statement is a computation which sets M to the largest of the variables A, B, and C as follows:

```
IF ((A ≥ B) ∧ (A ≥ C)) THEN; M ← A; END;
ELSE;
IF ((B ≥ A) ∧ (B ≥ C)) THEN; M ← B; END;
ELSE; M ← C ; END;
END;
```

In general, if $\mathcal{T}_1$ and $\mathcal{T}_2$ are arbitrary PL programs, and $\mathcal{E}$ is any expression, then

$$\begin{aligned}&\text{IF } \mathcal{E} \text{ THEN; } \mathcal{T}_1 \text{ END;}\\ &\qquad\text{ELSE; } \mathcal{T}_2 \text{ END;}\end{aligned}$$

may be implemented in PL as

$$\begin{aligned}&V \leftarrow \neg\,\mathcal{E};\\ &\text{LOOP } V;\ \mathcal{T}_2 \text{ END;}\\ &V \leftarrow \neg V;\\ &\text{LOOP } V;\ \mathcal{T}_1 \text{ END;}\end{aligned}$$

Notice that the IF statement may be implemented without using the GOTO statement, though, of course, a GOTO statement may be a part of $\mathcal{T}_1$ or $\mathcal{T}_2$.

Another useful programming operation is to repeatedly execute a group of statements until some specified condition is met. An example is

```
Y ← X;
WHILE ((Y × Y) > X);
    Y ← ((Y + (X/Y))/2);
END;
```

which assigns to Y the integer part of $\sqrt{X}$. The symbol / denotes integer division in which the remainder is ignored.

The scope of a WHILE statement is analogous to the scope of a LOOP statement. Before the scope of the WHILE statement is executed, the value of the expression in the WHILE statement is checked. If it is 0, control is given to the first statement after the matching END. If the expression is not 0, the scope of the WHILE is executed and the value of the expression is checked again. Thus, in contrast to the LOOP statement, changes in the value of the WHILE expression do affect the number of times the scope of the WHILE is executed. It is quite possible that the execution of a WHILE loop will never terminate, as shown by the following program:

```
X ← 1;
WHILE X;
    X ← X + 1;
END;
```

The WHILE statement may be implemented in PL by replacing

$$\text{WHILE } \mathcal{E};\ \mathcal{S}\ \text{END};$$

with

$$\text{LOOP: IF } \mathcal{E}\ \text{THEN};\ \mathcal{S}\ \text{GOTO LOOP; END};$$

where LOOP is a label not used elsewhere in the program.

One other convenience is the STOP statement which may be considered to be an abbreviation of

```
GOTO STOP;
```

where the statement

```
STOP: STOP ← STOP;
```

is added at the end of the program.

By means of the examples given, the reader should be convinced that the following "extended" version of PL. while more convenient for expressing effective procedures, computes exactly the same class of functions as the PL programs.

$$
\begin{aligned}
\langle \textit{letter} \rangle &= \mathrm{A} \cup \mathrm{B} \cup \cdots \cup \mathrm{Z} \\
\langle \textit{digit} \rangle &= 0 \cup 1 \cup \cdots \cup 9 \\
\langle \textit{name} \rangle &= \langle \textit{letter} \rangle \cup \langle \textit{name} \rangle\langle \textit{digit} \rangle \cup \langle \textit{name} \rangle\langle \textit{letter} \rangle \\
\langle \textit{numeral} \rangle &= \langle \textit{digit} \rangle \cup \langle \textit{numeral} \rangle\langle \textit{digit} \rangle \\
\langle \textit{operation} \rangle &= + \cup \dot{-} \cup \times \cup / \cup = \cup \neq \cup > \cup \geq \cup < \cup \leq \cup \vee \cup \wedge \\
\langle \textit{expression} \rangle &= \langle \textit{name} \rangle \cup \langle \textit{numeral} \rangle \cup (\neg \langle \textit{expression} \rangle) \\
&\quad \cup (\langle \textit{expression} \rangle\langle \textit{operation} \rangle\langle \textit{expression} \rangle) \\
\langle \textit{assignment} \rangle &= \langle \textit{name} \rangle \leftarrow \langle \textit{expression} \rangle \\
\langle \textit{instruction} \rangle &= \langle \textit{assignment} \rangle \cup \mathrm{GOTO}\langle \textit{name} \rangle \cup \mathrm{STOP} \\
\langle \textit{label instruction} \rangle &= \langle \textit{name} \rangle{:}\langle \textit{instruction} \rangle; \cup \langle \textit{instruction} \rangle; \\
\langle \textit{loop} \rangle &= \mathrm{LOOP}\ \langle \textit{expression} \rangle; \cup \langle \textit{name} \rangle{:}\mathrm{LOOP}\langle \textit{expression} \rangle; \\
\langle \textit{if-then} \rangle &= \mathrm{IF}\ \langle \textit{expression} \rangle\ \mathrm{THEN}; \cup \langle \textit{name} \rangle{:}\mathrm{IF}\langle \textit{expression} \rangle \\
&\quad \mathrm{THEN}; \\
\langle \textit{while} \rangle &= \mathrm{WHILE}\ \langle \textit{expression} \rangle; \cup \langle \textit{name} \rangle{:}\mathrm{WHILE}\ \langle \textit{expression} \rangle; \\
\langle \textit{end} \rangle &= \mathrm{END}; \cup \langle \textit{name} \rangle{:}\mathrm{END}; \\
\langle \textit{program} \rangle &= \langle \textit{label instruction} \rangle \cup \\
&\quad \langle \textit{loop} \rangle\langle \textit{program} \rangle\langle \textit{end} \rangle \cup \\
&\quad \langle \textit{while} \rangle\langle \textit{program} \rangle\langle \textit{end} \rangle \cup \\
&\quad \langle \textit{if-then} \rangle\langle \textit{program} \rangle\langle \textit{end} \rangle \cup \\
&\quad \langle \textit{if-then} \rangle\langle \textit{program} \rangle\langle \textit{end} \rangle\ \mathrm{ELSE};\ \langle \textit{program} \rangle\langle \textit{end} \rangle \\
&\quad \cup \langle \textit{program} \rangle\langle \textit{program} \rangle
\end{aligned}
$$

Even this extended version of PL lacks many of the features of a good programming language. These features include subscripted variables, subroutines, more general LOOP statements, and facilities to handle character-oriented operations and special data structures, such as lists and trees. Some of these features are explored in the exercises and some will be discussed in later chapters.

Many professional programmers feel that programs containing GOTO statements are difficult to debug and difficult to modify. They prefer instead to control statement sequencing by using LOOP, IF, and WHILE statements, which more easily indicate the structure of a program. We have already demonstrated how to implement the WHILE statement in PL. It is also possible to prove that all GOTO and LOOP statements may be replaced by the use of WHILE statements (see Exercises 11–13, which contain some hints). There is no need for labels if there are no GOTO statements and it is possible to prove that the following programming language, which uses a restricted type of WHILE statement, has the same computational power as PL. This can be done by establishing the connection with the partial recursive functions (see Exercise 8 of Section 3.1), later shown to be equal to the PL-computable functions.

The BNF definition of ⟨*letter*⟩, ⟨*digit*⟩, ⟨*name*⟩, and ⟨*assignment*⟩ are as in the original definition of PL.

⟨*program*⟩ = ⟨*assignment*⟩;
  ∪ LOOP ⟨*name*⟩; ⟨*program*⟩ END;
  ∪ WHILE ⟨*name*⟩; ⟨*program*⟩ END;

The reader should compare this result with that of Exercises 12 and 13, where a more general WHILE statement permits the elimination of the LOOP statement.

It is interesting to determine the effect on computational power if certain programming features are added or deleted. The notation PL + {features} and PL − {features} will be used to denote the language obtained from PL by respectively adding to PL or removing from PL the named features. For example, we have already shown that PL + {IF} + {WHILE} is equivalent to PL. Since the IF statement was implemented without using the GOTO statement, PL − {GOTO} + {IF} is equivalent to PL − {GOTO}. On the other hand, while one can define the LOOP statement in PL − {LOOP} + {IF} (Exercise 9), this is not possible in PL − {LOOP, GOTO} + {IF} because in order to execute a LOOP statement one must be able to branch to the beginning of the scope of the loop.

EXERCISES

1. Complete the proof of Theorem 2.1 by showing that $\zeta() = 0$ and $\iota(x) = x$ are PL-computable.

2. Show that the function

$$\mathrm{sign}(x) = \begin{cases} 1 & \text{if } x > 0 \\ 0 & \text{if } x = 0 \end{cases}$$

is PL-computable.

3. Show that the following computations may be performed in PL without using a GOTO statement:

a. Z ← X × Y;   multiplication

b. Z ← X/Y;   integer division with X/0 = 0

c. Z ← X = Y;   where $X = Y$ is $\begin{cases} 1 & \text{if } X = Y \\ 0 & \text{if } X \neq Y \end{cases}$

d. Z ← X ≠ Y;

e. $Z \leftarrow X < Y$;

f. $Z \leftarrow X \geq Y$;

g. $Z \leftarrow X > Y$;

h. $Z \leftarrow X \wedge Y$; where $X \wedge Y = \begin{cases} 1 & \text{if } X > 0 \text{ and } Y > 0 \\ 0 & \text{if } X = Y = 0 \end{cases}$

i. $Z \leftarrow X \supset Y$; where $X \supset Y = \begin{cases} 1 & \text{if } X = 0 \text{ or } Y > 0 \\ 0 & \text{if } X > 0 \text{ and } Y = 0 \end{cases}$

4. Write PL programs to compute the following functions:

a. $f(x) = 2^x$

b. $f(x,y) = 2^{2^{\cdot^{\cdot^{2^x}}}}\Big\}y$ that is, $f(x,0) = x$, $f(x, y+1) = 2^{f(x,y)}$

c. $f(x) = \begin{cases} 1 & \text{if } x \text{ is a prime number} \geq 2 \\ 0 & \text{otherwise} \end{cases}$

d. $f(x,y) =$ (xth prime number, yth prime number) where 2 is the zeroth prime number

5. Complete the proof of Theorem 2.2 by showing that the repetition of a PL-computable function is PL-computable.

6. Suppose program $\mathcal{T}$ computes $f: W^r \rightarrow W^s$. Explain how to modify $\mathcal{T}$ to get a sequence of statements to replace

$$(V_1, \ldots, V_s) \leftarrow f(U_1, \ldots, U_r);$$

where $V_1, \ldots, V_s, U_1, \ldots, U_r$ are arbitrary PL variables.

7. Consider the statements

$$\text{FOR X} = 5 \text{ STEP 2 TO 10; } \mathcal{T} \text{ END;}$$

which successively executes program $\mathcal{T}$ with X having values 5, 7, 9 and then transfers control to the next statement. Give a BNF definition for the FOR statement and a PL implementation of it. Also consider the case where arbitrary arithmetic expressions are permitted in place of the numerals. What problems must be dealt with in this case?

8. Give a BNF definition of a PL version of the FORTRAN DO statement (that is using PL labels) and show how it may be implemented in PL. Indicate those syntactic features which cannot be described in BNF.

9. Show that the LOOP statement can be implemented in PL − {LOOP} + {IF}, where the IF statement is of the form

$$\text{IF X} = \text{Y THEN; } \mathcal{T} \text{ END;}$$

10. An occurrence of a GOTO statement is said to be a *forward jump* in case the named statement occurs after the GOTO in the program, otherwise the occurrence of the GOTO is a *backward jump*. Show that forward jumps can be implemented in PL − {GOTO}.

11.$^{\Delta}$ Prove that each function computed by a PL program is computed by a PL program containing at most one occurrence of the GOTO statement.

12. a. Show that the function $X \dot{-} 1$ can be implemented in PL − {LOOP, GOTO} + {WHILE} where the WHILE statement has the form

$$\text{WHILE } X \neq Y;\ \mathcal{T}\ \text{END};$$

b. Show that the LOOP statement can be implemented in PL − {LOOP, GOTO} + {WHILE}, even if only the restricted form of the WHILE statement given in part a is permitted.

13. Prove that PL − {LOOP,GOTO} + {WHILE} is equivalent to PL.
Hint: Use the result of Exercise 11, replace the single GOTO with a WHILE statement, and use Exercise 12 to eliminate LOOP statements.

14. Show that the only assignment statements necessary in PL are $V \leftarrow 0$; and $V \leftarrow V + 1$; where V is a variable.

2.3 Church's Thesis and an Undecidable Problem

A function $f: W^r \to W^s$ is *effectively computable* if there is an effective procedure (also called a *program*) which, given $(x_1,\ldots,x_r) \in W^r$, eventually halts and outputs $f(x_1,\ldots,x_r)$ in case $(x_1,\ldots,x_r) \in \text{dom}\, f$, and never halts otherwise.

Algorithmic languages, as discussed in Chapter 1, are formal systems for characterizing the effectively computable functions. In this chapter we have considered a simple algorithmic language. Additional examples will be studied in later chapters. The main result will be that all of these systems are equivalent; that is, a function may be described in one system iff it is describable in all of them. This rather startling result has led to the general acceptance of a conjecture, usually called *Church's thesis* because it was first proposed by Church [1936a], to the effect that a *total* function is effectively computable iff it is PL-computable (recursive, Markov-algorithm-computable, etc.). Of course the notion of effective computability is not mathematical in nature and hence Church's thesis can never be proved. One of our reasons for proving the equivalence of several different algorithmic languages is to provide evidence for accepting Church's thesis. Each of these languages was designed to capture the intuitive meaning of effectiveness. However, despite the extreme differences in approach, the languages are equivalent. Furthermore no one has been able to obtain an algorithmic language capable of defining a non-PL-computable effectively computable function. Indeed many attempts have resulted in systems less powerful than those mentioned above.

A natural generalization of Church's thesis, which originally dealt only with total functions, is that a function is PL-computable iff it is effectively computable. Throughout this book we will use the term *Church's thesis* to apply to this more general proposition.

We shall occasionally use Church's thesis to infer the PL-computability of functions or procedures for which intuitively effective computation procedures have been described. This will simplify the proofs and render them somewhat more readable. Such applications of Church's thesis can be replaced by a formal definition of a PL program for computing the required function. The reader should interpret these uses of Church's thesis merely as a labor-saving device and not as an essential element of the proofs. In Chapter 5 we will formally show how to construct the required PL programs.

By definition, a set S is countable if there *exists* a 1-1 correspondence between S and the natural numbers or, equivalently, the set W (see Section 1.8). Hence if S is countable, there is an enumeration a_0, a_1, a_2, ... of S. This *does not* necessarily mean that it is possible to *effectively enumerate* the set S, that is, there need not exist an effective enumeration procedure which successively generates members of S in such a way that each member of S is eventually generated. Later in this section we give an example of a countable set which cannot be effectively enumerated. A cardinality argument that such a set exists goes as follows: There are only a countable number of effective procedures for enumerating sets. Hence only a countable number of sets may be effectively enumerated. However, there are an uncountable number of subsets of W, so there are enumerable subsets of W which cannot be effectively enumerated. This distinction between enumerability and effective enumerability is extremely important.

The next theorem illustrates the use of Church's thesis. The proof involves an effective enumeration of a subset of the PL programs.

THEOREM 2.3. There is a PL-computable total function that is not PL − {GOTO}-computable.

Proof. Let $\mathcal{T}_0$, $\mathcal{T}_1$, ... be an effective enumeration of all PL − {GOTO} programs The enumeration may be done effectively by first listing all required one-symbol programs, then all required two-symbol programs, and so on. At the nth stage list all words of length n which are syntactically correct PL − {GOTO} programs. Every PL − {GOTO} program will be listed by this procedure because there are only a finite number of program symbols. The procedure is effective because we can effectively decide if a given word is a syntactically correct PL − {GOTO} program.

Let $f_i: W \to W$ be the function with one input and one output computed by $\mathcal{T}_i$.

Define $\bar{f}$ by

$$\bar{f}(x) = f_x(x) + 1$$

where $\bar{f}$ is effectively computable as follows. Given input x, obtain $\mathcal{T}_x$ and execute it with x as the initial value of X1; $\mathcal{T}_x$ eventually stops because it does not contain any GOTO statements. The value of Y1 will be $f_x(x)$. Add one to the result to obtain $\bar{f}(x)$.

Since $\bar{f}$ is effectively computable, it is PL-computable by Church's thesis. However $\bar{f}$ is not PL – {GOTO}-computable because by the construction, for each x, $\bar{f}(x) \neq f_x(x)$ and $\{f_x\}$ contains every single-input, single-output function computed by a PL – {GOTO} program. ▮

The proof of Theorem 2.3 illustrates two important proof techniques, the use of Church's thesis and the Cantor diagonal method. The diagonal method was used to construct the function $\bar{f}$ and Church's thesis was used to infer that the effectively computable function $\bar{f}$ can be computed by a PL program.

Some proofs using the diagonal method were given in Section 1.8. Diagonal constructions are often of the form:

> Let $g_0, g_1, g_2, \ldots$ be an enumeration of (definitions of) functions. Define a function $\bar{g}$ such that $\bar{g} \notin \{g_x\}$ by forcing $\bar{g}$ to differ from each g_x on argument x in some desired manner.

The function $\bar{g}$ is defined by considering the diagonal $g_0(0), g_1(1), g_2(2), \ldots$ (see Figure 2-1). The specific scheme used to define $\bar{g}$ will depend on the properties which $\bar{g}$ is to have

$g_0(0)$	$g_0(1)$	$g_0(2)$	$g_0(3) \ldots$
$g_1(0)$	$g_1(1)$	$g_1(2)$	$g_1(3) \ldots$
$g_2(0)$	$g_2(1)$	$g_2(2)$	$g_2(3) \ldots$
$g_3(0)$	$g_3(1)$	$g_3(2)$	$g_3(3) \ldots$
$\vdots$			

FIGURE 2-1. **List of functions $g_0, g_1, \ldots$.**

In order to infer the effective computability of a function $\bar{g}$ obtained from $\{g_x\}$ by a diagonal argument, two conditions must be satisfied. First, the listing must be effective, which means that the process of enumerating definitions $d_0, d_1, d_2, \ldots$ of $g_0, g_1, g_2, \ldots$ is effective. Second, $g_x(x)$ must be effectively computable from x and its definition d_x. These effectiveness conditions are satisfied in the proof of Theorem 2.3 where the function definitions $\mathcal{P}_0, \mathcal{P}_1, \ldots$ are PL – {GOTO} programs. The PL – {GOTO} programs may be effectively enumerated by the method described in the proof of Theorem 2.3. Moreover, PL – {GOTO} programs halt for all inputs so the output $f_x(x)$ of the xth program on input x can be effectively computed. By defining $\bar{f}(x)$ to equal $f_x(x) + 1$ we guarantee that $\bar{f}$ is different from f_x, the function computed by the xth PL – {GOTO} program $\mathcal{P}_x$. We say that $\bar{f}$ is defined by *diagonalizing* over $\{f_x\}$.

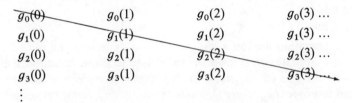

In the following, an effective definition of a function, that is, a definition which gives an effective method for computing the function, will be called

a *presentation.* PL programs are examples of presentations. To simplify the text we will often refer to an effective enumeration $g_0, g_1, \ldots$ of functions when we actually mean an effective enumeration $\mathcal{T}_0, \mathcal{T}_1, \ldots$ of presentations, where each $\mathcal{T}_i$ is a presentation of the function g_i. We will also say that $g_0, g_1, \ldots$ (or $\mathcal{T}_0, \mathcal{T}_1, \ldots$) is an *effective enumeration of some set S of functions* if each g_i is in S and each function in S appears at least once in the enumeration $g_0, g_1, \ldots$.

A diagonal argument may be noneffective if one wishes merely to infer the existence of a function not in a given set of functions. This is illustrated by the next theorem.

THEOREM 2.4. There is total function which is not PL-computable.

Proof. Let $f_0, f_1, \ldots$ be an enumeration of the PL-computable total functions $f_i: W \to W$. Such an enumeration exists because there are a countable number of PL programs. Define $\bar{f}$ by

$$\bar{f}(x) = f_x(x) + 1$$

The function $\bar{f}$ is total because each f_x is total but $\bar{f} \notin \{f_i\}$ so $\bar{f}$ is not PL-computable. ▮

COROLLARY 2.5. There is a total function which is not effectively computable.

Proof. Church's thesis. ▮

The enumeration used in Theorem 2.4 is not effective and indeed a proof similar to that of Theorem 2.4 also can be used to show that no such effective enumeration exists (see Exercise 1). However a noneffective enumeration is sufficient to prove the theorem because the function $\bar{f}$ defined is not effectively computable. Actually a somewhat more general theorem is proved by precisely the same method as in Theorem 2.4.

THEOREM 2.6. If $f_0, f_1, f_2, \ldots$ is any enumeration of total functions such that $f_i: W \to W$ for each $i = 0, 1, 2, \ldots$, then there is a total $\bar{f}: W \to W$ such that $f \notin \{f_i\}$. ▮

Theorem 2.6 states that the set of total functions from W into W is not countable.

According to Theorem 2.4, there is a total function which is not computed by a PL program. However, the theorem provides no information as to the characteristics of such a function. The next theorem uses Church's thesis and a diagonal argument to prove that a specific total function is not PL-computable. In Chapter 5 we shall give a proof which does not involve Church's thesis.

Let $f_0, f_1, \ldots$ be an effective enumeration of the PL-computable functions with one input and one output. This enumeration may be obtained, as in the proof of Theorem 2.3, by effectively enumerating all PL programs.

THEOREM 2.7. The function h defined by

$$h(x) = \begin{cases} 1 & \textit{if } x \in \operatorname{dom} f_x \\ 0 & \text{otherwise} \end{cases}$$

is not computed by a PL program.

Proof. Assume h is PL-computable and hence effectively computable. Define the function g by "diagonalizing" over $\{f_x\}$

$$g(x) = \begin{cases} f_x(x) + 1 & \text{if } h(x) = 1 \\ 0 & \text{if } h(x) = 0 \end{cases}$$

Since h is effectively computable, the function g is effectively computable. To compute $g(x)$, first compute $h(x)$. If $h(x) = 1$, obtain a presentation of f_x, that is, a program $\mathcal{T}_x$ which computes f_x. Since $h(x) = 1$, $f_x(x)$ is defined, and so $\mathcal{T}_x$ halts on input x. Then $g(x) = f_x(x) + 1$. If $h(x) = 0$, then $g(x) = 0$. Notice that in either case g differs from f_x on input x.

Since g is effectively computable, it is PL-computable by Church's thesis. Hence there is a y such that $g = f_y$, since $f_0, f_1, f_2, \ldots$ is an enumeration of all single-input, single-output PL-computable functions. Then

$$f_y(y) = g(y) = \begin{cases} f_y(y) + 1 & \text{if } h(y) = 1 \\ 0 & \text{if } h(y) = 0 \end{cases}$$

Since f_y is total, $y \in \operatorname{dom} f_y$, so $h(y) = 1$ and $f_y(y) = f_y(y) + 1$, which is a contradiction, so we must conclude that h is not PL-computable. ∎

The diagonal argument of Theorem 2.7 is somewhat more sophisticated than that of previous theorems. Here h is used to determine if $x \in \operatorname{dom} f_x$. If yes, then $g(x) = f_x(x) + 1$ and otherwise $g(x) = 0$. In either case, $g(x)$ is different from $f_x(x)$ so $g \neq f_x$ for any x. But the assumption that h is PL-computable leads to the conclusion that g *is* PL-computable and total, a contradiction since $\{f_x\}$ contains all PL-computable functions. Therefore we may conclude that h is not PL-computable.

Church's thesis was used in the proof of Theorem 2.7 to infer that g is computed by a PL program. The reader who is experienced in programming techniques should have little difficulty defining such a program.

COROLLARY 2.8. There is no effective procedure which, given an arbitrary PL program $\mathcal{T}_x$, decides whether $\mathcal{T}_x$ halts on input x. ∎

The problem of deciding for arbitrary x and y whether $y \in \operatorname{dom} f_x$ is called the *halting problem* because if f_x is presented by a program $\mathcal{T}_x$, then $y \in \operatorname{dom} f_x$ iff $\mathcal{T}_x$ halts on input y. Theorem 2.7 and Church's thesis imply that the halting problem is undecidable.

THEOREM 2.9. The functions g_1 and g_2 defined by

$$g_1(x,y) = \begin{cases} 1 & \text{if } y \in \operatorname{dom} f_x \\ 0 & \text{otherwise} \end{cases}$$

and

$$g_2(x) = \begin{cases} 1 & \text{if } f_x \text{ is PL-computable and total} \\ 0 & \text{otherwise} \end{cases}$$

are not PL-computable.

Proof. The proof for g_2 is similar to that of Theorem 2.7. If g_1 were PL-computable, then the function h of Theorem 2.7 would also be PL-computable, since $h(x) = g_1(x,x)$. ▮

The next corollary follows immediately by Church's thesis.

COROLLARY 2.10. The functions g_1 and g_2 of Theorem 2.9 are not effectively computable. ▮

Theorems 2.7 and 2.9 provide examples of interesting undecidable problems. To emphasize the importance of these results, we interpret them for programs written in any programming language which includes the features of PL.

THEOREM 2.11. The following problems are undecidable:

a. Given an arbitrary program $\mathcal{P}$ and input y, does $\mathcal{P}$ halt on input y?
b. Given an arbitrary program, does it halt on all inputs? Conversely, is there an input which causes the program to enter an infinite loop? ▮

Theorem 2.11 does not rule out the possibility of effectively deciding the halting problem for particular programs or sets of programs. It merely states that there is no general procedure which works for all programs. Moreover it is important to note that Theorem 2.11 is only true if no limit is imposed on program execution time and if an unlimited amount of storage is available. In PL, the second condition is satisfied by permitting variables to have arbitrarily large values. In FORTRAN a program may assume the existence of an unlimited supply of secondary storage such as tapes, cards, etc.

Let $f_0, f_1, \ldots$ be an effective enumeration of the PL-computable functions $f_i\colon W \to W$ for $i \geq 0$. By the extension of Church's thesis this is also an effective enumeration of the effectively computable functions. The function k given by

$$k(x) = \begin{cases} 1 & \text{if } x \in \operatorname{dom} f_x \\ \uparrow & \text{otherwise} \end{cases}$$

is effectively computable: Given x, obtain the program $\mathcal{P}_x$ which computes f_x. Execute $\mathcal{P}_x$ on input x, $\mathcal{P}_x$ will halt iff $x \in \operatorname{dom} f_x$. If $\mathcal{P}_x$ halts, $k(x) = 1$, otherwise the process never terminates. Note that

$$\operatorname{dom} k = \{x \mid x \in \operatorname{dom} f_x\}$$

Hence while there is no effective procedure for deciding whether or not an arbitrary x is in $\operatorname{dom} f_x$ (Theorem 2.7), there is an effective procedure which will eventually supply an affirmative answer in case x is in $\operatorname{dom} f_x$. This illustrates the essential difference between effective procedures and algorithms. An algorithm always halts, whereas an effective procedure will only halt on inputs which are in the domain of the function being computed. Hence an effective procedure (program) for computing a function $f: W^r \to W^s$ is an algorithm iff $\operatorname{dom} f = W^r$.

The function

$$k(x) = \begin{cases} 1 & \text{if } x \in \operatorname{dom} f_x \\ \uparrow & \text{otherwise} \end{cases}$$

can be effectively computed; there is an effective procedure which, given x, outputs 1 if $x \in \operatorname{dom} k$. If $x \notin \operatorname{dom} k$, then *no* output is produced since the effective procedure does not halt. The function

$$h(x) = \begin{cases} 1 & \text{if } x \in \operatorname{dom} f_x \\ 0 & \text{if } x \notin \operatorname{dom} f_x \end{cases}$$

is not effectively computable, since an effective procedure for computing h must supply an output for any input. By Theorem 2.7, this is impossible. Notice that an effective procedure for computing k provides partial information about membership in $H = \operatorname{dom} k = \{x \mid x \in \operatorname{dom} f_x\}$; if $x \in H$, we eventually find out, but if $x \notin H$, then no information is obtained. Furthermore, we cannot predict in advance whether an answer is forthcoming.

By Theorem 2.9 there is no way of deciding whether an arbitrary input is in the domain of an effective procedure. If it is, then this is eventually discovered, while if not, no information is obtained. Hence while there are effective procedures which are not algorithms, there is no effective procedure for deciding whether an arbitrary effective procedure is an algorithm.

There are many interesting computable functions which are not total. In Chapter 6 we will study such functions with emphasis on properties of their domains.

EXERCISES

1. Use a diagonal argument to prove that if $f_0, f_1, \ldots$ is any effective enumeration of a set of effectively computable total functions, then there is an effectively computable total function which is not in $\{f_i\}$. Infer that the PL-computable total functions cannot be effectively enumerated.

2. Give a procedure for effectively enumerating the nontotal PL-computable functions—that is, effectively enumerate a sequence $\mathcal{P}_0, \mathcal{P}_1, \ldots$ of presentations such that each nontotal PL-computable function is computed by some $\mathcal{P}_i$ in the list and every $\mathcal{P}_i$ listed computes a function which is not total.
Hint: Begin with an effective enumeration of all PL programs. Then modify each program so that all and only nontotal PL-computable functions are computed by the modified programs.

3.$^{\Delta}$ Give an effective enumeration of the set of functions $f: W — W$ computed by PL programs but not by PL $-$ {GOTO} programs.
Hint: Begin with an effective enumeration $\mathcal{P}_0, \mathcal{P}_1, \ldots$ of all PL programs. Modify $\mathcal{P}_i$ to a program $\mathcal{P}_i'$ satisfying these conditions: $\mathcal{P}_i'$ computes a total function iff $\mathcal{P}_i$ computes a total function, say f_i, and f_i is not computed by any PL $-$ {GOTO} program. Then combine with the enumeration of Exercise 2.

4. Prove Theorem 2.9.

5. Prove that the function k given by

$$k(x) = \begin{cases} 1 & \text{if } x \in S \\ \uparrow & \text{if } x \notin S \end{cases}$$

is effectively computable in case S is any of the sets $\{x \mid 5 \in \text{dom} f_x\}$, $\{x \mid 5 \in \text{ran} f_x\}$, or $\{x \mid f_x(y) = y, \text{ for some } y\}$, where $f_0, f_1, \ldots$ is an effective enumeration of the PL-computable functions.
Caution: For the last two parts recall that $f_x(y)$ need not be defined for all y.

2.4 History

The BNF notation was used in Naur[1960] to describe the syntax of the ALGOL 60 programming language. The language PL is an extension (GOTO statement, labels) of the LOOP language of Meyer and Ritchie [1967a,b]. The relationships discussed in Section 2.2 between the various types of programming language statements were studied in Constable and Borodin [1972].

Church first proposed identifying effective computability with the functions computed by various formal models in 1935. A detailed statement of Church's thesis may be found in Church [1936a]. The diagonal method was invented by Cantor [1874] to study properties of real numbers. The more sophisticated use of diagonalization described in Section 2.3 was first used by Gödel [1931] in his proof of the incompleteness of first-order arithmetic. Kleene [1936a], Turing [1936], and Church [1936a] all contain proofs of the undecidability of problems which are equivalent to the halting problem.

CHAPTER 3

Recursive Functions

The PL-computable functions are all intuitively computable, and PL programs are effective procedures. In this chapter we describe a second formalism for characterizing the effectively computable functions. The partial recursive functions defined by this formalism are the same as the functions computed by PL programs. Half of this assertion has already been proved as Theorems 2.1 and 2.2; the proof of the converse will be completed in Chapter 5.

The class of primitive recursive functions, a subclass of the partial recursive functions, will be defined and characterized as those functions which are PL − {GOTO}-computable. This provides a correspondence between some of the PL statement types and the operations used to define the partial recursive functions.

The class of partial recursive functions is defined inductively by specifying a set of initial functions and four operations for obtaining additional functions from those already defined. The initial functions will be effectively computable and the functions obtained by applications of the four operations will also be effectively computable, hence all partial recursive functions will be effectively computable.

3.1 Primitive Recursive and Partial Recursive Functions

The syntax for the definitions of primitive recursive and partial recursive functions will not be formally described since it is similar to standard mathematical notation. Similarly we will not specify exactly the way that the functions are to be evaluated. One obvious method parallels the inductive definition of a function. For example, if f is defined from g and h, then g and h are computed before f.

The initial functions used to define the primitive recursive and partial recursive functions are the following functions which were defined in Section 1.6. Recall the convention that $W = \Sigma^*$ for a finite alphabet Σ.

$\pi: W \to W^0$	$\pi(x) = ()$	the projection function
$\iota: W \to W$	$\iota(x) = x$	the identity function
$\zeta: W^0 \to W$	$\zeta(\,) = 0$	the zero function
$\varsigma: W \to W$	$\varsigma(x) = x + 1$	the successor function

Also recall the definitions of composition, combination, exponentiation, and repetition given by

$$f \circ g(x) = f[g(x)]$$

$$(f \times g)(x) = (fx, gx)$$

$$f^{\#}(x, y) = \overbrace{f \circ \cdots \circ f}^{y \text{ times}}(x)$$

$$f^{\nabla}(x, y) = x'$$

where k is the smallest value such that

$$f^k(x, y) = (x', 1) \text{ for some } x'.$$

These operations were defined in Section 1.7.

A function $f: W^r \to W^s$ is *partial recursive* in Σ if it is one of the functions π, ι, ζ, ς in Σ or can be obtained from these functions by a finite number of compositions, combinations, exponentiations, or repetitions. A function f is *recursive* in Σ if it is partial recursive in Σ and total ($\text{dom} f = W^r$).

Our definition of the partial recursive functions is representation independent. That is, the set of partial recursive definitions is the same for any Σ. However, it is important to keep in mind that the actual manipulations of words required in order to compute a partial recursive function will depend on the representation chosen. For example, $\varsigma(112) = 113$ in Σ_3 but $\varsigma(112) = 121$ in Σ_2. We continue to use the convention that if functions in Σ are being considered, then a number written in standard base 10 notation is an abbreviation for the word in Σ^* which represents that number.

Our definition of partial recursive differs from the traditional definition in three ways. First, we use the operations exponentiation and repetition rather than the more usual operations primitive recursion (see Section 3.2) and minimization (see Section 3.4). Later in this chapter we will show that exponentiation is equivalent to primitive recursion and repetition is equivalent to minimization. We have chosen to use exponentiation and repetition first, because of their simplicity relative to the other two operations and second, because they more closely parallel programming language constructs (LOOP-END, WHILE-END) than do the other two.

A second difference is that we deal with functions having multiple inputs and multiple outputs whereas the usual definition only specifies functions having a single output. To accomplish this we have added the operation of *combination* which does not appear in the traditional definition. By so doing we have been able to greatly simplify the set of base functions which in the traditional definition includes the countable set of functions $\{{}_ip_r(x_1,\ldots,x_r) = x_i \,|\, r \geq 1,\ 1 \leq i \leq r\}$. We believe that our definition comes closer to providing an appropriate formalism for the study of functions computed by computer programs.

Our most important break with tradition is in our use of partial recursive functions in Σ rather than partial recursive functions on N, the natural numbers. We have chosen to deal with functions in Σ because computing always involves manipulations of data. Moreover computer scientists are interested in algorithms, such as for parsing, which are defined directly in terms of words rather than numbers and which have no convenient number theoretic definition. Of course there is a close connection between number theoretic functions and functions which manipulate representations of numbers. A discussion of this relationship can be found in Section 3.7. It is interesting to note that because of the representation-independent form of partial recursive definitions, much of our development (Chapters 6, 8) closely parallels the traditional presentation.

The partial recursive functions in Σ can also be characterized as the smallest class containing π, ι, ζ, and ς, and which is closed under the operations of composition, combination, exponentiation, and repetition.

A particularly important subclass of the recursive functions in Σ is the class of *primitive recursive functions* in Σ, the smallest class containing π, ι, ζ, and ς which is closed under composition, combination, and exponentiation.

In the following, references to the alphabet Σ wil be omitted unless the particular alphabet chosen is of importance to the discussion. Hence we will often refer to "partial recursive", "recursive", and "primitive recursive" functions.

If f and g are recursive or primitive recursive, then so are $f \circ g$, $f \times g$, and $f^{\#}$; however, the repetition f^{∇} of f is partial recursive, but might not be recursive or primitive recursive. Since there are recursive functions which are not primitive recursive (by Theorem 2.3, Church's thesis, and Theorem 3.3), repetition is necessary to obtain all of the recursive functions.

Before proceeding, the reader is urged to review Theorems 2.1 and 2.2 and thereby be convinced that each partial recursive function is effectively computable.

For each $r \geq 0$, let $\iota_r(x) = x$, for $x \in W^r$. Each of the functions ι_r will be called an *identity function.*

Call $\delta: W \to W^2$ the *diagonalization function,* where $\delta(x) = (x,x)$. For $r \geq 1$, let $\delta_r(x_1,\ldots,x_r) = (x_1,\ldots.x_r,x_r)$, which defines a function that adds a copy of the last argument.

For $r \geq 2$ and $1 \leq j < r$, call ${}_j\xi_r: W^r \to W^r$ an *exchange function*, where

$${}_j\xi_r(x_1,\ldots,x_j,x_{j+1},\ldots,x_r) = (x_1,\ldots,x_{j+1},x_j,\ldots,x_r)$$

The function ${}_j\xi_r$ exchanges the arguments in positions j and $j+1$. For each $r \geq 1$, call $\pi_r: W^r \to W^{r-1}$ a *projection function*, where

$$\pi_r(x_1,\ldots,x_r) = (x_1,\ldots,x_{r-1})$$

All of these functions have the property that each output value is simply one of the input values. This motivates the following definition:

A *rearranging function* is any total function $f: W^r \to W^s$, $r, s \geq 0$, given by

$$f(x_1,x_2,\ldots,x_r) = (x_{i_1},x_{i_2},\ldots,x_{i_s})$$

where each i_j, $1 \leq j \leq s$, is an integer between 1 and r.

Example.

a. for ι_r, $i_1 = 1$, $i_2 = 2,\ldots,i_r = r$
b. for δ_r, $i_1 = 1$, $i_2 = 2,\ldots,i_r = i_{r+1} = r$
c. for ${}_j\xi_r$, $i_1 = 1$, $i_2 = 2,\ldots,i_j = j+1$, $i_{j+1} = j,\ldots,i_r = r$
d. for π, $s = 0$ so there is nothing to specify; for π_r, $r \geq 2$, $i_1 = 1,\ldots,i_{r-1} = r-1$
e. note that the functions ς and ζ are *not* rearranging functions

THEOREM 3.1. Every rearranging function is primitive recursive.

Proof. The function $\iota_0 = \pi \circ \zeta$ is primitive recursive and $\iota_{r+1} = \iota \times \iota_r$ so ι_r is primitive recursive for all r by induction on r.

To show that ${}_1\xi_2(x,y) = (y,x)$ is primitive recursive, let $f(x,y) = (\varsigma \times \iota)(x,y) = (x+1,y)$. Then $f^{\#}(x,y,z) = (x+z,y)$. Also $(\zeta \times \iota \times \iota)(x,y) = (0,x,y)$, so that $f^{\#} \circ (\zeta \times \iota \times \iota)(x,y) = f^{\#}(0,x,y) = (0+y,x) = (y,x)$. Thus ${}_1\xi_2 = (\varsigma \times \iota)^{\#} \circ (\zeta \times \iota \times \iota)$, which is primitive recursive by definition. Finally ${}_i\xi_r = \iota_{i-1} \times {}_1\xi_2 \times \iota_{r-i-1}$.

The diagonalization function δ is primitive recursive because

$$\delta = (\varsigma \times \varsigma)^{\#} \circ (\zeta \times \zeta \times \iota) \quad \text{and} \quad \delta_r = \iota_{r-1} \times \delta$$

We leave it as an exercise to prove that every rearranging function can be expressed as a composition of the functions ι_r, ${}_i\xi_r$, δ_r, and π_r, and is therefore primitive recursive. For example, if $f(x_1,x_2,x_3,x_4) = (x_2,x_4,x_2)$, then $f = {}_1\xi_3 \circ \delta_2 \circ {}_1\xi_2 \circ \pi_3 \circ {}_2\xi_3 \circ {}_1\xi_3 \circ \pi_4 \circ {}_3\xi_4$. ∎

Rearranging functions which copy several values are useful. For example, they may be used to show that $\langle f,g \rangle$ is primitive recursive whenever f and g are primitive recursive. Recall that $\langle f,g \rangle(x) = (fx,gx)$.

THEOREM 3.2. If $f: W^r \to W^s$ and $g: W^r \to W^t$ are primitive recursive, recursive, or partial recursive, then so is $\langle f,g \rangle: W^r \to W^{s+t}$.

Proof. Let $h(x_1,\ldots,x_r) = (x_1\ldots,x_r,x_1,\ldots,x_r)$, then $\langle f,g \rangle = (f \times g) \circ h$. ∎

Example. The function $f(x_1,x_2) = (x_2 + 2,1,x_2)$ is primitive recursive, since

$$f = \langle(\varsigma \circ \varsigma) \times (\varsigma \circ \zeta), \iota\rangle \circ (\pi \times \iota)$$

A schematic representation of f is shown in Figure 3-1.

Rearranging functions may also be used to allow any argument (not just the last one) to control the exponentiation operation. This is equivalent to allowing the use of any variable in a PL program LOOP statement. For example, if $f(x,y,z)$ is primitive recursive, then so are $f^w(x,y,z)$, $f^x(x,y,z)$, $f^y(x,y,z)$, and $f^z(x,y,z)$.

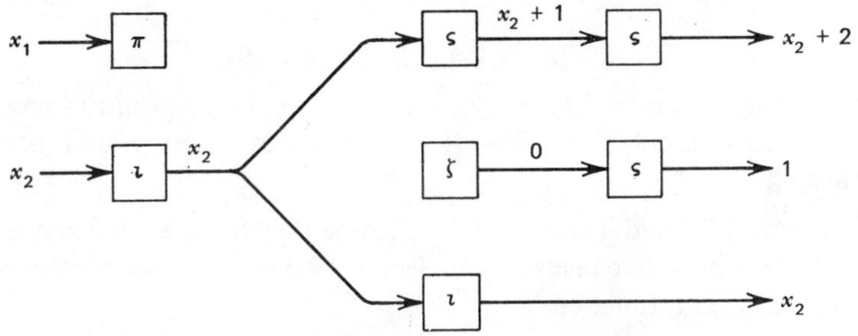

FIGURE 3-1. **Schematic representation of** $f = \langle(\varsigma \circ \varsigma) \times (\varsigma \circ \zeta), \iota\rangle \circ (\pi \times 2)$.

THEOREM 3.3. A function $f: W^r \to W^s$ is computable by a PL – {GOTO} program iff f is primitive recursive.

Proof. The PL – {GOTO} computability of each primitive recursive function was proved as part of the proof of Theorem 2.2. Let $\mathcal{T}$ be a PL – {GOTO} program and let $V_1, V_2, \ldots, V_t$ be a list of all variables referenced by $\mathcal{T}$ which includes the input/output variables X1, ..., Xr and Y1, Y2, ..., Ys. To simplify the notation slightly, let $V_1, \ldots, V_r$ be the input variables X1, ..., Xr and let $V_{r+1}, \ldots, V_{r+s}$ be the output variables Y1, ..., Ys. Let $f(x_1,\ldots,x_t)$ be the values of the variables $V_1, \ldots, V_t$ after the program halts, for any initial values $x_1, \ldots, x_t$ of the variables. The function f is primitive recursive. The proof is by induction on the number of statements in $\mathcal{T}$.

If the program contains only one statement, then f is given by:

a. $f(x_1,\ldots,x_i,\ldots,x_t) = (x_1,\ldots,0,\ldots,x_t)$ if the statement is $V_i \leftarrow 0$. In this case, $f = \iota_{i-1} \times (\zeta \circ \pi) \times \iota_{t-i}$
b. $f(x_1,\ldots,x_i,\ldots,x_t) = (x_1,\ldots,\varsigma(x_j),\ldots,x_t)$ if the statement is $V_i \leftarrow V_j + 1$ Then $f = (\iota_{i-1} \times \varsigma \times \iota_{t-i}) \circ g$ where $g(x_1,\ldots,x_i,\ldots,x_t) = (x_1,\ldots,x_j,\ldots,x_t)$. is a rearranging function.
c. $f(x_1,\ldots,x_i,\ldots,x_t) = (x_1,\ldots,x_j,\ldots,x_t)$ if the statement is $V_i \leftarrow V_j$. Thus f is the function g of part b. Each of these functions is primitive recursive.

If the program contains more than one statement, there are two cases to consider. If the first and last statements of the program are LOOP V_i and the *matching* END, and if g is the function computed by the program consisting of all but the first and last statements, then $f = g^{\#}$, the exponentiation of g, using the ith argument to determine the number of times g is to be applied. If the first and last statements are not a matching LOOP-END pair, then the statements of the program can be divided at some point into two smaller subprograms (see the syntax for PL programs given in Section 2.1). The entire program then computes the composition of the functions computed by the two smaller segments.

Finally, the input function

$$\alpha_r(x_1,\ldots,x_r) = (x_1,\ldots,x_r,\overbrace{0,\ldots,0}^{t-r})$$

and the output function $\omega_s(y_1,\ldots,y_t) = (y_{r+1},\ldots,y_{r+s})$ are primitive recursive, hence the function $\omega_s \circ f \circ \alpha_r\colon W^r \to W^s$ computed by the program is primitive recursive. ▌

By Theorem 3.3 and Theorem 2.3 we know that there is a recursive function that is not primitive recursive. In Sections 3.5 and 10.3 we give an explicit definition of such a function.

EXERCISES

1. Complete the proof of Theorem 3.1.

2. Prove directly that all constant functions are primitive recursive.

3. Prove that if $f \times g$ is primitive recursive, then so is f. If $f \circ g$ is primitive recursive, are f and g primitive recursive?

4. Prove directly that $f(x_1,x_2,x_3) = (x_3 + 4, x_1, 7, x_2)$ is primitive recursive.

5. Prove directly that $f(x,y) = x^y$ is primitive recursive.

6. Call $f \times \imath$ and $\imath \times f$ the *right* and *left cylindrification* of f. Show that the primitive recursive functions can be defined as the smallest class containing π, ζ, and ς which is closed under composition, cylindrification, and exponentiation.

7. Assume $f\colon W^{r+1} \to W^r$ is partial recursive and $f(x,1) = x$. Show that there is a partial recursive function $g\colon W^{r+1} \to W^{r+1}$ such that $f = g^{\triangledown}$.

8. Show that a function f is partial recursive iff it is computed by a program in the language without labels described at the end of Section 2.2. Note that the condition which determines termination of a WHILE statement differs from that of the repetition operation.

3.2 Recursion

It is often convenient to define functions using some form of induction scheme. In this section we give a general scheme of this type which we call recursion. Of particular interest is a form of recursion called primitive recursion, which is usually used instead of exponentiation to define the primitive recursive functions. We have chosen to use exponentiation because it is a simpler operation than primitive recursion and corresponds directly to the PL LOOP statement.

Let $d: W \to W$ be a total function with the property that $d(y) < y$ for each $y > 0$. Let $e: W^r \to W^r$, $g: W^r \to W^s$ and $h: W^{r+1+s} \to W^s$ be arbitrary functions. Then $f: W^{r+1} \to W^s$ is defined by *recursion* from d, e, g, and h if

$$f(x,0) = g(x)$$
$$f(x,y) = h[x,y,f(ex,dy)] \qquad \text{for } y > 0$$

If a function f is defined by recursion and there are computer programs available to compute the functions d, e, g, and h, then one way to compute $f(x,y)$ is to carry out the following instructions:

1. if $y = 0$, then compute $g(x)$
2. if $y > 0$, then first compute $x' = e(x)$ and $y' = d(y)$, then compute $z = f(x', y')$, and finally compute $h(x,y,z)$.

The most direct method of implementing such a program requires a system which permits a subroutine to invoke itself. These "recursive" calls are usually implemented by means of a push-down stack which keeps track of various values which must be restored when control returns to a higher level of execution—that is, when execution of the current subroutine ends and control returns to the subroutine which invoked it. To compute $f(x,y)$ as required by instruction 2 above, a subroutine must first compute $f(x',y')$. In fact, it will be the same subroutine which is computing $f(x,y)$. The values of x and y (and possibly some information about where to return when $f(x',y')$ is computed) are saved on a push-down stack and are later used to compute $h(x,y,z)$ after $z = f(x',y')$ is computed. From a logical standpoint this "recursive" subroutine feature of programming languages is equivalent to the availability of a push-down stack. However, it is sometimes a great convenience for a programmer to be able to use "recursive" subroutines.

The requirement that $d(y) < y$, for all $y > 0$, ensures that instruction 1 will eventually apply and the computation will terminate. Therefore, if f is defined by recursion from d, e, g, and h, which are all effectively computable, then f is effectively computable.

If e, g and h are not total functions, then $(x,y) \in \operatorname{dom} f$ iff all function values required by the evaluation method described above are defined. For example, if $d(y) > 0$ and $d \circ d(y) = 0$, then $f(x,y)$ is defined iff

$$e(x),\ e \circ e(x)$$
$$g \circ e \circ e(x)$$
$$h[ex,dy,g \circ e \circ e(x)]$$
$$h\{x,y,h[ex,dy,g \circ e \circ e(x)]\}$$

are all defined.

If $d(y) = y \dot{-} 1$ and e is the identity function, the recursion scheme becomes

$$f(x,0) = g(x)$$
$$f(x,y) = h[x,y,f(x,y \dot{-} 1)] \qquad \text{for } y > 0$$

and f is said to be defined by *primitive recursion*. The second line of the recursion scheme is often written

$$f(x,y+1) = h'[x,y,f(x,y)] \qquad \text{for } y \geq 0$$

where $h'(x,y,z) = h(x,y+1,z)$.

THEOREM 3.4. Every primitive recursive function can be obtained by applying the operations of composition, combination, and primitive recursion to the initial functions π, ι ζ, and ς—that is, each function defined by exponentiation from a primitive recursive function may also be defined by primitive recursion from primitive recursive functions.

Proof. Let $f: W^r \to W^r$ be primitive recursive. Then $f^{\#}: W^{r+1} \to W^r$ is defined by primitive recursion from f, ι_r, and $h = (\pi \times \cdots \times \pi \times f)$ as follows

$$f^{\#}(x,0) = \iota_r(x)$$
$$f^{\#}(x,y) = h[x,y,f^{\#}(x,y \dot{-} 1)] \qquad \text{for } y > 0$$

that is,

$$f^{\#}(x,0) = x$$
$$f^{\#}(x,y) = f[f^{\#}(x,y \dot{-} 1] \qquad \text{for } y > 0 \ \blacksquare$$

If f is defined by primitive recursion from g and h, it is possible to compute f in a more efficient manner than the "recursive" method described above. To illustrate this method, suppose

$$f(x,0) = g(x)$$
$$f(x,y) = h[x,y,f(x,y \dot{-} 1)] \qquad y > 0$$

then

$$f(x,3) = h(x,3,h(x,2,h(x,1,gx)))$$

Now $f(x,3)$ can be calculated by first calculating $f(x,0) = g(x)$ and successively "building" the values of $f(x,1)$, $f(x,2)$, and $f(x,3)$ from the values already computed. The successive values obtained are

$$f(x,0) = g(x)$$
$$f(x,1) = h(x,1,gx)$$
$$f(x,2) = h(x,2,h(x,1,gx))$$
$$f(x,3) = h(x,3,h(x,2,h(x,1,gx)))$$

If g and h are primitive recursive, then by Theorem 3.3 there are PL − {GOTO} programs which compute them. If f is defined by primitive recursion from g and h, then f is computed by the following program and hence is also primitive recursive:

```
(Y1,...,Ys) ← g(X1,...,Xr);
LOOP X(r + 1);
    Y ← Y + 1;
    (Y1,...,Ys) ← h(X1,...,Xr,Y,Y1,...,Ys);
END;
```

Together with Theorem 3.4, this proves that the class of primitive recursive functions is the smallest class containing the initial functions π, ι, ς, and ζ, which is closed under composition, combination, and primitive recursion.

We also want to show that the classes of recursive functions and partial recursive functions are closed under primitive recursion. Many theorems hold for the primitive recursive, recursive, and partial recursive functions, while other results hold for different combinations of the classes of primitive recursive, partial recursive, or recursive functions, so the following convention is useful: "If f is (primitive/partial) recursive, then g is (primitive/partial) recursive" means that if f is primitive recursive, partial recursive, or recursive, then g is primitive recursive, partial recursive, or recursive, respectively.

THEOREM 3.5. If $f: W^{r+1} \to W^s$ is defined by primitive recursion from (primitive/partial) recursive functions $g: W^r \to W^s$ and $h: W^{r+1+s} \to W^s$, then f is (primitive/partial) recursive.

Proof. The proof is an analog of the proof already given for primitive recursive functions. The exponentiation operation replaces the LOOP-END statements in the PL program. Notice that we cannot prove the theorem by building a PL program to compute f because we have not shown that every PL-computable function is partial recursive.

Let $k(x,y,z) = (x,y+1,h(x,y,z))$. If $p: W^{r+1+s} \to W^{r+1}$ is the projection function $p(x,y,z) = (x,y)$, for $(x,y,z) \in W^{r+1+s}$ (recall the convention that $(x,y,z) \in W^{r+1+s}$ means that $x \in W^r$, $y \in W$, and $z \in W^s$), then $k = \langle(\iota_r \times \varsigma) \circ p, h\rangle$, which is (primitive/partial) recursive by Theorems 3.1 and 3.2. The function k is shown in Figure 3-2.

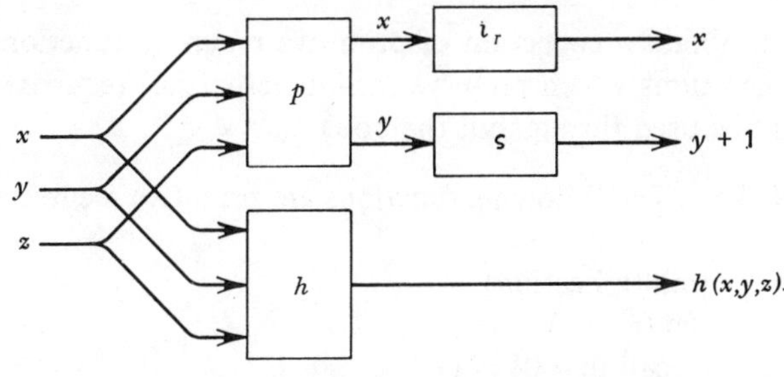

FIGURE 3-2. **Schematic representation of** $k = \langle(\iota_r \times \varsigma) \circ p, h\rangle$.

It is claimed that $k^y(x,1,gx) = (x,y+1,f(x,y))$. The proof is by induction on y.

$k^0(x,1,gx) = (x,1,gx)$	by the definition of exponentiation
$= (x,0+1,f(x,0))$	by the definition of f
$k^{y+1}(x,1,gx) = k[k^y(x,1,gx)]$	by the definition of exponentiation
$= k[x,y+1,f(x,y)]$	by the induction hypothesis
$= (x,y+2,h[x,y+1,f(x,y)])$	by the definition of k
$= (x,y+1+1,f(x,y+1))$	by the definition of f

If $p':W^{r+1+s} \to W^s$ is the projection function $p'(x,y,z) = z$, then $f(x,y) = p' \circ k^y(x,1,gx)$, which is (primitive/partial) recursive. More precisely, $f(x,y) = p' \circ k^{\#} \circ [\langle \iota_r \times (\varsigma \circ \zeta), g \rangle \times \iota](x,y)$, which illustrates how Theorem 3.2 is used. The way f is constructed is shown in Figure 3-3. ∎

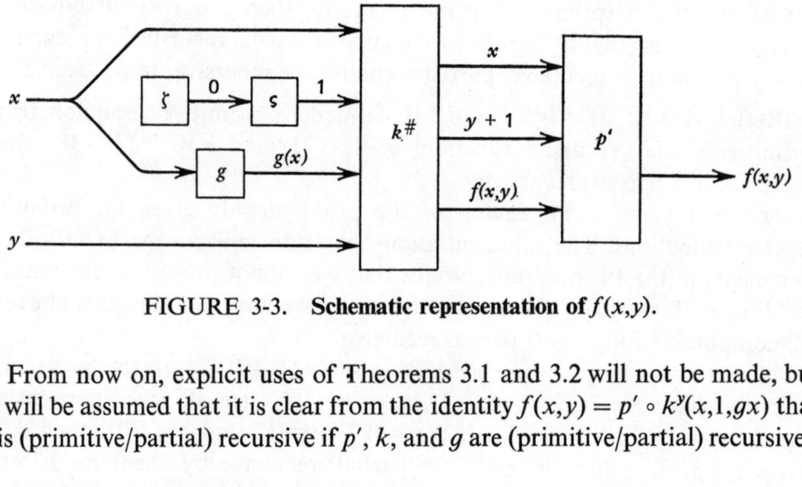

FIGURE 3-3. **Schematic representation of $f(x,y)$.**

From now on, explicit uses of Theorems 3.1 and 3.2 will not be made, but it will be assumed that it is clear from the identity $f(x,y) = p' \circ k^y(x,1,gx)$ that f is (primitive/partial) recursive if p', k, and g are (primitive/partial) recursive.

3.3 Closure Properties

It is useful to obtain a collection of primitive recursive functions and some additional operations which preserve (primitive/partial) recursiveness. These functions will be used throughout the book.

THEOREM 3.6. The following functions are primitive recursive.

a. $x + y$
b. $x \times y$ (multiplication)
c. x^y (let $0^0 = 1$)
d. $x!$ (recall that $0! = 1$)

e. $x \dot{-} y = \begin{cases} x - y & \text{if } x \geq y \\ 0 & \text{if } x < y \end{cases}$

f. $\text{sign}(x) = \begin{cases} 1 & \text{if } x > 0 \\ 0 & \text{if } x = 0 \end{cases}$

g. $\neg x = \begin{cases} 1 & \text{if } x = 0 \\ 0 & \text{if } x > 0 \end{cases}$

h. $x \vee y = \begin{cases} 1 & \text{if } x > 0 \text{ or } y > 0 \\ 0 & \text{if } x = 0 \text{ and } y = 0 \end{cases}$

i. $x \wedge y = \begin{cases} 1 & \text{if } x > 0 \text{ and } y > 0 \\ 0 & \text{if } x = 0 \text{ or } y = 0 \end{cases}$

j. $x \supset y = \begin{cases} 1 & \text{if } x = 0 \text{ or } y > 0 \\ 0 & \text{if } x > 0 \text{ and } y = 0 \end{cases}$

k. $x < y = \begin{cases} 1 & \text{if } x < y \\ 0 & \text{if } x \geq y \end{cases}$

The functions $>$, $\geq$, $\leq$ are similarly defined.

l. $\text{eq}(x,y) = \begin{cases} 1 & \text{if } x = y \\ 0 & \text{if } x \neq y \end{cases}$

The function eq(x,y) will often be written $x = y$.

Proof.

a. $x + y = \varsigma^y(x)$
b. $x \times 0 = 0 \quad x \times (y + 1) = (x \times y) + x$
e. Let $f(0) = 0$, $f(x + 1) = x$, then $f(x) = x \dot{-} 1$ and f is primitive recursive; now $x \dot{-} 0 = x$ and $x \dot{-} (y + 1) = f(x \dot{-} y) = (x \dot{-} y) \dot{-} 1$
f. $\text{sign}(0) = 0 \quad \text{sign}(x + 1) = 1$
g. $\neg x = 1 \dot{-} \text{sign}(x)$
h. $x \vee 0 = \text{sign}(x) \quad x \vee (y + 1) = 1$
i. $x \wedge 0 = 0 \quad x \wedge (y + 1) = \text{sign}(x)$
j. $x \supset y = (\neg x) \vee y$
k. $x < y = \text{sign}(y \dot{-} x)$
$x \leq y = x < (y + 1)$
l. $\text{eq}(x,y) = (x \leq y) \wedge (y \leq x)$ ▮

It is also possible to show that each of these functions is primitive recursive by constructing a PL – {GOTO} program that computes it. We have given direct proofs in order to illustrate the use of exponentiation and primitive recursion.

Any function whose value is either 1 or 0 can be thought of as the characteristic function of some set. For example, the sign function is the characteristic function of the set $\{x \mid x \neq 0\}$. The values of the functions $\wedge$, $\vee$, and $\neg$ are also always either 1 or 0 and so define sets.

A characteristic function may also be thought of as a *predicate* or statement about members of W under the interpretation that if the value of the function is 1, the statement is *true* and if the value of the function is 0, the statement is *false*. Thus the expression sign(x) may also be thought of as the statement that x is not 0. In this manner $\wedge$, $\vee$, and $\neg$ may be read as "and", "or", and "not". If $f(x)$ is a predicate and $g(y,z)$ is another predicate, then $f(x) \wedge \neg g(y,z)$ says that f is true for x, and g is false for y and z. Note that values ≥ 1 are treated as true and 0 is treated as false. The equivalent expressions

$$\text{sign}(x) \wedge \neg (y < x)$$

and

$$x \wedge (x \leq y)$$

say that x is not 0 and $x \leq y$, that is, $0 < x \leq y$.

THEOREM 3.7 If $f: W^{r+1} \to W$ and $g: W^r \to W$ are (primitive/partial) recursive, then so are

a. $\sum_{i=0}^{g(x)} f(x,i) = f(x,0) + f(x,1) + \cdots + f(x,gx)$

b. $\prod_{i=0}^{g(x)} f(x,i) = f(x,0) \times f(x,1) \times \cdots \times f(x,gx)$

c. $\bigvee_{i=0}^{g(x)} f(x,i) = 0 \vee f(x,0) \vee f(x,1) \vee \cdots \vee f(x,gx)$

d. $\bigwedge_{i=0}^{g(x)} f(x,i) = 1 \wedge f(x,0) \wedge f(x,1) \wedge \cdots \wedge f(x,gx)$

Note that if either f or g is not a total function, then these four functions are defined for argument x iff $x \in \text{dom } g$ and $(x,i) \in \text{dom } f$, for all $i \leq g(x)$.
Proof. a. Let $h(x,0) = f(x,0)$, $h(x,k+1) = h(x,k) + f(x,\varsigma(k))$. Then $h(x,k) = \sum_{i=0}^{k} f(x,i)$, hence $\sum_{i=0}^{g(x)} f(x,i) = h(x,gx)$. The proofs of b, c, and d are similar. ∎

If $f(x,i)$ is a predicate involving x and i, then $\bigvee_{i=0}^{g(x)} f(x,i)$ can be read as "there exists an $i \leq g(x)$ such that $f(x,i)$ is true" and $\bigwedge_{i=0}^{g(x)} f(x,i)$ can be read as "for all $i \leq g(x)$, $f(x,i)$ is true."

THEOREM 3.8. If $f: W^r \to W$ and $g: W^s \to W^t$ are (primitive/partial) recursive, then so is $f \to g: W^{r+s} \to W^t$ defined by

$$(f \to g)(x,y) = \begin{cases} (0,\ldots,0) & \text{if } f(x) = 0 \\ g(y) & \text{if } f(x) > 0 \\ \uparrow & \text{if } f(x)\uparrow \end{cases}$$

Proof. Let $h(0,y) = (0,\ldots,0) \in W^t$, $h(x + 1,y) = g(y)$. Then h is (primitive/partial) recursive and

$$h(x,y) = \begin{cases} (0,\ldots,0) & \text{if } x = 0 \\ g(y) & \text{if } x > 0 \end{cases}$$

Thus $(f \to g)(x,y) = h(fx,y)$. ▮

The function $(f \to g)(x,y)$ will usually be written $f(x) \to g(y)$, which might be interpreted as 0 if $f(x)$ is "false" (that is, 0); as $g(y)$ if $f(x)$ is "true"; and as undefined if $f(x)$ is undefined. Note also that if $f(x) > 0$ and $g(y)$ is undefined, then $f(x) \to g(y)$ is undefined, but if $f(x) = 0$ and $g(y)$ is undefined, $(f \to g)(x,y) = 0$. The funtion $(f \to g)(x,y)$ is not equal to $\text{sign}(fx) \times g(y)$ because $\text{sign}(fx) \times g(y)$ is undefined whenever $g(y)$ is undefined, even if $f(x) = 0$. This is due to our convention that composition of functions is defined only in case both components of the composition are defined. The function h avoids this problem, because if $f(x) = 0$, then only $h(0,y)$ need be computed by our convention specifying the domain of functions defined by recursion.

In the proof of Theorem 3.8, the function h is defined by primitive recursion on the first argument. This is permissible since the rearranging functions are all primitive recursive.

THEOREM 3.9. If f_1, f_2, g_1, g_2 are (primitive/partial) recursive functions, so is

$$f(x) = \begin{cases} f_1(x) & \text{if } g_1(x) = g_2(x) \\ f_2(x) & \text{if } g_1(x) \neq g_2(x) \end{cases}$$

Proof. $f(x) = [\text{eq}(g_1x,\ g_2x) \to f_1(x)] \oplus [\neg\text{eq}(g_1x,\ g_2x) \to f_2(x)]$, where $\oplus$ is vector addition, which is primitive recursive (see Exercise 6). ▮

If either $g_1(x)$ or $g_2(x)$ is not defined, $f(x)$ is not defined. If $g_1(x) = g_2(x)$, then $f(x)$ is defined iff $f_1(x)$ is defined. If $g_1(x) \neq g_2(x)$, then $f(x)$ is defined iff $f_2(x)$ is defined.

Theorem 3.9 will be used in a very informal manner. For example, the function

$$f(x) = \begin{cases} 2 \times x & \text{if } x > 3 \\ x + 4 & \text{if } x \leq 3 \end{cases}$$

is primitive recursive by Theorem 3.9, where $f_1(x) = 2 \times x$, $f_2(x) = x + 4$, $g_1(x) = x > 3$, and $g_2(x) = 1$.

EXERCISES

1. Complete the proof of Theorem 3.6.

2. Prove the following identities

a. $\text{sign} = \neg \circ \neg$

b. $\neg = \neg \circ \text{sign} = \text{sign} \circ \neg$

c. $x \wedge y = y \wedge x$
d. $x \vee y = y \vee x$
e. $x \wedge (y \vee z) = (x \wedge y) \vee (x \wedge z)$
f. $x \vee (y \wedge z) = (x \vee y) \wedge (x \vee z)$
g. $\neg(x \vee y) = (\neg x) \wedge (\neg y)$
h. $\neg(x \wedge y) = (\neg x) \vee (\neg y)$
i. $(x \wedge (x \supset y)) \supset y = [\varsigma \circ \zeta \circ (\pi \times \pi)](x,y) = 1$ (*modus ponens*)

3. The functions $\wedge$, $\vee$, and $\neg$ are characteristic functions of what sets?

4. Show that the class of partial recursive functions is the smallest class containing the functions π, ι, ζ, ς, and eq, which is closed under composition, combination, and repetition. Equivalently, show that if PL statements of the form

IF $X = Y$ THEN; GOTO ⟨name⟩; END;

are allowed, then the LOOP-END statements are not necessary.

5. Show that $x \otimes (x_1,\ldots,x_r) = (x \times x_1,\ldots,x \times x_r)$ (scalar multiplication) is primitive recursive.

6. Show that $(x_1,\ldots,x_r) \oplus (y_1,\ldots,y_r) = (x_1 + y_1,\ldots,x_r + y_r)$ (vector addition) is primitive recursive.

7. Prove that if $g_i{:}W^r \rightarrow W^s$, $0 \leq i < k$, and $h{:}W^{r+1+s} \rightarrow W^s$ are primitive recursive, then so is f: $W^{r+1} \rightarrow W^s$, where $f(x,y) = g_y(x)$, $y < k$ and $f(x,y) = h[x,y,f(x,y \dot{-} k)]$, $y \geq k$.

8. Show that

$$f(x,y) = \underbrace{2^{2^{\cdot^{\cdot^{\cdot^{2^y}}}}}}_{x+1 \text{ times}}$$

is primitive recursive.

9. Complete the proof of Theorem 3.7. Give a reasonable definition for

$$g(x,y) = \bigvee_{i=x}^{y} f(i)$$

where there is a possibility that $x > y$. Prove that if f is (primitive/partial) recursive, then so is g. Consider the analogous problems for $\wedge$, Π, and Σ.

10. Construct a primitive recursive function f such that for each y, $f(x) = y$ for infinitely many x.

11. Prove that if f_1,f_2: $W^r \rightarrow W$ are primitive recursive, then so is $f(x) = \max\{f_1(x), f_2(x)\}$.

12. Suppose functions f_1 and f_2 are defined by

$$f_1(x,0) = g_1(x)$$
$$f_2(x, 0) = g_2(x)$$
$$f_1(x, y+1) = h_1[x, y, f_1(x,y), f_2(x,y)]$$
$$f_2(x, y+1) = h_2[x, y, f_1(x, y), f_2(x,y)]$$

whese g_1, g_2, h_1, and h_2 are primitive recursive. Prove that f_1 and f_2 are primitive recursive.

13. Suppose f is defined by

$$f(x,0) = g(x) \qquad f(x, y+1) = f[f(x,y), y]$$

where g is primitive recursive. Show that f is primitive recursive.

3.4 Minimization

If $f: W^{r+1} \to W$ is a function, define

$$A_x = \{y \mid f(x,y) = 1 \text{ and } f(x,y') \text{ is defined for each } y' < y\}$$

Let $\min(A_x)$ be the smallest member of A_x under the ordering $<$, provided $A_x \neq \varnothing$. Define the *minimization* of f to be the function μf: $W^r \to W$ given by

$$(\mu f)(x) = (\mu y)[f(x,y)] = \begin{cases} \min(A_x) & \text{if } A_x \neq \varnothing \\ \uparrow & \text{if } A_x = \varnothing \end{cases}$$

Thus $(\mu y)[f(x,y)]$ may be calculated by computing $f(x,0)$, $f(x,1)$, ... until one of the values is 1. The computation will never be completed if there is an attempt to compute $f(x,y)$ using a value of y for which the function is not defined, or if $f(x,y) = 1$ for no value of y.

Example. If $f(x,y) = \text{eq}(x, 3 \times y)$, then

$$(\mu f)(x) = \begin{cases} \dfrac{x}{3} & \text{if } x \text{ is divisible by } 3 \\ \uparrow & \text{otherwise} \end{cases}$$

Example. Let

$$f(x,y) = \begin{cases} 1 & \text{if } x + y \text{ is even} \\ \uparrow & \text{otherwise} \end{cases}$$

then $(\mu f)(0) = 0$, since $f(0,0) = 1$, but $(\mu f)(1)$ is undefined because $f(1,0)$ is undefined, even though $f(1,1) = 1$.

THEOREM 3.10. If f is partial recursive, then μf is partial recursive.

Proof. Let $h(x,y,z) = (x, y+1, f(x,y+1))$. Then it can be proved by induction (see Exercise 1) that

$$h^k[x,0,f(x,0)] = \begin{cases} (x,k,f(x,k)) & \text{if } f(x,k') \text{ is defined for all } k' \leq k \\ \uparrow & \text{otherwise} \end{cases}$$

Hence

$$h^\nabla[x,0,f(x,0)] = \begin{cases} (x, k_0) & \text{where } k_0 = \min(A_x) \text{ if } A_x \neq \varnothing \\ \uparrow & \text{otherwise} \end{cases}$$

Thus $\mu f = p \circ h^\nabla \circ \langle \iota \times \zeta, f \circ (\iota \times \zeta) \rangle$ where p is the projection function from $W^{r+1} \to W^1$. ▮

In the traditional definition of minimization $A_x = \{y \mid f(x,y) = 1\}$. With this definition, Theorem 3.10 is no longer true, as will be shown in Section 6.2. For this reason, minimization is usually restricted to only total functions. This raises another difficulty because it will also be shown (Section 6.4) that there is no algorithm which will determine whether or not a given function is total. This means that with this definition there would be no effective way of deciding when minimization applied to a partial recursive function would yield a partial recursive function. This difficulty is not too serious because we will prove in Section 5.4 that any partial recursive function can be defined using minimization (or repetition) only once, so that all partial recursive functions are obtained by applying minimization (or repetition) only to primitive recursive functions.

The traditional definition of partial recursive functions uses the operation of minimization in place of repetition. Theorem 3.10 and Exercise 3 show that the definitions are equivalent.

If $f: W^{r+1} \to W$ and $g: W^r \to W$ are total functions, then $\mu fg: W^r \to W$, the *bounded minimization* of f and g, is defined by

$$(\mu fg)(x) = (\mu y \leq gx)[f(x,y)] = \begin{cases} \min(A_x^g) & \text{if } A_x^g \neq \varnothing \\ 0 & \text{if } A_x^g = \varnothing \end{cases}$$

where

$$A_x^g = \{y \mid y \leq gx, f(x,y) = 1\}$$

THEOREM 3.11. If f and g are (primitive) recursive, so is μfg.

Proof. First, suppose $A_x^g \neq \varnothing$ and $y_0 = \min(A_x^g)$.

If

$$h(x,y) = \neg \bigvee_{v=0}^{y} [f(x,v) = 1] = \begin{cases} 1 & \text{if } y < y_0 \\ 0 & \text{if } y \geq y_0 \end{cases}$$

then

$$y_0 = \sum_{y=0}^{g(x)} h(x,y) = (\mu fg)(x)$$

However, the function

$$h'(x) = \bigvee_{v=0}^{g(x)} [f(x,v) = 1] = \begin{cases} 1 & \text{if } A_x^g \neq \varnothing \\ 0 & \text{if } A_x^g = \varnothing \end{cases}$$

tests whether or not $A_x^g = \varnothing$ and so $(\mu fg)(x) = h'(x) \to \sum_{y=0}^{g(x)} h(x,y)$. ∎

THEOREM 3.12. The following functions are primitive recursive.

a. x/y, the largest integer less than or equal to x/y. Let $x/0 = 0$.

b. $\text{rem}(x,y)$, the remainder when x is divided by y

c. $y \mid x = \begin{cases} 1 & \text{if } y \text{ divides } x, \text{ that is, } x \text{ is divisible by } y \\ 0 & \text{otherwise} \end{cases}$

d. $\text{prime}(x) = \begin{cases} 1 & \text{if } x \text{ is a prime} \\ 0 & \text{otherwise} \end{cases}$

e. prime#(x), the xth prime, where prime#$(0) = 2$, prime#$(1) = 3$, prime#$(2) = 5, \ldots$

f. $\exp(x,i) = e_i$ if $x = \prod_{i=0}^{\infty} \text{prime\#}(i)^{e_i}$

Proof.

a. $x/y = y \rightarrow (\mu z \leq x)[y \times (z+1) > x]$

b. $\text{rem}(x,y) = x \dot{-} [(x/y) \times y]$

c. $y|x = \neg\text{rem}(x,y)$

d. $\text{prime}(x) = x > 1 \wedge \bigwedge_{y=0}^{x \dot{-} 1} [(y > 1) \supset \neg(y|x)]$

e. From number theory it is known that prime#$(x+1) \leq [\text{prime\#}(x)]! + 1$, let $g(x) = (\mu y \leq x! + 1)[y > x \wedge \text{prime}(y)]$; then prime#$(0) = 2$ and prime#$(x+1) = g[\text{prime\#}(x)]$

f. Exercise 5. ▮

EXERCISES

1. Prove that

$$h^k(x, 0, f(x,0)) = \begin{cases} (x, k, f(x,k)) & \text{if } f(x,k') \text{ is defined for all } k' \leq k \\ \uparrow & \text{otherwise.} \end{cases}$$

where h is the function defined in Theorem 3.10.

2. Define $A_x = \{y | f(x,y) = 1\}$ and redefine minimization using this A_x. With this definition of minimization, prove that if f is recursive, then μf is partial recursive.

3. Show that the class of partial recursive functions may be defined by replacing repetition with minimization (as defined in the text), that is, show that repetition can be expressed in terms of minimization.

4. Prove that if $f: W \rightarrow W$ is a recursive bijection, then so is f^{-1}.

5. If x is written in the form $x = 2^{e_0}3^{e_1}5^{e_2}7^{e_3}11^{e_4}13^{e_5}17^{e_6}\ldots$, where $e_i \geq 0$, it has been decomposed into its prime factors. For example, e_3 is the number of times 7, the third prime divides x. Show that $\exp(x,i) = e_i$ is primitive recursive.

6. Prove directly that if f and g are total and are computed by PL or PL $-$ {GOTO} programs, then so is μfg.

7. Give a definition of μfg that will apply if either f or g is partial recursive. Give a definition with the property that the partial recursive functions are closed under this operation.

8. Exhibit a function $g(x,y)$ which is not total, but $(\mu y)[g(x,y)]$ is total.

9. Show that $\lfloor\sqrt{x}\rfloor$, the largest integer less than or equal to $\sqrt{x}$, is primitive recursive. Also show that $f(x, p, q) = \lfloor\sqrt[q]{x^p}\rfloor = \lfloor x^{p/q}\rfloor$ is primitive recursive.

3.5 Recursion Revisited

Recall that $f:W^{r+1} \to W^s$ is defined by recursion from $d:W \to W$, $e:W^r \to W^r$, $g:W^r \to W^s$, and $h:W^{r+1+s}$ if

$$f(x,0) = g(x)$$
$$f(x,y) = h[x,y,f(ex,dy)] \qquad \text{for} \quad y > 0$$

where d is total and $d(y) < y$, for each $y > 0$.

To see how $f(x,y)$ can be computed, suppose $d(y) > 0$, $d^2(y) > 0$, and $d^3(y) = 0$, then

$$f(x,y) = h(x,y,h(ex,dy,h(e^2x,d^2y,g \circ e^3(x)))).$$

First, compute $(\mu w \leq y)[d^w(y) = 0]$ which is 3 in this case. Then compute $g \circ e^w(x)$, and "build" the value of $f(x,y)$ by applying h to the appropriate arguments. If programs are available to compute d, e, g, and h, the following PL program computes f.

```
Y ← X(r + 1);
W ← (μW ≤ Y)[d^W(Y) = 0];
(TX1,...,TXr) ← e^W(X1,...,Xr);
(Y1,...,Ys) ← g(TX1,...,TXr);
LOOP W;
    W ← W ∸ 1;
    (TX1,...,TXr) ← e^W(X1,...,Xr);
    TY ← d^W(Y);
    (Y1,...,Ys) ← h(TX1,...,TXr,TY,Y1,...,Ys);
END;
```

Using Theorem 3.3, the program shows that the class of primitive recursive functions is closed under recursion. Since we have not yet proved that every PL-computable function is partial recursive, we cannot use the program above to infer that f is (partial) recursive in case d,e,g, and h are (partial) recursive. To prove the result for the recursive and partial recursive functions, the same computation can be expressed directly in terms of functions as was done for the proof of Theorem 3.5.

THEOREM 3.13. If f is defined by recursion from (primitive/partial) recursive functions, d, e, g, and h, then f is (primitive/partial) recursive.

Proof. Let $c(y) = (\mu w \leq y)[d^w(y) = 0]$. Note that $c(y) = 0$ iff $y = 0$ since $dy < y$ for all $y > 0$. By the definition of recursion, d is total. If d is (primitive) recursive, then the function c is (primitive) recursive by Theorem 3.11. Let

$$k(w,x,y,z) = (w \dot{-} 1,x,y,h[e^w(x),d^w(y),z])$$

For every x, y, and $w \leq c(y)$,

$$(*) \quad k^w[cy \dot{-} 1,x,y,g \circ e^{cy}(x)] = (cy \dot{-} 1 \dot{-} w,x,y,f[e^{cy \dot{-} w}(x), d^{cy \dot{-} w}(y)])$$

The formula $(*)$ is proved by induction on w, For $w = 0$.

$$\begin{aligned} k^0(cy \dot{-} 1,x,y,g \circ e^{cy}(x)) &= (cy \dot{-} 1,x,y,g \circ e^{cy}(x)) \\ &= (cy \dot{-} 1,x,y,f[e^{cy}(x),0]) \\ &= (cy \dot{-} 1,x,y,f[e^{cy}(x),d^{cy}(y)]) \end{aligned}$$

If $(*)$ holds for some $w < c(y)$, then

$$\begin{aligned} &k^{w+1}(cy \dot{-} 1,x,y,g \circ e^{cy}(x)) \\ &= k \circ k^w(cy \dot{-} 1,x,y,g \circ e^{cy}(x)) \\ &= k(cy \dot{-} 1 \dot{-} w,x,y,f[e^{cy \dot{-} w}(x),d^{cy \dot{-} w}(y)]) \\ &= (cy \dot{-} 1 \dot{-} w \dot{-} 1,x,y,h[e^{cy \dot{-} (w+1)}(x),d^{cy \dot{-} (w+1)}(y), \\ &\quad f[e \circ e^{cy \dot{-} (w+1)}(x), d \circ d^{cy \dot{-} (w+1)}(y)]]) \\ &= (cy \dot{-} 1 \dot{-} (w+1),x,y,f[e^{cy \dot{-} (w+1)}(x),d^{cy \dot{-} (w+1)}(y)]) \end{aligned}$$

Thus with $w = c(y)$,

$$\begin{aligned} p \circ k^{cy}[cy \dot{-} 1,x,y,g \circ e^{cy}(x)] &= p(cy \dot{-} 1 \dot{-} cy,x,y,f[e^{cy \dot{-} cy}(x),d^{cy \dot{-} cy}(y)]) \\ &= p[0,x,y,f(x,y)] \\ &= f(x,y) \end{aligned}$$

where $p: W^{1+r+1+s} \to W^s$ is a projection function. ▮

From Theorem 3.13, it might appear that almost any reasonable induction scheme would define only primitive recursive functions from given primitive recursive functions. This is not true. The function known as Ackermann's function defined by

$$\begin{aligned} a(0,y) &= y + 1 \\ a(x+1,0) &= a(x,1) \\ a(x+1,y+1) &= a[x,a(x+1,y)] \end{aligned}$$

is not primitive recursive.

It is generally fairly difficult to prove that a given function is recursive, but not primitive recursive, but we can explore one possible method of constructing such a proof. If there is a recursive function that is not primitive recursive, then there must be functions $f(x,y)$ and $f'(x)$, where f is primitive recursive, and $f'(x) = (\mu y)[f(x,y)]$ is recursive, but not primitive recursive. If there were a primitive recursive function g such that $f'(x) \leq g(x)$, for each x, then $f'(x) = (\mu y \leq g(x))[f(x,y)]$, and so f' would be primitive recursive by bounded minimization. Thus for each primitive recursive function g, there must be an

x such that $f'(x) > g(x)$. This provides the motivation for attempting to prove the following proposition about Ackermann's function.

THEOREM 3.14. For each primitive recursive function g, there is an x such that $a(x,x) > g(x)$.

Proof. A proof will be given in Chapter 10 for a function quite similar to Ackermann's function. ▌

COROLLARY 3.15. a. The function $f(x) = a(x,x)$ is not primitive recursive.

b. Ackermann's function is not primitive recursive. ▌

Of course, it still must be demonstrated that Ackermann's function is recursive. This is probably most easily done by writing a PL program to compute it and then using a result of Chapter 5 which shows that every PL-computable function is partial recursive.

For each fixed k, $a(k,y)$ is a primitive recursive function of y (Exercise 3). Moreover, as k increases, the value of $a(k,y)$ grows extremely fast (see Exercise 1). For example,

$$a(4,y) > 2^{\cdot^{\cdot^{\cdot^{2}}}} \Big\}\text{-}y \text{ times}$$

The function $a(x,x)$ grows faster than $a(k,y)$ for any k and indeed faster than any primitive recursive function; that is, for each primitive recursive function $g(x)$, there is a constant c such that $a(x,x) > g(x)$ for $x \geq c$.

Since each PL instruction can add at most 1, any program that computes $a(x,y)$ requires $a(x,y)$ steps, so it surely is not practical to compute even $a(4,y)$. In Chapter 9, we will show that a function is primitive recursive iff it can be computed by a PL program whose computation time is bounded by a primitive recursive function. Hence the computation time for any nonprimitive recursive function must grow faster than, for example, $a(4,y)$, which is primitive recursive. This should help to convince the reader that all practical computing involves primitive recursive functions.

EXERCISES

1. If x is a constant 0, in Ackermann's function, $a(0,y)$ is the successor function $y + 1$. What is the value of $a(1,y)$, $a(2,y)$, $a(3,y)$ for a given y? What about $a(n,y)$ for fixed n?

2. Calculate $a(3,2)$, where a is Ackermann's function.

3. Prove that for any constant x, $a(x,y)$ is a primitive recursive function of y.

4. Construct a PL program that computes Ackermann's function.

5.△ Assume that the primitive recursive functions d_i, $1 \le i \le k$, each satisfy $d_i(0) = 0$ and $d_i(x) < x$, for $x > 0$. Show that f is primitive recursive if defined using primitive recursive functions g and h by the formulas

$$f(0, y) = g(y)$$
$$f(x,y) = h[x,y,f(d_1x,y),\ldots,f(d_kx,y)]$$

Hint: Use the function exp(x,i) of Theorem 3.12f.

6. Use the result of Exercise 5 to show that $f(n) =$ the nth number in the Fibonacci sequence 0, 1, 1, 2, 3, 5, 8, ... is primitive recursive. Alternatively, define a PL − {GOTO} program which computes f.

7. Let $c_0, \ldots, c_{k-1}, a_1, \ldots, a_k$ be given constants. Show that the function defined by

$$f(n) = c_n, \qquad 0 \le n < k$$
$$f(n) = a_1 \times f(n-1) + a_2 \times f(n-2) + \cdots + a_k \times f(n-k) \qquad n \ge k$$

is primitive recursive.

3.6 Recursion on the Length of a Word

Most of the functions discussed so far are "numerical" or "logical" in the sense that the words in Σ may be thought of as representations of integers or of the truth values "true" and "false". It is important to show that some of the "character" functions, such as the reversal function and concatenation, are also primitive recursive. Most of these functions are conveniently defined by induction on the length of a word. Theorem 3.17 proves that functions defined this way are primitive recursive. Two simple character manipulating functions needed to prove the theorem can be defined in terms of the functions already shown to be primitive recursive.

In the following we assume without loss of generality, that $\Sigma = \{1,2,\ldots,n\}$ and that the bijection $v: W \to N$ defined in Chapter 1 by

$$v(\sigma_k \cdots \sigma_1 \sigma_0) = \sigma_k \times n^k + \cdots + \sigma_1 \times n + \sigma_0$$

describes how words of Σ^* represent numbers.

THEOREM 3.16. The following two functions are primitive recursive.

a. $\text{trim}(x) = \begin{cases} x' & \text{if } x = x'\sigma, \quad \sigma \in \Sigma \\ 0 & \text{if } x = 0 \end{cases}$

b. $\text{lastletterof}(x) = \begin{cases} \sigma & \text{if } x = x'\sigma, \quad \sigma \in \Sigma \\ 0 & \text{if } x = 0 \end{cases}$

Proof. In the n-adic notation specified by the mapping v, the last symbol is eliminated by subtracting 1 and dividing by n. Thus $\text{trim}(x) = (x \dot{-} 1)/n$ and $\text{lastletterof}(x) = x \dot{-} [\text{trim}(x) \times n]$. ∎

THEOREM 3.17. If $g:W^r \to W^s$ and $h_\sigma:W^{r+1+s} \to W^s$, $\sigma \in \Sigma$, are each (primitive/partial) recursive, then so is f defined recursively from g and the h's by

$$f(x,0) = g(x)$$
$$f(x,y\sigma) = h_\sigma[x,y,f(x,y)]$$

Proof. If $d(y) = \text{trim}(y)$, then $d(y) < y$ for $y > 0$. Let $e(x) = \imath(x) = x$. Let

$$h(x,y,z) = \sum_{\sigma \in \Sigma} [(\text{lastletterof}(y) = \sigma) \to h_\sigma(x,\text{trim}(y),z]$$

Then $f(x,0) = g(x)$ and

$$f(x,y\sigma) = h_\sigma[x,y,f(x,y)]$$
$$= h(x,y\sigma,f[e(x),d(y\sigma)])$$

so f may be defined by recursion from d, e, g, and h. Thus f is (primitive/partial) recursive by Theorem 3.13. ∎

Note that when $\Sigma = \Sigma_1$, recursion on the length of the word is exactly the same as primitive recursion, since $y\sigma = y \cdot 1 = y + 1$.

THEOREM 3.18. The following functions are primitive recursive.

a. $R_\sigma(x) = x \cdot \sigma$, the σth right successor function, $\sigma \in \Sigma$

b. $L_\sigma(x) = \sigma \cdot x$, the σth left successor function, $\sigma \in \Sigma$

c. $x \cdot y$, concatenation

d. ρ, the reversal function

e. $\text{chop}(x) = \begin{cases} x' & \text{if } x = \sigma x', \quad \sigma \in \Sigma \\ 0 & \text{if } x = 0 \end{cases}$

f. $\text{length}(x)$, the number of letters in the word x

g. $\text{occurrences}(w,x)$, the number of times that x occurs as a subword of w.

h. $x \preccurlyeq w = \begin{cases} 1 & \text{if } x \text{ is a subword of } w \\ 0 & \text{otherwise} \end{cases}$

i. $U(w,x) = \begin{cases} u & \text{if } u \text{ is the shortest word such that } w = u \cdot x \cdot v \text{ for some } v \\ 0 & \text{if } \neg(x \preccurlyeq w) \end{cases}$

j. $V(w,x) = \begin{cases} v & \text{if } u \text{ is the shortest word such that } w = u \cdot x \cdot v \\ 0 & \text{if } \neg(x \preccurlyeq w) \end{cases}$

k. $\text{replace}(w,x,y) = \begin{cases} u \cdot y \cdot v & \text{if } u \text{ is the shortest word such that } w = u \cdot x \cdot v \\ w & \text{if } \neg(x \preccurlyeq w) \end{cases}$

l. $\text{part}(w,x,k)$, the subword of w which is between the kth and the $(k+1)$st *disjoint* occurrence of x in w as w is scanned from left to right. If there are less than $k+1$ disjoint occurrences of x in w, then $\text{part}(w,x,k) = 0$

m. $\chi_{W^r}(x) = \begin{cases} 1 & \text{if } x \in W^r \\ 0 & \text{if } x \notin W^r \end{cases}$

is primitive recursive in Σ', where $\Sigma \subseteq \Sigma'$ and $W = \Sigma^*$.

Proof. Assume Σ has n members.

a. $R_\sigma(x) = n \times x + \sigma$

b. $L_\sigma(x) = \sigma \cdot x$ using part c

c. $x \cdot 0 = x \qquad x \cdot (y\sigma) = R_\sigma(x \cdot y)$

d. $\rho(0) = 0 \qquad \rho(x\sigma) = \sigma \cdot \rho(x)$

e. $\text{chop} = \rho \circ \text{trim} \circ \rho$

f. $\text{length}(0) = 0$, $\text{length}(x\sigma) = \text{length}(x) + 1$

g. $\text{occurrences}(0,x) = \neg x$

$\text{occurrences}(w\sigma, x) = \bigvee_{y=0}^{w\sigma} (yx = w\sigma) + \text{occurrences}(w,x)$

h. $x \preccurlyeq w = \bigvee_{u=0}^{w} \bigvee_{v=0}^{w} (u \cdot x \cdot v = w) = \text{sign}[\text{occurrences}(w,x)]$

i. $U(w,x) = (\mu u \leq w)[\bigvee_{v=0}^{w} (u \cdot x \cdot v = w)]$

j. $V(w,x) = (\mu v \leq w)[U(w,x) \cdot x \cdot v = w]$

k. $\text{replace}(w,x,y) = \begin{cases} U(w,x) \cdot y \cdot V(w,x) & \text{if } x \preccurlyeq w \\ w & \text{otherwise} \end{cases}$

l. $\text{part}(w,x,0) = U(w,x)$

$\text{part}(w,x,k+1) = \text{part}[V(w,x),x,k]$

m. $\chi_W(0) = 1$

$$\chi_W(x\sigma) = \begin{cases} \chi_W(x) & \text{if } \sigma \in \Sigma \\ 0 & \text{if } \sigma \in \Sigma' - \Sigma \end{cases}$$

and

$$\chi_{W_r}(x_1,\ldots,x_r) = \bigwedge_{i=1}^{r} \chi_W(x_i) \quad \blacksquare$$

Note that the definition of part is by recursion on k, not on the length of x. It uses the recursion scheme discussed in the previous section with $e(w,x) = (V(w,x),x)$ and $d(k) = k \dot{-} 1$.

EXERCISES

1. Prove that the class of primitive recursive functions is closed under the "left" recursion scheme

$$f(0,y) = g(y)$$
$$f(\sigma x,y) = h_\sigma[x,y,f(x,y)]$$

Hint: Use the reversal function ρ as in the proof for the function chop.

2. Prove that $f(w,x) =$ the number of disjoint occurrences of x as a subword of w, is primitive recursive. For example

$$f(12121,\ 121) = 1$$

3. Prove that $\overline{V}(w,x) =$ the smallest $v \leq w$ such that there is a $u \geq 0$ satisfying $w = u \cdot x \cdot v$, is primitive recursive. Let $\overline{V}(w,x) = 0$ if $\neg(x \preccurlyeq w)$.

4. Prove that $f(i,j,x) =$ result of switching the ith and jth characters of x is primitive recursive. Let $f(i,j,x) = 0$ if $i = 0$ or $j = 0$ or length(x) is less than the maximum of i and j.

5. Prove that L_σ^{-1} and ε defined by

$$L_\sigma^{-1}(x) = \begin{cases} x' & \text{if } x = \sigma x' \\ \uparrow & \text{otherwise} \end{cases}$$

and

$$\varepsilon(x) = \begin{cases} 0 & \text{if } x = 0 \\ \uparrow & \text{otherwise} \end{cases}$$

are partial recursive in Σ_n.

6. Prove that $f: W^2 \to W$ given by

$$f(x, y) = \begin{cases} 1 & \text{if occurrences}(x,\sigma) = \text{occurrences}(y,\sigma) \text{ for all } \sigma \in \Sigma \\ 0 & \text{otherwise} \end{cases}$$

is primitive recursive.

3.7 Relationships between Functions in Different Alphabets

The class of (primitive/partial) recursive functions has been defined for an arbitrary, but fixed, finite alphabet Σ. Some very important connections between functions in different alphabets will now be stated. These results are proved in the appendix at the end of this chapter, because the proofs are a little tedious (though straightforward) and would detract from the presentation if given at this point. Throughout this section, assume that $W = \Sigma^*$, and $W' = (\Sigma')^*$.

THEOREM 3.19. Let $\Sigma \subseteq \Sigma'$. If $f: W^r \to W^s$ is (primitive/partial) recursive in Σ, then the function $\bar{f}:(W')^r \to (W')^s$ defined by

$$\bar{f}(x) = \begin{cases} f(x) & \text{if } x \in W^r \\ (0,\ldots,0) & \text{if } x \in (W')^r - W^r \end{cases}$$

is (primitive/partial) recursive in Σ'. The function $\bar{f}$ is called the *null extension* of f. ∎

Let $\nu: W \to N$ and $\nu': W' \to N$ be the bijections defined in Section 1.4. Then $\kappa = \nu^{-1} \circ \nu'$ is a bijection between W' and W. The combination $\kappa \times \kappa \times \cdots \times \kappa$, a bijection between $(W')^r$ and W^r, will also be denoted κ.

The function κ will be used throughout this book to denote the translation of words from one alphabet to another. The reader should note that there is a different κ for each pair of alphabets Σ' and Σ.

The function κ is defined as a mapping from W' to W. Strictly speaking, our definition of the primitive recursive functions included only functions with inputs and outputs from the same alphabet, but if $W \subseteq W'$, then κ^{-1}

can be extended to a total function from W' to W' by assigning the value 0 for $x \in W' - W$. Also κ determines a function from W' to W' since $\kappa(W') = W \subseteq W'$. Both of these functions are primitive recursive.

THEOREM 3.20. For $\Sigma \subseteq \Sigma'$, the function $\kappa: W' \to W$ and the function $\overline{\kappa^{-1}}$ defined by

$$\overline{\kappa^{-1}}(x) = \begin{cases} \kappa^{-1}(x) & \text{if } x \in W \\ 0 & \text{if } x \in W' - W \end{cases}$$

are primitive recursive in Σ'. ▮

If $f: W^r \to W^s$ is a function, then

$$f' = \kappa^{-1} \circ f \circ \kappa: (W')^r \to (W')^s$$

is called the *conjugate* of f in Σ'. See Figure 3-4. Also if $f = \kappa \circ f' \circ \kappa^{-1}$, then f is the conjugate of f'. The conjugate of the conjugate of f is f, since $\kappa \circ \kappa^{-1}$ is the identity function.

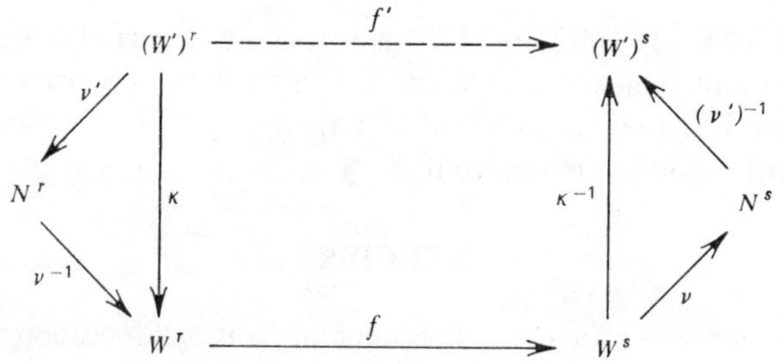

FIGURE 3-4. **Conjugate functions.**

THEOREM 3.21. If f is a (primitive/partial) recursive function in Σ expressed in terms of π, ι, ζ, and ς using the operations composition, combination, exponentiation, and repetition, then $f' = \kappa^{-1} \circ f \circ \kappa$, the conjugate of f in Σ', can be expressed in exactly the same way, where the functions and operations are appropriately interpreted in Σ'. ▮

Theorem 3.21 is actually a statement of the fact that the initial functions π, ι, ζ, and ς, and the operations composition, combination, exponentiation, and repetition are defined in such a way as to be independent of the particular alphabet Σ.

COROLLARY 3.22. $f: W^r \to W^s$ is (primitive/partial) recursive in Σ iff its conjugate f' is (primitive/partial) recursive in Σ'. ▮

If $f: W^r \to W^s$, then f and $f' = \nu \circ f \circ \nu^{-1}: N^r \to N^s$ can also be called conjugates. An analog of Theorem 3.21 holds for f and f', where $f': N^r \to N^s$ is defined to be (primitive/partial) recursive using the obvious analogs of π, ι, ζ, and ς, and the operations of composition, combination, exponentiation, and repetition for the natural numbers. In fact, the functions $f: N^r \to N$ traditionally defined to be (primitive/partial) recursive are precisely those which are conjugates of some (primitive/partial) recursive function in an alphabet Σ.

The conjugate of each of the "numerical" functions defined in Theorem 3.6 is the same function in any other alphabet. For example, the conjugate of multiplication in Σ_n is multiplication in Σ_m. On the other hand, concatenation in Σ_m is not the conjugate of concatenation in Σ_n, because $x \cdot y = m^{\text{length}(y)} \times x + y$ in Σ_m and $x \cdot y = n^{\text{length}(y)} \times x + y$ in Σ_n.

In order to show that a certain function is (primitive/partial) recursive in Σ, it is sometimes convenient to describe a computation in which some of the intermediate results contain symbols not in the alphabet Σ. The next theorem shows that (primitive/partial) recursive computations in the larger alphabet may be used. This theorem will be used often and the statement of the theorem should be studied carefully.

THEOREM 3.23. If $f(W')^r \to (W')^s$ is a (primitive/partial) recursive function in Σ', an alphabet which contains Σ and f has the property that for all $x \in W^r$, $f(x) \in W^s$, that is, $f(W^r) \subseteq W^s$, then $f \mid W^r$, the restriction of f to W^r, is (primitive/partial) recursive in Σ. ▮

EXERCISES

1. Prove that the conjugate of multiplication in Σ_2 is multiplication in Σ_3.

2. Show by counterexample that the conjugate of the successor function R_2 in Σ_2 is not the successor function R_2 in Σ_3.

3. For $m \geq n$, let $\kappa: \Sigma_m^* \to \Sigma_n^*$ be the function defined in this section. Prove $\kappa(x) \geq x$, for all $x \in \Sigma_m^*$, where the order is defined by treating $\kappa(x)$ as a member of Σ_m^*, which is possible since $\Sigma_n^* \subseteq \Sigma_m^*$. Infer that $\kappa^{-1}(y) \leq y$, for all $y \in \Sigma_n^*$.

4. For $m \geq 1$, let $\kappa: \Sigma_m^* \to \Sigma_1^*$. Show that $\kappa^{-1}(y) = \text{length}\ (y)$, for $y \in \Sigma_1^*$, where length is the length function defined in Σ_m.

3.8 The Pairing Function

Theorem 3.21 asserts that it does not matter which alphabet is used to define the class of partial recursive functions. There is a similar result which says that the member of arguments does not really matter either. This result is achieved by defining a primitive recursive bijection between W^r and W, for $r \geq 1$.

The definition of the pairing function $\beta: W^2 \rightarrow W$ is motivated by Figure 3-5 which shows the value of β for some pairs (x,y).

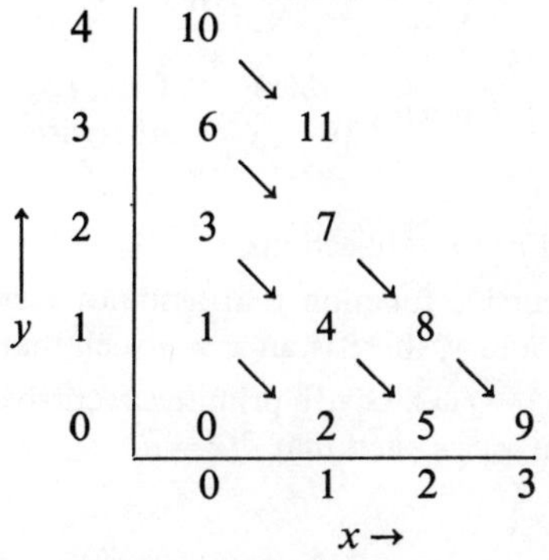

FIGURE 3-5. **The pairing function.**

Let

$$\beta(x,y) = \sum_{i=0}^{x+y} i + x = x + \tfrac{1}{2}(x+y) \times (x+y+1)$$

From Figure 3-5, it is clear that β is a bijection. From its definition, it is primitive recursive. To prove that β^{-1} is primitive recursive, let $\beta^{-1} = \langle \beta', \beta'' \rangle$ and observe that $\beta(x,y) \geq x$ and $\beta(x,y) \geq y$, so that $x = \beta(\beta' x, \beta'' x) \geq \beta' x$, hence $\beta' x \leq x$. Similarly $\beta'' x \leq x$. Thus $\beta'(x) = (\mu y \leq x)[\bigvee_{z=0}^{x} \beta(y,z) = x]$ and $\beta''(x) = (\mu y \leq x)[\beta(\beta' x, y) = x]$, which are primitive recursive by Theorem 3.11.

Let $\beta_1 = \iota: W \rightarrow W$, $\beta_{r+1} = \beta \circ (\beta_r \times \iota)$, that is $\beta_{r+1}(x_1, \ldots, x_r, x_{r+1}) = \beta[\beta_r(x_1, \ldots, x_r), x_{r+1}]$.

THEOREM 3.24. Let r, $s \geq 1$. The functions β_r and β_r^{-1} are primitive recursive bijections between W^r and W. The function $f: W^r \rightarrow W^s$ is (primitive/partial) recursive iff $f' = \beta_s \circ f \circ \beta_r^{-1}: W \rightarrow W$ is (primitive/partial) recursive.
Proof. The second part follows immediately from the fact that β_s and β_r^{-1} are primitive recursive. The proof that β_r and β_r^{-1} are bijections is left as an exercise. ▮

Define ${}_i\beta_r: W \rightarrow W$ by

$${}_i\beta_r(x) = x_i \qquad \text{where } \beta_r(x_1, \ldots, x_r) = x$$

It is easy to show that each ${}_i\beta_r$ is primitive recursive (see Exercise 1). The functions β_r, ${}_i\beta_r$, $1 \leq i \leq r$, can be used to implement subscripted variables in PL (see Section 3.9).

EXERCISES

1. Prove that ${}_i\beta_r$ is primitive recursive for $r \geq 1$, $1 \leq i \leq r$. Prove that $\bar{\beta}: W^3 \rightarrow W$ defined by

$$\bar{\beta}(i, r, x) = \begin{cases} {}_i\beta_r(x) & \text{if } 1 \leq i \leq r \\ 0 & \text{otherwise} \end{cases}$$

is primitive recursive.

2. Prove that β, β_r, and β_r^{-1} are bijections.

3. Give a primitive recursive function that assumes every value infinitely many times, that is, for each n and y, there is an $x > n$ such that $f(x) = y$.

4. Define $\partial fx = f(x+1) \dot{-} f(x)$. Give a primitive recursive function f such that for all n and all d, there is an $x > n$ such that $\partial fx = d$.

3.9 Coding

There are various methods by which a finite set of words can be coded as a single word, either of the same or of a different alphabet. In this section, we discuss several techniques for coding and show how they may be used to extend PL. An important characteristic of each of these methods is that the processes which encode and decode data items are all effective.

Recall the pairing functions ${}_i\beta_r$ and β_r which satisfy for $r \geq 1$, $1 \leq i \leq r$ and all $x, x_1, \ldots, x_r \in W$

$${}_i\beta_r(x) = x_i \quad \text{iff} \quad \beta_r(x_1, \ldots, x_r) = x$$

The function β_r encodes an r-tuple of members of W into a single member of W. The function ${}_i\beta_r$ can then be used to decode this word and to obtain the ith component of the coded word. By Exercise 1 of Section 3.8, ${}_i\beta_r: W \rightarrow W$ and $\beta_r: W^r \rightarrow W$ are primitive recursive for $r \geq 1$, $1 \leq i \leq r$. Hence the pairing functions provide an effective coding technique.

The pairing functions may be used to implement subscripted variables in PL. First add to PL a new statement with syntax:

$$\langle dimension \rangle = \text{DIMENSION } \langle list \rangle;$$
$$\langle list \rangle = \langle name \rangle\ (\langle name \rangle) \mid \langle list \rangle \langle list \rangle$$

A dimension statement may appear wherever a PL statement is permitted. It serves as an abbreviation for a group of legal PL statements and is to be replaced by this group of statements before the program is executed. We give the PL implementation for the DIMENSION statement by showing how a particular statement is handled.

The statement DIMENSION X(Y); when executed with Y $= k$ causes an array X(0),...,X(k) to be established with X(i) $= 0$ for $i \leq k$ X is called a *subscripted variable.* Unlike the FORTRAN DIMENSION statement, this

PL DIMENSION statement causes storage to be allocated *dynamically*, that is, during execution of the program. Different executions of the statement DIMENSION X(Y); may cause different sized arrays to be established, since the value of Y may change.

An occurrence of X(Z), where Z is any unsubscripted variable, is interpreted as a reference to the Zth member of the array $\{X(i) \mid i \leq k\}$. A subscripted variable may be used wherever an ordinary variable is permitted, except as a subscript. All occurrences of subscripted variables are replaced by legal PL statements before the program is executed.

Subscripting is implemented by coding the array X(0), ..., X(k) by $\beta_{k+2}[0,X(0),\ldots,X(k)]$, which for $k = 2$ equals $\beta_2(\beta_2(\beta_2(0,X(0)),X(1)),X(2))$.

The extra 0 eliminates the need to consider some special cases. All DIMENSION statements and occurrences of subscripted variables may be replaced as follows:

1. Replace DIMENSION X(Y); by X ← 0; DIMX ← Y; where DIMX is not used elsewhere in the original program. Note that $0 = \beta_{k+2}(0,\ldots,0)$ for all k.
2. Replace V ← X(Z); by

    Q ← X; COUNT ← DIMX $\dot{-}$ Z;
    LOOP COUNT;
    Q ← ${}_1\beta_2$(Q);
    END;
    V ← ${}_2\beta_2$(Q);

An error check for Z ≤ DIMX can also be added if desired. The names COUNT and Q may not appear in the original program.

3. Replace X(Z) ← V; by

    COUNT ← DIMX $\dot{-}$ Z;
    Q ← X; R ← 0;
    LOOP COUNT;
    R ← β_2(R,${}_2\beta_2$(Q));
    Q ← ${}_1\beta_2$(Q);
    END;
    Q ← β_2(${}_1\beta_2$(Q),V);
    LOOP COUNT;
    Q ← β_2(Q,${}_2\beta_2$(R));
    R ← ${}_1\beta_2$(R);
    END;
    X ← Q;

The names COUNT, R, and Q should not appear in the original program.

4. Replace LOOP X(Z); by V ← X(Z); LOOP V; and proceed as in 2.
5. The remaining PL statements are similar to 2 and 3 above.

As with the PL extensions discussed in Chapter 2, care must be exercised to use new names which do not already appear in the program. Also labels on statements containing subscripted variables should appear on the first replacement statement. While we have not done so, various checks for errors can be easily built into the implementation.

The implementation is completed by replacing statements of the form $V \leftarrow f(Z_1,\ldots,Z_k)$ by the PL code which sets V to $f(Z_1,\ldots,Z_k)$. All functions used are primitive recursive and are therefore also PL $-$ {GOTO}-computable.

The above implementation does not allow the use of subscripted variables as subscripts. The extension to include this feature is a little more complicated but presents no additional technical problems.

A second coding technique is based on the prime decomposition theorem of number theory which states that every number $x > 1$ has a unique representation of the form $\text{prime}\#(0)^{e_0} \times \cdots \times \text{prime}\#(j)^{e_j}$, for some $e_0, \ldots, e_j \geq 0$ ($\text{prime}\#(i)$ is the ith prime number). This method is often called *Gödel numbering* because it was first used by Gödel to prove that first-order number theory is incomplete.

The Gödel number $\text{gn}(x_0,\ldots,x_{r-1})$ of an r-tuple $(x_0,x_1,\ldots,x_{r-1}) \in W^r$, $r \geq 0$, is given by $\text{gn}(\,) = 1$ and

$$\text{gn}(x_0,\ldots,x_{r-1}) = \prod_{i=0}^{r \dot{-} 1} \text{prime}\#(i)^{x_i+1}$$

For example, $\text{gn}(6,8,0,3,0) = 2^7 \times 3^9 \times 5 \times 7^4 \times 11$.

This defines a mapping from all tuples of words in W into W, that is

$$\text{gn}\colon \bigcup_{r=0}^{\infty} W^r \to W$$

The mapping is 1-1 by the prime decomposition theorem but is not onto.

For $0 \leq i < r$, $x_i = \exp[\text{gn}(x_0,\ldots,x_{r-1}), i] \dot{-} 1$. Note that by Exercise 5 of Section 3.4 and Theorem 3.12, exp and prime# are primitive recursive.

For fixed r, both β_r and gn are effective 1-1 mappings from W^r into W. Both have been very important in the development of the theory of computation.

Subscripting in PL may be implemented by encoding the values X(0), ..., X(k) as the Gödel number $\text{gn}(\text{X}(0),\ldots,\text{X}(k)) = \prod_{i=0}^{k} \text{prime}\#(i)^{\text{X}(i)+1}$

1. replace DIMENSION X(Y); by

$$\text{X} \leftarrow \prod_{i=0}^{\text{Y}} \text{prime}\#(i);\ \text{DIMX} \leftarrow \text{Y};$$

2. replace V $\leftarrow$ X(Z); by V $\leftarrow$ exp(X,Z) $\dot{-}$ 1;

3. replace X(Z) ← V; by

$$\text{IF Z} \neq 0 \text{ THEN; X} \leftarrow \prod_{i=0}^{Z \dot{-} 1} (\text{prime}\#(i)^{\exp(X,i)}) \times \text{prime}\#(Z)^{V+1}$$

$$\times \prod_{i=Z+1}^{\text{DIMX}} (\text{prime}\#(i)^{\exp(X,i)}); \text{ END;}$$

$$\text{ELSE; X} \leftarrow 2^{V+1} \times \prod_{i=1}^{\text{DIMX}} (\text{prime}\#(i)^{\exp(X,i)}); \text{ END;}$$

4. replace LOOP X(Z); by
   COUNT ← exp(X,Z) $\dot{-}$ 1;
   LOOP COUNT;
5. the remaining cases are handled similarly

Gödel numbers may also be used to code finite sequences of r-tuples of words. If $S_i = ({}_ix_0,\ldots,{}_ix_{r-1})$, then

$$\overline{\text{gn}}(S_0,\ldots,S_{k-1}) = \prod_{i=0}^{k \dot{-} 1} \text{prime}\#(i)^{\text{gn } S_i}$$

One problem with this scheme is that it is not possible to distinguish the Gödel numbers of r-tuples of words from those of sequences of r-tuples of words. This problem is left as Exercise 1.

The original use of Gödel numbers was to code words in Σ^* as numbers. For example, if $\Sigma = \{a,b,c\}$, then a correspondence between Σ and numbers, say $a \leftrightarrow 1$, $b \leftrightarrow 2$, $c \leftrightarrow 3$, was defined. Then the Gödel number of $x = abcbb$ would be $2^1 \times 3^2 \times 5^3 \times 7^2 \times 11^2$. A method for coding words as numbers was necessary because only functions on the natural numbers were considered. Since our functions are defined as mappings from words to words, it is not necessary to code single words; words are already permissible inputs to functions. For this reason, we discuss Gödel numbering as a method for coding an r-tuple of words by a single word.

Also of interest are methods of coding which use one alphabet to encode words on another alphabet. For example, the bijection $\kappa: W \to W'$ provides an effective coding of W in terms of W', that is, for $x \in W$, $\kappa(x) \in W'$ is a coding of x in W'. The function κ converts the W representation of $\nu(x)$ into the W' representation of $\nu(x)$.

The words in any alphabet can be coded in terms of a two-letter alphabet. For example, let $\Sigma = \{a_1,a_2,a_3\}$. The function g as defined below provides a 1-1 effective map from Σ^* into $\{a,b\}^*$.

$$g(0) = 0$$
$$g(a_i) = ab^ia,\ 1 \leq i \leq 3$$
$$g(xa_i) = g(x)\cdot g(a_i),\ x > 0,\ 1 \leq i \leq 3$$

For example, $g(a_2a_2a_1a_3) = abbaabbaabaabbba$. This coding scheme will be important in Chapter 5.

Concatenation can be used to code finite subsets of Σ^* as single members of $(\Sigma \cup \{\$\})^*$ (assuming $\$ \notin \Sigma$). For example, $V = \{x_1, x_2, x_3\} \subseteq \Sigma^*$ can be encoded as $x_1\$x_2\$x_3\$$.

EXERCISES

1. Define a Gödel numbering $\overline{\text{gn}}:[\cup_{r=0}^{\infty} W^r \cup (\cup_{k=0}^{\infty} (\cup_{r=0}^{\infty} W^r)^k)] \to W$ which is 1-1.

2. A queue Q is a (possibly empty) linear list of data items $d_0 \cdots d_k$ which may be accessed as follows:

a. an item d may be added to the rear of Q to obtain $d\, d_0 \cdots d_k$.

b. the item d_k may be removed from the front of the queue leaving $d_0 \cdots d_{k-1}$

Implement queues in PL by adding the following statements: QUEUE Q initializes Q as an empty queue; V ←FRONT (Q) removes an item from the front of Q and assigns it to the variable V; REAR(Q) ← V adds V to the rear of Q. Show how these additions can be implemented in PL.

3.10 Recursive Sets

A set $A \subseteq W^r$ is defined to be (*primitive*) *recursive* iff its characteristic function

$$\chi_A(x) = \begin{cases} 1 & \text{if } x \in A \\ 0 & \text{if } x \notin A \end{cases}$$

is (primitive) recursive. Since a characteristic function and a "predicate" are exactly the same thing, A is recursive iff the predicate which states "$x \in A$" is recursive.

THEOREM 3.25. Suppose A, $B \subseteq W^r$, $C \subseteq W^s$ and $f: W^r \to W^s$ are all (primitive) recursive.

a. $\varnothing$ and W^r are primitive recursive

b. $A \cup B$ is (primitive) recursive

c. $A \cap B$ is (primitive) recursive

d. $\bar{A} = W^r - A$ is (primitive) recursive

e. all finite sets are primitive recursive

f. all cofinite sets (complements of finite sets) are primitive recursive

g. $A \cdot B$ is (primitive) recursive if $r = 1$

h. A^* and A^+ are (primitive) recursive if $r = 1$

i. $A \times C$ is (primitive) recursive

j. $f^{-1}(C) = \{x \in W^r \mid f(x) \in C\}$ is primitive recursive.

Proof.

a. $\chi_\varnothing = 0$, $\chi_{W^r} = 1$

b. $\chi_{A \cup B} = \chi_A \vee \chi_B$

c. $\chi_{A \cap B} = \chi_A \wedge \chi_B$
d. $\chi_{\bar{A}} = \neg \chi_A$
e. if A is the finite set $\{x_1, x_2, \ldots, x_k\}$, then $\chi_A(x) = \text{eq}(x,x_1) \vee \cdots \vee \text{eq}(x,x_k)$
f. this follows from d and e
g. $\chi_{A \cdot B}(x) = \bigvee_{u=0}^{x} \bigvee_{v=0}^{x} [\chi_A(u) \wedge \chi_B(v) \wedge u \cdot v = x]$
h. let $f(x,0) = \neg x, f(x,k+1) = \bigvee_{u=0}^{x} \bigvee_{v=0}^{x} [\chi_A(u) \wedge f(v,k) \wedge u \cdot v = x]$,

then $f(x,k)$ is the characteristic function of $A(k) = \overbrace{A \cdots A}^{k}$ (recall that $A(0) = \{0\}$), thus $\chi_{A^*}(x) = \bigvee_{k=0}^{\text{length}(x)} f(x,k)$ (see Exercise 1)
i. $\chi_{A \times W^r} = \chi_A \circ p$, where $p(x,y) = x$ and $A \times C = (W^r \times C) \cap (A \times W^s)$
j. $\chi_{f^{-1}(C)} = \chi_C \circ f$, since $x \in f^{-1}(C)$ iff $f(x) \in C$ ▮

By Church's thesis, a set is recursive iff its characteristic function is effectively computable. Hence recursive sets are precisely those sets whose membership problems can be effectively decided, that is, there is an effective procedure which, given an arbitrary $x \in W^r$, eventually stops and indicates whether or not x is in the set.

The symmetry indicated by Theorem 3.25d between the decision problem of a recursive set and its complement is extremely important. The set $H = \{x \mid f_x(x) \text{ is defined}\}$, where $\{f_x\}$ is an effective enumeration of the PL-computable functions, is an example of a nonrecursive set admitting a procedure which, for an arbitrary x, eventually halts and says "yes" if $x \in H$, but never halts if $x \notin H$. Much of the theory of decidability is based on the difference between these two types of procedures.

EXERCISES

1. If m is the length of x, prove that $x \in A^*$ iff $x \in A(k)$ for some $k \leq m$. This problem is the same as Exercise 1g of Section 1.4.

2. The alert reader may have realized that we now have two different definitions of "recursive function", since a function was defined as a set of input/output pairs (x,y). Fortunately, the two definitions are consistent. Let $f: W^r \to W^s$ be any total function. Let $A = \{(x,y) \mid f(x) = y\}$. The set A is sometimes called the *graph* of f. The way we have defined function, A and f are exactly the same set, but we use the letter A to emphasize that we are thinking of f as a set of ordered pairs. Prove that f is a recursive function iff A is a recursive set, that is, χ_A is recursive.

3.11 History

The functions that are now called "primitive recursive" were called "recursive" by Gödel [1931, 1934] when he used them to show that for any logical system satisfying certain reasonable conditions, there are true propositions about arithmetic that are not provable in the system. In these two papers, Gödel also used the coding scheme discussed in Section 3.9, now called "Gödel numbering" or "arithmetization". The name "primitive recursive" was first used in Kleene [1936a].

The primitive recursive functions had been studied prior to Gödel by Dedekind [1888], Hilbert [1926], Ackermann [1928], and others. The paper by Ackermann contains a proof that there is an intuitively computable total (that is, recursive) function which is not primitive recursive. This function, now called Ackerman's function was discussed in Section 3.5. A proof that it is not primitive recursive is given in Chapter 10.

Following a suggestion of Herbrand, Gödel [1934] used systems of equations to define a class of functions properly containing the primitive recursive functions which he called "general recursive" but which are now called "recursive". Kleene [1936a] used Gödel numbering to prove that there is no effective procedure for deciding whether such an arbitrary system of equations defines a general recursive function. This is equivalent to the nonexistence of an algorithm for deciding whether an arbitrary partial recursive function is recursive (see Chapter 6).

As mentioned previously, our definitions of the (primitive/partial) recursive functions differ in several respects from those originally given by Gödel, Herbrand, and Kleene. A proof that the recursive functions (on natural numbers) could be defined from the initial functions $\varsigma(x) = x + 1$, $z(x) = 0$ and ${}_ip_r(x_1, \ldots, x_r) = x_i$, $r \geq 1$, $1 \leq i \leq r$ using primitive recursion, composition, and minimization was given by Kleene [1936a]. A study of recursive functions with *words* for inputs and outputs was made by Asser [1960]. Eilenberg and Elgot [1970] discussed recursive functions with multiple outputs and also developed the idea of replacing minimization and primitive recursion with the simpler operations repetition and exponentiation.

The equivalence between the primitive recursive functions and the PL $\dot{-}$ {GOTO}-computable functions was proved in Meyer and Ritchie [1967a,b]. Further results of this type are discussed in Chapter 10.

There are two excellent document source books for studying the early development of the theory of computation: Davis [1965] and Van Heijenoort [1967]. Many of the papers referenced above are contained in these books.

APPENDIX: PROOFS OF THEOREMS IN SECTION 3.7

Throughout the appendix, we assume without loss of generality that each alphabet Σ is $\Sigma_n = \{1,2,\ldots,n\}$, for some n. Let $W_n = \Sigma_n^*$ and $\nu_n: W_n \to N$.

THEOREM 3.19. Let $m \geq n$. The null extension of a (primitive/partial) recursive function in Σ_n is (primitive/partial) recursive in Σ_m.

Proof. The proof is by induction on the structure of its definition. If f is $\imath$, then

$$\bar{\imath}(x) = \chi_{W_n}(x) \to x$$

which is primitive recursive in Σ_m by Theorems 3.8 and 3.18m. More precisely, we perhaps could write

$$_n\bar{\iota}(x) = \chi_{W_n}(x) \rightarrow {}_m\iota(x)$$

where $_n\iota$ and $_m\iota$ are the identity functions in Σ_n and Σ_m, respectively.

If f is the zero function ζ, or the projection function π in Σ_n, then $\bar{f}$ is the zero function or projection function in Σ_m, that is, $_n\bar{\zeta} = {}_m\zeta$ and $_n\bar{\pi} = {}_m\pi$.

If f is the successor function ς in Σ_n and σ' denotes the next larger digit after σ, then

$$\bar{f}(0) = 1$$

$$\bar{f}(x\sigma) = \begin{cases} \chi_{W_n}(x) \rightarrow x \cdot \sigma' & \text{if } \sigma < n \\ \chi_{W_n}(x) \rightarrow \bar{f}(x) \cdot 1 & \text{if } \sigma = n \\ 0 & \text{if } n < \sigma \leq m \end{cases}$$

Note that for $m > n$,

$$_n\bar{\varsigma} \neq \chi_{W_n} \rightarrow {}_m\varsigma$$

If $f = g \circ h$ where $h: W_n^r \rightarrow W_n^s$ and $g: W_n^s \rightarrow W_n^t$ are (primitive/partial) recursive in Σ_n, then by the induction hypothesis, $\bar{g}$ and $\bar{h}$ are (primitive/partial) recursive in Σ_m and so is $\bar{f}$ since

$$\bar{f} = \chi_{W_n{}^r} \rightarrow \bar{g} \circ \bar{h}$$

Similarly, if $f = g \times h$ where $g: W_n^r \rightarrow W_n^s$ and $h: W_n^t \rightarrow W_n^u$, then

$$\bar{f} = \chi_{W_n{}^{r+t}} \rightarrow \bar{g} \times \bar{h}$$

and if $f = g^\nabla$ where $g: W_n^{r+1} \rightarrow W_n^{r+1}$, then

$$\bar{f} = \chi_{W_n{}^{r+1}} \rightarrow \bar{g}^\nabla$$

The case $f = g^\#$ is more difficult as illustrated by the following example: Let $g(x) = x \cdot 1$ in Σ_1, then $g^\#(0,11) = 11$ in Σ_1. Also in Σ_2

$$\bar{g}(x) = \begin{cases} x \cdot 1 & \text{if } x \in \Sigma_1^* \\ 0 & \text{if } x \notin \Sigma_1^* \end{cases}$$

Thus $\bar{g}^\#(0,11) = 111$ in Σ_2, since $\nu_2(11) = 3$, but $\overline{g^\#}(0,11) = 11$.
However, we may define $\bar{f} = \overline{g^\#}$ by recursion as follows:
Let $x^- = (\mu z \leq x)[{}_n\bar{\varsigma}(z) = x]$. We already know that the null extension of the successor function in Σ_n is primitive recursive in Σ_m thus x^- is primitive recursive in Σ_m by Theorem 3.11 and satisfies

a. $x^- = 0$ if $x \in W_m - W_n$ or $x = 0$
b. $_n\varsigma(x^-) = x$ if $x \in W_n$ and $x \neq 0$

Now define

$$h(x,0) = x$$
$$h(x,y) = \bar{g} \circ h(x,y^-)$$

using recursion (Theorem 3.13) in Σ_m. Then

$$\overline{g^{\#}}(x,y) = \chi_{W_n{}^{r+1}}(x,y) \to h(x,y) \quad \blacksquare$$

The following lemma is needed for the proofs of Theorems 3.20 and 3.23.

LEMMA 3.26 Let $m \geq n \geq j$ and $\kappa = \nu_j^{-1} \circ \nu_m : W_m \to W_j$. Then $\kappa | W_n$ and

$$\overline{(\kappa | W_n)^{-1}}(x) = \begin{cases} \kappa^{-1}(x) & \text{if } x \in \kappa(W_n) \\ 0 & \text{if } x \notin \kappa(W_n) \end{cases}$$

are both primitive recursive in W_n.

Proof. Define $g: W_n \to W_n$ as follows:

$$g(0) = 0$$
$$g(x\sigma) = m \times g(x) + \sigma$$

If the word $x \in W_n$ is treated as the m-adic representation of a number r, then $g(x)$ is the n-adic representation of r. Define $h: W_n \to W_n$ by

$$h(0) = 0$$
$$h(x) = h[(x \dot{-} 1)/j] \cdot [1 + \text{rem}(x \dot{-} 1, j)]$$

If x is the n-adic representation of r, then $h(x)$ is the j-adic representation of r. Thus, $(\kappa | W_n)(x) = h \circ g(x)$. Also

$$\overline{(\kappa | W_n)^{-1}}(y) = (\mu x \leq y)[(\kappa | W_n)(x) = y]$$

The proof that $\overline{(\kappa | W_n)^{-1}}(y) \leq y$ is Exercise 3 of Section 3.7. $\blacksquare$

THEOREM 3.20. For any $m \geq j \geq 1$, the function $\kappa: W_m \to W_j$ and $\overline{\kappa^{-1}}$, where

$$\overline{\kappa^{-1}}(x) = \begin{cases} \kappa^{-1}(x) & \text{if } x \in W_j \\ 0 & \text{if } x \in W_m - W_j \end{cases}$$

are primitive recursive in Σ_m.

Proof. Let $m = n$ in Lemma 3.26. The lemma will be used with $n = j$ in the proof of Theorem 3.23. $\blacksquare$

THEOREM 3.21. If f is a (primitive/partial) recursive function in Σ_n expressed in terms of π, ι, ζ, and ς using the operations composition, combination, exponentiation, and repetition, then the conjugate of f (either in N or any other alphabet) can be expressed in exactly the same way.

Proof. The theorem is first proved for $f: N^r \to N^s$ and its conjugate $f' = \nu^{-1} \circ f \circ \nu: W^r \to W^s$ in an arbitrary alphabet Σ. Then the result follows for conjugate functions in two different alphabets because they are both conjugates of the same function in N.

The conjugates of the initial functions are the same initial functions. For example, if f is the successor function in N, then $f'(x) = \nu^{-1} \circ f \circ \nu(x) = \nu^{-1}(\nu x + 1) = \nu^{-1} \circ \nu \circ \varsigma(x) = \varsigma(x)$, the successor function in Σ.

The conjugate of $f \circ g$ is $f' \circ g'$. The conjugate of $f \times g$ is $f' \times g'$. Suppose $(x,y) = g^y(x)$ in N. Then

$$\begin{aligned} f'(x,y) &= \nu^{-1} \circ f \circ \nu(x,y) \\ &= \nu^{-1} \circ f(\nu x, \nu y) \\ &= \nu^{-1} \circ g^{\nu y}(\nu x) \\ &= \nu^{-1} \circ \overbrace{g \circ g \circ \cdots \circ g}^{\nu y \text{ times}}(\nu x) \\ &= (\nu^{-1} \circ g \circ \nu) \circ \cdots \circ (\nu^{-1} \circ g \circ \nu)(x) \\ &= (g')^y(x), \text{ where } g' = \nu^{-1} \circ g \circ \nu \end{aligned}$$

Finally, if $f = g^\nabla$, then $f' = (g')^\nabla$ since $x = 1$ iff $\nu(x) = 1$. ▮

THEOREM 3.23. Let $m \geq n$. If $f: W_m^r \to W_m^s$ is a (primitive/partial) recursive function in Σ_m and $f(W_n^r) \subseteq W_n^s$, then $f | W_n^r$ is (primitive/partial) recursive in Σ_n.

Proof. To simplify things slightly, assume $r = s = 1$. Let $\kappa: W_m \to W_n$. The conjugate $\kappa \circ f \circ \kappa^{-1}$ is then (primitive/partial) recursive in Σ_n by Theorem 3.21. Letting $j = n$ in Lemma 3.26, the function

$$\overline{(\kappa | W_n)^{-1}} \circ \kappa \circ f \circ \kappa^{-1} \circ (\kappa | W_n)$$

is (primitive/partial) recursive in Σ_n. This function is $f | W_n$. For $x \in W_n$,

$$\kappa^{-1} \circ (\kappa | W_n)(x) = \kappa^{-1} \circ \kappa(x) = x$$

Since $f(W_n) \subseteq W_n$, $f(x) \in W_n$, which means $\kappa \circ f(x) \in \kappa(W_n)$, so that

$$\overline{(\kappa | W_n)^{-1}} \circ \kappa \circ f(x) = \kappa^{-1} \circ \kappa \circ f(x) = f(x) \quad ▮$$

CHAPTER 4

Machine Languages

In Chapters 2 and 3, two algorithmic languages, PL and the definition scheme for the partial recursive functions, were presented. A common characteristic of these languages is that they are defined in a representation-independent fashion. That is, the classes of PL programs and partial recursive definitions do not depend on the alphabet chosen. Of course, the actual transformations performed by a PL program will vary with the alphabet so that the same program computes a different function $f: W^r \to W^s$ for each Σ. In this chapter we consider algorithmic languages which are designed for machines having fixed memory characteristics. Statements in these languages must explicitly specify how words stored in the machine's memory are to be manipulated. Languages of this type are often referred to as machine languages.

Results in this chapter show that every function computed by a PL program (and therefore every partial recursive function) can be computed by programs for each of the three machines considered. In Chapter 5 we will complete the chain of inclusions by showing that each function computed by a machine language program for these machines is computed by a labeled Markov algorithm and that each function computed by a labeled Markov algorithm is partial recursive.

4.1 Machines and Programs

In simplistic terms a digital computer consists of a collection of memory registers and some instructions which can test and modify the data stored in these registers. In addition, a computer has input and output facilities for transferring information between the registers of the machine and the outside world. The definition of a machine given here is designed to capture the basic properties of these features and yet be simple enough to allow us to study the formal properties of machines.

A *machine* in the alphabet Σ consists of a set of *memory registers* each of which can contain an arbitrary member of $W = \Sigma^*$, a set X of *memory con-*

figurations, a set $\mathfrak{R}$ of *instructions* where each $f \in \mathfrak{R}$ is a function $f: X \to X$, an *input function* $\alpha: W^r \to X$, and an *output function* $\omega: X \to W^s$. Each member of X, that is, each memory configuration, is one possible collection of information that may be stored in the memory registers. For example, if there are two memory registers and, if $X = W \times W$, then $(x_1,x_2) \in X$ represents $x_1 \in W$ stored in register 1 and $x_2 \in W$ stored in register 2. The instructions of a machine are functions, not necessarily total, whose arguments and values are memory configurations. For example, if $X = W \times W$, and $\imath$ and R_σ are as defined in Chapters 1 and 3, then $\imath \times R_\sigma$ is an instruction which adds σ to the right end of the word stored in register 2. The input function maps an r-tuple of input words into a memory configuration while the output function maps a memory configuration into an s-tuple of output words. The input and output functions need not be total.

Associated with each machine is an algorithmic language as in Chapter 1. For the machines we will study, these "machine languages" are computationally equivalent to PL. The main difference between such machine languages and so called higher level languages such as PL, ALGOL, or FORTRAN is that the former are intimately involved with the characteristics of a particular machine whereas the latter are to some extent machine-independent. Of course the distinction blurs when one considers micro-programmed computers having programmer defined machine languages.

In the following definition of a program, each instruction will have a label, which may or may not be different from all other instruction labels in the program. Associated with each instruction will also be the label of the next instruction to be executed. Each triple consisting of a label, an instruction, and the label of the next instruction to be executed is called a *statement*.

A *program* for a machine is a system $\mathcal{T} = \langle \mathfrak{L}, I, S, T\rangle$, where $\mathfrak{L}$ is a finite set of instruction *labels*, $I \subseteq \mathfrak{L}$ is a set of *initial labels*, $S \subseteq \mathfrak{L} \times \mathfrak{R} \times \mathfrak{L}$ is a finite set of *statements*, and $T \subseteq \mathfrak{L}$ is a set of *terminal labels*.

Recall that $L_\sigma(x) = \sigma x$, so L_σ^{-1} is the function characterized by

$$L_\sigma^{-1}(x) = \begin{cases} x' & \text{if } x = \sigma x' \\ \uparrow & \text{otherwise} \end{cases}$$

The function R_σ^{-1} is defined similarly.

Define the function ε by

$$\varepsilon(x) = \begin{cases} 0 & \text{if } x = 0 \\ \uparrow & \text{otherwise} \end{cases}$$

Example. Consider a one-register machine where $X = W_2 = \Sigma_2^*$ and $\mathfrak{R} = \{L_1^{-1}, L_1, \varepsilon\}$. Let $\mathcal{T}$ be the program $\langle \mathfrak{L}, I, S, T\rangle$ where $\mathfrak{L} = \{1,2,3\}$, $I = \{1\}$, $S = \{(1,L_1^{-1},1), (1,\varepsilon,2), (2,L_1,2), (2,L_1^{-1},3)\}$, and $T = \{3\}$.

It is often convenient to represent a program with a labeled directed graph. Figure 4-1 shows a graph representation of the program $\mathfrak{T}$ described above. In the graph, the nodes represent the instruction labels of the program and the edges of the graph are labeled with the corresponding instructions from $\mathfrak{R}$. Initial labels are shown with a small arrow pointing to them and terminal labels are shown with a small arrow pointing away.

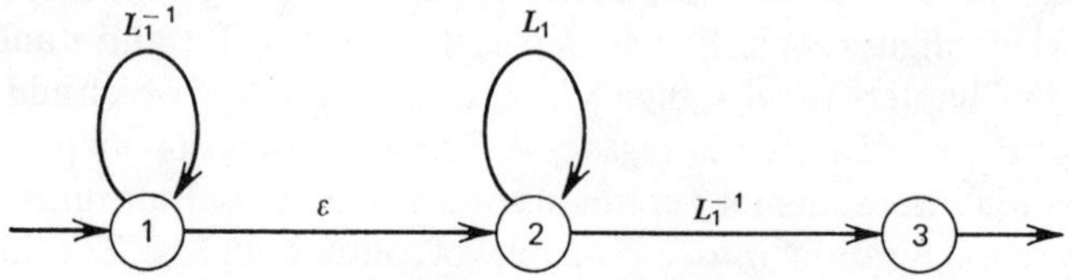

FIGURE 4-1. **Graphical representation of a program.**

There are some similarities between the graphical representation of a program as described above and flow charts for computer programs. For example, if there are two or more instructions with the same label, they will show up in a graph as multiple edges leaving a single node. This indicates a "branch", a point in the program at which a decision is made. On the other hand, computations are usually displayed within the nodes of a flow chart but occur on the edges of the graphs discussed here.

A *path* of length k is a sequence of statements of the form $p = (l_0,f_1,l_1)(l_1,f_2,l_2)\cdots(l_{k-1},f_k,l_k)$. Each label by itself is considered to be a path of length 0. The *computation* of the path p is $|p| = f_k \circ\cdots\circ f_1$. The computation of a path of length 0 is the identity function on X. The computation of a path applied to a memory configuration gives a value only if the initial configuration is in the domain of the computation. A path is *successful* if $l_0 \in I$ and $l_k \in T$.

Each program $\mathfrak{T}$ defines a relation $|\mathfrak{T}| = \{(x,y) | x,y \in X$ and there is a successful path p, $|p| = f_k \circ\cdots\circ f_1$ and $y = f_k \circ\cdots\circ f_1(x)\}$. Thus $(x,y) \in |\mathfrak{T}|$ means that for some successful path p, if the initial contents of the registers of the machine were $x \in X$, then the contents of the registers would be y when the program reached the terminal label at the end of the path.

Note that $|\mathfrak{T}|$ need not be a function, since for two different values of y, (x,y) may be in the relation $|\mathfrak{T}|$. It is possible to think of two distinct computations as being performed by different copies of the same program at different times. There is no interaction between the different executions of the program. For the program in Figure 4-1, both (111,1) and (111,11) are in $|\mathfrak{T}|$. In particular note that if the single register contains $1 \cdot x$, for some $x \in W_2$, at label 2, then either L_1 or L_1^{-1} can be applied with control transferring to label 2 or label 3, respectively. Also, for no y is $(22, y)$ in $|\mathfrak{T}|$, since no statement with label 1 contains an instruction having 22 in its domain.

This nondeterministic model of a machine can behave in a way that, it is hoped, real machines never behave. In some areas of computability theory, programs which compute two different y values for a given x play an important role, but with one or two exceptions, we will not discuss such programs in this book. However, in Theorem 7.6, we will prove one result that is expected from Church's thesis: Allowing nondeterministic programs does not increase the computing power of any device that already can compute all partial recursive functions.

In the previous example, $|\mathfrak{T}| = \{(x,y) \mid x,y \in W_1\} = W_1^2$. To show that $(111,11) \in |\mathfrak{T}|$, consider the path $p = (1,L_1^{-1},1)(1,L_1^{-1},1)(1,L_1^{-1},1)(1,\varepsilon,2)$ $(2,L_1,2)(2,L_1,2)(2,L_1,2)(2,L_1^{-1},3)$. Then $|p| = L_1^{-1} \circ L_1^3 \circ \varepsilon \circ (L_1^{-1})^3$ and $|p|$ $(111) = (11)$.

Example. Consider a two-register machine where $X = W \times W$ and $W = \Sigma_2^*$. Let $\mathfrak{R} = \{\iota \times L_\sigma^{-1},\ R_\sigma^{-1} \times \iota \mid \sigma \in \Sigma_2\} \cup \{\varepsilon \times \iota,\ \iota \times \varepsilon\}$ and let $\mathfrak{T}$ be the program shown in Figure 4-2. In this case $|\mathfrak{T}| = \{((x,y),(0,0)) \mid x = \rho y\}$.

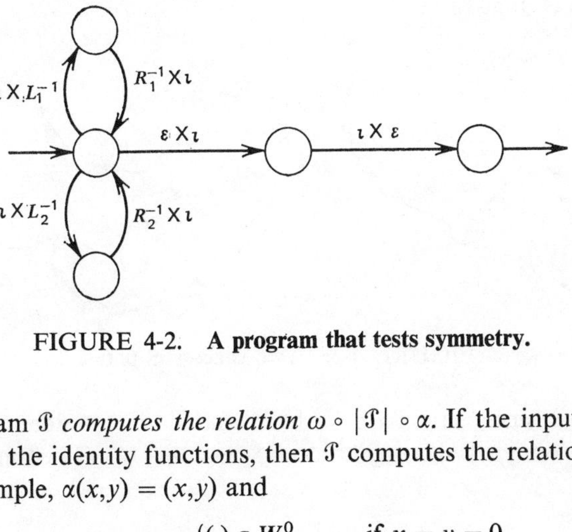

FIGURE 4-2. **A program that tests symmetry.**

The program $\mathfrak{T}$ *computes the relation* $\omega \circ |\mathfrak{T}| \circ \alpha$. If the input and output functions are the identity functions, then $\mathfrak{T}$ computes the relation $|\mathfrak{T}|$.

If, for example, $\alpha(x,y) = (x,y)$ and

$$\omega(x,y) = \begin{cases} (\,) \in W^0 & \text{if } x = y = 0 \\ \uparrow & \text{otherwise} \end{cases}$$

then the program $\mathfrak{T}$ shown in Figure 4-2 computes the relation $\omega \circ |\mathfrak{T}| \circ \alpha = \{(x,y) \mid x = \rho(y)\}$.

A program $\mathfrak{T}$ is *deterministic* if (a) it has one initial label, and (b) whenever (l,f_1,l_1) and (l,f_2,l_2) are distinct statements of $\mathfrak{T}$, then $\operatorname{dom} f_1 \cap \operatorname{dom} f_2 = \varnothing$. Part a means that all computations begin at the same label and part b means that for any memory configuration and any label, at most one instruction having that label is applicable to the memory configuration. Neither of the examples given is deterministic. An *exit* program is a program which does not contain statements of the form (l_1,f,l_2) with l_1 a terminal label.

LEMMA 4.1. If p_1 and p_2 are distinct successful paths of a deterministic exit program $\mathcal{I}$, then $\text{dom}\,|p_1| \cap \text{dom}\,|p_2| = \varnothing$.

Proof. If two paths are distinct, then since they must both begin at the single initial label, one must be an initial segment of the other or they must branch at some point. Since $\mathcal{I}$ is an exit program, the first alternative cannot hold. Thus, the situation must be as illustrated in Figure 4-3. Let $f = |p|$, $f_1' = |p_1'|, f_2' = |p_2'|$. Then $f_1 = f_1' \circ f = |p_1|$ and $f_2 = f_2' \circ f = |p_2|$. The following assertions are true for any functions:

a. $\text{dom}\,(g \circ h) \subseteq \text{dom}\,h$,
b. If $\text{dom}\,h_1 \cap \text{dom}\,h_2 = \varnothing$, then $\text{dom}\,(g_1 \circ h_1) \cap \text{dom}\,(g_2 \circ h_2) = \varnothing$, which follows from a.
c. If $\text{dom}\,g_1 \cap \text{dom}\,g_2 = \varnothing$, then $\text{dom}\,(g_1 \circ h) \cap \text{dom}\,(g_2 \circ h) = \varnothing$, since $x \in \text{dom}\,(g_1 \circ h) \cap \text{dom}\,(g_2 \circ h)$ implies $h(x) \in \text{dom}\,g_1 \cap \text{dom}\,g_2$, which is impossible.

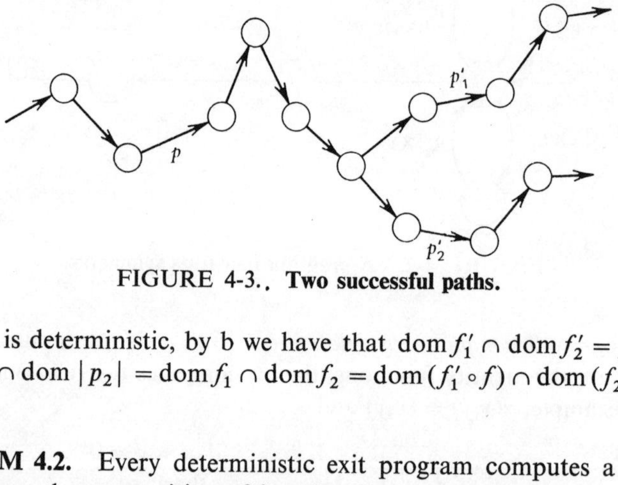

FIGURE 4-3.. **Two successful paths.**

Since $\mathcal{I}$ is deterministic, by b we have that $\text{dom}\,f_1' \cap \text{dom}\,f_2' = \varnothing$. Hence $\text{dom}\,|p_1| \cap \text{dom}\,|p_2| = \text{dom}\,f_1 \cap \text{dom}\,f_2 = \text{dom}\,(f_1' \circ f) \cap \text{dom}\,(f_2' \circ f) = \varnothing$ by c. ▮

THEOREM 4.2. Every deterministic exit program computes a function.

Proof. Since the composition of functions is a function, the computation of any successful path must be a function. By Lemma 4.1, the domains of all successful paths must be disjoint, hence $|\mathcal{I}|$ is a function which immediately implies that $\omega \circ |\mathcal{I}| \circ \alpha$ is also a function. ▮

A *complete* program is a deterministic exit program which has the additional property that for each nonterminal label l, $\cup\,\text{dom}\,f = X$, where the union is taken over all f such that (l,f,l') is a program statement for some label l'.

This means that each label is a terminal label or else there is exactly one applicable instruction for each possible configuration of the registers. Real computer programs should be complete, that is, each statement should specify a single unambiguous operation which can be performed regardless of the value of the variables in the program. To ensure that this will be true, the definition of computer instructions must indicate what action is to be taken in special cases such as division by 0 or the taking of the logarithm of a negative number. In the following sections we will be primarily concerned with complete programs.

EXERCISES

1. Construct deterministic exit programs for a machine, with a single memory register, in Σ_2, with instruction set $\{L_1^{-1}, L_2^{-1}, R_1^{-1}, R_2^{-1}, \varepsilon\}$, which compute the functions:

a. $\{(x,0) \mid x = \rho x\}$
b. $\{(x,0) \mid \text{length}(x) \text{ is even}\}$

Let $\alpha(x) = \omega(x) = x$.

2. Which of the following is true and which is false?

a. $\iota = L_\sigma \circ L_\sigma^{-1}$
b. $\iota = L_\sigma^{-1} \circ L_\sigma$

3. Construct programs for a two-register machine in Σ_2 which compute the functions $f: W^2 \to W$ given by

a. $\{((x,y), x \cdot y)\}$
b. $\{((x,x),0)\}$

The instruction set is

$$\mathcal{R} = \{(f \times g) \mid f,g \in \{R_1, L_1, R_2, L_2, R_1^{-1}, L_1^{-1}, R_2^{-1}, L_2^{-1}, \varepsilon\}\}$$

Let $\alpha(x,y) = (x,y)$ and $\omega(x,y) = y$.

4.2 The Unlimited-Register Machine

One characteristic of digital computers is that there is a fixed finite bound on the number of symbols which can be stored in any single memory register. Moreover, the computer itself usually has only a finite number of registers. However information can usually be stored on magnetic tapes, disks, and drums, so the machine theoretically has available unlimited storage areas, although in practice, utilization of large amounts of this "auxiliary" storage becomes quite impractical. In the first type of machine which we will study, an unlimited amount of storage area is obtained by assuming that the machine has as many registers as are ever needed and that any finite string of symbols can be stored in each register.

The *unlimited-register machine* (URM) in Σ consists of a countable set of registers with memory configurations $X = W^\infty = W \times W \times \cdots$ and instruction set $\mathfrak{R} = \{{}_kL_\sigma^{-1},\ {}_kR_\sigma,\ {}_k\varepsilon \mid k \geq 0,\ \sigma \in \Sigma\}$, where

$$
\begin{aligned}
{}_kL_\sigma^{-1} &= \iota_k \times L_\sigma^{-1} \times \iota_\infty \\
{}_kR_\sigma &= \iota_k \times R_\sigma \times \iota_\infty \\
{}_k\varepsilon &= \iota_k \times \varepsilon \times \iota_\infty
\end{aligned}
$$

and ι_∞ means $\iota \times \iota \times \cdots$.

The instruction ${}_kL_\sigma^{-1}$ deletes symbol σ at the left of register k if it is there, ${}_kR_\sigma$ writes σ at the right in register k, and ${}_k\varepsilon$ checks whether or not register k is empty (contains the null word). To simplify the notation, when $\Sigma = \Sigma_1$, the URM instructions will be written as ${}_kR$, ${}_kL^{-1}$ and ${}_k\varepsilon$ for $k \geq 0$.†

The input and output functions for a URM are defined by $\alpha_r(x_1,\ldots,x_r) = (0,x_1,\ldots,x_r,0,0,\ldots)$ and $\omega_s(y_0,y_1,\ldots,y_s,y_{s+1},\ldots) = (y_1,\ldots,y_s)$.

All URM programs will be complete. Since instructions in $\mathfrak{R}$ with different "k" values, that is, referring to different registers, have nondisjoint domains, the completeness property implies that two such instructions cannot have the same label. Moreover since ${}_kR_\sigma$ is total and the domains of ${}_k\varepsilon$ and ${}_kL_\sigma^{-1}$ are disjoint, if there is more than one statement with a given label, the instructions in the statements must belong to the set $\{{}_k\varepsilon,\ {}_kL_\sigma^{-1} \mid \sigma \in \Sigma\}$, with none of them appearing more than once, of course.

In the next section we show that every function computed by a PL program can be computed by a URM program; in fact, a URM program in Σ_1. The remainder of this section is devoted to the definition of some useful URM programs. In this discussion we adopt a notation which is closer to that used in real programming languages. For each label l, we write all statements having that label without parentheses on a single line labeled l. The label of the next instruction to be executed is omitted if this instruction is on the following line. Thus

1 h
3 k
2 f 3, g 1

will be written in place of $\{(1,h,3), (3,k,2), (2,f,3), (2,g,1)\}$.

Note that the line 2 f 3, g 1 is very much like an IF...THEN...ELSE statement of a programming language. If the program is deterministic, then

† URM memory registers are logically equivalent to the type of data structure which is often referred to as a queue. A queue is a linear list of data items having the property that all data is added at one end and removed from the other end. Our later results will show that the computational power of the URM is not diminished as a result of this restricted form of register access.

both f and g cannot be applicable and so $2\,f\,3,\ g\,1$ says "if f is applicable, compute f and go to 3, otherwise if g is applicable, compute g and go to 1". If the program is complete, exactly one of the instructions f or g must be applicable.

Note that a computation becomes undefined if a line which does not contain an instruction that is defined on the current register contents is reached. For example, if line 3 is reached and k is not defined on the current memory configuration, then the computation becomes undefined. Also recall that for a computation to be successful the last line reached must have a terminal label.

Many programming languages include features which facilitate the naming of sequences of instructions to be used more than once in a program. This name is then written in place of the entire set of instructions. In addition, each time the name is written, it may be possible to include variables, called *parameters*, which are to be given specific values, called *arguments*. The group of instructions and variable parameters is called a *macro definition*, or simply a *macro*, and the associated name is the macro name. It is important to keep in mind that the name of a macro is nothing more than an abbreviation for the instructions in the macro definition. It is convenient to use macros when writing URM programs. We adopt the following conventions for these macros.

1. Macro usage may not be recursive. For example, if macro B is mentioned in macro A, then the former cannot reference the latter. In general if A_1 references A_2, ..., A_{n-1} references A_n, then A_n cannot reference A_i for $1 \le i \le n$.

2. After macro references are replaced by the corresponding instructions, resolve location label conflicts. For example, if macro A is referenced at location l of a program, change each instruction label i of A to $l.i$. Repeat the process for all macros B referenced in A. If a macro B is referenced at location l of a program or macro, then a transfer to l is interpreted as a transfer to the first instruction of B. Of course all references in a program to locations whose names have been changed must also be changed.

3. A macro definition may contain variables (parameters) ranging over register names. Each macro reference in a program must then specify names of registers to be used in place of these variables by the instructions of the macro. Programs may *not* contain variables ranging over register names.

Some useful URM macros follow. To simplify the notation we write

$$l\ {}_kL_\sigma^{-1}\ l.\sigma \qquad \sigma \in \Sigma$$

for

$$l\ {}_kL_{\sigma_1}^{-1}\ l.\sigma_1,\ \ldots,\ {}_kL_{\sigma_m}^{-1}\ l.\sigma_m \qquad \text{where } \Sigma = \{\sigma_1, \ldots, \sigma_m\}$$

TABLE 4-1. Useful URM Macros[a]

Macro name		Macro definition	
1. l clear(k) l'		$l\ {}_k\varepsilon\ l',\ {}_kL_\sigma^{-1}\ l$	$\sigma \in \Sigma$
2. l conc(k,j) l'	$j \neq k$	$l\ {}_j\varepsilon\ l',\ {}_jL_\sigma^{-1}\ l.\sigma$	$\sigma \in \Sigma$
		$l.\sigma\ {}_kR_\sigma\ l$	$\sigma \in \Sigma$
3. l move(k,j) l'	$j \neq k$	l clear(k)	
		$l.1$ conc(k,j) l'	
4. l copy(k,j) l'		l clear(k)	
	$j \neq 0,\ k \neq 0,\ j \neq k$	$l.1$ clear(0)	
		$l.2\ {}_j\varepsilon\ l.2.1,\ {}_jL_\sigma^{-1}\ l.3.\sigma$	$\sigma \in \Sigma$
		$l.2.1$ move(j, 0) l'	
		$l.3.\sigma\ {}_0R_\sigma\ l.4.\sigma$	$\sigma \in \Sigma$
		$l.4.\sigma\ {}_kR_\sigma\ l.2$	$\sigma \in \Sigma$
5. $l\ {}_kL_\sigma\ l'$	$k \neq 0$	l clear(0)	
		$l.1\ {}_0R_\sigma$	
		$l.2$ conc(0, k)	
		$l.3$ move(k, 0) l'	

[a] Explanation:

1. The macro clear(k) sets register k to 0.
2. If $j \neq k$, conc(k,j) concatenates the contents of register j to the right end of register k. Register j is set to 0.
3. If $j \neq k$, move(k,j) sets the contents of register k to equal the contents of register j. Register j is set to 0.
4. The macro copy(k,j) is the same as move(k,j) except that register j is not changed. Since register 0 is set to 0, copy(k,j) is correct only if $j \neq 0$ and $k \neq 0$. The use of move requires $j \neq k$.
5. For $k \neq 0$, ${}_kL_\sigma$ concatenates σ to the left end of the word in register k.

Example. The macro call 5 move(6,2) 8 is expanded as follows:

Step 1. 5 clear(6)
5.1 conc(6,2) 8

Step 2. $5\ {}_6\varepsilon\ 5.1,\ {}_6L_\sigma^{-1}\ 5 \qquad \sigma \in \Sigma$
$5.1\ {}_2\varepsilon\ 8,\ {}_2L_\sigma^{-1}\ 5.1.\sigma \qquad \sigma \in \Sigma$
$5.1.\sigma\ {}_6R_\sigma\ 5.1 \qquad \sigma \in \Sigma$

Notice that there are *no* variables in a URM program. Moreover, each URM program uses a fixed, finite number of registers.

The line l stop indicates that l is a terminal label. If it is part of an exit program, then there will be no other statements with label l.

Example. Let $f = \langle(\iota \times (R_1 \circ \zeta)), R_2\rangle$, or less formally, $f(x) = (x,1,x \cdot 2)$. The function $f\colon W \to W^3$ is computed by the program

1 copy(3,1)
2 ${}_2R_1$
3 ${}_3R_2$
4 stop

There is one interesting feature of most digital computers that is not shared by the URM. Generally, programs as well as data are stored in the computer's memory. This gives machine language programs the capability of modifying themselves during execution. This capability is often cited as one of the most significant features of the earlier digital computers, and in fact allowed programmers to write some very clever machine language programs. With the widespread use of index registers and higher level languages, this feature is no longer very important. Indeed, programs which modify themselves are often avoided because they are difficult to debug and almost incapable of being understood by anyone except their creators.

It is not too difficult to alter the definition of the URM so that the program is stored in registers of the machine. It is convenient to assume that the alphabet Σ is large enough so that the instructions ${}_k\varepsilon$, ${}_kL_\sigma^{-1}$, and ${}_kR_\sigma$ can be represented as words in Σ^*. Some convention must be made which specifies the first instruction to be executed. The labels in the program should be integers which correspond to the register numbers of the machine. With these definitions appropriately made, it is not too difficult to show that any computation made by a stored program can be simulated by some URM as originally defined (see Exercise 4). This is to be expected since, as we shall prove in the next section, URM programs can compute all PL-computable functions, which implies by Church's thesis that the URM can compute all functions which are effectively computable. A stored program URM surely cannot compute functions which are not effectively computable.

EXERCISES

1. Exhibit a complete URM program to compute
  a. addition in Σ_2
  b. multiplication in Σ_1
  c. the reversal function ρ in Σ_2
  d. the function $f(x) = 3 \times x$ in Σ_3.

2. Prove that all functions computed by the URM in Σ_n are computable by the URM in Σ_1 if the input and output functions are changed to $\alpha(x_1,\ldots,x_r) = (0,\kappa x_1,\ldots,\kappa x_r,0,\ldots)$ and $\omega(y_0,y_1,\ldots,y_s,\ldots) = (\kappa^{-1}y_1,\ldots,\kappa^{-1}y_s)$ where $\kappa = \nu_1^{-1} \circ \nu_n$ and $\nu_1\colon W_1 \to N$, $\nu_n\colon W_n \to N$ are the bijections defined in Section 1.4.

3. Write and run an actual computer program which will simulate the unlimited register machine in Σ_2. Note carefully the ways in which the program is restricted from running an arbitrary URM program (for example, the number of available registers may be finite).

4. Show that a stored URM program can be simulated by an ordinary URM program. Make an outline of the proof without writing down all of the details. See the discussion at the end of this section.

Hint: Use a fixed number of URM registers to simulate the registers referred to by the stored URM program.

5. What is the effect of the macros

a. conc(j,j)

b. move(0,0)

c. copy(0,j)

6. How many complete URM programs in Σ_n are there which (a) use all of the labels from the set $\{1,\ldots,k\}$, and (b) never refer to a register number greater than or equal to m?

7. How many URM programs $\mathfrak{P}$ in Σ_n are there which satisfy the conditions of Exercise 6 except that $\mathfrak{P}$ may be nondeterministic?

4.3 A Compiler for PL Programs

Chapter 2 contains a proof that each partial recursive function is PL-computable. Later results will show that all functions computed by a URM are partial recursive. If each function computed by a PL program can also be computed by a URM program, then it will follow that a function is PL-computable iff it is partial recursive. One way to show that each function computed by a PL program is also computed by a URM program is to give a procedure which translates PL programs into "equivalent" URM programs. Such a procedure may be called a *compiler*, just as a program which translates BASIC, FORTRAN, COBOL, ALGOL, or PL/1 into machine instructions for a particular computer is called a compiler. In this section we describe a compiler which translates PL programs into programs for the URM in Σ_1. A similar procedure for translating PL programs into programs for the URM in Σ_n can be given (see Exercise 1). The procedure will be slightly more complicated due to the fact that adding and subtracting 1 in Σ_n is a bit more difficult than in Σ_1.

The description of the compiler is quite informal. To illustrate how the compiler works, we will apply the steps of the compilation process to the simple PL program

```
Y1 ← X1;
LOOP X2;
Z ← 0;
LOOP Y1;
```

```
Y1 ← Z;
Z ← Z + 1;
END;
END;
```

which computes

$$Y1 \leftarrow X1 \dot{-} X2$$

To compile a program for the URM in Σ_1 carry out the following steps. The PL program is assumed to be syntactically correct.

Step 1. Replace all variable names in the PL program by the names X_1, X_2, … . As a convenience, replace all variables X1, X2, …, Xj in the program by $X_1, \ldots, X_j$ and all variables Y_1, Y2, …, Yk by $X_{j+1}, \ldots, X_{j+k}$. The variable X_k will be stored in register k of the URM.

Step 2. Place labels 1, 2, … on sequential statements, changing the label of each GOTO statement accordingly. These labels will be the labels of the translated URM statements.

Steps 1 and 2 applied to the sample program yield

$$
\begin{aligned}
&1{:}\, X_3 \leftarrow X_1;\\
&2{:}\, \text{LOOP } X_2;\\
&3{:}\, X_4 \leftarrow 0;\\
&4{:}\, \text{LOOP } X_3;\\
&5{:}\, X_3 \leftarrow X_4;\\
&6{:}\, X_4 \leftarrow X_4 + 1;\\
&7{:}\, \text{END};\\
&8{:}\, \text{END};
\end{aligned}
$$

Step 3. Record the value of $m = \max\{k \mid X_k \text{ occurs in the program}\}$. In the example $m = 4$. At any point in the translation process $m + 1$ will be the lowest numbered register available for use. Replace each program statement by URM instructions or macros according to the following rules:

a. replace $l{:}X_k \leftarrow 0$ by l clear(k)

b. replace $l{:}X_k \leftarrow X_j + 1$ by

$$
\left.\begin{array}{r} l \text{ copy}(k,j) \\ l.1\ {}_kR \end{array}\right\} \quad \text{if } k \neq j
$$

$$
l\ {}_kR \qquad \text{if } k = j
$$

c. replace $X_k \leftarrow X_j$ by

$$
\begin{array}{rl} l \text{ copy}(k,j) & \text{if } k \neq j \\ l \text{ clear}(0) & \text{if } k = j \end{array}
$$

d. for the statement l: LOOP X_k, find the matching statement l': END and change it to l': END l. Increase the value of m by one and replace the statement l: LOOP X_k by the URM instructions

$$l \text{ copy}(m, k)$$
$$l.1 \ {}_m\varepsilon \ l'+1, {}_mL^{-1} l+1$$

e. replace the statement l': END l by l' clear(0) $l.1$ whose only function is to transfer control back to $l.1$

f. replace the statement l: GOTO l' by l clear(0) l'

Step 3 applied to the sample program yields

1	copy(3,1)
2	copy(5,2)
2.1	${}_5\varepsilon$ 9, ${}_5L^{-1}$ 3
3	clear(4)
4	copy(6,3)
4.1	${}_6\varepsilon$ 8, ${}_6L^{-1}$ 5
5	copy(3,4)
6	${}_4R$
7	clear(0) 4.1
8	clear(0) 2.1

Step 4. Add instructions to move the values of all of the variables Y1, Y2, ... that appear in the program into registers 1, 2, ..., then clear all other registers, and finally add a stop statement (the single terminal label of the URM program).

By Step 4 the following statements would be added to the sample program, since the value of the program variable Y1 is stored in register 3.

9	copy(1,3)
10	clear(2)
11	clear(3)
12	clear(4)
13	clear(5)
14	clear(6)
15	stop

THEOREM 4.3. Every function computed by a PL program is also computed by a complete URM program.

Proof. Observe that the compiler discussed in this section always produces a complete URM program. Compilers for the URM in Σ_n, $n > 1$, can be similarly specified. ▮

We have shown (with Exercise 1) that every PL-computable function in Σ_n is computable by the URM in Σ_n. If we utilize different input and output functions, then we can show that every PL-computable function in Σ_n can be computed by the URM in Σ_1. To accomplish this, let $\alpha_r'(x_1,\ldots,x_r) = (0,\kappa x_1,\ldots,\kappa x_r,0,\ldots,0)$ and $\omega_s(y_0,y_1,\ldots,y_s,\ldots) = (\kappa^{-1}y_1,\ldots,\kappa^{-1}y_s)$ where $\kappa: W_n \to W_1$ is the bijection defined in Section 3.7. (See Exercise 5 of Section 4.4.)

EXERCISES

1. Specify a compiler which translates a PL program into a URM program in Σ_2 which computes the same function as the original PL program. Also explain how to do it in Σ_n.

2. Implement the compiler of Exercise 1 as a real computer program. Include features to check for correct syntax. Combine this program with a URM simulator (see Exercise 3 in Section 4.2) to allow PL programs to be executed.

3. Extend the compiler given in the text to permit IF and WHILE statements and arbitrary arithmetic expressions.

4. Let $\mathcal{T}$ be a PL program and let $N(\mathcal{T})$ be the number of registers used by the URM program compiled from $\mathcal{T}$ by the compiler above. Give a formula for $N(\mathcal{T})$ as a function of the structure of $\mathcal{T}$. Explain how to modify the compiler so as to minimize the number of registers required to deal with LOOP and END statements.

4.4 The Single-Register Machine

The *single-register machine* (SRM) in Σ is a URM in Σ with only one register. The set X is W and the set of machine instructions is $\mathcal{R} = \{L_\sigma^{-1}, R_\sigma, \varepsilon\}$. If an SRM program is to compute a function $f: W^r \to W^s$, then the r inputs, the s outputs, and all intermediate results must somehow be stored in the one register. One way to accomplish this is to add a new symbol \$ to the alphabet Σ and use it to separate words consisting of the other symbols. Functions in Σ will be computed by the SRM in $\Sigma \cup \{\$\}$.

Assume from now on that $\$ \notin \Sigma$. Let $\Sigma' = \Sigma \cup \{\$\}$ and $W' = (\Sigma')^*$. The symbol \$ will act as a separator between words in $W = \Sigma^*$. The input function for the SRM in Σ' is $\alpha_r: W^r \to W'$ given by

$$\alpha_r(x_1,\ldots,x_r) = x_1\$x_2\$\cdots x_r\$$$

The output function $\omega_s: W' \to W^s$ is given by

$$\omega_s(y_1\$y_2\$\cdots\$y_t\$u) = \begin{cases} (y_1,y_2,\ldots,y_s) & \text{if } t \geq s \\ (y_1,y_2,\ldots,y_t,0,\ldots,0) & \text{if } t < s \end{cases}$$

where $y_1, \ldots, y_t, u \in W$.

Note that $\omega_s(y) = (\text{part}(y,\$,0),\ldots,\text{part}(y,\$,s \dot{-} 1))$, where part is the function defined in Section 3.6.

As an illustration, the exchange function $\xi(x_1,x_2) = (x_2,x_1)$ in Σ_2 is computed by

$$\begin{array}{ll} 1 & L_\$^{-1}\,3,\, L_1^{-1}\,2.1,\, L_2^{-1}\,2.2 \\ 2.1 & R_1\,1 \\ 2.2 & R_2\,1 \\ 3 & R_\$ \\ 4 & \text{stop} \end{array}$$

or more simply by

$$\begin{array}{ll} 1 & \text{shift} \\ 2 & \text{stop} \end{array}$$

where shift is a macro described below.

If the separator symbol is added to the alphabet, an SRM can compute any function that can be computed by a URM. However, the additional character \$ is not necessary as long as the original alphabet contains at least two characters. This can be accomplished by changing the input/output functions to encode words in W into words in W_1, using the second letter as a word separator (see Exercise 4). The one letter SRM cannot compute all partial recursive functions with one input and one output (see Exercises 2 and 3), which contrasts with the URM case (see Exercise 5).

THEOREM 4.4. If $\mathcal{T}$ is a URM program in Σ and m is greater than the largest register number referenced in the program $\mathcal{T}$, then there is an SRM program $\mathcal{T}'$ in Σ', such that $|\mathcal{T}|(0,x_1,\ldots,x_m,0,\ldots) = (y_0,y_1,\ldots,y_m,0,0,\ldots)$ iff $|\mathcal{T}'|(\$x_1\$\cdots x_m\$) = (y_0\$y_1\$\cdots y_m\$)$. Furthermore, if $\mathcal{T}$ is complete, then $\mathcal{T}'$ is also complete.

Proof. The SRM program $\mathcal{T}'$ will simulate a URM statement which references register k by *shifting* the word $x_0\$\cdots x_k\$\cdots x_m\$$ until it is in the form $x_k\$\cdots x_m\$x_0\$\cdots x_{k-1}\$$, modify x_k appropriately, and then shift the word back to its original position. The following SRM macros do the shifting:

$$\begin{array}{lll} l\ \text{shif}\ l' & l\ L_\$^{-1}\,l',\ \varepsilon\ l,\ L_\sigma^{-1} l.\sigma & \sigma \in \Sigma \\ & l.\sigma\ R_\sigma\ l & \sigma \in \Sigma \end{array}$$

The macro shif transforms $x_0\$x_1\$\cdots x_m\$$ into $x_1\$\cdots x_m\$x_0$.

$$\begin{array}{lll} l\ \text{shift}\ l' & l & \text{shif} \\ & l.1 & R_\$\ l' \end{array}$$

The macro shift transforms $x_0\$x_1\$\cdots x_m\$$ into $x_1\$\cdots x_m\$x_0\$$

$$\begin{array}{lll} l\ \text{shift}(k)\ l' & l & \text{shift} \\ k \geq 1 & l.2 & \text{shift} \\ & \vdots & \\ & l.k & \text{shift}\ l' \end{array}$$

Since there are always exactly $m+1$ \$'s in the register of the SRM, shift$(m+1)$ has no affect on the contents of the register. The statement shift$(m+1+k)$ will be used instead of shift(k) to handle the special case $k=0$.

Let the labels of $\mathcal{T}'$ be the labels of $\mathcal{T}$ plus the new labels needed to construct additional macros. Let the initial and terminal labels of $\mathcal{T}'$ be the same as the initial and terminal labels of $\mathcal{T}$. For each line of $\mathcal{T}$ include in $\mathcal{T}'$ the appropriate line described here.

URM		SRM	
l	${}_kR_\sigma\ l'$	l	shift$(m+1+k)$
		$l.1$	shif
		$l.2$	R_σ
		$l.3$	$R_\$$
		$l.4$	shift$(m-k)\ l'$
l	${}_kL_\sigma^{-1}l'$	l	shift$(m+1+k)$
		$l.1$	$L_\sigma^{-1}\ l.2.\sigma$
		$l.2.\sigma$	shift$(m+1-k)\ l'$
l	${}_k\varepsilon\ l'$	l	shift$(m+1+k)$
		$l.1$	$L_\$^{-1}l.2,\ \varepsilon\ l$
		$l.2$	$R_\$$
		$l.3$	shift$(m-k)\ l'$

The resulting program $\mathcal{T}'$ simulates $\mathcal{T}$ in the manner required by the statement of the theorem. We leave it to the reader to show that $\mathcal{T}'$ is complete if $\mathcal{T}$ is. ▮

THEOREM 4.5. Every function $f: W^r \to W^s$ computed by a complete URM program in Σ is computed by a complete SRM program in $\Sigma' = \Sigma \cup \{\$\}$.

Proof. Let f be computed by the complete URM program $\mathcal{T}$. Let $m = 1 + \max\{p,r,s\}$, where p is the largest register referenced by $\mathcal{T}$. Let $\mathcal{T}'$ be the SRM constructed using Theorem 4.4 and let $\mathcal{T}''$ consist of $\mathcal{T}'$ with the statements

$$\begin{array}{rl} 1 & R_\$ \\ 2 & R_\$ \\ & \vdots \\ m-r+1 & R_\$ \\ m-r+2 & \text{shift}(m) \end{array}$$

added at the beginning, all stop statements replaced by shift$(m+1)\ l$, where l is a new label, and the statements

$$\begin{array}{lll} l & L_\$^{-1}l',\ \varepsilon\ l,\ L_\sigma^{-1}l & \sigma \in \Sigma \\ l' & \text{stop} & \end{array}$$

added at the end of the program. Then $f(x_1,\ldots,x_r) = (y_1,\ldots,y_s)$ iff $|\mathcal{T}|(0,x_1,\ldots,x_r,0,0,\ldots) = (y_0,y_1,\ldots,y_s,y_{s+1},\ldots)$ for some y_0, $y_{s+1},\ldots$ iff $|\mathcal{T}'|(\$x_1\$\cdots x_r\$\$\cdots\$) = (y_0\$y_1\$\cdots y_s\$y_{s+1}\$\cdots y_m\$)$ iff $|\mathcal{T}''|(x_1\$\cdots x_r\$) = (y_1\$\cdots y_s\$y_{s+1}\$\cdots y_m\$)$ iff $f = \omega_s \circ |\mathcal{T}''| \circ \alpha_r$.

Since the URM program $\mathcal{T}$ is complete, the SRM program $\mathcal{T}''$ simulating $\mathcal{T}$ will be also. The procedure given for constructing $\mathcal{T}''$ may specify that certain SRM statements are to be included more than once. For example, if $\mathcal{T}$ contains the statements

$$7 \;\, {}_5L_1^{-1}\; 9,\;\, {}_5L_2^{-1}\; 6$$

then $\mathcal{T}'$ will contain the statements

7 shift($m + 1 + 5$)
7.1 L_1^{-1} 7.2.1
7.2.1 shift($m + 1 - 5$) 9
7 shift($m + 1 + 5$)
7.1 L_2^{-1} 7.2.2
7.2.2 shift($m + 1 - 5$) 6

which is identical to the set of statements

7 shift($m + 1 + 5$)
7.1 L_1^{-1} 7.2.1, L_2^{-1} 7.2.2
7.2.1 shift($m + 1 - 5$) 9
7.2.2 shift($m + 1 - 5$) 6

(Recall that machine instructions may be written in any order, since each instruction has its own goto label.) ▌

EXERCISES

1. Exhibit an SRM program to compute
  a. the diagonalization function $\delta(x) = (x,x)$ in Σ_3
  b. addition in Σ_1
  c. the reversal function ρ in Σ_2.

2. Show that it is not possible to give an SRM program $\mathcal{T}$ *in* Σ_1 such that $|\mathcal{T}|(1^k) = (1^{2k})$.

3. Characterize the total functions $|\mathcal{T}|$, where $\mathcal{T}$ is an SRM program in Σ_1.

4. Let $\alpha' : W_n^r \to W_1$ be given by $\alpha'(x_1,\ldots,x_r) = \kappa(x_1)\cdot\$\cdot\kappa(x_2)\cdot\$\cdots\kappa(x_r)\cdot\$$ where $\kappa = \nu_1^{-1} \circ \nu_n$. Let ω' be an appropriate corresponding output function. Using these input/output functions for the SRM, show that any partial recursive function $f : W_n^r \to W_n^s$ can be computed by the SRM in Σ_1, that is, $f = \omega' \circ |\mathcal{T}| \circ \alpha'$ for some SRM program $\mathcal{T}$ in Σ_1.

5. For the URM in Σ_1, let $\alpha'(x_1,\ldots,x_r) = (0,\kappa x_1,\ldots,\kappa x_r,0,0,\ldots)$ and define a corresponding output function where $\kappa = \nu_1^{-1} \circ \nu_n$. Using these input/output functions show that all partial recursive functions $f: W_n^r \to W_n^s$ can be computed by the URM in Σ_1.

6. Prove that each partial recursive function in Σ is computed by a deterministic exit SRM program in Σ' which does not contain the ε instruction.

4.5 The Turing Machine

The URM and SRM discussed in the preceding sections permit access only to data symbols at the left and right ends of the words stored in the registers. It is natural to consider machines which allow "local" access to any symbols of the stored words. One possible physical model for the storage medium of such a machine is a computer tape rather than a register. A machine with several tapes could move them back and forth, examining and possibly changing at each instant those tape symbols which are under the read/write heads. Usually there is one read/write head per tape as illustrated in Figure 4-4.

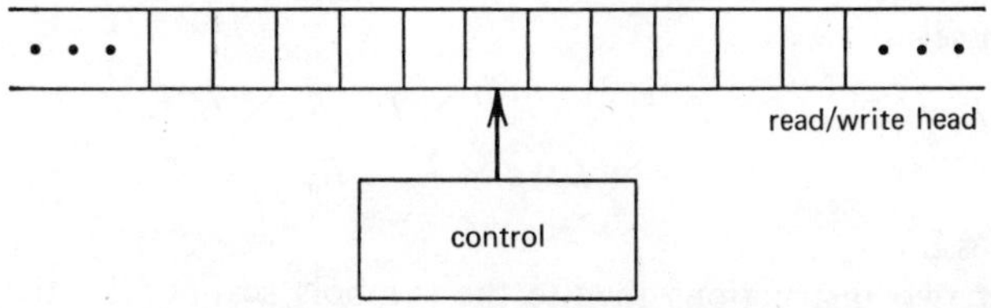

FIGURE 4-4. **Schematic representation of the Turing machine.**

This type of machine was first studied by the British mathematician Turing. Because of its simplicity it has provided an important formalization of the notion of effective computation and has played a central role in the development of the theory of algorithms.

Traditionally a Turing machine program (usually called simply a Turing machine) is described as a set of quintuples of the form $(q, \sigma, \sigma', M, q')$. The q and q' are called states of the machine and replace our labels. The symbol M stands for a move, which may be R or L (and sometimes C) meaning move right or left (or do not move). The symbol σ represents the symbol on the square of the tape scanned by the machine and σ' is to be written in its place. As an example, the quintuple (q, a, b, R, q') indicates that if the machine is in state q and a is the symbol scanned on the tape, replace the a with the symbol b, move to the right one tape square, and go to state q'. A quadruple scheme is also used where an instruction may specify a new symbol to be written on the tape or a move, but not both.

It is desirable to include Turing machines within the previously given formal definition of machines. With this goal in mind, note that a tape and its associated read/write head are logically equivalent to two registers, where the symbol at one end of each register is accessible as shown in Figure 4-5. The content of the tape is then the concatenation of the words stored in the two registers, with register 0 on the left and register 1 on the right. The instruction set for the Turing machine restricts access to the two registers in a way that imitates the operations which can be executed with a tape.

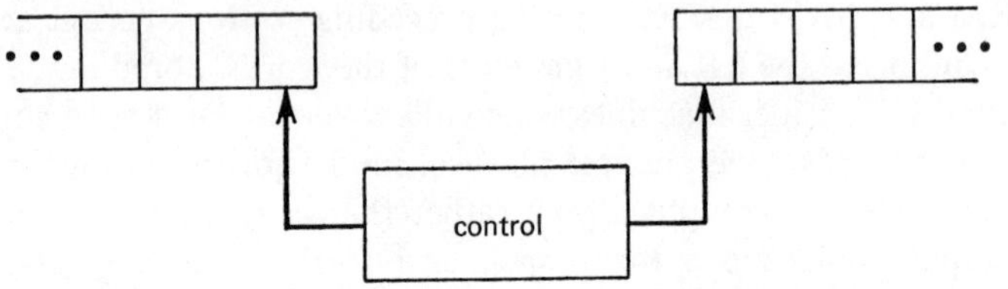

FIGURE 4-5. **Register representation of the Turing machine.**

The *Turing machine* (TM) in Σ is a two-register machine ($X = W^2$) with instruction set

$$\mathfrak{R} = \{\iota \times (L_\tau \circ L_\sigma^{-1}), (R_\tau \circ R_\sigma^{-1}) \times \iota, R_\sigma^{-1} \times L_\sigma, R_\sigma \times L_\sigma^{-1}, \\ \varepsilon \times L_\sigma, \varepsilon \times L_\sigma^{-1}, R_\sigma \times \varepsilon, R_\sigma^{-1} \times \varepsilon, \varepsilon \times \iota, \iota \times \varepsilon\}$$

where $\sigma, \tau \in \Sigma$.

The first two instructions rewrite the symbols scanned by the TM head, the leftmost symbol in register 1 and the rightmost symbol in register 0. The next two instructions shift the TM tape one square right and one square left, respectively. The remaining instructions modify and test the ends of the tape.

The input and output functions for the TM are

$$\alpha_r(x_1,\cdots,x_r) = (0,x_1\$x_2\$\cdots x_r\$)$$

and

$$\omega_s(x,y_1\$y_2\$\cdots\$y_t\$z) = \begin{cases}(y_1,\ldots,y_s) & \text{if } s \le t \\ (y_1,\ldots,y_t,0,\ldots,0) & \text{if } s > t\end{cases}$$

where $z \in \Sigma^*$ and $y_i \in \Sigma^*$ for $i = 1,\ldots,t$. The input is encoded with \$'s between arguments and put into register 1 (the right register), from which the output is also taken. Thus a TM program $\mathcal{P}$ in $\Sigma \cup \{\$\}$ computes $f: W^r \to W^s$ if $|\mathcal{P}|(0,x_1\$\cdots x_r\$) = (w,y)$ for some w and y such that $\omega_s(w,y) = (y_1,y_2,\ldots,y_s) = f(x_1,\ldots,x_r)$.

Many different types of Turing machines have been studied. However, with respect to the class of functions which can be computed, each of these has been shown to be equivalent to the model defined above. Our model has a single two-way unbounded tape, that is, a tape which may be arbitrarily extended on the left and on the right. Actually there is no restriction to the TM's power if only one-way unbounded tapes are used (see Exercise 3). On the other hand, we may show that TM with $n > 1$ tapes are equivalent to the single tape machine (see Exercise 4).

Two convenient TM macros are

l shiftleft l'	$l\ R_\sigma \times L_\sigma^{-1}\ l'$	$\sigma \in \Sigma$
l shiftright l'	$l\ R_\sigma^{-1} \times L_\sigma\ l'$	$\sigma \in \Sigma$

The macro shiftleft shifts one symbol from the left end of register 1 to the right of register 0. This is equivalent to the traditional TM shifting its tape one square to the left.

Example. The following TM program in Σ_3' computes the successor function ς in Σ_3.

1 shiftleft 1, $\iota \times \varepsilon$ 2
2 shiftright (shift the $)
3 $(R_2 \circ R_1^{-1}) \times \iota$ 5, $(R_3 \circ R_2^{-1}) \times \iota$ 5, $(R_1 \circ R_3^{-1}) \times \iota$ 4, $\varepsilon \times L_1$ 6
4 shiftright 3
5 shiftright 5, $\varepsilon \times \iota$ 6
6 stop

Example. The following TM program in Σ_2' computes concatenation in Σ_2 by deleting the $ between the arguments.

1 $R_1 \times L_1^{-1}$ 1, $R_2 \times L_2^{-1}$ 1, $R_\$ \times L_\$^{-1}$ 2
2 shiftright
3 $(R_1 \circ R_1^{-1}) \times \iota$ 4.1, $(R_2 \circ R_2^{-1}) \times \iota$ 4.2, $\varepsilon \times L_\$^{-1}$ 6
4.1 $\iota \times (L_1 \circ L_\$^{-1})$ 5
4.2 $\iota \times (L_2 \circ L_\$^{-1})$ 5
5 $(R_\$ \circ R_1^{-1}) \times \iota$ 2, $(R_\$ \circ R_2^{-1}) \times \iota$ 2
6 stop

THEOREM 4.6. For each SRM program $\mathcal{T}$ in Σ, there is a TM program $\mathcal{T}'$ in Σ such that $|\mathcal{T}|(x) = (y)$ iff $|\mathcal{T}'|(0,x) = (0,y)$.

Proof. Let the labels of $\mathcal{T}'$ be those of $\mathcal{T}$ plus whatever other labels are needed. The initial and terminal labels of $\mathcal{T}'$ are the same as the initial and terminal labels of $\mathcal{T}$. For each statement in $\mathcal{T}$, let $\mathcal{T}'$ have the statements shown in the following table:

SRM		TM
$l\ L_\sigma^{-1}\ l'$	l	$\varepsilon \times L_\sigma^{-1}\ l'$
$l\ R_\sigma\ l'$	l	shiftleft l, $R_\sigma \times \varepsilon\ l.1$
	$l.1$	shiftright $l.1$, $\varepsilon \times \iota\ l'$
$l\ \varepsilon\ l'$	l	$\iota \times \varepsilon\ l'$

The proof is completed by noting that register 0 is empty before and after each SRM instruction is simulated. ▮

THEOREM 4.7. Each function $f: W^r \to W^s$ in Σ computed by a complete SRM program in $\Sigma' = \Sigma \cup \{\$\}$ is also computed by a complete TM program in Σ'. ▮

COROLLARY 4.8. Every partial recursive function in Σ is computed by a TM program in $\Sigma \cup \{\$\}$. ▮

The examples above indicate the complexity of TM programs even for very simple functions. Moreover the TM though capable of computing every partial recursive function, in many ways is not a good model of a real computer. It is important primarily because of the central role it has played in the development of computability theory.

EXERCISES

1. Exhibit a TM program to compute
   a. the diagonalization function δ in Σ_3
   b. the exchange function ξ in Σ_1
   c. the reversal function ρ in Σ_2
   d. addition in Σ_2
   e. multiplication in Σ_1
   f. $f(x) = \begin{cases} 1 & \text{if } x \text{ is divisible by 3} \\ 0 & \text{otherwise} \end{cases}$ in Σ_2

2. Show that the partial functions $\iota \times L_\sigma$, $\iota \times L_\sigma^{-1}$, $R_\sigma \times \iota$, and $R_\sigma^{-1} \times \iota$ can be expressed in terms of the TM instructions. Show that a machine with

$$X = W^2 \text{ and } \mathcal{R} = \{R_\sigma \times \iota,\ R_\sigma^{-1} \times \iota,\ \iota \times L_\sigma,\ \iota \times L_\sigma^{-1},\ \iota \times \varepsilon,\ \varepsilon \times \iota\}$$

is equivalent in computational power to the TM.

3. Show that the TM with a single one-way unbounded tape and

$$\mathcal{R} = \{\iota \times (L_\tau \circ L_\sigma^{-1}),\ (R_\tau \circ R_\sigma^{-1}) \times \iota,\ R_\sigma \times L_\sigma^{-1},$$
$$R_\sigma^{-1} \times L_\sigma,\ R_\sigma \times \varepsilon,\ R_\sigma^{-1} \times \varepsilon,\ \iota \times \varepsilon,\ \varepsilon \times \iota\}$$

is equivalent to the two-way unbounded model.

4. Define a three-tape TM model and prove that it is equivalent to the one-tape model.

4.6 Sets Accepted by Machines

One way that a program can define a set is to compute its characteristic function. There is another more general way that a program can determine a set. A machine program $\mathcal{T}$ *halts* on input x if $x \in \operatorname{dom} |\mathcal{T}|$, that is, if when the program starts at an initial label with x in the machine registers, there is some computation that leads to a terminal label. For input and output functions $\alpha_r: W^r \to X$ and $\omega: X \to W^0$, the program $\mathcal{T}$ is said to *accept* or *recognize*, or *define* the set or language $L(\mathcal{T}) = \{x \in W^r \mid x \in \text{dom}\,(\omega \circ |\mathcal{T}| \circ \alpha_r)\}$.

One possible output function is the *total* function $\omega: X \to W^0$ which has constant value (), that is, the single member of W^0. In this case $L(\mathcal{T}) = \{x \in W^r \mid x \in \text{dom}\,(|\mathcal{T}| \circ \alpha_r)\}$. This output function will be used in the following discussion.

The deterministic (but not complete) SRM program in Σ_1'

$$\begin{array}{ll} 1 & L_\$^{-1}\ 3,\ L_1^{-1}\ 2 \\ 2 & L_1^{-1}\ 1 \\ 3 & \text{stop} \end{array}$$

halts on all words in $(\Sigma_1')^* = \{\$,1\}^*$ of the form $(11)^k\$x$, $k \geq 0$. For $r = 1$, $L(\mathcal{T}) = (11)^*$, for $r = 2$, $L(\mathcal{T}) = (11)^* \times W_1$.

The URM program in Σ_2'

$$\begin{array}{ll} 1 & {}_1L_1^{-1}\ 2.1,\ {}_1L_2^{-1}\ 2.2,\ {}_1\varepsilon\ 3 \\ 2.1 & {}_2L_1^{-1}\ 1 \\ 2.2 & {}_2L_2^{-1}\ 1 \\ 3 & {}_2\varepsilon\ 4 \\ 4 & \text{stop} \end{array}$$

halts on all inputs $(x_1,x_2,\ldots)$ such that $x_1 = x_2$, so for $r = 2$, $L(\mathcal{T}) = \{(x,y) \mid x = y\}$. For $r = 1$, $L(\mathcal{T}) = \{0\}$.

Sets accepted by URM programs are called *recursively enumerable* and are discussed in Chapter 6.

Several types of machines with computational power less than the URM, SRM and TM have been studied extensively. The three most common are the linear-bounded automaton, the push-down automaton, and the finite automaton.

A *linear-bounded automaton* is a two-register machine with instruction set $\mathcal{R} = \{\iota \times L_\sigma^{-1},\ R_\sigma \times L_\tau^{-1},\ R_\sigma^{-1} \times L_\tau,\ \iota \times \varepsilon,\ \varepsilon \times \iota\}$. The linear-bounded automaton, like the TM is traditionally described as a one-tape machine. The machine can shift the tape back and forth changing and deleting symbols, but can never increase the total number of symbols on the tape (that is, in the two registers). The input function is the same as the TM's input function.

A *push-down automaton* is a two-register machine, with instruction set $\mathcal{R} = \{\iota \times L_\sigma^{-1},\ R_\sigma \times \iota,\ R_\sigma^{-1} \times \iota,\ \iota \times \varepsilon,\ \varepsilon \times \iota\}$. The lefthand register is called a *push-down stack*. The machine may write or delete symbols from the push-down stack, but may only read from the input tape (the righthand register). The input function is the same as the TM's input function. The concept of a push-down stack has played an important role in the description of translators for computer programming languages.

The following push-down automaton program accepts the set of balanced strings of parentheses (and). A string of parentheses is balanced if there are the same number of left and right parentheses and if, scanning the string from left to right, the number of right parentheses scanned never exceeds the number of left parentheses.

$$
\begin{array}{ll}
1 & \iota \times L_{\$}^{-1}\,4,\ \iota \times L_{(}^{-1}\,2,\ \iota \times L_{)}^{-1}\,3 \\
2 & R_{(} \times \iota\ 1 \\
3 & R_{(}^{-1} \times \iota\ 1 \\
4 & \varepsilon \times \iota\ 5 \\
5 & \text{stop}
\end{array}
$$

Note that this program is a deterministic exit program. The program operates as follows: if a left parenthesis is leftmost in the input register, put it onto the push-down stack; if a right parenthesis is leftmost in the input register, the balancing left parenthesis is removed from the stack. When the separator $ is encountered, the stack is checked to see if it is empty.

A *finite automaton* is a one-register machine with instructions $\{L_\sigma^{-1}\}$. The input function is $\alpha_r(x_1,\ldots,x_r) = x_1\$\cdots x_r\$$.

A finite automaton program which accepts the empty set $\varnothing$ is the program

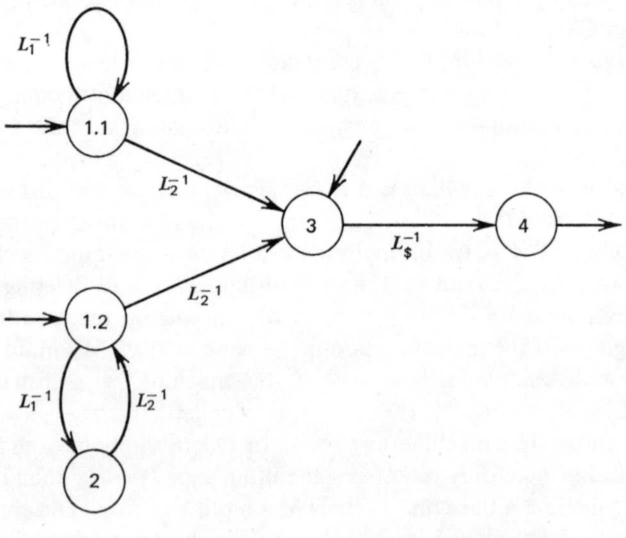

FIGURE 4-6. **A finite automaton program that accepts** $0` \cup (1^* \cup (12)^*)2$.

with no statements, or any program with no initial labels or no terminal labels. A nondeterministic program accepting the set $0 \cup (1^* \cup (12)^*)2$ is

$$\begin{array}{ll} 1.1 & L_1^{-1}\ 1.1,\ L_2^{-1}\ 3 \\ 1.2 & L_1^{-1}\ 2,\ L_2^{-1}\ 3 \\ 2 & L_2^{-1}\ 1.2 \\ 3 & L_\$^{-1}\ 4 \\ 4 & \text{stop} \end{array}$$

where 1.1, 1.2, and 3 are initial labels. The graphical representation of this program is given by Figure 4-6.

Nondeterministic programs for each of these machines play a very important role. The reader is referred to the list of references for more information about these machines.

EXERCISES

1. Write finite automaton programs that accept the sets

a. Σ_2^*

b. $\{(x,y) \in W^2 \mid x \in 1^*,\ y \in 2^*\}$

c. $\Sigma_2^* 12 \Sigma_2^*$

d. $(1^* \cup 22)^*$

2. Write a pushdown automaton program which accepts the set $\{x \cdot \rho(x) \mid x \in \Sigma^*\}$. *Hint:* the program will be nondeterministic.

3. Write a deterministic pushdown automaton program which accepts the set $\{1^n \cdot 2^n \mid n \geq 0\}$.

4. Write a deterministic finite automaton program which accepts the set

$$0 \cup (1^* \cup (1^*2)^*)1, \text{ the set } 0 \cup (1^* \cup (12)^*)^*1.$$

5. Write a linear-bounded automaton program which accepts the set $\{1^{2^n} \mid n \geq 0\}$.

6. Write a TM program that accepts the set

$$\{x \in \Sigma_2^* \mid \text{length}(x) \text{ is even}\}.$$

4.7 History

The idea of defining effective computability via a model of a computing device was introduced independently by Turing [1936] and Post [1936]. Turing [1937] contains a proof of the equivalence of Turing's model to another model for effective computability, the λ-definable functions of Church and Kleene (see Chapter 11). The idea of using a machine model might seem quite natural for a modern computer scientist, but the reader should remember that there were no digital computers as we now know them in 1936. The importance of the role of the TM in the development of computability theory is illustrated in the text of Davis [1958] and by the large amount of work which has been devoted to studying this machine model.

The URM and SRM were introduced by Shephardson and Sturgis [1963]. They also proved the equivalence of the URM- and SRM-computable functions to the partial recursive functions. Modern computers resemble the URM more closely than they resemble the TM; hence the URM provides a more natural model of the computing process than does the TM. However, just as higher level languages are more convenient than machine or assembly languages for writing algorithms, PL programs and the labeled Markov algorithms to be discussed in Chapter 5 provide a nicer framework for investigating computable functions than do TM or URM programs.

We have included this chapter on machines, not only because of the historical interest and the similarities with actual computers, but also because the definition of machine given provides a framework within which to study other important kinds of machines, such as the linear-bounded automaton, push-down automaton, and finite automaton. This unifying definition was given by Eilenberg [1973] and his book investigates properties of these machines in detail.

CHAPTER 5

Labeled Markov Algorithms

In this chapter we present an algorithmic language in which general word transformations may be conveniently described. The programs, called labeled Markov algorithms (LMA), of this language contain instructions which operate by first locating and then changing a given subword of an input word. Since LMA's operate directly on words and since each LMA is itself a word, it is not too difficult to construct an LMA which, given an input $x \cdot y$, interprets x as an LMA which is to be simulated on input y. The "universal" LMA obtained in this way has many important applications. For example, it is used to prove that the halting problem is undecidable without appealing to Church's thesis.

Labeled Markov algorithms compute all and only partial recursive functions. In this chapter we complete the proof of the equivalence of the algorithmic languages considered by showing that each function computed by a TM program is computed by an LMA and each function computed by an LMA is partial recursive. The latter involves defining a partial recursive function which describes the operation of an LMA. The universal function plays an important role in this proof.

5.1 Basic Properties

When writing programs to process words in the alphabet Σ, it is often not only convenient but also essential to be able to use some symbols other than those in Σ. We will call these additional symbols *auxiliary symbols*. In the following Φ will always denote the union of Σ and some set of auxiliary symbols.

A *labeled Markov algorithm* (LMA) $\mathcal{A}$ in the alphabet Φ is a nonempty ordered list of statements of the form

$$\begin{aligned} 0&: x_0 \to y_0 \,/l_0; \\ 1&: x_1 \to y_1 \,/l_1; \\ 2&: x_2 \to y_2 \,/l_2; \\ &\vdots \\ k&: x_k \to y_k \,/l_k; \end{aligned}$$

The numbers to the left of the colon are called *labels*. The $l_0, l_1, \ldots, l_k$ to the right of the slash must also be numbers. The symbol l_i is called the *goto* part of the statement $i\colon x_i \to y_i \,/l_i$. Each x_i and y_i must be a member of Φ^*. The statement $i\colon x_i \to y_i \,/l_i$ is applied to a word $w \in \Phi^*$ as follows: If $x_i \preccurlyeq w$ (x_i is a subword of w), first replace the *leftmost* occurrence of x_i in w by y_i and then apply the statement with label l_i to the word obtained. If x_i is not a subword of w, leave w unchanged and apply the next statement (the one with label $i + 1$) to w. The program begins by executing the statement with label 0 and terminates if n is designated as the label of the next statement and n is greater than the label of the last statement of the LMA.

Notice that $x \to y$ is applied to w by replacing the leftmost occurrence of x. If $w = u \cdot x \cdot v$, the leftmost x has been located if for no word $u' \prec u$ can w be written $w = u' \cdot x \cdot v'$. The result of applying $x \to y$ to word w is exactly described by the value of the function replace(w,x,y). See Theorem 3.18.

Example.

$$0\colon 0 \to 1 \,/1;$$

This LMA consists of a single statement. For a given word w, this LMA writes a 1 to the left of w and halts. Recall that $w = 0 \cdot w$, so the null word 0 " occurs " at the left end of every word.

Example.

$$\begin{aligned} 0&\colon 0 \to a \,/1;\\ 1&\colon a1 \to 1a \,/1;\\ 2&\colon a2 \to 2a \,/1;\\ 3&\colon a \to 2 \,/73; \end{aligned}$$

Suppose $w \in \{1,2\}^*$. Then this program writes the symbol a at the left of w, then using statements 1 and 2 moves the a to the right end, after which it is changed to 2. The net effect is to write the symbol 2 at the right end, computing $R_2(w)$.

Notice that it is harder for an LMA to compute R_σ than to compute L_σ. This is due to the fact that the leftmost occurrence of a subword is always the one replaced.

As with other programming schemes, it is convenient to introduce abbreviations when writing LMA's. Statements 1 and 2 in the second example could be abbreviated by

$$1\colon a\sigma \to \sigma a \,/1; \qquad \sigma \in \{1,2\}$$

Abbreviations of this type will be used only if the order of the abbreviated rules does not affect the final result of the computation.

Each algorithm $\mathcal{A}$ in Φ defines a function $|\mathcal{A}|:\Phi^* \to \Phi^*$. If $\mathcal{A}$ is applied to the word w and halts with $\mathcal{A}$ transformed to z, then $|\mathcal{A}|(w) = z$. If the computation does not terminate, $|\mathcal{A}|(w)$ is undefined.

For alphabet Σ, let $\Sigma' = \Sigma \cup \{\$\}$ and $\Sigma' \subseteq \Phi$. Input and output functions for an LMA can be defined by using the input function and the null extension of the output function for the SRM.

$$\alpha_r(x_1,\ldots,x_r) = x_1\$ \cdots x_r\$ \qquad \text{where } x_i \in \Sigma^* \text{ for } i = 1, \ldots, r$$

$$\omega_s(y) = \begin{cases} (\text{part}(y, \$, 0),\ldots,\text{part}(y, \$, s \dot{-} 1)) & \text{if } y \in (\Sigma')^* \\ (0,\ldots,0) & \text{if } y \in \Phi^* - (\Sigma')^* \end{cases}$$

Note that $\alpha_0() = 0$ and $\omega_0(y) = ()$.

The LMA $\mathcal{A}$ *computes* the function $\omega_s \circ |\mathcal{A}| \circ \alpha_r : W^r \to W^s$, r, $s \geq 0$. Thus the first algorithm computes the function L_1 if $r = s = 1$, and $f(x_1, x_2) = (1 \cdot x_1, x_2, 0)$ if $r = 2$ and $s = 3$. The second LMA computes R_2 and also the function $f(x_1,x_2) = (x_1 \cdot 2, x_2, 0)$.

Example. Let $\Sigma = \{1,2\}$, $\Phi = \Sigma \cup \{\$, a, b\}$.

$$\begin{array}{ll} 0: 0 \to a\ /1; & \\ 1: a\sigma \to \sigma b \sigma a\ /1; & \sigma \in \{1,2\} \\ 2: a \to 0\ /3; & \\ 3: \sigma\tau b \to \tau b \sigma\ /3; & \sigma, \tau \in \{1,2\} \\ 4: b \to 0\ /4; & \end{array}$$

For the word $112 \in \Sigma^*$, $\alpha_1(112) = 112\$$ and the algorithm applied to this input would produce $112\$ \Rightarrow a112\$ \Rightarrow 1b1a12\$ \Rightarrow 1b11b1a2\$ \Rightarrow 1b11b12b2a\$ \Rightarrow 1b11b12b2\$ \Rightarrow 1b1b112b2\$ \Rightarrow 1b1b12b12\$ \Rightarrow 1b1b2b112\$ \Rightarrow 11b2b112\$ \Rightarrow 112b112\$ \Rightarrow 112112\$$.

This algorithm computes the function $f(x) = x \cdot x$. A slight modification of this LMA will compute the diagonalization function $\delta(x) = (x,x)$. See Exercise 2a.

When constructing LMA's to compute certain functions, it is convenient to be able to use additional auxiliary symbols. For one later theorem, it will be necessary to know that no more than two auxiliary symbols are ever needed. (Actually, only one is necessary; see Exercises 1 and 2 of Section 5.2.)

LEMMA 5.1. If $\mathcal{A}$ is an LMA in the alphabet: Φ, $\Phi \supseteq \Sigma'$, then there is an LMA $\mathcal{A}'$ in $\Phi' = \Sigma' \cup \{a,b\}$, such that for all $x \in (\Sigma')^*$, if $|\mathcal{A}|(x) \in (\Sigma')^*$, then $|\mathcal{A}|(x) = |\mathcal{A}'|(x)$.

Proof. Let $\Phi = \Sigma' \cup \{\phi_1, \phi_2, \ldots, \phi_k\}$. Code ϕ_i by $\bar{\phi}_i = ab^i a$, $1 \leq i \leq k$. Define

$$\bar{0} = 0 \qquad \overline{x\sigma} = \begin{cases} \bar{x}\sigma & \text{if } \sigma \in \Sigma' \\ \bar{x}\bar{\sigma} & \text{if } \sigma \in \Phi - \Sigma' \end{cases}$$

The word $\bar{x}$ is obtained from x by replacing each symbol ϕ_i by the word ab^ia. Let $\mathcal{A}'$ be the LMA obtained from $\mathcal{A}$ by changing all rules $i\colon x_i \to y_i\ /l_i$ to $i\colon \bar{x}_i \to \bar{y}_i\ /l_i$. There is a 1-1 correspondence between computations in $\mathcal{A}$ and computations in $\mathcal{A}'$, starting with a word x in $(\Sigma')^*$. A statement $\bar{x} \to \bar{y}$ in $\mathcal{A}'$ will be applicable to $\bar{w}$, producing $\bar{z}$ iff the statement $x \to y$ in $\mathcal{A}$ is applicable to w, producing z. ▌

EXERCISES

1. Show the step-by-step computation of the following LMA when applied to the word $w = 221$.

$$
\begin{aligned}
&0{:}0 \to c/1;\\
&1{:}c1 \to 1ac/1;\\
&2{:}c2 \to 2bc/1;\\
&3{:}c \to 0/4;\\
&4{:}\tau\sigma \to \sigma\tau/4; \qquad \tau \in \{a,b\},\ \sigma \in \{1,2\}\\
&5{:}a \to 1/5;\\
&6{:}b \to 2/6;
\end{aligned}
$$

2. Construct LMA's to compute
- a. the diagonalization function δ in Σ_2
- b. the projection function π in Σ_2
- c. the zero function ζ in Σ_2
- d. concatenation in Σ_2
- e. the reversal function in Σ_2
- f. addition in Σ_2
- g. multiplication in Σ_1

3. Suppose LMA's to compute $f\colon W^r \to W^s$ and $g\colon W^s \to W^r$ are given. Explain how to construct an LMA to compute
- a. the composition $g \circ f$
- b. the combination $f \times g$
- c. the repetition of f (assume $r = s$)
- d. the exponentiation of f (assume $r = s$)

4. Construct an LMA in $\Sigma_2' = \{\$,1,2\}$ such that $|\mathcal{A}|(x_1\$x_2\$) = x_1\$x_2 1\$$, $x_1,x_2 \in \Sigma_2^*$.

5. Construct an LMA in $\Sigma_1' = \{\$,1\}$ such that $|\mathcal{A}|(x_1\$x_2\$) = x_1\$x_2 1\$$, where $x_1,x_2 \in \Sigma_1^*$.

6. Find a recursive function $f\colon \Sigma_1^* \to \Sigma_1^*$ in Σ_1 such that $f \neq |\mathcal{A}|$ for any LMA $\mathcal{A}$ in Σ_1.

7.[Δ] Characterize the set of total functions $|\mathcal{A}|\colon \Sigma_1^* \to \Sigma_1^*$ where $\mathcal{A}$ is an LMA in Σ_1.

8. Markov originally defined a *normal algorithm* (now called a *Markov algorithm*) as an ordered list of rules of the form

$$x_0 \to y_0$$
$$x_1 \to \cdot y_1$$
$$x_2 \to \cdot y_2$$
$$\vdots$$
$$x_k \to y_k$$

The rules are searched for the first one, say $x_i \to y_i$, which is applicable to the given word w. This rule is applied to the leftmost occurrence of x_i in w. Then the rules are again tested, beginning with rule 0. The computation terminates if a rule with a period after the arrow (a terminal rule) is applied. If no rule is applicable the computation does not "halt", but enters an "infinite loop".

a. Given a Markov algorithm $\mathcal{A}$, let $\mathcal{A}'$ be $\mathcal{A}$ with the rule $0 \to 0$ added at the end. Show that $|\mathcal{A}| = |\mathcal{A}'|$ and some rule of $\mathcal{A}'$ will always be applicable.

b. The following Markov algorithm in $\Sigma \cup \{a,b,c\}$ computes $f(x) = x \cdot x$ in Σ

$$\begin{array}{rlr} \sigma\tau b & \to \tau b\sigma & \sigma,\tau \in \Sigma \\ a\sigma & \to \sigma b\sigma a & \sigma \in \Sigma \\ b & \to c & \\ c & \to 0 & \\ a & \to \cdot\, 0 & \\ 0 & \to a & \end{array}$$

Notice that the order of the rules is quite critical. Write Markov algorithms to compute the functions listed in Exercise 2.

c. Show that each Markov algorithm can be simulated by an LMA.
Hint: Simply add the appropriate label and goto for each rule.

d. Show that each LMA can be simulated by a Markov algorithm.
Hint: Add symbols to the alphabet to control the sequencing of statements of the Markov algorithm.

5.2 Labeled Markov Algorithm Simulation of Turing Machine Programs

The next result shows that each function computed by a TM program can also be computed by an LMA. From this it follows that all partial recursive functions are computable by an LMA.

THEOREM 5.2 For each deterministic exit TM program $\mathcal{T} = \langle \mathcal{L}, l_0, S, T \rangle$ in Σ', there is an LMA $\mathcal{A}$ in $\Sigma' \cup \{a,b\}$ such that for each $x \in (\Sigma')^*$, $|\mathcal{A}|(x) = y$ iff $|\mathcal{T}|(0,x) = (w,y)$ for some w.

Proof. Let $\Phi = \Sigma' \cup \{|, [,]\}$. Assume A, B, C, D, and E are not labels of $\mathcal{T}$. The LMA is constructed by first writing the following statements, where l_0 is the initial label of $\mathcal{T}$:

$$\begin{array}{ll} A\!: 0 \to]\ /B; & \\ B\!:]\sigma \to \sigma]\ /B; & \sigma \in \Sigma' \\ C\!: 0 \to [|\ /l_0; & \end{array}$$

Next add one LMA statement for each statement of $\mathcal{T}$ according to the following table:

$\mathcal{T}$	$\mathcal{A}$
$l \quad \iota \times (L_\tau \circ L_\sigma^{-1}) \quad l'$	$l\colon |\sigma \to |\tau\ /l';$
$l \quad (R_\tau \circ R_\sigma^{-1}) \times \iota \quad l'$	$l\colon \sigma| \to \tau|\ /l';$
$l \quad R_\sigma^{-1} \times L_\sigma \quad l'$	$l\colon \sigma| \to |\sigma\ /l';$
$l \quad R_\sigma \times L_\sigma^{-1} \quad l'$	$l\colon |\sigma \to \sigma|\ /l';$
$l \quad \varepsilon \times L_\sigma \quad l'$	$l\colon [| \to [|\sigma\ /l';$
$l \quad \varepsilon \times L_\sigma^{-1} \quad l'$	$l\colon [|\sigma \to [|\ /l';$
$l \quad R_\sigma \times \varepsilon \quad l'$	$l\colon |] \to \sigma|]\ /l';$
$l \quad R_\sigma^{-1} \times \varepsilon \quad l'$	$l\colon \sigma|] \to |]\ /l';$
$l \quad \varepsilon \times \iota \quad l'$	$l\colon [| \to [|\ /l';$
$l \quad \iota \times \varepsilon \quad l'$	$l\colon |] \to |]\ /l';$

Suppose there are k TM statements with the same label l. Place the corresponding LMA statements together in any order and change the labels of all but the first statement to $l.1$, $l.2$, ... and add a statement $l.k\colon 0 \to 0\ /l.k$ so that the LMA will enter an infinite loop if no instruction in $\mathcal{T}$ with label l is applicable to the TM register contents when the statement with label l is reached. Since $\mathcal{T}$ is deterministic, the order of the individual LMA statements within a group derived from TM statements with the same label is not important because at most one can be applicable. Also, the ordering of the groups of statements within the LMA is not important because each TM statement contains an explicit goto part.

For each terminal label l of $\mathcal{T}$, add to the LMA the statement

$$l\colon 0 \to 0\ /D;$$

and finally add the statements

$$\begin{aligned} &D\colon [\sigma \to [\ /D; \qquad \sigma \in \Sigma' \\ &E\colon [| \to 0\ /F; \\ &F\colon] \to 0\ /F; \end{aligned}$$

The final task is to relabel the statements of the LMA 0, 1, 2, ... and change the goto parts appropriately.

For $x \in (\Sigma')^*$, $\mathcal{A}$ begins its computation by applying statement A yielding $]x$. Statement B is applied repeatedly yielding $x]$ and then statement C gives $[|x]$, at which point step-by-step simulation of the TM program begins. If (x,y) is stored in the registers of the TM and a statement of $\mathcal{T}$ is executed which changes the registers to (x',y'), then the corresponding statement of the LMA will transform the word $[x|y]$ into $[x'|y']$.

If the TM program halts, then the LMA will branch to statement D which will change the word $[x|y]$ to $[|y]$. Finally, statements E and F remove the symbols [,], and | and the program halts.

The proof is completed by observing that according to Lemma 5.1 only two auxiliary symbols are required. ▮

Example. Let $\mathcal{T}$ be the following TM program in $\Sigma_2' = \Sigma_2 \cup \{\$\}$ which computes concatenation in Σ_2 (see Section 4.5 for an alternate method for computing concatenation on the TM).

1	$R_1 \times L_1^{-1}\,1, R_2 \times L_2^{-1}\,1, \iota \times (L_1 \circ L_\$^{-1})\,2$
2	$(R_1 \circ R_1^{-1}) \times \iota\,3.1, (R_2 \circ R_2^{-1}) \times \iota\,3.2, \varepsilon \times L_1^{-1}\,5, \varepsilon \times L_2^{-1}\,5$
3.1	$\iota \times (L_1 \circ L_1^{-1})\,4, \iota \times (L_1 \circ L_2^{-1})\,4$
3.2	$\iota \times (L_2 \circ L_1^{-1})\,4, \iota \times (L_2 \circ L_2^{-1})\,4$
4	$R_1^{-1} \times L_1\,2, R_2^{-1} \times L_2\,2$
5	stop

The resulting LMA before the last relabeling step is as follows:

A:	$0 \to]$	$/B$;	
B:	$]\sigma \to \sigma]$	$/B$;	$\sigma \in \Sigma_2'$
C:	$0 \to [|$	$/1$;	
1:	$|1 \to 1|$	$/1$;	
1.1:	$|2 \to 2|$	$/1$;	
1.2:	$|\$ \to |1$	$/2$;	
1.3:	$0 \to 0$	$/1.3$;	
2:	$1| \to 1|$	$/3.1$;	
2.1:	$2| \to 2|$	$/3.2$;	
2.2:	$[|1 \to [|$	$/5$;	
2.3:	$[|2 \to [|$	$/5$;	
2.4:	$0 \to 0$	$/2.4$;	
3.1:	$|1 \to |1$	$/4$;	
3.1.1:	$|2 \to |1$	$/4$;	
3.1.2:	$0 \to 0$	$/3.1.2$;	
3.2:	$|1 \to |2$	$/4$;	
3.2.1:	$|2 \to |2$	$/4$;	
3.2.2:	$0 \to 0$	$/3.2.2$;	
4:	$1| \to |1$	$/2$;	
4.1:	$2| \to |2$	$/2$;	
4.2:	$0 \to 0$	$/4.2$;	
5:	$0 \to 0$	$/D$;	
D:	$[\sigma \to [$	$/D$;	$\sigma \in \Sigma_2'$
E:	$[| \to 0$	$/F$;	
F:	$] \to 0$	$/F$;	

THEOREM 5.3. Each function $f: W^r \to W^s$, where $W = \Sigma^*$, computed by a TM program $\mathcal{T}$ in $\Sigma \cup \{\$\}$ is computed by some LMA in $\Sigma \cup \{\$,a,b\}$.

Proof. $f(x_1,\ldots,x_r) = (y_1,\ldots,y_s)$ iff $|\mathcal{T}|(0,\alpha_r(x)) = (w,y)$ for some w, where $\omega_s(y) = (y_1,\ldots,y_s)$. Hence by Theorem 5.2, there is an LMA in $\Sigma' \cup \{a,b\}$ such that $|\mathcal{A}|(\alpha_r(x)) = y$, so $f = \omega_s \circ |\mathcal{A}| \circ \alpha_r$, which means $\mathcal{A}$ computes f. ▌

EXERCISES

1. Show that each function $f: W^r \to W^s$ computed by a TM program in $\Sigma \cup \{\$\}$ is computed by an LMA in $\Sigma \cup \{\$,|\}$; that is, only *one* auxiliary symbol is required. *Hint:* carefully code [,],| as members of $\{|\}^*$.

2. Assume $\Sigma = \{1,2,\ldots,n\}$ and define $g:(\Sigma \cup \{\$\})^* \to \{1,\$\}^*$ by

$$g(i) = \$1^i\$ \qquad i \in \Sigma$$
$$g(\$) = \$1^{n+1}\$$$
$$g(x\sigma) = g(x)g(\sigma) \qquad \text{for } \sigma \in \Sigma \cup \{\$\}$$

Assume that the LMA input function is $\alpha_r': W^r \to \{1,\$\}^*$ defined by

$$\alpha_r'(x_1,\ldots,x_r) = g(x_1)g(\$)\cdots g(\$)g(x_r)g(\$)$$

Define a corresponding output function ω_s' and show that with these input/output functions every function $f: W^r \to W^s$ computed by an LMA can be computed by an LMA in $\{1,\$\}$—that is, every function computed by an LMA can be computed by an LMA with a two-letter alphabet given suitable input and output functions.

3.$^{\Delta}$ Show that there do not exist input and output functions α' and ω' which enable the LMA in Σ_1 to compute all functions $f:\Sigma_1^* \to \Sigma_1^*$ computed by LMA's. Compare with Exercise 2.

*5.3 SNOBOL

The programming language SNOBOL (*S*tri*N*g-*O*riented sym*BO*lic *L*anguage), developed by computer scientists at Bell Telephone Laboratories, has been strongly influenced by Markov algorithms. In turn, our definition of LMA's incorporates some of the ideas which were introduced by the designers of SNOBOL in order to obtain a more useful programming language than the language of Markov algorithms.

SNOBOL is a very elegant language, with many sophisticated features for processing both words and numerical data; however, a small subset of SNOBOL is quite similar to the class of LMA's. In order to demonstrate the similarity, a description of this subset of SNOBOL will be given.

In SNOBOL a blank symbol is used both to separate a label from the rest of the statement and to designate the concatenation operation. There is no restriction on the order in which labels appear and a statement need not have a label. Character strings are designated by enclosing them in quotation marks. As with most languages, there are variables to which strings may be assigned. Character strings not enclosed in quotes are used as names for these variables. The two types of statements considered are *assignment* statements and *replacement* statements, which correspond to the replacement rules of an LMA. The goto part of a statement may contain either a *success* or a *fail* branch as shown in the following example of a program which computes the reversal of any word in {A,B}* provided as input.

```
       X = "L" INPUT;
       Y = " ";
RPT    X "LA" = "L"          :F(TRYB);
       Y = "A" Y             :S(RPT)F(RPT);
TRYB   X "LB" = "L"          :F(DONE);
       Y = "B" Y             :S(RPT)F(RPT);
DONE   OUTPUT = Y;
END
```

The first statement containing the special name INPUT reads a word from an input card, concatenates the character L to its left end and assigns the result to the variable X. The next statement assigns the null word to Y. The statement labeled RPT checks for an occurrence of the subword LA; if it occurs, it is replaced by the word L and an A is concatenated to the left end of Y. If LA does not occur, the statement with label TRYB performs a similar check for LB. When all letters A and B have been deleted from X, the statement with label DONE prints the value of Y by assigning it to the special variable OUTPUT. The last statement of a SNOBOL program is always a null statement with label END.

Note that the letter L will occur at most once in X, always at the left end, so there can be at most one occurrence of LA or LB. If there were two or more occurrences of LA, SNOBOL would execute the statement labeled RPT by replacing the leftmost occurrence of LA by L.

To further illustrate how SNOBOL programs are executed, consider the following two statements:

```
LABELA  X  Y    = Z  "V"  :S(ABC);
LABELB  X  "Y" = Z  Z  :S(ABC)F(DEF);
```

Let value(V) be the word which is the value of the variable V. The first statement replaces the leftmost occurrence of value(Y) in value(X) (if such exists) by value(Z) concatenated with the character V to obtain the new value of X. If value(Y) occurs as a subword of value(X), the next statement executed is the one with label ABC, otherwise the program statement following the one having label LABELA is executed next. The second statement replaces the leftmost occurrence (if such exists) of the *character* Y in value(X) with value(Z) · value(Z). If $Y \preccurlyeq$ value(X), then statement ABC is executed next, otherwise statement DEF is executed next.

The following is a formal description of the syntax of a subset of SNOBOL using the BNF described in Section 2.1.

⟨*blanks*⟩ = any string of one or more blanks
⟨*letter*⟩ = A ∪ B ∪ C ∪ ··· ∪ Y ∪ Z
⟨*digit*⟩ = 0 ∪ 1 ∪ 2 ∪ ··· ∪ 9
⟨*char*⟩ = ⟨*letter*⟩ ∪ ⟨*digit*⟩
⟨*word*⟩ = ⟨*char*⟩ ∪ ⟨*word*⟩⟨*char*⟩
⟨*variable*⟩ = ⟨*letter*⟩ ∪ ⟨*variable*⟩⟨*char*⟩
⟨*term*⟩ = ⟨*variable*⟩ ∪ "⟨*word*⟩" ∪ " "
⟨*exp*⟩ = ⟨*term*⟩ ∪ ⟨*exp*⟩⟨*blanks*⟩⟨*term*⟩
⟨*label*⟩ = ⟨*word*⟩⟨*blanks*⟩ ∪ ⟨*blanks*⟩
⟨*goto*⟩ = :S(⟨*word*⟩) ∪ :F(⟨*word*⟩) ∪ :S(⟨*word*⟩)F(⟨*word*⟩) ∪ ⟨*blanks*⟩
⟨*body*⟩ = ⟨*variable*⟩⟨*blanks*⟩⟨*exp*⟩⟨*blanks*⟩ = ⟨*blanks*⟩⟨*exp*⟩
  ∪ ⟨*variable*⟩⟨*blanks*⟩ = ⟨*blanks*⟩⟨*exp*⟩
⟨*statement*⟩ = ⟨*label*⟩⟨*body*⟩; ∪ ⟨*label*⟩⟨*body*⟩⟨*goto*⟩;
⟨*program*⟩ = END ∪ ⟨*statement*⟩⟨*program*⟩

Each LMA can easily be rewritten as a SNOBOL program. As an example, the LMA in Section 5.1 which computes $f(x) = x \cdot x$ can be directly translated into the following SNOBOL program

```
    W = INPUT;
0   W " " = "A" :S(1);
1   W "A1 " = " 1B1A" :S(1);
2   W "A2 " = " 2B2A" :S(1);
3   W "A" = " " :S(4);
4   W " 11B " = " 1B1 " :S(4);
5   W " 12B " = " 2B1 " :S(4);
6   W " 21B " = " 1B2 " :S(4);
7   W " 22B " = " 2B2 " :S(4);
8   W " B " = " " :S(8);
    OUTPUT = W;
END
```

It is fairly tedious just to prove that each function computed by even the simple SNOBOL programs described here is also computed by an LMA. One complicating factor is the possibility of using several variable names in one program; an LMA computes with only one word at a time. One way to handle this problem is to add new auxiliary symbols to the LMA alphabet which are used to delimit the values of the SNOBOL program's variables the way that \$ is used in the SRM to separate the several input arguments. The string which the LMA processes will then contain the current values of all of the SNOBOL program's variables, delimited by special symbols. It is also possible to use the fact that each function computable by a SNOBOL program is intuitively computable, hence by Church's thesis it is computable by an LMA.

In order to get a better idea of the excellent facility for string-manipulating computations provided by the SNOBOL language, the interested reader should consult the text by Griswold, Poage, and Polonsky [1971].

EXERCISES

1. Sketch a proof that each function computed by a SNOBOL program is also computed by an LMA.

2. Write SNOBOL programs to compute

a. addition in Σ_2

b. multiplication in Σ_1

c. $f(x) = \begin{cases} \text{YES} & \text{if } x \text{ is a palindrome } [x = \rho(x)] \\ \text{NO} & \text{otherwise} \end{cases}$

d. $f(x) = x$ with all occurrences of DAMN replaced by DXXX

3. Assume that the SNOBOL statement

$$X = Y + Z$$

adds the values of Y and Z, using decimal notation. Strings of digits are treated as numbers by this statement. Write a SNOBOL program to count the number of times the letter E occurs in an input word.

5.4 Partial Recursiveness of Functions Computed by Labeled Markov Algorithms

In this section, we complete the loop in Figure 5-1, thereby proving the equivalence of the various computational schemes which have been discussed.

Actually we will prove much more than the assertion that each function computed by an LMA is partial recursive. It will be shown that the function $f(m,x) = |\mathcal{A}_m|(x)$ is partial recursive, where $\mathcal{A}_0, \mathcal{A}_1, \mathcal{A}_2, \ldots$ is a list of all

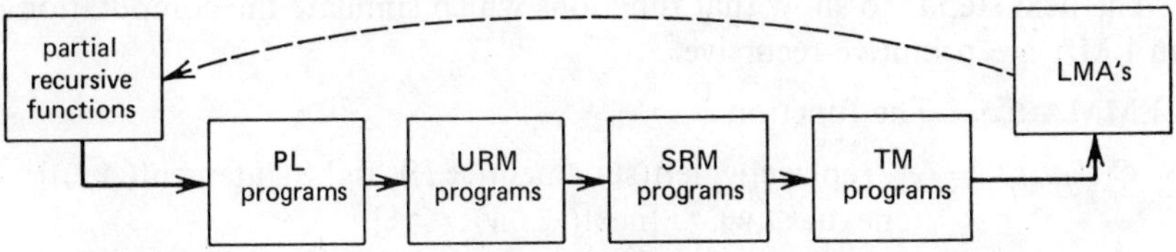

FIGURE 5-1. **Equivalent characterizations of the partial recursive functions.**

LMA's in some alphabet Φ. In a sense f simulates the computation of any LMA in Φ. Since it will follow that a function is partial recursive iff it is computed by an LMA, the function f can be computed by an LMA. Hence for any Φ there is an LMA which can simulate all LMA's in Φ, a *universal* LMA. Similarly it will be shown that there are universal URM programs, SRM programs, TM programs, and PL programs.

The list $\mathcal{A}_0, \mathcal{A}_1, \mathcal{A}_2, \ldots$ is also a list of all partial recursive functions in some alphabet Σ where $\Sigma \cup \{\$\} \subseteq \Phi$, namely the functions in Σ computed by $\mathcal{A}_0, \mathcal{A}_1, \mathcal{A}_2, \ldots$. This particular listing of the partial recursive functions in Σ will be very important in later chapters.

Suppose $\mathcal{A}$ is an LMA in the alphabet $\Phi = \Sigma \cup \{\$,a,b\}$ which computes a function in Σ. Let $\Psi = \Phi \cup \{\rightarrow,/,:,;\}$, where the four new special symbols are not in Φ. The semicolon is used to separate LMA statements in $\mathcal{A}$. Each LMA in Φ is then simply a word in Ψ^*. The next results show that functions which analyze an LMA into its component statements and statement parts are primitive recursive. To avoid confusion about which base is used for arithmetic operations, the labels witll be represented in "tally" or "unary" notation as members of Σ_1^*.

THEOREM 5.4. The following functions are primitive recursive in Ψ.

a. $\text{size}(\mathcal{A}) = \text{occurrences}(\mathcal{A},;) \dot{-} 1$
b. $\text{statement}(\mathcal{A},l) = \text{part}[\mathcal{A},;,\text{length}(l)]$
c. $\text{label}(s) = U(s,:)$
d. $\text{left}(s) = U[V(s,:),\rightarrow]$
e. $\text{right}(s) = U[V(s,\rightarrow),/]$
f. $\text{goto}(s) = V(s,/)$
g. $\text{next}(\mathcal{A},l,w) = \begin{cases} \text{goto}[\text{statement}(\mathcal{A},l)] & \text{if left}[\text{statement}(\mathcal{A},l)] \preccurlyeq w \\ l \cdot 1 & \text{otherwise} \end{cases}$

Proof. Theorem 3.18. ∎

If $\mathcal{A} \in \Psi^*$ is an LMA, then size($\mathcal{A}$) is one less than the number of statements, which is the number of 1's in the label of the last statement. The value of statement($\mathcal{A}$,l) is the lth statement of $\mathcal{A}$. If s is the statement $l{:}\, x \rightarrow y\, /l'$ and w is the word $\mathcal{A}$ is operating on, then label(s) $= l$, left(s) $= x$, right(s) $= y$, goto(s) $= l'$, and next($\mathcal{A}$,l,w) is the label of the next instruction to be executed.

The next step is to show that functions which simulate the computation of an LMA are primitive recursive.

LEMMA 5.5. The function

$$C(\mathcal{A}w,,l,t) = (\mathcal{A}, \text{replace}[w, \text{left}(\text{statement}(\mathcal{A},l)), \text{right}(\text{statement}(\mathcal{A},l))], \\ \text{next}(\mathcal{A},l,w), \neg\, [\text{next}(\mathcal{A},l,w){:}\preccurlyeq \mathcal{A}])$$

is primitive recursive in Ψ. ∎

The function C simulates the computation of the LMA $\mathcal{A}$ for one "step", namely, the execution of the single statement with label l applied to the word w. The new output value of t is 1 if the algorithm halts after execution of the statement and is 0 otherwise. Note that since LMA statements are labeled $0, 1, 11, \ldots$ in sequence, $\neg\,[\text{next}(\mathcal{A},l,w) : \preccurlyeq \mathcal{A}]$ is 1 iff the next statement to be executed does not occur in the LMA. To simulate the entire computation of $\mathcal{A}$ on input w, set l and t initially to 0 and repeat C until $t = 1$. In short, compute $C^{\nabla}(\mathcal{A},w,0,0)$.

THEOREM 5.6. Each function $f: W^r \to W^s$, $W = \Sigma^*$, computed by an LMA is partial recursive in Σ.

Proof. Let $f: W^r \to W^s$ be computed by an LMA. Then by Lemma 5.1, f is computed by some LMA $\mathcal{A} \in \Psi^*$ in $\Phi = \Sigma \cup \{\$,a,b\} \subset \Psi$. For this fixed $\mathcal{A}$

$$|\mathcal{A}| : \Phi^* \to \Phi^*$$

may be defined as

$$|\mathcal{A}|(w) = p \circ C^{\nabla}(\mathcal{A},w,0,0)$$

where $p(\mathcal{A},w,l,t) = w$. Since C is primitive recursive in Ψ, $p \circ C^{\nabla}(\mathcal{A},w,0,0)$ is partial recursive in Ψ. But $|\mathcal{A}|(w) \in \Phi^*$ whenever $w \in \Phi^*$, so $|\mathcal{A}|$ is partial recursive in Φ by Theorem 3.23. But $\mathcal{A}$ computes f so

$$f = \omega_s \circ |\mathcal{A}| \circ \alpha_r$$

where ω_s and α_r are the LMA output and input functions. Since ω_s and α_r, the null extension of α_r to Φ, are primitive recursive in Φ and

$$f = \omega_s \circ |\mathcal{A}| \circ \alpha_r : W^r \to W^s$$

f is partial recursive in Σ by Theorem 3.23. ▮

COROLLARY 5.7. To define any partial recursive function, the operation of repetition (or minimization) is needed only once, that is, every partial recursive function is of the form $g \circ h^{\nabla}$, where g and h are primitive recursive. In the definition of the partial recursive functions, the operation of repetition (or minimization) may be restricted to apply to primitive recursive functions. Also, any partial recursive function may be computed by a PL program with only a single GOTO statement.

Proof. Repetition is used only once in the proof of Theorem 5.6. The resolution of difficulties arising due to the fact that h: $W^r \to \Phi^*$ and g: $\Phi^* \to W^s$ is left to the reader. ▮

THEOREM 5.8. A function f is partial recursive iff it is computed by the URM, the SRM, the TM, an LMA, or a PL program. ▮

The next goal is to give an effective listing $\mathcal{A}_0, \mathcal{A}_1, \ldots$ of all LMA's over a fixed alphabet $\Phi = \Sigma \cup \{\$,a,b\}$, thus obtaining an effective listing of the partial recursive functions in Σ.

LEMMA 5.9. The set $S = \Sigma_1^*:\Phi^* \to \Phi^*/\Sigma_1^*$ of legal LMA statements is primitive recursive in Ψ. Recall that labels are members of Σ_1^*.
Proof. Theorem 3.18. ▮

LEMMA 5.10. The set $A \subseteq \Psi^*$ of LMA's in Φ is primitive recursive in Ψ.

Proof. $\chi_A(\mathcal{A}) = \bigwedge_{k=0}^{\text{size}(\mathcal{A})} (\text{statement}(\mathcal{A},1) \in S \wedge \text{label}[\text{statement}(\mathcal{A},1^k)] = 1^k)$
$\wedge$ last letter of$(\mathcal{A}) = ;$ ▮

Let $\bar{\kappa}$ be the null extension of the bijection $\kappa: \Sigma^* \to \Psi^*$. Define the function

$$\mathcal{A}(m) = \begin{cases} \kappa(m) & \text{if } m \in \Sigma^* \text{ and } \kappa(m) \in A, \text{ the set of LMA's in } \Phi \\ 0:0 \to 0/0; & \text{otherwise} \end{cases}$$

LEMMA 5.11. The function $\mathcal{A}$ is primitive recursive in Ψ.
Proof. Immediate from Lemma 5.10 and the fact that κ and χ_{Σ^*} are primitive recursive in Ψ. ▮

For each $m \in \Sigma^*$, $\mathcal{A}(m) \in \Psi^*$ is an LMA; and for each LMA $m' \in \Psi^*$, there is an $m \in \Sigma^*$, namely $m = \kappa^{-1}(m')$, such that $\mathcal{A}(m) = m'$. Thus, as m ranges over all values in Σ^*, $\mathcal{A}(m)$ ranges over all LMA's which compute with alphabet Φ. *Theorem* 5.8 *thus implies that a function is partial recursive in* Σ *iff it is computed by* $\mathcal{A}(m)$, *for some* $m \in \Sigma^*$.

Define ${}^r_s\varphi_m = \omega_s \circ |\mathcal{A}(m)| \circ \alpha_r$. Let $\varphi_m(x) = {}^1_1\varphi_m(x)$. Since a function is partial recursive in Σ iff it is computed by an LMA in Φ, a function $f: W^r \to W^s$ is partial recursive in Σ iff $f = {}^r_s\varphi_m$ for some $m \in \Sigma^*$. The value of m is called an *index* for the function f. This indexing for the partial recursive functions in Σ will be used throughout the remainder of the book.

THEOREM 5.12. Every partial recursive function f has infinitely many indices.
Proof. Let $\mathcal{A}$ be an LMA which computes f. Increase all labels and goto's in $\mathcal{A}$ by k and add the statements $i:0 \to 0/k$, $0 \leq i < k$ at the beginning of $\mathcal{A}$. For each k, the resulting LMA also computes f, thus there are infinitely many LMA's which compute f. This method of finding additional LMA's which compute f is known as *padding.* ▮

Define $T_r(m,x,k)$, called the *T-predicate*, to be the predicate which states that the LMA $\mathcal{A}(m)$ in $\Phi = \Sigma \cup \{\$,a,b\}$ halts on input $x \in W^r$ in *exactly k* steps. A "step" is the execution of one statement of the LMA. There is a different T-predicate for each r and Σ.

THEOREM 5.13. The T-predicate is primitive recursive in Σ.

Proof. First note that $T_r : \Sigma^{1+r+1} \to \{0,1\}$. The value of T_r is given by

$$T_r(m,x,k) = p \circ C^k[\mathcal{A}(m), \alpha_r(x),0,0] \wedge \bigwedge_{j=0}^{k \dot{-} 1} \neg (p \circ C^j[\mathcal{A}(m),\alpha_r(x),0,0])$$

where p is the projection function whose value is the last argument. Note that $T_r(m,x,0) = 0$, since each LMA has at least one statement and hence cannot halt in 0 steps. Theorem 3.23 is used implicitly. ∎

The function $(\mu k)T_r(m,x,k)$ equals the number of instructions executed by $\mathcal{A}(m)$ before halting when started on input x. A definition of ${}^r_s\varphi_m$ which uses minimization instead of repetition is

$${}^r_s\varphi_m(w) = \omega_s \circ p \circ C^{(\mu k)T_r(m,\,x,\,k)}(\mathcal{A}(m),\alpha_r(x),0,0)$$

where C is as in Lemma 5.5 and $p(\mathcal{A},w,k,t) = w$. Hence every partial recursive function can be defined using a single application of minimization and primitive recursive functions.

EXERCISES

1. Suppose i is an index for f and j is an index for g, that is, $f = \varphi_i$ and $g = \varphi_j$. Explain how to find an index for $g \circ f$.

2. What is the function φ_0? In Σ_1, find the smallest m such that $\varphi_m \neq \varphi_0$.

3. Let

$$f(m,x) = \begin{cases} 1 & \text{if } \mathcal{A}(m) \text{ halts in } x \text{ or fewer steps on input } x \\ 0 & \text{if } \mathcal{A}(m) \text{ halts after more than } x \text{ steps on input } x \\ \uparrow & \text{if } \mathcal{A}(m) \text{ does not halt on input } x \end{cases}$$

Show that $f(m,x)$ is partial recursive.

5.5 Universal Functions and Programs

Theorem 5.8 asserts that the functions computed by the URM, SRM, TM, LMA's, and PL programs are the partial recursive functions. A somewhat stronger statement has actually been proved. This chapter and the previous two explain precisely how to construct a URM, SRM, TM or PL program, or an LMA to compute any given partial recursive function. Using Church's thesis, it follows that there is a recursive function f, such that if x is a description of a partial recursive function (that is, a partial recursive definition), then $f(x)$ is a description of a TM to compute the function x. To prove this formally, a scheme for describing partial recursive functions as words in some alphabet would have to be devised. The alphabet would include, among others, the symbols ζ, π, (,), and $\circ$. For example if $x = (\zeta \circ \pi)$, then the value of $f(x)$ would be a TM program which computes $\zeta \circ \pi$. In fact, for any two of the algorithmic languages discussed, a similar recursive function exists. For example, a function which, given an index m of an LMA, outputs a partial recursive definition of $\omega_s \circ |\mathcal{A}(m)| \circ \alpha_r$, is easily shown to be recursive by the results of the previous section.

The proof that each function in Σ computed by an LMA is partial recursive in Σ exhibits a single partial recursive function (for each r and s) $f(m,x) = \omega_s \circ |\mathcal{A}(m)| \circ \alpha_r(x)$, which simulates the action of $\mathcal{A}(m)$ on input x. Such a function is called a *universal function*, because, in a sense, the function f can compute all partial recursive functions in Σ. The LMA which computes $f(m,x)$ is a universal LMA because, treating the first argument as a description of another LMA, $\mathcal{A}(m)$, it simulates the computation $\mathcal{A}(m)$ would make with input x. Note that f is computed by an LMA in

$$\Phi = \Sigma \cup \{\$,a,b\}.$$

The existence of a universal program should not surprise computer scientists. A program which will compile and execute any FORTRAN program is a universal FORTRAN program. The compiler itself could be written in FORTRAN if that were desirable. The user of such a program provides as input a FORTRAN program (the first argument of the universal program) and the data which is to be treated as input for the FORTRAN program.

In the programming language LISP, it is particularly easy to write a universal LISP program which will simulate any other LISP program. Indeed, an important feature of the LISP language is that there is no distinction between programs and their data.

A universal URM (SRM, TM, PL) program is one which accepts as its first argument a description of some URM (SRM, TM, PL) program and simulates the computation of that program with input consisting of the remaining arguments. The following discussion informally demonstrates that there is a universal SRM program. The proofs for the URM, TM, and PL would be similar.

Let $g(\mathcal{T})$ be the LMA which simulates the computation of the SRM program $\mathcal{T}$, that is $|g(\mathcal{T})|(x) = |\mathcal{T}|(x)$. This chapter and the previous one explain how to compute g, so it is recursive. The function $f(g(\mathcal{T}),x)$, where f is a universal function, is partial recursive, so some SRM program $\overline{\mathcal{T}}$ must compute it. Thus $|\overline{\mathcal{T}}|(\mathcal{T},x) = |g(\mathcal{T})|(x) = |\mathcal{T}|(x)$, which means $\overline{\mathcal{T}}$ is a universal SRM program.

The LMA's have been given the special status of providing the indices of the partial recursive functions. It is important to observe that any of the other algorithmic languages considered would serve equally well in this regard. All results proved about the partial recursive functions using this particular indexing could also be proved using any other suitable indexing.

EXERCISE

1. List some properties that any "suitable" indexing should have.

5.6 A Function that Is Not Recursive

It is now possible to explicitly describe a function and a set which are not recursive. Consider the function

$$h(x) = \begin{cases} 1 & \text{if } \varphi_x(x)\downarrow \\ 0 & \text{otherwise} \end{cases}$$

The function h is 1 for input x if the LMA $\mathcal{A} = \mathcal{A}(x)$ halts on input x, that is, $\mathcal{A}$ halts on an input consisting of its own description (index) x.

THEOREM 5.14. The function h is not recursive.

Proof. This proof is a formal version of the diagonalization argument presented in Section 2.3. Suppose h is recursive and define $g(x) = h(x) \rightarrow (\varphi_x(x) + 1)$, where $\varphi_x(x) = \omega_1 \circ |\mathcal{A}(x)| \circ \alpha_1(x)$, that is,

$$g(x) = \begin{cases} \varphi_x(x) + 1 & \text{if } h(x) = 1 \\ 0 & \text{if } h(x) = 0 \end{cases}$$

If h is recursive, then so is $g(x)$, because $\varphi_x(x)$ will always be defined when $h(x) = 1$. Let m be an index for g, so that $g = \varphi_m$. Then $h(m) = 1$, since g is recursive, which means that $\varphi_m(m) = g(m) = \varphi_m(m) + 1$, which is absurd. The assumption that h is recursive must be false. ▮

COROLLARY 5.15. The set $H = \{x \mid \varphi_x(x)\downarrow\}$ is not recursive.

Proof. $h(x) = \chi_H(x)$. ▮

Recall that in Section 2.3 Church's thesis was used to infer the PL-computability (and hence the recursiveness) of the function g of Theorem 5.14. This is no longer necessary because we have now (in effect) shown that there is a PL program which simulates the computation of other programs, that is, which computes the function $f(m,x) = \varphi_m(x) = \omega_1 \circ |\mathcal{A}(m)| \circ \alpha_1(x)$. The function g may be defined by

$$g(x) = h(x) \rightarrow \omega_1 \circ |\mathcal{A}(x)| \circ \alpha_1(x)$$

which is recursive if h is recursive and hence PL-computable if h is PL-computable.

The problem of calculating the characteristic function of a particular set is called the *decision problem* for that set. A set with a nonrecursive characteristic function is said to be *undecidable* or *unsolvable*. Similarly a nonrecursive predicate is also called undecidable. Corollary 5.15 states that the set H is undecidable.

COROLLARY 5.16. The function

$$h'(x,y) = \begin{cases} 1 & \text{if } \varphi_x(y)\downarrow \\ 0 & \text{otherwise} \end{cases}$$

is not recursive.

Proof. If h' is recursive, then so is h, since $h(x) = h'(x, x)$. ▮

Corollary 5.16 may be interpreted to say that there is no program which will accept as input any program x (say, written in FORTRAN) and any data y, and decide whether or not program x will halt using input y. The decision problem for $\{(x,y) \mid \varphi_x(y)\downarrow\}$ is generally called the *halting problem*. Corollary 5.16 states that the halting problem is undecidable.

There are many other interesting problems which are undecidable. Some of these will be discussed in Chapter 6. For example, it will be shown that there is no program which will decide whether a given program x will halt for *all* inputs.

The *completion* of a function f is defined to be

$$\bar{f}(x) = \begin{cases} f(x) & \text{if } f(x)\downarrow \\ 0 & \text{otherwise} \end{cases}$$

COROLLARY 5.17. There is a partial recursive function whose completion is not recursive.

Proof. Let

$$f(x) = \begin{cases} 1 & \text{if } x \in H \\ \uparrow & \text{if } x \notin H \end{cases}$$

then $f(x) = \varphi_x(x) + 1 \dot{-} 1$ so it is partial recursive, but the completion of f is the function $h = \chi_H$. ▮

EXERCISES

1. Given any total function f that is not recursive, show that $A = \{x \mid f(x) > 0\}$ may or may not be a recursive set.

2. If, for all x for which f is defined, g is also defined and $f(x) = g(x)$, then g is an *extension* of f, written $f \subseteq g$. The completion of a function f is one possible extension. Exhibit a partial recursive function which does not have a recursive extension.
Hint: Give a partial recursive f such that if g is a total recursive extension of f, then by computing g, the halting problem can be solved.

3. Show that $\{x \mid \varphi_x \text{ recursive}\}$ is not recursive.

4. Show that the partial recursive function

$$g(x) = \begin{cases} 1 & \text{if } \varphi_x(x)\downarrow \\ \uparrow & \text{otherwise} \end{cases}$$

cannot be defined by applying minimization to a primitive recursive function, that is, $g(x) \neq (\mu k) f(x,k)$ for any primitive recursive f. Compare this with the results at the end of Section 5.4.

5.7 The Index and Recursion Theorems

In this section we present two results which have many applications in recursive function theory. Both are related to the indexing of the partial recursive functions introduced in Section 5.4.

As before let Σ be a fixed alphabet, $\Sigma' = \Sigma \cup \{\$\}$, $\Phi = \Sigma \cup \{\$,a,b\}$, and $\Psi = \Phi \cup \{:,\rightarrow,/,;\}$.

Suppose $f(x,y)$ is a partial recursive function. If x has some fixed value, say $x = x_0$, then $g(y) = f(x_0,y)$ is a partial recursive function with argument y. The index theorem states that an index for g can be effectively computed, given an index for f. The main part of the proof of the theorem is contained in the following lemma. Recall that labels are Σ_1^*.

LEMMA 5.18. There is a function $K(\mathcal{A},x)$, primitive recursive in Ψ, such that if $\mathcal{A}$ is an LMA and x and y are in $(\Sigma')^*$, then $K(\mathcal{A},x)$ is also an LMA and $|K(\mathcal{A},x)|(y) = |\mathcal{A}|(x \cdot y)$.

Proof. The function K performs the following computation, given input $\mathcal{A}$ and x:

a. Increase the label and goto part of each statement of $\mathcal{A}$ by 1.
b. Put the statement $0: 0 \rightarrow x/1;$ at the beginning of the modified version of $\mathcal{A}$.

The resulting LMA $\mathcal{A}'$ is the value of $K(\mathcal{A},x)$ and satisfies $|\mathcal{A}'|(y) = |\mathcal{A}|(x \cdot y)$. A formal primitive recursive definition of K is given by

$$K(0,x) = 0: 0 \rightarrow x\,/1;$$

$$K(\mathcal{A}\sigma,x) = \begin{cases} K(\mathcal{A},x)\cdot 1 \cdot \sigma & \text{if } \sigma = \text{ : or } \sigma = \text{ ;} \\ K(\mathcal{A},x)\cdot\sigma & \text{otherwise} \end{cases}$$ ∎

Example. Suppose $\mathcal{A}$ is the LMA

$$\begin{aligned} &0:\ \ 0 \rightarrow a\,/1; \\ &1: a1 \rightarrow 1a\,/1; \\ &2: a2 \rightarrow 2a\,/1; \\ &3:\ \ a \rightarrow 2\,/73; \end{aligned}$$

where $\Sigma = \{1, 2\}$. If $x = 11\$$, then $\mathcal{A}' = K(\mathcal{A},x)$ is the LMA

$$\begin{aligned} &0:\ \ 0 \rightarrow 11\$\,/1; \\ &1:\ \ 0 \rightarrow a\,/2; \\ &2: a1 \rightarrow 1a\,/2; \\ &3: a2 \rightarrow 2a\,/2; \\ &4:\ \ a \rightarrow 2\,/74; \end{aligned}$$

For input $y = 221\$$, the computation of $|\mathcal{A}'|(y)$ is $221\$ \Rightarrow 11\$221\$ \Rightarrow a11\$221\$ \Rightarrow 1a1\$221\$ \Rightarrow 11a\$221\$ \Rightarrow 112\$221\$$. The computation of $\mathcal{A}$ with input $x \cdot y = 11\$221\$$ is identical, starting with the second step.

THEOREM 5.19 (the index theorem). For each $r \geq 0$, there is a primitive recursive function $K_r : W^{1+r} \to W, W = \Sigma^*$, such that for all r, r', s, and m, ${}^{r+r'}_{s}\varphi_m(x,y) = {}^{r'}_{s}\varphi_{K_r(m,x)}(y)$.

Proof. Let $K_r(m, x) = \kappa^{-1} \circ K[\mathcal{A}(m), \alpha_r(x)]$, where K is the function defined in Lemma 5.18 and where κ is the bijection $\kappa : \Sigma^* \to \Psi^*$ discussed in Section 3.7. Then

$$\begin{aligned}
{}^{r'}_{s}\varphi_{K_r(m,x)}(y) &= \omega_s \circ |\mathcal{A}[K_r(m,x)]| \circ \alpha_{r'}(y) \\
&= \omega_s \circ |\mathcal{A} \circ \kappa^{-1} \circ K[\mathcal{A}(m),\alpha_r(x)]| \circ \alpha_{r'}(y) && \text{by the definition of } K_r \\
&= \omega_s \circ |K[\mathcal{A}(m),\alpha_r(x)]| \circ \alpha_{r'}(y) && \text{by the definitions of } \mathcal{A} \text{ and } \kappa \\
&= \omega_s \circ |\mathcal{A}(m)|[\alpha_r(x) \cdot \alpha_{r'}(y)] && \text{by Lemma 5.18} \\
&= \omega_s \circ |\mathcal{A}(m)| \circ \alpha_{r+r'}(x,y) && \text{by the definition of } \alpha \\
&= {}^{r+r'}_{s}\varphi_m(x,y) \quad \blacksquare
\end{aligned}$$

The function $K_r(m,x)$ merely obtains an index of an LMA which first adds the r-tuple x to its input string and then simulates the LMA $\mathcal{A}(m)$ on the new input.

In order to prove the index theorem using an indexing that is not based on LMA's, it may be necessary to have a different function $K_{rr'}$ for each pair of values r, $r' \geq 0$. Indeed, the index theorem is traditionally called the *S-m-n* theorem and is stated as follows: For each m, $n \geq 0$, there is a primitive recursive function ${}_mS_n$ satisfying ${}^{m+n}_{1}\varphi_i(x,y) = {}^{n}_{1}\varphi_{{}_mS_n(i,\,x)}(y)$.

The following proposition illustrates how the index theorem can be applied.

THEOREM 5.20. There is a primitive recursive function $f(x,y)$ such that

$$\varphi_{f(x,y)} = \varphi_y \circ \varphi_x$$

Given indices x and y for functions, the value of $f(x,y)$ is an index for the composition of the functions.

Proof. Let $g(x,y,z) = \varphi_y \circ \varphi_x(z)$. The function g is partial recursive, since $g(x,y,z) = \omega_1 \circ |\mathcal{A}(y)| \circ \alpha_1[\omega_1 \circ |\mathcal{A}(x)| \circ \alpha_1(z)]$. Let m_0 be an index for the function g, that is, $g = {}^{3}_{1}\varphi_{m_0}$, and let $f(x,y) = K_2(m_0,x,y)$. Then $\varphi_{f(x,y)}(z) = \varphi_{K_2(m_0,x,y)}(z) = {}^{3}_{1}\varphi_{m_0}(x,y,z) = g(x,y,z) = \varphi_y \circ \varphi_x(z)$. $\blacksquare$

Theorem 5.20 asserts simply that there is a primitive recursive and hence an effectively computable way to combine two programs to produce a third which computes the composition of the functions computed by the two given programs. Note that in the proof of Theorem 5.20, the use of the index theorem can be replaced by an appeal to Church's thesis; given x and y (that is, descriptions of LMA's which compute φ_x and φ_y), we may effectively describe an LMA which computes $\varphi_y \circ \varphi_x$. But then by Church's thesis there is a recursive function f such that, for any x, y, $f(x,y)$ is an index of $\varphi_y \circ \varphi_x$, that is, $\varphi_{f(x,y)} = \varphi_y \circ \varphi_x$. This is somewhat weaker than the above proof because Church's thesis does not permit us to infer the primitive recursiveness of a function.

Tedious proofs that a function is recursive are often simplified by the use of Church's thesis. An example is the function that produces an equivalent TM, given a description of a URM. Often the use of Church's thesis merely replaces an application of the index theorem. These situations are easy to identify. As an example, rather than stating that the function $f(x)$, defined implicitly by

$$\varphi_{f(x)}(y) = 2 \times \varphi_x(y)$$

is recursive by Church's thesis, the recursiveness of f may be inferred by appealing to the index theorem (see Exercise 2). Recursive functions will be defined throughout the text using equations similar to the one given above.

A *fixed point* of a function f is an argument x such that x and $f(x)$ are indices of the same function, that is, $\varphi_x = \varphi_{f(x)}$. An important result asserts that every recursive function has a fixed point. Moreover a fixed point for a total function may be effectively obtained, given an index of the function. That is, there is a recursive function g which has the property that $g(m)$ is the fixed point of the function φ_m, provided φ_m is total.

THEOREM 5.21 (the recursion theorem). There is a primitive recursive function g such that if φ_m is total, then $\varphi_{\varphi_m[g(m)]} = \varphi_{g(m)}$. Note this does *not* mean that $\varphi_m[g(m)] = g(m)$!

Proof. Let

$$k(m,y,x) = \begin{cases} \varphi_{\varphi_m[K_1(y,y)]}(x) & \text{if } \varphi_m[K_1(y,y)]\downarrow \\ \uparrow & \text{otherwise} \end{cases}$$

To compute k, the first argument m is treated as a program which is applied to the value of $K_1(y,y)$. If this calculation terminates, the output is also treated as a program, which is executed with input x.

Let q be an index for k, so that ${}_1^3\varphi_q = k$. Then by the index theorem

$$\varphi_{K_1[K_1(q,m),y]}(x) = {}_1^3\varphi_q(m,y,x) = \begin{cases} \varphi_{\varphi_m[K_1(y,y)]}(x) & \text{if } \varphi_m[K_1(y,y)]\downarrow \\ \uparrow & \text{otherwise} \end{cases}$$

Let φ_m be total and fix $y = h(m) = K_1(q,m)$. Then

$$\varphi_{K_1(hm,hm)}(x) = \begin{cases} \varphi_{\varphi_m[K_1(hm,hm)]}(x) & \text{if } \varphi_m[K_1(hm,hm)]\downarrow \\ \uparrow & \text{otherwise} \end{cases}$$

But by assumption φ_m is total so

$$\varphi_{K_1(hm,hm)}(x) = \varphi_{\varphi_m[K_1(hm,hm)]}(x)$$

which means that $g(m) = K_1(hm,hm) = K_1[K_1(q,m), K_1(q,m)]$ is the required fixed point. ▮

To illustrate further the usefulness of Church's thesis we present another less formal proof of the recursion theorem. The use of Church's thesis in this proof can easily be eliminated by an appeal to the index theorem (Exercise 6).

THEOREM 5.22 (recursion theorem restated). Let f be a recursive function. Then there is an index m_0 such that

$$\varphi_{f(m_0)} = \varphi_{m_0}$$

Moreover m_0 may be effectively obtained from an index of f.

Proof. Define

$$a_y(x) = \begin{cases} \varphi_{\varphi_y(y)}(x) & \text{if } \varphi_y(y)\downarrow \\ \uparrow & \text{otherwise} \end{cases}$$

Given y, we can effectively describe a procedure for computing a_y. First compute $\varphi_y(y)$. If an answer is obtained, then compute $\varphi_{\varphi_y(y)}(x)$.

By Church's thesis there is a recursive function k such that

$$\varphi_{k(y)}(x) = a_y(x) = \begin{cases} \varphi_{\varphi_y(y)}(x) & \text{if } \varphi_y(y)\downarrow \\ \uparrow & \text{otherwise} \end{cases}$$

Since $f \circ k$ is recursive, given indices for f and k we can effectively obtain an index for $f \circ k$; call it index$[f \circ k]$. Let $m_0 = k(\text{index}[f \circ k])$

$$\begin{aligned} \varphi_{m_0} &= \varphi_{k(\text{index}[f \circ k])} \\ &= \varphi_{\varphi_{\text{index}[f \circ k]}(\text{index}[f \circ k])} && \text{since } f \circ k \text{ is total} \\ &= \varphi_{f \circ k(\text{index}[f \circ k])} \\ &= \varphi_{f(m_0)} \end{aligned}$$

Hence $m_0 = k(\text{index}[f \circ k])$ is the required fixed point. By the above comments, m_0 may be effectively obtained from an index for f. ▮

The recursion theorem can be used to construct some interesting recursive functions. One example is given by Theorem 5.23.

THEOREM 5.23. There is an LMA which prints its own description, given any input.

Proof. Define f by $\varphi_{f(x)}(y) = x$, that is, $f(x) = K_1(e, x)$, where e is an index for the projection function $p(x,y) = x$. Since $f(x)$ is recursive, by the recursion theorem there is an m_0 such that $\varphi_{f(m_0)} = \varphi_{m_0}$, hence $\varphi_{m_0}(y) = \varphi_{f(m_0)}(y) = m_0$.

The function φ_{m_0} is a function whose constant value is its index m_0. The LMA which computes φ_{m_0} always outputs its own description. The word m_0 is called a "description" of the LMA because the LMA with index m_0 is $\mathcal{A}(m_0)$. ∎

THEOREM 5.24. There is a URM (SRM, TM, PL) program which outputs its own description, given any input.

Proof. The proof utilizes a function $g(\mathcal{T})$, whose value is an LMA which simulates the computation of the program $\mathcal{T}$ (Exercise 4). ∎

The recursion theorem can be used to justify nontrivial recursive definitions; indeed, this use is to some extent responsible for its being called the recursion theorem. As a further example. let us show that there is an LMA computing φ_m which on input y outputs the value $\varphi_y(m)$, that is, φ_m simulates φ_y on the former's own index. First define k recursive by

$$\varphi_{k(x)}(y) = \varphi_y(x)$$

By the recursion theorem there is a fixed point m such that

$$\varphi_m(y) = \varphi_{k(m)}(y) = \varphi_y(m)$$

as required.

This is a rather strange recursive definition of a function φ_m, whose value on input y depends on the computation of φ_y on input m and hence on φ_m itself.

EXERCISES

1. Show that for each $r, s, t \geq 0$, there is a primitive recursive function $f(x,y)$, such that ${}^{r}_{t}\varphi_{f(x,y)} = {}^{s}_{t}\varphi_y \circ {}^{r}_{s}\varphi_x$.

2. Show that there is a primitive recursive function f such that $\varphi_{f(x)}(y) = 2 \times \varphi_x(y)$.

3. Show that for each $r > 0$ there is a primitive recursive function f such that ${}^{r+1}_{r}\varphi_{f(x)} = {}^{r+1}_{r+1}\varphi^{\nabla}_{x}$.

4. Prove Theorem 5.24.

5. Discuss the possibility of an LMA $\mathcal{A} \in \Psi^*$ outputting the string $\mathcal{A}$ itself, rather than a "description" m, where $\mathcal{A} = \mathcal{A}(m)$.

6. Eliminate the use of Church's thesis in the second proof of the recursion theorem (Theorem 5.22).

7. Show that there is an x such that $\varphi_x(y) = (y \times x) + y$ for all y.

8. Write a nontrivial computer program which outputs itself, for example, a FORTRAN program which outputs a word which equals the concatenation of the statements of the program.

9. Let q be an index for the function k as in the proof of Theorem 5.21. Show that $g(m) = K_2[q,m,K_1(q,m)]$ is also a fixed point of each total function φ_m.

10. Show that there is an x such that $\varphi_x(y) = x^2$ for all y.

11.$^{\Delta}$ Show that there are x and y in W, $x \neq y$, such that dom $\varphi_x = \{y\}$ and dom $\varphi_y = \{x\}$.

12. Show that for each recursive f there is a 1-1 recursive g such that for all i, $g(i)$ is a fixed point of f, that is,

$$\varphi_{f[g(i)]} = \varphi_{g(i)} \qquad \text{for all } i$$

13. Show that there is a primitive recursive function f such that if φ_m is a recursive bijection, then $\varphi_{f(m)} = \varphi_m^{-1}$.

5.8 History

Markov algorithms were originally called "normal algorithms" by Markov [1954]. The form of his normal algorithms is discussed in Exercise 8 of Section 5.1. Our LMA's are motivated by Markov's normal algorithms, the SNOBOL programming language of Farber, Griswold, and Polonsky [1964] (see also Griswold, Poage and Polonsky [1971]), and the programmed grammars of Rosenkranz [1969]. The SNOBOL language, a portion of which is discussed in Section 5.3, was developed at the Bell Telephone Laboratories in 1962 to facilitate the writing of compilers. It was based on an earlier language COMIT, developed by Yngve [1957] primarily for use in investigating linguistic problems. In Rosenkranz [1969], programmed grammars, Markov algorithms with labels, were investigated. They later were used by Galler and Perlis [1970] as a basic model for the computation process.

The universal TM program (Section 5.5) was given in Turing [1936]. At the same time Kleene [1936a] defined the T-predicate (Section 5.4) and later showed that it could be used to obtain a universal partial recursive function [1943]. The characterization of the partial recursive functions using the T-predicate and one application of minimization given at the end of Section 5.4 is also in Kleene [1943].

The undecidability of the halting problem in essentially the form given in Section 5.6 was proved by Kleene [1936a]. Similar undecidability results were obtained at about the same time by Church [1936a] for the Λ-calculus, and by Turing [1936] for TM programs which output potentially infinite sequences.

The index and recursion theorems of Section 5.7 are due to Kleene [1938].

CHAPTER 6

Recursively Enumerable Sets

A program can define a set by computing its characteristic function. The sets definable in this way are the recursive sets discussed in Section 3.10. The concept of a program accepting a set was discussed in Section 4.6. In this chapter we discuss sets which can be defined by programs which enumerate the set by printing its members. It turns out that the effectively enumerable sets (those enumerated by some effective procedure) are exactly the same as the ones which are accepted by some program. In this chapter we will give several examples of sets which are not recursive and sets which are not effectively enumerable.

6.1 Programs that Enumerate Sets

Suppose statements of the form

PRINT X;

which causes the value of the variable X to be printed, are allowed in PL programs as discussed in Chapter 2. Further suppose that all variables of a PL program have value 0 before execution of the program begins. As the program is being executed, a value may be printed from time to time. A set A is PL-*enumerable* if there is a PL program which prints only members of A and each member of A is eventually printed.

Example. The set of Fibonacci numbers {1,2,3,5,8,13,...} is enumerated by the program

```
A ← 0;  B ← 1;
REPEAT:  B ← A + B;  A ← B ∸ A;
         PRINT B;
         GOTO REPEAT;
```

This program never halts. Each member of the Fibonacci set will eventually be printed by the program, but at no time will all of the members have been printed, since the set is infinite.

Example. The set $W = \Sigma^*$ is enumerated by the program

```
A ← 0;
REPEAT:  PRINT A;
         A ← A + 1;  GOTO REPEAT;
```

Example. The set $A = \{0,1,6\}$ is enumerated by the program

```
A ← 0;     B ← 1;  C ← 6;  PRINT C;
REPEAT:  PRINT B;        PRINT A;
         GOTO REPEAT;
```

and the program

```
A ← 0;  PRINT A;  A ← 6;  PRINT A;
A ← 1;  PRINT A;  STOP;
```

The first program prints members of the set more than once, which is allowed.

Example. The empty set is enumerated by the program

```
X ← X;
```

and the program

```
HERE:  GOTO HERE;
```

Each PL-enumerable set is effectively enumerable in the sense of Chapter 2. Moreover, we can use Church's thesis to infer that every effectively enumerable set is PL-enumerable. In the remainder of this section we will not distinguish between PL-enumerability and effective enumerability.

It is not difficult to see that each recursive set must be effectively enumerable. If A is recursive, then there is a program which will set Y equal to 1 if $X \in A$ and 0 otherwise. Let the statement Y ← A(X); stand for the program which calculates the characteristic function of A. Then A is enumerated by the program

```
X ← 0;
CHECK:  Y ← A(X);
        LOOP Y;
          PRINT X;
        END;
        X ← X + 1; GOTO CHECK;
```

On the other hand, there are effectively enumerable sets which are not recursive. An informal proof of this fact was given at the end of Section 2.3. A formal proof must be delayed until Section 6.2. The existence of such sets becomes plausible if we consider the process by which a program enumerates a set A. How could we decide whether x is in A, given the program? One way is to start running the program to see if it ever prints x. If it does, then x is in A and the problem is solved. However, if x is not in A, the enumerating program will never print it, but at no time can we be sure that the value of x will never be printed.

If A is the range of a recursive function, then the set $A = \{f(0), f(1), f(2), \ldots\}$ can be enumerated by a program which successively calculates and prints $f(x)$, for $x = 0, 1, 2, \ldots$. This observation motivates the formal definition of recursively enumerable sets given in the next section. Recursive enumerability is a formalization of the intuitive notion of effective enumerability. It will be shown that the function f can always be chosen to be primitive recursive and even 1-1 if A is infinite.

EXERCISES

1. Write a program which enumerates
  a. the even numbers
  b. the prime numbers
  c. all words in W_2 which end with 1

2. Given programs to enumerate A and B, explain informally how to construct a program to enumerate $A \cup B$, that is, show that the effectively enumerable sets are closed under set union. Do the same for $A \cap B$, $A \cdot B$, and A^*.

3. Show informally that A is recursive iff both A and its complement are effectively enumerable.

4. Assume there is a set A that is effectively enumerable but not recursive. Use the result of Exercise 3 to show that the complement of A is not recursive.

6.2 Properties of Recursively Enumerable Sets

A set $A \subseteq W^s$ is *recursively enumerable* (r.e.) if A is the range of some partial recursive function.

THEOREM 6.1. $A \subseteq W^s$ is r.e. iff $\beta_s(A) \subseteq W$ is r.e., where β_s is the bijection from W^s to W.
Proof. Let $f\colon W^r \to W^s$. $A = \operatorname{ran} f$ iff $\beta_s(A) = \operatorname{ran}(\beta_s \circ f)$. ▮

THEOREM 6.2. $A \subseteq W^s$ is r.e. iff $A = \operatorname{ran} f$, for some partial recursive $f\colon W \to W^s$.
Proof. Suppose $A = \operatorname{ran}(g)$, $g\colon W^r \to W^s$. Let $f = g \circ \beta_r^{-1}\colon W \to W^s$, then $A = \operatorname{ran} g = \operatorname{ran}(g \circ \beta_r^{-1}) = \operatorname{ran} f$, since β_r is a bijection. ▮

Theorem 6.3 gives several characterizations of the recursively enumerable sets. Two of them involve new concepts.

Let f be any function and define

$$\bigvee_y f(x,y) = \begin{cases} 1 & \text{if } f(x,y) \neq 0 \text{ for some } y \\ 0 & \text{otherwise} \end{cases}$$

As a predicate $\bigvee_y f(x,y)$ asserts that there exists a y such that $f(x,y)$ is true. Even if f is recursive, $\bigvee_y f(x,y)$ may not be partial recursive (see Exercise 5). For example, if h is defined by

$$h(x) = \begin{cases} 1 & \text{if } \varphi_x(x)\downarrow \\ 0 & \text{otherwise} \end{cases}$$

then $h(x) = \bigvee_y T(x,x,y)$, which is total but not recursive and hence not partial recursive. Before proceeding the reader should carefully note the differences between $\bigvee_y f(x,y)$ and $(\mu y)f(x,y)$. The former does not specify a computation procedure and is always total whereas the latter does specify a computation procedure and may not be total even if f is total. For f partial recursive, $(\mu y)f(x,y)$ is partial recursive whereas $\bigvee_y f(x, y)$ need not be partial recursive even if f is recursive.

Let $A \subseteq W^s$ and define $\iota_A: W^s \to W^s$ by

$$\iota_A(x) = \begin{cases} x & \text{if } x \in A \\ \uparrow & \text{if } x \notin A \end{cases}$$

THEOREM 6.3. $A \subseteq W^s$ is r.e. iff

a. $A = \operatorname{ran} f$, f partial recursive
b. $A = \varnothing$ or $A = \operatorname{ran} f$, f primitive recursive
c. $A = \varnothing$ or $A = \operatorname{ran} f$, f recursive
d. A is finite or $A = \operatorname{ran} f$, f recursive and 1-1
e. $A = \operatorname{dom} f$, f partial recursive
f. $\chi_A(x) = \bigvee_y f(x,y)$, f recursive
g. ι_A is partial recursive

In a, b, c, and d, the function f may be chosen as a mapping from W to W^s. In e, the function f may be chosen to be a mapping from W^s to W^0.

Proof. The proofs that the domain of each function used in a–d and the range of the function in e may be W and W^0, respectively, are similar to the proofs of Theorems 6.1 and 6.2. In order to simplify the notation, we will assume that $s = 1$. Theorem 6.1 may then be used to prove the more general case.

Part a implies b: Suppose $A = \operatorname{ran} \varphi_m$ and $A \neq \varnothing$, with element $y_0 \in A$. The construction of a primitive recursive f with $A = \operatorname{ran} f$ is a little tricky. The idea is to have the function f simulate the computation of φ_m for a certain input for a specified number of steps. If the computation produces a value, it is taken as the value of f. If the computation does not halt in the number of steps simulated, f is given the value $y_0 \in A$. For each input x, the inverse of the pairing function β is used to determine an input to φ_m and the number of steps to be simulated; as x assumes all values, each input for φ_m is simulated for each possible number of steps as shown in Figure 6-1. Recall that $\beta(\beta'x,\beta''x) = x$.

$\beta''x =$ number of steps						value of x
5	15					
4	10	16				
3	6	(11)	17	...		
2	(3)	7	12	18		
1	1	4	8	13		
0	0	2	5	9	14	
	0	1	2	3	...	$\beta'x =$ input to φ_m

FIGURE 6-1. **Number of steps in the computation of φ_m.**

On input 11 to f, the computation of $\varphi_m(1)$ is simulated for 3 steps; on input 3 the computation of $\varphi_m(0)$ is simulated for 2 steps (see the circled entries in Figure 6-1). At each step of the simulation, the primitive recursive T-predicate discussed in Section 5.4 is used to test if the computation terminates. For example, if the computation of $\varphi_m(3)$ requires exactly 2 steps, then

$$T(m,3,2) = T[m, \beta'(18), \beta''(18)] = 1$$

The required function f is calculated by simulating the calculation of $\varphi_m(\beta'x)$ for $\beta''x$ steps. If the computation halts at the last step, the value of f is taken to be $\varphi_m(\beta'x)$, otherwise it is y_0. More precisely,

$$f(x) = \begin{cases} \omega \circ p \circ C^{\beta''x}[\mathcal{A}(m),\alpha(\beta'x),0,0] & \text{if } T(m,\beta'x,\beta''x) = 1 \\ y_0 & \text{otherwise} \end{cases}$$

where α and ω are the LMA input/output functions, $p(x_1,x_2,x_3,x_4) = x_2$, and C is as in Lemma 5.5.†

If $y \in A = \text{ran } \varphi_m$, then there are values w and k such that $y = \varphi_m(w)$ and the computation takes exactly k steps, hence if $x = \beta(w,k)$, $w = \beta'x$, and $k = \beta''x$, then $f(x) = \varphi_m(w) = y$, which means $y \in \text{ran} f$. Conversely, if $y \in \text{ran} f$, either $y = y_0 \in A$ or $y = f(x) = \varphi_m(\beta'x)$, so $y \in \text{ran } \varphi_m = A$.

Part b implies c: Every primitive recursive function is recursive.

† Notice that f cannot be defined by

$$f(x) = [T(m, \beta'x, \beta''x) \rightarrow \varphi_m(\beta'x)] + [\neg T(m, \beta'x, \beta''x) \rightarrow y_0]$$

because, if φ_m is not primitive recursive, this does not show that f is primitive recursive, but only that f is recursive.

Part c implies d: Suppose A is infinite. Then by the assumption, since $A \neq \varnothing$, $A = \operatorname{ran} g$, g recursive, that is, $A = \{g(0), g(1), \ldots\}$. A function f can be constructed such that $f(0), f(1), \ldots$ is also an enumeration of A, consisting of the sequence $g(0)$, $g(1)$, ..., with repetitions deleted.

The first step is to define a function k with the property that $k(t)$ is the position in the sequence $g(0)$, $g(1)$, ... where the tth new element appears. Let

$$k(0) = 0$$

$$k(t+1) = (\mu x)[x > kt \wedge \bigwedge_{u=0}^{kt} (gu \neq gx)]$$

The function k is defined for each t because $A = \operatorname{ran} g$ is infinite. The composition $f = g \circ k$ is the required 1-1 recursive function.

The values that k will assume are shown for one typical function g in Table 6-1.

TABLE 6-1. Values of the function k.

x	0	1	2	3	4	5	6	7	8
$g(x)$	7	7	3	4	9	3	4	1	3
t	0		1	2	3			4	
$k(t)$	0		2	3	4			7	

Part d implies e: If A is finite, then χ_A is recursive. Let

$$f(x) = (\mu y)[\chi_A(x)] = \begin{cases} 0 & \text{if } x \in A \\ \uparrow & \text{otherwise} \end{cases}$$

If $A = \operatorname{ran} g$, and g is 1-1 and recursive, then let

$$f(x) = (\mu y)[g(y) = x] = \begin{cases} g^{-1}(x) & \text{if } x \in A \\ \uparrow & \text{otherwise} \end{cases}$$

In either case f is partial recursive and $\operatorname{dom} f = A$.

Part e implies f: Suppose $A = \operatorname{dom} \varphi_m$, then $\chi_A(x) = \bigvee_y T(m,x,y)$.

Part f implies g: Suppose $\chi_A(x) = \bigvee_y f(x,y)$ with f recursive, then

$$\begin{aligned} \iota_A(x) &= 0 \times (\mu y)[f(x,y) > 0] + x \\ &= \begin{cases} x & \text{if } (\mu y)[f(x,y) > 0] \text{ is defined} \\ \uparrow & \text{otherwise} \end{cases} \end{aligned}$$

Thus ι_A is partial recursive if f is recursive.

Part g implies a: $A = \operatorname{ran} \iota_A$. ∎

THEOREM 6.4. There is an r.e. set which is not recursive.

Proof. The set $H = \{x \mid x \in \text{dom } \varphi_x\}$, shown to be nonrecursive in Section 5.6, is r.e. by Theorem 6.3f, since $\chi_H(x) = \bigvee_k T(x,x,k)$. ▮

THEOREM 6.5. A set is r.e. iff it is accepted by a TM program, a URM program, an SRM program, or a PL program.

Proof. Using any output function which is total, the set accepted by a program is dom φ_m, where φ_m is the function computed by the program. The theorem follows from Theorem 6.3e and the equivalence of TM, URM, SRM, and PL programs to LMA's. ▮

Theorems 6.3 and 6.5 say that a program may define a set by treating the members of the set as input or by producing the members of the set as output. For TM, URM, SRM, and PL programs, the sets defined are the same, namely the r.e. sets.

If both A and its complement $\bar{A}$ are r.e., a method for computing $\chi_A(x)$ is to simultaneously run the programs which enumerate A and $\bar{A}$. The value x must eventually be printed by one of them, indicating the correct value for $\chi_A(x)$. This intuitive argument is made precise in the proof of the following theorem.

THEOREM 6.6. A set A is recursive iff both A and $\bar{A}$ are r.e.

Proof. If A is recursive, then χ_A is recursive and so $\iota_A(x) = x + (\mu y)[\chi_A(x)]$ is partial recursive. Hence A is r.e. by Theorem 6.3g. Also if A is recursive, then $\bar{A}$ is recursive and so $\bar{A}$ is r.e. by the same argument.

Conversely, if A and $\bar{A}$ are r.e., then by Theorem 6.3f, there are recursive functions f and g such that

$$\chi_A(x) = \bigvee_y f(x,y)$$

and

$$\chi_{\bar{A}}(x) = \bigvee_y g(x,y)$$

Let $h(x) = (\mu y)[f(x,y) \vee g(x,y)]$. The function h is total since either $x \in A$ $x \notin A$. Then $\chi_A(x) = \text{sign} \circ f(x,hx)$. ▮

COROLLARY 6.7. The set $\bar{H} = \{x \mid x \notin \text{dom } \varphi_x\}$ is not r.e.

Proof. By Theorem 6.4, H is r.e. If $\bar{H}$ were also r.e., then by Theorem 6.6, H would be recursive, contradicting Corollary 5.15. ▮

Theorem 6.3 indicates that for each infinite r.e. set A, a function can be found so that $f(0), f(1), \ldots$ is an enumeration of A and f can be chosen to be either primitive recursive or 1-1 recursive. However, it is not always possible to enumerate A in order by having $f(0) < f(1) < f(2) < \cdots$. If such an enumeration of A is available, then A is recursive, because $\chi_A(x)$ can be effectively computed by enumerating A in order until a member of A is printed which is either x or larger than x. If x is printed, then $x \in A$. If a $y > x$ is printed without x being printed, then $x \notin A$. It is interesting that this argument does not apply to a finite set A, because if x is larger than any member of A, no $y > x$ will ever be printed; but, of course, all finite sets are recursive.

THEOREM 6.8. $A \subseteq W$ is recursive iff A is finite or $A = \operatorname{ran} f$, where f is a strictly increasing recursive function.

Proof. If A is recursive and infinite, let

$$f(0) = (\mu y)[\chi_A(y)]$$
$$f(x+1) = (\mu y)[y > f(x) \wedge \chi_A(y)]$$

The values $f(0), f(1), \ldots$ are all members of A in ascending order.

For the converse, if A is finite, it is recursive by Theorem 3.25. Assume A is infinite and is the range of a 1-1 increasing recursive function f. Let $h(x) = (\mu y)[f(y) \geq x]$. Then

$$\chi_A(x) = \begin{cases} 1 & \text{if } f(hx) = x \\ 0 & \text{if } f(hx) > x \end{cases} \blacksquare$$

Theorems 6.3, 6.6, and 6.8 emphasize the distinction between the recursive sets and the r.e. sets. For a recursive set A, there is an effective procedure which will determine whether a given x is a member of A. For a r.e. set B, there is a *partial* procedure which gives the correct answer for an $x \in B$, but gives no answer if $x \notin B$.

When minimization was defined in Section 3.4, it was mentioned that if $\mu f(x)$ were defined to be the minimum of the set $\{y \mid f(x,y) = 1\}$, then there would be partial recursive functions f such that μf would not be partial recursive. An example can now be given. The set $H = \{x \mid x \in \operatorname{dom} \varphi_x\}$ is r.e., hence ι_H is partial recursive by Theorem 6.3g. Define f by

$$f(0) = (\mu y)[\iota_H(y) = y]$$
$$f(x+1) = (\mu y)[y > f(x) \wedge \iota_H(y) = y]$$

using the modified definition of μ. Then $f(0), f(1), \ldots$ is an enumeration of H in ascending order. If f is recursive, then H is recursive by Theorem 6.8. Hence f is not recursive, and since f is total, it is also not partial recursive.

If our definition of minimization is used, then the f defined above does not provide an enumeration of H since by our definition, to compute $(\mu y)\, g(x,y)$, it is necessary to successively compute $g(x,0)$, $g(x,1)$, ... until a value is found equal to 1. If in the process of computing successive values of g, an attempt is made to compute $g(x,k)$ where $g(x,k)$ is undefined, then $(\mu y)\, g(x,y)$ is undefined. In fact, if $0 \notin \operatorname{dom} \varphi_0$, then $\iota_H(0)$ is undefined, and so $f(0)$ is undefined. This means that f is nowhere defined.

EXERCISES

1. Show that A is r.e. iff $A = \text{dom } f$, for some 1-1 partial recursive f.

2. A set $D \subseteq W$ is called an *initial segment* if $x \in D$ and $x' < x$ imply $x' \in D$. An initial segment is either all of W or of the form $\{x \mid x < k\}$ for some k. (For $k = 0$ $\{x \mid x < k\} = \varnothing$.) Show that A is r.e. iff $A = \text{ran } f$, where f is 1-1 partial recursive and $\text{dom } f$ is an initial segment.

3. Show that A is recursive iff $A = \text{ran } f$, where f is 1-1 partial recursive, strictly increasing, and $\text{dom } f$ is an initial segment (see Exercise 2).

4. Prove that every infinite r.e. set contains an infinite recursive subset.

5. Give conditions on f which guarantee that $\bigvee_y f(x,y)$ is recursive.

6. Let $f: W^r \to W^s$ be any total function. To emphasize the fact that f is a set of ordered pairs, let $A = f = \{(x,y) \mid fx = y\}$ as was done in Exercise 2 of Section 3.10. Show that if A is r.e., then $\bar{A}$ is also r.e. Use Exercise 2 of Section 3.10 to infer that f is a recursive function iff A is recursive iff A is r.e.

7. Let $f: W^r \to W^s$ be any function. Let A be as defined in Exercise 6. Prove that f is partial recursive iff A is r.e.

8. Let f be an increasing partial recursive function, that is, $f(x)\downarrow$, $f(y)\downarrow$ and $x < y$ imply that $f(x) < f(y)$. Is $\text{ran } f$ recursive?

9. Prove that φ_m is recursive iff there is a recursive g such that for all x the LMA $\mathcal{A}(m)$ halts in exactly $g(x)$ steps on input x.

10. Show that if $f: W \to W$ is a 1-1 partial recursive function, then f^{-1} is also partial recursive.

6.3 An Indexing of the Recursively Enumerable Sets

Theorem 6.3e shows that $A \subseteq W^r$ is r.e. iff it is the domain of a partial recursive function. Define ${}^rD_m = \text{dom}({}^r_1\varphi_m)$, $D_m = \text{dom } \varphi_m$. The set D_m is called the mth r.e. set and m is called an *index* for D_m. The set D_m is the set accepted by a program which computes φ_m. Since A is r.e. iff $A = \text{ran } f$, for some partial recursive f, it would also be possible to let m be an index for $\text{ran } \varphi_m$. However, it is somewhat more convenient to use domains. For instance, the relation

$$\chi_{D_m}(x) = \bigvee_y T(m,x,y)$$

given by the proof of Theorem 6.3f is very useful.

The r.e. sets are closed under union and intersection. In addition, it is possible to compute an index for $A \cup B$, given indices for A and B.

THEOREM 6.9. There are primitive recursive functions union and intersection, such that

$$D_{\text{union}(x,y)} = D_x \cup D_y$$

and

$$D_{\text{intersection}(x,y)} = D_x \cap D_y$$

Proof. Let

$$f(x,y,z) = \varphi_x(z) + \varphi_y(z)$$

which is defined iff $z \in D_x \cap D_y$. For each fixed x and y, $f(x,y,z)$ is a function of z only; an index for that function can be computed using the index theorem. Let m be an index for f so that $f = {}_1^3\varphi_m$. Then $\varphi_{K_2(m,x,y)}(z) = {}_1^3\varphi_m(x,y,z) = f(x,y,z)$. If intersection$(x,y) = K_2(m,x,y)$, then

$$D_{\text{intersection}(x,y)} = \{z \mid f(x,y,z)\downarrow\} = D_x \cap D_y.$$

The proof that union(x,y) is primitive recursive is left as Exercise 2. ▌

COROLLARY 6.10. The intersection or union of any finite number of r.e. sets is r.e. ▌

THEOREM 6.11. There are primitive recursive functions image(x,y) and preimage(x,y) such that $\varphi_x(D_y) = D_{\text{image}(x,y)}$ (see Figure 6-2) and $\varphi_x^{-1}(D_y) = D_{\text{preimage}(x,y)}$ (see Figure 6-3). Thus the image and preimage of any r.e. set under a partial recursive function are r.e.

Proof. Let

$$f(x,y,z) = \begin{cases} z & \text{if } \varphi_x(v) = z \text{ and } \varphi_y(v)\downarrow \text{ for some } v \\ \uparrow & \text{otherwise} \end{cases}$$

Exercise 3 is to prove that $f(x,y,z)$ is partial recursive. For a fixed x and y, $f(x,y,z)\downarrow$ iff $z \in \varphi_x(D_y) = \varphi_x(D_x \cap D_y)$.

Let m be an index for f, then $\varphi_{K_2(m,x,y)}(z) = {}_1^3\varphi_m(x,y,z) = f(x,y,z)$. Let image$(x,y) = K_2(m,x,y)$, then $z \in \varphi_x(D_y)$ iff $f(x,y,z)\downarrow$ iff $z \in D_{K_2(m,x,y)}$ iff $z \in D_{\text{image}(x,y)}$. The proof that preimage(x,y) is primitive recursive is left as Exercise 4. ▌

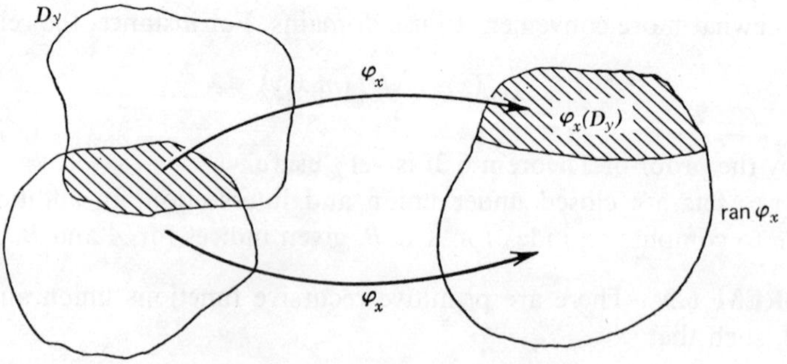

FIGURE 6-2. **Diagram of $\varphi_x(D_y)$.**

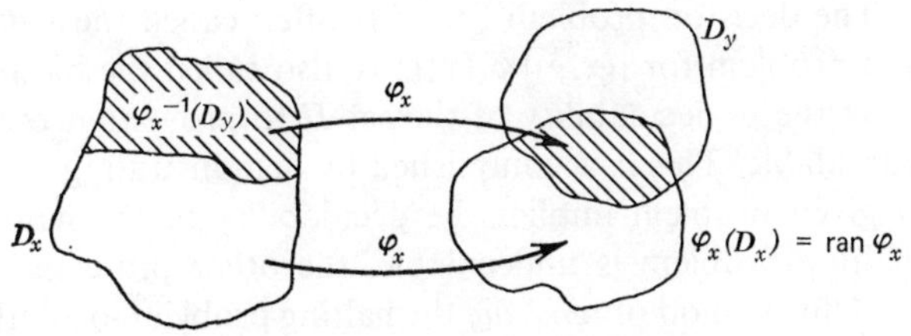

FIGURE 6-3. **Diagram of $\varphi_x^{-1}(D_y)$.**

EXERCISES

1. Prove that each r.e. set has infinitely many indices.

2. Prove that there is a primitive recursive function union(x,y), such that

$$D_{\text{union}(x,y)} = D_x \cup D_y.$$

3. Show that

$$f(x,y,z) = \begin{cases} z & \text{if } \varphi_x(v) = z \text{ and } \varphi_y(v)\downarrow \text{ for some } v \\ \uparrow & \text{otherwise} \end{cases}$$

is partial recursive.

4. Prove that there is a primitive recursive function preimage(x,y) such that

$$\varphi_x^{-1}(D_y) = D_{\text{preimage}(x,y)}$$

5. Prove that a countable union of r.e. sets need not be r.e. What about a countable intersection?

6. A set $A \subseteq W$ is *immune* if it is infinite and has no infinite r.e. subset. Prove:

a. no immune set is r.e.
b. there is an r.e. set A such that $\bar{A}$ is immune
c. there is a set A such that A and $\bar{A}$ are immune
d. every infinite set is a union of two immune sets

7.a. Show that there is a primitive recursive function f such that $D_{f(x)} = \{x^2\}$, the set containing the single element x^2.

b. Show that there exists an x such that $D_x = \{x^2\}$.

6.4 Undecidable Problems

The *decision problem* for a set $A \subseteq W^r$ is the problem of effectively determining whether or not an arbitrary x belongs to A. By Church's thesis, a set is decidable iff it is recursive, that is, has a recursive characteristic function. Section 5.6 contains a proof that the set $H = \{x \mid \varphi_x(x)\downarrow\}$ is not recursive, hence it is undecidable by Church's thesis. This means that there is no algorithm for deciding if $x \in \text{dom}\, \varphi_x$, or equivalently, for deciding if the LMA $\mathcal{A}(x)$ halts on input x. The decision problem for H is often called the *halting problem*. (The decision problem for $\{(x,y) \mid \varphi_x(y)\downarrow\}$ is also called the halting problem.)

We may use the undecidability of the set H to prove that other problems are also undecidable. This is accomplished by demonstrating that the decidability of a given problem implies the decidability of the halting problem. Since the halting problem is undecidable, the other problem must also be undecidable. This method of *reducing* the halting problem to another problem, in order to prove the undecidability of the latter, is one of the most important methods for proving undecidability. Indeed, almost all undecidability proofs either directly or indirectly involve a reduction of the halting problem to some other problem.

Another undecidable problem is that of determining whether or not an arbitrary partial recursive function is total, or equivalently, whether a program always halts, regardless of the input data. This is expressed formally by the assertion that the set $\{x \mid \varphi_x \text{ is total}\}$ is not recursive. The problem of determining whether or not a given program halts for at least one input is also undecidable. These and related results are contained in the following theorem, the proof of which illustrates the method of reduction.

THEOREM 6.12. The following sets and their complements are not recursive:

$$H = \{x \mid x \in D_x\}$$

$$\begin{array}{ll} A_1 = \{x \mid D_x = \varnothing\} & A_2 = \{x \mid \operatorname{ran} \varphi_x = \varnothing\} \\ A_3 = \{x \mid D_x \text{ is finite}\} & A_4 = \{x \mid \operatorname{ran} \varphi_x \text{ is finite}\} \\ A_5 = \{x \mid \varphi_x \text{ is total}\} & A_6 = \{x \mid \operatorname{ran} \varphi_x = \Sigma^*\} \\ A_7 = \{x \mid x_0 \in D_x\} & A_8 = \{x \mid x_0 \in \operatorname{ran} \varphi_x\} \end{array}$$

For A_7 and A_8, x_0 is an arbitrary fixed word.

Proof. We show that the computation of χ_H can be reduced to the computation of each χ_{A_i}. Let

$$f(x,y) = 0 \times \varphi_x(x) + y = \begin{cases} y & \text{if } x \in H \\ \uparrow & \text{if } x \notin H \end{cases}$$

and let $h(x) = K_1(m,x)$, where m is an index for the function f, so that $\varphi_{h(x)}(y) = f(x,y)$ by the index theorem of Chapter 5. If $x \in H$, then $\varphi_{h(x)} = \imath$, the identity function. If $x \notin H$, then $\varphi_{h(x)}$ is the function which is nowhere defined. Thus $x \in H$ iff $\varphi_x(x)\downarrow$ iff $\varphi_{h(x)} = \imath$ iff $h(x) \notin A_1$, and so $\chi_H(x) = \neg\chi_{A_1}[h(x)]$. If A_1 were recursive, then χ_H would also be recursive, which contradicts Corollary 5.15, that is, if we could decide membership in A_1, then we could decide whether $h(x)$ is in A_1 for an arbitrary x. But $h(x)$ is in A_1 iff x is not in H, so the recursiveness of the decision problem for A_1 would imply the recursiveness of the decision problem for H, a contradiction. Therefore the decision problem for A_1 is not recursive.

Since $A_2 = \bar{A}_1$, it also is not recursive. Each of the other sets is not recursive because

$$x \in H \text{ iff } h(x) \notin A_3$$
$$x \in H \text{ iff } h(x) \notin A_4$$
$$x \in H \text{ iff } h(x) \in A_5$$
$$x \in H \text{ iff } h(x) \in A_6$$
$$x \in H \text{ iff } h(x) \in A_7$$
$$x \in H \text{ iff } h(x) \in A_8$$

Since the complement of each recursive set is also recursive, the complement of each set $A_1, A_2, \ldots, A_8$ must also be nonrecursive. ▮

If it can be shown that any of the sets A_i is r.e., then it must follow that its complement is not r.e., since if both a set and its complement are r.e., then the set must be recursive (Theorem 6.6).

COROLLARY 6.13. The sets $\bar{A}_1$, $\bar{A}_2$, A_7, and A_8 are r.e., so the sets A_1, A_2, $\bar{A}_7$, and $\bar{A}_8$ are not r.e.

Proof. Let $f(x) = (\mu k)[T(x,\beta' k,\beta'' k)]$, where $\beta(\beta' x, \beta'' x) = x$ is the pairing function. Then $\operatorname{dom} f = \bar{A}_1$, since $x \notin A_1$ iff for some u, $u \in D_x$ iff for some u and some number of steps v, $T(x,u,v)$ is true iff for $k = \beta(u,v)$, $T(x, \beta' k, \beta'' k)$ iff $x \in \operatorname{dom} f$. Since $\bar{A}_1 = \operatorname{dom} f$ and f is partial recursive, $\bar{A}_1$ is r.e. by Theorem 6.3e. Since A_1 is not recursive, A_1 must not be r.e.

Since $A_2 = \bar{A}_1$, it is also not r.e. If $f(x) = \varphi_x(x_0)$, then $\operatorname{dom} f = A_7$, so A_7 is r.e., hence $\bar{A}_7$ is not. The proof that $\bar{A}_8$ is not r.e. is left as Exercise 1. ▮

In Theorem 6.12, the proofs that $A_1, A_2, \ldots, A_8$ are not recursive are all essentially the same. This suggests that there might be a single general theorem that includes each of the special sets in Theorem 6.12. Some definitions are needed before this general result can be stated.

Let $m \approx m'$ mean $\varphi_m = \varphi_{m'}$, that is, m and m' are indices of the same partial recursive function.

THEOREM 6.14. The relation $\approx$ is an equivalence relation.

Proof. Exercise 2. ▮

A set A is a *function index set* if for each m and m', $m \in A$ and $m \approx m'$ imply that $m' \in A$. If A contains one index for a partial recursive function, then it must contain all indices for that function. Each of the sets except H in Theorem 6.12 is a function index set.

Since a function is a set of ordered pairs, $\varphi_m \subseteq \varphi_{m'}$ means that if $x \in \text{dom } \varphi_m$, then $x \in \text{dom } \varphi_{m'}$ and $\varphi_m(x) = \varphi_{m'}(x)$.

THEOREM 6.15 (Rice). If A is a function index set and there are indices $m \in A$ and $m' \in \bar{A}$ such that $\varphi_m \subseteq \varphi_{m'}$, then A is not r.e.

Proof. Assume A is a function index set, $m \in A$, $m' \in \bar{A}$, and $\varphi_m \subseteq \varphi_{m'}$. Define the recursive function f by

$$\varphi_{f(x)}(y) = \begin{cases} \varphi_m(y) & \text{if } x \notin H \\ \varphi_{m'}(y) & \text{if } x \in H \end{cases}$$

The function $\varphi_{f(x)}$ is computed by simultaneously computing $\varphi_x(x)$ and $\varphi_m(y)$. If the computation $\varphi_x(x)$ halts ($x \in H$), then also stop computing $\varphi_m(y)$ and compute $\varphi_{m'}(y)$. If the computation of $\varphi_m(y)$ halts before the computation of $\varphi_x(x)$, then take the value of $\varphi_m(y)$ as the answer. Note that in this case, $\varphi_m(y)$ is the correct answer, even if $x \in H$, since if $\varphi_m(y)$ is defined, $\varphi_m(y) = \varphi_{m'}(y)$.

A partial recursive definition of $\varphi_{f(x)}$ is given as follows: Let e stand for $(\mu w)[T(m,y,w) \vee T(x,x,w)]$. Then

$$\varphi_{f(x)}(y) = [T(m,y,e) \rightarrow \varphi_m(y)] + [\neg T(m,y,e) \rightarrow \varphi_{m'}(y)].$$

The function f is recursive by the index theorem. If $x \notin H$, then $f(x) \approx m \in A$, hence $f(x) \in A$, since A is a function index set. If $x \in H$, then $f(x) \approx m' \notin A$ so $f(x) \notin A$. Hence $x \in \bar{H}$ iff $f(x) \in A$, and so $\iota_{\bar{H}}(x) = 0 \times \iota_A(fx) + x$. If A were r.e., then $\bar{H}$ would also be r.e. by Theorem 6.3g. A similar argument may be made using Theorem 6.11 and the fact that $\bar{H} = f^{-1}(A)$. ∎

The proof that A is not r.e. could be given less formally by the following argument. Suppose A were r.e. Then $\bar{H}$ could be enumerated by simultaneously enumerating $f(0), f(1), f(2), \ldots$ and A. Each value of x with the property that $f(x)$ appears in the enumeration of A would be enumerated as a member of $\bar{H}$.

The proof of Theorem 6.15 involves a modified form of reduction. Here the recursive enumerability of the set $\bar{H}$ is reduced to the recursive enumerability of the set A, that is, if A were r.e., then $\bar{H}$ would also be r.e. Since $\bar{H}$ is not r.e., we may conclude that A is not r.e. The method of reduction, in its various forms, is an extremely important tool in computability theory. Hence the reader would be well-advised to review the various instances of reduction which have been used in this section. We will discuss reduction in a general framework in Chapter 8.

COROLLARY 6.16. If A is a function index set, then A is recursive iff $A = \varnothing$ or $A = \Sigma^*$.

Proof. Suppose A is a function index set, $A \neq \varnothing$, and $A \neq \Sigma^*$, then either A or $\bar{A}$ contains all indices of the function $f = \varnothing$ which is nowhere defined. Since $\varnothing \subseteq \varphi_x$, for all x, the result follows from Theorem 6.15. ∎

COROLLARY 6.17. The following are nontrivial function index sets and so neither they nor their complements are recursive. Again, x_0 is fixed, but arbitrary.

a. the sets $A_1, A_2, \ldots, A_8$ of Theorem 6.12
b. $A_9 = \{x \mid D_x \text{ is recursive}\}$
c. $A_{10} = \{x \mid \varphi_x = \varphi_{x_0}\}$
d. $A_{11} = \{x \mid \varphi_x \text{ a bijection}\}$
e. $A_{12} = \{x \mid \varphi_x \text{ is primitive recursive}\}$
f. $A_{13} = \{x \mid \varphi_x(y) = \varphi_{x_0}(y) \text{ for some } y\}$ ▮

COROLLARY 6.18. The set $A_{14} = \{(x,y) \mid \varphi_x = \varphi_y\}$ is not recursive.

Proof. For a fixed m, $A_{10} = \{x \mid \varphi_x = \varphi_m\}$ is a nontrivial function index set and so is not recursive. If A_{14} were recursive, then membership of x in A_{10} could be computed by testing whether (x,m) is in A_{14}; hence the decision problem for A_{10} is reducible to the decision problem for A_{14}. Since A_{10} is not recursive, neither is A_{14}. ▮

Corollary 6.18 states that it is impossible to effectively decide whether two given programs compute the same function.

Rice's theorem has been used to show that A_1–A_{14} and their complements are not recursive. We are also interested in determining which of these sets are r.e. These results are summarized in Table 6-2. The letter Y indicates

TABLE 6-2. Summary of Results on Recursive Enumerability[a]

Set B	B	$\overline{B}$
$H = \{x \mid \varphi_x(x)\downarrow\}$	Y	N
$A_1 = \{x \mid D_x = \varnothing\}$	N-R	Y
$A_2 = \{x \mid \text{ran } \varphi_x = \varnothing\}$	N-R	Y
$A_3 = \{x \mid D_x \text{ finite}\}$	N-R	N
$A_4 = \{x \mid \text{ran } \varphi_x \text{ finite}\}$	N-R	N
$A_5 = \{x \mid \varphi_x \text{ total}\}$	N	N-R
$A_6 = \{x \mid \text{ran } \varphi_x = \Sigma^*\}$	N	N-R
$A_7 = \{x \mid x_0 \in D_x\}$	Y	N-R
$A_8 = \{x \mid x_0 \in \text{ran } \varphi_x\}$	Y	N-R
$A_9 = \{x \mid D_x \text{ recursive}\}$	N-R	N-R
$A_{10} = \{x \mid \varphi_x = \varphi_{x_0}\}$, φ_{x_0} total	N	—
$A_{10} = \{x \mid \varphi_x = \varphi_{x_0}\}$, φ_{x_0} not total	N-R	—
$A_{10} = \{x \mid \varphi_x = \varphi_{x_0}\}$, $\varphi_{x_0} = \varnothing$	—	Y
$A_{10} = \{x \mid \varphi_x = \varphi_{x_0}\}$, $\varphi_{x_0} \neq \varnothing$	—	N-R
$A_{11} = \{x \mid \varphi_x \text{ a bijection}\}$	N	N-R
$A_{12} = \{x \mid \varphi_x \text{ primitive recursive}\}$	N	N-R
$A_{13} = \{x \mid \varphi_x(y) = \varphi_{x_0}(y), \text{ for some } y\}$, φ_{x_0} total	Y	N-R
$A_{14} = \{(x,y) \mid \varphi_x = \varphi_y\}$	N	N

[a] Key: Y = r.e., N = not r.e., R = not r.e. by Rice's theorem.

that the set is r.e. while N indicates that it is not r.e. An R means that the nonrecursive enumerability of the set follows by Rice's theorem. Notice that there are four entries in the table for A_{10}. This is necessary because the properties of A_{10} and its complement depend on the value of x_0.

We have already shown that $\bar{A}_1$, $\bar{A}_2$, and A_7 are r.e. The proofs that A_8, $\bar{A}_{10}$ for $\varphi_{x_0} = \varnothing$, and A_{13} are r.e. are left as exercises. The next corollary is proved by applying Rice's theorem.

COROLLARY 6.19. The following sets are not r.e.: A_1, A_2, A_3, A_4, $\bar{A}_5$ $\bar{A}_6$ $\bar{A}_7$ $\bar{A}_8$ A_9, $\bar{A}_9$, A_{10} for φ_{x_0} not total, $\bar{A}_{10}$ for $\varphi_{x_0} \neq \varnothing$, $\bar{A}_{11}$, $\bar{A}_{12}$, and $\bar{A}_{13}$.

Proof. Consider $\bar{A}_{12} = \{x \mid \varphi_x \text{ not primitive recursive}\}$. The nowhere defined function, $\varphi_y = \varnothing$ is in $\bar{A}_{12}$, while $\varphi_z = \iota$ is in A_{12}. Since $\varphi_y \subseteq \varphi_z$, by Rice's theorem $\bar{A}_{12}$ is not r.e. The remaining parts are left as an exercise. ∎

The sets $\bar{A}_3$, $\bar{A}_4$, A_5, A_6, A_{10} for φ_{x_0} total, A_{11}, A_{12}, A_{14}, and $\bar{A}_{14}$ are also not r.e., but Rice's theorem does not provide the proof. The next theorem contains a proof for some of these sets.

THEOREM 6.20. The sets $\bar{A}_3$, $\bar{A}_4$, A_5, A_6, A_{10} for φ_{x_0} total, A_{11}, and A_{12} are not r.e.

Proof. The proof for A_5 goes as follows: If $A_5 = \{x \mid \varphi_x \text{ total}\}$ is r.e., then by Theorem 6.3c there is a recursive f such that $A_5 = \operatorname{ran} f$. Then $g(x) = \varphi_{fx}(x) + 1$ is recursive. Let m be an index for g. By the definition of f, there is a y such that $f(y) = m$. Then

$$\varphi_{fy}(y) = \varphi_m(y) = g(y) = \varphi_{fy}(y) + 1.$$

Therefore, it follows that $A_5 \neq \operatorname{ran} f$, and so A_5 is not r.e. Note that this is a formal version of Exercise 1 in Section 2.3.

To prove that A_{10} is not r.e. when φ_{x_0} is total, define

$$\varphi_{f(x)}(y) = \begin{cases} \varphi_{x_0}(y) & \text{if } \neg \bigvee_{k=0}^{y} T(x,x,k) \\ \uparrow & \text{otherwise} \end{cases}$$

If $x \in H$, then $T(x,x,y_0)$ for some $y_0 \geq 0$ and

$$\varphi_{f(x)}(y) = \begin{cases} \varphi_{x_0}(y) & \text{if } y < y_0 \\ \uparrow & \text{otherwise} \end{cases}$$

If $x \notin H$, then $\varphi_{f(x)}(y) = \varphi_{x_0}(y)$ for all y. Thus $f(x) \in A_{10}$ iff $f(x) \approx x_0$ iff $x \in \bar{H}$, and as before, the recursive enumerability of A_{10} would imply that $\bar{H}$ is recursively enumerable.

We can show that $\bar{A}_3$, $\bar{A}_4$, A_6, A_{11}, and A_{12} are not r.e. by replacing $\varphi_{x_0}(y)$ in the proof above for A_{10} by the identity function, $\iota(y) = y$. ∎

Before proceeding, it is useful to again review the important method of reduction which has been extensively used in this section. Given two sets A and B, we say that (the decision problem for) A is reducible to (the decision problem for) B, written $A \leq B$, if the recursiveness of B implies the recursiveness of A. The proofs in this section all involve a special type of reducibility, called strong reducibility, which is discussed in Chapter 8. A set A is strongly reducible to a set B if there is a recursive f such that $x \in A$ iff $f(x) \in B$, for all x. If f exists, then to decide whether $x \in A$ for an arbitrary x, compute $f(x)$ and decide whether it is in B. Hence if B is recursive, then so is A.

If $A \leq B$, then the decision problem for B is at least as difficult as the decision problem for A. Hence if A is not recursive, then B is also not recursive. Similarly if A is strongly reducible to B and A is not r.e., then B is not r.e. In the proof of Theorem 6.20 we showed that A_{10} for φ_{x_0} total is not r.e. by exhibiting a recursive f such that $x \in \overline{H}$ iff $f(x) \in A_{10}$, that is, by showing that the recursive enumerability of $\overline{H}$ is reducible to the recursive enumerability of A_{10}.

Define $m \sim m'$ to mean $D_m = D_{m'}$, that is, m and m' are indices of the same recursively enumerable set.

A set A is a *set index set* if for each m and m', $m \in A$ and $m \sim m'$ imply $m' \in A$. If A contains one index for a given r.e. set, then it must contain all of them.

Each of the sets A_1, A_2, A_3, A_5, A_7, A_9 is a set index set. The remaining A_i's are not set index sets. For example, consider $A_6 = \{x \mid \text{ran } \varphi_x = \Sigma^*\}$. Let $\varphi_u(y) = y$, $\varphi_w(y) = 0$ for all y. Then $u \in A_6$, $D_u = D_w$ but $w \notin A_6$ so A_6 is not a set index set. The next theorems are easy to prove.

THEOREM 6.21. Every set index set is a function index set. ▌

THEOREM 6.22. There is a function index set which is not a set index set. ▌

THEOREM 6.23. A set index set A is recursive iff $A = \varnothing$ or $A = \Sigma^*$.
Proof. Apply Corollary 6.16 and Theorem 6.21. ▌

EXERCISES

1. Prove that $A_8 = \{x \mid x_0 \in \text{ran } \varphi_x\}$ is r.e. Infer that its complement is not r.e.

2. Prove that if $m \approx m'$ iff $\varphi_m = \varphi_{m'}$, then $\approx$ is an equivalence relation.

3. Let $[m] = \{m' \mid m \approx m'\}$ be the unique equivalence class to which m belongs. Show that A is a function index set iff it is the union of equivalence classes.

4. Prove that the complement of a function index set is also a function index set.

5. Prove that if A is not r.e. and there is a recursive function f such that $x \in A$ iff $f(x) \in B$, then B is not r.e.

6. Prove that $\{m \mid \varphi_m \text{ is a constant function}\}$ is not recursive. Is it r.e.?

7. Prove analogs of Exercises 2, 3, and 4 for the relation $\sim$, given by $m \sim m'$ iff $D_m = D_{m'}$.

8. Prove that none of the equivalence classes of $\sim$ is r.e.

9. Prove that every set index set is also a function index set, but not every function index set is a set index set.

10. Demonstrate how Rice's theorem is applied to each of the sets of Corollary 6.19.

11. Prove that $\bar{A}_{10} = \{x \mid \varphi_x \neq \varphi_{x_0}\}$, where $\varphi_{x_0} = \varnothing$, is r.e.

12. Prove that $A_{14} = \{(x,y) \mid \varphi_x = \varphi_y\}$ and $\bar{A}_{14}$ are not r.e.

13. Prove that $\{(x,y) \mid \varphi_x(y)\downarrow\}$ is r.e. but not recursive.

14. Show that there is no r.e. set A having the following properties:

a. for each $x \in A$, φ_x is recursive

b. for every recursive function f, there is an $x \in A$ such that $\varphi_x = f$

15. Show that there is an r.e. set A having the following properties:

a. for each $x \in A$, D_x is recursive

b. for every recursive set D, there is an $x \in A$ such that $D = D_x$

Is there a recursive set having the above properties? Explain the difference between Exercises 14 and 15.

16$^{\Delta}$. Can a set which contains one index for each partial recursive function be recursive? r.e.?

17. Show that there is no recursive function g satisfying: If D_x is recursive, then $\varphi_{g(x)} = \chi_{D_x}$, that is, there is no effective procedure which, given an index of a partial recursive function whose domain is recursive, obtains an index of the characteristic function of the domain.

18. Show that

$$\{x \mid \varphi_x \text{ total and } \bigvee_w \bigwedge_y [\varphi_x(y) \leq w]\}$$

is not r.e. Clearly explain the reduction involved.

19. Let A be an arbitrary r.e. set. Show that A is reducible to H.

20. Prove that $\bigcup_{x \in A} D_x$ is r.e. if A is r.e., but $\bigcap_{x \in A} D_x$ need not be r.e. even if A is recursive.

21. Show that for any r.e. sets A and B, there are r.e. sets A' and B' such that $A' \subseteq A$, $B' \subseteq B$, $A' \cup B' = A \cup B$, and $A' \cap B' = \varnothing$.

6.5 Effective Enumerability of Sets of Functions

A set of partial recursive functions $\mathcal{F}$ is effectively enumerable if there is an effectively enumerable set of programs (effective procedures) $\{\mathcal{T}_i\}$ satisfying:

1. each function in $\mathcal{F}$ is computed by a program in $\{\mathcal{T}_i\}$
2. each program in $\{\mathcal{T}_i\}$ computes a function in $\mathcal{F}$

$\{\mathcal{T}_i\}$ is said to be an *effective enumeration* of $\mathcal{F}$.

In the following let $\mathcal{F}_P$, $\mathcal{F}_R$ and $\mathcal{F}_{PM}$ stand for the classes of partial recursive, recursive, and primitive recursive functions $f: W \to W$, respectively. Results of Section 2.3 showed that $\mathcal{F}_R$ is not effectively enumerable. On the other hand, it is easy to give an effective enumeration of $\mathcal{F}_P$ (for example, by listing all PL programs) or of $\mathcal{F}_{PM}$.

If $\mathcal{F}_1$ and $\mathcal{F}_2$ are sets of functions, then $\mathcal{F}_1 - \mathcal{F}_2$ is the set of functions which are in $\mathcal{F}_1$ but not in $\mathcal{F}_2$.

We wish to show that $\mathcal{F}_P - \mathcal{F}_R$ and $\mathcal{F}_P - \mathcal{F}_{PM}$ are both effectively enumerable. To simplify the discussion we only consider functions with one input and one output. The reader should, before proceeding with the proofs, note that the following statements are not inconsistent.

a. $\mathcal{F}_P - \mathcal{F}_R$ is effectively enumerable
b. $\{x \mid \varphi_x \in \mathcal{F}_P - \mathcal{F}_R\}$ is *not* effectively enumerable

The set of b is a function index set and by results of the previous section is not effectively enumerable. The difference is that an effective enumeration of $\mathcal{F}_P - \mathcal{F}_R$ need not include more than one program for each function in $\mathcal{F}_P - \mathcal{F}_R$ (though it may contain many more) whereas an effective enumeration of $\{x \mid \varphi_x \in \mathcal{F}_P - \mathcal{F}_R\}$ is an effective enumeration of *all* programs which compute functions in $\mathcal{F}_P - \mathcal{F}_R$.

THEOREM 6.24. $\mathcal{F}_P - \mathcal{F}_R$ is effectively enumerable.

Proof. Let $\mathfrak{I}_0, \mathfrak{I}_1, \mathfrak{I}_2, \ldots$ be an effective enumeration of all PL programs. For $n,i \geq 0$, let $\mathfrak{I}(i,n)$ be the program

$$\text{L: IF X1} = n \text{ THEN; GOTO L; END;}$$
$$\mathfrak{I}_i$$

$\mathfrak{I}_i$ and $\mathfrak{I}(i,n)$ perform the same computation except possibly for input $\text{X1} = n$ on which $\mathfrak{I}(i,n)$ does not halt.

The program $\mathfrak{I}(i,n)$ is not defined for $\text{X1} = n$ so it computes a partial recursive function which is not recursive. Conversely let $f: W \to W$ be partial recursive but not recursive. Then there is a $\mathfrak{I}_i$ which computes f and an input $\text{X1} = n$ on which $\mathfrak{I}_i$ does not halt. The program $\mathfrak{I}(i,n)$ computes f.

The required effective enumeration is

$$\mathfrak{I}[\beta'(0),\beta''(0)],\ \mathfrak{I}[\beta'(1),\beta''(1)],\ldots$$

where $\beta: W^2 \to W$ given by $\beta[\beta'(x),\beta''(x)] = x$ is the pairing function of Section 3.8. ▌

THEOREM 6.25. If $\mathcal{F}$ is any effectively enumerable set of recursive functions, then $\mathcal{F}_P - \mathcal{F}$ is effectively enumerable.

Proof. Assume $\mathcal{T}_0, \mathcal{T}_1, \mathcal{T}_2, \ldots$ is an effective enumeration of $\mathcal{F}_P$ where $\mathcal{T}_i$ computes g_i and $\mathcal{R}_0, \mathcal{R}_1, \mathcal{R}_2, \ldots$ is an effective enumeration of $\mathcal{F}$ where $\mathcal{R}_i$ computes $f_i \in \mathcal{F}$. Define the program $\mathcal{T}'_i$ computing g'_i as follows:

1. Read input x. Go to 2.
2. Compute $g_i(x)$. Go to 3.
3. Set j to 0. Go to 4.
4. Compute $f_x(j)$ and $g_i(j)$. Go to 5.
5. If $g_i(j) = f_x(j)$, then add 1 to j and go to 4. If $g_i(j) \neq f_x(j)$, then go to 6.
6. Output $g_i(x)$.

Assume $\mathcal{T}'_i$ computes the function g'_i. If $g_i(x)$ is undefined, then $\mathcal{T}'_i$ never leaves step 2 so $g'_i(x)$ is undefined. If $g_i(x)$ is defined, then $g'_i(x)$ is defined only if a j such that $g_i(j) \neq f_x(j)$ is found while executing steps 4 and 5, that is, in case g_i differs from f_x.

If g'_i is total, then $g_i = g'_i$, g_i is total and for each x, $g_i \neq f_x$. Conversely if g_i is total and $g_i \neq f_x$ for each x, then $g_i = g'_i$ so g'_i is total. Hence each function in $\mathcal{F}_R - \mathcal{F}$ is computed by some $\mathcal{T}'_i$. Of course $\{g'_i\}$ includes many nontotal functions. The required effective enumeration is obtained by enumerating

$$\{\mathcal{T}'_i\} \cup \{\mathcal{T}(i,n)\}$$

where $\{\mathcal{T}(i,n)\}$ is as in the proof of Theorem 6.24. ▌

COROLLARY 6.26. $\mathcal{F}_P - \mathcal{F}_{PM}$ is effectively enumerable. ▌

The set $\mathcal{F}_P - \mathcal{F}$ is effectively enumerable for each effectively enumerable $\mathcal{F} \subseteq \mathcal{F}_R$. However for $\mathcal{F}$ effectively enumerable, $\mathcal{F}_R - \mathcal{F}$ can never be effectively enumerable (see Exercise 1).

EXERCISES

1. Prove that for no effectively enumerable set $\mathcal{F} \subseteq \mathcal{F}_R$ can $\mathcal{F}_R - \mathcal{F}$ be effectively enumerable.

2. Prove that $\{f \mid f \in \mathcal{F}_P,\ 5 \in \operatorname{dom} f\}$, $\{f \mid f \in \mathcal{F}_P,\ \operatorname{dom} f \text{ finite}\}$, and $\{f \mid f \in \mathcal{F}_P,\ 5 \in \operatorname{ran} f\}$ are effectively enumerable.

3. Is $\{f \mid \operatorname{dom} f \text{ infinite},\ f \in \mathcal{F}_P\}$ effectively enumerable?

4. Prove Theorems 6.24 and 6.25 for functions with an arbitrary number of inputs and outputs.

5. Is Theorem 6.25 true if $\mathcal{F} \subseteq \mathcal{F}_P$?

6. Show that $\{f \mid f$ primitive recursive and 1-1$\}$ is effectively enumerable. Is $\{f \mid f$ recursive and 1-1$\}$ effectively enumerable?

7.[Δ] Let $\{\mathcal{T}_i\}$ be an effective enumeration of all PL$-$\{GOTO\} programs, where $\mathcal{T}$ computes f_i: $W \to W$.

a. is it possible to decide for arbitrary i and j whether $f_i = f_j$?

b. is there an effectively enumerable set A satisfying

(1) $\bigwedge_i \bigvee_j [f_i = f_j \wedge j \in A]$

(2) $\bigwedge_i \bigwedge_j [i \in A \wedge j \in A \supset f_i \neq f_j]$

6.6 Finite Sets

Occasionally an effective procedure is described in the following way: "Enumerate the set A and apply procedure $\mathcal{T}$ to each of the elements enumerated". We then claim that the whole procedure is an algorithm provided that A is finite and $\mathcal{T}$ is an algorithm. Actually, to decide when the procedure terminates, we need to know not only that A is finite, but also when the enumeration of A has been completed. Suppose we are using some procedure to enumerate A and all we know is that A is finite. Furthermore, suppose the procedure enumerates three elements, then runs one million steps without enumerating any new elements. The results of the previous section indicate that, in general, there is no way to tell whether the procedure will ever enumerate any more elements. Compare the two procedures given in Section 6.1, which enumerate the set $A = \{0,1,6\}$.

In previous sections we have considered various methods of describing sets. For example, a characteristic function defines the set of inputs for which the function has value 1. Also, a set may be defined as the domain or range of some function. The way a set is presented is extremely important; for example, a recursive characteristic function provides more information about a recursive set than a partial recursive function whose domain is the set. The former permits one to effectively decide membership in the set whereas the latter provides only partial information about membership. In fact, there is no effective procedure for going from an index of a partial recursive function to an algorithm for computing the characteristic function of the domain, even if the domain is known to be recursive and so has a recursive characteristic function (see Exercise 17 of Section 6.4).

For finite sets, even characteristic functions provide less information than may be obtained from other methods of presentation. For example, given an index of a characteristic function of a finite set, there is no effective procedure for determining the number of elements in the set or for enumerating the set in such a way as to be able to effectively decide when the enumeration is complete. These facts will be proved in this section. We then show how to effectively describe finite sets in a way which permits recovery of all pertinent information. This method of presentation will be useful in Chapter 8.

Let cd A denote the number of elements in a finite set A.

THEOREM 6.27. There is no partial recursive function f, such that if φ_j is the characteristic function of some finite set A, then $f(j) = \text{cd } A$.

Proof. Define the primitive recursive function g by

$$\varphi_{g(m)}(k) = T(m,m,k)$$

Then $\varphi_{g(m)} = \chi_{A_m}$, where cd $A_m = 1$ if $m \in H$, and cd $A_m = 0$ if $m \notin H$. If there were a partial recursive function f as described, then $f \circ g = \chi_H$, which contradicts the fact that H is not recursive. ▮

THEOREM 6.28. There is a primitive recursive function index such that if $\varphi_m = \chi_A$ for some finite set A, then index(m) is an index for A, that is, $A = D_{\text{index}(m)}$.

Proof. Let

$$\varphi_{\text{index}(m)}(x) = \begin{cases} 1 & \text{if } \varphi_m(x) = 1 \\ \uparrow & \text{otherwise} \end{cases} \quad ▮$$

COROLLARY 6.29. There is no partial recursive function f such that if $D_m = A$ for a finite set A, then $f(m) = \text{cd } A$.

Proof. If there were such an f, then $f \circ \text{index}$ would satisfy the conditions of Theorem 6.27. ▮

It is also true that there is no effective way to find an index for the characteristic function of a finite set A, given an m such that $D_m = A$ (see Exercise 1). Thus while it is possible to effectively go from a characteristic function of a finite set to an index for the set, the opposite is not true; hence recursive characteristic functions provide more information about finite sets than do partial recursive functions.

We now provide a description of each finite set A which has the property that cd A can be effectively calculated from the description.

Let $F_m = \{x \mid \exp(m,x) > 0\}$, where $\exp(m,x)$ is the exponent of the xth prime in the prime decomposition of m.

Example. If $m = 2^5 \times 7 \times 11^2$, then $F_m = \{0,3,4\}$.

THEOREM 6.30. The function

$$f(m,x) = \begin{cases} 1 & \text{if } x \in F_m \\ 0 & \text{if } x \notin F_m \end{cases}$$

is primitive recursive.

Proof. $f(m,x) = \text{prime}\#(x) \mid m$ ▮

COROLLARY 6.31. There is a primitive recursive function χindex such that

$$\varphi_{\chi\text{index}(m)} = \chi_{F_m}$$

Proof. $\varphi_{\chi\text{index}(m)}(x) = f(m,x)$, where f is as in Theorem 6.30. ▮

THEOREM 6.32. For each finite set $A \subseteq W$, there is an m such that $A = F_m$.
Proof. Let $A = \{x_1,x_2,\ldots,x_k\}$. Then $A = F_m$, where

$$m = \prod_{i=1}^{k} \text{prime}\#(x_i). \ \blacksquare$$

LEMMA 6.33. If $x \in F_m$, then $x \leq m$.
Proof. Exercise 3. ▮

THEOREM 6.34. There is a primitive recursive function $\text{cd}(m)$ such that $\text{cd}(m) = \text{cd}\ F_m$.

Proof. $\text{cd}(m) = \sum_{x=0}^{m} f(m,x)$,
where f is the function in Theorem 6.30. ▮

COROLLARY 6.35. There is no partial recursive function f, such that if $\varphi_m = \chi_A$ for a finite set A, then $A = F_{f(m)}$.
Proof. Theorems 6.27 and 6.34. ▮

EXERCISES

1. Show that there is no partial recusive function f such that if $D_m = A$ for some finite set A, then $\varphi_{f(m)} = \chi_A$.
2. Show that there is no partial recursive function f such that if D_m is recursive, then $D_{f(m)} = \overline{D}_m$.
3. Prove that $x \leq m$ for all $x \in F_m$.
4. Prove that for each finite set A, there are infinitely many m such that $A = F_m$.
5. Let $A = \{x_1,\ldots,x_k\}$ with $x_1 < x_2 < \cdots < x_k$. Let $m = 2^{x_1} + 2^{x_2} + \cdots + 2^{x_k}$ be the *canonical index* of A. Show that this indexing satisfies the properties stated in Theorems 6.30–6.34 and has the additional property that each finite set has exactly one index. Let $\varnothing$ have index 0.
6. Show that there exists an m such that $D_m = F_m$.

6.7 History

Kleene [1936a], Turing [1936], and Church [1936a] contain the earliest proofs of the nonrecursiveness of problems related to the halting problem. The basic properties of the r.e. sets were first investigated by Kleene [1943] and Post [1943, 1944]. In 1943, Kleene proved his enumeration theorem (Theorem 6.3f in the text), which states that for each m,

$$\chi_{D_m}(x) = \bigvee_p T(m,x,p)$$

Post developed the various concepts of reducibility discussed in this chapter and in Chapter 8 as well as proving such basic results as "a set is recursive iff it and its complement are r.e."

The general method via function index sets for obtaining undecidability results (Theorem 6.15) is due to Rice [1953, 1956]. Related results may be found in Dekker and Myhill [1958]. The effective enumerability of classes of functions is studied (in effect) in the above papers and in Landweber and Robertson [1972].

CHAPTER 7

Formal Languages

In our terminology, a language is nothing more than a subset of $W = \Sigma^*$, the set of words over some finite alphabet Σ. Of particular interest, because of their relationship to effective computability, are the r.e. languages. Indeed, all programming languages belong to a subset of the primitive recursive languages called the context-sensitive languages.

Previous chapters have considered various equivalent methods of defining or presenting an r.e. language. Examples are as the domain or the range of a partial recursive function or as the set of inputs on which a PL program halts. In this chapter we study another method for presenting languages. A grammar will be a set of rules for generating the words of a language. The most general types of grammars are capable of generating all r.e. languages. Grammars are extremely important in computer science because by restricting in a natural manner the type of rules permitted, one obtains classes of grammars which generate the context-free and context-sensitive languages. Both of these classes are used extensively in the study and definition of programming languages. The BNF grammars used in Section 2.1 to define the language PL and in Section 5.3 to define a subset of SNOBOL are examples of context-free grammars.

We will prove some of the general properties of these systems, show how they are used in logic, and investigate some of their decidable and undecidable properties.

7.1 Post Production Systems

A *Post production system* (PPS) in the alphabet Σ is a system $\mathcal{S} = \langle \Sigma, \Phi, R, S \rangle$, where

1. Φ is a finite alphabet containing Σ; the members of Σ are called *terminal* symbols and the members of Φ-Σ are called *nonterminal* or *auxiliary* symbols
2. $S \subseteq \Phi^*$ is a finite set of *axioms* or *start words*; when S contains a single nonterminal symbol, this symbol will also be denoted by S

3. R is a finite set of *rewrite* or *production rules* of the form

$$x_0\boxed{i_1}x_1\boxed{i_2}\cdots\boxed{i_k}x_k \rightarrow y_0\boxed{j_1}\cdots\boxed{j_{k'}}y_{k'}$$

where each x and each y is a member of Φ^*, $i_1, \ldots, i_k, j_1, \ldots, j_{k'}$ are numbers, and each number j on the right side of the rule is one of the i's on the left.

For a PPS $\mathcal{S}$ and words x and y in Φ^*, $x \Rightarrow y$, or y is *directly derivable* from x, means that there is a way of filling in the boxes of some rule in R with words in Φ^* so that boxes with the same number receive identical words and the result is x on the left side and y on the right. We also say that the rule *applied* to x yields y. As an example, for $\Phi = \{a,b\}$, $abaabaaa \Rightarrow abaab$ using the rule $ab\boxed{1}\,b\boxed{1}\,a\boxed{2} \rightarrow \boxed{2}\,ab\boxed{1}\,b$, where aa is placed in box 1 and 0 is placed in box 2.

Several words may be directly derivable from a single word x, even if only one rule is used. For example, by using the rule $\boxed{1}\,\boxed{2} \rightarrow \boxed{2}\,\boxed{1}$, where $x_0 = x_1 = x_2 = y_0 = y_1 = y_2 = 0$, each of the words aba, baa, and aab may be directly derived from aba. Another example is provided by the rule $ab\boxed{1}\,b\boxed{1}\,a\boxed{2} \rightarrow \boxed{2}\,ab\,\boxed{2}\,ab\boxed{1}\,b$, which applied to $abbaabbaaa$ yields $abbaaaababbaaaabb$ ($\boxed{1} = 0$, $\boxed{2} = abbaaa$) and $ababbaab$ ($\boxed{1} = baa$, $\boxed{2} = 0$). Note that in this example $\boxed{1}$ cannot equal $baab$.

If $x = w_0 \Rightarrow w_1 \Rightarrow \cdots \Rightarrow w_m = y$, then y is *derivable* from x, written $x \overset{*}{\Rightarrow} y$, and $w_0 \Rightarrow w_1 \Rightarrow \cdots \Rightarrow w_m$ is a *derivation of length m* of y from x. Note that $x \overset{*}{\Rightarrow} x$ for each x by a derivation of length 0. Let $|\mathcal{S}| = \{x \in \Phi^* \mid s \overset{*}{\Rightarrow} x$, for some $s \in S\}$, which is the set of words derivable from an axiom of $\mathcal{S}$. Then $L(\mathcal{S}) = |\mathcal{S}| \cap \Sigma^*$ is the *language generated by* $\mathcal{S}$. The language generated by $\mathcal{S}$ contains all words consisting of only terminal symbols which can be derived from an axiom of $\mathcal{S}$.

Example. $\Sigma = \{1\}$, $\Phi = \Sigma \cup \{a,b\}$. Let $\mathcal{S}$ be the system with a single axiom $ab1$ and rules

$$a\boxed{1}\,b\boxed{2} \rightarrow a\boxed{2}\,b\boxed{1}\,\boxed{2}$$

$$a\boxed{1}\,b\boxed{2} \rightarrow \boxed{1}$$

In this case $L(\mathcal{S})$ is the set of Fibonacci numbers 0, 1, 2, 3, 5, 8, 13, ... written in base 1 or "tally" notation. The set $|\mathcal{S}|$ contains all words of the form af_kbf_{k+1} and f_k, where f_k is the kth Fibonacci number. A derivation of 111 is $ab1 \Rightarrow a1b1 \Rightarrow a1b11 \Rightarrow a11b111 \Rightarrow a111b11111 \Rightarrow 111$.

Example. Let $\Phi = \Sigma = \{(,)\}$. Let $\mathcal{S}$ be the system with a single axiom 0 (the null word) and rule $\boxed{1}\,\boxed{2} \rightarrow \boxed{1}\,(\,)\boxed{2}$. The rule says that a pair of parentheses may be introduced at any place in a word. The language $L(\mathcal{S})$ is the set of balanced strings of parentheses. The following is a derivation of (()())()

in which the new pair of parentheses introduced at each step is shown in bold face type: $0 \Rightarrow \mathbf{()} \Rightarrow (\mathbf{()}) \Rightarrow (()\mathbf{()}) \Rightarrow (()())\mathbf{()}$.

A PPS is called a *grammar* if each rule is of the form $\boxed{1}\, x\boxed{2} \rightarrow \boxed{1}\, y\boxed{2}$. The rules of a grammar will be written in the form $x \rightarrow y$. In a grammar, the rule $x \rightarrow y$ may be applied to any word of the form $u \cdot x \cdot v$ to yield $u \cdot y \cdot v$. Notice that grammar rules differ from the rules of a LMA in that grammar rules are not required to replace the leftmost occurrence of a word. Moreover, LMA's precisely specify which production is to be applied at each step, whereas any rule of a grammar may be applied at any step. The motivation for these differences is that LMA's were used to compute functions whereas grammars generate sets of words. It is possible to design grammars so that at most one word is directly derivable from any given word. If in addition the set of axioms is allowed to be infinite, then the notion of a grammar computing a function can be defined. If this is done correctly, then all partial recursive functions can be computed by grammars.

The BNF definitions discussed in Chapter 2 are examples of grammars. Symbols such as ⟨*name*⟩ should be thought of as single nonterminal symbols. Each rule is of the form

$$\boxed{1}\, A\boxed{2} \rightarrow \boxed{1}\, y\boxed{2}$$

written $A = y$, where A is a nonterminal symbol. The notation $A = y_1 \cup y_2 \cup \cdots \cup y_m$ is an abbreviation for the m rules $A \rightarrow y_1$, $A \rightarrow y_2$, ..., $A \rightarrow y_m$.

The BNF grammars have the property that the left side of each rule is a word of length one. Such grammars are called *context-free* (see Section 7.7).

A grammar which has the property that $y \rightarrow x$ is also a rule if $x \rightarrow y$ is a rule, is called a *Thue system* after the Norwegian mathematician Thue. For this reason grammars are sometimes called *semi-Thue systems.*

THEOREM 7.1. For each PPS (grammar) $\mathcal{S}$, it is possible to effectively find another system (grammar) $\mathcal{S}'$ with a single start symbol, such that $L(\mathcal{S}') = L(\mathcal{S})$.

Proof. Let $\mathcal{S} = \langle \Sigma, \Phi, R, S \rangle$. Assume S' is some symbol which is not used in the system $\mathcal{S}$, that is, $S' \notin \Phi$. Let $\mathcal{S}' = \langle \Sigma, \Phi', R', \{S'\} \rangle$, where $\Phi' = \Phi \cup \{S'\}$, and $R' = R \cup \{S' \rightarrow s \mid s \in S\}$. Then $s \Rightarrow w_1 \Rightarrow \cdots \Rightarrow w_m = x$ in $\mathcal{S}$ iff $S' \Rightarrow s \Rightarrow w_1 \Rightarrow \cdots \Rightarrow w_m = x$ in $\mathcal{S}'$. Thus $L(\mathcal{S}') = L(\mathcal{S})$. ▮

EXERCISES

1. Let $\Sigma = \{1, a, b, c, +, =\}$, $\Phi = \Sigma \cup \{|\}$.
What is the language of the PPS with the following axioms and rules?

a. axiom: 11
 rule: $\boxed{1} \rightarrow \boxed{1}\, 11$

b. axiom: 11
   rule: $\boxed{1} \to \boxed{1}\boxed{1}$

c. axiom: $+=$
   rules: $\boxed{1} + \boxed{2} = \boxed{3} \to \boxed{1}\,1 + \boxed{2} = \boxed{3}\,1$
   $\boxed{1} + \boxed{2} = \boxed{3} \to \boxed{2} + \boxed{1} = \boxed{3}$

d. axiom: $|$
   rules: $\boxed{1} \,|\, \boxed{1} \to \boxed{1}\, a \,|\, \boxed{1}\, b$
   $\boxed{1} \,|\, \boxed{1} \to \boxed{1}\boxed{1}$

e. axiom: $||$
   rules: $\boxed{1} \,|\, \boxed{2} \,|\, \boxed{3} \to \boxed{1}\, a \,|\, \boxed{2}\, b \,|\, c\boxed{3}$
   $\boxed{1} \,|\, \boxed{2} \,|\, \boxed{3} \to \boxed{1}\boxed{2}\boxed{3}$

2. Let $\Sigma = \{a,b\}$, $\Phi = \Sigma \cup \{|, A, B\}$. What is the language generated by the grammars with the following axioms and rules?

a. axiom: 0
   rules: $0 \to a$ (that is, $\boxed{1}\boxed{2} \to \boxed{1}\, a \boxed{2}$)
   $0 \to b$

b. axiom: ab
   rules: $a \to aa$
   $b \to bb$

c. axioms: a, bab, $ababa$
   rule: $b \to a$

d. axiom: A
   rules: $A \to aAa$
   $A \to bAb$
   $A \to 0$

e. axiom: A
   rules: $A \to (A)A$
   $A \to 0$

f. axiom: $||$
   rules: $| \to a|A$
   $| \to b|B$
   $Aa \to aA$
   $Ab \to bA$
   $Ba \to aB$
   $Bb \to bB$
   $A| \to a|$
   $B| \to b|$
   $| \to 0$

3. Given a PPS $\mathcal{S}$, show how to construct a system $\mathcal{S}'$ such that $L(\mathcal{S}') = \rho[L(\mathcal{S})] = \{x \mid \rho(x) \in L(\mathcal{S})\}$.

4. Given PPS's $\mathcal{S}_1$ and $\mathcal{S}_2$, show how to construct $\mathcal{S}'$, such that $L(\mathcal{S}') = L(\mathcal{S}_1) \cup L(\mathcal{S}_2)$ and $\mathcal{S}''$ such that $L(\mathcal{S}'') = L(\mathcal{S}_1) \cdot L(\mathcal{S}_2)$.

5. Construct PPS's $\mathcal{S}$ so that

a. $L(\mathcal{S}) = \{a^p b^q \mid p \geq q \geq 0\}$

b. $L(\mathcal{S}) = \{a^p b^q c^r \mid p = q \text{ or } q = r\}$

c. $L(\mathcal{S}) = \{a^p b^{2p} \mid p \geq 0\}$

d. $L(\mathcal{S}) = \{x \cdot c \cdot y \mid x \preccurlyeq y,\ x,y \in \{a,b\}^*\}$
e. $L(\mathcal{S}) = \{a^{2p}b^{3q} \mid p, q \geq 0\}$
f. $L(\mathcal{S}) = \{a^{2^p + 3^q} \mid p, q \geq 0\}$
g. $L(\mathcal{S}) = \{a^{p^2} \mid p \geq 1\}$
h. $L(\mathcal{S}) = \{a^p \mid p \text{ prime}\}$

7.2 Recursive Enumerability of Each Language

Since the definition of recursive enumerability is supposed to coincide with the intuitive notion of effective enumerability, it is to be expected that the language generated by each PPS is r.e. This will be proved in this section.

THEOREM 7.2. For each PPS $\mathcal{S} = \langle \Sigma, \Phi, R, S \rangle$, the set of derivations in $\mathcal{S}$ is primitive recursive in $\Psi = \Phi \cup \{\Rightarrow\}$.

Proof. First, the predicate $d_r(x,y)$, which states that y is directly derivable from x using rule r, is primitive recursive. To illustrate, suppose rule r is

$$x_0 \boxed{1} x_1 \boxed{2} x_2 \boxed{2} x_3 \rightarrow y_0 \boxed{2} y_1 \boxed{2} y_2,$$

then

$$d_r(x,y) = \bigvee_{u_1=0}^{x} \bigvee_{u_2=0}^{x} [x = x_0u_1x_1u_2x_2u_2x_3 \wedge y = y_0u_2y_1u_2y_2]$$

Thus the predicate

$$x \Rightarrow y = \bigvee_{r \in R} d_r(x,y)$$

which asserts that y is directly derivable from x, is primitive recursive. Let $\Psi = \Phi \cup \{\Rightarrow\}$. If a word z is of the form $w_0 \Rightarrow w_1 \Rightarrow \cdots \Rightarrow w_m \in \Psi^*$, where each w is in Φ^*, then recall that occurrences$(z,\Rightarrow) = m$ and part$(z \cdot \Rightarrow,\Rightarrow,k) = w_k$, $0 \leq k \leq m$. Thus

$$\text{deriv}(z) = \left(\bigwedge_{k=0}^{\text{occurrences}(z,\Rightarrow) \dot{-} 1} [\text{part}(z \cdot \Rightarrow,\Rightarrow,k) \Rightarrow \text{part}(z \cdot \Rightarrow,\Rightarrow,k+1)] \right)$$
$$\vee\ [\text{occurrences}(z,\Rightarrow) = 0]$$

asserts that z is a derivation in $\mathcal{S}$ and is primitive recursive. ▮

Informally, our method for enumerating members of $L(\mathcal{S})$ is to successively examine each word $z \in \Psi^*$ to see if it is a derivation. If z is a derivation, w_0 is an axiom, and w_m, the last word of the derivation, contains only terminal symbols, then print w_m.

THEOREM 7.3. For each PPS $\mathcal{S}$, $L(\mathcal{S})$ is r.e.

Proof. If $A = L(\mathcal{S})$, then

$$\chi_A(x) = \bigvee_{z} [\text{deriv}(z) \wedge \text{part}(z \cdot \Rightarrow, \Rightarrow, 0) \in S$$
$$\wedge\ \text{part}(z \cdot \Rightarrow,\Rightarrow,\text{occurrences}(z,\Rightarrow)) = x]$$

hence $L(\mathcal{S})$ is r.e. by Theorem 6.3f. ▮

EXERCISES

1. Given a PPS $\mathcal{S}$, and given $x \Rightarrow y$, calculate a bound on the length of y in terms of $\mathcal{S}$ and the length of x.

2. Let B_k be the set of words derivable from some axiom of $\mathcal{S}$ in k steps or less (that is, by a derivation of length k or less). Use the result of Exercise 1 to show that B_k is primitive recursive, for each k.

3. Use the result of Exercise 2 to provide another proof that $L(\mathcal{S})$ is r.e.

4. Prove that

$$C_k = \{w \mid w \in L(\mathcal{S}) \wedge \text{length}(w) = k\}$$

is r.e. for any PPS $\mathcal{S}$ and any $k \geq 0$. Is it recursive?

7.3 A Grammar for Each Recursively Enumerable Set

A set is r.e. iff it is $L(\mathcal{S})$ for some PPS $\mathcal{S}$. In fact, each r.e. set is the language of some grammar. In this section, we complete the proof of these facts.

All of the machine programs considered in Chapter 4 were deterministic. However, the original definition of a machine program did not require determinism; several instructions of a program having the same label might be applicable to the given words. The following result is just as easy to prove if nondeterministic TM programs are considered. The fact that each set accepted by a nondeterministic program is also accepted by a deterministic program is also proved. This result is again expected, since deterministic programs accept all r.e. sets.

THEOREM 7.4. For every nondeterministic TM program $\mathcal{T}$, a grammar $\mathcal{S}$ can be constructed such that $L(\mathcal{S})$ is the subset of W accepted by $\mathcal{T}$. That is, $x \in L(\mathcal{S})$ iff program $\mathcal{T}$ halts with input x.

Proof. A grammar $\mathcal{S}$ can be constructed which simulates the computational steps of the TM in *reverse order*. Thus the grammar will generate a word x iff the TM program accepts it.

Let $\mathcal{L}$ be the set of labels in the TM program $\mathcal{T}$. Let $\Phi = \Sigma \cup \{\$\} \cup \{I, T, [,]\} \cup \mathcal{L}$, where $\Sigma' = \Sigma \cup \{\$\}$ is the alphabet of the TM. Construct $\mathcal{S}$ as follows:

axiom: $[T]$

rules:	$T \to \sigma T$	$\sigma \in \Sigma \cup \{\$\}$
	$T \to T\sigma$	$\sigma \in \Sigma \cup \{\$\}$
	$T \to l$	for each terminal label l of $\mathcal{T}$

For each instruction of $\mathcal{T}$ include rules in $\mathcal{S}$ according to the following table:

$\mathcal{T}$	$\mathcal{S}$
$l \quad \iota \times (L_\tau \circ L_\sigma^{-1}) \quad l'$	$l'\tau \to l\sigma$
$l \quad (R_\tau \circ R_\sigma^{-1}) \times \iota \quad l'$	$\tau l' \to \sigma l$
$l \quad R_\sigma^{-1} \times L_\sigma \quad l'$	$l'\sigma \to \sigma l$
$l \quad R_\sigma \times L_\sigma^{-1} l'$	$\sigma l' \to l\sigma$
$l \quad \varepsilon \times L_\sigma \quad l'$	$[l'\sigma \to [l$
$l \quad \varepsilon \times L_\sigma^{-1} l'$	$[l' \to [l\sigma$
$l \quad R_\sigma \times \varepsilon \quad l'$	$\sigma l'] \to l]$
$l \quad R_\sigma^{-1} \times \varepsilon \quad l'$	$l'] \to \sigma l]$
$l \quad \varepsilon \times \iota \quad l'$	$[l' \to [l$
$l \quad \iota \times \varepsilon \quad l'$	$l'] \to l]$

Finally add rules $[l \to I$ for each initial label l of $\mathcal{T}$

$I\sigma \to \sigma I \qquad \sigma \in \Sigma$

$I\$] \to 0$

Observe that a derivation in $\mathcal{S}$ must begin with $[T] \Rightarrow \cdots \Rightarrow [uTv] \Rightarrow [ul'v]$, where $u, v \in (\Sigma')^*$ and l' is a terminal label. At this point, the derivation must simulate in reverse order the computational steps of the TM program. If the TM has u and v in its registers, executes the statement with label l, leaves u' and v' in the registers, and is to execute next the statement with label l', then $[ulv]$ is derivable in one step from $[u'l'v']$. For the derivation to end with a word $x \in \Sigma^*$, the last steps must be in the form $[lx\$] \Rightarrow Ix\$] \Rightarrow \cdots \Rightarrow xI\$] \Rightarrow x$, where l is an initial label. Thus $x \in L(\mathcal{S})$ iff for some $u, v \in (\Sigma')^*$, some initial label l, and some terminal label l', $[ul'v] \overset{*}{\Rightarrow} [lx\$]$. This will happen, iff $|\mathcal{T}|(0,x\$) = (u,v)$, that is, the program $\mathcal{T}$ halts when started with 0 in one register and $\alpha_1(x) = x\$$ in the other. ▮

THEOREM 7.5. A set $A \subseteq W$ is r.e. iff $A = L(\mathcal{S})$ for some PPS $\mathcal{S}$.

Proof. It has already been shown that every r.e. set is accepted by a deterministic TM program. The theorem follows immediately from Theorems 7.3 and 7.4. ▮

THEOREM 7.6. Every set accepted by a nondeterministic TM (URM, SRM) program is also accepted by a deterministic TM(URM, SRM) program.

Proof. This result follows from Theorems 7.4 and 7.5. To prove the assertion for URM and SRM programs, observe that the simulations of URM and SRM programs by TM programs, as given in Theorems 4.4 and 4.6 are valid for nondeterministic programs. ▮

THEOREM 7.7. If $A = L(\mathcal{S})$ for some PPS, then a grammar $\mathcal{S}'$ can be constructed so that $A = L(\mathcal{S}')$.
Proof. This follows from the proofs of Theorems 7.3–7.5. ▮

Theorem 7.4 shows how to effectively construct a grammar $\mathcal{S}$ which generates any given r.e. set, that is, generates D_m, for any given m. Thus problems concerning indices for partial recursive functions can be reduced to problems about production systems, providing the proof of several undecidable properties of the production systems.

THEOREM 7.8. The following properties of production systems and grammars are undecidable:

a. $L(\mathcal{S}) = \varnothing$
b. $L(\mathcal{S})$ is finite
c. $L(\mathcal{S}) = \Sigma^*$
d. $x_0 \in L(\mathcal{S})$, where x_0 is a fixed but arbitrary word in Σ^*
e. $L(\mathcal{S}_1) = L(\mathcal{S}_2)$
f. $L(\mathcal{S}_1) \subseteq L(\mathcal{S}_2)$

Proof. Given x, construct a grammar such that $L(\mathcal{S}) = D_x$, according to the procedures given in Theorem 7.4. If any of the properties a, b, c, d, e, or *f* are decidable, then so is the corresponding property of D_x, which contradicts results contained in Section 6.4. ▮

EXERCISES

1. Construct grammars for each of the languages generated by the PPS's given in Exercise 1 of Section 7.1.

2. Sketch a proof of Theorem 7.6 which involves only concepts related to TM programs, that is, one that could be presented in Chapter 4.

3. Sketch a direct proof (one using only concepts related to PPS's) of Theorem 7.7.

*7.4 Normal Systems

A PPS is a *normal system* if all rules are of the form

$$x\boxed{1} \rightarrow \boxed{1}y$$

Rules of this type will be written simply as $x\square \rightarrow \square y$, which says that if x occurs at the beginning of a word, the x may be deleted and y added at the end, that is, $x \cdot z$ yields $z \cdot y$.

Example. If $\Phi = \Sigma = \{1\}$, $\mathcal{S}$ has one axiom 11 and one rule $1\square \rightarrow \square 111$, then $L(\mathcal{S}) = \{1^{2n} \mid n \geq 1\}$.

Example. If $\Sigma = \{1\}$ and $\Phi = \{1,a\}$, $\mathcal{S}$ has the axiom $a1$ and rules $a\Box \to \Box a$, $1\Box \to \Box 11$, and $a\Box \to \Box$, then $L(\mathcal{S}) = \{1^{2^n} | n \geq 1\}$. A derivation of 1^4 is

$$a1 \Rightarrow 1a \Rightarrow a11 \Rightarrow 11a \Rightarrow 1a11 \Rightarrow a1111 \Rightarrow 1111$$

A normal system works very much like an SRM program, reading and deleting at the left end of a word and writing at the right end. It is thus not surprising that a normal system can be constructed to simulate the computational steps of an SRM program in reverse order, the way a grammar simulates the computation of a TM program.

THEOREM 7.9. For every SRM program $\mathcal{T}$, a normal system $\mathcal{S}$ can be constructed such that $L(\mathcal{S})$ is the subset of W accepted by $\mathcal{T}$.

Proof. Let $\mathcal{L}$ be the set of labels of $\mathcal{T}$. Let $\Phi = \Sigma \cup \{\$\} \cup \mathcal{L} \cup \{T,]\}$, where $\Sigma \cup \{\$\}$ is the alphabet of the SRM. Construct $\mathcal{S}$ as follows:

axiom: $T]$

rules:	$T\Box \to \Box T\sigma$	$\sigma \in \Sigma \cup \{\$\}$
	$T\Box \to \Box l'$	for each terminal label l' of $\mathcal{T}$
	$\tau\Box \to \Box\tau$	$\tau \in \Phi$

For each instruction in $\mathcal{T}$, add rules to $\mathcal{S}$ according to the following table:

$\mathcal{T}$	$\mathcal{S}$
$l \;\; L_\sigma^{-1} \;\; l'$	$l'\Box \to \Box l\sigma$
$l \;\; R_\sigma \;\; l'$	$\sigma]l'\Box \to \Box]l$
$l \;\; \varepsilon \;\; l'$	$l']\Box \to \Box l]$

Finally, add rules $\$]l\Box \to \Box$ for each initial label l. It is claimed that $|\mathcal{T}|(x\$) = y$ iff $T] \overset{*}{\Rightarrow} Ty] \overset{*}{\Rightarrow} l'y] \overset{*}{\Rightarrow} lx\$] \overset{*}{\Rightarrow} \$]lx \Rightarrow x$, for some initial label l and terminal label l'. ▮

COROLLARY 7.10. A set $A \subseteq W$ is r.e. iff $A = L(\mathcal{S})$ for some normal system $\mathcal{S}$. ▮

COROLLARY 7.11. Every set generated by a PPS is also generated by some normal system. ▮

EXERCISES

1. Sketch a direct proof of Corollary 7.11.
2. Construct normal systems for each of the languages generated by the PPS's given in Exercise 1 of Section 7.1.

*7.5 Production Rules with Multiple Antecedents

Sometimes it is useful to consider production systems in which a derivation says that a word y is derivable only if several words $x_1, \ldots, x_k$ have already been derived. One such rule might say that whenever words x_1 and x_2 are generated, then their concatenation $x_1 \cdot x_2$ may also be generated. This rule could be written

$$\left.\begin{array}{l}\boxed{1}\\ \boxed{1}\end{array}\right\} \to \boxed{1}\,\boxed{2}$$

Rules such as these with more than one word on the left side are called *multiple antecedent* rules.

Example. Let $\Sigma = \{a\}$, $\Phi = \{a,2,3\}$.

axioms: $2a$, $3a$

rules:

$$2\boxed{1} \to 2\boxed{1}\,\boxed{1}$$
$$3\boxed{1} \to 3\boxed{1}\,\boxed{1}\,\boxed{1}$$
$$\left.\begin{array}{l}2\boxed{1}\\ 3\boxed{2}\end{array}\right\} \to \boxed{1}\,\boxed{2}$$

In this case $L(\mathcal{S}) = \{a^{2^p+3^q} \mid p, q \geq 1\}$. A derivation of $a^{17} = a^{2^3+3^2}$ is

$$\left.\begin{array}{r}2a \Rightarrow 2aa \Rightarrow 2aaaa \Rightarrow 2aaaaaaaa\\ 3a \Rightarrow 3aaa \Rightarrow 3aaaaaaaaa\end{array}\right\} \Rightarrow a^{17}$$

The definition of a derivation needs to be modified to state that $w_0 \Rightarrow w_1 \Rightarrow \cdots \Rightarrow w_m$ is a derivation if each w_i is either an axiom or directly derivable from *some* of the previous w's by one of the production rules. The proof of Theorem 7.3 can be appropriately modified to show that each set generated by a PPS with multiple antecedent rules is r.e. The details of this modification are left as Exercise 1.

The syntax of formal systems for mathematical logic is often specified by rules which correspond directly to production rules with more than one antecedent. This will be illustrated by examining the propositional calculus in detail. First, an informal description of the syntax of propositional calculus, similar to what might be found in a logic textbook, is given. Then, an equivalent formal description as a PPS follows.

The Propositional Calculus

1. There are a countable number of *proposition* or *statement letters*, $p_0, p_1, p_2, \ldots$.
2. A is a formula iff
   a. it is a proposition letter, or
   b. it is $\neg A'$, A' a formula, or
   c. it is $(A' \supset A'')$, A', A'' formulas

3. An *axiom* is a word of one of the following three forms, where A, B, and C are formulas

a. $(A \supset (B \supset A))$
b. $((A \supset (B \supset C)) \supset ((A \supset B) \supset (A \supset C)))$
c. $((\neg B \supset \neg A) \supset (A \supset B))$

4. There is one *rule of inference*, called *modus ponens*, which says that formula B is derivable from formulas A and $(A \supset B)$.

5. A *proof* is a sequence of formulas such that each is either an axiom or can be derived from two previous members of the sequence using the rule of inference, *modus ponens*.

6. A formula A is a *theorem* iff A is the last formula of some proof.

The following PPS generates the set of theorems of propositional calculus. Thus the set of theorems is r.e. It will not be proved here, but it is known that the set of theorems is the same as the set of formulas, called *tautologies*, with all "true" entries in their truth table. Thus the set of theorems is also recursive; a way to decide whether a given formula is a theorem is to construct its truth table and see whether or not it contains all "true" entries.

A production system for propositional calculus:

Let $\Sigma = \{p, 1, \neg, \supset, (,)\}$ and $\Phi = \Sigma \cup \{P, F, T, A\}$.

Note that the propositional calculus has infinitely many axioms and a production system $\mathcal{S}$ can have only finitely many axioms. Thus, the axioms of propositional calculus must be derived words in $\mathcal{S}$.

Let $\mathcal{S}$ have the single axiom Pp and production rules as follows:

1. $Pp\boxed{1} \rightarrow Pp1\boxed{1}$

2. $P\boxed{1} \rightarrow F\boxed{1}$

$F\boxed{1} \rightarrow F\neg\boxed{1}$

$\left.\begin{matrix} F\boxed{1} \\ F\boxed{2} \end{matrix}\right\} \rightarrow F(\boxed{1} \supset \boxed{2})$

3. $\left.\begin{matrix} F\boxed{1} \\ F\boxed{2} \end{matrix}\right\} \rightarrow A(\boxed{1} \supset (\boxed{2} \supset \boxed{1}))$

$\left.\begin{matrix} F\boxed{1} \\ F\boxed{2} \\ F\boxed{3} \end{matrix}\right\} \rightarrow A((\boxed{1} \supset (\boxed{2} \supset (\boxed{3})) \supset ((\boxed{1} \supset \boxed{2} \supset)(\boxed{1} \supset \boxed{3})))$

$\left.\begin{matrix} F\boxed{1} \\ F\boxed{2} \end{matrix}\right\} \rightarrow A((\neg\boxed{2} \supset \neg\boxed{1}) \supset (\boxed{1} \supset \boxed{2}))$

4. $\left.\begin{matrix} T\boxed{1} \\ T(\boxed{1} \supset \boxed{2}) \\ F\boxed{1} \\ F\boxed{2} \end{matrix}\right\} \rightarrow T\boxed{2}$

5. $A\boxed{1} \rightarrow T\boxed{1}$

6. $T\boxed{1} \rightarrow \boxed{1}$

The following facts are claimed. Recall that $x \in |\mathcal{S}|$ iff $x \in \Phi^*$ is derivable from the axioms.

1. $Px \in |\mathcal{S}|$ iff x is a propositional variable $x = p11 \cdots 11$.
2. $Fx \in |\mathcal{S}|$ iff x is a formula.
3. $Ax \in |\mathcal{S}|$ iff x is an axiom.
4, 5. $Tx \in |\mathcal{S}|$ iff x is a theorem.
6. Thus, $x \in L(\mathcal{S})$ iff x is a theorem.

It is usually a requirement of any formal system of logic that the set of formulas and the set of proofs be recursive and that the set of theorems be r.e. The predicate calculus discussed in Section 7.9 is an extension of the propositional calculus which has the property that the set of theorems is not recursive.

EXERCISES

1. Prove that a PPS which may have rules with more than one antecedent generates an r.e. set.

2. In the production system $\mathcal{S}$ which generates the theorems of propositional calculus, show a derivation of the theorem $(\neg\neg p11 \supset \neg\neg p11)$.

3. Show that the antecedents $F\boxed{1}$ and $F\boxed{2}$ are not necessary in rule 4 corresponding to *modus ponens*.

7.6 The Post Correspondence Problem

In addition to the halting problem, there is one other undecidable problem, called the *Post correspondence problem* (PCP) which is frequently used to obtain undecidability results. In this section we prove that the PCP is undecidable. Applications to problems for context-free grammars are given in Section 7.8.

Let A and B be two finite lists of words in Σ^*; $A = x_1, x_2, \ldots, x_k$ and $B = y_1, y_2, \ldots, y_k$. Each pair (A, B) defines an *instance* of the PCP. We say that an instance PCP(A, B) of the PCP has a *solution* if there are numbers $i_1, i_2, \ldots, i_m$, $m \geq 1$, such that $x_{i_1} \cdot x_{i_2} \cdots x_{i_m} = y_{i_1} \cdot y_{i_2} \cdots y_{i_m}$.

Example.

i	x_i	y_i
1	1	111
2	1211	12
3	112	2

A solution of this instance of the PCP is $x_2x_1x_1x_3 = 121111112 = y_2y_1y_1y_3$.

Example.

i	x_i	y_i
1	12	121
2	211	11
3	121	211

If there is a solution, then $i_1 = 1$, since the first row of the table is the only one containing words which begin with the same symbol. The solution must be of the form $12 \cdots = 121 \cdots$, which means that x_{i_2} must begin with the symbol 1. If $i_2 = 1$, then

$$x_1x_1 \cdots = 1212 \cdots \neq 121121 \cdots = y_1y_1 \cdots$$

With $i_2 = 3$, $x_1x_3 = 12121$ and $y_1y_3 = 121211$. By exactly the same argument $i_3, i_4, \cdots$ must all be 3 and therefore there is no solution to this instance of the PCP.

Some additional notation is convenient. If the lists A and B each have k words, let $\Psi = \{1,2,\ldots,k\}$ and for each $t \in \Psi^*$, $t = i_1 \cdots i_m$, let $A(t) = x_{i_1} \cdots x_{i_m}$ and $B(t) = y_{i_1} \cdots y_{i_m}$. The PCP for A and B then may be stated: Does there exist a $t \in \Psi^+$ such that $A(t) = B(t)$? In the first example, $t = 2113$ is a solution.

The PCP itself is: Does there exist an algorithm which will decide whether or not a given instance of the PCP has a solution? Before proving that the answer is no, it is convenient to show that a closely related problem is not decidable.

Each pair of lists A and B and words a, b, c, and d define an instance MPCP(A,B,a,b,c,d) of the *modified Post correspondence problem.* There is a solution to MPCP(A,B,a,b,c,d) if for some $t \in \Psi^*$, $a \cdot A(t) \cdot c = b \cdot B(t) \cdot d$. Note that the words a, b, c, and d can occur only at the ends of the solution unless they also happen to be in one of the lists A or B. An instance of the MPCP is, in effect, an instance of the PCP, with the additional requirements that the solution begin with a and b and end with c and d.

The MPCP can be shown undecidable by showing that the problem of deciding whether $0 \in L(\mathcal{S})$, for an arbitrary grammar $\mathcal{S}$, can be reduced to it.

LEMMA 7.12. The MPCP is undecidable.

Proof. Let $\mathcal{S} = \langle \Sigma, \Phi, R, S \rangle$ be any grammar with a single axiom $S \in \Phi$ (see Theorem 7.1). Let

$$a = 0 \qquad c = \$$$
$$b = \$S \qquad d = 0$$

where $ is a symbol that is not in Φ. Construct lists A and B as follows:

A	B	
x_i	y_i	for each rule $x_i \to y_i$ in R
σ	σ	for each $\sigma \in \Phi \cup \{\$\}$

It is claimed that

$$w \in |\mathcal{S}| \text{ iff } a \cdot A(t) = x \text{ and } b \cdot B(t) = x \cdot \$ \cdot w \quad \text{for some } x \in (\Phi \cup \{\$\})^* \text{ and some } t \in \Psi^* \tag{7-1}$$

First, if $w \in |\mathcal{S}|$, then there is a derivation

$$S = w_0 \Rightarrow w_1 \Rightarrow \cdots \Rightarrow w_{m-1} \Rightarrow w_m = w$$

It is not difficult to show that there is a t such that

$$a \cdot A(t) = \$w_0\$w_1\$ \cdots \$w_{m-1}$$

and (7-2)

$$b \cdot B(t) = \$w_0 = \$w_1\$ \cdots \$w_{m-1}\$w_m$$

Conversely, if $a \cdot A(t) = x$ and $b \cdot B(t) = x \cdot \$ \cdot w$ are written in the form of (7-2), with $\$ \not\leqslant w_i$, $0 \leq i < m$, then $\$ \not\leqslant w$, since for any t, $a \cdot A(t)$ has exactly one less $ than $b \cdot B(t)$. It is not difficult to verify that $w_i \overset{*}{\Rightarrow} w_{i+1}$ in $\mathcal{S}$. It is possible that $w_i = w_{i+1}$ or that the derivation takes more than one step. Since $b = \$S$ and $a = 0$, this means that $w_0 = S$ and therefore $w = w_m \in |\mathcal{S}|$.

We now claim that MPCP(A,B,a,b,c,d) has a solution iff $0 \in L(\mathcal{S})$. Suppose the MPCP has solution

$$a \cdot A(t) \cdot c = 0 \cdot A(t) \cdot \$ = \$S \cdot B(t) \cdot 0 = b \cdot B(t) \cdot d$$

Then, for $x = a \cdot A(t)$,

$$a \cdot A(t) = x$$
$$b \cdot B(t) = b \cdot B(t) \cdot d = a \cdot A(t) \cdot c = x \cdot \$ = x \cdot \$ \cdot 0$$

and so $0 \in L(\mathcal{S})$, since $0 \in |\mathcal{S}|$ by (7-1). Conversely if $0 \in L(\mathcal{S})$, then by (7-1), there is a t such that $a \cdot A(t) = x$ and $b \cdot B(t) = x \cdot \$ \cdot 0$, hence $a \cdot A(t) \cdot c = x \cdot \$ = x \cdot \$ \cdot 0 \cdot 0 = b \cdot B(t) \cdot d$ is a solution of the MPCP.

The MPCP is undecidable, since $0 \in L(\mathcal{S})$ is undecidable (Theorem 7.8). ▮

LEMMA 7.13. The MPCP is reducible to the PCP; given an instance of the MPCP, one can effectively construct an instance of the PCP so that the PCP has a solution iff the MPCP has a solution.

Proof. Let # and / be symbols which do not occur in any pairs of the MPCP.

Define $(\sigma_1\sigma_2 \cdots \sigma_m)^\# = \sigma_1\#\sigma_2\# \cdots \sigma_m\#$ and $^\#(\sigma_1\sigma_2 \cdots \sigma_m) = \#\sigma_1\#\sigma_2 \cdots \#\sigma_m$. Let $0^\# = {}^\#0 = 0$. Construct the PCP as follows:

A	B	
$/ \cdot \# \cdot a^\#$	$/ \cdot {}^\#b$	
$x_i^\#$	$^\#y_i$	for each pair (x_i,y_i) of the MPCP
$c^\# \cdot /$	$^\#d \cdot \# \cdot /$	

Note that if the PCP has a solution, it must begin with the pair $(/\# a^\#, /^\#b)$ and end with the pair $(c^\#/, {}^\#d\#/)$. The symbol / is needed because a, b, c, and d may be 0. Thus the modified PCP has solution

$$ax_{i_1} \cdots x_{i_m}c = by_{i_1} \cdots y_{i_m}d$$

iff the PCP has solution

$$/\# a^\# x_{i_1}^\# \cdots x_{i_m}^\# c^\# / = /^\# b^\# y_{i_1} \cdots {}^\# y_{i_m} {}^\# d\#/ \tag{7-3}$$

We leave it to the reader to supply the tedious but trivial proof by cases that any solution to the PCP must be a concatenation of solutions of the form (7-3). To avoid a trivial special case assume that (0,0) is not a pair of the MPCP. Note that all rules $0 \to 0$ may be eliminated from a grammar without affecting the language generated. ∎

THEOREM 7.14. The PCP is undecidable.
Proof. Lemmas 7.12 and 7.13. ∎

Some applications of the undecidability of the PCP will be given in Section 7.8.

EXERCISES

1. Show that the PCP is reducible to the problem of deciding if $L(\mathcal{S}) = \varnothing$ by constructing, for each instance of the PCP, a production system $\mathcal{S}_{AB}$ such that $L(\mathcal{S}_{AB}) \neq \varnothing$ iff PCP(A,B) has a solution.

2. Show that the PCP is decidable if the lists are restricted to containing only words in the one-letter alphabet Σ_1.

3. Show that the PCP is decidable if the lists are restricted to contain exactly one pair of words.

4.$^\Delta$ Is the PCP undecidable if the lists are restricted to contain at most two pairs of words? This is an open problem!

5.$^\Delta$ Let $A = \{x_1,\ldots,x_k\}$ and $B = \{y_1,\ldots,y_k\}$ be the same as in the PCP. Call a pair of sequences $i_1, \ldots, i_n$, and $j_1, \ldots, j_m$, $n, m > 0$ such that $x_{i_1} \cdots x_{i_n} = y_{j_1} \cdots y_{j_m}$ a solution of (A,B). Show that the problem of deciding whether an arbitrary (A,B) has a solution in this sense is decidable. Note that (A,B) has a solution iff $A^+ \cap B^+ \neq \varnothing$.

6. Show that the following instance of the PCP has no solution.

	A	B
i	x_i	y_i
1	12	121
2	12	212
3	122	22
4	121	211

7. Find a solution to the following PCP.

	A	B
i	x_i	y_i
1	1	111
2	12111	12
3	12	2

7.7 Context-Sensitive, Context-Free, and Linear Grammars

Two special types of PPS, grammars and normal systems, were studied in previous sections. Each of these is powerful enough to generate all r.e. sets. There are some interesting classes of grammars which do not generate all r.e. sets.

A grammar is *context-sensitive* if each rule $x \to y$ has the property that $\text{length}(x) \le \text{length}(y)$.

Example. Let $\Sigma = \{a,b,c\}$, $\Phi = \Sigma \cup \{B\}$. The set $\{a^n b^n c^n \mid n \ge 1\}$ is generated by the context-sensitive grammar with single axiom abc and rules $ab \to aabbB$, $Bb \to bB$, and $Bc \to cc$.

The grammar with axiom 0 and single rule $0 \to ()$ is another example of a context-sensitive grammar which generates the set of balanced strings of parentheses.

The original definition of context-sensitive grammars required that all rules be of the form $uAv \to uyv$, where $u, v, y \in \Phi^*$, $\text{length}(y) \ge 1$ and $A \in \Phi - \Sigma$. The name "context-sensitive" then reflects the fact that the symbol A may be replaced by y only if it appears in the context of u and v. A proof that the two definitions are equivalent is left as an exercise.

A grammar is *context-free* if each rule $x \to y$ satisfies $\text{length}(x) = 1$. It is not necessary to do so, but most definitions also restrict the left side of the rule to be a nonterminal symbol.

Example. The grammar with axiom S and rules $S \to aSb$ and $S \to 0$ generates the set $\{a^n b^n \mid n \geq 0\}$.

These grammars are called context-free because a production $x \to y$ specifies that x may be replaced by y regardless of the symbols preceding or following x.

Many other examples of context-free grammars, including the BNF grammars, have been given previously.

A grammar is *left-linear* (*right-linear*) if all of the rules are of the form $A \to xB$ ($A \to Bx$) or $A \to y$, where x and y are members of Σ^* and A and B are nonterminal symbols. The rules are called linear because only one nonterminal can appear on the right side of a rule.

Example. Let $\Sigma = \{a,b,1,2\}$ and $\Phi = \Sigma \cup \{V\}$. Let $\mathcal{S}$ have axiom V and rules

$$V \to a$$
$$V \to b$$
$$V \to Va$$
$$V \to Vb$$
$$V \to V1$$
$$V \to V2$$

In this case $\mathcal{S}$ is right-linear and generates the set of words in Σ^* that begin with a letter, a or b.

The context-sensitive, context-free, and left-linear (right-linear) grammars and the context-sensitive, context-free, and left-linear (right-linear) languages generated by them have many interesting properties. A few of the important ones are stated below; proofs may be found in some of the references.

1. A language is left-linear iff it is right-linear.

2. Each left-linear (right-linear) language is a context-free language; each context-free language is context-sensitive; each context-sensitive language is primitive recursive. The inclusions are all proper.

3. All three classes of languages are closed under union and concatenation. The context-sensitive and left-linear classes, but not the context-free class, are closed under intersection. The class of left-linear languages is closed under complementation; the class of context-free languages is not closed under complementation; and it is not known whether the class of context-sensitive languages is closed under complementation. The complement problem is one of the most fundamental and difficult open problems in the theory of computation.

4. A set is accepted by a finite automaton iff it is a left-linear language; a set is accepted by a nondeterministic push-down automaton iff it is context-free; a set is accepted by a nondeterministic linear-bounded automaton iff it is context-sensitive. See Section 4.6.

EXERCISES

1. Exhibit a left-linear or right-linear grammar which generates each of the sets given in Exercise 1 of Section 4.6.

2. Exhibit context-free grammars that generate the following subsets of $\{a,b,c\}^*$

a. $\{a^p b^q c^r \mid p = q \text{ or } q = r\}$

b. $\{a^p b^q \mid 0 \leq p \leq q \leq 3p\}$

c. $\{x \cdot y \mid \rho(x) \preccurlyeq y,\ x,y \in \{\text{a, b}\}^*\}$

d. $\{x \mid \text{occurrences}(x,a) = \text{occurrences}(x,b)\}$

3. The set $\{a^n b^n \mid n \geq 1\}$ is context-free but not left-linear. The set $\{a^n b^n c^n \mid n \geq 1\}$ is context-sensitive but not context-free. Show that $\{a^n b^n c^n d^n \mid n \geq 1\}$ is also context-sensitive.

4. Exhibit context-sensitive grammars that generate the following subsets of $\{a,b,c\}^*$

a. $\{x \cdot \dot{x} \mid x \in \{a,b\}^*\}$

b. $\{x \mid \text{occurrences}(x,a) = \text{occurrences}(x,b) = \text{occurrences}(x,c)\}$

5. Prove that for a context-sensitive grammar $\mathcal{S}$, $0 \in L(\mathcal{S})$ iff 0 is an axiom of $\mathcal{S}$. Some definitions of context-sensitive grammars arbitrarily exclude 0 as an axiom, so that $L(\mathcal{S}) \subseteq \Sigma^+$.

6. Show that each context-sensitive language is generated by a grammar with rules of the form $uAv \rightarrow uyv$, where $u, v \in \Phi^*$, $y \in \Phi^+$, and $A \in \Phi - \Sigma$.

7.8 Some Undecidable Properties of Grammars

The context-free languages are particularly important in computing science because they are often used to formally describe the syntax of programming languages. The BNF description of PL given in Section 2.1 is in fact a context-free grammar, where each object of the form ⟨*name*⟩ is considered to be a single nonterminal symbol. Thus it is of practical interest to know that it is not possible to effectively decide such questions as whether a given context-free grammar is ambiguous or if two given context-free grammars generate the same language. Before exploring these problems, we will show that there are some problems concerning the context-sensitive and context-free grammars which are decidable. Note that all of these problems are undecidable for general grammars.

THEOREM 7.15. Given a context-sensitive grammar in Σ and $x \in \Sigma^*$, it is possible to effectively decide whether $x \in L(\mathcal{S})$; in fact, $L(\mathcal{S})$ is a primitive recursive set.

Proof. Let $\mathcal{S} = \langle \Sigma, \Phi, R, S \rangle$. For each $m, n \geq 0$, define the sets ${}_nA_m$ by

$${}_nA_0 = \{s \in S \mid \text{length}(s) \leq n\}$$

$${}_nA_{m+1} = {}_nA_m \cup \{y \mid \text{length}(y) \leq n \text{ and } x \Rightarrow y \text{ for some } x \in {}_nA_m\}$$

By definition ${}_nA_0 \subseteq {}_nA_1 \subseteq \cdots \subseteq (\{0\} \cup \Phi \cup \Phi^2 \cup \cdots \cup \Phi^n)$, which has $1 + k + k^2 + \cdots + k^n < k^{n+1}$ elements, where k is the number of symbols in Φ. Hence for some $m_0 < k^{n+1}$, ${}_nA_{m_0} = {}_nA_{m_0+1} = \cdots$.

We claim that $x \in |\mathcal{S}|$ and length(x) $\leq n$ iff $x \in {}_nA_m$ for some m. Clearly every member of ${}_nA_m$ is in $|\mathcal{S}|$ and has length less than or equal to n. Conversely, if $s \Rightarrow w_1 \Rightarrow \cdots \Rightarrow w_m = x$ for some $s \in S$, then, since $0 \leq \text{length}(s) \leq \text{length}(w_1) \leq \cdots \leq \text{length}(w_m) \leq n$, $s \in {}_nA_0$, $w_1 \in {}_nA_1$, ... and $w_m = x \in {}_nA_m$. Thus if

$$A(n,0,y) = \chi_S(y) \wedge \text{length}(y) \leq n$$

$$A(n,m+1,y) = A(n,m,y) \vee \left(\text{length}(y) \leq n \wedge \bigvee_{x=0}^{y \cdot y} [x \Rightarrow y \wedge A(n,m,x)]\right)$$

then

$$A(n,m,y) = \begin{cases} 1 & \text{if } y \in {}_nA_m \\ 0 & \text{if } y \notin {}_nA_m \end{cases}$$

and $A(n,m,y)$ is a primitive recursive function because $x \Rightarrow y$ is primitive recursive for any grammar (Section 7.2). If $x \Rightarrow y$ in a context-sensitive grammar, then length(x) $\leq$ length(y) and so $x \leq y \cdot y$ (but it is not necessarily the case that $x \leq y$).

Thus $\chi_{L(\mathcal{S})}(y) = \chi_{\Sigma^*}(y) \wedge A[\text{length}(y), k^{\text{length}(y)+1}, y]$ is primitive recursive. ▌

Each r.e. set is generated by some grammar. However, context-sensitive languages are all primitive recursive, so not every recursive set is a context-sensitive language. In fact, there are primitive recursive sets which are not context-sensitive languages (Exercise 5). The only restriction on context-sensitive grammars is that the production rules may not be length decreasing, that is, each rule $x \to y$ must satisfy length(x) $\leq$ length(y). Hence the ability to delete or erase symbols is a very important feature of grammars.

THEOREM 7.16. There is an effective procedure for deciding whether the language generated by an arbitrary context-free grammar $\mathcal{S}$ is the empty set, that is, the emptiness problem for context-free grammars is decidable.

Proof. Let $\mathcal{S} = \langle \Sigma, \Phi, R, S \rangle$. By Theorem 7.1 we may assume that S is a single nonterminal symbol. Define sets

$$A_0 = \varnothing$$

$$A_{m+1} = A_m \cup \{\sigma \in \Phi - \Sigma \mid \sigma \Rightarrow x, x \in (\Sigma \cup A_m)^*\}$$

By definition $A_0 \subseteq A_1 \subseteq A_2 \subseteq \cdots \subseteq \Phi - \Sigma$. Since Φ is a finite set, there must be some m_0 less than or equal to the number of elements in $\Phi - \Sigma$ such that $A_{m_0} = A_{m_0+1} = A_{m_0+2} = \cdots$. The procedure is thus to construct the finite sets A_0, A_1, ..., until two successive sets A_m and A_{m+1} are equal. Then $L(\mathcal{S}) \neq \varnothing$ iff $S \in A_m$. The proof of this last assertion is left as an exercise. ▌

It is interesting to note that the emptiness problem for context-sensitive grammars is not decidable. This is proved as Theorem 7.23.

THEOREM 7.17. There is an effective procedure for deciding whether a given context-free grammar generates the null word.

Proof. The proof is similar to the proof of Theorem 7.15 and is left as an exercise. ▌

THEOREM 7.18. Given a context-free grammar, one can effectively construct another context-free grammar which generates the same set, but contains no rules of the form $\sigma \to 0$.

Proof. The required procedure is to decide, for each σ, whether $\sigma \overset{*}{\Rightarrow} 0$, using the procedure of Theorem 7.17. Then delete all such rules and for each rule in which σ occurs on the right side, say $\sigma' \to x\sigma y$, introduce a new rule $\sigma' \to xy$ (unless $x = y = 0$). If the right side contains several occurrences of the same or different symbols σ with $\sigma \overset{*}{\Rightarrow} 0$, then a new rule must be introduced for each possible combination of deletions. For example, if $\sigma' \to \sigma a \sigma$ is a rule and $\sigma \overset{*}{\Rightarrow} 0$ in the original grammar, then the rules

$$\sigma' \to \sigma a \sigma$$
$$\sigma' \to a \sigma$$
$$\sigma' \to \sigma a$$
$$\sigma' \to a$$

would all appear in the new grammar. Also if 0 is generated by the given grammar, it must be an axiom of the new grammar. The details of this proof are also left as an exercise. ▌

COROLLARY 7.19. For each context-free and left (right)-linear grammar $\mathcal{S}$, $L(\mathcal{S})$ is context-sensitive and therefore primitive recursive. Hence $x \in L(\mathcal{S})$ can be effectively decided for $\mathcal{S}$ an arbitrary context-free, left-linear, or right-linear grammar.

Proof. Given a context-free grammar, the grammar constructed in Theorem 7.18 is both context-free and context-sensitive. Also, each left (right)-linear grammar is context-free. ▌

We now prove that some problems about context-sensitive and context-free grammars are undecidable by showing that if they were decidable, then the PCP would also be decidable, that is, the PCP is reducible to each of them.

Let (A,B) be an instance of the PCP, where $A = x_1, \ldots, x_k$, $B = y_1, \ldots, y_k$, and $x_i, y_i \in \Sigma^*$, $1 \le i \le k$. Assume Σ does *not* contain the symbols $1, 2, \ldots, k$, so that $\Sigma_k = \{1,2,\ldots,k\}$ and Σ are disjoint. Define two grammars $\mathcal{S}_A = \langle \Sigma \cup \Sigma_k, \Phi_A, R_A, S_A \rangle$ and $\mathcal{S}_B = \langle \Sigma \cup \Sigma_k, \Phi_B, R_B, S_B \rangle$, where

$$\Phi_A = \Sigma \cup \Sigma_k \cup \{S_A\}$$
$$\Phi_B = \Sigma \cup \Sigma_k \cup \{S_B\}$$

R_A consists of the rules

$$S_A \to x_\sigma S_A \sigma \qquad \sigma \in \Sigma_k$$
$$S_A \to x_\sigma \sigma \qquad \sigma \in \Sigma_k$$

and R_B consists of the rules

$$S_B \to y_\sigma S_B \sigma \qquad \sigma \in \Sigma_k$$
$$S_B \to y_\sigma \sigma \qquad \sigma \in \Sigma_k$$

The grammars $\mathcal{S}_A$ and $\mathcal{S}_B$ are both context-sensitive and context-free. If $L_A = L(\mathcal{S}_A)$ and $L_B = L(\mathcal{S}_B)$, it is easy to see that

$$L_A = \{x_{\sigma_1} \cdots x_{\sigma_m} \sigma_m \cdots \sigma_1 \mid m \geq 1, \sigma_i \in \Sigma_k, 1 \leq i \leq m\}$$

and

$$L_B = \{y_{\sigma_1} \cdots y_{\sigma_m} \sigma_m \cdots \sigma_1 \mid m \geq 1, \sigma_i \in \Sigma_k, 1 \leq i \leq m\}$$

LEMMA 7.20. PCP(A,B) has a solution iff $L_A \cap L_B \neq \varnothing$.
Proof. PCP(A,B) has a solution iff there is a $t = \sigma_1 \cdots \sigma_m \in \Sigma_k^+$ such that $x = x(t) = x_{\sigma_1} \cdots x_{\sigma_m} = y_{\sigma_1} \cdots y_{\sigma_m} = y(t) = y$ iff $x \cdot \rho(t) = y \cdot \rho(t) \in L_A \cap L_B$. ▮

THEOREM 7.21. It is impossible to effectively decide if $L(\mathcal{S}_1) \cap L(\mathcal{S}_2) = \varnothing$, given two arbitrary context-free or context-sensitive grammars $\mathcal{S}_1$ and $\mathcal{S}_2$.
Proof. Given a PCP(A,B), construct the grammars $\mathcal{S}_A$ and $\mathcal{S}_B$. By Lemma 7.20, $L(\mathcal{S}_A) \cap L(\mathcal{S}_B) \neq \varnothing$ iff PCP(A,B) has a solution, thus if one could decide if $L(\mathcal{S}_A) \cap L(\mathcal{S}_B) = \varnothing$, one could also decide if PCP(A,B) has a solution. ▮

THEOREM 7.22. Given context-sensitive grammars $\mathcal{S}_1$ and $\mathcal{S}_2$, one may effectively construct a context-sensitive grammar $\mathcal{S}$ such that $L(\mathcal{S}) = L(\mathcal{S}_1) \cap L(\mathcal{S}_2)$.
Proof. The proof is fairly complicated, but may be found in Hopcroft and Ullman [1969]. ▮

Theorem 7.22 is not true for the context-free grammars. For example, there are context-free grammars $\mathcal{S}_1$ and $\mathcal{S}_2$ such that

$$L(\mathcal{S}_1) = \{a^i b^n c^n \mid n \geq 0, i \geq 0\}$$

and

$$L(\mathcal{S}_2) = \{a^n b^n c^i \mid n \geq 0, i \geq 0\}$$

However, $L(\mathcal{S}_1) \cap L(\mathcal{S}_2) = \{a^n b^n c^n \mid n \geq 0\}$ is context-sensitive, but not context-free. The next theorem together with Theorem 7.16 indicates another difference between context-free and context-sensitive grammars.

THEOREM 7.23. The emptiness problem for context-sensitive grammars is undecidable.

Proof. Given a PCP(A,B), construct a context-sensitive grammar $\mathcal{S}$ such that $L(\mathcal{S}) = L(\mathcal{S}_A) \cap L(\mathcal{S}_B)$. Then PCP($A$,$B$) has a solution iff $L(\mathcal{S}) \neq \varnothing$. If $L(\mathcal{S}) = \varnothing$ were decidable, then the PCP would also be decidable. ∎

A context-free grammar derivation is *leftmost* if there are no consecutive steps in the derivation of the form

$$u\sigma_1 v\sigma_2 w \Rightarrow u\sigma_1 v y_2 w \Rightarrow u y_1 v y_2 w \tag{7-4}$$

using rules $\sigma_1 \to y_1$ and $\sigma_2 \to y_2$. Given any derivation, a leftmost derivation of the same word may be obtained by replacing all subderivations of the form (7-4) by

$$u\sigma_1 v\sigma_2 w \Rightarrow u y_1 v\sigma_2 w \Rightarrow u y_1 v y_2 w$$

It must be verified that, after some finite number of changes, a leftmost derivation is obtained.

For a context-free grammar whose rules are all of the form $\sigma \to y$, σ a nonterminal symbol, a leftmost derivation of a terminal word is one in which the leftmost nonterminal symbol is replaced at each step.

A word which has more than one leftmost derivation in $\mathcal{S}$ is said to be *ambiguous* with respect to $\mathcal{S}$. An ambiguous grammar is one whose language contains an ambiguous word. This definition captures the idea that a word with two different leftmost derivations has two different "interpretations" or "meanings" in the language.

Note that the grammars $\mathcal{S}_A$ and $\mathcal{S}_B$ defined previously are unambiguous grammars.

Example. The grammar

$$\mathcal{S} = \langle \{a\}, \{S,A,a\}, \{S \to A,\ A \to a\}, \{A, S\} \rangle$$

is ambiguous because each of the following is a leftmost derivation of a.

$$S \Rightarrow A \Rightarrow a$$
$$A \Rightarrow a$$

Example. Consider the following grammar which generates some simple arithmetic expressions without parentheses.

$$\langle \textit{variable} \rangle = A \cup B \cup \cdots \cup Z$$
$$\langle \textit{op} \rangle = + \cup - \cup \times \cup /$$
$$\langle \textit{exp} \rangle = \langle \textit{variable} \rangle \cup \langle \textit{exp} \rangle\, \langle \textit{op} \rangle\, \langle \textit{exp} \rangle$$

The grammar is ambiguous because the following are both leftmost derivations of the expression $A + B \times C$.

$$\begin{aligned}\langle exp\rangle &\Rightarrow \langle exp\rangle\ \langle op\rangle\ \langle exp\rangle\\ &\Rightarrow \langle variable\rangle\ \langle op\rangle\ \langle exp\rangle\\ &\overset{*}{\Rightarrow} A + \langle exp\rangle\ \langle op\rangle\ \langle exp\rangle\\ &\overset{*}{\Rightarrow} A + B \times C\\ \langle exp\rangle &\Rightarrow \langle exp\rangle\ \langle op\rangle\ \langle exp\rangle\\ &\Rightarrow \langle exp\rangle\ \langle op\rangle\ \langle exp\rangle\ \langle op\rangle\ \langle exp\rangle\\ &\overset{*}{\Rightarrow} A + B \times C\end{aligned}$$

If the multiplicative operations $\times$ and $/$ are to have precedence over the additive operations $+$ and $-$, then the first derivation given above is the "correct" one and the following unambiguous grammar correctly generates the same set of expressions.

$$\begin{aligned}\langle variable\rangle &= A \cup B \cup \cdots \cup Z\\ \langle add\text{-}op\rangle &= + \cup -\\ \langle mul\text{-}op\rangle &= \times \cup /\\ \langle mul\text{-}exp\rangle &= \langle variable\rangle \cup \langle variable\rangle\ \langle mul\text{-}op\rangle\ \langle mul\text{-}exp\rangle\\ \langle exp\rangle &= \langle mul\text{-}exp\rangle \cup \langle mul\text{-}exp\rangle\ \langle add\text{-}op\rangle\ \langle exp\rangle\end{aligned}$$

The definition of ambiguity given can be fairly easily extended to arbitrary grammars, but we will only be interested in ambiguity in context-free grammars.

THEOREM 7.24. It is undecidable whether a given context-free grammar is ambiguous.

Proof. Given PCP(A,B), construct the unambiguous grammars $\mathcal{S}_A$ and $\mathcal{S}_B$ as previously described and then construct $\mathcal{S} = \langle \Sigma \cup \Sigma_k, \Phi, R, S\rangle$, where $\Phi = \Sigma \cup \Sigma_k \cup \{S, S_A, S_B\}$ and $R = R_A \cup R_B \cup \{S \to S_A,\ S \to S_B\}$. Note that $L(\mathcal{S}) = L(\mathcal{S}_A) \cup L(\mathcal{S}_B)$. It is claimed that $\mathcal{S}$ is ambiguous iff $L_A \cap L_B \neq \varnothing$. If $L_A \cap L_B = \varnothing$, then each $x \in L(\mathcal{S})$ is in L_A or L_B, but not both. Suppose $x \in L_A$, but $x \notin L_B$, then there is only one derivation of x, namely $S \Rightarrow S_A \overset{*}{\Rightarrow} x$, where $S_A \overset{*}{\Rightarrow} x$ is the unique derivation of x in S_A. If $x \in L_B$, but not L_A, the situation is similar. If $L_A \cap L_B \neq \varnothing$, then there is some x with derivations $S_A \overset{*}{\Rightarrow} x$ in $\mathcal{S}_A$ and $S_B \overset{*}{\Rightarrow} x$ in $\mathcal{S}_B$. Thus x has two derivations, $S \Rightarrow S_A \overset{*}{\Rightarrow} x$ and $S \Rightarrow S_B \overset{*}{\Rightarrow} x$, in $\mathcal{S}$ and so $\mathcal{S}$ is ambiguous. Thus $\mathcal{S}$ is ambiguous iff PCP(A,B) has a solution and a procedure for deciding ambiguity of $\mathcal{S}$ would yield a procedure for deciding if PCP(A,B) has a solution. ▮

Since the purpose of this section has been to illustrate various decidable problems concerning grammars and to show how PCP can be used to prove some undecidability results, we have presented only a few results and the proofs have been somewhat sketchy. Table 7-1 summarizes some decidable

TABLE 7-1. Status of Decision Problems for Left (Right)-Linear, Context-Free, Context-Sensitive, and Arbitrary Grammars

Problem	Left-(Right)-linear	Context-free	Context-sensitive	Arbitrary Grammar
Is $L(\mathcal{S}_1) \cup L(\mathcal{S}_2)$ generated by a grammar of the same type?	Y	Y	Y	Y
Is $L(\mathcal{S}_1) \cdot L(\mathcal{S}_2)$ generated by a grammar of the same type?	Y	Y	Y	Y
Is $L(\mathcal{S}_1) \cap L(\mathcal{S}_2)$ generated by a grammar of the same type?	Y	U	Y	Y
Is $\Sigma^* - L(\mathcal{S})$ generated by a grammar of the same type?	Y	U	?	U
Is $x \in L(\mathcal{S})$?	D	D	D	U
Is $L(\mathcal{S}) = \varnothing$?	D	D	U	U
Is $L(\mathcal{S}_1) = L(\mathcal{S}_2)$ or $L(\mathcal{S}_1) \subseteq L(\mathcal{S}_2)$?	D	U	U	U
Is $L(\mathcal{S}_1) \cap L(\mathcal{S}_2) = \varnothing$	D	U	U	U

[a] The symbol Y means the answer to the question is yes, D means decidable, U means undecidable, and ? means that the status of the problem is not known.

and undecidable properties of grammars. The table illustrates that almost all problems concerning arbitrary grammars are undecidable and almost all problems concerning left (right)-linear grammars are decidable. We cannot give the proof here, but there is one interesting problem about left (right)-linear grammars which is undecidable. Given grammars $\mathcal{S}_1$ and $\mathcal{S}_2$, define $f_i(x)$, $i = 1, 2$, to be the number of leftmost derivations of x in grammar $\mathcal{S}_i$. The undecidable problem is: Is $f_1(x) \le f_2(x)$, for all $x \in \Sigma^*$? The problem of determining if $f_1 = f_2$ is decidable.

EXERCISES

1. Complete the proof of Theorem 7.16, that is, show that $L(\mathcal{S}) \neq \varnothing$ iff $S \in A_m$.

2. Why does the proof of Theorem 7.16 not provide an effective procedure for deciding, for a context-sensitive grammar, if $L(\mathcal{S}) = \varnothing$?

3. Prove Theorem 7.17.

4. Complete the proof of Theorem 7.18.

5. Prove that there is a primitive recursive set that is not context-sensitive.

6. Show how to construct left-linear, right-linear, context-free, context-sensitive, and arbitrary grammars that generate $L(\mathcal{S}_1) \cup L(\mathcal{S}_2)$ and $L(\mathcal{S}_1) \cdot L(\mathcal{S}_2)$, given grammars $\mathcal{S}_1$ and $\mathcal{S}_2$ of the same type.

*7.9 The Undecidability of the Predicate Calculus

In this section we will show that there is no algorithm for deciding if a given formula is a theorem of the first-order predicate calculus with equality. This is proved by showing that the halting problem for the SRM is reducible to the decision problem for the predicate calculus. It is assumed that the reader is familiar with the basic properties of the predicate calculus as developed in a text such as Kleene [1967], Mendelson [1964], or Margaris [1967]. However, the following definitions are particularly pertinent and so are reviewed.

A formula A is *provable* or is a *theorem* if there is a sequence of formulas $A_1, \ldots, A_k$ such that each A_i is either an axiom or follows from previous formulas in the sequence by one of the rules of inference. A *sentence* is a formula with no free variables. A *matrix* is a formula with no quantifiers. If a sentence S contains predicate symbols $P_1, \ldots, P_k$ and function symbols $f_1, \ldots, f_j$ (we treat constants as zero-place functions), then an *interpretation* of S is a system $\langle D, \bar{P}_1, \ldots, \bar{P}_k, \bar{f}_1, \ldots, \bar{f}_j \rangle$, where D is a nonempty set and each $\bar{P}_i(\bar{f}_i)$ is a predicate (function) with the appropriate number of inputs from D. A sentence S is *satisfiable* if there is an interpretation of S under which S is true; such an interpretation is called a *model* of S. A sentence S is *valid* if every interpretation of S is a model of S. If $\langle D, \bar{P}_1, \ldots, \bar{P}_k, \bar{f}_1, \ldots, \bar{f}_j \rangle$ and $\langle D', \bar{P}'_1, \ldots, \bar{P}'_k, \bar{f}'_1, \ldots, \bar{f}'_j \rangle$ are interpretations then $h: D \to D'$ is a *homomorphism* if

1. $h(D) = D'$ (h is onto)
2. for $1 \le i \le k$ and all $x_1, \ldots, x_r \in D$, $\bar{P}_i(x_1, \ldots, x_r)$ is true iff $\bar{P}'_i(hx_1, \ldots, hx_r)$ is true
3. for $1 \le i \le j$ and all $x_1, \ldots, x_r \in D$, $h \circ \bar{f}_i(x_1, \ldots, x_r) = \bar{f}'_i(hx_1, \ldots, hx_r)$

THEOREM 7.25 (Gödel). A sentence is provable iff it is valid. ▌

THEOREM 7.26. A sentence S is valid iff $\neg S$ is not satisfiable. ▌

COROLLARY 7.27. $\{S \mid S \text{ is provable}\}$ is recursive iff $\{S \mid S \text{ is satisfiable}\}$ is recursive. ▌

THEOREM 7.28. There is no algorithm which decides whether a given complete SRM program halts if started with the null word in the SRM register. See Theorems 6.5 and 6.12. ▌

THEOREM 7.29. Let M be a matrix containing the variables $x_1,\ldots,x_k$ and let $S = \forall x_1 \cdots \forall x_k M$. Suppose $\langle D,\ldots\rangle$ and $\langle D',\ldots\rangle$ are interpretations of S and $h:D \rightarrow D'$ is a homomorphism. If $\langle D',\ldots\rangle$ is a model of S, then so is $\langle D,\ldots\rangle$.
Proof. Exercise 1. ▮

We now specify an effective procedure which, given any complete SRM program $\mathfrak{I}$, produces a sentence that is satisfiable iff $\mathfrak{I}$ does not halt when started on the null word. If the set of satisfiable sentences were decidable, then the halting problem for SRM's would be also, that is, the set of SRM programs which halt on the null word is reducible to the set of satisfiable sentences.

A complete SRM program may only contain sets of instructions in one of the following three forms:

$$l\ \varepsilon\ l_\varepsilon,\ L_\sigma^{-1} l_\sigma \qquad \sigma \in \Sigma$$
$$l\ R_\sigma\ l'$$
$$l \text{ stop}$$

Given a complete SRM program $\mathfrak{I}$, associate with each label a distinct k-tuple of T's and F's (for true and false), where 2^k is greater than or equal to the number of labels in $\mathfrak{I}$. Let the initial label be represented by (T,T,...,T). Do the same for the members of $\Sigma \cup \{0\}$, using (F,F,...,F) as the representation of the null word 0. From now on, when we say that l is a label or that σ is a member of $\Sigma \cup \{0\}$, we mean l or σ is the tuple of T's and F's corresponding to a label or a member of $\Sigma \cup \{0\}$.

Construct formulas Delete, Print, Stop, Write, and Goto involving l and σ and the propositional connectives $\wedge$, $\vee$, $\neg$, $\supset$, and $\leftrightarrow$ such that:

Delete(l) is true iff l is the label of a "delete and test" instruction.
Print(l) is true iff l is the label of a "print" instruction.
Stop(l) is true iff l is the label of a "stop" instruction.
Write(l) = σ if l is the label of an R_σ instruction.
Goto(l,σ) = l' if

$l\ L_\sigma^{-1} l'$ is in $\mathfrak{I}$ and $\sigma \in \Sigma$, or
$l\ R_{\sigma'}\ l'$ is in $\mathfrak{I}$ for some $\sigma' \in \Sigma$, or
$l\ \varepsilon\ l'$ is in $\mathfrak{I}$ and $\sigma = 0$

Example. Let $\Sigma = \{1,\$\}$ and let $\mathfrak{I}$ be the program

1 $R_\$$ 2
2 $L_1^{-1}1,\ L_\$^{-1}\ 2,\ \varepsilon\ 3$
3 stop

Represent labels and members of $\Sigma \cup \{0\}$ as pairs according to the following tables.

l	l_1	l_2
1	T	T
2	T	F
3	F	T

σ	σ_1	σ_2
\$	T	T
1	T	F
0	F	F

Then Delete(l) = T iff $l = 2$, that is, $l = (l_1, l_2) = (\text{T}, \text{F})$, so Delete($l$) = $l_1 \wedge \neg l_2$. Similarly Print(l) $= l_1 \wedge l_2$ and Stop(l) $= \neg l_1 \wedge l_2$. If $l = 1$, then Write(l) must be the representation of \$, which is (T,T). Thus Write is actually a pair of formulas. Since it does not matter what values Write(l) assumes if $l \neq 1$, we may choose Write(l) $= (l_1 \vee \neg l_1, l_1 \vee \neg l_1)$. The construction of the formula Goto(l,σ) is aided by Table 7-2.

TABLE 7-2. Truth Table for Goto

l	l_1	l_2	σ_1	σ_2	σ	l'	l'_1	l'_2
	T	T	T	T	\$	2	T	F
1	T	T	T	F	1	2	T	F
	T	T	F	T				
	T	T	F	F	0	2	T	F
	T	F	T	T	\$	2	T	F
2	T	F	T	F	1	1	T	T
	T	F	F	T				
	T	F	F	F	0	3	F	T
	F	T	T	T	\$			
3	F	T	T	F	1			
	F	T	F	T				
	F	T	F	F	0			
	F	F	T	T	\$			
	F	F	T	F	1			
	F	F	F	T				
	F	F	F	F	0			

One possible choice is Goto(l,σ) $= (l_2 \vee \sigma_1, \neg l_2 \wedge \neg \sigma_2)$. If the value of $l' =$ Goto(l,σ) is not specified in Table 7-2 for certain values of l and σ, then any value may be assigned.

In the formula A to be constructed, there are four predicate symbols, R, L, E, and S. In order to motivate the particular choice of A, it should be noted at this time that these predicates will be interpreted in the following way:

$R(t,p)$: the letter in position p of the SRM register at time t
$L(t)$: the label of the instruction of $\mathfrak{T}$ being executed at time t
$E(t)$: the letter in position 0 (the left end) of the register at time t
$S(t,p)$: the size (length) of the word in the SRM register at time t is p

By "the letter in position p" we mean the pth letter from the left of the word in the SRM register. If p is greater than or equal to the length of the word in the register, then "the letter in position p" means 0.

Note that if the letters of Σ are represented as k-tuples of T's and F's, then $R(t,p)$ stands for a k-tuple of predicates R_1, R_2, ..., R_k. The formula $\neg R_1(t,p) \wedge \cdots \wedge \neg R_k(t,p)$ will be abbreviated as Rempty(t,p). Similarly E stands for a k-tuple of predicates E_1, ..., E_k and $\neg E_1(t) \wedge \cdots \wedge \neg E_k(t)$ will be abbreviated as Eempty(t). If labels are represented as j-tuples, then L stands for a j-tuple of predicates L_1, ..., L_j and $L_1(t) \wedge \cdots \wedge L_j(t)$ will be abbreviated as Linitial(t).

The symbol $^+$ stands for a unary function which will be interpreted as the successor function $\varsigma(x) = x + 1$. The symbol 0 is a constant (or zero-place function) which will be interpreted as the null word.

To construct the formula A, form the conjunction of the following formulas:

Initial conditions:

$$S(0,0) \wedge \neg S(0,p^+) \wedge \text{Rempty}(0,p) \wedge \text{Linitial}(0)$$

End letter:

$$E(t) \leftrightarrow R(t,0)$$

Register modification:

$$\text{Delete}(Lt) \supset [R(t^+,p) \leftrightarrow R(t,p^+)]$$
$$[\text{Print}(Lt) \wedge S(t,p)] \supset [R(t^+,p) \leftrightarrow \text{Write}(Lt)]$$
$$[\text{Print}(Lt) \wedge \neg S(t,p)] \supset [R(t^+,p) \leftrightarrow R(t,p)]$$

Length modification:

$$[\text{Delete}(Lt) \wedge \text{Eempty}(t)] \supset [S(t^+,p) \leftrightarrow S(t,p)]$$
$$[\text{Delete}(Lt) \wedge \neg\text{Eempty}(t)] \supset [S(t^+,p) \leftrightarrow S(t,p^+)]$$
$$\text{Print}(Lt) \supset [S(t^+,p^+) \leftrightarrow S(t,p)]$$
$$\text{Print}(Lt) \supset \neg(t^+,0)$$

Next statement:

$$Lt^+ \leftrightarrow \text{Goto}(Lt,Et)$$

Does not halt:

$$\neg\text{Stop}(Lt)$$

LEMMA 7.30. The sentence $\forall t\, \forall p\, A(0,t,t^+,p,p^+)$ is satisfiable in $\langle W,0,\varsigma\rangle$ iff R, L, E, and S are interpreted as above on this page and $\mathfrak{T}$ does not halt when started with the null word in the SRM register.

Proof. If R, L, E, and S are interpreted as described on p. 186, then certainly the sentence $\forall t \, \forall p \, A(0,t,t^+,p,p^+)$ is true if $\mathfrak{T}$ does not halt when started with 0 in the SRM register. The converse is proved by induction on t. The initial conditions determine the values of $S(0,p)$ and $R(0,p)$, for all p, and the value of $L(0)$. The formula $E(t) \leftrightarrow R(t,0)$ determines the value of $E(0)$. Since $L(0)$ must be the initial label, $\neg\text{Stop}(Lt)$ means that $L(0)$ is not the label of a stop instruction.

By the induction hypothesis, any interpretation in $\langle W,0,\varsigma\rangle$ of R, L, E, and S must have the correct values at time t, and $\mathfrak{T}$ does not halt at time t. The "next statement", "length modification", and "register modification" components of A ensure that the values of any interpretations of L, S, and R will have the same values as described on p. 186 for $t^+ = t + 1$. The formula $E(t) \leftrightarrow R(t,0)$ determines the value of E at t^+ and $\neg\text{Stop}(Lt)$ implies that $\mathfrak{T}$ does not halt at time t^+. It is important to note that exactly one of the formulas Delete, Print, and Stop will be true for each Lt; since $\neg\text{Stop}(Lt)$ is true for each t, exactly one of the two formulas Delete(Lt) or Print(Lt) must be true for each t. ▌

We now want to make two modifications to A without changing the lemma just proved. The first modification eliminates all occurrences of p^+.

Introduce a new predicate R' and conjoin to A the formula

$$R'(p,t) \leftrightarrow R(p,t^+)$$

(notice the reversal of the letters p and t), and replace all occurrences of $R(t,p^+)$ in A with $R'(t,p)$. Also introduce a new predicate S', conjoin to A the formula

$$S'(p,t) \leftrightarrow S(p,t^+)$$

and

replace $S(0,p^+)$ with $S'(0,p)$,
replace $S(t,p^+)$ with $S'(t,p)$,
replace $S(t^+,p^+)$ with $S'(t^+,p)$

The result is a formula having the form $A'(0,t,t^+,p)$.

The second modification is made so that the constant symbol 0 occurs only once. Introduce a new predicate Z, conjoin to A' the formula

$$Z0 \wedge \neg Zt^+$$

replace $S(0,0) \wedge \neg S'(0,p) \wedge \text{Rempty}(0,p) \wedge \text{Linitial}(0)$ with $Zt \supset [S(t,t) \wedge \neg S'(t,p) \wedge \text{Rempty}(t,p) \wedge \text{Linitial}(t)]$. Also replace $E(t) \leftrightarrow R(t,0)$ with $Zp \supset [E(t) \leftrightarrow R(t,p)]$ and replace $\text{Print}(Lt) \supset \neg S(t^+,0)$ with $[\text{Print}(Lt) \wedge Zp] \supset \neg S(t^+,p)$.

The result has the form

$$\forall t\, \forall p\, [Z0 \wedge M(t,t^+,p)]$$

which is equivalent to

$$Z0 \wedge \forall t\, \forall p\, M(t,t^+,p)$$

where M is a matrix involving only the terms t, t^+, and p. This formula is satisfiable in $\langle W,0,\varsigma\rangle$ iff R, L, E, S are interpreted as before, R', S' and Z are interpreted in the obvious way, and $\mathcal{T}$ does not halt, starting with the null word.

LEMMA 7.31. For any matrices $Z(x)$ and $M(t,u,p)$

$$\exists x\, Z(x) \wedge \forall t\, \exists u\, \forall p\, M(t,u,p) \tag{7-5}$$

is satisfiable iff

$$Z(0) \wedge \forall t\, \forall p\, M(t,t^+,p) \tag{7-6}$$

is satisfiable in $\langle W,0,\varsigma\rangle$.

Proof. Assume P_1, P_2, ..., P_k are the predicates which occur in Z or M and assume that $\langle D,\bar{P}_1,\ldots,\bar{P}_k\rangle$ is a model of (7-5). Formula (7-5) asserts that there is an element a in D and a function $f(t)$ which, for each $t \in D$, gives a $u \in D$ such that $Z(a) \wedge \forall t\, \forall p\, M(t,ft,p)$ is true, that is, $\langle D,a,f,\bar{P}_1,\ldots,\bar{P}_k\rangle$ is a model of (7-6). (The function f is often called a Skolem function.)

Let $\bar{\bar{D}} = \{a,fa,ffa,\ldots\}$, which is the smallest set containing a which is closed under f. Let $\bar{\bar{f}} = f\,|\,\bar{\bar{D}}$ and $\bar{\bar{P}}_i = \bar{P}_i\,|\,(\bar{\bar{D}})^r$, where r is the number of inputs for P_i. Since (7-6) is a universally quantified matrix, $\langle\bar{\bar{D}},a,\bar{\bar{f}},\bar{\bar{P}}_1,\ldots,\bar{\bar{P}}_k\rangle$ is also a model of (7-6).

Define $h\colon W \to \bar{\bar{D}}$ by

$$h(m) = f^m(a)$$

Note that h is onto $\bar{\bar{D}}$, $h(0) = a$, and $h(\varsigma t) = h(t+1) = f(ht)$.

Define

$$P_i^*(x_1,\ldots,x_r) = \bar{\bar{P}}_i(hx_1,\ldots,hx_r)$$

With these definitions h is a homomorphism from $\langle W,0,\varsigma,P_1^*,\ldots,P_k^*\rangle$ onto $\langle\bar{\bar{D}},a,\bar{\bar{f}},\bar{\bar{P}}_1,\ldots,\bar{\bar{P}}_k\rangle$ and so $\langle W,0,\varsigma,P_1^*,\ldots,P_k^*\rangle$ also satisfies (7-6) by Theorem 7.29.

For the converse, it is obvious that any interpretation which satisfies (7-6) also satisfies (7-5). ▮

THEOREM 7.32. The predicate calculus is undecidable.

Proof. Given any SRM program $\mathcal{T}$, construct formula (7-5)

$$\exists x\, Z(x) \wedge \forall t\, \exists u\, \forall p\, M(t,u,p)$$

which, by Lemma 7.31, is satisfiable iff (7-6) is satisfiable in $\langle W,0,\varsigma\rangle$ iff $\mathcal{P}$ does not halt when started with the null word in the SRM register, by Lemma 7.30. Since the halting problem (on the null input) for SRM programs is undecidable, the set of satisfiable sentences is also not recursive. By Corollary 7.27, it follows that the set of provable sentences is also not recursive. ∎

EXERCISES

1. Prove Theorem 7.29.
2. Construct the formula

$$Z(0) \wedge \forall t\, \forall p\, M(t,t^+,p)$$

for the example SRM program given between Theorem 7.29 and Lemma 7.30 in this section.

7.10 History

The theory of formal languages, as presented in this chapter, was developed initially by Post [1943], although some of the basic ideas may be found in Thue [1914]. Post's 1943 paper discusses his "canonical systems", now called Post canonical systems or Post production systems, and also the normal systems of Section 7.4. A proof of the unsolvability of the PCP appeared in Post [1946].

The special types of grammars discussed in Section 7.7 were defined and first investigated by the mathematical linguist Chomsky [1959]. He was motivated by the problem of developing a formal grammar for English and other natural languages. Interesting properties of the context-sensitive, context-free, and linear languages have been investigated by many people. Two texts containing many of these results are those of Eilenberg [1973] and Hopcroft and Ullman [1969]. Many of the undecidable properties of these grammars were first investigated by Bar-Hillel, Perles, and Shamir [1961].

The undecidability of the predicate calculus was first proved by Church [1936b]. The proof given in Section 7.9 is a modification of the one given by Büchi [1962], who used TM programs rather than SRM programs.

The undecidable property of left (right)-linear grammars mentioned at the end of Section 7.8 is due to Eilenberg [1973]. There is an interesting connection with the open problem given as Exercise 4 of Section 7.6, because Eilenberg proved his undecidability result by reducing the PCP to it. In the reduction, there is a correspondence between the number of rules in the PCP and the size of the terminal alphabet of the grammar. If the problem of Exercise 4 is undecidable, then Eilenberg's problem will be undecidable with a two-letter alphabet.

CHAPTER 8

Reducibility

The method of reduction discussed in Chapter 6 is not only a useful tool for proving that various problems are undecidable but also is a means by which the difficulty of undecidable problems may be compared. For example, if problem P is reducible to problem P', that is, the solvability of P' implies the solvability of P, then P' is at least as difficult as P. If P is reducible to P' and P' is reducible to P, then P and P' are equivalent with respect to level or degree of difficulty. Notice that all recursive problems are equivalent in this sense. Unfortunately, this is not true for r.e. problems. In this chapter we prove an important theorem which states that there are r.e. sets whose decision problems are not related in the above sense. The proof uses an ingenious method, called a priority argument, to enumerate the required r.e. sets. This method has important applications in abstract complexity theory (see Chapter 9) as well as in computability theory.

8.1 Programs with Oracles

Let $f: W^r \rightarrow W^s$ be any function, not necessarily PL-computable. Suppose statements of the form

$$(V_1,\ldots,V_s) \leftarrow f(U_1,\ldots,U_r); \tag{8-1}$$

are allowed in PL programs, with the interpretation that if $(U_1,\ldots,U_r) \in \operatorname{dom} f$, then the statement assigns to the variables $V_1, \ldots, V_s$ the value of the function f applied to the variables $U_1, \ldots, U_r$. If $f(U_1,\ldots,U_r)$ is undefined, then control never exits from (8-1).

If f is a PL-computable function, then the statement (8-1) may be replaced by legal PL statements. If not, then it is possible to use (8-1) to construct programs which compute non-PL-computable functions. For example, the program

$$\text{Y1} \leftarrow \chi_H(\text{X1});$$

computes the characteristic function of the nonrecursive set H. Since H is not recursive, neither is χ_H.

If the program $\mathcal{T}$ computes the function g and $\mathcal{T}$ contains statements of the form (8-1) for some f, then (the problem of computing) g is reducible to (the problem of computing) f. That is, if f is PL-computable, then g is also PL-computable. Of course, if f is not PL-computable, then there is no effective procedure for executing $\mathcal{T}$. Indeed, "programs" which contain statements of the form (8-1) do not in general define effective procedures, that is, they are not really programs. However, it is still possible to study the mathematical properties of such programs. One merely assumes that there is a method for evaluating (8-1), possibly by obtaining the answer from some external source or *oracle*. Since we are interested in the relative difficulty of undecidable problems, the properties of the oracle are not important; all that matters is that it supplies the correct answers (of course in a noneffective nonobservable manner). Given the existence of an oracle for a function f, we may then study the class of functions computable with the assistance of such an oracle.

A function is *f-PL-computable* if it is computable by a PL program in which statements of the form (8-1) are allowed.

THEOREM 8.1. If f is PL-computable, then a function is f-PL-computable iff it is PL-computable.

Proof. Each occurrence of a statement which consults the oracle can be replaced by ordinary PL statements. ▮

The notion of f-computability can also be defined for machine programs, LMA's, and the partial recursive functions. Let us first consider the partial recursive functions.

A function is *f-partial recursive* if it is one of the functions f, π, ς, ι, or ζ, or is obtained from these functions by a finite number of the operations composition, combination, exponentiation, or repetition. If g is f-partial recursive, we write $g \leq f$ and say that g is *reducible* to f. A function is *f-recursive* if it is f-partial recursive and total.

THEOREM 8.2. The class of f-partial recursive functions is the smallest class containing f and all of the partial recursive functions which is closed under the operations of composition, combination, exponentiation, and repetition.

Proof. Exercise 1. ▮

THEOREM 8.3. If f is partial recursive, then g is f-partial recursive iff g is partial recursive.

Proof. Exercise 2. ▮

THEOREM 8.4. If g is partial recursive, then g is f-partial recursive for every function f, that is, $g \leq f$, for all f.

Proof. Immediate from the definition of $g \leq f$. ▮

If $g \leq f$ and if there is some way to compute f, then there is a way to compute g. Thus, in one sense, g is no more difficult to compute than f. That is the intuitive meaning of the relation $\leq$. If $g \leq f$, this does not imply that a particular program for computing g is any simpler than a program for f; such questions dealing with the difficulty of computations will be discussed in Chapters 9 and 10.

THEOREM 8.5. For all functions, f, $f \leq f$.

Proof. Trivially, f is f-partial recursive. ▮

THEOREM 8.6. If $f \leq g$ and $g \leq h$, then $f \leq h$.

Proof. The function g can be expressed in terms of h, the initial functions ζ, ς, ι, π and the operations composition, combination, repetition, and exponentiation. Similarly, f can be expressed in terms of g. In the expression for f, replace all occurrence of g by the expression for g which involves h. The result will be an expression for f involving h (but not g). Thus $f \leq h$. ▮

Theorems 8.5 and 8.6 assert that the relation $\leq$ is reflexive and transitive.

The next result states that we need to consider only oracles with a single input and output.

THEOREM 8.7. If $f: W^r \to W^s$, $r,s \geq 1$, then there is an $f': W \to W$ such that $g \leq f$ iff $g \leq f'$.

Proof. Let $f' = \beta_s \circ f \circ \beta_r^{-1}$, where β_r and β_s are the appropriate pairing functions defined in Section 3.8. Then $f' \leq f$, and also $f \leq f'$, since $f = \beta_s^{-1} \circ f' \circ \beta_r$. The theorem follows from Theorem 8.6. ▮

We now consider the extension of other algorithmic languages to include programs which consult oracles. Suppose the instruction $f \times \iota_\infty = f \times \iota \times \iota \times \cdots$ is added to the instruction set of the URM. Call this new machine the *f-URM*. The new instruction causes f to be applied to the word stored in register 0 and the result is left in register 0. By Theorem 8.7, we need to consider only oracle instructions applicable to a single register. Functions computed by an f-URM program are called *f-URM-computable*.

We may also allow a LMA to consult an oracle. Interpret the instruction

$$k{:}/l; \tag{8-2}$$

applied to the word x to yield $f(x')\$y$ if $x = x'\$y$ and \$ does not occur in x', that is, $\$ \not\leq x'$. The statement with label l is then executed. If $\$ \not\leq x$ or $f(x')$ is undefined, then the instruction is undefined and the computation "hangs up" at that point.

The language of f-LMA's is obtained from the language of LMA's by permitting the use of statements of the form (8-2).

As was done in Chapter 5, the f-LMA's may be effectively enumerated; indeed, a primitive recursive function $\mathcal{A}: \Sigma^* \to \Psi^*$, where $\Psi = \Sigma \cup \{\$, a, b, :,$

$\rightarrow$,/,;}, may be defined with the property that $\mathcal{A}(0)$, $\mathcal{A}(1)$, ... is an enumeration of all f-LMA'S. Recall that $\mathcal{A}$ was originally defined as

$$\mathcal{A}(m) = \begin{cases} \kappa(m) & \text{if } \kappa(m) \text{ is an LMA} \\ 0{:}0 \rightarrow 0/0; & \text{otherwise} \end{cases}$$

where κ is the bijection from Σ^* to Ψ^*. The new $\mathcal{A}$ is defined similarly except that some words $\kappa(m) \in \Psi^*$ that were previously not LMA's are now f-LMA's. Let ${}^r_s\varphi^f_m$ be the function with r inputs and s outputs computed by the f-LMA $\mathcal{A}(m)$. Let $\varphi^f_m = {}^1_1\varphi^f_m$.

All of the results obtained so far can be easily generalized to theorems about f-computability. The proofs given need only some minor modifications and additions to apply to the generalized theorems. We give a sample of some of the important generalizations. The reader is urged to carefully generalize the proof of a few of these results.

THEOREM 8.8. A function g is f-partial recursive iff it is computed by an f-PL program, an f-LMA, the f-URM, the f-SRM, or the f-TM.
Proof. The definition of the f-SRM and f-TM is left as Exercise 4. See Theorem 5.8. ▮

Let

$$T^f_r(m,x,k) = \begin{cases} 1 & \text{if the } m\text{th } f\text{-LMA halts in exactly} \\ & k \text{ steps on input } x \in W^r \\ 0 & \text{otherwise} \end{cases}$$

THEOREM 8.9. The function T^f_r is f-primitive recursive.
Proof. The definition of f-primitive recursive is similar to f-partial recursive except that repetition is not allowed. See Theorem 5.13. ▮

THEOREM 8.10. For each r, there is a primitive recursive function K'_r, such that for all r', s, m, x, y, and all functions $f: W \rightarrow W$,

$${}^{r+r'}_{s}\varphi^f_m(x,y) = {}^{r'}_{s}\varphi^f_{K'r(m,x)}(y)$$

Note that K'_r is independent of f.
Proof. See Theorem 5.19, the index theorem. ▮

A set $A \subseteq W^r$ is *f-recursive* if χ_A is f-recursive, or equivalently if $\chi_A \leq f$ (χ_A is f-partial recursive), because χ_A is always total. A set A is *f-recursively enumerable* if $A = \operatorname{ran} g$, for some f-partial recursive function g. Intuitively, a set A is f-recursive if the effective computability of f implies the effective solvability of the decision problem for A. Similarly, A is f-r.e. if A can be effectively enumerated by PL programs containing statements of form $Y \leftarrow f(X)$.

THEOREM 8.11. $A \subseteq W^r$ is f-r.e. iff

a. $A = \text{ran}\, g$, g f-partial recursive
b. $A = \emptyset$ or $A = \text{ran}\, g$, g f-primitive recursive
c. $A = \emptyset$ or $A = \text{ran}\, g$, g f-recursive
d. A is finite or $A = \text{ran}\, g$, g f-recursive and 1-1
e. $A = \text{dom}\, g$, g f-partial recursive
f. $\chi_A(x) = \bigvee_y g(x,y)$, g f-recursive
g. ι_A is f-partial recursive
h. A is accepted by an f-TM program, an f-SRM program, or an f-PL program

Proof. See Theorems 6.3 and 6.5. ▮

THEOREM 8.12. A set $A \subseteq W^r$ is f-recursive iff both A and $\bar{A}$ are f-r.e.
Proof. See Theorem 6.6. ▮

Let $D_m^f = \text{dom}\, \varphi_m^f$. Then D_0^f, D_1^f, D_2^f, ... is an enumeration of all of the f-r.e. subsets of W. Let $H^f = \{x \mid x \in D_x^f\} = \{x \mid \varphi_x^f(x)\downarrow\}$.

THEOREM 8.13. For each function f, H^f is f-.r.e., but not f-recursive. Also $\overline{H^f}$ is not f-.re.
Proof. See Corollary 5.15, Theorem 6.4, and Corollary 6.7. ▮

If B is χ_A-recursive (or χ_A-r.e.) for some set A, then we say that B is *A-recursive* (or *A-r.e.*). If B is A-recursive, we write $B \leq A$ instead of $\chi_B \leq \chi_A$. We also write H^A instead of H^{χ_A}. Using this notation, the following facts (except for g) follow immediately from or are restatements of theorems already established.

THEOREM 8.14. Let $A \subseteq W^r$, then

a. there is a set $A' \subseteq W$ such that $B \leq A'$ iff $B \leq A$
b. $\bar{A} \leq A$
c. $B \leq A$ if B is recursive; in particular. $\emptyset \leq A$.
d. $B \leq \emptyset$ iff B is recursive
e. H^A is A-r.e. and $\overline{H^A}$ is not A-r.e.
f. $H^A \nleq A$; in particular $H \nleq \emptyset$, since $H^{\emptyset} = H$
g. $A \leq H^A$
h. $B \leq A$ iff B is A-r.e. and $\bar{B}$ is A-r.e.

Proof of g. Given x, obtain an A-LMA with index $f(x)$ which halts on all inputs or no inputs depending on whether or not $x \in A$. Then $x \in A$ iff $f(x) \in H^A$ iff $\varphi_{f(x)}^A(fx)\downarrow$. ▮

The next theorem will be only used once later (see Theorem 8.51), but should help the reader to understand how LMA's with oracles perform computations.

We restrict our attention to oracles for sets. Suppose an LMA oracle computes the characteristic function of a set A. For a given input to the LMA, we can effectively simulate the computation of the LMA until an instruction to compute χ_A is reached. At that point, we can record the input w to the oracle and proceed to simultaneously simulate two computations, one based on the assumption that $\chi_A(w) = 1$ and one based on the assumption that $\chi_A(w) = 0$. Either of these computations may in turn reach a point at which the oracle is consulted and the simulation process branches again. The simulation of an LMA computing with input x is shown schematically in Figure 8-1.

From time to time, one of the branches of the simulated computation may terminate. At that point, we may record the finite set F_u, consisting of all inputs to the oracle which produced a "yes" answer and F_v, the finite set of inputs to the oracle yielding a "no" answer (see Section 6.6). In Figure 8-1,

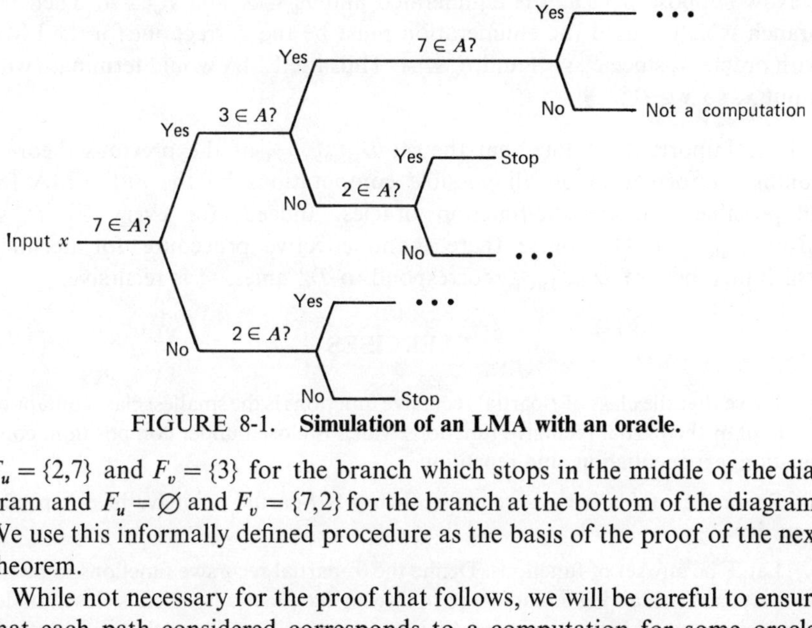

FIGURE 8-1. **Simulation of an LMA with an oracle.**

$F_u = \{2,7\}$ and $F_v = \{3\}$ for the branch which stops in the middle of the diagram and $F_u = \varnothing$ and $F_v = \{7,2\}$ for the branch at the bottom of the diagram. We use this informally defined procedure as the basis of the proof of the next theorem.

While not necessary for the proof that follows, we will be careful to ensure that each path considered corresponds to a computation for some oracle. This means that if at one point on a path an answer from the oracle is assumed for some y then all later answers for y along the path must be the same as the first one, that is, $F_u \cap F_v = \varnothing$. For example, the path in Figure 8-1 with answers 7-yes, 3-yes, 7-no cannot be a computation.

THEOREM 8.15. There is a recursive function simulate such that $x \in D_m^A$ iff for some terminating computation branch as described above, $F_u \subseteq A$, $F_v \subseteq \bar{A}$ and $\beta_3(x,u,v) \in D_{\mathbf{simulate}(m)}$.

Proof. Given a χ_A-LMA with oracle A and an input x, the procedure described above may be effectively specified. This procedure may be modified to "simultaneously" simulate computations for all inputs by first simulating one step with input 0, then one step for inputs 0 and 1, then one step for inputs 0, 1, 2, etc. This trick was used in the proof of Theorem 6.3. Whenever any branch of a computation with input x stops, then $\beta_3(x,u,v)$ is enumerated, where u and v are indices for the finite sets F_u and F_v described previously. Thus simulate(m), an index for the set enumerated, may be effectively found given m. By Church's thesis, simulate(m) is recursive.

Suppose $x \in D_m^A$, then eventually the simulation process will complete the simulation of the "correct" branch of the computation for input x. The correct branch is, of course, the one for which the computation simulated is identical to that which would really be made by the LMA with oracle A. In this case $F_u \subseteq A$, $F_v \subseteq \bar{A}$, and $\beta_3(x,u,v)$ is enumerated as required.

Now suppose $\beta_3(x,u,v)$ is enumerated and $F_u \subseteq A$ and $F_v \subseteq \bar{A}$. Then the branch which caused the enumeration must be the correct one for the LMA with oracle A, since $F_u \subseteq A$ and $F_v \subseteq \bar{A}$. Thus the LMA would terminate with input x, so $x \in D_m^A$. ∎

It is important to note that the set $D_{\text{simulate}(m)}$ of the previous theorem contains information on all possible computations by the mth LMA for all possible characteristic-function oracles. Indeed, for every A, $D_m^A \subseteq {}_1\beta_3(D_{\text{simulate}(m)})$. Of course there is no effective procedure for deciding which members of $D_{\text{simulate}(m)}$ correspond to D_m^A unless A is recursive.

EXERCISES

1. Prove that the class of f-partial recursive functions is the smallest class containing f and all of the partial recursive functions which is closed under composition, combination, exponentiation, and repetition.

2. Prove that if f is partial recursive, then g is f-partial recursive iff g is partial recursive.

3. Let $\mathfrak{F}$ be any set of functions. Define the $\mathfrak{F}$-partial recursive functions to be the smallest class containing $\mathfrak{F}$ and the partial recursive functions which is closed under composition, combination, exponentiation, and repetition. Show that if $\mathfrak{F}$ is finite, there is a single function f such that a function is $\mathfrak{F}$-partial recursive iff it is f-partial recursive.

4. Give the instruction set $\mathfrak{R}$ for an f-SRM and an f-TM.

5. Assume $A \cup B = W$ for r.e. sets A and B. Show that $A \leq A \cap B$. What if $A \cap B = \varnothing$?

6. Write a PL program which computes $\chi_{\bar{H}}$ using a χ_H oracle, that is, show that $\bar{H}$ is χ_H-PL-computable.

8.2 Degrees

In this section we will consider only reducibility of sets. The results given may easily be generalized to arbitrary total functions. Whenever possible, we will refer to the sets, rather than their characteristic functions, using A is B-recursive, $A \leq B$, and A is B-r.e. in place of χ_A is χ_B-recursive, $\chi_A \leq \chi_B$, and χ_A is χ_B-r.e., respectively.

Recall that $\leq$ is reflexive and transitive, but not symmetric, since $\emptyset \leq H$, but $H \nleq \emptyset$. Given any reflexive and transitive relation, there is always a natural way to define an equivalance relation: Let $A \equiv B$ mean $A \leq B$ and $B \leq A$.

THEOREM 8.16. $\equiv$ is an equivalence relation.

Proof. Exercise 1. ▮

The equivalence class $d(A) = \{B \mid B \equiv A\}$ to which a set A belongs is called the *Turing degree of unsolvability* of A, or simply the *degree* of A.

If $A \leq B$ but $B \nleq A$, that is, $A \not\equiv B$, then we write $A < B$.

THEOREM 8.17. If $A < B \leq C$ or $A \leq B < C$, then $A < C$.

Proof. Let $A < B \leq C$. Then $A \leq B$ and $B \leq C$, so $A \leq C$ by the transitivity of $\leq$ (Theorem 8.6). If $C \leq A$, then by the same theorem $B \leq A$, contrary to assumption. Thus $A < C$. The second part is proved similarly. ▮

THEOREM 8.18. If $A \equiv A'$, $B \equiv B'$, and $A \leq B$ (or $A < B$), then $A' \leq B'$ (or $A' < B'$).

Proof. Exercise 2. ▮

By Theorem 8.18, it makes sense to extend the orderings $<$ and $\leq$ to degrees. Define $d(A) \leq d(B)$ to mean $A \leq B$. Theorem 8.18 says that the definition does not depend upon which members A and B of the degrees are used.

The next theorem follows immediately from results already observed in Section 8.1.

THEOREM 8.19. Let $A \subseteq W^r$ be an arbitrary set.

a. $d(B) \leq d(A)$ for any recursive set B
b. $d(\emptyset) = d(A)$ iff A is recursive
c. there is an $A' \subseteq W$ such that $d(A) = d(A')$
d. $d(H^A) > d(A)$ ▮

THEOREM 8.20. There is a smallest degree, but no largest degree.

Proof. The set of recursive sets $d(\emptyset)$ is a smallest degree, but for each A, $d(H^A) > d(A)$, so that, for no A, can $d(A)$ be a largest degree. ▮

In Section 8.4 we will prove that there are r.e. sets which are incomparable under the ordering $\leq$, that is, neither $A \leq B$ nor $B \leq A$. However, for any two sets A and B there is a third set C such that $A \leq C$ and $B \leq C$. Such a C is called an *upper bound* for A and B (with respect to $\leq$). In fact, any two sets A and B also have a least upper bound, that is, there is a C such that if $A \leq C'$ and $B \leq C'$ for some C', then $C \leq C'$. Note that the least upper bound is not unique since, if C is a least upper bound of A and B and $C' \equiv C$, then C' is also a least upper bound.

THEOREM 8.21. Any two sets A and B have a least upper bound with respect to the ordering $\leq$.

Proof. First suppose $A, B \subseteq W$. The construction of a least upper bound C is motivated by the problem of the innkeeper with an infinite number of rooms, all full. Suppose an infinite number of new guests arrive; what can he do to accomodate them? The answer is to have each guest in the inn move to a room whose number is double the number of his present room. The guest in room 1 moves to room 2; the guest in room 2 moves to room 4, etc. The new guests may then occupy rooms 1, 3, 5, ...

Define $A \sqcup B = (2 \times A) \cup (2 \times B + 1) = \{y \mid y = 2x, x \in A\} \cup \{y \mid y = 2x + 1, x \in B\}$. ($A$ corresponds to the old guests, B to the new arrivals.) We now prove that $A \sqcup B$ is a least upper bound for A and B. $\chi_A(x) = \chi_{A \sqcup B}(2x)$, which is $A \sqcup B$-recursive. Similarly $B \leq A \sqcup B$. Suppose C is some upper bound for A and B. Since

$$\chi_{A \sqcup B}(x) = \begin{cases} \chi_A(x/2) & \text{if } 2 \mid x \\ \chi_B((x \dot{-} 1)/2) & \text{if } \neg(2 \mid x) \end{cases}$$

and χ_A and χ_B are C-recursive, so is $A \sqcup B$, that is, $A \sqcup B \leq C$.

Now suppose A and B are arbitrary subsets of W^r. Then by Theorem 8.14a, there are sets $A', B' \subseteq W$, such that $A \equiv A'$ and $B \equiv B'$ and $A' \sqcup B'$ is a least upper bound for A and B. ▌

COROLLARY 8.22. For any sets A and B, $d(A \sqcup B)$ is a unique least upper bound for $d(A)$ and $d(B)$.

Proof. Exercise 3. ▌

Although there is no maximal set under the ordering $\leq$, there is an r.e. set which is maximal among all r.e. sets. Such an r.e. set is called *complete*. More generally, a set C is *A-complete* if C is A-r.e. and for all sets B, B is A-r.e. implies $B \leq C$.

THEOREM 8.23. The set H^A is A complete; in particular, H is complete.

Proof. Let B be any A-r.e. set with index m, that is, $B = D_m^A$. By the index theorem, there is a primitive recursive function f such that

$$\varphi_{f(x)}^A(y) = \varphi_m^A(x) \qquad \text{for all } y$$

Then $f(x) \in H^A$ iff $\varphi^A_{f(x)}(fx)\downarrow$ iff $\varphi^A_m(x)\downarrow$ iff $x \in D^A_m = B$. Thus $\chi_B(x) = \chi_{H^A} \circ f(x)$ and so B is H^A-recursive, that is, $B \leq H^A$. ∎

We have just proved that if B is r.e., then $B \leq H$. Note that the converse is false, since $\overline{H} \leq H$, but $\overline{H}$ is not r.e.

If A is recursive, then $A \equiv \varnothing$. If A is r.e. but not recursive, then $\varnothing < A \leq H$. A natural question is: Are there any sets A such that $\varnothing < A < H$? This is known as *Post's Problem* and in Section 8.4 we will show that there are such sets.

EXERCISES

1. Show that $A \equiv B$ iff $A \leq B$ and $B \leq A$ is an equivalence relation.

2. Show that $A \equiv A'$, $B, \equiv B'$, and $A\,B \leq$ imply $A' \leq B'$.

3. Show that $d(A \sqcup B)$ is a unique least upper bound for $d(A)$ and $d(B)$.

4. Show that, for any sets A and B, if the *symmetric difference* $A \,\Delta\, B = (A - B) \cup (B - A)$ is finite, then $A \equiv B$.

5. Give sets A, B, and C such that A is B-r.e. and B is C-r.e., but A is not C-r.e.

8.3 Strong Reducibility

In Theorem 6.12, we showed that H is reducible to several sets A by exhibiting a recursive function h such that $x \in H$ iff $h(x) \in A$. Since $\chi_H = \chi_A \circ h$, H is A-recursive. In general A is *strongly reducible* to B, written $A \leq_s B$, if $\chi_A = \chi_B \circ f$ for some recursive f. If, in addition, f can be chosen to be a 1-1 function, then A is 1-*reducible* to B and we write $A \leq_1 B$. Also define

$$A \equiv_s B \text{ if } A \leq_s B \text{ and } B \leq_s A$$
$$A \equiv_1 B \text{ if } A \leq_1 B \text{ and } B \leq_1 A$$

It is easy to verify that $\equiv_1$ and $\equiv_s$ are equivalence relations. The equivalence classes of $\equiv_s$ ($\equiv_1$) are called s-*degrees* (1-*degrees*) *of unsolvability*.

Strong reducibility is a common and useful type of reducibility in recursion theory as well as in other branches of mathematics. If A is strongly reducible to B via the recursive function f, then to decide whether an arbitrary x is in A, it is sufficient to decide membership in B for a single effectively determined value $f(x)$. With general reducibility, to answer membership questions about A, an oracle for B may have to be consulted arbitrarily often. In addition, it is not even possible to decide which questions, after the first one, will be asked of the oracle, since program branches can depend upon the oracle's answers.

In this section, we will be interested in relationships between the various types of reducibility only for r.e. sets. These problems were first considered by Post, who hoped to obtain a type of reducibility for which all nonrecursive r.e. sets would be equivalent. He was able to demonstrate that this was not true for strong reducibility, 1-reducibility and another type of reducibility, called truth-table reducibility, which we will not consider. For general reducibility ($\leq$), Post was unable to either prove or disprove the equivalence of all nonrecursive r.e. sets. A proof that they are not all equivalent will be given in the next section.

The following theorem states some easily proved facts about strong reducibility.

THEOREM 8.24.

a. if $A \leq_1 B$, then $A \leq_s B$
b. if $A \leq_s B$, then $A \leq B$
c. $\leq_1$ and $\leq_s$ are reflexive and transitive
d. $\equiv_1$ and $\equiv_s$ are equivalence relations
e. for each $A \subseteq W^r$, $r > 0$, there is a set $A' \subseteq W$ such that $A' \equiv_1 A$, and hence $A' \equiv_s A$
f. there are sets A and B such that $A \leq_s B$, but $A \nleq_1 B$
g. if $A \leq_s B$ or $A \leq_1 B$ and B is recursive, then A is recursive
h. if $A \leq_s B$ or $A \leq_1 B$ and B is r.e., then A is r.e.
i. if $A \leq_s B$, then $\bar{A} \leq_s \bar{B}$; also if $A \leq_1 B$, then $\bar{A} \leq_1 \bar{B}$
j. there are recursive sets A and B and nonrecursive sets A and B such that neither $A \leq_s B$ nor $B \leq_s A$ (hence neither $A \leq_1 B$ nor $B \leq_1 A$)
k. there is an r.e. set A such that $A \nleq_s \bar{A}$ (and hence $A \nleq_1 \bar{A}$)

Proof. Parts a–d follow immediately from the definitions.

e. let $A' = \beta_r(A)$
f. let $A = \{0,1\}$ and $B = \{1\}$, let $h(x) = (x \leq 1)$; then $\chi_A = \chi_B \circ h$; on the other hand if $\chi_A = \chi_B \circ h$ for some h, then $h(0) = h(1) = 1$, since $x \in A$ iff $h(x) \in B$ and $B = \{1\}$; thus h cannot be 1-1
g. if $\chi_A = \chi_B \circ f$, f is recursive, and χ_B is recursive, then χ_A is recursive
h. if $A \leq_s B$ then $\chi_A = \chi_B \circ f$, f recursive; if B is r.e., then $\chi_B(x) = \bigvee_y g(x, y)$ for some recursive g, by Theorem 6.3f; then $\chi_A(x) = \chi_B \circ f(x) = \bigvee_y g(fx,y)$, so A is also r.e. by Theorem 6.3f
i. if $\chi_A = \chi_B \circ f$, then $\chi_{\bar{A}} = \neg \circ \chi_A = \neg \circ \chi_B \circ f = \chi_{\bar{B}} \circ f$
j. the recursive sets $\varnothing$ and W are incomparable; by (*h*), $\bar{H} \nleq_s H$ and so by (i), $H \nleq_s \bar{H}$, neither H nor $\bar{H}$ is recursive
k. as shown in (j), $H \nleq_s \bar{H}$. ▮

An r.e. set B is *s-complete* (*1-complete*) if $A \leq_s B$ ($A \leq_1 B$), for each r.e. set A.

THEOREM 8.25. H is s-complete.

Proof. Let A be r.e. with index m, that is, $A = D_m$. Define the primitive recursive function f by

$$\varphi_{f(x)}(y) = \begin{cases} 1 & \text{if } \varphi_m(x)\downarrow \\ \uparrow & \text{otherwise} \end{cases}$$

Then $f(x) \in H$ iff $\varphi_{f(x)}(fx)\downarrow$ iff $\varphi_m(x)\downarrow$ (by the definition of f) iff $x \in D_m = A$. Thus $\chi_A = \chi_H \circ f$ and $A \leq_s H$. The same proof was used in Theorem 8.23 to show that H^A is A-complete. ▮

Instead of showing directly that H is 1-complete, we will give another characterization of the class of 1-complete subsets of W and show that H is in this class.

An r.e. set $C \subseteq W$ is *creative* if there is a recursive function f such that if $D_x \subseteq \bar{C}$, then $f(x) \in \bar{C} - D_x$ (see Figure 8-2).

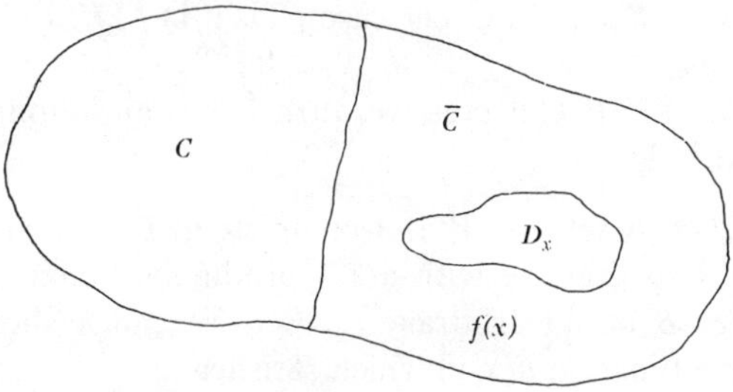

FIGURE 8-2. **A creative set.**

Recall that an r.e. set C is recursive iff $\bar{C}$ is r.e., that is, $\bar{C} = D_x$, for some x. For each x which is a candidate as an index for $\bar{C}$ in the sense that $D_x \subseteq \bar{C}$, the function f produces a value $f(x) \in \bar{C} - D_x$, which shows that $\bar{C}$ is not r.e. For this reason, f is sometimes called a *productive* function.

THEOREM 8.26. H is creative.
Proof. For $D_x \subseteq \bar{H}$, $\imath(x) = x \in \bar{H} - D_x$, so the identity function is a productive function for H. ▮

We will prove that a set $A \subseteq W$ is s-complete iff A is 1-complete iff A is creative, but first the following lemma is needed.

LEMMA 8.27. Each creative set C has a 1-1 productive function.
Proof. Let C be creative and let f be the recursive productive function such that $D_x \subseteq \bar{C}$ implies $f(x) \in \bar{C} - D_x$. Define $g(x,y)$ recursive so that

$$D_{g(x,0)} = D_x$$
$$D_{g(x,y+1)} = D_{g(x,y)} \cup \{f \circ g(x,y)\}$$

Since C is creative, if $D_x \subseteq \bar{C}$, then

$$D_x = D_{g(x,0)} \subset D_{g(x,1)} \subset \cdots \subset \bar{C}$$

where $\subset$ denotes proper containment (that is, $A \subset B$ iff $A \subseteq B$ and $A \neq B$).

For each x such that $D_x \subseteq \bar{C}$, the set

$$A(x,y) = \{f \circ g(x,0),\ldots,f \circ g(x,y)\}$$

contains $y + 1$ distinct members of $\bar{C} - D_x$. Define a 1-1 recursive function f' by

$$f'(0) = f(0)$$

$$f'(x+1) = \begin{cases} \text{smallest member of} & \\ A(x+1, x+1) - \{f'(0), \ldots, f'(x)\} & \text{if such exists} \\ \max\{f'(0), \ldots, f'(x)\} + 1 & \text{otherwise} \end{cases}$$

If $D_{x+1} \subseteq \bar{C}$, then there are $x + 2$ distinct members of $\bar{C} - D_{x+1}$ in $A(x + 1, x + 1)$, so the first alternative in the definition of $f'(x + 1)$ applies and $f'(x + 1) \in \bar{C} - D_{x+1}$. In either case $f'(x + 1) \notin \{f'(0), \ldots, f'(x)\}$, so that f' is 1-1. ∎

COROLLARY 8.28. If C is creative, then $\bar{C}$ has an infinite r.e. subset.

Proof. Exercise 2. ∎

THEOREM 8.29. A set $C \subseteq W$ is 1-complete iff C is creative.

Proof. Assume C is creative with a 1-1 productive function f as given by Lemma 8.27. Let B be an arbitrary r.e. set. We must show that $B \leq_1 C$. Define a recursive function $g(x,y)$ which satisfies

$$D_{g(x,y)} = \begin{cases} \{f(x)\} & \text{if } y \in B \\ \varnothing & \text{if } y \notin B \end{cases}$$

For each fixed value of y, $g(x,y)$ is a function of x alone. By the recursion theorem there is a fixed point x_y such that

$$\varphi_{x_y} = \varphi_{g(x_y,y)}$$

Also, for each y, the fixed point can be effectively calculated from y and so by Church's thesis (or Exercise 4), there is a recursive function $e(y)$ such that

$$\varphi_{g(ey,y)} = \varphi_{e(y)}$$

For each y, $g(x,y)$ has an infinite number of fixed points x_y satisfying $\varphi_{x_y} = \varphi_{g(x_y,y)}$ (see Exercise 12 of Section 5.7 or the proof of the recursion theorem). Hence e can be chosen 1-1. Thus

$$D_{e(y)} = D_{g(ey,y)} = \begin{cases} \{f(ey)\} & \text{if } y \in B \\ \varnothing & \text{if } y \notin B \end{cases}$$

Since f is the productive function for the creative set C,

$$D_{e(y)} \subseteq \bar{C} \text{ implies } f(ey) \in \bar{C} - D_{e(y)}$$

Now if $y \in B$, then $D_{e(y)} = \{f(ey)\}$. In this case $f(ey)$ cannot be a member of $\bar{C} - D_{e(y)}$, so $D_{e(y)}$ is not a subset of $\bar{C}$. Since $D_{e(y)}$ consists of the single element $f(ey)$, $f(ey)$ must be a member of C. On the other hand, if $y \notin B$, then $D_{e(y)} = \varnothing \subseteq \bar{C}$, hence $f(ey) \in \bar{C} - D_{e(y)} = \bar{C}$.

Therefore, $y \in B$ iff $f \circ e(y) \in C$, so $B \leq_1 C$ via the function $f \circ e$, which is 1-1, since f and e are both 1-1 (see Exercise 5).

For the converse, assume C is 1-complete. Then $H \leq_1 C$. Suppose f is a 1-1 recursive function satisfying $x \in H$ iff $f(x) \in C$. By Theorem 6.11, there is a recursive g such that for all x and y,

$$D_{g(x,y)} = \varphi_y^{-1}(D_x)$$

Let m be an index for f so that $f = \varphi_m$. We show that $h(x) = f[g(x,m)]$ is a productive function for C. Let $D_x \subseteq \bar{C}$,

then $f^{-1}(D_x) \subseteq \bar{H}$ by the definition of f
hence $\varphi_m^{-1}(D_x) \subseteq \bar{H}$ since $\varphi_m = f$
hence $D_{g(x,m)} \subseteq \bar{H}$ by the definition of g
hence $g(x,m) \in \bar{H} - D_{g(x,m)}$ since $\imath$ is a productive function for H
hence $f[g(x,m)] \in \bar{C} - D_x$ by the definition of f and g (Note that $D_{g(x,m)} = \varphi_m^{-1}(D_x) = f^{-1}(D_x)$ to show that $f[g(x,m)] \notin D_x$.)

Thus $D_x \subseteq \bar{C}$ implies $h(x) = f[g(x,m)] \in \bar{C} - D_x$, so C is creative. ▮

COROLLARY 8.30. A set $C \subseteq W$ is s-complete iff C is creative.
Proof. Exercise 6. ▮

COROLLARY 8.31. H is 1-complete. ▮

The s-degrees and 1-degrees can be ordered in a natural way since they are the equivalence classes of $\equiv_s$ and $\equiv_1$, respectively. Theorem 8.29 and Corollary 8.30 state that under each of these orderings, the creative sets form a maximal r.e. degree.

To show that there is more than one nonrecursive r.e. s-degree (1-degree), we must exhibit a nonrecursive r.e. set which is not creative. To accomplish this, define a *simple* set to be an r.e. set S such that $\bar{S}$ is infinite and $\bar{S}$ contains no infinite r.e. subset. By Corollary 8.28, the complement of every creative set contains an infinite r.e. subset, hence no simple set is creative. We now show that there is a simple set.

THEOREM 8.32. There is a simple set.
Proof. Let f be the function defined by

$$f(x) = \beta'[(\mu y)[\beta' y > 2x \wedge T(x,\beta' y,\beta'' y)]]$$

where β is the pairing function and $\beta(\beta' x, \beta'' x) = x$. Let $S = \text{ran } f$, which is r.e. since f is partial recursive. Since $f(x) > 2x$ (if it is defined), S contains at most x members of the set $\{0, 1,\ldots,2x\}$, for any x, so $\bar{S}$ is infinite. Let D_x be any infinite r.e. set. There is a smallest y such that $\beta' y > 2x$, $\beta' y \in D_x$ and $T(x,\beta' y,\beta'' y)$. Then $f(x) = \beta' y$, so $\beta' y \in S$ and D_x is not a subset of $\bar{S}$. Therefore S is simple. ▮

The simple set S exhibited in Theorem 8.32 satisfies $S \leq_s H$, since H is s-complete, but $H \not\equiv_s S$, since S is not creative. Thus there are at least two s-degrees (and also two 1-degrees). The next theorem indicates that $\leq_s$ and $\leq_1$ differ on the nonrecursive r.e. sets.

THEOREM 8.33. Let S be simple.

a. $S \equiv_s S \times W$
b. $S \leq_1 S \times W$, but $S \times W \nleq_1 S$
c. $S \times W$ is not creative

Proof. Exercise 7. ▮

The properties of $\leq_s$ and $\leq_1$ are summarized in Figure 8-3. As indicated in Figure 8-3, all of the nonrecursive r.e. sets considered in this section are equivalent with respect to general reducibility ($\leq$). A proof that not all nonrecursive r.e. sets are equivalent with respect to general reducibility (Post's problem) is given in the next section.

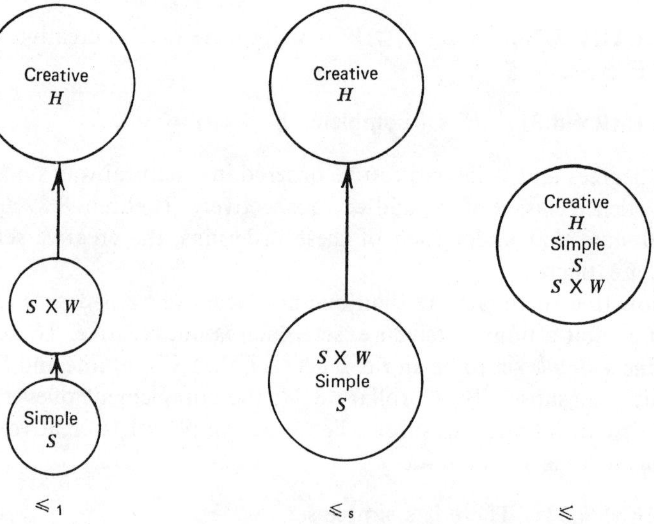

FIGURE 8-3. **Partial representation of $\leq_1$, $\leq_s$, and $\leq$.**

EXERCISES

1. Prove or disprove: For each set $A \subseteq W^r$, $r > 0$, there is a set $A' \subseteq W$ such that

a. $A' \equiv_1 A$
b. $A' \equiv_s A$

(see Theorem 8.24e)

2. Prove that although the complement of a creative set cannot be r.e., it always contains an infinite r.e. subset (Corollary 8.28).

3. Prove in detail that if B is r.e. and f is recursive, then there is a recursive function $g(x,y)$ such that

$$D_{g(x,y)} = \begin{cases} \{f(x)\} & \text{if } y \in B \\ \varnothing & \text{if } y \notin B \end{cases}$$

(see Theorem 8.29)

4. Let $g(x,y)$ be recursive. Without appealing to Church's thesis, prove that there is a recursive function e such that

$$\varphi_{g(ey,y)} = \varphi_{e(y)}$$

for all y (see Theorem 8.29).

5. Prove that if f and g are 1-1, then so is $f \circ g$.

6. Prove that $C \subseteq W$ is s-complete iff C is creative (see Corollary 8.30).

7. Prove Theorem 8.33.

8. Characterize $\leq_1$, $\leq_s$, and $\leq$ on the recursive sets.

9. Recall that $H = \{x \mid x \in \text{dom } \varphi_x\}$. Let $H' = \{x \mid x \in \text{ran } \varphi_x\}$.

a. show that H' is r.e. but not recursive

b. which of the following are true?

i. $H \equiv H'$

ii. $H \equiv_s H'$

iii. $H \equiv_1 H'$

10. Show that $\overline{H} \leq_s \{x \mid \varphi_x \text{ total}\}$.

11. Show that $\{m \mid D_m \text{ infinite}\} \equiv_s \{m \mid \varphi_m \text{ total}\}$.

12. Show that if A is r.e. and $A \leq_s \overline{A}$, then A is recursive.

13. Assume $A \cup B = W$ and $A \cap B \neq \varnothing$ for r.e. sets A and B. Show that

$$A \leq_s A \cap B.$$

14. Let A, B be arbitrary finite sets.

a. under what conditions is $A \equiv_1 B$?

b. under what conditions is $A \equiv_s B$?

c. show that there are recursive functions f_1 and f_s such that

$$f_1(u,v) = \begin{cases} 1 & \text{if } F_u \equiv_1 F_v \\ 0 & \text{otherwise} \end{cases}$$

$$f_s(u,v) = \begin{cases} 1 & \text{if } F_u \equiv_s F_v \\ 0 & \text{otherwise} \end{cases}$$

(see Section 6.6).

8.4 Post's Problem

In 1944 Post posed the question of whether or not there is a set A such that $\varnothing < A < H$. This became known as *Post's problem*. Since every r.e. set is H-recursive, a negative solution would imply that all nonrecursive r.e. sets have the same degree of undecidability, namely $d(H)$, the degree of H. Unfortunately this is not the case and indeed the order structure of degrees of r.e.

sets is quite complicated. Post's problem was solved independently in 1956 by Friedberg and Muchnik. We will prove their main theorem, which states that there are nonrecursive r.e. sets A and B such that $A \nleq B$ and $B \nleq A$, that is, the degrees of A and B are incomparable. Because $A \leq H$ and $B \leq H$, this immediately implies that $\varnothing < A < H$ and $\varnothing < B < H$. The proof is fairly difficult, involving a completely new proof procedure called a priority argument. Before presenting it, we will investigate how one might prove that $A \nleq B$ for an r.e. set A.

If a set A is r.e., we can prove that it is not recursive by showing that $\bar{A}$ is not r.e., that is, $\bar{A} \neq D_m$, for each m.

LEMMA 8.34. If a set A is r.e., then A is not recursive iff for each m, there is an x such that $x \in A$ iff $x \in D_m$.

Proof. A is not recursive iff $\bar{A} \neq D_m$ for all m. Now $\bar{A} \neq D_m$ iff $x \in \bar{A}$ and $x \in \bar{D}_m$ or else $x \in A$ and $x \in D_m$, for some x iff ($x \in A$ iff $x \in D_m$), for some x. ▮

Thus an r.e. set A is not recursive iff there is a function which, given m, produces an $x = f(m)$ such that $x \in A$ iff $x \in D_m$. Note that the function f need not be effective. If there is a recursive f, then A is *effectively nonrecursive*. The function f may also be called *productive*, although it satisfies conditions that are slightly different from those required of a productive function in Section 8.3. For each m, $f(m)$ is a counterexample to the claim that $\bar{A} = D_m$.

If A is r.e. it is also B-r.e. and so A is B-recursive iff $\bar{A}$ is B-r.e. By the same reasoning as before, to show that A is not B-recursive, we must exhibit a function f such that for all m, $f(m) \in A$ iff $f(m) \in D_m^B$. The Friedberg–Muchnik theorem is proved by exhibiting two r.e. sets A and B, with A not B-recursive and B not A-recursive. Thus we need functions f and g such that for all m, $f(m) \in A$ iff $f(m) \in D_m^B$ and $g(m) \in B$ iff $g(m) \in D_m^A$. The reason that the proof of the theorem is difficult is that the functions f and g cannot be recursive, as shown by the next theorem.

THEOREM 8.35. If A and B are r.e. and A is effectively non-B-recursive, then B is recursive.

Proof. Using the index theorem, define the recursive function g by

$$\varphi_{g(x)}^B(y) = \begin{cases} 1 & \text{if } x \notin B \\ \uparrow & \text{if } x \in B \end{cases}$$

Then

$$D_{g(x)}^B = \begin{cases} W & \text{if } x \notin B \\ \varnothing & \text{if } x \in B \end{cases}$$

Note that $\varphi_{g(x)}^B(y)$ is a B-partial recursive function, but $g(x)$ is recursive (in fact primitive recursive).

Let f be the recursive function which satisfies $f(x) \in A$ iff $f(x) \in D_x^B$. Then

$$\begin{aligned} & f \circ g(x) \in A & \\ \text{iff} \quad & f \circ g(x) \in D_{g(x)}^B & \text{by the definition of } f \\ \text{iff} \quad & D_{g(x)}^B = W & \text{since } D_{g(x)}^B = \varnothing \text{ or } W \\ \text{iff} \quad & x \notin B & \text{by the definition of } g \end{aligned}$$

Thus $\chi_{\bar{B}} = \chi_A \circ f \circ g$, that is, $\bar{B} \leq_s A$. By assumption, A and B are r.e. Thus $\bar{B}$ is r.e. by Theorem 8.24h, and hence B is recursive since B and $\bar{B}$ are both r.e. ▮

THEOREM 8.36 (Friedberg-Muchnik). There are r.e. sets A and B which are incomparable with respect to the ordering $\leq$.

Proof. Consider the following procedure for effectively enumerating the sets A and B. The final values assigned to f and g are to satisfy

$$f(m) \in A \text{ iff } f(m) \in D_m^B$$

and

$$g(m) \in B \text{ iff } g(m) \in D_m^A$$

```
f(0) ← 0;
g(0) ← 0;
α ← 1;
β ← 1;
A ← ∅;
B ← ∅;
For k = 1 to ∞;
  f(k) ← α;
  α ← α + 1;
  For j = 0 to k;
    Simulate the enumeration of D_j^B for k steps, recording {b_1,...,b_q},
    which are determined to be not in B by consulting the "oracle"
    for the finite set B during the enumeration of D_j^B;
    For each x in D_j^B enumerated;
      If f(j) = x and x ∉ A then go to OUTA;
    Next x;
  Next j;
  Go to BK;
  OUTA: Output x as a member of A;
  A ← A ∪ {x};
  β ← max{β; b_1 + 1, ..., b_q + 1};
```

```
For i = j to k ∸ 1;

   g(i) ← β;
   β ← β + 1;
Next i;
BK:   g(k) ← β;
β ← β + 1;

For j = 0 to k;
  Simulate the enumeration of D_j^A for k steps, recording {a_1,...,a_p}
  found to be not in A during the enumeration;
  For each y in D_j^A enumerated;
    If g(j) = y and y ∉ B then go to OUTB;
  Next y;
Next j;
Go to NEXTK;
OUTB: Output y as a member of B;
B ← B ∪ {y};
α ← max{α, a_1 + 1,...,a_p + 1};

For i = j + 1 to k;

   f(i) ← α;
   α ← α + 1;

Next i;
NEXTK: Next k;
```

This combination of programming-like statements and English describes an effective procedure for enumerating sets A and B which never terminates. The only problem concerns the statement "Simulate the enumeration of D_j^B for k steps. . . ." Observe that B is finite at each stage of the procedure and for a *finite* set B (in fact, any recursive set B), it is possible to effectively simulate the calculation of any B-LMA. If $T^B(j, \beta'k, \beta''k) = 1$ and $x = \beta'(k)$, then we say that x is produced at the kth step in the enumeration of D_j^B.

The procedure enumerates two sets A and B. These are the two sets required by the theorem. The members of A are enumerated by the statement OUTA and the members of B are enumerated by the statement OUTB.

The values of $f(i)$ and $g(i)$ may change as the program is executed, but the final values assigned define functions f and g, which are the functions needed to show that $A \not\leq B$ and $B \not\leq A$. It is crucial that, for each i, there is a certain point during the execution of the program, after which the values of $f(i)$ and $g(i)$ never change, that is, the values of $f(i)$ and $g(i)$ change at most a finite number of times. To prove this, let us examine the procedure in more detail.

The variable α has the smallest value which is not in A, is not assigned as a value to f, and has not caused the oracle to give a "no" answer when a set D_j^A enumerates a y which is added to B. The value of β is analogous. After the initial steps of the procedure are executed, the situation is as follows

i	0	$\alpha = \beta = 1$
$f(i)$	0	
$g(i)$	0	$A = B = \varnothing$

For $k = 1$, the assignments

$$f(1) \leftarrow 1$$
$$\alpha \leftarrow 2$$

are made and the enumeration of D_0^B and D_1^B are simulated for 1 step. ($B = \varnothing$ at this point.) Assume nothing is enumerated, causing a transfer to the label BK. Then the assignments

$$g(1) \leftarrow 1$$
$$\beta \leftarrow 2$$

are made. Also assume the simulations of the enumerations of D_0^A and D_1^A produce nothing. Then k is increased to 2 and the process is repeated. Suppose this continues with $k = 2, 3, \ldots, 17$, without the portions of the program labeled OUTA and OUTB being executed. The status of the program is as follows

i	0	1	$\cdots$	17	$\alpha = \beta = 18$
$f(i)$	0	1	$\cdots$	17	
$g(i)$	0	1	$\cdots$	17	$A = B = \varnothing$.

For $k = 18$, $f(18)$ is given the value 18 and α is increased to 19. Next, D_0^B is enumerated for 18 steps; suppose 17 and 3 are enumerated, and during the computation the oracle gives a no answer when asked if $b \in B$ for $b = 6$, 2, and 3. This is summarized by

D_0^B	x's	17 3
	b's	6 2 3

For each x enumerated $f(0) \neq x$, so $j = 1$ is considered next. Suppose the enumeration of D_1^B yields

D_1^B	x's	4 1 12
	b's	3 31

Now $f(1) \neq 4$, but $f(1) = 1$ and $1 \notin A$, so there is a branch to label OUTA. The value $x = 1$ is enumerated as a member of A, β is assigned the value $\max\{18,4,32\} = 32$, and the values of $g(1), g(2), \ldots, g(17)$ are changed to 32, 33, ..., 48, respectively, leaving β with the value 49. The status of the program is now

i	0	1	2	⋯	17	18
$f(i)$	0	1	2	⋯	17	18
$g(i)$	0	32	33	⋯	48	

$\alpha = 19$
$\beta = 49$
$A = \{1\}$
$B = \varnothing$

As the statement with label BK is executed, $g(18)$ is given the value 49 and β is increased to 50. Suppose the enumeration of D_0^A and D_1^A produce nothing of interest, but the enumeration of D_2^A yields

D_2^A	y's	6	33	4
	a's	19	11	164

Since $g(2) = 33$ and $33 \notin B$, 33 is added to B and output as a member of B, α is assigned the value $\max\{19,20,12,165\} = 165$, the values of $f(3), f(4), \ldots, f(18)$ are changed to 165, 166, ..., 180, respectively, leaving α with the value 181. As the large k-loop begins again with $k = 19$, the status of the program is

i	0	1	2	3	4	⋯	17	18
$f(i)$	0	1	2	165	166	⋯	179	180
$g(i)$	0	32	33	34	35	⋯	48	49

$\alpha = 181$
$\beta = 50$
$A = \{1\}$
$B = \{33\}$

Note that the i-loop after the statement labeled OUTA runs from $i = j$ to $k - 1$. Thus the value of $g(i)$ can change at step k only if $j \leq i < k$ and $f(j) = x$ is added to the set A. Similarly, the i-loop after the statement labeled OUTB runs from $i = j + 1$ to k, so the value of $f(i)$ can change at step k only if $j < i \leq k$ and $g(j) = y$ is added to the set B. Thus, the value of $f(0)$ never changes and the value of $g(0)$ can change only if $f(0) = 0$ is added to the set A. This can occur only once. Suppose $p(i)$ and $q(i)$ represent the number of different values that $f(i)$ and $g(i)$, respectively, may assume. Then, as we have observed, $p(0) = 1$ and $q(0) \leq 2$. In general $q(i) \leq 1 + \sum_{j \leq i} p(j)$, which represents the value originally assigned plus at most the number of different values assumed by $f(0), f(1), \ldots, f(i)$. Similarly $p(i + 1) \leq 1 + \sum_{j \leq i} q(j)$. Table 8-1 shows the maximum possible values for $p(i)$ and $q(i)$. Note that the numbers in the table are the members of the Fibonacci sequence.

TABLE 8-1. The Maximum Number of Values for $f(i)$ and $g(i)$

i	0	1	2	3	
$p(i)$	1	3	8	21	...
$q(i)$	2	5	13	34	

Since $f(i)$ and $g(i)$ change at most a finite number of times for each i, the procedure defines two functions f and g, whose values $f(i)$ and $g(i)$ are given by the final values assigned. Recall that the functions f and g are not recursive. The procedure given does not yield an effective method for calculating f or g because there is no effective way of deciding, at any step k, whether any $f(i)$ or $g(i)$ has been assigned its final value.

For i fixed, we now let $f(i)$ and $g(i)$ denote the final values assigned to $f(i)$ and $g(i)$ and let A and B denote the sets enumerated by the program. In order to show that $A \not\leq B$ and $B \not\leq A$, we show that

$$f(i) \in A \text{ iff } f(i) \in D_i^B$$

and

$$g(i) \in B \text{ iff } g(i) \in D_i^A$$

Suppose $f(i) = x \in A$, then $f(i) = x$ was added to A at some step k. If $\{b_1,\ldots,b_q\}$ were the values found to be not in B when x was enumerated as a member of D_i^B, then β was immediately assigned a value greater than $\max\{b_1,\ldots,b_q\}$. Thus for $i' \geq i$, $g(i')$ is given a value $\beta > \max\{b_1,\ldots,b_q\}$ and if it is changed, it can only be increased, because β is never decreased. For $i' < i$, if $g(i')$ is later added to B, the value of $f(i)$ would be changed, contrary to the assumption that $f(i)$ is the final value. Thus, since only values of g are added to B, $b_1,\ldots,b_q$ will never be added to B, and so the questions about membership in B that were obtained during the enumeration of D_i^B at step k will never change. Thus $f(i) \in D_i^B$.

Conversely, if $f(i) \in D_i^B$, then eventually $f(i)$ will have its final value and eventually B will have enough members to allow the oracle to answer the questions in the correct way to enumerate $f(i)$, and therefore $f(i)$ will be added to A eventually.

Similarly $g(i) \in B$ iff $g(i) \in D_i^A$. Thus A and B are r.e., but $A \not\leq B$ and $B \not\leq A$. ▌

The proof given in the Friedberg–Muchnik theorem is called a *priority* argument, because, when necessary, values of f and g having lower priority are changed. In the proof, for fixed j, each $g(i)$, $i \geq j$ has lower priority than

$f(j)$. Similarly, for fixed j, each $f(i)$, $i > j$, has lower priority than $g(j)$. Priority arguments are used frequently to prove sophisticated theorems in recursive function theory.

COROLLARY 8.37. There is an r.e. set A such that $\varnothing < A < H$.
Proof. Let A and B be the same as in Theorem 8.36. Since A is r.e. and H is complete, $\varnothing < A \leq H$. If $H \leq A$, then $B \leq H$ implies $B \leq A$, which is false. Hence $H \nleq A$, and so $A < H$. ▮

COROLLARY 8.38. There are at least four r.e. degrees,
Proof. $d(\varnothing)$, $d(A)$, $d(B)$, $d(H)$ are all distinct. ▮

The next result is much stronger, but will not be proved here.

THEOREM 8.39. Let $\mathcal{O}$ be any partial ordering of a countably infinite set and let A be any r.e. nonrecursive set. Then there is a collection of r.e. sets, all reducible to A, whose partial ordering under $\leq$ is isomorphic to $\mathcal{O}$.
Proof. See Sacks [1963]. ▮

Example. A partial ordering $\leq$ may be defined on $W \times W$ by

$$(a,b) \leq (c,d) \quad \text{iff } a \leq c \text{ and } b \leq d$$

In this ordering $(3,9) \leq (4,12)$, but $(6,8)$ and $(4,9)$ are incomparable. By Theorem 8.39, there is an infinite collection of r.e. sets A_{ij}, $i, j \geq 0$, such that $A_{ij} \leq H$, for all $i, j \geq 0$ and

$$A_{ij} \leq A_{i'j'} \quad \text{iff } i \leq i' \text{ and } j \leq j'$$

Example. For each rational number r, there is an r.e. set $A_r \leq H$ and these sets satisfy $A_r \leq A_{r'}$ iff $r \leq r'$.

*8.5 The Arithmetic Hierarchy

We have already observed that a set is f-r.e. iff its characteristic function can be expressed in the form $\bigvee_y g(x,y)$, where g is f-recursive. In fact, if $A = {}_1^r D_m^f$, then $\chi_A(x) = \bigvee_y T_r^f(m,x,y)$, where T_r^f is the T-predicate for the f-partial recursive functions (see Theorem 8.9). We will how explore this kind of relationship in more detail.

Throughout this section all functions f considered will be total with ran $f \subseteq \{0,1\}$, that is, characteristic functions of sets. As in previous chapters, we identify the word 1 with the truth value "true" and the word 0 with the truth value "false". The reader may interpret $f(x) = \chi_A(x)$ either as the value of the characteristic function of A on x or as the truth value of the predicate

"$x \in A$". One consequence of this restriction is that for $f: W^r \to \{0,1\}$, if $f = \chi_A$, then $\neg f = \chi_{W^r - A}$.

We will say that a function is f-r.e. if it is the characteristic function of some f-r.e. set.

Define

$$f(x) = \bigwedge_y g(x,y) = \begin{cases} 1 & \text{if } g(x,y) = 1 \text{ for all } y \\ 0 & \text{if } g(x,y) = 0 \text{ for some } y \end{cases}$$

Throughout this section, statements of the form

$$\bigvee_y f(x,y) = 1$$

are to stand for

$$\left[\bigvee_y f(x,y)\right] = 1, \text{ not } \bigvee_y [f(x,y) = 1].$$

THEOREM 8.40. $\neg \bigwedge_y g(x,y) = \bigvee_y \neg g(x,y)$.

Proof. $\neg \bigwedge_y g(x,y) = 0$

iff $\bigwedge_y g(x,y) = 1$	by the definition of $\neg$
iff $g(x,y) = 1$	for all y, by the definition of $\bigwedge$
iff $\neg g(x,y) = 0$	for all y
iff $\bigvee_y \neg g(x,y) = 0$	by the definition of $\bigvee$

The theorem follows from the observation that both sides of the proposed equality have a value which is either 1 or 0. ▮

Let $\sqcup_0$ be the set of all recursive functions $f: W^r \to \{0,1\}$, $r \geq 1$. Let

$$\sqcap_k = \{f \mid f = \neg g, g \in \sqcup_k\}$$

and

$$\sqcup_{k+1} = \{f \mid f(x) = \bigvee_y g(x,y), g \in \sqcap_k\}.$$

The collection of all functions in either $\sqcup_k$ or $\sqcap_k$ for some $k \geq 0$ is the set $\bigcup_{k=0}^{\infty} (\sqcup_k \cup \sqcap_k)$ and is called the *arithmetic hierarchy*. Note that $\sqcap_0 = \sqcup_0$, since if g is recursive, then so is $\neg g$. Note also that $\sqcup_1$ consists of the characteristic functions of the r.e. sets and $\sqcap_1$ consists of the characteristic functions of sets whose complements are r.e.

THEOREM 8.41. For $k \geq 0, \sqcap_{k+1} = \{f | f(x) = \bigwedge_y g(x, y), g \in \sqcup_k\}$.

Proof. $f(x) = \bigwedge_y g(x, y), g \in \sqcup_k$

iff $f(x) = \neg \bigvee_y \neg g(x,y), g \in \sqcup_k$	by Theorem 8.40
iff $f(x) = \neg \bigvee_y g'(x,y), g' \in \sqcap_k$	by the definition of $\sqcap_k$
iff $f(x) = \neg g''(x), g'' \in \sqcup_{k+1}$	by the definition of $\sqcup_{k+1}$
iff $f \in \sqcap_{k+1}$	by the definition of $\sqcap_{k+1}$ ▮

LEMMA 8.42. a. If $g(x,y) \in \sqcup_k$ $(g(x,y) \in \sqcap_k)$ and f is recursive, then $g(x,fx) \in \sqcup_k$ $(g(x,fx) \in \sqcap_k)$.

b. If $\bigvee_z g(x,y,z) \in \sqcup_{k+1}$, then $\bigvee_y \bigvee_z g(x,y,z) \in \sqcup_{k+1}$. If $\bigwedge_z g(x,y,z) \in \sqcap_{k+1}$, then $\bigwedge_y \bigwedge_z g(x,y,z) \in \sqcap_{k+1}$.

Proof. a. Exercise 4.

b. If $\bigvee_z g(x,y,z) \in \sqcup_{k+1}$, then $g \in \sqcap_k$ and $\bigvee_y \bigvee_z g(x,y,z) = \bigvee_u g(x,\beta' u,\beta'' u) \in \sqcup_{k+1}$ by part a. The remaining part is similar. ▮

THEOREM 8.43. A function f is in the arithmetic hierarchy iff it can be expressed in the form

$$f(x) = \mathop{\mathsf{X}}_{x_1} \mathop{\mathsf{X}}_{x_2} \cdots \mathop{\mathsf{X}}_{x_k} g(x,x_1,x_2,\ldots,x_k)$$

where each X is the operation $\bigvee$ or $\bigwedge$ and g is a recursive characteristic function. Furthermore, if $f \in \sqcup_k$, then

$$f(x) = \bigvee_{x_1} \bigwedge_{x_2} \cdots \mathop{\mathsf{X}}_{x_k} g(x,x_1,\ldots,x_k)$$

where X is $\bigwedge$ if k is even and X is $\bigvee$ if k is odd, and if $f \in \sqcap_k$, then

$$f(x) = \bigwedge_{x_1} \bigvee_{x_2} \cdots \mathop{\mathsf{X}}_{x_k} g(x,x_1,\ldots,x_k)$$

where X is $\bigvee$ if k is even and X is $\bigwedge$ if k is odd.

Proof. If f is in the arithmetic hierarchy, then by the definition of $\sqcup_{k+1}$ and the characterization of $\sqcap_{k+1}$ given by Theorem 8.41, f can be expressed in one of the above forms where the operations alternate between $\bigwedge$ and $\bigvee$. If $f(x)$ is expressed in the form

$$f(x) = \mathop{\mathsf{X}}_{x_1} \cdots \mathop{\mathsf{X}}_{x_k} g(x,x_1,\ldots,x_k),$$

then Lemma 8.42 can be used to "collapse" adjacent occurrences of $\bigwedge$'s or $\bigvee$'s. ▮

Example.

$$\bigwedge_t \bigvee_u \bigvee_v \bigvee_w \bigwedge_y \bigwedge_z g(t,u,v,w,x,y,z) = \bigwedge_t \bigvee_u \bigwedge_y g(t, {}_1\beta_3 u, {}_2\beta_3 u, {}_3\beta_3 u, x, {}_1\beta_2 y, {}_2\beta_2 y)$$

which is in $\sqcap_3$.

LEMMA 8.44. Let f be any function $f: W^r \to \{0,1\}$. Let $f'(x,y) = f(x)$ so that $f': W^{r+1} \to \{0,1\}$. Then $\bigvee_y f'(x,y) = \bigwedge_y f'(x,y) = f(x)$.

Proof. $\bigvee_y f'(x,y) = 0$ iff $f'(x,y) = 0$, for all y iff $f(x) = 0$. Also $\bigwedge_y f'(x,y) = 1$ iff $f'(x,y) = 1$ for all y iff $f(x) = 1$. ▮

THEOREM 8.45. $\sqcup_k \cup \sqcap_k \subseteq \sqcup_{k+1} \cap \sqcap_{k+1}$.

Proof. Suppose $f \in \sqcup_k$ and k is odd. Then $f(x) = \bigvee_{x_1} \bigwedge_{x_2} \cdots \bigvee_{x_k} g(x,x_1,\ldots,x_k)$, where g is recursive. Let

$$g'(x,x_0,x_1,\ldots,x_k) = g(x,x_1,\ldots,x_k)$$

for all x_0.

Then by Lemma 8.44 $f(x) = \bigvee_{x_1} \bigwedge_{x_2} \cdots \bigvee_{x_k} \bigwedge_{x_0} g'(x,x_0,x_1,\ldots,x_k)$, which is a member of $\sqcup_{k+1}$. Also if

$$f'(x,x_0) = \bigvee_{x_1} \cdots \bigvee_{x_k} g'(x,x_0,x_1,\ldots,x_k)$$

then

$$\begin{aligned} f(x) &= \bigvee_{x_1} \cdots \bigvee_{x_k} g(x,x_1,\ldots,x_k) \\ &= \bigvee_{x_1} \cdots \bigvee_{x_k} g'(x,x_0,x_1,\ldots,x_k) \qquad \text{for all } x_0 \\ &= f'(x,x_0) \qquad \text{for all } x_0 \end{aligned}$$

Hence

$$f(x) = \bigwedge_{x_0} f'(x,x_0) = \bigwedge_{x_0} \bigvee_{x_1} \cdots \bigvee_{x_k} g'(x,x_0,x_1,\ldots,x_k)$$

which is a member of $\sqcap_{k+1}$.

If $f \in \sqcap_k$ or k is even, the proof is similar. ▮

Thus

$$\sqcup_0 \subseteq \sqcup_1 \subseteq \cdots \qquad \text{and} \qquad \sqcap_0 \subseteq \sqcap_1 \subseteq \cdots$$

so we have two hierarchies of sets of functions. Since $\sqcup_k \subseteq \sqcap_{k+1}$ and $\sqcap_k \subseteq \sqcup_{k+1}$, the two sequences are intimately connected. We will prove later that we have a true hierarchy in the sense that for each k there are functions in $\sqcup_{k+1}$ that are not in $\sqcup_k$ and functions in $\sqcap_{k+1}$ that are not in $\sqcap_k$. Moreover, for $k > 0$, $\sqcap_k - \sqcup_k \neq \varnothing$, $\sqcup_k - \sqcap_k \neq \varnothing$, and

$$(\sqcup_{k+1} \cap \sqcap_{k+1}) - (\sqcup_k \cup \sqcap_k) \neq \varnothing.$$

We now show where (the characteristic functions of) several familiar sets fall in the arithmetic hierarchy. Recall that T is primitive recursive, where $T(m,x,k) = 1$ iff the LMA $\mathcal{A}(m)$ halts in exactly k steps on input x. The letters used to name sets in the following examples correspond to Table 6-2 on p. 149.

Example. $\chi_H(x) = \bigvee_y T(x,x,y)$, thus $H \in \sqcup_1$ (that is, $\chi_H \in \sqcup_1$), and so H is r.e. as we already know. Since $\bar{H}$ is not r.e., $H \in \sqcup_1 - \sqcap_1$.

Example. For $A_7 = \{m \mid x_0 \in D_m\}$, $\chi_{A_7}(m) = \bigvee_k T(m,x_0,k)$ and so $A_7 \in \sqcup_1$ also, as was proved in Section 6.4. Since $\bar{A}_7$ is not r.e., $A_7 \in \sqcup_1 - \sqcap_1$.

Example. For $A_1 = \{m \mid D_m = \varnothing\}$, $\chi_{A_1}(m) = \bigwedge_x \neg \bigvee_k T(m,x,k)$, that is, for each input x, $\mathcal{A}(m)$ does not halt in any number k of steps. However

$$\begin{aligned} \bigwedge_x \neg \bigvee_k T(m,x,k) &= \bigwedge_x \bigwedge_k \neg T(m,x,k) \qquad \text{by Theorem 8.40} \\ &= \bigwedge_x \neg T(m,\beta' x,\beta'' x) \end{aligned}$$

so $A_1 \in \sqcap_1$, that is, A_1 is the complement of an r.e. set, as we also proved in Section 6.4. Since A_1 is not r.e., $A_1 \in \sqcap_1 - \sqcup_1$.

Example. Let $A_3 = \{m \mid D_m \text{ finite}\}$. Now D_m is finite iff there is some x_0, such that for $x > x_0$, $x \notin D_m$, that is, $\mathcal{A}(m)$ does not halt on input x. Thus $\chi_{A_3}(m) = \bigvee_{x_0} \bigwedge_x \bigwedge_k [x > x_0 \supset \neg T(m,x,k)]$. Collapsing the adjacent occurrences of $\bigwedge$, we see that $A_3 \in \sqcup_2$. We proved in Section 6.4 that neither A_3 nor its complement is r.e., hence we know that $A_3 \notin \sqcup_1 \cup \sqcap_1$.

Example. For $A_5 = \{m \mid D_m = W\} = \{m \mid \varphi_m \text{ is total}\}$, $\chi_{A_5}(m) = \bigwedge_x \bigvee_k T(m,x,k)$, so $A_5 \in \sqcap_2$.

Example. Let $A_9 = \{m \mid D_m \text{ is recursive}\}$. Since each D_m is r.e., D_m is recursive iff $\bar{D}_m$ is r.e. iff $\bar{D}_m = D_{m'}$ for some m'. Now $\bar{D}_m = D_{m'}$ provided $x \in \bar{D}_m$ iff $x \in D_{m'}$ for all x. Furthermore $x \in \bar{D}_m$ iff $\neg T(m,x,k)$ for all k, and $x \in D_{m'}$ iff $T(m',x,k')$ for some k'. If we write $x \leftrightarrow y$ for the primitive recursive function $(x \supset y) \wedge (y \supset x)$, then

$$\chi_{A_9}(m) = \bigvee_{m'} \bigwedge_x \left[\bigwedge_k \neg T(m,x,k) \leftrightarrow \bigvee_{k'} T(m',x,k') \right].$$

It is possible to prove that

$$\bigwedge_{k} \neg T(m,x,k) \leftrightarrow \bigvee_{k'} T(m',x,k')$$
$$= \bigwedge_{k_2} \bigwedge_{k_2'} \bigvee_{k_1} \bigvee_{k_1'} \left([\neg T(m,x,k_1) \supset T(m',x,k_1')] \wedge [T(m',x,k_2') \supset \neg T(m,x,k_2)] \right)$$

(See Exercise 1). Thus

$$\chi_{A_9}(m) = \bigvee_{m'} \bigwedge_{x} \bigwedge_{k_2} \bigwedge_{k_2'} \bigvee_{k_1} \bigvee_{k_1'} f(m,m',x,k_2,k_2',k_1,k_1') = \bigvee_{m'} \bigwedge_{x} \bigvee_{k} f'(m,m',x,k,)$$

for some recursive function f'. Thus $A_9 \in \sqcup_3$.

In each of these cases, we may prove that no sharper estimate is possible (see Rogers [1967]). For example, for $A_9 = \{m \mid D_m \text{ is recursive}\}$, shown to be in $\sqcup_3$, $A_9 \notin \sqcup_2$ and $A_9 \notin \sqcap_3$.

Figure 8-4 is a schematic representation of the arithmetic hierarchy. Note that it is completely symmetric; the negation of any function on the left side is on the right side and vice-versa.

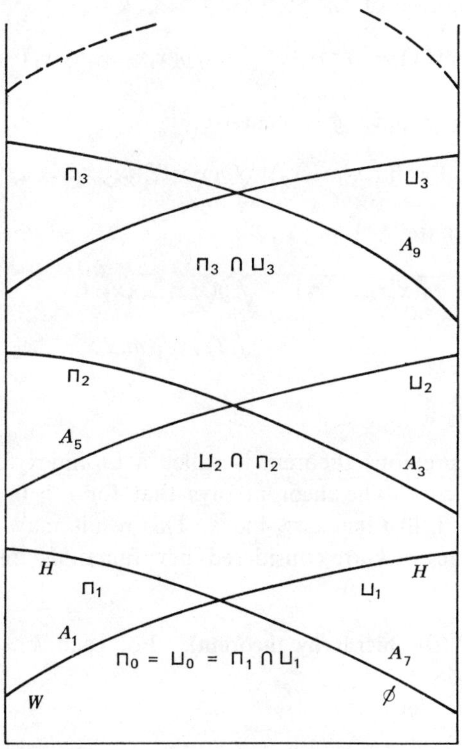

FIGURE 8-4. **The arithmetic hierarchy.**

The fact that $x \in {}^rD_m$ iff $\bigvee_k T_r(m,x,k)$ allowed us to use the T-predicate to provide an indexing for all of the r.e. sets. Since $f \in \sqcup_1$ iff f is the characteristic function of an r.e. set, this same scheme is an indexing of all functions in $\sqcup_1$, that is, $f: W^r \to \{0,1\}$ is in $\sqcup_1$ iff there is an m such that

$$f(x) = \bigvee_k T_r(m,x,k)$$

Since $\neg f \in \sqcap_1$ iff $f \in \sqcup_1$, the same m is an index for a function in $\sqcap_1$.

The following theorem shows that this concept can be extended to any part of the arithmetic hierarchy.

THEOREM 8.46. For each $k > 0$ and $f: W^r \to \{0,1\}$, $f \in \sqcup_k$ iff

$$f(x) = \bigvee_{x_k} \neg \cdots \neg \bigvee_{x_2} \neg \bigvee_{x_1} T_{r+k-1}(m,x,x_k,\ldots,x_2,x_1)$$

for some m.

Proof. First observe that if $f(x)$ can be expressed in the above form, then $f \in \sqcup_k$ by the definition of $\sqcup_k$. Suppose $f \in \sqcup_k$, $k > 0$. Then

$$f(x) = \bigvee_{x_k} \neg \cdots \neg \bigvee_{x_2} \neg \bigvee_{x_1} g(x,x_k,\ldots,x_2,x_1)$$

for some recursive g. Since g is recursive,

$$A = \{(x,x_k,\ldots,x_2) \mid \bigvee_{x_1} g(x,x_k,\ldots,x_2,x_1) = 1\}$$

is an r.e. subset of W^{r+k-1} and so

$$\begin{aligned} \chi_A(x,x_k,\ldots,x_2) &= \bigvee_{x_1} g(x,x_k,\ldots,x_2,x_1) \\ &= \bigvee_{x_1} T_{r+k-1}(m,x,x_k,\ldots,x_2,x_1) \end{aligned}$$

for some index m. ▮

The m in the previous theorem is called a $\sqcup_k$-index for f. It is also a $\sqcap_k$-index for $\neg f \in \sqcap_k$. The theorem says that for $k > 0$, $f \in \sqcup_k$ iff f has a $\sqcup_k$-index and $f \in \sqcap_k$ iff f has a $\sqcap_k$-index. This result may be used to show that as larger values of k are considered, new functions are found in the sets $\sqcup_k$ and $\sqcap_k$.

THEOREM 8.47 (the hierarchy theorem). For each $k > 0$, $\sqcup_k - \sqcap_k \neq \varnothing$ and $\sqcap_k - \sqcup_k \neq \varnothing$.

Proof. For $x \in W$, let

$$f(x) = \bigvee_{x_k} \neg \cdots \neg \bigvee_{x_1} T_{1+k-1}(x,x,x_k,\ldots,x_2,x_1)$$

which is a member of $\sqcup_k$. Suppose $f \in \sqcap_k$, then by the previous theorem, f has a $\sqcap_k$-index, that is,

$$f(x) = \neg \bigvee_{x_k} \neg \cdots \neg \bigvee_{x_1} T_{1+k-1}(m,x,x_k,\ldots,x_2,x_1)$$

But this implies that $f(m) = \neg f(m)$. Thus $f \notin \sqcap_k$, that is, $f \in \sqcup_k - \sqcap_k$. Also $\neg f \in \sqcap_k - \sqcup_k$. Note that this is actually a diagonal argument. The definition of f ensures that f will differ from the mth member of $\sqcap_k$ on input m. ▮

COROLLARY 8.48. $\sqcup_{k+1} - \sqcup_k \neq \emptyset$ and $\sqcap_{k+1} - \sqcap_k \neq \emptyset$.

Proof. There is a function $f \in \sqcup_k - \sqcap_k$. Since $\sqcup_k \subseteq \sqcap_{k+1}$ by Theorem 8.45, $f \in \sqcap_{k+1} - \sqcap_k$. The other part is proved similarly. ▮

For the final main theorem of this chapter which shows a relationship between reducibility and the arithmetic hierarchy, some identities are needed.

THEOREM 8.49.

a. $$\left[\bigvee_x f(x,y)\right] \vee g(y) = \bigvee_x [f(x,y) \vee g(y)]$$

b. $$\left[\bigvee_x f(x,y)\right] \wedge g(y) = \bigvee_x [f(x,y) \wedge g(y)]$$

c. $$\left[\bigwedge_x f(x,y)\right] \vee g(y) = \bigwedge_x [f(x,y) \vee g(y)]$$

d. $$\left[\bigwedge_x f(x,y)\right] \wedge g(y) = \bigwedge_x [f(x,y) \wedge g(y)]$$

Proof. For part c,

$$\left[\bigwedge_x f(x,y)\right] \vee g(y) = 1$$

iff $g(y) = 1$ or, for all x, $f(x,y) = 1$
iff for all x, $g(y) = 1$ or $f(x,y) = 1$
iff $\bigwedge_x [f(x,y) \vee g(y)] = 1$.

Parts a, b, and d are similar. ▮

THEOREM 8.50. For each recursive function $f: W^{1+1+r} \to \{0,1\}$, there are recursive functions f' and f'' such that

a. $$\bigwedge_{x=0}^{a} \bigvee_y f(x,y,z) = \bigvee_y \bigwedge_{x=0}^{a} f'(x,y,z)$$

b. $$\bigvee_{x=0}^{a} \bigwedge_y f(x,y,z) = \bigwedge_y \bigvee_{x=0}^{a} f''(x,y,z)$$

Proof. Let ${}_x\beta_{a+1}$ be the xth coordinate of the inverse of the pairing function β_{a+1}, so that $\beta_{a+1}({}_1\beta_{a+1}y, {}_2\beta_{a+1}y, \ldots, {}_{a+1}\beta_{a+1}y) = y$. Recall that ${}_u\beta_v(w)$ is a recursive function of u, v, and w.

For part a, let $f'(x,y,z) = f(x, {}_{x+1}\beta_{a+1}y, z)$. Suppose $\bigwedge_{x=0}^{a} \bigvee_y f(x,y,z) = 1$. Then for all $x \leq a$, there is a y such that $f(x,y,z) = 1$, that is, there exist $y_0, y_1, \ldots, y_a$ such that

$$f(0,y_0,z) = f(1,y_1,z) = \cdots = f(a,y_a,z) = 1$$

Let $\bar{y} = \beta_{a+1}(y_0,y_1,\ldots,y_a)$, then $f(0,{}_1\beta_{a+1}\bar{y},z) = f(1,{}_2\beta_{a+1}\bar{y},z) = \cdots = f(a,{}_{a+1}\beta_{a+1}\bar{y},z) = 1$, that is,

$$\bigwedge_{x=0}^{a} f(x,{}_{x+1}\beta_{a+1}\bar{y},z) = \bigwedge_{x=0}^{a} f'(x,\bar{y},z) = 1$$

Thus

$$\bigvee_y \bigwedge_{x=0}^{a} f'(x,y,z) = 1$$

Conversely, if $\bigwedge_{x=0}^{a} f'(x,\bar{y},z) = 1$ for some $\bar{y}$, then for each $x \leq a$, let $y_x = {}_{x+1}\beta_{a+1}\bar{y}$. Then $f(x,y_x,z) = f(x,{}_{x+1}\beta_{a+1}\bar{y},z) = f'(x,\bar{y},z) = 1$, for all $x \leq a$. Hence $\bigwedge_{x=0}^{a} \bigvee_y f(x,y,z) = 1$.

For part b,

$$\bigvee_{x=0}^{a} \bigwedge_y f(x,y,z) = \neg \bigwedge_{x=0}^{a} \neg\neg \bigvee_y \neg f(x,y,z) \qquad \text{by Exercise 2h in Section 3.3 and Theorem 8.40}$$

$$= \neg \bigwedge_{x=0}^{a} \bigvee_y \neg f(x,y,z) \qquad \text{since } \neg \circ \neg = \iota$$

$$= \neg \bigvee_y \bigwedge_{x=0}^{a} \neg f''(x,y,z) \qquad \text{for some } f'', \text{ by part a}$$

$$= \bigwedge_y \bigvee_{x=0}^{a} f''(x,y,z) \quad \blacksquare$$

Recall that for each A, $H^A = \{x \mid x \in D_x^A\}$ is A-r.e., but not A-recursive. Thus we may define a sequence of sets, each (as we will show) higher in the arithmetic hierarchy than its predecessor. Let

$$H_0 = \varnothing$$
$$H_{k+1} = H^{H_k}$$

We already know that $H_0 = \varnothing < H_1 \doteq H < H_2 < H_3 < \cdots$. The following theorem shows a relationship between the sets H_k and the arithmetic hierarchy.

THEOREM 8.51. For each $k \geq 0$, $f \in \sqcup_{k+1}$ iff f is H_k-r.e., that is, f is the characteristic function of an H_k-r.e., set.

Proof. We already know that $f \in \sqcup_1$ iff f is r.e. (f is the characteristic function of an r.e. set). We now prove the theorem by induction on k. Assume that $f \in \sqcup_{k+1}$ iff f is H_k-r.e.

Suppose $f \in \sqcup_{k+2}$, then $f(x) = \bigvee_y \neg g(x,y)$, for some $g \in \sqcup_{k+1}$ which, by the induction hypothesis, implies g is H_k-r.e. Thus $g \leq H^{H_k} = H_{k+1}$, since by Theorem 8.23, H^{H_k} is H_k-complete. Thus $\neg g \leq H_{k+1}$ also, that is, $\neg g$ is H_{k+1}-recursive, which implies by Theorem 8.11 that $f(x) = \bigvee_y \neg g(x,y)$ is H_{k+1}-r.e.

For the converse, suppose $f(x)$ is H_{k+1}-r.e., that is, f is the characteristic function of $D_m^{H_{k+1}}$ for some m. By Theorem 8.15,

$$f(x) = \bigvee_u \bigvee_v \Big([\beta_3(x,u,v) \in D_{\text{simulate}(m)}] \wedge [F_u \subseteq H_{k+1}] \wedge [F_v \subseteq \bar{H}_{k+1}] \Big)$$

We now consider each of the bracketed terms. First

$$\begin{aligned} \beta_3(x,u,v) \in D_{\text{simulate}(m)} &= \bigvee_y T[\text{simulate}(m), \beta_3(x,u,v), y] \\ &= \bigvee_y T'(m,x,u,v,y) \qquad \text{where } T' \text{ is recursive} \end{aligned}$$

Since H_{k+1} is H_k-r.e., $H_{k+1} \in \sqcup_{k+1}$ by the induction hypothesis, which means that

$$\chi_{H_{k+1}}(w) = \bigvee_{w_{k+1}} \bigwedge_{w_k} \cdots \bigtimes_{w_1} g(w,w_1,\ldots,w_{k+1})$$

where g is recursive and $\bigtimes$ is $\bigwedge$ if k is odd and $\bigtimes$ is $\bigvee$ if k is even.

Then, recalling that all members of F_u are $\leq u$, $F_u \subseteq H_{k+1}$ iff

$$\begin{aligned} \bigwedge_{w=0}^{u} (w \in F_u \supset w \in H_{k+1}) &= \bigwedge_{w=0}^{u} (w \notin F_u \vee w \in H_{k+1}) \\ &= \bigwedge_{w=0}^{u} [w \notin F_u \vee \bigvee_{w_{k+1}} \bigwedge_{w_k} \cdots \bigtimes_{w_1} g(w,w_1,\ldots,w_{k+1})] \end{aligned}$$

which may be further transformed using the identities of Theorems 8.49 and 8.50 and the recursiveness of $w \notin F_u$ to

$$\begin{aligned} &\bigwedge_{w=0}^{u} \bigvee_{w_{k+1}} \bigwedge_{w_k} \cdots \bigtimes_{w_1} [w \notin F_u \vee g(w,w_1,\ldots,w_{k+1})] \\ &= \bigvee_{w_{k+1}} \bigwedge_{w_k} \cdots \bigtimes_{w_1} \bigwedge_{w=0}^{u} g'(u,w,w_1,\ldots,w_{k+1}) \\ &= \bigvee_{w_{k+1}} \bigwedge_{w_k} \cdots \bigtimes_{w_1} h(u,w_1,\ldots,w_{k+1}) \end{aligned}$$

where g' and h are recursive.

Similarly, since $\overline{H}_{k+1} \in \sqcap_{k+1}$,

$$F_v \subseteq \overline{H}_{k+1} \text{ iff } \bigwedge_{w'_{k+1}} \bigvee_{w'_k} \cdots \mathop{\mathsf{X}}_{w'_1} h'(v,w,\ldots,w'_{k+1}),$$

where h' is recursive and where $w_1, \ldots, w_{k+1}, w'_1, \ldots, w'_{k+1}, u, v,$ and y are all distinct variables.

Thus $f(x)$ is of the form

$$\begin{aligned}
f &= \bigvee \bigvee [(\bigvee T') \wedge (\overbrace{\bigvee \bigwedge \cdots \mathsf{X}}^{k+1} h) \wedge (\overbrace{\bigwedge \bigvee \cdots \mathsf{X}}^{k+1} h')] \\
&= \bigvee \bigvee \bigvee [T' \wedge (\bigvee \bigwedge \cdots \mathsf{X} h) \wedge (\bigwedge \bigvee \cdots \mathsf{X} h')] \\
&= \bigvee \bigvee \bigvee \bigvee [T' \wedge (\overbrace{\bigwedge \cdots \mathsf{X}}^{k} h) \wedge (\overbrace{\bigwedge \bigvee \cdots \mathsf{X}}^{k+1} h')] \\
&= \bigvee \bigwedge [T' \wedge (\overbrace{\bigvee \cdots \mathsf{X}}^{k-1} h) \wedge (\overbrace{\bigvee \cdots \mathsf{X}}^{k} h')] \\
&\ \ \vdots \\
&= \overbrace{\bigvee \bigwedge \cdots \mathsf{X}}^{k+1} [T' \wedge h \wedge \mathsf{X} h'] \\
&= \overbrace{\bigvee \bigwedge \cdots \mathsf{X}}^{k+2} [T' \wedge h \wedge h']
\end{aligned}$$

Hence $f \in \sqcup_{k+2}$. ∎

COROLLARY 8.52. $f \in \sqcup_{k+1} \cap \sqcap_{k+1}$ iff $f \leq H_k$.

Proof. $f \in \sqcup_{k+1} \cap \sqcap_{k+1}$ iff f and $\neg f$ are both H_k-r.e., iff f is H_k-recursive. ∎

COROLLARY 8.53. $H_{k+1} \in \sqcup_{k+1} - \sqcap_{k+1}$ and $\overline{H}_{k+1} \in \sqcap_{k+1} - \sqcup_{k+1}$ (see Theorem 8.47, the hierarchy theorem).

Proof. H_{k+1} is H_k-r.e. (hence in $\sqcup_{k+1}$), but not H_k-recursive (hence not in $\sqcap_{k+1} \cap \sqcup_{k+1}$). ∎

COROLLARY 8.54. For $k > 0$, $f \in \sqcup_k$ iff $f \leq_1 H_k$

Proof. Exercise 8. ∎

Corollary 8.52 and Corollary 8.54 illustrate the difference between $\leq$ and $\leq_1$, in particular the greater generality of $\leq$. By Corollary 8.52, H_k and $\leq$ characterize $\sqcup_{k+1} \cap \sqcap_{k+1}$ while by Corollary 8.54, H_k and $\leq_1$ characterize only $\sqcup_k$.

It should be noted that everything in this section can be translated into results about the first-order theory of elementary arithmetic. Each function $f\colon W^r \to \{0,1\}$ corresponds to a predicate, the functions $\wedge$, $\vee$, and $\neg$ correspond to the propositional connectives "and", "or", and "not", and $\bigwedge_x$ and $\bigvee_x$ correspond to the universal and existential quantifiers, respectively. In logic, a predicate is called *arithmetic* if it can be expressed in the predicate calculus using only recursive predicates. Thus the arithmetic predicates correspond to the functions in the arithmetic hierarchy (see Exercise 3).

There is also a similarity between the arithmetic hierarchy and the Borel hierarchy of subsets of real numbers. In the Borel hierarchy the open sets correspond to $\sqcup_1$, the r.e. sets. In the usual topology for the real numbers a set is open if it is a union of open intervals of the form $\{x \mid a < x < b\}$. A closed set is a complement of an open set and so the class of closed sets corresponds to $\sqcap_1$. Countable unions of closed sets correspond to members of $\sqcup_2$, and so on. The sets corresponding to the recursive sets in $\sqcup_0 \cap \sqcap_0$ are those which are both closed and open. The empty set and the set of all real numbers are the only sets which are both open and closed.

EXERCISES

1. Use Theorems 8.40 and 8.49 and the fact that $x \supset y = \neg x \vee y$ to prove

$$\left[\bigwedge_x fx \supset \bigvee_y gy\right] \wedge \left[\bigvee_y gy \supset \bigwedge_x fx\right] = \bigwedge_{x_2} \bigwedge_{y_2} \bigvee_{x_1} \bigvee_{y_1} [(fx_1 \supset gy_1) \wedge (gy_2 \supset fx_2)]$$

2. Prove parts a, b, and d of Theorem 8.49.

3. Show that the arithmetic hierarchy is the smallest class of functions which contains the recursive functions and is closed under the operations of $\vee$, $\wedge$, $\neg$, $\bigvee_x$, and $\bigwedge_x$; that is, show that any function g in this class is in the arithmetic hierarchy by showing that g can be written in *prenex normal form* as $\mathsf{X} \cdots \mathsf{X} f$, where each X is $\bigvee_x$ or $\bigwedge_x$ and f is recursive.

4. Prove Lemma 8.42a.

5. Locate each of the sets A_1–A_{14} of Section 6.4 in the arithmetic hierarchy. Note that Corollaries 8.52 and 8.54 can be useful in this regard.

6. $H_2 = H^H$ and $H_3 = H^{H_2} = H^{(H^H)}$. Let $H_3' = H_2^H = (H^H)^H$. Is $H_3' \equiv H_3$?

7. Show that the set

$$\{m \mid \varphi_m \text{ total and there is a } y_m \text{ such that } \varphi_m(x) \leq y_m \text{ for all } x\}$$

is in $\sqcup_3 \cap \sqcap_3$.

8. Prove Corollary 8.54.

8.6 History

The basic reference for the topic of reducibility is Post [1944]. In that paper, Post discussed general reducibility or Turing reducibility, strong reducibility (often called many-to-one or m-1 reducibility), truth-table reducibility, complete sets, simple sets, and creative sets. In the same paper, he posed what is now called Post's problem (Section 8.4). This problem was solved independently by Friedberg [1957] and Muchnik [1956]. The priority method developed by Friedburg and Muchnik to solve Post's problem has many important applications in recursion theory and complexity theory (see Chapter 9).

The basic result that alternating quantifiers applied to recursive functions (predicates) yields a hierarchy as well as the characterization using the T-predicate of the classes $\sqcup_k$ and $\sqcap_k$ (Theorem 8.46) are due to Kleene [1943]. The relationship between the Turing degrees and the classes $\sqcup_k$ and $\sqcap_k$ (Theorem 8.51, Corollary 8.52) is due to Kleene [1952] and Post [1948]. The books by Rogers [1967] and Sacks [1963] contain a great deal of information on the arithmetic hierarchy.

CHAPTER 9

Complexity of Computations

Every day computing problems rarely approach the borderline between effective and noneffective computability. Indeed it is probably the case that actual problems are always primitive recursive. Hence while it is important to understand the limits of effective computability in order to discourage attempts to design general systems for deciding things like the equivalence of programs, there are other questions of more pressing concern to the computer scientist. For example, given that a function is effectively computable, an important practical question arises as to how difficult the function is to compute, as measured by some criterion such as the amount of time or storage required. Complexity criteria of this type are called *dynamic measures* of complexity. Also of importance are questions dealing with *static measures* of complexity such as the size of programs for computing a given function.

Relative to the various complexity criteria, we may consider such significant and difficult questions as whether one function is more complex than another function, whether one algorithm is better than another algorithm for computing a given function, or whether a function has a best algorithm. In this chapter we present an axiomatic approach to the study of the complexity of functions and algorithms. One appealing aspect of this approach is that it is possible to obtain results which are true of all common notions of complexity and of all algorithmic languages. A disadvantage is that in order to obtain this level of applicability, we must sacrifice the ability to analyze properties which are peculiar to any one algorithmic language or group of algorithmic languages.

9.1 Axioms for Dynamic Complexity Measures

Let $\mathfrak{L}_1$ and $\mathfrak{L}_2$ be algorithmic languages and let $\{f_i\}$ and $\{g_i\}$ be effective enumerations of the (functions $f_i: W \to W$, $g_i: W \to W$ computed by the) programs of $\mathfrak{L}_1$ and $\mathfrak{L}_2$, respectively. Then $\langle \mathfrak{L}_1, \{f_i\} \rangle$ is *recursively isomorphic* to $\langle \mathfrak{L}_2, \{g_i\} \rangle$ if:

1. There is a 1-1 recursive h such that for arbitrary $j \geq 0$,

$$g_{h(j)} = f_j$$

2. There is a 1-1 recursive k such that for arbitrary $j \geq 0$,

$$f_{k(j)} = g_j$$

The languages discussed in Chapters 2–5 (PL, partial recursive definitions, URM programs, SRM programs, TM programs, LMA's) are recursively isomorphic. Indeed the proofs given of their computational equivalence provide the necessary 1-1 effective procedures for converting a program of one language into an equivalent program of any other of these languages. In the following we will restrict our attention to languages which are recursively isomorphic to the language of LMA's.

It is not difficult to see that if $\mathfrak{L}$ is recursively isomorphic to the language of LMA's, then the results of Chapters 5 and 6 are true of $\mathfrak{L}$. For example, $\mathfrak{L}$ admits a universal program; the index and recursion theorems are true in $\mathfrak{L}$; the undecidable properties of LMA's discussed in Chapter 6 are also undecidable when interpreted in $\mathfrak{L}$; programs of $\mathfrak{L}$ compute all and only partial recursive functions; and the operation of "padding" can be done effectively in $\mathfrak{L}$, that is, there is an effective procedure which given an index i of a program in $\mathfrak{L}$ obtains an index $j > i$ such that the jth and ith programs of $\mathfrak{L}$ compute the same function.

LEMMA 9.1. If $\langle \mathfrak{L}, \{f_i\} \rangle$ is recursively isomorphic to $\langle \mathfrak{L}_{\text{LMA}}, \{\varphi_i\} \rangle$, where $\mathfrak{L}_{\text{LMA}}$ is the language of LMA's, then there is a recursive bijection h such that $\varphi_i = f_{h(i)}$ for all i.

Proof. The proof follows directly from the definition of recursive isomorphism and the fact that padding can be done in $\mathfrak{L}_{\text{LMA}}$, and $\mathfrak{L}$. The completion of the proof is left as Exercise 1. ∎

Lemma 9.1 allows us, without loss of generality, to always use the standard effective enumeration $\{\varphi_i\}$, where $\varphi_i: W \to W$ is the function computed by the LMA with index i. For a language $\mathfrak{L}$, φ_i will be the function computed by the program with index $h(i)$ of $\mathfrak{L}$, where h is the bijection of Lemma 9.1 between $\mathfrak{L}_{\text{LMA}}$ and $\mathfrak{L}$. The program of $\mathfrak{L}$ with index $h(i)$ will be referred to as the program of $\mathfrak{L}$ with index i or the ith program of $\mathfrak{L}$. In this manner, all effective enumerations of languages other than $\mathfrak{L}_{\text{LMA}}$ are reordered to correspond to the ordering of $\mathfrak{L}_{\text{LMA}}$ and the recursive bijection of Lemma 9.1.

To simplify the notation, we will consider only functions having a single input and a single output. The results of Section 3.8 pertaining to the pairing function imply that this is not a significant restriction.

Let $\mathfrak{L}$ be an algorithmic language which is recursively isomorphic to the language of LMA's. A *measure* of *computational complexity*, a *complexity measure*, or simply a *measure* (with respect to $\mathcal{L}$) is a set of partial recursive functions $\mathcal{C} = \{C_i\}$ satisfying the following axioms:

AXIOM 9.2. For each i, dom C_i = dom φ_i.

AXIOM 9.3. There is a recursive M such that for all $i,x,y \geq 0$

$$M(i,x,y) = \begin{cases} 1 & \text{if } C_i(x) = y \\ 0 & \text{otherwise} \end{cases}$$

If $\mathcal{C} = \{C_i\}$ is a complexity measure, then each C_i is called a *complexity* or *cost* function.

Example. Consider the language of LMA's in $\Sigma \cup \{\$,a,b\}$ which compute functions in Σ. The following are complexity measures.

a. the set $\mathcal{T} = \{T_i\}$ where $T_i(x)$ is the number of instructions executed by the ith LMA on input x in case $x \in$ dom φ_i, and $T_i(x)$ is undefined if $x \notin$ dom φ_i; this measure is called the *standard time measure*

b. the set $\mathcal{S} = \{L_i\}$ where $L_i(x)$ is the length of the longest word generated by the ith LMA on input x if $x \in$ dom φ_i, and $x \notin$ dom L_i if $x \notin$ dom φ_i; this measure is called the *standard storage measure*

Example. Let $G_i(x)$ be the number of times the ith PL program executes a GOTO statement when started on an input x in the domain of φ_i. If $x \notin$ dom φ_i, then $x \notin$ dom G_i.

The reader may verify that the above examples satisfy the axioms for complexity measures. Before proceeding to study the properties of measures, we give some examples of sets $\{C_i\}$ which do not satisfy the axioms.

Example. Let $\mathcal{L}$ be the language of LMA's.

a. if $\{C_i\}$ is given by $C_i = \varphi_i$ for all i, then Axiom 9.2 but not Axiom 9.3 is satisfied

b. if $\{C_i\}$ is given by $C_i(x) = 0$ for all i and x, then Axiom 9.3 but not Axiom 9.2 is satisfied

c. let $C_i(x)$ be the number of times the first instruction of the ith LMA is executed on input x in case $x \in$ dom φ_i; if $x \notin$ dom φ_i, then $x \notin$ dom C_i; Axiom 9.2 but not Axiom 9.3 is satisfied

The reader may verify that each of the examples is not a complexity measure.

Axiom 9.2 states that the cost of the computation of the ith program on input x is defined iff the ith program halts on input x. Axiom 9.3 says that we can effectively decide if the computation of a given program on a given input has a given cost. Intuitively this means that as a computation proceeds, it is possible to successively rule out larger and larger cost values. It would be somewhat unrealistic if a rather arduous computation were to have a low cost. This is surely not true of our usual notions of complexity. For example, the amount of time and storage used (by a program which is not in an infinite loop) both increase as a computation proceeds.

It is difficult to conceive of a realistic complexity criterion which does not possess the minimal properties expressed by the axioms. Indeed, all of our usual notions of dynamic complexity satisfy the axioms. Unfortunately the converse is not true. Due to the weakness of the axioms it is possible to define complexity measures which satisfy the axioms but which are not at all realistic. However, it is important to stress that if a given property is true for all measures, then it is also true of our usual complexity criteria. Despite the weakness of the axioms, we can still prove some rather surprising results for all measures of complexity.

EXERCISES

1. Prove that if $\langle \mathfrak{L}, \{f_i\}\rangle$ is recursively isomorphic to $\langle \mathfrak{L}_{LMA}, \{\varphi_i\}\rangle$, then

a. $\mathfrak{L}$ has a universal function

and

b. padding can be done effectively in $\mathfrak{L}$

2. Complete the proof of Lemma 9.1.

3. Prove that the standard time measure $\{T_i\}$, the standard storage measure $\{L_i\}$, and $\{G_i\}$ defined in this section for PL programs, are measures of complexity.

4. Prove that the following $\{C_i\}$ are not complexity measures:

a. $C_i = \varphi_i$ for all i

b. $C_i(x) = 0$ for all i and x

c.
$$C_i(x) = \begin{cases} \text{the number of times the first instruction of the } i\text{th LMA is} \\ \quad \text{executed on input } x, \text{ if } x \in \text{dom } \varphi_i \\ \uparrow \text{ if } x \notin \text{dom } \varphi_i. \end{cases}$$

5. Show that every cost function C is of the form

$$C(x) = (\mu y) f(x,y)$$

for some recursive f. Compare with the end of Section 5.4 and Exercise 4 of Section 5.6 which show that while every partial recursive function can be defined using primitive recursive functions and a *single* application of minimization, there are partial recursive functions g such that $g \neq \mu f$ for any recursive f.

9.2 Properties of Complexity Measures

Given a program $\mathcal{P}$ of a programming language such as PL, ALGOL, or FORTRAN and a finite set $A \subseteq W$, it is often possible to obtain another program $\mathcal{P}'$ satisfying:

1. $\mathcal{P}'$ computes the same function as $\mathcal{P}$
2. for all $x \in A$, the computation of $\mathcal{P}'$ on x is more efficient than that of $\mathcal{P}$ on x in terms of some criterion such as execution time

This "speed-up" can be accomplished by inserting instructions at the beginning of $\mathcal{P}$ which check whether the input is in the finite set A and, if it is, "look up" the correct output value. For example, if $A = \{x_1,\ldots,x_n\}$ and if $\mathcal{P}$ outputs y_i on input x_i for $1 \leq i \leq n$, then $\mathcal{P}'$ could be the program

$$\text{IF X1} = x_1 \text{ THEN; Y1} \leftarrow y_1\text{; STOP; END;}$$
$$\vdots$$
$$\text{IF X1} = x_n \text{ THEN; Y1} \leftarrow y_n\text{; STOP; END;}$$

This ability to use table look-up to simplify the computation of a function on a finite set of inputs indicates that the complexity of a function should not depend entirely on the efficiency of a particular program on a particular finite set of inputs. Along these lines many of the theorems to be proved in this chapter will involve properties of functions or algorithms which hold for all but a finite number of inputs.

One criticism of this approach is that in solving real problems we are never interested in more than a finite set of inputs. Moreover, input size is usually bounded by the size of the computer's memory, by the requirements of a particular implementation of an algorithmic language, or by some other restriction. Hence by eliminating consideration of a finite set of inputs one might eliminate consideration of all computations which are of interest or which can actually be executed on a particular computer.

A response to this criticism is that algorithms are finite presentations of functions which, in general, are infinite objects. The elimination of a finite portion of an infinite object should not greatly affect its mathematical properties. Analogous situations may be found in probability theory where events having probability 0 are often ignored; in the definition of such basic mathematical concepts as the limit point; and in the branch of complexity theory which analyzes the limiting behavior (the behavior as input size or number of inputs increase) of algorithms for such tasks as sorting or matrix multiplication. Moreover, as mentioned above, one may use table look-up to obtain maximum efficiency for any particular finite input set.

We leave it to the reader to judge for himself the merits of the above arguments. We will present the axiomatic theory in order to give the reader some idea of the type of results which can be obtained via a language-independent approach, and because several of the results have, in addition to their mathematical content, interesting implications for programming languages.

The following terminology and notation is used throughout this chapter. All functions considered are total. Let $P(\,)$ denote a property of members of W or of *recursive* functions on W; $P(x)$ is true *almost everywhere* (a.e.) or for *almost all* x means that $P(x)$ is true for all but a finite set of $x \in W$; $P(x)$ is true *infinitely often* (i.o.) or for *infinitely many* x means that for each $y \in W$ there is an $x \in W$ such that $x \geq y$ and $P(x)$ is true. The property $P(f)$ is true for *sufficiently large functions* f means that there is a function g such that if $f(x) \geq g(x)$ for all x, then $P(f)$ is true; $P(f)$ is true for *arbitrarily large* functions f means that for each function g there is a function f such that $f(x) \geq g(x)$ for all x and $P(f)$ is true. The notation max A means the largest member of A if A is finite but nonempty and 0 if A is empty; min A is similarly defined.

The algorithm φ_i is *less complex* than the algorithm φ_j if $C_i(x) \leq C_j(x)$ a.e. The function f is *less complex* than the function g if there is an i satisfying $\varphi_i = f$ and

$$C_i(x) \leq C_j(x) \text{ a.e.}$$

whenever $\varphi_j = g$.

The next lemma shows that all measures of complexity are recursively related. Recall that $\max \varnothing = \min \varnothing = 0$.

LEMMA 9.4. If $\{C_i\}$ and $\{C_i'\}$ are measures of complexity, then there is a recursive function g such that for all i for which φ_i is recursive and all $x \geq i$

$$C_i(x) \leq g[x, C_i'(x)]$$

and

$$C_i'(x) \leq g[x, C_i(x)]$$

Proof. Define g by

$$g(x,y) = \max \{C_j(x), C_j'(x) \mid j \leq x \wedge [C_j(x) \leq y \vee C_j'(x) \leq y]\}$$

The function g is recursive because by Axiom 9.3, $C_j(x) \leq y$ and $C_j'(x) \leq y$ can be effectively decided for arbitrary j, x, and y. Moreover, by Axiom 9.2, $C_j(x)$ is defined iff $C_j'(x)$ is defined, so that a calculation of $C_j(x)$ or $C_j'(x)$ is necessary only in cases where it is known that the calculation will terminate. Finally the value of x is a bound on the number of times a cost function must be evaluated to compute $g(x,y)$.

If $\varphi_i(x)$ is defined, then both $C_i(x)$ and $C_i'(x)$ are defined. If, in addition, $x \geq i$, then

$$\begin{aligned} g[x, C_i'(x)] &= \max \{C_j(x), C_j'(x) \mid j \leq x \wedge [C_j(x) \leq C_i'(x) \vee C_j'(x) \leq C_i'(x)]\} \\ &\geq C_i(x) \end{aligned}$$

Similarly $g[x, C_i(x)] \geq C_i'(x)$ for $x \geq i$ in case $\varphi_i(x)\downarrow$. ∎

In the above proof, the argument x serves as a bound on the number of cost functions which must be evaluated to compute g. This plus the fact that $C_j(x)$ and $C_j'(x)$ are included in the computation of $g(x,y)$ only in case one is $\leq y$, which means that both are defined, imply that g is recursive.

If $C_i(x) \geq x$ and $C_i'(x) \geq x$ for all x, then a bit stronger version of Lemma 9.4 can be proved.

COROLLARY 9.5. Let $\{C_i\}$ and $\{C_i'\}$ be measures satisfying $C_i(x) \geq x$ and $C_i'(x) \geq x$ for all i and x. Then there is a recursive g such that for all i and $x \geq i$ for which $\varphi_i(x)\downarrow$

$$C_i(x) \leq g[C_i'(x)]$$
$$C_i'(x) \leq g[C_i(x)]$$

Proof. Exercise 1. ∎

The restriction that $C_i(x) \geq x$ may be interpreted as meaning that cost increases with input size. This is quite realistic. For example, if inputs are given in base 1 and either time or storage is taken as the complexity criterion, then $C_i(x) \geq x$ means that enough time or storage to permit a complete scan of the input x is always required. For base n, $C_i(x) \geq \log_n x =$ length x would suffice. Actually the corollary holds, with minor modification, for any increasing f where $C_i(x) \geq f(x)$ for all i and x.

Lemma 9.4 is quite useful. It allows us in many cases to extend theorems proved for particular measures to all measures. Its statement may be interpreted as saying that if f and h have the same complexity in one measure, then they have "almost" (*modulo g*) the same complexity in any other measure.

Also useful is the following lemma which states that for any measure there is an effective procedure which, given a cost function C_i, obtains an index j such that $\varphi_j = C_i$.

LEMMA 9.6. If $\mathcal{C} = \{C_i\}$ is a measure, then there is a recursive d, which depends on $\mathcal{C}$, such that

$$\varphi_{d(i)} = C_i \qquad \text{for all } i$$

Proof. Let $\{C_i\}$ be a measure and let $M(i,x,y)$ be the recursive function given by Axiom 9.3. Define h by

$$h(i,x) = (\mu y)[M(i,x,y)]$$
$$= C_i(x)$$

Since h is partial recursive, there is an index m such that

$${}^2_1\varphi_m(i,x) = h(i,x)$$

and by the index theorem

$$\varphi_{K_1(m,i)}(x) = h(i,x) = C_i(x)$$

Thus $d(i) = K_1(m,i)$ is the required function. ∎

This section concludes with two simple, though interesting, theorems on properties of measures.

THEOREM 9.7. Let $\{C_i\}$ be any measure. For each recursive f there is a recursive g such that for all i, if $\varphi_i = g$, then

$$C_i(x) > f(x) \qquad \text{for all } x \geq i$$

Proof. The proof is a diagonalization over the class of functions φ_i such that $C_i(x) \leq f(x)$ for some $x \geq i$. Let f be recursive and define g by

$$g(x) = \max\{\varphi_j(x) + 1 \mid j \leq x \wedge C_j(x) \leq f(x)\}$$

Now note that if $C_i(x) \leq f(x)$ for some $x \geq i$, then for the smallest $x \geq i$ at which this occurs, $g(x) \geq \varphi_i(x) + 1 > \varphi_i(x)$. Hence for any index i such that $g = \varphi_i$ it follows that $C_i(x) > f(x)$ for all $x \geq i$. ▮

Theorem 9.7 says that for any measure there are functions of arbitrary complexity. In particular, for any recursive function f there is a recursive function g which cannot be computed by any program which, for infinitely many x, executes fewer than $f(x)$ instructions on input x. We leave it as Exercise 4 to show that the a.e. condition of Theorem 9.7 cannot be omitted.

The next theorem states that the complexity of algorithms cannot in general be recursively related to the values of the functions computed by the algorithms. The proof is left as Exercise 2.

THEOREM 9.8. Let $\{C_i\}$ be any measure. Then there is no recursive b such that for all i

$$C_i(x) \leq b[\varphi_i(x), x] \text{ a.e. } ▮$$

EXERCISE

1. Prove Corollary 9.5.

2. Prove Theorem 9.8.
Hint: Consider 0–1 valued functions.

3. Let $\{C_i\}$ be any measure. Prove that for each recursive f and recursive g there is a j such that $\varphi_j = g$ and $C_j(x) > f(x)$ for almost all x, that is, for any function there are arbitrarily bad algorithms. Use the recursion theorem to eliminate the a.e. condition. (This theorem is well known to students and instructors of programming.)

4. Show that Theorem 9.7 without the a.e. condition is not true of the standard LMA time or storage measures.

9.3 Complexity Classes of Recursive Functions

Let g be a *recursive* function and $\mathcal{C} = \{C_i\}$ a measure of complexity. The $\mathcal{C}$ *complexity class* of g, $\mathfrak{R}_g^{\mathcal{C}}$ is defined by

$$\mathfrak{R}_g^{\mathcal{C}} = \{f \mid f \text{ recursive and for some } i, f = \varphi_i \text{ and } C_i(x) \leq g(x) \text{ a.e.}\}.$$

The complexity class $\mathcal{R}_g^{\mathcal{C}}$ contains all recursive functions whose complexity, relative to $\mathcal{C}$, is bounded by the recursive function g. The superscript $\mathcal{C}$ will often be omitted when the meaning is clear from the context.

Theorem 9.7 shows that, with respect to any measure, there are functions of arbitrary complexity. This means, for example, that for any recursive g, there is a recursive f such that any PL program for computing f must execute more than $g(x)$ instructions on all but a finite number of inputs x. Theorem 9.7 may be restated as follows where $\subset$ denotes proper inclusion.

THEOREM 9.9. For any measure $\mathcal{C}$ and recursive g_1, there is a recursive g_2 such that $\mathcal{R}_{g_1} \subset \mathcal{R}_{g_2}$. ▮

Hence for any recursive g_1, there exists an infinite sequence $g_1, g_2, \ldots$ of recursive functions satisfying $\mathcal{R}_{g_1} \subset \mathcal{R}_{g_2} \subset \mathcal{R}_{g_3} \subset \cdots$. An obvious question is whether there is a uniform effective procedure for obtaining larger complexity classes. A negative answer is given by the following theorem (see Figure 9-1).

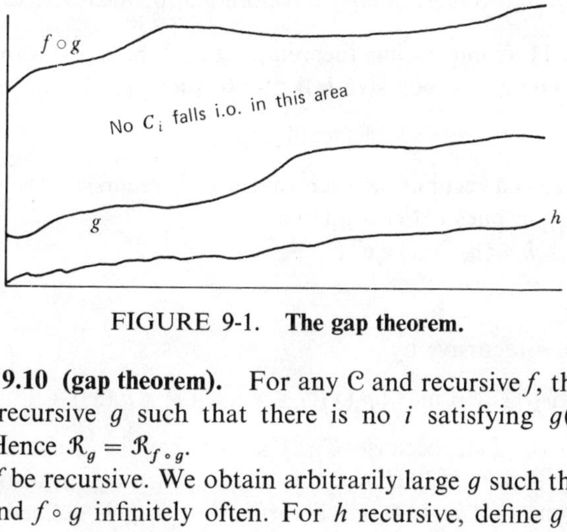

FIGURE 9-1. **The gap theorem.**

THEOREM 9.10 (gap theorem). For any $\mathcal{C}$ and recursive f, there are arbitrarily large recursive g such that there is no i satisfying $g(x) \leq C_i(x) \leq f \circ g(x)$ i.o. Hence $\mathcal{R}_g = \mathcal{R}_{f \circ g}$.

Proof. Let f be recursive. We obtain arbitrarily large g such that no C_i falls between g and $f \circ g$ infinitely often. For h recursive, define $g \geq h$ recursive by

$$g(0) = h(0)$$

$$g(x) = (\mu w)[w \geq h(x) \wedge \neg \bigvee_{i=0}^{x} w \leq C_i(x) \leq f(w)] \qquad \text{for } x > 0$$

First note that $g \geq h$ and that g is recursive because the condition in the brackets can be effectively evaluated and the required w always exists. For example, $w = \max\{h(x), \max\{C_i(x) + 1 \mid i \leq x \wedge C_i(x)\downarrow\}\}$ works, though the computation of $g(x)$ may halt before reaching this value for w. For $x \geq i$, the definition of g ensures that either $C_i(x) < g(x)$, $f[g(x)] < C_i(x)$ or $C_i(x)\uparrow$. Therefore $\mathcal{R}_g = \mathcal{R}_{f \circ g}$. The details are left to the reader. ▮

The gap theorem says that for any measure there are arbitrarily large complexity gaps, that is, regions in which no cost functions are found. We may interpret this as saying that the cost functions are "sparse" in the recursive functions. Moreover, no recursive f can have the property that $\mathcal{R}_g \subset \mathcal{R}_{f \circ g}$ for all recursive g. The gaps occur at arbitrarily high levels of complexity so no such f exists even if only sufficiently large g are considered. As an example, consider the PL time measure (number of instructions executed). For any recursive f and h, there is a recursive $g \geq h$ such that no PL program executes between g and $f \circ g$ instructions on more than a finite number of inputs. Experienced programmers will probably find this difficult to accept.

Though it is not possible to uniformly obtain larger complexity classes for all recursive functions, there are interesting sets of functions which do admit such a procedure. An r.e. set $\mathcal{G} = \{g_i\}$ of partial recursive functions is *measured* if there is an effective procedure for deciding for arbitrary i, x, and y whether $g_i(x) = y$. Note that this is, in effect, Axiom 9.3 for measures of complexity.

THEOREM 9.11 (compression theorem). Let $\mathcal{C}$ be a measure and $\{g_i\}$ a measured set. There is a recursive $h: W^2 \to W$ such that for all *recursive* g_i

$$\mathcal{R}_{g_i} \subset \mathcal{R}_{h \circ \langle g_i, \iota \rangle}$$

Moreover, there is a recursive k such that if g_i is recursive, then

a. $\varphi_j = \varphi_{k(i)}$ implies $C_j(x) > g_i(x)$ a.e.

b. $C_{k(i)}(x) \leq h \circ \langle g_i, \iota \rangle(x)$ a.e.

so that

c. $\varphi_{k(i)} \in \mathcal{R}_{h \circ \langle g_i, \iota \rangle} - \mathcal{R}_{g_i}$

Proof. Define k recursive by

$$\varphi_{k(i)}(x) = \max \{\varphi_j(x) \mid j \leq x \wedge C_j(x) \leq g_i(x)\} + 1$$

If $g_i(x)\downarrow$, then $\varphi_{k(i)}(x)\downarrow$ because $C_j(x) \leq g_i(x)$ can be decided and if true, then $\varphi_j(x)\downarrow$ by Axiom 9.2. Hence if g_i is total, then $\varphi_{k(i)}$ is also total. In the following assume that g_i is total. The function $\varphi_{k(i)}$ is defined by diagonalization so as to differ from any function φ_j satisfying $C_j(x) \leq g_i(x)$ i.o. Therefore $\varphi_{k(i)} \notin \mathcal{R}_{g_i}$ and $\varphi_j = \varphi_{k(i)}$ implies $C_j(x) > g_i(x)$ a.e. Now define h by

$$h(y,x) = \max \{C_{k(j)}(x) \mid g_j(x) = y,\ j \leq x\}$$

The function h is recursive because $\{g_i\}$ measured implies $g_j(x) = y$ is decidable and $g_j(x) = y$ implies $g_j(x)\downarrow$ which by the above implies $C_{k(j)}(x)\downarrow$. Then for g_i total

$$\begin{aligned} h[g_i(x),x] &= \max \{C_{k(j)}(x) \mid g_j(x) = g_i(x) \wedge j \leq x\} \\ &\geq C_{k(i)}(x) \qquad \text{for } x \geq i \end{aligned}$$

so $\varphi_{k(i)} \in \mathcal{R}_{h \circ \langle g_i, \iota \rangle}$ which completes the proof. ∎

COROLLARY 9.12. If $\mathcal{G}$ is measured, then there is a recursive h such that for recursive g, if $g \in \mathcal{G}$ and $g \geq \iota$, then $\mathcal{R}_g \subset \mathcal{R}_{h \circ g}$.
Proof. Exercise 1. ▌

The compression theorem allows us to uniformly, for each g_i, obtain a function whose complexity is compressed between g_i and $h \circ \langle g_i, \iota \rangle$. The ability to decide whether $g_i(x) = y$ for functions g_i of a measured set is a very strong condition. It enables us to define $\varphi_{k(i)}$ in the proof of the compression theorem by uniformly diagonalizing out of $\mathcal{R}_{g_i}$. This is not possible in general for r.e. sets of functions as seen by the gap theorem.

For any measure, the set of cost functions is a measured set by Axiom 9.3 and Lemma 9.6. This implies the next result.

COROLLARY 9.13. For any measure $\mathcal{C}$ there is a recursive h such that if C_i is total, then $\mathcal{R}_{C_i} \subset \mathcal{R}_{h \circ \langle C_i, \iota \rangle}$. Similarly there is an h such that for $C_i \geq \iota$ and C_i total, $\mathcal{R}_{C_i} \subset \mathcal{R}_{h \circ C_i}$. ▌

The next theorem is proved by an application of the priority method discussed in Section 8.4. A set $\mathcal{F}$ of partial recursive functions is said to be *class determining* for a measure $\mathcal{C}$ if for every recursive f there is a recursive $g \in \mathcal{F}$ such that $\mathcal{R}_g = \mathcal{R}_f$, that is, if $\mathcal{F}$ contains a *name* for each $\mathcal{C}$ complexity class.

THEOREM 9.14 (honesty theorem). Every measure $\mathcal{C}$ has a class determining measured set $\mathcal{F}$. Furthermore, there is an effective procedure which, given an index of a recursive f, finds an index of a recursive $g \in \mathcal{F}$ such that $\mathcal{R}_f = \mathcal{R}_g$.
Proof. In the following, we adopt the convention that "undefined" is greater than all defined values, that is, $f(x) \leq h(x)$ if either $h(x)\uparrow$ or $h(x)\downarrow$ and $f(x) \leq h(x)$ in the usual sense.

We give a procedure which for any partial recursive ψ produces a partial recursive ψ' such that $\psi'(x) = y$ can be effectively decided and for all i, $C_i(z) \leq \psi(z)$ a.e. iff $C_i(z) \leq \psi'(z)$ a.e. The procedure is uniform in ψ so that there is a recursive g such that if $\psi = \varphi_e$, then $\psi' = \varphi_{g(e)}$. Note that $\varphi_{g(e)}$ will not necessarily be total even if φ_e is total. We later show how to obtain a g' from g such that φ_e total implies $\varphi_{g'(e)}$ total and $\{\varphi_{g'(e)}\}$ is still a measured set satisfying for all i and e, $C_i(z) \leq \varphi_{g'(e)}(z)$ a.e. iff $C_i(z) \leq \varphi_e(z)$ a.e., so for φ_e total, $\mathcal{R}_{\varphi_e} = \mathcal{R}_{\varphi_{g'(e)}}$.

Recall the pairing function $\beta: W^2 \to W$ and the functions $\beta': W \to W$, $\beta'': W \to W$ of Section 3.8 which satisfy $\beta[\beta'(x), \beta''(x)] = x$ for all x. From the definition of β it follows that $\beta(x,y) < \beta(x,y+1)$ for all x and y. This fact is used in the following.

The procedure for computing ψ', given a procedure that computes ψ, maintains a queue of indices of functions. Let q_j, $j \geq 0$, be the index in position j on the queue. Associated with each index i is a value pop(i) which will be either 0 or 1 and will change during the execution of the procedure. If pop(i) = 1 at Stage n, then the index i is requesting to be "serviced" at Stage n. The value of pop(i) is set to 1 when it is discovered that $C_i(u) > \psi(u)$ for some u. This represents a request to set $C_i(v) > \psi'(v)$ for some v. The nth stage, $n \geq 0$, of the procedure for computing $\psi' = \varphi_{g(e)}$, where $\psi = \varphi_e$, is given by:

Stage *n*.

a. put n on the bottom of the queue (that is, $q_n \leftarrow n$); set x to $\beta'(n)$,y to $\beta''(n)$
b. if $C_e(x) = y$ (recall $\varphi_e = \psi$), then for $0 \leq i \leq n$, if $C_i(x) > \psi(x)$, set pop(i) to 1
c. if $\psi'(x)$ has already been defined at an earlier stage, go to Stage $n + 1$
d. find the least $k \leq n$ (if any) such that
   i. pop(q_k) = 1
   ii. $C_{q_k}(x) > y$
   iii. for all $j < k$, pop(q_j) = 0 implies $C_{q_j}(x) \leq y$

If k exists, define $\psi'(x) = y$, set pop(q_k) to 0, put the index q_k on the bottom of the queue and go to Stage $n + 1$. If no such k exists, go directly to Stage $n + 1$.

For any $\varphi_e = \psi$ and any $n \geq 0$, Stage n in the computation of ψ' is effective and will terminate. In particular, note that in part b, if $C_e(x) = y$, then $\psi(x)\downarrow$ by Axiom 9.2 for measures. Condition c guarantees that if $\psi'(x)$ is defined, it is defined at only one stage so ψ' is well defined. Furthermore, the procedure is uniform in e so $\psi' = \varphi_{g(e)}$ for some recursive g. By condition d, if $\psi'(x)$ is defined, it is defined at Stage $n = \beta[x,\psi'(x)]$, so to decide if $\psi'(x) = y$ we need only run the procedure to Stage $\beta(x,y)$. Hence $\{\psi'\}$ is a measured set. It only remains to show that for each i, $C_i(z) \leq \psi$ a.e. iff $C_i(z) \leq \psi'(z)$ a.e. The proof divides into cases depending on the final position of the integer i on the queue. If i reaches a final location on the queue, then we say that i is stable; otherwise i is unstable.

Case 1. i is unstable

Since i does not stabilize, it must be moved to the bottom of the queue infinitely often by step d. But step d defines $\psi'(x) = y < C_i(x)$ and hence $C_i(z) > \psi'(z)$ i.o. In addition, step d sets pop(i) to 0, so for d to again move i to the bottom, pop(i) must be reset to 1. This only occurs when it is discovered that $C_i(x) > \psi(x)$ for some x. Since this can occur only once for each x, that is, at stage $\beta[x,C_e(x)]$, we have $C_i(z) > \psi(z)$ i.o.

Case 2. i is stable

Since i is stable, pop(i) must eventually stabilize at either 0 or 1.

Case 2a. pop(i) stable at 0

Since pop(i) can be set to 1 only finitely often by b, $C_i(z) \leq \psi(z)$ a.e. There is some stage after which i, all indices above i on the queue, and their pop values are stable. Hence for all but a finite number of arguments x in the domain of ψ', $\psi'(x)$ is defined via d using an index below i on the queue. Then by diii, for each such x, $C_i(x) \leq \psi'(x)$. For x not in the domain of ψ', $C_i(x) \leq \psi'(x)$ by convention. Hence $C_i(x) \leq \psi'(x)$ a.e.

Case 2b. pop(i) stable at 1

Consider any x such that i, all indices above i on the queue, and their pop values have stabilized at Stage $\beta(x,0)$ and all later stages. By Case 2a we may assume $C_j(x) \leq \min\{\psi(x),\psi'(x)\}$ for all j above i on the queue having pop(j) = 0. Let

$$m = \max\{C_j(x) \mid j \text{ above } i \text{ on queue, pop(j)} = 0\}$$

Then $m \leq \min\{\psi(x),\psi'(x)\}$ so if m is infinite, both $\psi(x)$ and $\psi'(x)$ are undefined, so $C_i(x) \leq \psi(x)$ and $C_i(x) \leq \psi'(x)$. Suppose m is finite. Since β is increasing in its second argument, $\beta(x,m)$ is the earliest stage at which $\psi'(x)$ could be defined without violating diii and the assumption that the queue has stabilized at $\beta(x,0)$. Note that $\psi'(x)$ *cannot* be defined before Stage $\beta(x,0)$. If $\psi'(x)$ was defined at Stage $\beta(x,y)$, $y < m$, then $C_j(x) > y = \psi'(x)$ for some j above i with pop(i) = 0 which contradicts diii. But i has also stabilized by Stage $\beta(x,0)$, so i must fail to satisfy dii at Stage $\beta(x,m)$. Thus $C_i(x) \leq m \leq \min\{\psi(x),\psi'(x)\}$. Since the above is true for almost all x, we have $C_i(z) \leq \psi(z)$ a.e. and $C_i(z) \leq \psi'(z)$ a.e.
Therefore

$$C_i(z) \leq \psi(z) \text{ a.e. iff } i \text{ is stable iff } C_i(z) \leq \psi'(z) \text{ a.e.} \tag{9-1}$$

Recall that $\varphi_e = \psi$ and $\varphi_{g(e)} = \psi'$.
It only remains to modify g so that φ_e total implies $\varphi_{g'(e)}$ total. Define g' by

$$\varphi_{g'(e)}(x) = \min\{\varphi_{g(e)}(x), \varphi_e(x) + C_e(x)\} \tag{9-2}$$

Since $\varphi_{g(e)}(x) = y$ and $C_e(x) = y$ are decidable and $C_e(x)\downarrow$ implies $\varphi_e(x)\downarrow$, g' is recursive and $\varphi_{g'(e)}(x) = y$ is decidable so $\{\varphi_{g'(e)}\}$ is a measured set. Furthermore, if φ_e is total, then so is $\varphi_{g'(e)}$. We leave it to the reader to use (9-1) and (9-2) to show that for all i and e, $C_i(z) \leq \varphi_e(z)$ a.e. iff $C_i(z) \leq \varphi_{g'(e)}(z)$ a.e., so for φ_e total, $\mathfrak{R}_{\varphi_e} = \mathfrak{R}_{\varphi_{g'(e)}}$. ∎

If we view g as a name for the complexity class $\mathfrak{R}_g$, then the honesty theorem states that there is a "good" set of names for the complexity classes of $\mathfrak{C}$. Intuitively, a name g_i in a measured set $\{g_i\}$ is *honest* because its value at x is recursively related to the complexity of computing $g_i(x)$ (g_i need not be total). This follows immediately from the decidability of $g_i(x) = y$ for arbitrary x and y.

For any measure $\mathfrak{C}$, consider the following implications of the gap, compression, and honesty theorems. By the honesty theorem there is a class determining measured set $\mathcal{F}$ for $\mathfrak{C}$. By Corollary 9.12 of the compression theorem, there is a recursive h such that for sufficiently large $g \in \mathcal{F}$ $(g(x) \geq x)$, $\mathcal{R}_g \subset \mathcal{R}_{h \circ g}$. But the gap theorem says that there are arbitrarily large recursive f such that $\mathcal{R}_f = \mathcal{R}_{h \circ f}$. For such an f, choose $g_f \in \mathcal{F}$ satisfying $\mathcal{R}_{g_f} = \mathcal{R}_f$. But then

$$\mathcal{R}_{h \circ f} = \mathcal{R}_f = \mathcal{R}_{g_f} \subset \mathcal{R}_{h \circ g_f}$$

that is, f, g_f, and $h \circ f$ are all names of the same class while $h \circ g_f$ is the name of a larger class. This is perhaps an indication that names belonging to the measured set $\mathcal{F}$ have more desirable properties than do arbitrary names.

The gap, compression, and honesty theorems are examples of the type of theorems which are obtained via the axiomatic approach to complexity theory. Additional properties of complexity measures and classes are considered in the next section.

EXERCISES

1. Prove Corollary 9.12.

2. Prove that for any measure there is a recursive h such that if φ_i is total, then $\mathcal{R}_{\varphi_i(x)} \subset \mathcal{R}_{h(i,x)}$. Compare with the gap theorem.

3. Define $\mathcal{R}_g$ for g total but not necessarily recursive, in the obvious way. Prove that there is a nonrecursive g such that $\mathcal{R}_g \neq \mathcal{R}_f$ for any recursive f.

4. Consider the standard LMA storage measure and let g be primitive recursive. Prove that every function in $\mathcal{R}_g$ is primitive recursive. Show that this is not true for arbitrary measures.

9.4 Properties of Complexity Classes

Several properties of complexity classes and measures, some of which are possible candidates for axioms, are considered in this section. As we shall see, the original axioms do not restrict the set of complexity measures to those which are justifiable on an intuitive basis. The discovery of additional axioms which would achieve this goal is an important open problem in axiomatic complexity theory.

Recall that a set $\mathcal{F}$ of partial recursive functions is r.e. if there is an r.e. set $A \subseteq W$ such that

$$\mathcal{F} = \{\varphi_m | m \in A\}$$

For some measures, all complexity classes are r.e. Furthermore, for any measure $\mathcal{C}$ and sufficiently large functions f, $\mathcal{R}_f^{\mathcal{C}}$ is r.e. Some of the theorems which follow give conditions which guarantee that complexity classes will be r.e. We first give an example of a measure which has a non-r.e. class.

THEOREM 9.15. For any recursive f, there is a measure $\mathcal{C}$ such that $\mathfrak{R}_f^{\mathcal{C}}$ is not r.e.

Proof. Let $\mathcal{C}' = \{C_i'\}$ be a measure and f a recursive function. Let $\{i_0, i_1, \cdots\}$ be a recursive set of indices satisfying $\varphi_{i_j}(x) = j$ for all j and x. Define $\mathcal{C} = \{C_i\}$ as follows:

$$C_i(x) = C_i'(x) + f(x) + 1 \text{ if } i \notin \{i_0, i_1, \cdots\}$$

$$C_{i_j}(x) = \begin{cases} f(x) & \text{if } \neg \bigvee_{y=0}^{x} T(j,j,y) \\ f(x) + 1 & \text{otherwise} \end{cases}$$

where T is the T-predicate defined in Section 5.4.

The reader may verify that $\{C_i\}$ is a measure. Moreover,

$$\begin{aligned} C_{i_j}(x) \le f(x) \text{ a.e. iff } & C_{i_j}(x) = f(x) && \text{for all } x \\ \text{iff } & \neg \bigvee_{y=0}^{x} T(j,j,y) && \text{for all } x \\ \text{iff } & \neg T(j,j,y) && \text{for all } y \\ \text{iff } & j \notin \text{dom } \varphi_j \\ \text{iff } & j \in \overline{H} \end{aligned}$$

If $\mathfrak{R}_f^{\mathcal{C}} = \{\varphi_{i_j} \mid j \in \overline{H}\}$ were r.e., then $\{j \mid \varphi_{i_j} \in \mathfrak{R}_f^{\mathcal{C}}\} = \overline{H}$ would be r.e. Therefore $\mathfrak{R}_f^{\mathcal{C}}$ is not r.e. ▮

A complexity class $\mathfrak{R}_f$ is *finitely invariant* if $g \in \mathfrak{R}_f$ and $g(x) = h(x)$ a.e. imply that $h \in \mathfrak{R}_f$. The functions h and g are said to be *finite variants* of each other if $h(x) = g(x)$ a.e.

It is reasonable to expect that complexity classes should be finitely invariant, since a finite portion of a function should not greatly affect the function's complexity. All cost functions of the standard storage measure satisfy $L_i(x) \ge \text{length}(x) + 1$. This may be used to prove the next theorem.

THEOREM 9.16. Every complexity class of the standard storage measure is finitely invariant.

Proof. Exercise 1. ▮

An analogous result holds for the standard time measure $\mathcal{T} = \{T_i\}$.

THEOREM 9.17. If $f(x) \ge \text{length}(x) + 1$ for all x, then $\mathfrak{R}_f^{\mathcal{T}}$ is finitely invariant.

Proof. Exercise 1. ▮

The next theorem links finite invariance with recursive enumerability of classes.

THEOREM 9.18. If $\mathfrak{R}_f$ contains all finite variants of some recursive h, then $\mathfrak{R}_f$ is r.e. Hence if $\mathfrak{R}_f$ is finitely invariant, then $\mathfrak{R}_f$ is r.e.

Proof. If $\mathfrak{R}_f$ is empty, then it is trivially r.e. Let $h \in \mathfrak{R}_f$ be as in the statement of the theorem and define g recursive by

$$\varphi_{g(i,u)}(x) = \begin{cases} \varphi_i(x) & \text{if } \bigwedge_{y=0}^{x} \Big([y \leq u \wedge C_i(y) \leq u] \vee C_i(y) \leq f(y)\Big) \\ h(x) & \text{otherwise} \end{cases}$$

We claim that $\mathfrak{R}_f = \{\varphi_m \mid m \in \text{ran } g\}$ so $\mathfrak{R}_f$ is r.e. Let $m = g(i,u)$. First note that h total, f total, Axiom 9.2, and Axiom 9.3 imply that φ_m is total. The first possibility is that the first alternative is always used so $\varphi_m = \varphi_{g(i,u)} = \varphi_i$ in which case $C_i(y) \leq f(y)$ for $y > u$, so $\varphi_m \in \mathfrak{R}_f$. If the second alternative is used a.e., then $\varphi_m(x) = h(x)$ a.e. so $\varphi_m \in \mathfrak{R}_f$ because $h \in \mathfrak{R}_f$ and $\mathfrak{R}_f$ contains all finite variants of h.

Conversely if $e \in \mathfrak{R}_f$, then there is an i and a v such that $\varphi_i = e$ and $C_i(x) \leq f(x)$ for $x \geq v$. Let $u = \max\{v, \max\{C_i(y) \mid y \leq v\}\}$. Then $\varphi_{g(i,u)} = \varphi_i = e$. ∎

Theorems 9.16–9.18 imply the following theorem.

THEOREM 9.19. a. $\mathfrak{R}_f^{\mathcal{S}}$ is r.e. for all f.
b. $\mathfrak{R}_f^{\mathcal{T}}$ is r.e. for $f(x) > \text{length}(x)$. ∎

The next theorem indicates that finite invariance is not a consequence of the axioms. One reason for including the proof is to indicate to the reader how one may define measures which satisfy the axioms but which do not correspond to our standard notions of complexity. Theorem 9.20 is also an illustration of the failure of the axioms to adequately restrict the class of measures.

THEOREM 9.20. There is a measure $\mathcal{C} = \{C_i\}$ such that for arbitrarily large f, $\mathfrak{R}_f^{\mathcal{C}}$ is not finitely invariant.

Proof. The desired $\{C_i\}$ is obtained by modifying $\mathcal{S} = \{L_i\}$, the standard storage measure. By the honesty theorem (Theorem 9.14), there is a class determining measured set $\mathcal{G} = \{g_i\}$ for $\mathcal{S}$. By a suitable modification of the proof of the compression theorem (Exercise 2), for g_i recursive there are recursive h and k satisfying:

a. $\varphi_{k(i)}(x) = 0$ if $x = \text{prime}\,\#\,(i)^j$ for some $j > 0$ and $\varphi_{k(i)}(x) > 0$ otherwise

b. $\varphi_{k(i)} \in \mathfrak{R}^{\mathcal{S}}_{h \circ \langle g_i, \imath \rangle} - \mathfrak{R}^{\mathcal{S}}_{g_i}$

c. $L_{k(i)}(x) \leq h \circ \langle g_i, \imath \rangle(x)$ a.e.

Padding can be used to make k increasing. Now define a measure $\mathcal{C} = \{C_i\}$ as follows:

Method for computing $C_j(x)$.

```
IF j ∉ ran k THEN; C_j(x) ← L_j(x); STOP; END;
IF j = k(i) THEN;
    y ← 0;
    A: IF g_i(x) = y THEN;
            IF y ≤ L_k(i)(x) ≤ h(y,x) THEN;
                C_k(i)(x) ← y; STOP; END;
                ELSE; C_k(i)(x) ← L_k(i)(x); STOP; END;
    END;
    IF L_k(i)(x) = y THEN; C_k(i)(x) ← L_k(i)(x); STOP; END;
    y ← y + 1; GOTO A;
END;
```

The proof that $\mathcal{C}$ is a measure is left as Exercise 4. In essence, for g_i recursive, the above construction sets $\mathcal{R}_{g_i}^{\mathcal{C}}$ to $\mathcal{R}_{g_i}^{\mathcal{S}}$ plus some subset of $\{\varphi_{k(e)}\}$ which includes $\varphi_{k(i)}$ but no finite variants of $\varphi_{k(i)}$. Hence $\mathcal{R}_{g_i}^{\mathcal{C}}$ is not finitely invariant. To see this note that if $i \neq j$, then $\varphi_{k(i)}$ and $\varphi_{k(j)}$ are not finite variants of each other. Moreover, all classes of the standard storage measure are finitely invariant so no finite variant of $\varphi_{k(i)}$ is in $\mathcal{R}_{g_i}^{\mathcal{S}}$ because $\varphi_{k(i)} \notin \mathcal{R}_{g_i}^{\mathcal{S}}$.

Since $\mathcal{G}$ is class determining for $\mathcal{S}$, $\mathcal{G}$ contains arbitrarily large recursive functions. ▮

Notice that $\{g_i\}$ in the above proof may not be class determining for $\{C_i\}$ so the proof of Theorem 9.20 does not yield a measure none of whose classes is finitely invariant. The proof illustrates how one may somewhat arbitrarily modify the complexity of even an infinite set of functions to obtain new measures from a given measure (see Exercise 5).

If all finite variants of a single function belong to a complexity class, then the class is r.e. The next lemma implies that for any $\mathcal{C}$ and sufficiently large f, $\mathcal{R}_f^{\mathcal{C}}$ is r.e.

LEMMA 9.21. Let $\mathcal{C}$ be a measure. Then there is an f such that, for recursive g, if $g(x) = 0$ a.e. and $h \geq f$, then $g \in \mathcal{R}_h^{\mathcal{C}}$.

Proof. Let $\varphi_{i_0}, \varphi_{i_1}, \ldots$ be an effective enumeration of the a.e. 0 total functions, which are all recursive. Define f by $f(x) = \max\{C_{i_j}(x) \mid j \leq x\}$. Then for each j, $C_{i_j}(x) \leq f(x)$ a.e. so for $h \geq f$, $\varphi_{i_j} \in \mathcal{R}_h^{\mathcal{C}}$. ▮

COROLLARY 9.22. For every measure $\mathcal{C}$, $\mathcal{R}_f^{\mathcal{C}}$ is r.e. for sufficiently large functions f. ▮

We now consider various closure properties of complexity classes. First note that for any $\mathcal{C}$ and recursive f the complement of $\mathcal{R}_f^{\mathcal{C}}$, $\{g \mid g \notin \mathcal{R}_f^{\mathcal{C}}, g \text{ recursive}\}$ cannot be a complexity class (Exercise 6). The union of two complexity classes of a measure need not be a complexity class. Indeed, for every

$\mathcal{C}$, there are arbitrarily large f and g such that $\mathcal{R}_f^{\mathcal{C}} \cup \mathcal{R}_g^{\mathcal{C}}$ is not a complexity class. For intersection the situation is somewhat nicer. While there are measures $\mathcal{C}$ such that $\mathcal{R}_f^{\mathcal{C}} \cap \mathcal{R}_g^{\mathcal{C}}$ is not a complexity class for arbitrarily large f and g, there also measures in which complexity classes are closed under intersection. We omit proofs and examples of the above assertions and refer the reader to the references dealing with abstract complexity theory.

The next theorem provides a link between complexity theory and classical computability theory; its proof provides a simple example of an application of the priority method discussed in Chapter 8.

THEOREM 9.23 (union theorem). Let $\{C_i\}$ be a measure and $\{f_i\}$ an r.e. set of recursive functions such that $f_i(x) \le f_{i+1}(x)$ for all i and x. Then there is a recursive g such that $\mathcal{R}_g = \bigcup_i \mathcal{R}_{f_i}$.

Proof. Let $\{C_i\}$ be a measure and $\{f_i\}$ as above. The following effective procedure defines a recursive g so that for each j, $C_j(y) \le g(y)$ a.e. iff for some i, $C_j(y) \le f_i(y)$ a.e. Note that the computation of $g(x)$ requires the computation of $g(0), \ldots, g(x \dot{-} 1)$. To simplify matters the procedure given below successively computes $g(0), g(1), g(2), \ldots$.

Procedure for Computing g.

```
FOR x = 0 TO ∞;
    guess(x) ← x;
    α ← f_x(x);
    FOR i = 0 TO x;
      IF C_i(x) ≤ f_guess(i)(x) THEN; GOTO A; END;
      α ← min (α, f_guess(i)(x));
      guess(i) ← x;
   A: NEXT i;
   g(x) ← α;
NEXT x;
```

Assume $g(0), \ldots, g(x \dot{-} 1)$ have been defined. The computation of $g(x)$ begins by setting guess(x) to x. For $i \le x$, the value guess(i) represents a guess that $C_i(y) \le f_{\text{guess}(i)}(y)$ a.e. Whenever $C_i(x) > f_{\text{guess}(i)}(x)$, we will have $g(x) \le f_{\text{guess}(i)}(x) < C_i(x)$ and guess(i) will be increased to x.

We first show that for each j, $f_j(y) \le g(y)$ a.e. so $\bigcup_i \mathcal{R}_{f_i} \subseteq \mathcal{R}_g$. The value of g at x is

$$g(x) = \min\left\{\{f_x(x)\} \cup \{f_{\text{guess}(i)}(x) \mid i \le x, f_{\text{guess}(i)}(x) < C_i(x)\}\right\}$$

Assume $x \ge j$. For i satisfying $j \le i \le x$, guess$(i) \ge j$ so $f_{\text{guess}(i)}(x) \ge f_j(x)$. For $i < j$ such that guess$(i) \le j$, if $f_{\text{guess}(i)}(x)$ is used to compute $g(x)$, then guess(i) is reset to $x \ge j$. Hence there is an $\bar{x} \ge j$ such that for $x \ge \bar{x}$, no f_i

such that $i < j$ is used in the computation of $g(x)$. Since $f_k(y) \le f_{k+1}(y)$ for all k and y, we have $g(x) \ge f_j(x)$ for $x \ge \bar{x}$.

To prove the converse, show that $C_i(y) \le g(y)$ a.e. implies there is a j such that $C_i(y) \le f_j(y)$ a.e. Assume for $x \ge \bar{x} \ge i$, $C_i(x) \le g(x)$. But then for $x \ge \bar{x}$ the computation of $g(x)$ cannot discover that $C_i(x) > f_{\text{guess}(i)}(x)$ because this would imply $C_i(x) > f_{\text{guess}(i)}(x) \ge g(x)$. Hence for $x \ge \bar{x}$, guess(i) has a fixed value and $C_i(x) \le f_{\text{guess}(i)}(x)$. ∎

The above proof is an example of a priority argument because during the computation of $g(x)$, the smallest $f_{\text{guess}(i)}(x)$, $i \le x$, such that $C_i(x) > f_{\text{guess}(i)}(x)$, is found. Because of the condition on $\{f_i\}$, this involves finding the smallest guess(i) for which the above holds. This guess(i) has priority over larger values in that $g(x)$ is set to $f_{\text{guess}(i)}(x)$.

The next two theorems characterize the primitive recursive functions in terms of how difficult they are to compute. Let $\mathcal{C}^P = \{T_i^P\}$ be the time measure (number of instructions executed) for PL programs. Then φ_i is the function computed in T_i^P steps by the PL program corresponding to the ith LMA.

THEOREM 9.24. A function f is primitive recursive iff there is an i such that $\varphi_i = f$ and T_i^P is bounded by a primitive recursive function, that is, f is primitive recursive iff it can be computed by a PL program using a primitive recursive number of steps.

Proof. Assume f is primitive recursive. Then by Theorem 3.3 there is a PL − {GOTO} program $\mathcal{T}_i$ such that $\varphi_i = f$. Let COUNT be a variable not appearing in $\mathcal{T}_i$ (otherwise change this name in $\mathcal{T}_i$). Insert the statement

$$\text{COUNT} \leftarrow \text{COUNT} + 1;$$

before each statement of $\mathcal{T}_i$. Add

$$\text{COUNT} \leftarrow 0;$$

at the beginning, and

$$\text{Y1} \leftarrow \text{COUNT};$$

at the end. This gives a PL − {GOTO} program which computes T_i^P, so by Theorem 3.3, T_i^P is primitive recursive.

Conversely assume T_i^P is bounded by the primitive recursive function f and let $\mathcal{T}$ be a PL − {GOTO} program which sets a variable COUNT to f(X1) but which does not change the value of any other variables, that is, which leaves X1 unchanged and all other variables set to 0. We obtain a PL − {GOTO} program which computes φ_i. By the results of Section 2.2 (including Exercise 10), forward GOTO statements and IF statements can be implemented in PL − {GOTO}. Hence we may use these statements in eliminating backward GOTO statements. The solution is similar to that required for

Exercise 11 of Section 2.2. Because we have a bound on the number of steps $\mathcal{P}_i$ executes on input x (value of COUNT), a loop can be used instead of the GOTO of Exercise 11.

We describe a procedure for eliminating backward GOTO's in $\mathcal{P}_i$. The procedure is illustrated by showing how to eliminate the statement 5: GOTO 3; in the following program.

```
0: LOOP V;
1: V ← V + 1;
2: LOOP W;
3: U ← X + 1;
4: LOOP V;
5: GOTO 3;
6: END;
7: END;
8: END;
```

Assume $\mathcal{P}_i$ has k statements. Assign a label 0, ..., $k - 1$ to each statement and change all GOTO's accordingly. Backward GOTO's are eliminated by successive applications of the following procedure. Replace the backward GOTO j; by

$$\text{ALPHA}j \leftarrow 1;\ \text{GOTO FIND};$$

where ALPHAj and FIND are names not used elsewhere. If statement j is in the scope of some loops, then it is necessary to keep track of how many times these loops have been executed so that the proper loop index values can be restored after the GOTO j; is executed. This is accomplished by replacing each LOOP statement i: LOOP X; and its associated END statement k: END; of $\mathcal{P}_i$ by

$$\begin{aligned} i&: \text{TEMP}Xi \leftarrow X;\\ i'&: \text{LOOP TEMP}Xi; \end{aligned}$$

and

$$\begin{aligned} k&: \text{TEMP}Xi \leftarrow \text{TEMP}Xi \dot{-} 1;\\ &\ \ \text{END}; \end{aligned}$$

respectively where TEMPXi is a name not used elsewhere in the program and i' is a new label. Call this program $\mathcal{P}_i'$. For the example $\mathcal{P}_i'$ is

```
 0: TEMPV0 ← V;
 0': LOOP TEMPV0;
 1: V ← V + 1;
 2: TEMPW2 ← W;
 2': LOOP TEMPW2;
```

```
 3: U ← X + 1;
 4: TEMPV4 ← V;
4': LOOP TEMPV4;
 5: ALPHA3 ← 1;
    GOTO FIND;
 6: TEMPV4 ← TEMPV4 ∸ 1;
    END;
 7: TEMPW2 ← TEMPW2 ∸ 1;
    END;
 8: TEMPV0 ← TEMPV0 ∸ 1;
    END;
```

Now let $\bar{L}_0 = j$ and define $\bar{L}_{r+1}$ to be the label of the LOOP statement of $\mathcal{P}_i'$ (if any) with the smallest scope containing $\bar{L}_r$. Let $\bar{L}_0,\ldots,\bar{L}_t$ be the labels defined by this procedure. Then insert for each r, $1 \le r < t$,

IF ALPHAj = 1 THEN; GOTO $\bar{L}_{r-1}$; END;

after the LOOP statement having label $\bar{L}_r$. Replace the statement j:S; by j: ALPHAj ← 0; S; to obtain $\mathcal{P}_i''$. The final program is

$\mathcal{P}$
LOOP COUNT;
IF ALPHAj = 1 THEN; GOTO $\bar{L}_t$; END;
$\mathcal{P}_i''$
STOP;
FIND: END;

For example we obtain:

```
     𝒫
     LOOP COUNT;
     IF ALPHA3 = 1 THEN; GOTO 0'; END;
 0:  TEMPV0 ← V;
 0': LOOP TEMPV0;
     IF ALPHA3 = 1 THEN; GOTO 2'; END;
 1:  V ← V + 1;
 2:  TEMPW2 ← W;
 2': LOOP TEMPW2;
     IF ALPHA3 = 1 THEN; GOTO 3; END;
 3:  ALPHA3 ← 0;
     U ← X + 1;
 4:  TEMPV4 ← V;
 4': LOOP TEMPV4;
 5:  ALPHA3 ← 1;
     GOTO FIND;
```

```
      6: TEMPV4 ← TEMPV4 ∸ 1;
         END;
      7: TEMPW2 ← TEMPW2 ∸ 1;
         END;
      8: TEMPV0 ← TEMPV0 ∸ 1;
         END;
         STOP;
   FIND: END;
```

The proof is completed by noting that numerals can be implemented in PL − {GOTO} and that STOP is an abbreviation for a forward GOTO. ▌

Theorem 9.24 implies that the PL computation time for any nonprimitive recursive function must grow faster than any primitive recursive function such as

$$2^{\cdot^{\cdot^{2}}}\Big\} x$$

Hence nonprimitive recursive functions cannot be practically computed.

THEOREM 9.25. There is a recursive g such that $\mathcal{R}_g^{\mathcal{C}P}$ is equal to the class of primitive recursive functions.

Proof. Let $\{f_i\}$ be an effective enumeration of the primitive recursive functions, f_i. Define $\{f_i'\}$ by

$$f_i'(x) = \sum_{j=0}^{i} f_j(x)$$

The set $\{f_i'\}$ satisfies $f_i'(x) \leq f_{i+1}'(x)$ for all i and x so by the union theorem there is a recursive g such that

$$\mathcal{R}_g^{\mathcal{C}P} = \bigcup_i \mathcal{R}_{f'_i}^{\mathcal{C}P}$$

The proof is completed by observing that for any function h,
h is primitive recursive

iff $h \in \mathcal{R}_{f'_i}^{\mathcal{C}P}$ for some i by Theorem 9.24
iff $h \in \mathcal{R}_{f'_i}^{\mathcal{C}P}$ for some j because each f'_j is primitive recursive ▌

Theorem 9.25 is true of all the usual notions of dynamic complexity. Hence the primitive recursive functions are, in a very real sense, the least complex of the recursive functions. Unfortunately, it is easy to define a measure $\mathcal{C}$ such that for no recursive g does $\mathcal{R}_g^{\mathcal{C}}$ equal the primitive recursive functions (Exercise 7).

The property of the primitive recursive functions given by Theorems 9.24 and 9.25 is true of many interesting classes of functions. Such matters will be considered in more detail in Chapter 10.

EXERCISES

1. Prove Theorems 9.16 and 9.17.

2. Prove that if $\{g_i\}$ is a measured set and $\{C_i\}$ is a measure, then there are recursive functions h and k such that if g_i is recursive, then

a. $\varphi_{k(i)}(x) = 0$ if $x = \text{prime}\,\#(i)^j$ for some $j > 0$ and $\varphi_{k(i)}(x) > 0$ otherwise

b. $\varphi_{k(i)} \in \mathcal{R}_{h \circ \langle g_i, i \rangle} - \mathcal{R}_{g_i}$.

c. $C_{k(i)}(x) \leq h \circ \langle g_i, i \rangle(x)$ a.e.

Hint: Note that b only requires that for $\varphi_j = \varphi_{k(i)}$, $C_j(x) > g_i(x)$ i.o. This is weaker than the compression theorem.

3.[Δ] a. Prove that there is a measure such that there are arbitrarily large f and g for which $\mathcal{R}_f \cap \mathcal{R}_g$ is not a complexity class.

b. A measure has the *parallel computation property* if there is a recursive g satisfying

$$\varphi_{g(i,j)}(x) = \begin{cases} \varphi_i(x) & \text{if } C_i(x) \leq C_j(x) \\ \varphi_j(x) & \text{otherwise} \end{cases}$$

and $C_{g(i,j)} = \min\{C_i, C_j\}$. Show that if a measure has the parallel computation property, then its complexity classes are closed under intersection.

4. Prove that $\{C_i\}$ as defined in the proof of Theorem 9.20 is a measure of complexity.

5. Prove that if $\mathcal{F}$ is an r.e. set of recursive functions and g is recursive, then there is a measure $\mathcal{C}$ satisfying $\mathcal{F} = \mathcal{R}^{\mathcal{C}}$.

6. Prove that for any $\mathcal{C}$ and recursive f, $\{g \mid g \notin \mathcal{R}_f^{\mathcal{C}}, g \text{ recursive}\}$ cannot be a complexity class.

Hint: Use Corollary 9.22.

7. Define a measure $\mathcal{C}$ such that $\mathcal{R}_g^{\mathcal{C}}$ is not the class of primitive recursive functions for any recursive g.

8. Let $\{T_i\}$ be the standard LMA time measure. Show direcly that if T_i is primitive recursive, then so is φ_i.

Hint: Consider the role of minimization in the characterization of the partial recursive functions given at the end of Section 5.4.

9.[Δ] Prove that for any measure and any complexity class $\mathcal{R}_g$ there is a set S such that

a. $\bar{S}$ is r.e.

b. $\mathcal{R}_g = \{\varphi_e \mid e \in S\}$

10. Prove that the union of two complexity classes need not be a complexity class.

9.5 The Speedup Theorem

Does every function have a best algorithm with respect to a given measure of complexity? In this section, we demonstrate that best algorithms need not always exist. Indeed, for any measure of complexity and any "efficiency increment", there is a function whose algorithms can all be improved by the given increment. This precludes the possibility of always being able to find best algorithms. On the other hand, the function constructed in the proof of the speedup theorem is somewhat artificial. An interesting open problem in complexity theory is to characterize the set of recursive functions which have a best algorithm with respect to one of the standard mearures such as time or storage requirements.

THEOREM 9.26 (speedup theorem). Let $\{C_i\}$ be a measure of complexity. For any recursive $g: W^2 \to W$, there is a recursive f such that if $\varphi_i = f$, then there is a j such that $\varphi_j = f$ and $C_i(x) \geq g[x, C_j(x)]$ a.e., that is, the algorithm φ_j is better than φ_i by the amount specified by g.

As an example, let $g(x,y) = 2^y$ and let $\mathcal{C}^P = \{T_i^P\}$ be the PL time measure. Then there is an f such that if $\varphi_i = f$, there is a j such that $\varphi_j = f$ and $T_i^P(x) \geq 2^{T_j{}^P(x)}$ a.e., so $T_j^P(x) \leq \log_2 T_i^P(x)$ a.e. If $g(x,y) = 2^{2^y}$, then the f obtained has the property that if $\varphi_i = f$, then there is a j such that $\varphi_j = f$ and $T_j^P(x) \leq \log_2 \log_2 T_i^P$ a.e., so T_j^P is better than T_i^P by two binary orders of magnitude. It is important to note that while the speedup theorem is true for any measure and any recursive g, the function f is of a very special type. Unfortunately the a.e. condition cannot be omitted (Exercise 3).

Proof of the speedup theorem. The idea of the proof is to "simultaneously" define two fixed recursive functions φ_r and f_r which have the property that for each i such that $\varphi_i = f_r$,

$C_i(x) > \varphi_r(x \dot{-} i)$ a.e. and (9-3)

there is a j which satisfies $\varphi_j = f_r$ and $g[x, C_j(x)] \leq \varphi_r(x \dot{-} i)$ a.e. (9-4)
(see Figure 9-2).

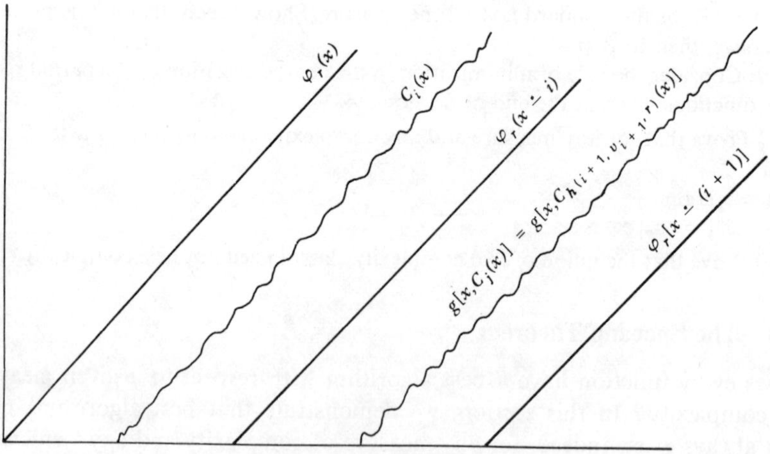

FIGURE 9-2. **The speedup theorem.**

The first step in the proof is to show that for any recursive φ_m, there is a recursive f_m which satisfies (9-3), that is, if $\varphi_i = f_m$, then $C_i(x) > \varphi_m(x \dot{-} i)$ a.e. In fact, for any recursive φ_m, we obtain an infinite set $\{h(u,v_u,m) \mid u \geq 0\}$ of indices for such an f_m. The recursive function h is defined by

$$\varphi_{h(u,v,m)}(x) = \varphi_{h(0,0,m)}(x)$$

if $u > 0$ and $x < v$. If $u = 0$ or $x \geq v$, then h is defined by

$$\varphi_{h(u,v,m)}(x) = \max\{0, \varphi_a(x) + 1\}$$

where a is the smallest index such that

1. $u \leq a \leq x$
2. $C_a(x) \leq \varphi_m(x \dot{-} a)$
3. a has not been used to compute $\varphi_{h(u,v,m)}(w)$ for $v \leq w < x$
4. a is not used to compute $\varphi_{h(0,0,m)}(w)$ for $w < v$

When the second alternative is applicable ($u = 0$ or $x \geq v$), the index a is said to be *used* to compute $\varphi_{h(u,v,m)}(x)$.

First observe that the computation of $\varphi_{h(0,0,m)}$ always involves the second alternative. Moreover, when $v = 0$, condition 4 is not relevant.

The second alternative in the definition of $\varphi_{h(u,v,m)}(x)$ is computed by computing $\varphi_m(0), \ldots, \varphi_m(x \dot{-} u)$ to check condition 2 (noting that $u \leq a \leq x$); $\varphi_{h(u,v,m)}(w)$ for $w < x$ to check condition 3; and $\varphi_{h(0,0,m)}(w)$ for $w < v$ to check condition 4. Thus $\varphi_{h(u,v,m)}(x)$ is undefined iff any of these are undefined. If all of these values are defined, then $\varphi_{h(u,v,m)}(x)$ is defined by Axioms 9.2 and 9.3. Hence if φ_m is total, so is $\varphi_{h(u,v,m)}$ for all u and v.

Now let φ_m be total and define $f_m = \varphi_{h(0,0,m)}$. By the definition of h, if $\varphi_i = f_m$, then $C_i(x) > \varphi_m(x \dot{-} i)$ a.e.

Also, for every u, there is a v_u such that $\varphi_{h(u,v_u,m)} = \varphi_{h(0,0,m)} = f_m$ (Exercise 1). Hence $\{h(0,0,m), h(1,v_1,m), h(2,v_2,m), \ldots\}$ is an infinite set of indices for f_m. In fact, as indicated in Figure 9-2 for the particular r to be defined (r will be a particular value of m), if $\varphi_i = f_r$, then $\varphi_{h(i+1,v_{i+1},r)} = f_r$ is the required g speedup of φ_i. Note that $\varphi_{h(u+1,v_{u+1},m)}$ can be computed faster than $\varphi_{h(u,v_u,m)}$ because the second alternative for $\varphi_{h(u+1,v_{u+1},m)}$ considers only values of a greater than u in the diagonalization, whereas $a \geq u$ must be considered to compute $\varphi_{h(u,v_u,m)}$.

For each total φ_m, we now have an f_m satisfying (9-3) ($\varphi_i = f_m$ implies $C_i(x) \geq \varphi_m(x \dot{-} i)$ a.e.). All that remains is to choose a particular value of m (call it r) which also satisfies (9-4). This is accomplished by defining φ_r so that for any u and v,

$$\varphi_r(x) > g[x + u \dot{-} 1, C_{h(u,v,r)}(x + u \dot{-} 1)] \text{ a.e.}$$

so that

$$\varphi_r(x \dot{-} i) \geq g[x + u \dot{-} (i+1), C_{h(u,v,r)}(x + u \dot{-} (i+1))] \text{ a.e.}$$

Then with $u = i + 1$ and $v = v_{i+1}$,

$$\varphi_r(x \dot{-} i) \geq g[x, C_{h(i+1, v_{i+1}, r)}(x)] \text{ a.e.}$$

where $\varphi_{h(i+1, v_{i+1}, r)} = f_r$ by Exercise 1. Again, notice that as u increases, each $\varphi_{h(u, v_u, r)}$ provides a faster way to compute f_r because the second alternative in the definition of $\varphi_{h(u, v_u, r)}$ only requires consideration of φ_a for $a \geq u$.

The definition of r involves the use of the recursion theorem (Theorem 5.21). First define the recursive function k by

$$\varphi_{k(m)}(0) = 0$$

$$\varphi_{k(m)}(x+1) = \begin{cases} \max\{g[x+u, C_{h(u,v,m)}(x+u)] \mid 0 \leq u, v \leq x\} \\ \qquad\qquad \text{if } \varphi_m(0)\downarrow \wedge \cdots \wedge \varphi_m(x)\downarrow \\ \uparrow \qquad\qquad \text{otherwise} \end{cases}$$

By the recursion theorem, k has a fixed point r. Thus

$$\varphi_r(0) = 0$$

$$\varphi_r(x+1) = \begin{cases} \max\{g[x+u, C_{h(u,v,r)}(x+u)] \mid 0 \leq u, v \leq x\} \\ \qquad\qquad \text{if } \varphi_r(0)\downarrow \wedge \cdots \wedge \varphi_r(x)\downarrow \\ \uparrow \qquad\qquad \text{otherwise} \end{cases}$$

A simple induction proof shows that φ_r is total (Exercise 2). The recursion theorem provided the transition from a partial recursive $\varphi_{k(m)}$ for each m to a recursive φ_r.

Now for i fixed such that $\varphi_i = f_r$ and for $x \geq \max\{(i+1)+(i+1), v_{i+1}+(i+1)\}$

$$\begin{aligned} \varphi_r(x \dot{-} i) &= \max\{g[x+u \dot{-} (i+1), C_{h(u,v,r)}(x+u \dot{-} (i+1))] \mid 0 \leq u, \\ &\qquad\qquad v \leq x \dot{-} (i+1)\} \\ &\geq g[x, C_{h(i+1, v_{i+1}, r)}(x)] \text{ taking } u = i+1 \text{ and } v = v_{i+1} \end{aligned}$$

so (9-4) is true of φ_r.

Again note that φ_r is defined so as to eventually be larger than enough values of $C_{h(u,v,r)}$ to ensure that (9-4) holds. The recursion theorem is used to force φ_r to be total. ▮

EXERCISES

1. Let h be as in the proof of the speedup theorem. Prove that for φ_m recursive and any u, there is a v_u such that $\varphi_{h(u, v_u, m)} = \varphi_{h(0,0,m)}$.

2. Prove that φ_r as defined in the proof of the speedup theorem is recursive.

3. Show that the speedup theorem cannot be strengthened by omitting the a.e. condition.

9.6 History

The axiomatic approach to complexity theory was developed by Blum [1967] in an attempt to unify previous results for particular measures of complexity. The speedup theorem and the compression theorem are contained in Blum's original paper.

Complexity classes for a particular complexity measure were first discussed in Hartmanis and Stearns [1965]. The properties of abstract complexity classes were studied in the following papers: the gap theorem in Borodin [1972], the honesty and union theorems in McCreight [1969] and McCreight and Meyer [1969], and the existence of non-r.e. complexity classes in Landweber and Robertson [1970, 1972] and Lewis [1970]. The proof given here of the honesty theorem is due to Meyer and Moll [1972]. Properties of complexity classes of arbitrary partial recursive functions were studied in Robertson [1971].

An interesting survey of results in abstract complexity theory containing additional references may be found in Hartmanis and Hopcroft [1971].

CHAPTER 10

Subrecursive Hierarchies

There are various criteria with respect to which one may study the complexity of recursive functions. For example, Chapter 9 dealt with dynamic complexity properties. In this chapter we show that there is a relationship between the dynamic complexity (execution time) and the static or structural complexity (depth of nesting of loops) of primitive recursive functions. We define a hierarchy $\mathfrak{L}_0 \subset \mathfrak{L}_1 \subset \mathfrak{L}_2 \cdots$ of the functions computed by PL − {GOTO} programs, that is, the primitive recursive functions, in terms of structural complexity. For $i \geq 2$, $\mathfrak{L}_i$ has the property that a function is in $\mathfrak{L}_i$ iff it can be computed by a PL − {GOTO} program whose execution time is bounded by a function in $\mathfrak{L}_i$. A new method called *majorization* is used both to prove results about this hierarchy and to later show that Ackermann's function is not primitive recursive. Similar methods can be used to extend this hierarchy beyond the primitive recursive functions. The last section presents another characterization of the classes $\mathfrak{L}_i$, $i \geq 2$, and discusses the properties of $\mathfrak{L}_2$, the class of *elementary functions*. The class $\mathfrak{L}_2$ is particularly important because by results of Section 10.1, all "practically computable" functions are in $\mathfrak{L}_2$.

10.1 A Hierarchy of Primitive Recursive Functions

In Section 3.1 we showed that PL − {GOTO} programs compute all and only primitive recursive functions. In the following we call such programs *loop programs*. A loop(i) program is a loop program having maximum depth of nesting i for LOOP-END pairs. That is, a loop(0) program is a PL program which contains no LOOP, END, or GOTO statements. Loop($i + 1$) programs are then defined recursively from loop(i) programs via the following BNF definition.

$$\langle \text{loop}(i+1) \rangle = \langle \text{loop}(i) \rangle \cup \text{LOOP}\langle \text{name} \rangle; \langle \text{loop}(i) \rangle \text{END}; \cup \langle \text{loop}(i+1) \rangle \langle \text{loop}(i+1) \rangle$$

Let $\mathfrak{L}_i$ be the class of functions computed by loop(i) programs. As mentioned above, all functions in $\mathfrak{L}_i$ are primitive recursive and $\bigcup_i \mathfrak{L}_i$ is the class of primitive recursive functions. In this section we show that for all i, $\mathfrak{L}_i \subset \mathfrak{L}_{i+1}$ where $\subset$ denotes proper inclusion. A more important result is that there is a relationship between dynamic complexity (execution time) and structural or static complexity (depth of nesting of loops) for functions computed by loop programs. Let $T_{\mathcal{P}}(x)$ be the number of PL statements executed by the loop program $\mathcal{P}$ on input $x \in W^r$ where END statements are executed each time the program reaches the end of a loop and LOOP statements are only executed when a loop is entered. We shall prove that, for $i \geq 2$, a function $f:W^r \to W^s$ is in $\mathfrak{L}_i$ iff there is a loop program $\mathcal{P}$ which computes f and a $g:W \to W$, $g \in \mathfrak{L}_i$, such that for all $x \in W^r$, $T_{\mathcal{P}}(x) \leq g(\max x)$. That is, a function can be computed by a loop(i) program ($i \geq 2$) iff it can be computed by any loop program whose execution time is bounded by a function in $\mathfrak{L}_i$.

By results of Sections 3.1 and 9.4, a function is primitive recursive iff it can be computed by a loop program iff it can be computed by a PL program whose execution time is bounded by a primitive recursive function. This type of relationship between structural (static) complexity and dynamic complexity is a characteristic of many interesting classes of functions including the classes $\mathfrak{L}_i$, for $i \geq 2$. We will say that a class $\mathcal{F}$ of recursive functions is *self-bounded* with respect to a measure of complexity $\{C_i\}$ and an algorithmic language $\mathfrak{L}$ provided that $\mathcal{F}$ satisfies: $f \in \mathcal{F}$ iff there is a $g \in \mathcal{F}$ and a program φ_i in the algorithmic language, such that φ_i computes f and $C_i \leq g$. The class $\mathfrak{L}_i$, $i \geq 2$, (class of primitive recursive functions) is self-bounded with respect to the PL time measure and the loop language (PL language).

The results for loop programs are obtained by defining a sequence of functions $f_0, f_1, f_2, \ldots, f_i: W \to W$, satisfying:

1. $f_i \in \mathfrak{L}_i - \mathfrak{L}_{i-1}$ for $i > 0$
2. for all $i \geq 1$ and all k, $f_i^k \in \mathfrak{L}_i$
3. for all i and all k, $f_{i+1}(x) > f_i^{k+1}(x) > f_i^k(x)$ a.e.
4. for $i \geq 2$ and $f: W^r \to W^s$, $f \in \mathfrak{L}_i$ iff there is a loop program $\mathcal{P}$ which computes f and a k such that $T_{\mathcal{P}}(x) \leq f_i^k(\max x)$ for all $x \in W^r$

For $i \geq 0$, the functions f_i are defined by

$$f_0(x) = \begin{cases} 1 & \text{if } x = 0 \\ 2 & \text{if } x = 1 \\ x + 2 & \text{if } x > 1 \end{cases}$$

$$f_{i+1}(x) = f_i^x(1)$$

Notice that

$$\begin{aligned} f_0(x) &= x + 2 && \text{for } x > 1 \\ f_1(x) &= 2 \times x && \text{for } x > 0 \\ f_2(x) &= 2^x && \text{for all } x \\ f_3(x) &= 2^{\cdot^{\cdot^{2}}}\}x && \text{for } x > 0 \end{aligned}$$

etc.

For the special case where $i = 1$ or $i = 2$ it is easy to see that $f_{i+1}(x) > f_i^k(x) + x$ a.e. for any fixed k. Hence if we can show that each function in $\mathfrak{L}_i$ has a computation time bounded by f_i^k for some k, it will then follow that $f_{i+1} \notin \mathfrak{L}_i$. One need only observe that to compute a function $h(x)$ requires a minimum of $h(x) - \max x$ steps, since a single PL statement can only increase a variable's value by 1. Since $f_{i+1}(x) > f_i^k(x) + x$ a.e. for any k, f_{i+1} cannot be computed in time f_i^k for any k.

The following lemma proves some useful properties of the set $\{f_i\}$.

LEMMA 10.1. For all k and all x

a. $f_i(x) \geq x + 1$ for all i
b. $f_i^k(x)$ is increasing in i, k, and x
c. $2 \times f_i^k(x) \leq f_i^{k+1}(x)$ for $i \geq 1$
d. $f_i^k(x) + x \leq f_i^{k+1}(x)$ for $i \geq 1$

Proof.

a. for $i = 0$, $f_0(x) \geq x + 1$. Assume the result holds for i; then $f_{i+1}(x) = f_i^x(1) \geq x + 1$ by the induction hypothesis.

b. Exercise 2.

c. for each $i \geq 1$, the result is obtained by induction on k. For $k = 0$, and all x,

$$\begin{aligned} 2 \times f_i^0(x) &= 2 \times x \\ &\leq f_1(x) && \text{definition of } f_1 \\ &\leq f_i^1(x) && \text{by b} \end{aligned}$$

Assume the results holds for k and all x. Then

$$\begin{aligned} 2 \times f_i^{k+1}(x) &= 2 \times f_i^k[f_i(x)] && \text{by the definition of exponentiation} \\ &\leq f_i^{k+1}[f_i(x)] && \text{by the induction hypothesis} \\ &= f_i^{k+2}(x) && \text{by the definition of exponentiation} \end{aligned}$$

d. this follows directly from a and c. ▮

Before proceeding let us adopt the convention that the argument x of $T_{\mathcal{P}}(x)$ will, unless otherwise specified, be the vector of initial values of *all* of the variables of $\mathcal{P}$. If $\mathcal{P}$ is computing $f: W^r \to W^s$, then all coordinates of x other than those which initially contain the r input values will initially have value 0 so that, in this case, the value of $T_{\mathcal{P}}(x)$ in effect depends only on the inputs to f.

THEOREM 10.2. Let $\mathcal{P} \in \text{loop}(i)$. Then there is a k which can be effectively found from $\mathcal{P}$ such that $T_{\mathcal{P}}(x) \leq f_i^k(\max x)$ for all x.

Proof. The proof is by induction on i. For $i = 0$, $\mathcal{P} \in \text{loop}(0)$ has no loops so $T_{\mathcal{P}}(x) = k$, the number of statements in $\mathcal{P}$. But $f_0^k(\max x) \geq k$ for all x.

Assume the theorem is true for all programs in loop(i) and let $\mathcal{P} \in$ loop ($i+1$). From the inductive definition of loop($i+1$) there are three cases.

Case 1. $\mathcal{P} \in$ loop(i). Then by the induction hypothesis, there is a k such that $T_{\mathcal{P}}(x) \leq f_i^k(\max x)$. But by Lemma 10.1b, $f_i^k \leq f_{i+1}^k$ so $T_{\mathcal{P}}(x) \leq f_{i+1}^k(\max x)$.

Case 2. $\mathcal{P}$ is of the form LOOP Y; $\mathcal{P}'$ END; where $\mathcal{P}' \in$ loop(i). There are two subcases:

Subcase 2a. $i > 0$. By the induction hypothesis there is a k such that if x is the vector of initial variable values when execution of $\mathcal{P}'$ begins, then $T_{\mathcal{P}'}(x) \leq f_i^k(\max x)$. Let $u = \max x$. The first execution of $\mathcal{P}'$ requires at most $f_i^k(u)$ steps so after this execution the maximum value of any variable is $f_i^k(u) + u \leq f_i^{k+1}(u)$ by Lemma 10.1d. The next execution of $\mathcal{P}'$ requires at most $f_i^k[f_i^{k+1}(u)]$ steps and gives maximum variable value

$$
\begin{aligned}
f_i^k[f_i^{k+1}(u)] + f_i^{k+1}(u) &\leq f_i^{k+1}[f_i^{k+1}(u)] \quad \text{by Lemma 10.1d}\\
&= f_i^{2(k+1)}(u)
\end{aligned}
$$

This is also a bound on the number of steps required for the first two executions of $\mathcal{P}'$. By induction one shows that the first j executions of $\mathcal{P}'$ require at most $f_i^{j(k+1)}(u)$ steps. The maximum number of executions of $\mathcal{P}'$ is u so the maximum number of steps required to execute $\mathcal{P}$ on input x is

$$
\begin{aligned}
T_{\mathcal{P}}(x) &\leq 1 + u + f_i^{u(k+1)}(u)\\
&\leq 1 + u + f_i^{u(k+1)}[f_i^u(1)] && \text{since } f_i^u(1) > u\\
&= 1 + u + f_i^{u(k+2)}(1)\\
&\leq 1 + u + f_i^{f_{i+1}^{k+1}(u)}(1) && \text{since } f_{i+1}^{k+1}(u) \geq f_1^{k+1}(u) = 2^{k+1}u \geq u(k+2)\\
&= 1 + u + f_{i+1}[f_{i+1}^{k+1}(u)]\\
&\leq f_{i+1}^{k+2}(u) + f_{i+1}^{k+2}(u) && \text{by Lemma 10.1a, 10.1b}\\
&\leq f_{i+1}^{k+3}(u) && \text{by Lemma 10.1c}
\end{aligned}
$$

Subcase 2b. The case $i = 0$ is left as an exercise.

Case 3. The case where $\mathcal{P}$ is the concatenation of a sequence $\mathcal{P}_1, \ldots, \mathcal{P}_l$ of programs such that $\mathcal{P}_j \in$ loop(i) or $\mathcal{P}_j$ is of the form in Case 2 is left as an exercise. ▮

The next two lemmas together with Theorem 10.2 establish the hierarchy result $\mathcal{L}_{i-1} \subset \mathcal{L}_i$.

LEMMA 10.3. For all i and k, $f_i^k(x) < f_{i+1}(x)$ a.e.

Proof. The proof is by induction on i. For $i = 0$ and $x > 2k$, $f_0^k(x) = x + 2k < 2x = f_1(x)$, for $x > 0$. Assume the result holds for i and prove it for $i+1$ by induction on k. If $k = 0$, then

$$
\begin{aligned}
f_{i+1}^0(x) &= x\\
&< f_{i+2}(x) \quad \text{for all } x \text{ by Lemma 10.1a}
\end{aligned}
$$

Assume the result holds for $i+1$ and k.

$$\begin{aligned}
f_{i+1}^{k+1}(x) &\le f_{i+1}^{k+1}[2(x \dot- 2)] && \text{for } x \ge 4 \text{ by Lemma 10.1b} \\
&= f_{i+1}^{k+1}[f_1(x \dot- 2)] \\
&\le f_{i+1}^{k+1}[f_{i+1}(x \dot- 2)] && \text{by Lemma 10.1b} \\
&= f_{i+1}^{2}[f_{i+1}^{k}(x \dot- 2)] \\
&< f_{i+1}^{2}[f_{i+2}(x \dot- 2)] \text{ a.e.} && \text{by the induction hypothesis on } k \text{ and Lemma 10.1b} \\
&= f_{i+2}(x) && \text{by the definition of } f_{i+2} \ \blacksquare
\end{aligned}$$

LEMMA 10.4. If $g \in \mathcal{L}_i$, $g: W^r \to W^s$, then $\max g(w) \le f_i^k(\max w)$ for some k and all $w \in W^r$.

Proof. First let $i > 0$. Since $g \in \mathcal{L}_i$, there is a $\mathcal{P} \in \text{loop}(i)$ which computes g. By Theorem 10.2, $T_{\mathcal{P}}(x) \le f_i^{k-1}(\max x)$ for some $k > 0$ where x is the vector of initial values of the variables of $\mathcal{P}$. When $\mathcal{P}$ computes g, all variables except the inputs of g are initially 0 so $\max w = \max x$. Moreover each PL statement can increase a variable by at most one. For $i > 0$ and all $w \in W^r$,

$$\begin{aligned}
\max g(w) &\le T_{\mathcal{P}}(x) + \max x \\
&\le f_i^{k-1}(\max x) + \max x && \text{by Theorem 10.2} \\
&\le f_i^{k}(\max x) && \text{by Lemma 10.1d} \\
&= f_i^{k}(\max w)
\end{aligned}$$

For $i = 0$,

$$\begin{aligned}
\max g(w) &\le T_{\mathcal{P}}(x) + \max x \\
&= k + \max x && \text{if } \mathcal{P} \text{ has } k \text{ statements} \\
&\le f_0^{k}(\max x) \\
&= f_0^{k}(\max w) \ \blacksquare
\end{aligned}$$

THEOREM 10.5. For $i > 0$, $f_i \in \mathcal{L}_i - \mathcal{L}_{i-1}$ so $\mathcal{L}_{i-1} \subset \mathcal{L}_i$.

Proof. For $i > 0$, $f_i(x) > f_{i-1}^k(x)$ a.e. for all k by Lemma 10.3. Hence by Lemma 10.4, f_i cannot be in $\mathcal{L}_{i-1}$. The proof is completed by showing that $f_i \in \mathcal{L}_i$ for all $i > 0$. We leave it to the reader to show that $f_0 \in \mathcal{L}_1 - \mathcal{L}_0$ (Exercise 4). ∎

If $f(x) < g(x)$ a.e., then g is said to *majorize* f. If g majorizes every $f \in \mathcal{F}$, then we say that g *majorizes* $\mathcal{F}$. The function f_{i+1} majorizes $\{f_i^k\}$ and hence by Lemma 10.4, $f_{i+1} \notin \mathcal{L}_i$. Moreover, f_{i+1} (actually $f_{i+1}(\max x)$) majorizes the execution times of functions in $\mathcal{L}_i$ as well as the maximum output values of the functions in $\mathcal{L}_i$ themselves. The process of majorization which has been illustrated in the above proof represents an alternate method to diagonalization for obtaining a function not in a given class. With majorization, a function is shown not to be in a given class of functions by demonstrating that it grows faster than (majorizes) every function in the given class. It is important to note that, though they have similar goals, diagonalization and majorization are different processes.

The next result completes the characterization of $\mathcal{L}_i$ in terms of execution times.

THEOREM 10.6. For $i \geq 2$, a function g is in $\mathcal{L}_i$ iff there is a loop program $\mathcal{P}$ which computes g and a k such that $T_{\mathcal{P}}(x) \leq f_i^k(\max x)$ for all vectors x of initial values of the variables of $\mathcal{P}$.

Proof. The proof for the implication from left to right follows immediately from Theorem 10.2. In the other direction, assume that $\mathcal{P}$ is a loop program and that $\mathcal{P}$ computes $g: W^r \to W^s$. Furthermore, assume that $\mathcal{P}$ uses the variables $U_1, \ldots, U_m$ and that $T_{\mathcal{P}}(U_1,\ldots,U_m) \leq f_i^k[\max(U_1,\ldots,U_m)]$ for all values of $U_1, \ldots, U_m$ satisfying $U_j = 0$ if $U_j \notin \{\text{X1},\ldots,\text{X}r\}$. As usual we use U_j for both the variable U_j and its value.

Let $\mathcal{P}$ be $S_1, \ldots, S_v$ where each S_j, $1 \leq j \leq v$, is a single statement of the loop program $\mathcal{P}$. The idea of the proof is to replace each S_j by a set of statements $\mathcal{S}_j$ which will be executed whenever S_j is to be executed. Each $\mathcal{S}_j$ will consist of one or more loops which will simulate the statement S_j and select the next statement to be executed. The total number of program steps to be simulated is computed by a loop(i) program $\mathcal{P}'$ which sets a variable T $\notin \{U_1,\ldots,U_m\}$ to a value greater than an equal to $f_i^k[\max(U_1,\ldots,U_m)]$. The program $\mathcal{P}'$ exists because $f_i^k(\max x) \leq f_i^k(\sum x) \in \mathcal{L}_i$ for $i \geq 1$ (Exercise 8).

For $1 \leq j \leq v$, the variable Vj is used to control sequencing of the subprogram $\mathcal{S}_j$. LOOP and END statements require additional variables to control looping. All of these variables initially have value 0.

The required loop(i) program which computes g is

$\mathcal{P}'$	set the counter T
V1 ← V1 + 1;	select first statement to be executed
LOOP T;	simulate $\mathcal{P}$
$\mathcal{S}_1$	
$\mathcal{S}_2$	
⋮	
$\mathcal{S}_v$	
END;	

where the subprograms $\mathcal{S}_1, \ldots, \mathcal{S}_v$ are specified as follows.

If S_j is an assignment statement, then $\mathcal{S}_j$ is

LOOP Vj;	
Vj ← 0;	
V(j + 1) ← 1;	select next statement
S_j	
END;	

If S_j is LOOP U; and the matching END is S_l, then $\mathcal{S}_j$ is

```
LOOP Vj;
    Vj ← 0;
    Rj ← 1;
    Cj ← U;                      Cj is the loop counter
END;
LOOP Rj;
    Rj ← 0;
    V(l + 1) ← 1;    tentatively select the statement after S_l
    Ej ← 0;
END;
LOOP Cj;                         if Cj = 0, S_{l+1} is executed next
    Cj ← Ej;                     if Cj > 0, decrease Cj by 1
    Ej ← Ej + 1;
    V(l + 1) ← 0;                select first statement of loop
    V(j + 1) ← 1;
END;
```

and the subprogram $\mathcal{S}_l$ for the END statement matching the LOOP statement S_j is

```
LOOP Vl;
    Vl ← 0;
    V(l + 1) ← 1;  if Cj = 0 select first statement after loop
END;
LOOP Cj;
    V(l + 1) ← 0;
    Rj ← 1;                  go back to beginning of the loop
END;
```

We leave it to the reader to verify that the subprograms operate as required. Note that $\mathcal{T}' \in \text{loop}(i)$ and the remainder of the modified program is in loop(2). Thus for $i \geq 2$, the program constructed is in loop(i). ▮

Since $f_i^k(\max x): W^r \to W$ is in $\mathcal{L}_i$ for $i \geq 2$ (Exercise 8) and since max $\circ\, h$ for each $h: W^r \to W^s$ in $\mathcal{L}_i$ is bounded by $f_i^k \circ \max$ for some k, we may restate Theorem 10.6 as follows.

COROLLARY 10.7. For $i \geq 2$, $g \in \mathcal{L}_i$ iff there is a loop program $\mathcal{T}$ which computes g and an $h \in \mathcal{L}_i$ such that $T_{\mathcal{T}}(x) \leq h(x)$ for all x. ▮

Theorem 10.6 does hold for $i = 0$ though a different proof is required. For $i = 1$, the theorem is false. The proofs are left as Exercise 5.

The proof of Theorem 10.6 implies that every function in $\mathcal{L}_i$, $i \geq 2$ can be computed by a program of the form $\mathcal{P}_1\mathcal{P}_2$ where $\mathcal{P}_2 \in$ loop(2) and $\mathcal{P}_1$ computes $f_i^k(\max x)$ for some k. The class $\mathcal{L}_2$ will be discussed in greater detail in Section 10.4. To indicate its importance, note that the T-predicate, $T(m,x,y)$, is in $\mathcal{L}_2$.

EXERCISES

1. Show that for each i there is no effective procedure for deciding whether an arbitrary loop program computes a function in $\mathcal{L}_i$.
Hint: Use the fact that the T-predicate is primitive recursive.

2. Complete the proof of Lemma 10.1 by showing that $f_i^k(x)$ is increasing in i, k, and x.

3. Complete the proof of Theorem 10.2.

4. Complete the proof of Theorem 10.5 by showing that for all $i > 0$, f_i can be computed by a loop(i) program. Also show that $f_0 \in \mathcal{L}_1 - \mathcal{L}_0$.

5.[Δ] Show that Theorem 10.6 is true for $i = 0$ but is not true for $i = 1$.

6. Show that $x \times y$ and x^y are in $\mathcal{L}_2 - \mathcal{L}_1$.

7. Show that for $i \geq 2$, $h_1(x,y) = \Sigma_{j=0}^{y}\, g(x,j)$ and $h_2(x,y) = \Pi_{j=0}^{y}\, g(x,j)$ are in $\mathcal{L}_i$ in case g is in $\mathcal{L}_i$.
Hint: Consider the number of steps required to compute h_1 and h_2.

8. Show that $f_i^k(\max x)\colon W^r \to W$ is in $\mathcal{L}_i$ for $i \geq 2$ and $f_i^k(\Sigma x) \in \mathcal{L}_i$ for $i \geq 1$.

9. Define $\mathcal{M}_0$ to be the smallest class of functions containing δ, ξ, ζ, ς, π, and ι which is closed under the operations of composition and combination. Let $\mathcal{M}_{i+1}$ be the smallest class containing $\mathcal{M}_i$ and $\{f^{\#} \mid f \in \mathcal{M}_i\}$ (recall that $f^{\#}$ is the exponentiation of f) which is closed under composition and combination. Show that for all $k \geq 0$, $\mathcal{L}_k = \mathcal{M}_k$, that is, k-fold nested exponentiation is equivalent to k-fold nested loops in PL $-$ {GOTO}.

10.[Δ] Define $\mathcal{R}_i$ to correspond to the definition of $\mathcal{M}_i$ in Exercise 9 but with exponentiation replaced by primitive recursion. How are the classes $\mathcal{L}_i$ related to the classes $\mathcal{M}_i$?

10.2 Loop(1) Programs

Loop programs compute all and only primitive recursive functions. In this section we characterize $\mathcal{L}_1$, the set of functions computed by loop(1) programs. This characterization is used in Tsichritzis [1970] to show that the equivalence problem for loop(1) programs—that is, the question of deciding whether two loop(1) programs compute the same function—is decidable. For $i \geq 2$, the equivalence problem for loop(i) programs is undecidable by results of Ritchie [1963] and Meyer and Ritchie [1967a,b].

The class of *simple* functions is the smallest class which contains the functions

$$\delta(x) = (x,x)$$
$$\xi(x,y) = (y,x)$$
$$\iota(x) = x$$
$$\pi(x) = ()$$
$$\zeta() = 0$$
$$\varsigma(x) = x + 1$$
$$x + y$$
$$x \dot{-} 1$$
$$x/k \qquad \text{for each constant } k \geq 1$$
$$\text{rem}(x,k) \qquad \text{for each constant } k \geq 1$$
$$\alpha: W^2 \to W \text{ given by } \alpha(x,y) = \neg x \to y = \begin{cases} y & \text{if } x = 0 \\ 0 & \text{if } x > 0 \end{cases}$$

and which is closed under the operations composition and combination. The main result of this section is that a function f is simple iff $f \in \mathfrak{L}_1$.

To motivate the choice of base functions, note that, with δ, π, ι, and ξ plus combination and composition, it is possible to define the rearranging functions of Section 3.1. These functions are precisely the functions computable by loop(0) programs using only the single statement type X ← Y; the addition of ζ and ς corresponds to adding the PL statements X ← 0 and X ← Y + 1, respectively. The remaining functions provide for simulating the mechanics of singly nested loops.

THEOREM 10.8. $\mathfrak{L}_0$ is the smallest class containing δ, ξ, ι, ζ, π, and ς which is closed under combination and composition.

Proof. The proof is left to the reader. ▌

THEOREM 10.9. A function $f: W^r \to W^s$ is in $\mathfrak{L}_0$ iff $f = \langle g_1,\ldots,g_s \rangle$ [recall $\langle g_1,\ldots,g_s\rangle(x) = (g_1x,\ldots,g_sx)$] where $g_i(x_1,\ldots,x_r) = x_l + k$ for some $k \in W$ and $1 \leq l \leq r$ or $g_i(x_1,\ldots,x_r) = k$ for some $k \in W$.

Proof. Exercise 1. ▌

COROLLARY 10.10. Every function in $\mathfrak{L}_0$ is simple.

Proof. Exercise 2. ▌

Theorem 10.9 states that a loop(0) program can only set a variable to a constant or to the initial value of some variable plus a constant.

The functions δ and ξ are included in the definition of simple functions so as to permit the definition of all multiple output functions computed by loop(0) programs. If they are omitted from the definition, then Corollary 10.10 is not true. For example, $\delta(x) = (x,x) \in \mathcal{L}_0$ but cannot be defined unless some mechanism for duplicating arguments is available (see Exercise 3). It was not necessary to include δ and ξ in the definition of the primitive recursive functions because they can be defined from the other initial primitive recursive functions via the use of exponentiation, composition, and combination. Half of the main result is given by the next theorem.

THEOREM 10.11. Every simple function is in $\mathcal{L}_1$.

Proof. ς, π, δ, ξ, ζ, ι, and $+$ are obviously in $\mathcal{L}_1$. The loop(1) program

```
Z ← 0;
LOOP X;
Y ← Z;
Z ← Z + 1;
END;
```

computes Y ← X $\dot{-}$ 1;.

The loop(1) program

```
Z ← Y;
LOOP X;
Z ← 0;
END;
```

computes Z ← α(X,Y);.

The functions x/k and rem(x,k) are left as Exercise 4.

If f and g are computed by loop(1) programs, then $f \circ g$ and $f \times g$ are easily seen to be computed by loop(1) programs. ∎

The other direction is somewhat more complicated.

THEOREM 10.12. Every function in $\mathcal{L}_1$ is simple.

Proof. Assume $f: W^r \to W^s$ is computed by the loop program $\mathcal{P}$ containing the variables $U[1]$, ..., $U[m]$. Note that the notation $U[i]$ is used instead of U_i so as to avoid the need for subscripted subscripts. Also assume that $U[1]$, ..., $U[m]$ includes X1, ..., Xr, Y1, ..., Ys even if these variables do not occur in $\mathcal{P}$. Furthermore, as a notational convenience assume

$$(U[1],\ldots,U[r]) = (\text{X1},\ldots,\text{X}r)$$
$$(U[r+1],\ldots,U[r+s]) = (\text{Y1},\ldots,\text{Y}s)$$

Then $\mathcal{P}$ is of the form

$$\begin{array}{c}\mathcal{P}_1\\ \mathcal{P}_2\\ \vdots\\ \mathcal{P}_v\end{array}$$

where each $\mathfrak{T}_i$ is either a loop or is an assignment statement. The function $f:W^r \to W^s$ computed by $\mathfrak{T}$ is

$$(\overbrace{\pi \times \cdots \times \pi}^{r} \times \overbrace{\iota \times \cdots \times \iota}^{s} \times \overbrace{\pi \times \cdots \times \pi}^{m \dot{-} (r+s)}) \circ g_v \circ \cdots \circ g_1 \circ (\overbrace{\iota \times \cdots \times \iota}^{r} \times \overbrace{\zeta \times \cdots \times \zeta}^{m \dot{-} r})$$

where $g_i : W^m \to W^m$ is computed by $\mathfrak{T}_i$ for $1 \le i \le v$. It only remains to show that each g_i is simple.

If $\mathfrak{T}_i$ is $U[j] \leftarrow 0$; then $g_i = \iota \times \cdots \times \iota \times (\zeta \circ \pi) \times \iota \times \cdots \times \iota$. The cases $U[j] \leftarrow U[l]$; and $U[j] \leftarrow U[l] + 1$; are left to the reader.

If $\mathfrak{T}_i$ is

LOOP $U[j]$;
$\mathfrak{T}'$
END;

then we must analyze how each variable changes as a result of $U[j]$ executions of $\mathfrak{T}'$. By Theorem 10.9, after one execution of $\mathfrak{T}'$, each $U[l]$ has value $k[l]$ or $U[p] + k[l]$ for some constant $k[l]$ and variable $U[p]$. In the second case we say that variable $U[p]$ *points to* variable $U[l]$. If we draw the directed graph having variables as nodes and an arrow from $U[p]$ to $U[l]$ in case variable $U[p]$ points to variable $U[l]$, then it is easy to see that each $U[l]$ falls into one and only one of the following four categories.

a. there are no arrows into $U[l]$ so $\mathfrak{T}'$ sets $U[l]$ to $k[l]$
b. $U[l]$ is in a cycle, that is, there are nodes $U[i_1]$, ..., $U[i_t]$, $t \ge 1$ and $U[i_q]$ points to $U[i_{q+1}]$ for $1 \le q < t$ and $U[i_t]$ points to $U[i_1]$
c. $U[l]$ is not in a cycle but there is a path from some node in a cycle to $U[l]$
d. there is a path from a node in category a above to $U[l]$

First note that $g_i = \langle h_1, \ldots, h_m \rangle$ for some h_1, ..., h_m and that if h_1, ..., h_m are simple, then so is $\langle h_1, \ldots, h_m \rangle$ (Exercise 7). Furthermore, note that each node has either zero or one node pointing to it.

For case a, $h_l = \iota \times \cdots \times \iota \times (\varsigma^{k[l]} \circ \zeta \circ \pi) \times \iota \times \cdots \times \iota$.

For case b, let $U[i_1]$, ..., $U[i_t]$ be a cycle. Let $u[i_1]$, ..., $u[i_t]$ be the initial values of $U[i_1]$, ..., $U[i_t]$, respectively. Without loss of generality we define h_{i_t}. After one execution of $\mathfrak{T}'$

$$\begin{aligned} U[i_t] &= u[i_{t-1}] + k[i_t] \\ U[i_{t-1}] &= u[i_{t-2}] + k[i_{t-1}] \\ &\vdots \\ U[i_2] &= u[i_1] + k[i_2] \\ U[i_1] &= u[i_t] + k[i_1] \end{aligned}$$

After the second execution of $\mathcal{S}'$

$$U[i_t] = u[i_{t-2}] + k[i_{t-1}] + k[i_t]$$
$$U[i_{t-1}] = u[i_{t-3}] + k[i_{t-2}] + k[i_{t-1}]$$
$$\vdots$$
$$U[i_1] = u[i_{t-1}] + k[i_t] + k[i_1]$$

It follows that after $u[j]$ executions of $\mathcal{S}'$

$$U[i_t] = h_{i_t}(u[1],\ldots,u[m])$$
$$= (u[j]/t)(k[i_1] + \cdots + k[i_t]) + \sum_{l=0}^{t \dot{-} 1} \alpha(\neg\, \text{eq}[\text{rem}(u[j],t), l], e_l)$$

where

$$\neg\text{eq}(x,l) = \begin{cases} 1 & \text{if } x \neq l \\ 0 & \text{if } x = l \end{cases}$$

is simple for each fixed l (Exercises 5 and 6) and

$$e_0 = u[i_t]$$
$$e_l = u[i_{t \dot{-} l}] + k[i_t] + \cdots + k[i_{t \dot{-} (l \dot{-} 1)}] \qquad \text{for } 0 < l \leq t \dot{-} 1$$

Note also that the index t of the above is a constant so that the summation is over a fixed number of terms. Hence h_{i_t} is simple.

Cases c and d are left as exercises. ∎

EXERCISES

1. Prove Theorem 10.9.

2. Prove Corollary 10.10.

3. Show that if δ and ξ are omitted from the definition of simple, then each $f: W^r \to W$, $f \in \mathfrak{L}_0$ is still simple.

4. Prove directly that x/k and rem(x,k) are in $\mathfrak{L}_1$.

5. Prove that the elementary logical functions $\wedge$, $\vee$, and $\neg$ are simple.

6. Show directly that $x \leq k$, $k \leq x$, $k \dot{-} x$, and eq(x,k) are simple, where k is a constant.

7. Show that the rearranging functions defined in Section 3.1 are all simple.

8. Complete the proof of Theorem 10.12.

10.3 A Function that Is Not Primitive Recursive

If e, d, g, and h are primitive recursive and $d(y) < y$ for all y, then the function f defined by the following recursion scheme was shown to be primitive recursive in Chapter 3.

$$f(x,0) = g(x)$$
$$f(x,y) = h[x,y,f(ex,dy)] \qquad y > 0$$

Ackermann [1928] used a more general type of recursion to define a nonprimitive recursive function. In this section we present a variant of Ackermann's function and use the results of Section 10.1 to show that it is not primitive recursive.

Define the function a by the recursion scheme

$$a(0,x) = f_0(x) = \begin{cases} 1 & \text{if } x = 0 \\ 2 & \text{if } x = 1 \\ x + 2 & \text{if } x > 1 \end{cases}$$

$$a(y + 1,0) = 1$$
$$a(y + 1,x + 1) = a[y,a(y + 1,x)]$$

THEOREM 10.13. For each i, $a(i,x) = f_i(x)$ where $\{f_i\}$ is the set of functions defined in Section 10.1.

Proof. The proof is by induction on i. For $i = 0$, $a(0,x) = f_0(x)$ by definition. Assume $a(i,x) = f_i(x)$ for all x. Then by induction on x, prove that $a(i + 1,x) = f_{i+1}(x)$ for all x. For $x = 0$,

$$a(i + 1,0) = 1 = f_i^0(1) = f_{i+1}(0)$$

Assume that $a(i + 1,x) = f_{i+1}(x)$. Then

$$\begin{aligned} a(i + 1,x + 1) &= a[i,a(i + 1,x)] \\ &= a[i,f_{i+1}(x)] && \text{by the induction hypothesis on } x \\ &= f_i[f_{i+1}(x)] && \text{by the induction hypothesis on } i \\ &= f_i[f_i^x(1)] && \text{by the definition of } f_{i+1} \\ &= f_i^{x+1}(1) \\ &= f_{i+1}(x + 1) && \text{by the definition of } f_{i+1} \end{aligned}$$ ▮

THEOREM 10.14. The function a is not primitive recursive.

Proof. If a were primitive recursive, then it would be in $\mathcal{L}_i$ for some i. Then by Lemma 10.4 there would be a k such that

$$a(y,x) \le f_i^k[\max(y,x)] \qquad \text{for all } y,x$$

This is not possible because for $y = i + 1$ and x sufficiently large

$$\begin{aligned} a(y,x) &= a(i + 1,x) \\ &= f_{i+1}(x) && \text{by Theorem 10.13} \\ &> f_i^k(x) && \text{by Lemma 10.3} \\ &= f_i^k[\max(i + 1,x)] \end{aligned}$$

Therefore a is not primitive recursive. ▮

The nonprimitive recursive function a is defined by majorization over the functions $\{f_j\}$. Since every primitive recursive function is bounded by some f_i, a also majorizes the primitive recursive functions, that is, grows faster than any primitive recursive function. The reader should compare the definition of a with the definition by diagonalization of a nonprimitive recursive function given in Section 2.3.

EXERCISES

1. Write a computer program to compute Ackermann's function. Compute $a(y,x)$ for a few *small* values of y and x.

Caution: Be sure to put a time limit on program execution time.

2. In Section 5.4 we showed that there is a partial recursive, universal function for partial recursive functions, that is, a partial recursive $F: W^2 \to W$ such that for all i and x, $F(i,x) = \varphi_i(x)$. Show that a universal function for primitive recursive functions cannot be primitive recursive, that is, the function G defined by

$$G(i,x) = \begin{cases} \varphi_i(x) & \text{if } i \text{ is the index of a PL} - \{\text{GOTO}\} \text{ program} \\ 0 & \text{otherwise} \end{cases}$$

is not primitive recursive where an indexing of PL programs as described in Exercise 3 is assumed.

3.[Δ] In Section 5.4 we showed that the function C which satisfies

$$\varphi_m(x) = \omega_1 \circ p \circ C^\nabla[\mathcal{A}(m), \alpha_1 x, 0, 0]$$

is primitive recursive where $\mathcal{A}(m)$ is the LMA with index m. A similar primitive recursive function $\bar{C}$ exists which satisfies

$$\varphi_m(x) = \bar{p} \circ \bar{C}^\nabla(m,x,0,0,0)$$

where $\bar{p} = \pi \times \pi \times \iota \times \pi$, an indexing of PL programs instead of LMA's is used, and each application of $\bar{C}$ simulates the execution of one instruction of the mth PL program. The arguments of $\bar{C}$ are as follows: m is the index of the mth PL program; the second argument at each step equals the value of the input variable X1; the third argument at each step equals the value of the output variable Y1; the fourth argument at each step is a coding of the variables of the mth PL program; and the last argument is set to 1 when the mth PL program halts, thus stopping the simulation. The function $\bar{p} \circ \bar{C}^\nabla$ is a universal function for the PL computable functions. Show that $\bar{C}$ is primitive recursive. Ritchie[1963] (in effect) proved that $\bar{C}$ is in $\mathcal{L}_2$.

A function H_i is said to be *almost universal* for $\mathcal{L}_i$ if for each m which is the index of a loop(i) program there is a k such that

$$\varphi_m(x) = H_i(k,m,x) \qquad \text{for all } x$$

Show that

a. an almost universal function for $\mathcal{L}_i$ cannot be in $\mathcal{L}_i$

b. for $i \geq 2$, there is an almost universal function for $\mathcal{L}_i$ in $\mathcal{L}_{i+1}$

Hint: See Exercise 9 of Section 10.1. Note that if m is an index of a loop(i) program, then for some k

$$\varphi_m(x) = \bar{p} \circ \bar{C}^{f_i^k(x)}(m,x,0,0,0)$$

If necessary, assume that $\bar{C} \in \mathfrak{L}_2$.

4. Use the fact that the function $\bar{C}$ described in Exercise 3 is known to be in $\mathfrak{L}_2$ to show that, for $i \geq 2$, there is no effective procedure for deciding whether two loop(i) programs compute the same function.

5. Ackermann's original nonprimitive recursive function was defined by

$$a'(0,y,z) = y + z$$

$$a'(x+1,0,z) = \begin{cases} 0 & \text{if } x = 0 \\ 1 & \text{if } x = 1 \\ z & \text{if } x > 1 \end{cases}$$

$$a'(x+1,y+1,z) = a'[x,a'(x+1,y,z),z]$$

Show that a' is not primitive recursive.
Hint: Consider the growth of $a''(x) = a'(x,x,x)$.

10.4 The Grzegorczyk Hierarchy

In Section 10.2 we gave a characterization of $\mathfrak{L}_1$ as the smallest class of functions containing certain initial functions which is closed under combination and composition. In Chapter 3 the primitive recursive functions were defined as the smallest class of functions containing ς, ι, π, and ζ which is closed under the operations composition, combination, and exponentiation. Since $\bigcup_i \mathfrak{L}_i$ equals the primitive recursive functions, a natural question is whether each class $\mathfrak{L}_i$ may be defined in the above manner. In this section we present such a characterization. The class $\mathfrak{L}_2$ is particularly important because it contains the function C and the T-predicate of Section 5.4 as well as all "practically computable" functions. The key to this characterization is in suitably restricting exponentiation so that not all primitive recursive functions can be defined.

The following operations on functions are considered.

A function $f: W^{r+1} \to W^r$ is defined by *limited exponentiation* (lim exp) from $h: W^r \to W^r$ and $j: W^{r+1} \to W$ if

$$f(x,y) = h^y(x)$$

and f satisfies

$$\max f(x,y) \leq j(x,y) \qquad \text{for all } x \in W^r,\ y \in W$$

A function $f: W^{r+1} \to W^s$ is defined by *limited recursion* (lim rec) from $g: W^r \to W^s$, $h: W^{r+1+s} \to W^s$ and $j: W^{r+1} \to W$ if

$$f(x,0) = g(x)$$
$$f(x,y+1) = h[x,y,f(x,y)]$$

and f satisfies

$$\max f(x,y) \le j(x,y) \qquad \text{for all } x \in W^r,\ y \in W$$

To simplify the notation in the following let $\mathcal{F} = \{\varsigma, \iota, \pi, \zeta, \delta, \xi, \max\}$ where $\max: W^2 \to W$ is defined by $\max(x,y) =$ maximum of x and y. Note that the maximum of $x = (x_1,\ldots,x_n)$ is also denoted $\max x$ and can be defined by $\max[x_1,\max(x_2,\ldots,\max(x_{n-1},x_n),\ldots)]$. Let $\mathcal{O}$ stand for the operations of composition and combination.

Let $\mathcal{E}'_i$ be the smallest class of functions containing $\mathcal{F}$ and the functions f_0 and f_i of Section 10.1 which is closed under the operations in $\mathcal{O}$ and limited exponentiation. We write this as

$$\mathcal{E}'_i = [\mathcal{F}, f_0, f_i; \mathcal{O}, \text{lim exp}]$$

The hierarchy $\mathcal{E}'_0 \subset \mathcal{E}'_1 \subset \mathcal{E}'_2 \cdots$ was first studied in somethat different form by Grzegorczyk [1953]. The class $\mathcal{E}_i$ was originally defined by

$$\mathcal{E}_i = [\mathcal{F}', g_i; \mathcal{O}', \text{lim rec}]$$

where only single output functions are considered; g_i is defined by

$$\begin{aligned} g_0(x,y) &= x + 1 \\ g_1(x,y) &= x + y \\ g_2(x,y) &= (x+1)(y+1) \\ &\vdots \\ g_{n+1}(x,0) &= g_n(x+1,x+1) \\ g_{n+1}(x,y+1) &= g_{n+1}[g_{n+1}(x,y),y] \qquad \text{for } n \ge 2 \end{aligned}$$

and $\mathcal{F}'$ contains ς, $p_1(x,y) = x$ and $p_2(x,y) = y$; and $\mathcal{O}'$ consists of composition, substitution of constants for variables, and identification of variables. For single output functions, $\mathcal{E}'_i = \mathcal{E}_{i+1}$ for $i \ge 2$ (Exercise 1). The difference in the two hierarchies stems from the fact that that, for $i \ge 2$, f_i and g_{i+1} grow at about the same rate.

Our first goal is to show that $\mathcal{E}'_i = \mathcal{L}_i$ for $i \ge 2$ and $\mathcal{E}'_i \subset \mathcal{E}'_{i+1}$ for all i.

THEOREM 10.15. $\mathcal{E}'_i \subset \mathcal{E}'_{i+1}$.

Proof. We first show that $\mathcal{E}'_i \subseteq \mathcal{E}'_{i+1}$ by showing that for each k and all $j \le k$, $f_j \in \mathcal{E}'_k$. The proof is by induction on $j \le k$. By definition $f_0 \in \mathcal{E}'_k$. Assume $f_j \in \mathcal{E}'_k$ for $j < k$. Then

$$\begin{aligned} f_{j+1}(x) &= f_j^x(1) \\ &= f_j^{\#} \circ ((\varsigma \circ \zeta) \times \iota)(x). \end{aligned}$$

and $f_{j+1}(x) \le f_k(x)$ for all x. Hence f_{j+1} is defined by limited exponentiation from functions known to be in $\mathcal{E}'_k$ so $f_{j+1} \in \mathcal{E}'_k$.

To show that $\mathcal{E}'_i \subset \mathcal{E}'_{i+1}$ note that for any $g \in \mathcal{E}'_i$ there is an l such that

$$\max g(x) \leq f_i^l(\max x) \qquad \text{for all } x \text{ (Exercise 4)}$$

But then, by Lemma 10.3, $f_{i+1} \in \mathcal{E}'_{i+1} - \mathcal{E}'_i$. ∎

THEOREM 10.16. $\mathcal{E}'_i \subseteq \mathcal{L}_i$ for $i \geq 2$.

Proof. Assume $i \geq 2$. The proof is by induction on the definition of $f \in \mathcal{E}'_i$. First note that $\mathcal{F} \subseteq \mathcal{L}_i$ for $i \geq 2$. Furthermore, $f_0 \in \mathcal{L}_i$, $f_i \in \mathcal{L}_i$, and $\mathcal{L}_i$ is obviously closed under composition and combination. It only remains to show that if $h, j \in \mathcal{L}_i$ and f is defined by

$$f(x,y) = h^y(x)$$

where

$$\max f(x,y) \leq j(x,y)$$

then $f \in \mathcal{L}_i$. Consider the PL program $\mathcal{P}$ defined by

LOOP Y;
$\mathcal{P}'$
END;

where $\mathcal{P}' \in \text{loop}(i)$ computes h, Y initially contains the value of y, and Y is not used in $\mathcal{P}'$. Furthermore, assume that all variables of $\mathcal{P}'$ other than those containing the outputs of h are set to 0 before $\mathcal{P}'$ terminates each time through the loop. Since $\mathcal{P}' \in \text{loop}(i)$, $j \in \mathcal{L}_i$, and $i \geq 2$, there are, by Theorem 10.6, constants k and l such that $T_{\mathcal{P}'}(x) \leq f_i^k$ (max x) and $j(x,y) \leq f_i^l[\max(x,y)]$. The first execution of $\mathcal{P}'$ requires at most $f_i^k(\max x)$ steps. Since $\max f(x,p) \leq f_i^l[\max(x,p)]$ for all x and p, and $\mathcal{P}'$ sets all nonoutput variables to 0, the $(p+1)$st execution of $\mathcal{P}'$, which computes $f(x,p+1) = h^{p+1}(x)$, takes at most $f_i^k[\max f(x,p)] \leq f_i^k(f_i^l[\max(x,p)])$ steps. The complete computation on input x, y takes at most

$$1 + y + \sum_{p=1}^{y} f_i^k\,(f_i^l[\max(x, p-1)])$$

steps. Hence

$$T_{\mathcal{P}}(x,y) \leq 1 + y + yf_i^{k+l}[\max(x,y)] \leq yf_i^{k+l+1}[\max(x,y)] + 1$$

We leave it for the reader to show (Exercise 2) that for $i \geq 2$ and all u and q.

$$uf_i^q(u) \leq f_i^{q+2}(u)$$

Therefore $T_{\mathcal{P}}(x,y) \leq f_i^{k+l+4}[\max(x,y)]$ so by Theorem 10.6, $f \in \mathcal{L}_i$. ∎

Notice that $\mathcal{E}'_0$ is not a subset of $\mathcal{L}_0$ because $f_0 \notin \mathcal{L}_0$. This follows from the inability to test inputs with loop(0) programs. We leave it to the reader (Exercise 3) to study the relationships between the classes $\mathcal{L}_0$, $\mathcal{L}_1$, $\mathcal{E}_0$, $\mathcal{E}_1$, $\mathcal{E}_2$, $\mathcal{E}'_0$, and $\mathcal{E}'_1$.

THEOREM 10.17. $\mathcal{L}_i \subseteq \mathcal{E}'_i$ for all i.

Proof. The proof is by induction on i. For $i = 0$, the result is obvious. Assume $\mathcal{L}_i \subseteq \mathcal{E}'_i$ and let $f \in \mathcal{L}_{i+1}$. Following the definition of loop($i + 1$) there are three cases.

Case 1. If $f \in \mathcal{L}_i$, then by the inductive hypothesis, $f \in \mathcal{E}'_i$ so by Theorem 10.15, $f \in \mathcal{E}'_{i+1}$.

Case 2. If f is computed by a loop($i + 1$) program $\mathcal{P}$ of form

LOOP Y;
$\mathcal{P}'$
END;

where $\mathcal{P}'$ computes $g \in \mathcal{L}_i$, then, by the induction hypothesis, $g \in \mathcal{E}'_i$ so $g \in \mathcal{E}'_{i+1}$ by Theorem 10.15 Moreover, $f(x,y) = g^y(x)$ and by results of Section 10.1, since $f \in \mathcal{L}_{i+1}$, there is a k such that

$$\max f(x,y) \leq f^k_{i+1}[\max(x,y)]$$

But $f^k_{i+1}[\max(x,y)]$ is in $\mathcal{E}'_{i+1}$ so f can be defined by limited exponentiation from functions in $\mathcal{E}'_{i+1}$ which gives $f \in \mathcal{E}'_{i+1}$.

Case 3. If f is computed by a loop($i + 1$) program $\mathcal{P}_1 \ldots \mathcal{P}_n$ where each $\mathcal{P}_i$ is either in loop(i) or of the form in Case 2, then the result follows directly via the use of composition. ▮

COROLLARY 10.18. For $i \geq 2$, $\mathcal{L}_i = \mathcal{E}'_i$. ▮

The class $\mathcal{E}'_2 = \mathcal{L}_2$ is often referred to as the class of *elementary functions.* We claim that all real problems are in fact elementary, that is, computable by loop(2) programs. To see this, note that by Theorem 10.6 a function is elementary iff it can be computed by a loop program whose computing time as a function of its inputs is bounded by f^k_2 for some k. If a function g is not elementary, then any loop program which computes g must, for any k, use more than

$$f^k_2(\max x) = \left.2^{2^{\cdot^{\cdot^{2^{\max x}}}}}\right\} k$$

steps on infinitely many inputs. It should be clear that this extraordinarily large computing time requirement precludes the computation of functions not in $\mathcal{L}_2$ by loop programs on any existing or planned digital computer. One might suggest that a more efficient method for computing g might be found if a more powerful language such as PL were used. However, a result of Constable and Borodin [1972] shows that if a primitive recursive function is computable by a PL program in time $T(x)$, then it can be computed by a loop program in time $T^2(x)$. Similar results hold even if all the language features discussed in Chapters 2 and 3 are permitted. Hence the use of PL or a similar language would not significantly modify the above comments on the impracticality of computing functions not in $\mathcal{E}_2'$.

A function $f:W^{r+1} \to W$ is defined by *bounded minimization* (bd min) from a function $h:W^{r+1} \to W$ if

$$f(x,y) = (\mu z \leq y)[h(x,z)]$$

A function $f:W^{r+1} \to W$ is defined by *limited summation* (lim sum) [*limited multiplication* (lim mult)] from the function $h:W^{r+1} \to W$ if

$$f(x,y) = \sum_{i \leq y} h(x,i) = h(x,0) + \cdots + h(x,y)$$

$$[f(x,y) = \prod_{i \leq y} h(x,i) = h(x,0) \times \cdots \times h(x,y)]$$

There are several equivalent definitions for the elementary functions. In particular the classes $\mathcal{C}_1$–$\mathcal{C}_6$ defined by

$$\mathcal{C}_1 = [\mathcal{F}, x^y; \mathcal{O}, \text{lim rec}]$$
$$\mathcal{C}_2 = [\mathcal{F}, x^y, x \dot{-} y; \mathcal{O}, \text{lim min}]$$
$$\mathcal{C}_3 = [\mathcal{F}, x^y, x \dot{-} y, x \times y; \mathcal{O}, \text{lim sum}]$$
$$\mathcal{C}_4 = [\mathcal{F}, x^y, x \dot{-} y, x \times y; \mathcal{O}, \text{lim mult}]$$
$$\mathcal{C}_5 = [\mathcal{F}, x + y, x \dot{-} y; \mathcal{O}, \text{lim sum, lim mult}]$$
$$\mathcal{C}_6 = [\mathcal{F}, x+y, x \times y, x/y; \mathcal{O}, \text{lim sum, lim mult}]$$

are all equal to $\mathcal{E}_2'$, the elementary functions.

EXERCISES

1. Show that $\mathcal{E}_i' = \mathcal{E}_{i+1}$ for $i \geq 2$, where only single-output functions are considered.

2. Show that for $i \geq 2$ and all u and q, $uf_i^q(u) \leq f_i^{q+2}(u)$.

3. Discuss the relationships between the classes $\mathcal{L}_0$, $\mathcal{L}_1$, $\mathcal{E}_0$, $\mathcal{E}_1$, $\mathcal{E}_2$, $\mathcal{E}_0'$, and $\mathcal{E}_1'$.

4. Show that for each $g \in \mathcal{E}_i'$ there is an l such that max $g(x) \leq f_i^l(\max x)$, for all x.

5. Show that for $i \geq 2$, $\mathcal{E}_i'$ ($\mathcal{L}_i$) is closed under limited recursion, bounded minimization, limited summation, and limited multiplication.

6.$^\Delta$ a. Show that $x + y$, $x \times y$, $x \dot{-} y$, x/y, and x^y are in $\mathcal{E}_2'$ ($\mathcal{L}_2$).
b. Show that each of the classes $\mathcal{C}_1, \ldots, \mathcal{C}_6$ is $\mathcal{E}_2'$.

10.5 History

Initial interest in hierarchies of functions stemmed from Hilbert's [1926] proposal that they might lead to a positive solution to the problem of the continuum (is cd $P(N)$ the next largest cardinality after $\aleph_0$?) and Ackermann's

[1928] use of a more general form of recursion than primitive recursion to obtain a nonprimitive recursive function. Early work on a syntactic approach to defining hierarchies (by defining classes which contain certain initial functions and are closed under various operations) may be found in Peter [1936], Grzegorczyk [1953], and Kleene [1952]. Peter used recursion schemes of increasing complexity to obtain a hierarchy the smallest class of which was the primitive recursive functions. Ackermann's function is in Peter's second smallest class. Grzegorczyk [1953] defined the hierarchy of Section 10.4 and showed that its union is the primitive recursive functions. The elementary functions ($\mathcal{E}_3 = \mathcal{L}_2$) were first defined and studied by Kalmar [1943] (see also Kleene [1952]). The various equivalent definitions of this class are given in Grzegorczyk [1953].

Recent interest in subrecursive hierarchies is due to the fact that they also can be defined by consideration of the computational complexity of functions. The relationship between the more traditional hierarchies and hierarchies based on complexity criteria was first investigated by Ritchie [1963] and Cobham [1964]. Ritchie's hierarchy, based on memory requirements, is a refinement of the class $\mathcal{L}_2(\mathcal{E}_3)$ of elementary functions. A hierarchy based on the number of jumps executed by a URM program, due to Cleave [1963], extends the Ritchie hierarchy through $\bigcup \mathcal{L}_i = \bigcup \mathcal{E}_i$, the primitive recursive functions. A later result of Constable [1968] uses random access devices to extend the Ritchie–Cleave hierarchy through the Peter hierarchy.

The loop hierarchy and its relation to Grzegorczyk's [1953] hierarchy were first studied by Meyer and Ritchie [1967a,b]. The proof that the functions in $\mathcal{L}_i$ are self-bounded with respect to the loop language and the PL time measure is due to Meyer and Ritchie [1967a,b]. A later result of Constable and Borodin [1972] shows that if a primitive recursive function is computed by an arbitrary PL program in time $T(x)$, then it can be computed by a loop program in time $c[T(x)]^2$ for some constant c.

The characterization of $\mathcal{L}_1$ in Section 10.2 is due to Tsichritzis [1970].

CHAPTER 11

Introduction to Combinatory Logic

by George W. Petznick

11.1 Introduction

Our subject has two independent beginnings. That these two different formulations are equivalent is, in a number of ways for the practical computer scientist, more interesting than the fact that both are equivalent to partial recursiveness. And that both starts strove for a reduction of the whole of logic to an extremely primitive framework is of some interest in view of the paradox that developed later.

The earlier of these two starts took place December 7, 1920 when Schönfinkel presented before the Göttingen Mathematical Society a number of rather elementary ideas for the reduction of the number of primitive notions of logic, until the goal, nothing less than the complete elimination of variables, was an accomplished fact. These ideas, which we shall consider first before discussing the later start, were subsequently written up by Behmann and published as Schönfinkel [1924].

Consider a function f or $f(x)$ or $y = f(x)$ of one variable x. In particular, consider the linguistic requirement that demands the description of a definite finite procedure by which, given a value $m \in \operatorname{dom} f$, the value $n \in \operatorname{ran} f$ such that $n = f(m)$, can be obtained in a finite number of steps or applications of the rules of the calculus as specified by the procedure. First of all, if $\hat{F}$ and $\hat{m}$ denote objects in the proposed calculus that represent in some way or another the function f of one variable and the positive integer m, respectively, then, following Schönfinkel [1924], we shall write $(\hat{F}\hat{m})$ instead of the more standard $f(m)$ and speak of the *application* of $\hat{F}$ to $\hat{m}$. For the sake of illustration, let us suppose that there are objects $\hat{1}, \hat{2}, \hat{3}, \ldots, \hat{m}, \widehat{m+1}, \ldots$ that represent the (positive) integers $1, 2, 3, \ldots, m, m+1, \ldots$, respectively. Now if there is an object $\hat{S}$ such that, for each (positive) integer m, it is the case that the combination $(\hat{S}\hat{m})$, the application of $\hat{S}$ to $\hat{m}$, may be reduced or transformed by the rules of procedure of the calculus to $\widehat{m+1}$, in symbols $(\hat{S}\hat{m}) \Rightarrow \widehat{m+1}$, then one is permitted by the intended interpretation to view the object $\hat{S}$ as a representation of the successor function S, $S(m) = m + 1$. Likewise, an object $\hat{\mathcal{T}}$ such that, for each (positive) integer m, $(\hat{\mathcal{T}}\hat{m}) \Rightarrow \widehat{m+2}$ may be viewed as a representation of the function $\mathcal{T}$ such that $\mathcal{T}(x) = x + 2$.

But being able to write $(\hat{S}(\hat{S}\hat{m})) \Rightarrow (\hat{S}\widehat{m+1}) \Rightarrow \widehat{m+2}$, because one will, by the rules of the calculus, be able "to replace a properly parenthesized component part of an object agreeing with the lefthand side of a known reduction by the corresponding righthand side to obtain an object to which the first reduces", does not yield a definition of $\hat{\mathcal{T}}$ in terms of $\hat{S}$. For the combination $(\hat{S}(\hat{S}\hat{m}))$ is not in the form of an application $(\hat{\mathcal{T}}\hat{m})$ of an object $\hat{\mathcal{T}}$ representing $\mathcal{T}$ to an object $\hat{m}$ representing the argument m. However, if we, along with Schönfinkel, postulate a primitive constant B with

RULE *B* 11.1. $$(((B\alpha)\beta)\gamma) \rightarrow (\alpha(\beta\gamma))$$

which is to be understood as yielding for objects $\hat{X}$, $\hat{Y}$, and $\hat{Z}$ the reduction $(((B\hat{X})\hat{Y})\hat{Z}) \Rightarrow (\hat{X}(\hat{Y}\hat{Z}))$, then we do obtain such a definition, namely $\hat{\mathcal{T}} \equiv ((B\hat{S})\hat{S})$, as $(\hat{\mathcal{T}}\hat{m}) \equiv (((B\hat{S})\hat{S})\hat{m}) \Rightarrow (\hat{S}(\hat{S}\hat{m})) \Rightarrow \widehat{m+2}$.

A moment's reflection will reveal that B does indeed model the law of composition for functions of one variable. But we do not want to get too far ahead of Schönfinkel's presentation.

The usual trick which permits functions of more than one variable to be treated in terms of functions of one variable is to view a function f or $f(x_1,\ldots,x_n)$ or $y = f(x_1,\ldots,x_n)$ of $n > 1$ variables $x_1, \ldots, x_n$ with domains $X_1, \ldots, X_n$ as a function f' of one variable x with the domain X that is the cartesian product of $X_1, \ldots, X_n$. But the trick does not suffice for our needs here, as an n-tuple is itself a function of n variables.

To understand the crucial idea of Schönfinkel, let us consider the function f of two variables x and y defined by $f(x,y) = x \div y$.† If we fix x, say $x = m$, then we obtain at once a function g_m of one variable y which is defined by $g_m(y) = m \div y$. If we permit functions of one variable in the ranges of functions of one variable, there is then no difficulty with the notion of the function h of one variable x which, to each value m, makes correspond the function g_m. In symbols $h(m) = g_m$, so that h may be defined parametrically by $h(x) = g_x$. Now, let $\hat{H}$ be an object, presumed to exist for the time being, that represents h. Then, in regard to the intended interpretation $(\hat{H}\hat{m}) \Rightarrow \hat{G}_m$ and $(\hat{G}_m\hat{n}) \Rightarrow \widehat{m \div n}$, where $\hat{G}_m$ is some object that may be viewed as representing, for the

† Since we are dealing with the positive integers only, we shall mean by "$x \div y$" the value 1, whenever $x \leq y$, and $1 + (x-y)$, otherwise.

positive integer m, g_m. Using again our earlier procedural rule, $((\hat{H}\hat{m})\hat{n}) \Rightarrow (\hat{G}_m\hat{n}) \Rightarrow \widehat{m \div n}$. The final step is now obvious: The object $\hat{H}$ is to be taken as a representation of f.

For the common binary operations of addition, subtraction, multiplication, and division, it is indeed just as if we were writing simple expressions like $x + y$, $x - y$, $x \times y$, and x/y in a prefixed notation, that is, $+xy$, $-xy$, $\times xy$, and $/xy$, respectively. To emphasize this, we may and shall abbreviate combinations by deleting left nests of properly paired parentheses—for example, we may and shall write $\hat{H}\hat{m}\hat{n}$, as well as $(\hat{H}\hat{m})\hat{n}$ and $(\hat{H}\hat{m}\hat{n})$, for the combination $((\hat{H}\hat{m})\hat{n})$ of the preceding paragraph.

Observe that the primitive constant B may be viewed as an (intuitive) function of three variables. Also note that (intuitive) functions of one variable may occur in the domains and ranges of (intuitive) functions of one variable. This is done so that we may view each and every object as representing an (intuitive) function of one variable.

The asymmetry of $\div$ suggests the following question: How may one obtain from $\hat{H}$ an object representing the function g defined by $g(x,y) = f(y,x) = y \div x$? The answer is that we shall, continuing to follow Schönfinkel, postulate another primitive constant C with Rule C.

RULE C 11.2. $$(((C\alpha)\beta)\gamma) \rightarrow ((\alpha\gamma)\beta)$$

For then, as $(((C\hat{H})\hat{m})\hat{n}) \Rightarrow ((\hat{H}\hat{n})\hat{m}) \Rightarrow \widehat{n \div m}$, we are at liberty, in regard to the intended interpretation, to view $(C\hat{H})$ as representing g.

How about the function f of two variables defined by $f(x,y) = (x + 1) \div y$? One may verify that

$$((((B\hat{H})\hat{S})\hat{m})\hat{n}) \Rightarrow ((\hat{H}(\hat{S}\hat{m}))\hat{n}) \Rightarrow ((\hat{H}\widehat{m + 1})\hat{n}) \Rightarrow \widehat{(m + 1) \div n}$$

so that $((B\hat{H})\hat{S})$ will suffice. How about $g(x,y) = x \div (y + 1)$? One may verify that

$$((B(CB\hat{S})\hat{H})\hat{m}\hat{n}) \Rightarrow (CB\hat{S}(\hat{H}\hat{m})\hat{n}) \Rightarrow (B(\hat{H}\hat{m})\hat{S}\hat{n})$$
$$\Rightarrow ((\hat{H}\hat{m})(\hat{S}\hat{n})) \Rightarrow ((\hat{H}\hat{m})\widehat{n + 1}) \Rightarrow \widehat{m \div (n + 1)}$$

and that

$$((C(B(C\hat{H})\hat{S}))\hat{m}\hat{n}) \Rightarrow (B(C\hat{H})\hat{S}\hat{n}\hat{m}) \Rightarrow (C\hat{H}(\hat{S}\hat{n})\hat{m})$$
$$\Rightarrow ((\hat{H}\hat{m})(\hat{S}\hat{n})) \Rightarrow ((\hat{H}\hat{m})\widehat{n + 1}) \Rightarrow \widehat{m \div (n + 1)}$$

so that *either* $(B(CB\hat{S})\hat{H})$ *or* $(C(B(C\hat{H})\hat{S}))$ will suffice. What about the function g of one variable defined by $g(x) = f(x,x) = (x + 1) \div x$? Here one encounters a problem. Informally, neither Rule B(11.1) nor Rule C(11.2) has a duplicative effect—B appears to rearrange the parentheses of an object, and C

appears to permute component parts of an object. Here, we require another primitive constant W with Rule W.

RULE W 11.3. $$((W\alpha)\beta) \to ((\alpha\beta)\beta)$$

With it, one sees that $(W((B\hat{H})\hat{\mathbb{S}}))$ suffices, as

$$((W((B\hat{H})\hat{\mathbb{S}}))\hat{m}) \Rightarrow ((((B\hat{H})\hat{\mathbb{S}})\hat{m})\hat{m}) \Rightarrow \widehat{(m+1) \div m}$$

in view of our earlier work with respect to f.

Throughout this chapter we use "hats" to obtain names of objects. For example, $\hat{F}$, $\hat{G}$, $\hat{H}$ for arbitrary objects; $\hat{1}$, $\hat{2}$, $\hat{3}$, $\hat{m}$, $\widehat{m+1}$ for *numerals*; $\hat{x}$, $\hat{y}$, $\hat{z}$ for *variables*; and $\hat{\zeta}_1$, $\hat{\zeta}_2$, $\hat{\zeta}_3$ for *indeterminates* (see below). It is important to note that $\hat{x}$ ($\hat{\zeta}_i$) is a generic name of a variable (indeterminate) and need not be a name for the specific variable x (the specific indeterminate ζ_i). Unless otherwise stated, distinct names for variables (indeterminates) should be presumed to name distinct variables (indeterminates), for example, $\hat{x} \neq \hat{y}$ ($\hat{\zeta}_1 \neq \hat{\zeta}_2$).

We now turn aside from special cases and consider the notion of *combinatorial completeness.*

We begin by introducing into the basic calculus *indeterminates*† $\zeta_1, \zeta_2, \ldots$ and adopting the notation $\hat{\mathcal{E}}[\hat{\zeta}_1,\ldots,\hat{\zeta}_n]$ to denote a combination among the component parts of which appear *one or more* occurrences of each of the *distinct* indeterminates $\hat{\zeta}_1, \ldots, \hat{\zeta}_n$. For example, we may write $\hat{\mathcal{E}}[\hat{\zeta}_1,\hat{\zeta}_2] \equiv ((\hat{H}(\hat{\mathbb{S}}\hat{\zeta}_1))\hat{\zeta}_2)$. The understanding is that, for objects $\hat{X}$ and $\hat{Y}$, $\hat{\mathcal{E}}[\hat{X},\hat{Y}] \equiv ((\hat{H}(\hat{\mathbb{S}}\hat{X}))\hat{Y})$. A calculus is *combinatorial complete* iff there is, for each possible combination $\hat{\mathcal{E}}[\hat{\zeta}_1,\ldots,\hat{\zeta}_n]$, an object $\hat{F}$ no component part of which is an occurrence of any of $\hat{\zeta}_1, \ldots, \hat{\zeta}_n$ such that $(\hat{F}\hat{\zeta}_1\cdots\hat{\zeta}_n) \Rightarrow \hat{\mathcal{E}}[\hat{\zeta}_1, \ldots, \hat{\zeta}_n]$. In case $\hat{\mathcal{E}}[\hat{\zeta}_1,\hat{\zeta}_2] \equiv ((\hat{H}(\hat{\mathbb{S}}\hat{\zeta}_1))\hat{\zeta}_2)$, we have seen that a possible $\hat{F}$ is $((B\hat{H})\hat{\mathbb{S}})$. In case $\hat{\mathcal{E}}[\hat{\zeta}_1] \equiv (\hat{H}(\hat{\mathbb{S}}\hat{\zeta}_1)\hat{\zeta}_1)$, we have seen that a possible $\hat{F}$ is $(W((B\hat{H}))\hat{\mathbb{S}})$.

Suppose that to B, C, and W one adds the primitive constant I with Rule I.

RULE I 11.4. $$(I\alpha) \to \alpha$$

Then there always is such an $\hat{F}$ for each $\hat{\mathcal{E}}[\hat{\zeta}_1,\ldots,\hat{\zeta}_n]$. This is remarkable because, as we shall see in Section 11.3, combinatorial completeness is decisive in proving that a calculus with objects that are combinations of the primitive

† An indeterminate differs from a variable in that, while the procedural rules of a calculus have something to say about variables (for example, just what objects may be substituted for just which instances of a variable), they have nothing whatever to say about indeterminates as entities distinct from arbitrary objects. Because in proving results *about* the calculus, inderminates seem to play a role not unlike variables, one must be on guard and realize that this appearance is due to that fact that, in the *meta-language* which is being used to talk about the given calculus, the indeterminates are often treated as variables, meta-variables, or semantic variables—as far as the given calculus is concerned!

constants B, C, W, and I, with their rules yielding the basic laws of reduction, is adequate for describing the partial recursive functions.

Let us now turn to consider the historically later, but nonetheless independent, start of Church.

In the early 1930's Church [1932] set forth, as the beginning of a very primitive foundation for logic, a lean formal system a central feature of which was a calculus—now known as the *lambda-calculus* or *λ-calculus*—for substitution processes. Displaying a sequence of objects of this calculus as possible representations of the positive integers, Church [1932] expressed the belief that the system was adequate for the description of partial recursive functions. This fact and the fact that the λ-calculus is equivalent to the *combinatory calculus* based on B, C, W, and I were established before the decade was over by Church's students Kleene and Rosser (see Kleene [1935, 1936a,b] and Rosser [1935]).

With our hindsight of the work of Schönfinkel, we are able to see that Church's system ensures the existence, for each combination $\hat{\mathcal{E}}[\zeta_1,\ldots,\zeta_n]$ in his calculus (extended with indeterminates ζ_1, ζ_2, ζ_3, ...) of an object $\hat{F}$ such that $(\hat{F}\hat{\zeta}_1\cdots\hat{\zeta}_n) \Rightarrow \hat{\mathcal{E}}[\hat{\zeta}_1,\ldots,\hat{\zeta}_n]$. This is achieved by the very simple expedient of introducing another operation (besides application) called *abstraction* which gives $\hat{F}$ immediately: For variables $\hat{x}_1$, ..., $\hat{x}_n$, suitably chosen from a postulated denumerable set of variables, $\hat{F} \equiv (\lambda\hat{x}_1,\ldots,\hat{x}_n.\hat{\mathcal{E}}[\hat{x}_1,\ldots,\hat{x}_n])$. That is, $(\lambda\hat{x}_1,\ldots,\hat{x}_n.\hat{\mathcal{E}}[\hat{x}_1,\ldots,\hat{x}_n])$ is the abstraction of $\hat{\mathcal{E}}[\hat{x}_1,\ldots,\hat{x}_n]$ with respect to the variables $\hat{x}_1$, ..., $\hat{x}_n$.† The rules of reduction for abstraction then will give $(\hat{F}\hat{\zeta}_1\cdots\hat{\zeta}_n) \equiv ((\lambda\hat{x}_1,\ldots,\hat{x}_n.\hat{\mathcal{E}}[\hat{x}_1,\ldots,\hat{x}_n])\hat{\zeta}_1\cdots\hat{\zeta}_n) \Rightarrow \hat{\mathcal{E}}[\hat{\zeta}_1,\ldots,\hat{\zeta}_n]$. It may be useful for computer scientists to think of $\hat{F}$ as a description of a procedure which involves the formal parameters $\hat{x}_1$, ..., $\hat{x}_n$. When $\hat{F}$ is applied to the arguments $\hat{\zeta}_1$, ..., $\hat{\zeta}_n$ (in programming terminology, when $\hat{F}$ is called with arguments $\hat{\zeta}_1$, ..., $\hat{\zeta}_n$), then occurrences of $\hat{x}_i$, $1 \le i \le n$, in $\hat{\mathcal{E}}[\hat{x}_1,\ldots,\hat{x}_n]$ are replaced by $\hat{\zeta}_i$ yielding $\hat{\mathcal{E}}[\hat{\zeta}_1,\ldots,\hat{\zeta}_n]$.

The crux of the matter here involves the rules of reduction (with respect to the operation of abstraction) by which it is verified that $(\hat{F}\hat{\zeta}_1\cdots\hat{\zeta}_n) \Rightarrow \hat{\mathcal{E}}[\hat{\zeta}_1,\ldots,\hat{\zeta}_n]$. Indeed, Church's rules constitute the first correct statement of substitution to be recognized historically as such.

The following examples illustrate applications of the rules of reduction with respect to abstraction:

$$((\lambda\hat{x}.(\hat{x}(\hat{y}\hat{x})))\hat{w}) \Rightarrow (\hat{w}(\hat{y}\hat{w}))$$

$$((\lambda\hat{x},\hat{y}.(\hat{x}(\hat{x}\hat{y})))\hat{v}\hat{w}) \Rightarrow (\hat{v}(\hat{v}\hat{w}))$$

$$((\lambda\hat{x}.(\hat{x}((\lambda\hat{y}.(\hat{x}\hat{y}))\hat{w})))\hat{v}) \begin{matrix} \nearrow (\hat{v}((\lambda\hat{y}.(\hat{v}\hat{y}))\hat{w})) \searrow \\ \searrow ((\lambda x.(\hat{x}(\hat{x}\hat{w})))\hat{v}) \nearrow \end{matrix} (\hat{v}(\hat{v}\hat{w}))$$

† We remind the reader of the restriction on $\hat{\mathcal{E}}[\hat{\zeta}_1,\ldots,\hat{\zeta}_n]$ that there be at least one occurrence of each of $\hat{\zeta}_1$, ..., $\hat{\zeta}_n$ in $\hat{\mathcal{E}}[\hat{\zeta}_1, \ldots, \hat{\zeta}_n]$.

The student who is familiar with the predicate calculus or with such programming languages as LISP or ALGOL will recognize that the above examples do not consider the problem of the conflict of variable names. To illustrate this difficulty, consider $((\lambda\hat{x}.(\lambda\hat{y}.(\hat{x}\hat{y})))\hat{y}\hat{z})$. It would be embarrassing if $((\lambda\hat{x}.(\lambda\hat{y}.(\hat{x}\hat{y})))\hat{y})$ reduced to $(\lambda\hat{y}.(\hat{y}\hat{y}))$, for then $((\lambda\hat{x}.(\lambda\hat{y}.(\hat{x}\hat{y})))\hat{y}\hat{z})$ would reduce to $(\hat{z}\hat{z})$, leading us to view $(\lambda\hat{x}.(\lambda\hat{y}.(\hat{x}\hat{y})))$ as a representation of a function f of two variables x and y given by $f(x,y) = (yy)$; that is, $f(x,y)$ is the application of y to itself. But we would also expect *and want* $((\lambda\hat{x}.(\lambda\hat{y}.(\hat{x}\hat{y})))\hat{w})$ $\Rightarrow (\lambda\hat{y}.(\hat{w}\hat{y}))$, so that $((\lambda\hat{x}.(\lambda\hat{y}.(\hat{x}\hat{y})))\hat{w}\hat{z}) \Rightarrow (\hat{w}\hat{z})$, leading us to view $(\lambda\hat{x}.(\lambda\hat{y}.(\hat{x}\hat{y})))$ as a representation of a function g of two variables x and y given by $g(x,y) = (xy)$, the application of x to y. Indeed, observing, for $\hat{\mathcal{E}}[\hat{\zeta}_1,\hat{\zeta}_2] \equiv (\hat{\zeta}_1\hat{\zeta}_2)$, $\hat{\mathcal{E}}[\hat{x},\hat{y}] \equiv (\hat{x}\hat{y})$, the corresponding $\hat{F}$ would be $(\lambda\hat{x},\hat{y}.(\hat{x}\hat{y}))$, which is $(\lambda\hat{x}.(\lambda\hat{y}.(\hat{x}\hat{y})))$, employing the exactly analogous trick here as Schönfinkel did to reduce functions of more than one variable to functions of one variable.

The source of the difficulty is easily pinpointed: One may not confuse the first two (reading left to right) instances of $\hat{y}$ in $((\lambda\hat{x}.(\lambda\hat{y}.(\hat{x}\hat{y})))\hat{y}\hat{z})$ with the third. Consequently, before one may carry out the indicated substitution of $\hat{y}$ for $\hat{x}$, one must change the first two instances of $\hat{y}$, the familiar operation known as "the change of (bound) variables", by means of an *α-reduction* $((\lambda\hat{x}.(\lambda\hat{y}.(\hat{x}\hat{y})))\hat{y}\hat{z}) \Rightarrow ((\lambda\hat{x}.(\lambda\hat{w}.(\hat{x}\hat{w})))\hat{y}\hat{z})$. Only then may one perform the indicated substitution of $\hat{y}$ for $\hat{x}$, the *β-reduction* $((\lambda\hat{x}.(\lambda\hat{w}.(\hat{x}\hat{w})))\hat{y}\hat{z}) \Rightarrow ((\lambda\hat{w}.(\hat{y}\hat{w}))\hat{z})$. Carrying out the β-reduction which is, in effect, the substitution of $\hat{z}$ for $\hat{w}$, $((\lambda\hat{w}.(\hat{y}\hat{w}))\hat{z}) \Rightarrow (\hat{y}\hat{z})$, one obtains the correct result $((\lambda\hat{x}.(\lambda\hat{y}.(\hat{x}\hat{y})))\hat{y}\hat{z})$ $\Rightarrow (\hat{y}\hat{z})$; $(\lambda\hat{x}.(\lambda\hat{y}.(\hat{x}\hat{y})))$ is a consistent representation of g, the function of two variables x and y given by $g(x,y) = (xy)$.

That this is not the only way the difficulty of the confusion of variables manifests itself is already evident in the above α-reduction: One is not free to choose $\hat{w} = \hat{x}$. Nor is it possible to effect the substitution of $\hat{y}$ for the fourth instance of $\hat{x}$ in $((\lambda\hat{x}.(\lambda\hat{w}.(\hat{x}((\lambda\hat{x}.\hat{x})\hat{w}))))\hat{y}\hat{z})$.

But let us leave these details to Section 11.2, noting here that the confusion of variables is often the source of difficulties that are euphemistically called "side effects" in higher level programming languages. The fact that the reduction rules of the λ-calculus are consistent, avoiding any possibility of confusing variables, is the essential result of the well-known Church–Rosser theorem, so-called after Church and Rosser [1936].

The Church–Rosser theorem states that a certain property, now known as the Church–Rosser property, holds. It we let $\Leftrightarrow$ denote the equivalence relation generated by $\Rightarrow$, this property is as follows:

CHURCH–ROSSER PROPERTY 11.5. If $\hat{M} \Leftrightarrow \hat{N}$, then there exists an object $\hat{Q}$ such that both $\hat{M} \Rightarrow \hat{Q}$ and $\hat{N} \Rightarrow \hat{Q}$.

It is no accident that this property is equivalent to the proposition that, if $\hat{P} \Rightarrow \hat{M}$ and $\hat{P} \Rightarrow \hat{N}$, then there exists a $\hat{Q}$ such that both $\hat{M} \Rightarrow \hat{Q}$ and $\hat{N} \Rightarrow \hat{Q}$.

That is, no matter what the algorithm for reduction of $\hat{P}$, be it one that yields $\hat{P} \Rightarrow \hat{M}$ or another that yields $\hat{P} \Rightarrow \hat{N}$, there are algorithms which, on the one hand, will yield $\hat{M} \Rightarrow \hat{Q}$ and, on the other hand, will yield $\hat{N} \Rightarrow \hat{Q}$. In still other, more familiar words to the computer scientist, reduction is "machine independent" or "implementation invariant".

Let us make this last point somewhat clearer. To do this, we need to divide our consideration between a combinatory calculus and a λ-calculus. On the one hand, in a combinatory calculus, an object $\hat{Z}$ is said to be in *normal form* just when no rule is applicable to any component of $\hat{Z}$, that is, $\hat{Z}$ is *irreducible*. On the other hand, in a λ-calculus, where one cares little about changes of (bound) variables, an object $\hat{Z}$ is said to be in *normal form* just when every object $\hat{Y}$ differing from $\hat{Z}$ only in the choice of bound variables can only be reduced via α-reductions.† In either kind of calculus, we say that an object $\hat{X}$ *possesses a normal form* just when there is an object $\hat{Z}$ which is in normal form (in that calculus) such that $\hat{X} \Leftrightarrow \hat{Z}$. Our point is that, if the object $\hat{P}$ above possesses a normal form $\hat{Z}$, then not only does the validity of the Church–Rosser property guarantee the uniqueness of $\hat{Z}$ (up to a change of bound variables for a λ-calculus), but it also ensures that $\hat{Q}$ may be taken to be $\hat{Z}$. If the machine algorithms are effective in discovering normal forms of objects possessing such, then they *all* arrive at the same object.

Returning to our historical sketch, the results of Church, Kleene, and Rosser confirmed what was already suspected by Schönfinkel: A theory of substitution is by itself sufficient as a formal system for partial recursive functions.

Indeed, to complete the examples herein (at least for a λ-calculus), if we, following Church [1932], take

$$\hat{1} \equiv (\lambda \hat{x}.(\lambda \hat{y}.(\hat{x}\hat{y})))$$

$$\hat{2} \equiv (\lambda \hat{x}.(\lambda \hat{y}.(\hat{x}(\hat{x}\hat{y}))))$$

$$\hat{3} \equiv (\lambda \hat{x}.(\lambda \hat{y}.(\hat{x}(\hat{x}(\hat{x}\hat{y})))))$$

and so forth, then we may take $(\lambda \hat{x}.(\lambda \hat{y}.(\lambda \hat{z}.(\hat{y}(\hat{x}\hat{y}\hat{z})))))$ as $\hat{\mathrm{S}}$. For example,

$$
\begin{aligned}
(\hat{\mathrm{S}}\hat{2}) &\equiv ((\lambda \hat{x}.(\lambda \hat{y}.(\lambda \hat{z}.(\hat{y}(\hat{x}\hat{y}\hat{z})))))\hat{2}) \Rightarrow (\lambda \hat{y}.(\lambda \hat{z}.(\hat{y}(\hat{2}\hat{y}\hat{z}))))\\
&\Rightarrow (\lambda \hat{u}.(\lambda \hat{v}.(\hat{u}(\hat{2}\hat{u}\hat{v})))) \equiv (\lambda \hat{u}.(\lambda \hat{v}.(\hat{u}((\lambda \hat{x}.(\lambda \hat{y}.(\hat{x}(\hat{x}\hat{y}))))\hat{u}\hat{v}))))\\
&\Rightarrow (\lambda \hat{u}.(\lambda \hat{v}.(\hat{u}((\lambda y.(\hat{u}(\hat{u}\hat{y})))\hat{v})))) \Rightarrow (\lambda \hat{u}.(\lambda \hat{v}.(\hat{u}(\hat{u}(\hat{u}\hat{v})))))\\
&\Rightarrow (\lambda \hat{x}.(\lambda \hat{y}.(\hat{x}(\hat{x}(\hat{x}\hat{y}))))) \equiv \hat{3}
\end{aligned}
$$

† A formal definition will be given in the section on other λ-calculi. See also Definition 11.50.

For the object $\hat{H}$ which represents the function f of two variables x and y given by $f(x,y) = x \div y$, we take the somewhat complicated object $(\lambda\hat{x}.(\lambda\hat{y}.(\hat{y}\hat{P}\hat{x})))$, where $\hat{P} \equiv (\lambda\hat{x}.(\hat{x}\hat{F}\hat{F}_0\hat{1}\hat{1}\hat{1}))$,

$$\hat{F} \equiv (\lambda\hat{w}.(\lambda\hat{x}.(\lambda\hat{y}.(\lambda\hat{z}.(\hat{w}(\hat{S}\hat{x})(\hat{y}(\lambda\hat{u}.\hat{u})\hat{x})(\hat{z}(\lambda\hat{u}.\hat{u})\hat{y}))))))$$

and

$$\hat{F}_0 \equiv (\lambda\hat{x}.(\lambda\hat{y}.(\lambda\hat{z}.(\hat{x}(\lambda\hat{u}.\hat{u})(\hat{y}(\lambda\hat{u}.\hat{u})\hat{z})))))$$

To bring these introductory remarks to a close, let us repeat that the intended interpretation is always to view an object, whether a combination of primitive constants of a combinatory calculus or a combination of variables and abstractions of combinations of a λ-calculus, as representing a function of one variable. This is true even for $\hat{1}$, $\hat{2}$, $\hat{3}$, ...; $\hat{n}$ abstracts the notion of the nth iterative application of a function f of one variable x to an argument,

$$f^{(n)}(x) = \overbrace{f(f(\cdots(f(x))\cdots))}^{nf\text{'s}}.$$

11.2 The Calculi

In the previous section, we distinguished two calculi, a combinatory calculus and a λ-calculus, together with their extensions by denumerably many indeterminates. We shall present herein not only their formal definitions, but also those of a number of other combinatory calculi and λ-calculi. For the sake of convenience, all will be formulated to include denumerably many indeterminates.

As each presentation is linguistic—the set of objects will be a distinguished subset of the set of words over some alphabet, and the basic rules of procedure will be given as relations on this distinguished subset—let us agree on some nomenclature in order to avoid repeating morphological details.

As the context will resolve any possible ambiguity between the name of a symbol of an alphabet and the name of a word which consists solely of that symbol, we shall use the former also as a name of the latter. We shall continue to use "hats" to obtain names of objects. Consequently, we shall write, for example, $(\hat{F}I)$, where $\hat{F}$ denotes an object or word, as the word that is the concatenation of a left parenthesis, the symbols of the word $\hat{F}$, the symbol I, and a right parenthesis.

We shall exploit parentheses in the familiar manner. Each word that is an object will admit a unique proper pairing of its left and right parentheses (even when abbreviated with the omission of any or all pairs of parentheses of a left nest of such) which will display the structure of the object. We refer to those parts or subwords of an object lying between properly paired parentheses (including the parentheses) as *components* of the object. These components are the *composite* components of the object; the *primitive* components are those parts or subwords consisting solely of a primitive constant symbol, an indeterminate symbol, or a variable symbol that does not lie between a λ to its left and a period to its right with no intervening parentheses, lambdas, or periods. These designations will be clear from the definitions of the objects. It should be noted, however, that the object itself is one of its components. If we wish to exclude this component from the discussion we shall refer to the *proper* components of an object. For example, we take as obvious

LEMMA 11.6. Let $\hat{P}$ and $\hat{Q}$ denote distinct components of an object $\hat{X}$. Then, exactly one of the following holds:

a. $\hat{P}$ is a proper component of $\hat{Q}$.
b. $\hat{Q}$ is a proper component of $\hat{P}$.
c. $\hat{P}$ and $\hat{Q}$ are nonoverlapping (no component of $\hat{X}$ is both a component of $\hat{P}$ and a component of $\hat{Q}$). ▮

We shall write, say, $\hat{G} \equiv (\hat{F}I)$ to indicate that we are defining $\hat{G}$ as the name of the object or word $(\hat{F}I)$ and $\hat{G} = (\hat{F}I)$ to state that the words $\hat{G}$ and $(\hat{F}I)$ are *equiform* (spelled the same). We continue to employ $\rightarrow$ in the statement of the rules of procedure (for example, Rule B: $(((B\alpha)\beta)\gamma) \rightarrow (\alpha(\beta\gamma))$). We shall also employ $\rightarrow$ for the basic relation of reduction as follows: First, let $\hat{P}$ and $\hat{Q}$ be objects such that $\hat{P} \rightarrow \hat{Q}$ is an instance of a rule (for example, in the case of Rule B, $\hat{P} \equiv (((B\hat{X})\hat{Y})\hat{Z})$ and $\hat{Q} \equiv (\hat{X}(\hat{Y}\hat{Z}))$, for some objects $\hat{X}$, $\hat{Y}$, and $\hat{Z}$). Next let $\hat{U}$, $\hat{V}$ be objects such that $\hat{P}$ is a component of $\hat{U}$ and $\hat{V}$ results if one replaces the component $\hat{P}$ of $\hat{U}$ by $\hat{Q}$. Then, we shall write $\hat{U} \rightarrow \hat{V}$. There will be no confusion since $\hat{P} \rightarrow \hat{Q}$ in either sense.

We obtain the other basic relations from the relation $\rightarrow$.

$(\underset{n}{\Longrightarrow})$ if $\hat{X} \rightarrow \hat{Y}$, then $\hat{X} \underset{n}{\Longrightarrow} \hat{Y}$ for each $n \geq 1$

for every $\hat{X}$, $\hat{X} \underset{n}{\Longrightarrow} \hat{X}$ for each $n \geq 0$

if $\hat{X} \underset{m}{\Longrightarrow} \hat{Y}$ and $\hat{Y} \underset{n}{\Longrightarrow} \hat{Z}$, then $\hat{X} \underset{m+n}{\Longrightarrow} \hat{Z}$

$(\Rightarrow)$ if, for some n, $\hat{X} \underset{n}{\Longrightarrow} \hat{Y}$, then $\hat{X} \Rightarrow \hat{Y}$

$(\Leftrightarrow)$ if $\hat{X} \Rightarrow \hat{Y}$, then $\hat{X} \Leftrightarrow \hat{Y}$

if $\hat{X} \Leftrightarrow \hat{Y}$, then $\hat{Y} \Leftrightarrow \hat{X}$

if $\hat{X} \Leftrightarrow \hat{Y}$ and $\hat{Y} \Leftrightarrow \hat{Z}$, then $\hat{X} \Leftrightarrow \hat{Z}$

Informally, if $\hat{X} \underset{n}{\Longrightarrow} \hat{Y}$, then $\hat{Y}$ is obtained from $\hat{X}$ by at most n "basic steps"; $\Rightarrow$ is the reflexive transitive closure of $\rightarrow$; and $\Leftrightarrow$ is the equivalence relation generated by $\Rightarrow$ (and thus by $\rightarrow$). We take as obvious Lemma 11.7.

LEMMA 11.7. Let $\hat{X}$ and $\hat{Y}$ be objects such that $\hat{Y}$ would result if one were to replace a component $\hat{P}$ of $\hat{X}$ by an object $\hat{Q}$. Then, if $\hat{P} \underset{n}{\Longrightarrow} \hat{Q}$ (alternatively, $\hat{P} \Rightarrow \hat{Q}$, $\hat{P} \Leftrightarrow \hat{Q}$), $\hat{X} \underset{n}{\Longrightarrow} \hat{Y}$ (respectively, $\hat{X} \Rightarrow \hat{Y}$, $\hat{X} \Leftrightarrow \hat{Y}$). ▮

We may write $\hat{Y} \leftarrow \hat{X}$ ($\hat{Y} \underset{n}{\Longleftarrow} \hat{X}$ and $\hat{Y} \Leftarrow \hat{X}$) as an alternative to $\hat{X} \rightarrow \hat{Y}$ ($\hat{X} \underset{n}{\Longrightarrow} \hat{Y}$ and $\hat{X} \Rightarrow \hat{Y}$). The following names for these relations will be used:

$\rightarrow$	contraction	$\leftarrow$	expansion
$\underset{n}{\Longrightarrow}$	reduction of length n	$\underset{n}{\Longleftarrow}$	expansion of length n
$\Rightarrow$	reduction	$\Leftarrow$	expansion
$\Leftrightarrow$	interconvertibility		

The Γ_I-Calculus. Of all the finite words over the

Γ_I-Alphabet

improper symbols:	(and)
constant symbols:	B, C, I, and W
indeterminate symbols:	$\zeta_0, \zeta_1, \zeta_2, \ldots$

we distinguish the following

Γ_I-Objects
These, divided into *primitive* and *composite* objects, are defined recursively as follows:

I-A. the words B, C, I, and W are primitive objects which we shall call the *primitive constants*
I-B. the words $\zeta_0, \zeta_1, \zeta_2, \ldots$ are primitive objects which we shall call the *indeterminates*
II. if $\hat{F}$ and $\hat{A}$ are objects, then $(\hat{F}\hat{A})$ is a composite object which we shall call the *application of $\hat{F}$ to $\hat{A}$*
III. the only words that are objects are just those given by clauses (I-A), (I-B), and (II)

for which we postulate the following

Γ_I-Rules

Rule B:	$(((B\alpha)\beta)\gamma) \rightarrow (\alpha(\beta\gamma))$
Rule C:	$(((C\alpha)\beta)\gamma) \rightarrow ((\alpha\gamma)\beta)$
Rule I:	$(I\alpha) \rightarrow \alpha$
Rule W:	$((W\alpha)\beta) \rightarrow ((\alpha\beta)\beta)$

This Γ_I-calculus is the combinatory calculus, or rather its extension by indeterminates, introduced in the previous section.

The abstraction algorithm for the Γ_I-calculus is given by:

Γ_I-ABSTRACTION ALGORITHM 11.8. Let $\hat{\mathcal{E}}[\hat{\zeta}]$ be an object with components equiform to an indeterminate $\hat{\zeta}$. Then, *the abstraction of* $\hat{\mathcal{E}}[\hat{\zeta}]$ *with respect to* $\hat{\zeta}$, in symbols $[\Lambda\hat{\zeta}:\hat{\mathcal{E}}[\hat{\zeta}]]$, is recursively defined as follows:

I. if $\hat{\mathcal{E}}[\hat{\zeta}] \equiv \hat{\zeta}$, then $[\Lambda\hat{\zeta}:\hat{\mathcal{E}}[\hat{\zeta}]] \equiv I$

II. if $\hat{\mathcal{E}}[\hat{\zeta}] \equiv (\hat{P}\hat{Q})$, then there are three cases:

- II-A. no component of $\hat{P}$ is equiform to $\hat{\zeta}$, but some component of $\hat{Q}$ is: $[\Lambda\hat{\zeta}:\hat{\mathcal{E}}[\hat{\zeta}]] \equiv ((B\hat{P})[\Lambda\hat{\zeta}:Q])$
- II-B. no component of $\hat{Q}$ is equiform to $\hat{\zeta}$, but some component of $\hat{P}$ is: $[\Lambda\hat{\zeta}:\hat{\mathcal{E}}[\hat{\zeta}]] \equiv ((C[\Lambda\hat{\zeta}:\hat{P}])\hat{Q})$
- II-C. a component of $\hat{P}$ and a component of $\hat{Q}$ is equiform to $\hat{\zeta}$: $[\Lambda\hat{\zeta}:\hat{\mathcal{E}}[\hat{\zeta}]] \equiv ((((B(BW))((BB)C))[\Lambda\hat{\zeta}:\hat{P}])[\Lambda\hat{\zeta}:\hat{Q}])$

A simple induction will show that no component of $[\Lambda\hat{\zeta}:\hat{\mathcal{E}}[\hat{\zeta}]]$ is equiform to $\hat{\zeta}$ so the combinatorial completeness of Γ_I will follow from:

PROPOSITION 11.9. Let $\hat{\mathcal{E}}[\hat{\zeta}]$ be an object with components equiform to an indeterminate $\hat{\zeta}$. Then, $([\Lambda\hat{\zeta}:\hat{\mathcal{E}}[\hat{\zeta}]]\hat{\zeta}) \Rightarrow \hat{\mathcal{E}}[\hat{\zeta}]$.

Proof. The proof is by induction on the number of components of $\hat{\mathcal{E}}[\hat{\zeta}]$. Basis step: $\hat{\mathcal{E}}[\hat{\zeta}]$ is a primitive object. Evidently, $\hat{\mathcal{E}}[\hat{\zeta}] \equiv \hat{\zeta}$. By definition, $[\Lambda\hat{\zeta}:\hat{\mathcal{E}}[\hat{\zeta}]] \equiv I$. That $([\Lambda\hat{\zeta}:\hat{\mathcal{E}}[\hat{\zeta}]]\hat{\zeta}) \Rightarrow \hat{\zeta}$ follows at once from Rule *I*. Induction step: $\hat{\mathcal{E}}[\hat{\zeta}]$ is a composite object $(\hat{P}\hat{Q})$. As there are components of $\hat{\mathcal{E}}[\hat{\zeta}]$ equiform to $\hat{\zeta}$, it cannot be that not one of the components of $\hat{P}$ or $\hat{Q}$ is equiform to $\hat{\zeta}$. So there are just three possibilities. First, no component of $\hat{P}$ is equiform to $\hat{\zeta}$, but some component of $\hat{Q}$ is. As the number of components of $\hat{Q}$ is less than the number of components of $(\hat{P}\hat{Q})$, $([\Lambda\hat{\zeta}:\hat{Q}]\hat{\zeta}) \Rightarrow \hat{Q}$ by the hypothesis of the induction. But then, as $[\Lambda\hat{\zeta}:\hat{\mathcal{E}}[\hat{\zeta}]] \equiv ((B\hat{P})[\Lambda\hat{\zeta}:\hat{Q}])$, we may compute

$$
\begin{aligned}
(((B\hat{P})[\Lambda\hat{\zeta}:\hat{Q}])\hat{\zeta}) &\Rightarrow (\hat{P}([\Lambda\hat{\zeta}:\hat{Q}]\hat{\zeta})) && \text{(Rule } B\text{)}\\
&\Rightarrow (\hat{P}\hat{Q}) && \text{(Induction Hypothesis with respect to } \hat{Q}\text{)}
\end{aligned}
$$

to verify that $([\Lambda\hat{\zeta}:\hat{\mathcal{E}}[\hat{\zeta}]]\hat{\zeta}) \Rightarrow \hat{\mathcal{E}}[\hat{\zeta}]$. Second, no component of $\hat{Q}$ is equiform to $\hat{\zeta}$, but some component of $\hat{P}$ is. As then $[\Lambda\hat{\zeta}:\hat{\mathcal{E}}[\hat{\zeta}]] \equiv ((C[\Lambda\hat{\zeta}:\hat{P}])\hat{Q})$, we may compute

$$
\begin{aligned}
(((C[\Lambda\hat{\zeta}:\hat{P}])\hat{Q})\hat{\zeta}) &\Rightarrow (([\Lambda\hat{\zeta}:\hat{P}]\hat{\zeta})\hat{Q}) && \text{(Rule } C\text{)}\\
&\Rightarrow (\hat{P}\hat{Q}) && \text{(Induction Hypothesis with respect to } \hat{P}\text{)}
\end{aligned}
$$

to again verify that $([\Lambda\hat{\zeta}:\hat{\mathcal{E}}[\hat{\zeta}]]\hat{\zeta}) \Rightarrow \hat{\mathcal{E}}[\hat{\zeta}]$. And third, components of $\hat{P}$ and components of $\hat{Q}$ are equiform to $\hat{\zeta}$. As then

$$[\Lambda\hat{\zeta}:\hat{\mathcal{E}}[\hat{\zeta}]] \equiv ((((B(BW))((BB)C))[\Lambda\hat{\zeta}:\hat{P}])[\Lambda\hat{\zeta}:\hat{Q}]),$$

we may compute

$$
\begin{aligned}
&(((((B(BW))((BB)C))[\Lambda\hat{\zeta}:\hat{P}])[\Lambda\hat{\zeta}:\hat{Q}])\hat{\zeta}) \\
&\quad \underset{1}{\Longrightarrow} ((((BW)(((BB)C)[\Lambda\hat{\zeta}:\hat{P}]))[\Lambda\hat{\zeta}:\hat{Q}])\hat{\zeta}) && \text{(Rule } B) \\
&\quad \underset{1}{\Longrightarrow} ((W((((BB)C)[\Lambda\hat{\zeta}:\hat{P}])[\Lambda\hat{\zeta}:\hat{Q}]))\hat{\zeta}) && \text{(Rule } B) \\
&\quad \underset{1}{\Longrightarrow} (((((((BB)C)[\Lambda\hat{\zeta}:\hat{P}])[\Lambda\hat{\zeta}:\hat{Q}])\hat{\zeta})\hat{\zeta}) && \text{(Rule } W) \\
&\quad \underset{1}{\Longrightarrow} ((((B(C[\Lambda\hat{\zeta}:\hat{P}]))[\Lambda\hat{\zeta}:\hat{Q}])\hat{\zeta})\hat{\zeta}) && \text{(Rule } B) \\
&\quad \underset{1}{\Longrightarrow} (((C[\Lambda\hat{\zeta}:\hat{P}])([\Lambda\hat{\zeta}:\hat{Q}]\hat{\zeta}))\hat{\zeta}) && \text{(Rule } B) \\
&\quad \underset{1}{\Longrightarrow} (([\Lambda\hat{\zeta}:\hat{P}]\hat{\zeta})([\Lambda\hat{\zeta}:\hat{Q}]\hat{\zeta})) && \text{(Rule } C) \\
&\quad \Rightarrow (\hat{P}([\Lambda\hat{\zeta}:\hat{Q}]\hat{\zeta})) && \text{(Induction Hypothesis with respect to } \hat{P}) \\
&\quad \Rightarrow (\hat{P}\hat{Q}) && \text{(Induction Hypothesis with respect to } \hat{Q})
\end{aligned}
$$

to once again verify that $([\Lambda\hat{\zeta}:\hat{\mathcal{E}}[\hat{\zeta}]]\hat{\zeta}) \Rightarrow \hat{\mathcal{E}}[\hat{\zeta}]$. ∎

Indeed, reviewing the foregoing proof, we have in fact proved

COROLLARY 11.10. Let $\hat{\mathcal{E}}[\hat{\zeta}]$ be an object with components equiform to an indeterminate $\hat{\zeta}$. If $\hat{\mathcal{E}}[\hat{A}]$ is the object which would result if each component of $\hat{\mathcal{E}}[\hat{\zeta}]$ equiform to $\hat{\zeta}$ were replaced by an object $\hat{A}$, then $([\Lambda\hat{\zeta}:\hat{\mathcal{E}}[\hat{\zeta}]]\hat{A}) \Rightarrow \hat{\mathcal{E}}[\hat{A}]$. ∎

Consider again the example in Section 11.1 wherein we arrived at an object $\hat{\mathcal{T}}$ to represent the function $\mathcal{T}(x) = x + 2$ from the object $\hat{\mathcal{S}}$ postulated to represent the successor function $\mathcal{S}(x) = x + 1$. As we want an object $\hat{\mathcal{T}}$ such that, for each positive integer m, $(\hat{\mathcal{T}}\hat{m}) \Rightarrow (\hat{\mathcal{S}}(\hat{\mathcal{S}}\hat{m}))$, we may take $\hat{\mathcal{T}} \equiv [\Lambda\hat{\zeta}:(\hat{\mathcal{S}}(\hat{\mathcal{S}}\hat{\zeta}))]$. We have from the Γ_I-Abstraction Algorithm that $[\Lambda\hat{\zeta}:(\hat{\mathcal{S}}(\hat{\mathcal{S}}\hat{\zeta}))] \equiv ((B\hat{\mathcal{S}})[\Lambda\hat{\zeta}:(\hat{\mathcal{S}}\hat{\zeta})]) \equiv ((B\hat{\mathcal{S}})((B\hat{\mathcal{S}})[\Lambda\hat{\zeta}:\hat{\zeta}])) \equiv ((B\hat{\mathcal{S}})((B\hat{\mathcal{S}})I))$. To check this, verifying Corollary 11.10 in this case, we simply compute as follows:

$$
\begin{aligned}
(((B\hat{\mathcal{S}})((B\hat{\mathcal{S}})I))\hat{m}) &\Rightarrow (\hat{\mathcal{S}}(((B\hat{\mathcal{S}})I)\hat{m})) && \text{(Rule } B) \\
&\Rightarrow (\hat{\mathcal{S}}(\hat{\mathcal{S}}(I\hat{m}))) && \text{(Rule } B) \\
&\Rightarrow (\hat{\mathcal{S}}(\hat{\mathcal{S}}\hat{m})) && \text{(Rule } I) \\
&\Rightarrow (\hat{\mathcal{S}}\widehat{m+1}) \Rightarrow \widehat{m+2} && \text{(Hypothesis for } \mathcal{S})
\end{aligned}
$$

That this choice of an object to represent $\mathcal{T}$ does not agree with that in Section 11.1 should be no cause for alarm, as we have already seen in Section 11.1 that there is indeed a choice—one of denumerably many in fact. Also, as might have been expected, one can usually do better than the above abstraction algorithm in arriving at simpler objects (in the sense of fewer components).

The Γ_K-Calculus. Of all the finite words over the

Γ_K-Alphabet

improper symbols:	(and)
constant symbols:	K and S
indeterminate symbols:	$\zeta_0, \zeta_1, \zeta_2, \ldots$

we distinguish the following

Γ_K-Objects

These, divided into *primitive* and *composite* objects, are defined recursively as follows:

I-A. the words K and S are primitive objects which we shall call the *primitive constants*

I-B. the words $\zeta_0, \zeta_1, \zeta_2, \ldots$ are primitive objects which we shall call the *indeterminates*

II. if $\hat{F}$ and $\hat{A}$ are objects, then $(\hat{F}\hat{A})$ is a composite object which we shall call the *application of* $\hat{F}$ *to* $\hat{A}$

III. the only words that are objects are just those given by clauses (I-A), (I-B), and (II)

for which we postulate the following

Γ_K-Rules

Rule K: $((K\alpha)\beta) \rightarrow \alpha$

Rule S: $(((S\alpha)\beta)\gamma) \rightarrow ((\alpha\gamma)(\beta\gamma))$

In order to see the relationship between Γ_K and Γ_I, let us observe, for arbitrary objects $\hat{X}$, $\hat{Y}$, and $\hat{Z}$, that

$$\begin{aligned}
&(((((S(KS))K)\hat{X})\hat{Y})\hat{Z}) \underset{4}{\Longrightarrow} (\hat{X}(\hat{Y}\hat{Z}))\\
&(((((S(K((SS)(KK))))((S(KK))S))\hat{X})\hat{Y})\hat{Z}) \underset{10}{\Longrightarrow} ((\hat{X}\hat{Z})\hat{Y})\\
&(((SK)K)\hat{X}) \underset{2}{\Longrightarrow} \hat{X}\\
&((((SS)(K((SK)K)))\hat{X})\hat{Y}) \underset{5}{\Longrightarrow} ((\hat{X}\hat{Y})\hat{Y})
\end{aligned} \qquad (11\text{-}1)$$

Consequently, as we may model Rules B, C, I, and W of Γ_I in Γ_K when we take $((S(KS))K)$, $((S(K((SS)(KK))))((S(KK))S))$, $((SK)K)$, and $((SS)(K((SK)K)))$ as representations of B, C, I, and W, respectively, Γ_K is at least as general as Γ_I.

Conversely, one may verify that a model of Rule S may be obtained for Γ_I when $[\Lambda\hat{\zeta}_1{:}[\Lambda\hat{\zeta}_2{:}[\Lambda\hat{\zeta}_3{:}((\hat{\zeta}_1\hat{\zeta}_3)(\hat{\zeta}_2\hat{\zeta}_3))]]]$ is taken as a representation of S. However, there is no possible representation for K! (One is *not* able to write $[\Lambda\hat{\zeta}_2{:}\hat{\zeta}_1]$—let alone $[\Lambda\hat{\zeta}_1{:}[\Lambda\hat{\zeta}_2{:}\hat{\zeta}_1]]$—as the object $\hat{\zeta}_1$, that is, the expression $\hat{\mathcal{E}}[\hat{\zeta}_2]$, does not possess a component equiform to $\hat{\zeta}_2$.) Unlike B, C, I, and W, the primitive constant K, or rather its rule, has a cancellative effect. This fact is reflected in the following (cf. 11.8)

Γ_K-ABSTRACTION ALGORITHM (Rosser [1935]) 11.11. Let $\hat{\mathcal{E}}[\hat{\zeta}]$ be any object. Then, *the abstraction of* $\hat{\mathcal{E}}[\hat{\zeta}]$ *with respect to an indeterminate* $\hat{\zeta}$, in symbols $\{\Lambda\hat{\zeta}{:}\hat{\mathcal{E}}[\hat{\zeta}]\}$ is recursively defined as follows:

I-A. if $\hat{\mathcal{E}}[\hat{\zeta}]$ does not possess a component equiform to $\hat{\zeta}$, then $\{\Lambda\hat{\zeta}{:}\hat{\mathcal{E}}[\hat{\zeta}]\} \equiv (K\hat{\mathcal{E}}[\hat{\zeta}])$

I-B. if $\hat{\mathcal{E}}[\hat{\zeta}] \equiv \hat{\zeta}$, then $\{\Lambda\hat{\zeta}{:}\hat{\mathcal{E}}[\hat{\zeta}]\} \equiv ((SK)K)$

II. if $\hat{\mathcal{E}}[\hat{\zeta}] \equiv (\hat{P}\hat{Q})$ possesses a component equiform to $\hat{\zeta}$, then $\{\Lambda\hat{\zeta}{:}\hat{\mathcal{E}}[\hat{\zeta}]\} \equiv ((S\{\Lambda\hat{\zeta}{:}\hat{P}\})\{\Lambda\hat{\zeta}{:}\hat{Q}\})$

for which we have (cf. Corollary 11.10)

PROPOSITION 11.12. Let $\hat{\mathcal{E}}[\hat{\zeta}]$ be any object. If $\hat{\mathcal{E}}[\hat{A}]$ is the object which would result if each component of $\hat{\mathcal{E}}[\hat{\zeta}]$ equiform to an indeterminate $\hat{\zeta}$ were replaced by an object $\hat{A}$, then $(\{\Lambda\hat{\zeta}{:}\hat{\mathcal{E}}[\hat{\zeta}]\}\hat{A}) \Rightarrow \hat{\mathcal{E}}[\hat{A}]$. ∎

So the difference between Γ_I and Γ_K is that the former, in not permitting the abstraction of an object with respect to an indeterminate unless that indeterminate occurs in the object, cannot represent all constant functions, while the latter, in permitting the abstraction of any object with respect to any indeterminate whatsoever, can represent every possible constant function. Yet, notwithstanding this essential difference, no one has found Γ_I to be any less general than Γ_K; Γ_I *is* adequate for the description of partial recursive functions.

For insight as to why this should be, let us see how one may obtain in Γ_I an object which will represent the constant function f defined by $f(x) = n$, for some positive integer n. We need an object $\hat{F}$ of Γ_I such that, for each positive integer m, $(\hat{F}\hat{m}) \Rightarrow \hat{n}$. We shall define $\hat{m}$ so that for any objects $\hat{X}$ and $\hat{Y}$, we shall have that $((\hat{m}\hat{X})\hat{Y}) \Rightarrow (\overbrace{\hat{X}(\ldots(\hat{X}}^{mX\text{'s}}\hat{Y})\ldots))$. Hence, for any object $\hat{Z}$, $((\hat{m}I)\hat{Z}) \Rightarrow \hat{Z}$, in view of Rule *I*. Consequently, we may take for $\hat{F}$ the object $((C((CI)I))\hat{n})$, for $(((C((CI)I))\hat{n})\hat{m}) \Rightarrow ((((CI)I)\hat{m})\hat{n}) \Rightarrow (((I\hat{m})I)\hat{n}) \Rightarrow ((\hat{m}I)\hat{n}) \Rightarrow \hat{n}$. Thus, as long as we know that the domain of f is to be $\{\hat{1},\hat{2},\hat{3},\ldots\}$, we may model K by $(C((CI)I))$.

Hence, while we shall work with Γ_K in the future because the lack of any restriction in forming the abstraction of an object with respect to an indeterminate gives a degree of freedom that yields simplification, we leave it for the reader to check (see, for example, Exercise 3 in Section 11.3) that all could be done in Γ_I.

Other Combinatory Calculi. The calculi Γ_I and Γ_K above are two of three classical combinatory calculi. The third, due to Rosser, is based upon two primitive constants I and J, where I is as above for Γ_I and J is postulated to have the rule $((((J\alpha)\beta)\gamma)\delta) \rightarrow ((\alpha\beta)((\alpha\delta)\gamma))$. In each of these three calculi, no primitive constant may be modeled or defined in terms of the others. In this they are by no means unique; however, the calculus based on I and J is considered the most primitive.

If one is not interested in independent primitive constants, all sorts of possible combinatory calculi are possible. For example, one may combine Γ_I and Γ_K to obtain a combinatory calculus based upon B, C, I, K, S, and W with the above postulated rules. A consequence of such a mixture is the possibility of obtaining much less complicated (in the sense of fewer components) objects for the abstraction of a given object with respect to a given indeterminate. The reader need only consider the frightening objects

$$[\Lambda\zeta_1:[\Lambda\zeta_2:[\Lambda\zeta_3:[\Lambda\zeta_4:[\Lambda\zeta_5:((\zeta_1((\zeta_2\zeta_4)\zeta_5))((\zeta_3\zeta_4)\zeta_5))]]]]]$$

and

$$\{\Lambda\zeta_1:\{\Lambda\zeta_2:\{\Lambda\zeta_3:\{\Lambda\zeta_4:\{\Lambda\zeta_5:((\zeta_1((\zeta_2\zeta_4)\zeta_5))((\zeta_3\zeta_4)\zeta_5))\}\}\}\}\}$$

which will arise in a discussion of the composition scheme for functions of two variables, namely to define a function φ of two variables in terms of the functions f, g, and h of two variables by $\varphi(x,y) = f(g(x,y), h(x,y))$. Yet, in the mixed calculus, we may proceed as follows (as we are employing here our convention concerning nests of left parentheses (see Section 11.1), the reader is advised to write out the abbreviated forms for Rule B and Rule S):

$$
\begin{aligned}
\hat{f}(\hat{g}\hat{x}\hat{y})(\hat{h}\hat{x}\hat{y}) &\Leftarrow B\hat{f}(\hat{g}\hat{x})\hat{y}(\hat{h}\hat{x}\hat{y}) && \text{(Rule } B)\\
&\Leftarrow S(B\hat{f}(\hat{g}\hat{x}))(\hat{h}\hat{x})\hat{y} && \text{(Rule } S)\\
&\Leftarrow BS(B\hat{f})(\hat{g}\hat{x})(\hat{h}\hat{x})\hat{y} && \text{(Rule } B)\\
&\Leftarrow B(BS(B\hat{f}))\hat{g}\hat{x}(\hat{h}\hat{x})\hat{y} && \text{(Rule } B)\\
&\Leftarrow S(B(BS(B\hat{f}))\hat{g})\hat{h}\hat{x}\hat{y} && \text{(Rule } S)\\
&\Leftarrow BS(B(BS(B\hat{f})))\hat{g}\hat{h}\hat{x}\hat{y} && \text{(Rule } B)\\
&\Leftarrow B(BS)B(BS(B\hat{f}))\hat{g}\hat{h}\hat{x}\hat{y} && \text{(Rule } B)\\
&\Leftarrow B(B(BS)B)(BS)(B\hat{f})\hat{g}\hat{h}\hat{x}\hat{y} && \text{(Rule } B)\\
&\Leftarrow B(B(B(BS)B)(BS))B\hat{f}\hat{g}\hat{h}\hat{x}\hat{y} && \text{(Rule } B)
\end{aligned}
$$

We thus obtain $(B(B(B(BS)B)(BS))B)$ as an abstraction of $(\zeta_1(\zeta_2\zeta_4\zeta_5)(\zeta_3\zeta_4\zeta_5))$ with respect to, in turn, ζ_5, ζ_4, ζ_3, ζ_2, and ζ_1 by a process that one may describe as the *discharging of indeterminates*, first $\hat{y}$, then $\hat{x}$, $\hat{h}$, $\hat{g}$, and finally $\hat{f}$.

There is, of course, nothing to prohibit one from postulating a primitive constant B_2 with the rule $(((((B_2\alpha)\beta)\gamma)\delta)\varepsilon) \rightarrow ((\alpha((\beta\delta)\varepsilon))((\gamma\delta)\varepsilon))$, nor any other primitive constant with associated rule which would facilitate the programming of a class of problems and improve the efficiency of the process of reduction as implemented by some kind of hardware or software. For example, in any practical application, one will want postulated primitive constants for numbers, for addition, etc.

However, to retain the spirit of combinatory calculi, one is constrained to rules that do not violate the Church–Rosser property. This topic we must leave for Section 11.5.

The Λ_I-and Λ_K-Calculi. Of all the finite words over the

Λ_K-Λ_I-Alphabet

improper symbols:	(, λ, ., and)
variable symbols:	$x_0, x_1, x_2, \ldots$
indeterminate symbols:	$\zeta_0, \zeta_1, \zeta_2, \ldots$

we distinguish the following

Λ_K-Objects
These, divided into *primitive* and *composite* objects, are defined recursively as follows:

I-A. the words $x_0, x_1, x_2, \ldots$ are primitive objects which we shall call the *variables*

I-B. the words $\zeta_0, \zeta_1, \zeta_2, \ldots$ are primitive objects which we shall call the *indeterminates*

II. if $\hat{F}$ and $\hat{A}$ are objects, then $(\hat{F}\hat{A})$ is a composite object which we shall call the *application of* $\hat{F}$ *to* $\hat{A}$

III. if $\hat{E}$ is an object and if $\hat{x}$ is a variable symbol, then $(\lambda\hat{x}.\hat{E})$ is a composite object which we shall call the (unrestricted) *abstraction of* $\hat{E}$ *with respect to the variable* $\hat{x}$

IV. the only words that are objects are just those given by clauses (I-A), (I-B), (II), and (III)

from which we shall shortly distinguish the Λ_I-objects.

But first, for both calculi, we need to define a number of concepts required for the statements of the rules for reduction. They are concerned with the *scope* of variables, in order that there shall be no confusion of variables.

BOUND AND FREE OCCURRENCES OF A VARIABLE. Let $\hat{E}$ be an object and $\hat{x}$ a variable. A component of $\hat{E}$ equiform to $\hat{x}$ is a *free* (*bound*) *occurrence of* $\hat{x}$ in $\hat{E}$ as given recursively by the following:

I. if $\hat{E} \equiv \hat{x}$, then the component $\hat{E}$ itself is a free occurrence of $\hat{x}$ in $\hat{E}$

II. if $\hat{E} \equiv (\hat{P}\hat{Q})$, then each component of $\hat{P}$ and $\hat{Q}$ (necessarily a component of $\hat{E}$) that is a free (bound) occurrence of $\hat{x}$ in $\hat{P}$ and $\hat{Q}$, respectively, is a free (bound) occurrence of $\hat{x}$ in $\hat{E}$

III-A. if $\hat{E} \equiv (\lambda\hat{x}.\hat{R})$, then each component of $\hat{R}$ (necessarily a component of $\hat{E}$) that is either a free or a bound occurrence of $\hat{x}$ in $\hat{R}$ is a bound occurrence of $\hat{x}$ in $\hat{E}$

III-B. if $\hat{E} \equiv (\lambda\hat{y}.\hat{R})$, where $\hat{y} \neq \hat{x}$, then each component of $\hat{R}$ (necessarily a component of $\hat{E}$) that is a free (bound) occurrence of $\hat{x}$ in $\hat{R}$ is a free (bound) occurrence of $\hat{x}$ in $\hat{E}$

IV. the only free (bound) occurrences of $\hat{x}$ in $\hat{E}$ are just those given by clauses I, II, III-A, and III-B

We shall leave for the reader the verification that each and every *component* of $\hat{E}$ equiform to $\hat{x}$ is either a free occurrence of $\hat{x}$ in $\hat{E}$ or a bound occurrence of $\hat{x}$ in $\hat{E}$, but not both. The proof of the following lemma is also left to the reader.

LEMMA 11.3. Let $\hat{P}$ and $\hat{Q}$ be components of an object $\hat{E}$ such that $\hat{Q}$ is a component of $\hat{P}$. If $\hat{X}$ is a component of $\hat{Q}$ equiform to a variable $\hat{x}$, then the following hold:

I. if $\hat{X}$ is a free occurrence of $\hat{x}$ in $\hat{P}$, then $\hat{X}$ is a free occurrence of $\hat{x}$ in $\hat{Q}$

II. if $\hat{X}$ is a bound occurrence of $\hat{x}$ in $\hat{Q}$, then $\hat{X}$ is a bound occurrence of $\hat{x}$ in $\hat{P}$ ▮

Consider, for example, the object $(((\lambda\hat{x}.(\lambda\hat{y}.(\hat{x}\hat{y})))\hat{y})\hat{z})$ of the introduction. Its components are as follows

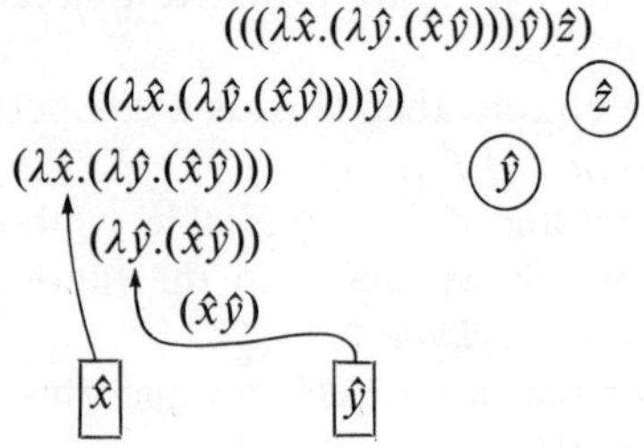

(11-2)

Those components enclosed in either a box or circle are the primitive components; they are all variables, either the variable $\hat{x}$, $\hat{y}$, or $\hat{z}$. Those enclosed in boxes are bound occurrences of the variable displayed within, while those enclosed in circles are free occurrences. The arrows point to what we shall call the *context* of the variable enclosed in the box from which the arrow emanates; all the components arrayed below it have the boxed component as a free occurrence, while those above it have it as a bound occurrence. All components arrayed above the encircled components have the encircled components as free occurrences. It is in this way that the two components equiform to $\hat{y}$ are distinguished—the one is bound to $(\lambda\hat{y}.(\hat{x}\hat{y}))$ and the other is free in $(((\lambda\hat{x}.(\lambda\hat{y}.(\hat{x}\hat{y})))\hat{y})\hat{z})$.

In passing, note the tree structure of the array (11-2) of the components of $(((\lambda\hat{x}.(\lambda\hat{y}.(\hat{x}\hat{y})))\hat{y})\hat{z})$. Note also that neither $\lambda\hat{x}.$, $\lambda\hat{y}.$, nor any part thereof, is a component of this object.

We may now distinguish the Λ_I-objects:

Λ_I-Objects

These are given exactly as the Λ_K-objects, but for clause III, which is to be replaced with:

III′. if $\hat{E}$ is an object possessing a free occurrence of a given variable $\hat{x}$, then $(\lambda\hat{x}.\hat{E})$ is a composite object which we shall call the (*restricted*) *abstraction of* $\hat{E}$ *with respect to the variable* $\hat{x}$

As the reader may already suspect, there is indeed a close relationship between the pairs of calculi Γ_I and Γ_K and Λ_I and Λ_K, a relationship which preserves the relationship between Γ_I and Γ_K discussed on pages 284-285. These relationships we shall investigate in Section 11.6. It is worthwhile repeating here that no one has yet done anything "meaningful" in Λ_K that could not also be done in Λ_I.

It is necessary to distinguish between bound and free occurrences of a variable in an object in order to carry out sequences of reductions based upon elementary substitution rules. For example, consider, in the informal manner of Section 11.1, the following reduction:

$$((\lambda\hat{x}.(\hat{x}\hat{x}))(\lambda\hat{y}.((\lambda\hat{z}.(\hat{y}\hat{z}))\hat{w}))) \Rightarrow ((\lambda\hat{y}.((\lambda\hat{z}.(\hat{y}\hat{z}))\hat{w}))(\lambda\hat{y}.((\lambda\hat{z}.(\hat{y}\hat{z}))\hat{w})))$$
$$\Rightarrow ((\lambda\hat{z}.((\lambda\hat{y}.((\lambda\hat{z}.(\hat{y}\hat{z}))\hat{w}))\hat{z}))\hat{w})$$

Here we have started with an object in which it is not really necessary to distinguish between the bound and free occurrences of a variable—in each component of $((\lambda\hat{x}.(\hat{x}\hat{x}))(\lambda\hat{y}.((\lambda\hat{z}.(\hat{y}\hat{z}))\hat{w})))$, the occurrences of any variable are either all free or all bound occurrences, if there are any such at all. But we have ended with an object in which it is of the utmost importance to distinguish between the bound and free occurrences of $\hat{z}$; for we shall want

$$((\lambda\hat{z}.((\lambda\hat{y}.((\lambda\hat{z}.(\hat{y}\hat{z}))\hat{w}))\hat{z}))\hat{w}) \Rightarrow ((\lambda\hat{y}.((\lambda\hat{z}.(\hat{y}\hat{z}))\hat{w}))\hat{w})$$

and *not* the object which would result if both the free and the bound occurrence of $\hat{z}$ in $((\lambda\hat{y}.((\lambda\hat{z}.(\hat{y}\hat{z}))\hat{w}))\hat{z})$ are replaced by $\hat{w}$.

Seeing that we must deal with such convoluted objects like the one arrived at above, we see that we must also deal with the contingencies already mentioned in Section 11.1 and displayed by the object $((\lambda\hat{y}.((\lambda\hat{z}.(\hat{y}\hat{z}))\hat{w}))\hat{z})$ above: We can not carry out the substitution of $\hat{z}$ for the free occurrence of $\hat{y}$ in the component $((\lambda\hat{z}.(\hat{y}\hat{z}))\hat{w})$, because it would become a bound occurrence of $\hat{z}$ in the component, indicating that its context had changed.

These remarks lead to the following definition:

FREE SUBSTITUTION. An object $\hat{A}$ is free for substitution for the free occurrences of a variable $\hat{x}$ in an object $\hat{E}$; in short, $\hat{A}$ *is free for* $\hat{x}$ *in* $\hat{E}$ just when each variable $\hat{y}$ that occurs free in $\hat{A}$ would be, at each of the free occurrences of $\hat{x}$ in $\hat{E}$, a free occurrence of $\hat{y}$.

We may now give the rules of these two calculi:

Λ_K- (Λ_I-) Rules

Rule α: $(\lambda\hat{x}.\hat{E}) \rightarrow (\lambda\hat{y}.\hat{F})$ provided that the variable $\hat{y}$ is such that (a) $\hat{y}$ differs from each variable that occurs free in $\hat{E}$, and (b) $\hat{y}$ is free for $\hat{x}$ in $\hat{E}$ and $\hat{F}$ is the object which would result if each free occurrence of $\hat{x}$ in $\hat{E}$ were replaced by $\hat{y}$

Rule β: $((\lambda\hat{x}.\hat{E})\hat{A}) \rightarrow \hat{R}$ provided that $\hat{A}$ is free for $\hat{x}$ in $\hat{E}$ and $\hat{R}$ is the object which would result if each free occurrence of $\hat{x}$ in $\hat{E}$ were replaced by $\hat{A}$

One may recognize in Rule α the familiar *change of dummy* (*bound*) *variables*, and one may appreciate that Rule β gives the elementary substitution operations from which, in conjunction with those given by Rule α, *all* others follow. Indeed, we do have the following:

Λ_K-ABSTRACTION ALGORITHM 11.14. Let $\hat{\mathcal{E}}[\hat{\zeta}]$ be any object. Then, *the abstraction of* $\hat{\mathcal{E}}[\hat{\zeta}]$ *with respect to an indeterminate* $\hat{\zeta}$ is $(\lambda\hat{x}.\hat{\mathcal{E}}[\hat{x}])$, where $\hat{x}$ is the first of the variables x_0, x_1, x_2, ... that (a) does not occur free in $\hat{\mathcal{E}}[\hat{\zeta}]$, and (b) would not be, at any of the components of $\hat{\mathcal{E}}[\hat{\zeta}]$ equiform to $\hat{\zeta}$, a bound occurrence of $\hat{x}$ (that is, abusing the terminology slightly, $\hat{x}$ is free for $\hat{\zeta}$ in $\hat{\mathcal{E}}[\hat{\zeta}]$).

Λ_I-ABSTRACTION ALGORITHM 11.15. This is just as the Λ_K-Abstraction Algorithm, but for the additional restriction on $\hat{\mathcal{E}}[\hat{\zeta}]$ that there be at least one component equiform to $\hat{\zeta}$.

And, it is easily verified that $((\lambda\hat{x}.\hat{\mathcal{E}}[\hat{x}])\hat{\zeta}) \Rightarrow \hat{\mathcal{E}}[\hat{\zeta}]$, where $\hat{\mathcal{E}}[\hat{\zeta}]$ and $(\lambda\hat{x}.\hat{\mathcal{E}}[\hat{x}])$ are as given in 11.14 or in 11.15. But clearly a much more general result holds. To state it, let us introduce the following terminology:

DEFINITION 11.16. α-interconvertibility $\approx$. Objects $\hat{X}$ and $\hat{Y}$ are *α-interconvertible*, in symbols $\hat{X} \approx \hat{Y}$, iff there are objects $\hat{Z}_0, \ldots, \hat{Z}_n$ $(0 \leq n)$ such that (a) $\hat{Z}_0 = \hat{X}$, (b) $\hat{Z}_n = \hat{Y}$, and (c), for $1 \leq j \leq n$, $\hat{Z}_{j-1} \rightarrow \hat{Z}_j$ solely on the basis of Rule α.

We leave it for the reader to check that α-interconvertibility is an equivalence relation. The more general result is the following:

PROPOSITION 11.17. Let $\hat{\mathcal{E}}[\hat{\zeta}]$ and $(\lambda\hat{x}.\hat{\mathcal{E}}[\hat{x}])$ be as given in 11.14, or in 11.15 alternatively. Then, for every object $\hat{A}$, there is an object $\hat{\mathcal{E}}'[\hat{\zeta}] \approx \hat{\mathcal{E}}[\hat{\zeta}]$ such that $((\lambda\hat{x}.\hat{\mathcal{E}}[\hat{x}])\hat{A}) \Rightarrow \hat{\mathcal{E}}'[\hat{A}]$.

Proof. With Rule α, change the bound variables of $\hat{\mathcal{E}}[\hat{\zeta}]$ so that no variable $\hat{y}$ which occurs free in $\hat{A}$ would be, at the components of $\hat{\mathcal{E}}'[\hat{\zeta}] \approx \hat{\mathcal{E}}[\hat{\zeta}]$ equiform to $\hat{\zeta}$, a bound occurrence of $\hat{y}$ in $\mathcal{E}'[\hat{\zeta}]$. Evidently, $((\lambda\hat{x}.\hat{\mathcal{E}}[\hat{x}])\hat{A}) \Rightarrow ((\lambda\hat{x}.\hat{\mathcal{E}}'[\hat{x}])\hat{A}) \Rightarrow \hat{\mathcal{E}}'[\hat{A}]$, the latter by Rule β. ∎

Comparing Λ_K and Λ_I with Γ_K and Γ_I, respectively, as long as we are careful to avoid all possibility of confusion in the choice of variables, the abstraction operation that is part and parcel of Λ_K and Λ_I gives at once what requires in Γ_K and Γ_I a nontrivial algorithm for the abstraction of an object with respect to a variable. But then, this is the price one must pay to eliminate variables and avoid entirely the troublesome problems associated with confusion of variables. The question is whether the price is worth it: Do the advantages accruing to a computer design based upon the simpler rules of Γ_K and Γ_I offset the advantages accruing to a computer design based upon the more sophisticated rules of Λ_K and Λ_I?

Other Λ-Calculi. The calculus Λ_I is that proposed by Church [1932]. It and the simple modification Λ_K are the basic Λ-calculi from which all others are derived by the addition of rules, some of which require the addition of primitive constants. Of course, we could add in this way the primitive constants B, C, I, K, S, and W and their associated rules of the basic combinatory calculi Γ_I and Γ_K. The resulting mixed calculus, which is not uninteresting, is usually referred to as a *combinatory logic*. We shall not quibble over the loose terminology: if the calculus has variables, an abstraction operation, and rules for them like Rule α and Rule β, it is a λ-calculus, no matter what other primitive constants and associated rules it may possess.

An often postulated rule is the following:

RULE η 11.18. $(\lambda\hat{x}.(\hat{Q}\hat{x})) \rightarrow \hat{Q}$ provided that $\hat{x}$ does not occur free in $\hat{Q}$.

This yields a form of extentionality. Certainly, if $\hat{F} \Leftrightarrow \hat{G}$, then $(\hat{F}\hat{X}) \Leftrightarrow (\hat{G}\hat{X})$, for every object $\hat{X}$. That is, under the intended interpretation, if two objects $\hat{F}$ and $\hat{G}$ representing two functions f and g, respectively, are such that $\hat{F}$ and $\hat{G}$ satisfy $\hat{F} \Leftrightarrow \hat{G}$, then necessarily, for all x, $f(x) = g(x)$. What about the converse? When does $(\hat{F}\hat{X}) \Leftrightarrow (\hat{G}\hat{X})$, for every object $\hat{X}$, ensure $\hat{F} \Leftrightarrow \hat{G}$?

Suppose $(\hat{F}\hat{X}) \Leftrightarrow (\hat{G}\hat{X})$, for every object $\hat{X}$. Let $\hat{x}$ be a variable that does not occur free in either $\hat{F}$ or $\hat{G}$. Certainly, $(\lambda\hat{x}.(\hat{F}\hat{x})) \Leftrightarrow (\lambda\hat{x}.(\hat{G}\hat{x}))$; but because of Rule η, both $(\lambda\hat{x}.(\hat{F}\hat{x})) \Rightarrow \hat{F}$ and $(\lambda\hat{x}.(\hat{G}\hat{x}) \Rightarrow \hat{G}$. Therefore, $\hat{F} \Leftrightarrow (\lambda\hat{x}.(\hat{F}\hat{x})) \Leftrightarrow (\lambda\hat{x}.(\hat{G}\hat{x})) \Leftrightarrow \hat{G}$.

That this may not happen in either Λ_I or Λ_K will be apparent from the choice $\hat{F} \equiv (\lambda\hat{x}.(\hat{Q}\hat{x}))$ and $\hat{G} \equiv \hat{Q}$, where $\hat{x}$ does not occur free in $\hat{Q}$, and the Church–Rosser property for Λ_I (or Λ_K). Note that, for any object $\hat{X}$, $(\hat{F}\hat{X}) \equiv ((\lambda\hat{x}.(\hat{Q}\hat{x}))\hat{X}) \Rightarrow (\hat{Q}\hat{X})$ follows at once from Rule β.

Turning to yet one more class of rules that are often postulated for λ-calculi, we require the following terminology: An object $\hat{X}$ is in *normal form* iff every object $\hat{Y} \approx \hat{X}$ is such that no rule other than Rule α is applicable to a component of $\hat{Y}$. Then, a rule that is typically postulated is that attributed to Church, namely, for a primitive constant δ:

RULE δ 11.19. For objects $\hat{M}$ and $\hat{N}$ in normal form having no free variables

$$((\delta\hat{M})\hat{N}) \to \begin{cases} (\lambda x_1.(\lambda x_2.(x_1(x_1 x_2)))) & \text{if } \hat{M} \approx \hat{N} \\ (\lambda x_1.(\lambda x_2.(x_1 x_2))) & \text{otherwise}\dagger \end{cases}$$

The restrictions on $\hat{M}$ and $\hat{N}$ are absolutely necessary in order for the Church–Rosser property to hold. First, consider the requirement that both $\hat{M}$ and $\hat{N}$ must be in normal form. Take $\hat{M} \equiv ((\lambda\hat{x}.\hat{x})(\lambda\hat{y}.\hat{y}))$ and $\hat{N} \equiv (\lambda\hat{z}.\hat{z})$. Here, $\hat{M} \Rightarrow \hat{N}$; yet $\hat{M}$ is *not* α-interconvertible with $\hat{N}$. If $((\delta\hat{M})\hat{N})$ reduced to $(\lambda\hat{x}_1.(\lambda\hat{x}_2.(\hat{x}_1(\hat{x}_1\hat{x}_2))))$, then, since $((\delta\hat{M})\hat{N}) \Rightarrow ((\delta\hat{N})\hat{N})$, and since $((\delta\hat{N})\hat{N}) \to (\lambda x_1.(\lambda x_2.(x_1 x_2)))$ *is* an instance of Rule δ, it would have to be that $(\lambda x_1.(\lambda x_2.(x_1 x_2)))$ and $(\lambda x_1.(\lambda x_2.(x_1(x_1 x_2))))$ are interconvertible. But, in view of the Church–Rosser property, this cannot be, for $(\lambda x_1.(\lambda x_2.(x_1 x_2)))$ and $(\lambda x_1.(\lambda x_2.(x_1(x_1 x_2))))$ are both in normal form, and yet are not α-interconvertible. Next, consider the requirement that neither $\hat{M}$ nor $\hat{N}$ may possess free occurrences of a variable. Take $\hat{M} \equiv (\lambda\hat{x}.(\hat{w}\hat{x}))$ and $\hat{N} \equiv (\lambda\hat{x}.\hat{x})$. Both $\hat{M}$ and $\hat{N}$ are in normal form, and neither is α-interconvertible with the other. If $((\delta\hat{M})\hat{N})$ reduced to $(\lambda x_1.(\lambda x_2.(x_1 x_2)))$, then $((\lambda\hat{w}.((\delta\hat{M})\hat{N}))(\lambda\hat{z}.\hat{z}))$ would reduce to $((\lambda\hat{w}.(\lambda x_1.(\lambda x_2.(x_1 x_2))))(\lambda\hat{z}.\hat{z})) \Rightarrow (\lambda x_1.(\lambda x_2.(x_1 x_2)))$. Since $((\lambda\hat{w}.((\delta\hat{M})\hat{N}))(\lambda\hat{z}.\hat{z})) \Rightarrow ((\delta(\lambda\hat{x}.((\lambda\hat{z}.\hat{z})\hat{x})))\hat{N}) \Rightarrow ((\delta(\lambda x.\hat{x}))\hat{N})$ and since $((\delta(\lambda\hat{x}.\hat{x}))\hat{N}) \to (\lambda x_1.(\lambda x_2.(x_1(x_1 x_2))))$ is an instance of Rule δ, it would have to be that $(\lambda x_1.(\lambda x_2.(x_1 x_2)))$ and $(\lambda x_1.(\lambda x_2.(x_1(x_1 x_2))))$ are interconvertible, because $((\lambda\hat{w}.((\delta\hat{M})\hat{N}))(\lambda\hat{z}.\hat{z}))$ reduces to both of these.

Let us take this opportunity to note the more standard names of λ-calculi in the literature. Our Λ_K- and Λ_I-calculi are often referred to as a "λ-*K*-calculus" and a "λ-*I*-calculus", respectively. A λ-calculus having also Rule η is often referred to as a "λ-η-calculus" and sometimes as a "λ-βη-calculus" to emphasize the existence of Rule β (Rule α being too obvious to mention usually). A λ-calculus having also Rule δ is often referred to as a "λ-δ-calculus" or a "λ-βδ-calculus". A λ-calculus having also both Rule η and Rule δ is often called a "full" λ-calculus, a "λ-ηδ-calculus" or a "λ-βηδ-calculus".

EXERCISES

1. Church [1932] set forth the following objects of Λ_I (and hence also of Λ_K) to represent the positive integers in the belief that they would prove adequate for a theory of functions:

$$\hat{1} \equiv (\lambda\hat{x}.(\lambda y.(\hat{x}\hat{y})))$$
$$\hat{2} \equiv (\lambda\hat{x}.(\lambda\hat{y}.(\hat{x}(\hat{x}\hat{y}))))$$
$$\hat{3} \equiv (\lambda\hat{x}.(\lambda\hat{y}.(\hat{x}(\hat{x}(\hat{x}\hat{y})))))$$

† The rather mysterious objects on the righthand side of Rule δ will be seen later to be the objects taken to represent the positive integers 2 and 1, respectively.

and so forth. Rosser, at the time a student of Church's, made the following discovery:

$$(\hat{2}\hat{3}) \Rightarrow \hat{9}$$

Verify this and then show, as did Rosser, that the following holds in general:

$$(\hat{m}\hat{n}) \Rightarrow \widehat{n^m}$$
$$((\lambda\hat{x}.(\lambda\hat{y}.(\lambda\hat{z}.((\hat{x}(\hat{y}\hat{z}))))))\hat{m}\hat{n}) \Rightarrow \widehat{m \times n}$$
$$((\lambda\hat{x}.(\lambda\hat{y}.(\lambda\hat{z}.(\lambda\hat{w}.((\hat{x}\hat{z})((\hat{y}\hat{z})w))))))\hat{m}\hat{n}) \Rightarrow \widehat{m+n}$$

Thus, one may take the following objects of Λ_I to represent the indicated functions on the positive integers:

exponentiation	$(\lambda\hat{x}.(\lambda\hat{y}.(\hat{x}\hat{y})))$
multiplication	$(\lambda\hat{x}.(\lambda\hat{y}.(\lambda\hat{z}.(\hat{x}(\hat{y}\hat{z})))))$
addition	$(\lambda\hat{x}.(\lambda\hat{y}.(\lambda\hat{z}.(\lambda w.((\hat{x}\hat{z})((\hat{y}\hat{z})\hat{w}))))))$

2. For convenience, let us operate in the mixed combinatory calculus with primitive constants B, C, I, K, S, and W. Then we may take

$$\hat{1} \equiv ((SB)(KI))$$
$$\hat{2} \equiv ((SB)((SB)(KI)))$$
$$\hat{3} \equiv ((SB)((SB)((SB)(KI))))$$

and so forth as representatives in this calculus for the positive integers, analogous to Church's numerals of the preceding exercise. Observe that for objects $\hat{x}$ and $\hat{y}$, $(\hat{1}\hat{x}\hat{y}) \Rightarrow (\hat{x}\hat{y})$, $(\hat{2}\hat{x}\hat{y}) \Rightarrow (\hat{x}(\hat{x}\hat{y}))$, $(\hat{3}\hat{x}\hat{y}) \Rightarrow (\hat{x}(\hat{x}(\hat{x}\hat{y})))$ and so forth. Hence our choices agree with those of the preceding exercise. Show that the following hold:

a. $(\hat{2}\hat{3})$ does not reduce to $\hat{9}$.

b. While $(\hat{2}\hat{3})$ does not reduce to $\hat{9}$, $((\hat{2}\hat{3})\hat{x}\hat{y})$ does reduce to

$$(\hat{x}(\hat{x}(\hat{x}(\hat{x}(\hat{x}(\hat{x}(\hat{x}(\hat{x}(\hat{x}\hat{y})))))))))$$

so that $(\hat{2}\hat{3})$ and $\hat{9}$ are different abstractions of the same expression.

c. The following objects may be taken to represent the indicated functions on the positive integers:

addition	$\hat{\oplus} \equiv ((CI)(SB))$
multiplication	$\hat{\otimes} \equiv ((B((CC)(KI)))((CB)\hat{\oplus}))$
exponentiation	$\hat{\Uparrow} \equiv (C((B(C((CC)((SB)(KI))))) \hat{\otimes}))$

3. Calculate, according to Rosser's abstraction algorithm 11.11, the objects of Γ_K denoted by:

a. $\hat{A}_n^m \equiv \{\Lambda\zeta_3{:}((\zeta_m\zeta_3)(\zeta_n\zeta_3))\}$, $1 \leq m, n$

b. $\hat{B}_m \equiv \{\Lambda\zeta_2{:}\hat{A}_2^m\} \equiv \{\Lambda\zeta_2{:}\{\Lambda\zeta_3{:}((\zeta_m\zeta_3)(\zeta_2\zeta_3))\}\}$, $1 \leq m$

c. $\hat{C} \equiv \{\Lambda\zeta_1{:}\hat{B}_1\} \equiv \{\Lambda\zeta_1{:}\{\Lambda\zeta_2{:}\{\Lambda\zeta_3{:}((\zeta_1\zeta_3)(\zeta_2\zeta_3))\}\}\}$

d. $\hat{E}_n \equiv \{\Lambda\zeta_3{:}(((SK)\zeta_3)(\zeta_n\zeta_3))\}$, $1 \leq n$

e. $\hat{F} \equiv \{\Lambda\zeta_2{:}\hat{E}_2\} \equiv \{\Lambda\zeta_2{:}\{\Lambda\zeta_3{:}(((SK)\zeta_3)(\zeta_2\zeta_3))\}\}$
f. $\hat{G} \equiv \{\Lambda\zeta_2{:}(\{\Lambda\zeta_0{:}\{\Lambda\zeta_3{:}((\zeta_0\zeta_3)(\zeta_2\zeta_3))\}\}(SK))\}$

Then verify the following:

a. Notwithstanding that $(\hat{C}\zeta_2)$ and $(\hat{C}\zeta_3)$ do not reduce to $\hat{B}_2$ and $\hat{B}_3$, respectively, and that $(\hat{C}\zeta_i\zeta_j)$, for $i = 3$ or $j = 3$, does not reduce to $\hat{A}^i_j$, it is still the case that, for *any* objects $\hat{X}$, $\hat{Y}$, and $\hat{Z}$, $(\hat{C}\hat{X}\hat{Y}\hat{Z}) \Rightarrow ((\hat{X}\hat{Z})(\hat{Y}\hat{Z}))$.
b. For each $n \geq 1$, $\hat{E}_n$ (alternatively, $\hat{F}$) differs from $\hat{A}^m_n$ (respectively, $\hat{B}_m$) in that *the* component of $\hat{A}^m_n$ (of $\hat{B}_m$) equiform to ζ_m is replaced by (SK).
c. It is not the case that $\hat{G}$ reduces to $\hat{F}$.

Finally, show that if one were to modify Rosser's abstraction algorithm 11.11 as follows, then a and c still hold while b fails:

(I-A′) if $\hat{\mathcal{E}}[\hat{\zeta}]$ is a primitive object different from $\hat{\zeta}$, then $\{\Lambda{:}\hat{\zeta}{:}\hat{\mathcal{E}}[\hat{\zeta}]\} \equiv (K\hat{\mathcal{E}}[\hat{\zeta}])$

(II′) if $\hat{\mathcal{E}}[\hat{\xi}] \equiv (\hat{P}\hat{Q})$, then $\{\Lambda\hat{\zeta}{:}\hat{\mathcal{E}}[\hat{\zeta}]\} \equiv ((S\{\Lambda\hat{\zeta}{:}\hat{P}\})\{\Lambda\hat{\zeta}{:}\hat{Q}\})$

11.3 Adequacy for Partial Recursiveness

In this section, we prove that the (unrestricted) combinatorially complete calculi Γ_K and Λ_K are adequate for an interpretation of partial recursive functions. (We leave for the reader the verification that such is also possible for the restricted calculi Γ_I and Λ_I as well. See Exercise 3.)

In order to give a treatment that is uniform, as well as general, let us introduce the following notation:

DEFINITION 11.20. Let $\langle\Lambda\hat{\zeta}_1,\ldots,\hat{\zeta}_n{:}\hat{\mathcal{E}}[\hat{\zeta}_1,\ldots,\hat{\zeta}_n]\rangle$ be, in the respective case, the following object:

(Γ_K) $\{\Lambda\hat{\zeta}_1{:}\{\ldots\{\Lambda\hat{\zeta}_n{:}\hat{\mathcal{E}}[\hat{\zeta}_1,\ldots,\hat{\zeta}_n]\}\ldots\}\}$ (cf. 11.11 the Γ_K-Abstraction Algorithm)

(Λ_K) $(\lambda\hat{x}_1.(\ldots(\lambda\hat{x}_n.\hat{\mathcal{E}}[\hat{x}_1,\ldots,\hat{x}_n])\ldots))$, where, for $j = n, n-1, \ldots, 1$, $\hat{x}_j$ is the first in the list of variables which differs from $\hat{x}_{j+1}, \ldots, \hat{x}_n$ and which does not occur in $(\lambda\hat{x}_{j+1}.(\ldots(\lambda\hat{x}_n.\hat{\mathcal{E}}[\hat{\zeta}_1,\ldots,\hat{\zeta}_j,\hat{x}_{j+1},\ldots,\hat{x}_n])\ldots))$ (cf. 11.14 the Λ_K-Abstraction Algorithm)

We intend to base the whole demonstration upon the following:

PROPOSITION 11.21. Let $\hat{X}_1, \ldots, \hat{X}_n$ be objects. And let $\hat{\mathcal{E}}[\hat{\zeta}_1,\ldots,\hat{\zeta}_n]$ and $\langle\Lambda\hat{\zeta}_1,\ldots,\hat{\zeta}_n{:}\hat{\mathcal{E}}[\hat{\zeta}_1,\ldots,\hat{\zeta}_n]\rangle$ be as given in Definition 11.20. Then,

$$(\langle\Lambda\hat{\zeta}_1,\ldots,\hat{\zeta}_n{:}\hat{\mathcal{E}}[\hat{\zeta}_1,\ldots,\hat{\zeta}_n]\rangle\hat{X}_1\cdots\hat{X}_n) \Rightarrow \hat{R}$$

where $\hat{R}$ is, in the respective situation, as follows:

(Γ_K) $\hat{R} \equiv \hat{\mathcal{E}}[\hat{X}_1,\ldots,\hat{X}_n]$

(Λ_K) $\hat{R} \equiv \hat{\mathcal{E}}'[\hat{X}_1,\ldots,\hat{X}_n]$, where $\mathcal{E}'[\hat{\zeta}_1,\ldots,\hat{\zeta}_n] \approx \mathcal{E}[\hat{\zeta}_1,\ldots,\hat{\zeta}_n]$

Proof. For Λ_K the result follows readily from Proposition 11.17. For Γ_K the result is not quite so easy. But it will follow easily from Proposition 11.12 and the following two results which we shall establish in Section 11.6:

a. Let $\hat{F}$ result from $\hat{E}$ by replacing each component of $\hat{E}$ equiform to distinct indeterminates $\hat{\zeta}_1, \ldots, \hat{\zeta}_n$ by indeterminates $\hat{\zeta}'_1, \ldots, \hat{\zeta}'_n$, respectively. Then, if $\hat{\zeta}'_1, \ldots, \hat{\zeta}'_n$ are different from each other and different from each indeterminate equiform to a component of $\hat{E}$,

$$\{\Lambda\hat{\zeta}_1{:}\ldots\{\Lambda\hat{\zeta}_n{:}\hat{E}\}\ldots\} = \Lambda\hat{\zeta}'_1{:}\ldots\{\Lambda\hat{\zeta}'_n{:}\hat{F}\}\ldots\}.$$

b. Let $\hat{\zeta}_y$ be an indeterminate different from $\hat{\zeta}_x$. Let $\hat{R}$ be the result of replacing each component of $\hat{E}$ equiform to $\hat{\zeta}_y$ by $\hat{A}$. And, let $\hat{T}$ be the result of replacing each component of $\{\Lambda\hat{\zeta}_x{:}\hat{E}\}$ equiform to $\hat{\zeta}_y$ by $\hat{A}$. Then, if $\hat{\zeta}_x$ is not equiform to a component of $\hat{A}$, $\hat{T} = \{\Lambda\hat{\zeta}_x{:}\hat{R}\}$.

Indeed, result a, which is Corollary 11.70, allows us to pick the indeterminates of the indicated abstractions in such a way that the replacement operation of Proposition 11.12 can be carried across the indicated abstractions by means of result b, which is Proposition 11.69. In other words, in the metacalculus for Γ_K in which we have the abstraction operation $\{\Lambda\hat{\zeta}{:}\text{—}\}$, we may operate in a way analogous to Λ_K with the abstraction operation $(\lambda\hat{x}.\text{—})$. This relationship is the subject of Section 11.6. ▮

In view of Definition 11.20, for each $2 \leq j \leq n$,

$$\langle\Lambda\hat{\zeta}_1,\ldots,\hat{\zeta}_{j-1}{:}\langle\Lambda\hat{\zeta}_j,\ldots,\hat{\zeta}_n{:}\hat{\mathfrak{E}}[\hat{\zeta}_1,\ldots,\hat{\zeta}_n]\rangle\rangle = \langle\Lambda\hat{\zeta}_1,\ldots,\hat{\zeta}_n{:}\hat{\mathfrak{E}}[\hat{\zeta}_1,\ldots,\hat{\zeta}_n]\rangle$$

This is, of course, none other than a restatement of Schönfinkel's idea for interpreting a function of several variables by means of functions of one variable. And, we shall exploit this fact in order to make clearer the presentation below. See, for example, Definition 11.26 and Lemma 11.27. It is by no means essential to the argument below; all that is required is that the calculus be combinatorially complete in the sense indicated in Proposition 11.21.

One final observation is useful before getting under way. Consider again Proposition 11.21 with respect to Λ_K. If no component of $\hat{\mathfrak{E}}[\hat{\zeta}_1,\ldots,\hat{\zeta}_n]$ that is an abstraction $(\lambda\hat{x}.\hat{E})$ has a component equiform to $\hat{\zeta}_1,\ldots,\hat{\zeta}_n$, then $\hat{R} \equiv \hat{\mathfrak{E}}[\hat{\zeta}_1,\ldots,\hat{\zeta}_n]$; that is $\hat{\mathfrak{E}}'[\hat{\zeta}_1,\ldots,\hat{\zeta}_n]$ may be taken to be $\hat{\mathfrak{E}}[\hat{\zeta}_1,\ldots,\hat{\zeta}_n]$.

Now, according to the classical definition of partial recursive functions (see, for example, Kleene [1952]), we are required:

I. To specify an object:
   1. $\hat{0}$ to represent the number zero
   2. $\hat{\mathfrak{S}}$ to represent the successor function

II. To produce objects:
   3. $\hat{\mathfrak{U}}^m_n$ to represent the projection functions: $\varphi(x_1,\ldots,x_n) = x_m$, where $1 \leq m \leq n$

III. To derive objects:
   4. $\hat{\mathfrak{C}}^m_n$ to model the composition schemes: for a given function f of $m \geq 1$ variables and m given functions $g_1,\ldots,g_m$ of $n \geq 1$ variables each, $\varphi(x_1,\ldots,x_n) = f(g_1(x_1,\ldots,x_n),\ldots,g_m(x_1,\ldots,x_n))$

5. $\widehat{\mathfrak{T}}_n$ to model the primitive recursion schemes: for a given function g of $n-1 \geq 0$ variables† and a given function h of $n+1$ variables, $\varphi(0,x_2,\ldots,x_n) = g(x_2,\ldots,x_n)$ and $\varphi(m+1,x_2,\ldots,x_n) = h(m,\varphi(m,x_2,\ldots,x_n),x_2,\ldots,x_n)$
6. $\widehat{\mathcal{M}}_n$ to model the minimization schemes: for a given f of $n+1 \geq 1$ variables $\varphi(x_1,\ldots,x_n) = \mu_y[f(y,x_1,\ldots,x_n) = 0]$; that is, if, for $z = 0,1,2,\ldots,m-1$, $f(z,x_1,\ldots,x_n) \neq 0$, and if $f(m,x_1,\ldots,x_n) = 0$, then $\varphi(x_1,\ldots,x_n) = m$.††

To settle I, we propose, following the original suggestion of Church [1932], the following choice:

DEFINITION 11.22. Numerals.

To represent zero: $\hat{0} \equiv \langle\Lambda\zeta_1,\zeta_2{:}\zeta_2\rangle$

To represent the successor function: $\hat{\mathfrak{S}} \equiv \langle\Lambda\zeta_1{:}\langle\Lambda\zeta_2,\zeta_3{:}(\zeta_2((\zeta_1\zeta_2)\zeta_3))\rangle\rangle$ so that

$$\hat{1} \equiv (\hat{\mathfrak{S}}\hat{0})$$
$$\hat{2} \equiv (\hat{\mathfrak{S}}\hat{1}) \equiv (\hat{\mathfrak{S}}(\hat{\mathfrak{S}}\hat{0}))$$
$$\hat{3} \equiv (\hat{\mathfrak{S}}\hat{2}) \equiv (\hat{\mathfrak{S}}(\hat{\mathfrak{S}}(\hat{\mathfrak{S}}\hat{0})))$$

and so forth.

For example, in Λ_K we have quite simply $\hat{0} \equiv (\lambda x_1.(\lambda x_0.x_0))$ and $\hat{\mathfrak{S}} \equiv (\lambda x_2.(\lambda x_1.(\lambda x_0.(x_1((x_2x_1)x_0)))))$. Here one may verify that $\hat{1} \equiv (\hat{\mathfrak{S}}\hat{0}) \Rightarrow (\lambda x_1.(\lambda x_0.(x_1x_0)))$, $\hat{2} \equiv (\hat{\mathfrak{S}}\hat{1}) \Rightarrow (\lambda x_1.(\lambda x_0.(x_1(x_1x_0))))$, and so forth. Indeed, we have the following general result:

LEMMA 11.23. For any objects $\hat{X}$ and $\hat{Y}$

$$((\hat{0}\hat{X})\hat{Y}) \Rightarrow \hat{Y}$$
$$((\widehat{n+1}\hat{X})\hat{Y}) \Rightarrow (\hat{X}((\hat{n}\hat{X})\hat{Y}))$$

so that

$$((\hat{n}\hat{X})\hat{Y}) \Rightarrow \overbrace{(\hat{X}(\ldots(\hat{X}}^{nX\text{'s}}\hat{Y})\ldots))$$

Proof. That $((\hat{0}\hat{X})\hat{Y}) \Rightarrow \hat{Y}$ is immediate from the definition of $\hat{0}$ as $\langle\Lambda\zeta_1,\zeta_2{:}\zeta_2\rangle$. Now, as $\widehat{n+1} \equiv (\hat{\mathfrak{S}}\hat{n})$, $((\widehat{n+1}\hat{X})\hat{Y}) \equiv (((\hat{\mathfrak{S}}\hat{n})\hat{X})\hat{Y})$. Since $(((\hat{\mathfrak{S}}\hat{n})\hat{X})\hat{Y}) \Rightarrow (\hat{X}((\hat{n}\hat{X})\hat{Y}))$ follows at once from the definition of $\hat{\mathfrak{S}}$ as $\langle\Lambda\zeta_1{:}\langle\Lambda\zeta_2,\zeta_3{:}(\zeta_2((\zeta_1\zeta_2)\zeta_3))\rangle\rangle$, $((\widehat{n+1}\hat{X})\hat{Y}) \Rightarrow (\hat{X}((\hat{n}\hat{X})\hat{Y}))$. ∎

† A function of 0 variables is understood to be a constant.

†† Note that $f(y,x_1,\ldots,x_n) = 0$, instead of $f(y,x_1,\ldots,x_n) = 1$, is used here. While the difference is inessential, initially it is a great convenience.

While Lemma 11.23 indicates that we are perhaps on the right track with the choices of Definition 11.22, we shall not really know until we are done whether or not they are, as claimed, "adequate".

We can quickly settle II with the following:

DEFINITION 11.24. Projection Functions. To represent the projection function $\varphi(x_1,\ldots,x_n) = x_m$ $(1 \leq m \leq n)$, take $\hat{\mathfrak{U}}_n^m \equiv \langle \Lambda\zeta_1,\ldots,\zeta_n{:}\zeta_m\rangle$.

LEMMA 11.25. For objects $\hat{X}_1,\ldots,\hat{X}_n$, $((\ldots(\hat{\mathfrak{U}}_n^m\hat{X}_1)\ldots)\hat{X}_n) \Rightarrow \hat{X}_m$ ∎

While the proof of this lemma offers no difficulty at all—it is immediate from the definition of $\hat{\mathfrak{U}}_n^m$ as $\langle \Lambda\zeta_1,\ldots,\zeta_n{:}\zeta_m\rangle$—it will be observed that the lemma is verifying that $\hat{\mathfrak{U}}_n^m$ does indeed possess the requisite property by which an object may be viewed as representing the projection function $\varphi(x_1,\ldots,x_n) = x_m$ $(1 \leq m \leq n)$.

At this point, let us recall our convention regarding parentheses in Section 11.1. With it, Lemma 11.25 could read "for objects $\hat{X}$ and $\hat{Y}$, $(\hat{\mathfrak{U}}_n^m\hat{X}_1\cdots\hat{X}_n) \Rightarrow \hat{X}_m$" by omitting all but the outermost pair of parentheses—the outermost we keep for the sake of clarity. We shall ruthlessly exploit this convention again and again below. It will help to recall that $(\hat{F}\hat{X}_1\cdots\hat{X}_n)$ is the analogue of the usual $f(x_1,\ldots,x_n)$.

Furthermore, we shall no longer explicitly display particular indeterminates; instead of writing $\langle \Lambda\zeta_1,\ldots,\zeta_n{:}\zeta_m\rangle$ as in Definition 11.24, we shall write $\langle \Lambda\hat{\zeta}_1,\ldots,\hat{\zeta}_n{:}\hat{\zeta}_m\rangle$, leaving for the reader explicit choices for $\hat{\zeta}_1$, ..., $\hat{\zeta}_n$ (provided the choices are different for different names). This we may do because of observation a of the proof of Proposition 11.21 for Γ_K and because of Rule α for Λ_k. We do this to avoid the need for subscripts on subscripts.

Now, we can, just as easily as with II, settle III-4 as follows:

DEFINITION 11.26. Composition Schemes. To model the composition scheme defined for given f and g_1, ..., g_m by

$$\varphi(x_1,\ldots,x_n) = f(g_1(x_1,\ldots,x_n),\ldots,g_m(x_1,\ldots,x_n))$$

take $\hat{\mathfrak{C}}_n^m \equiv \langle \Lambda\hat{\zeta}'_0,\hat{\zeta}'_1,\ldots,\hat{\zeta}'_m{:}\langle \Lambda\hat{\zeta}_1,\ldots,\hat{\zeta}_n{:}(\hat{\zeta}'_0(\hat{\zeta}'_1\hat{\zeta}_1\cdots\hat{\zeta}_n)\cdots(\hat{\zeta}'_m\hat{\zeta}_1\cdots\hat{\zeta}_n))\rangle\rangle$.

LEMMA 11.27. Let $\hat{F}$ and $\hat{G}_1$, ..., $\hat{G}_m$ be given objects. For objects $\hat{X}_1$, ..., $\hat{X}_n$, $((\hat{\mathfrak{C}}_n^m\hat{F}\hat{G}_1\cdots\hat{G}_m)\hat{X}_1\cdots\hat{X}_n) \Rightarrow (\hat{F}(\hat{G}_1\hat{X}_1\cdots\hat{X}_n)\cdots(\hat{G}_m\hat{X}_1\cdots\hat{X}_n))$. ∎

Again, while the proof of the lemma is immediate, we see that, if $\hat{F}$ represents f and $\hat{G}_1$, ..., $\hat{G}_m$ represent g_1, ..., g_m, respectively, then $(\hat{\mathfrak{C}}_n^m\hat{F}\hat{G}_1\cdots\hat{G}_m)$ will represent φ, where $\varphi(x_1,\ldots,x_n) = f(g_1(x_1,\ldots,x_n),\ldots,g_m(x_1,\ldots,x_n))$.

It is hard not to be surprised by the simplicity of the results so far. And yet, reflecting upon the pure substitutional character of the identity functions and the composition schemes, it is hard to remain surprised. Basically, we have not yet had to make use in any essential way of our choice of numerals. To settle III-5 and III-6, this is no longer the case.

To settle III-5, we begin with the special case $n = 0$ and observe that $\varphi(0) = g$ and $\varphi(m+1) = h(m,h(m-1,\ldots,h(1,h(0,g))\ldots))$. With this in mind, consider the following objects:

DEFINITION 11.28.

$$\hat{\mathscr{F}}_0 \equiv \langle \Lambda \hat{\zeta}_1, \hat{\zeta}_2, \hat{\zeta}_3 : \hat{\zeta}_3 \rangle$$
$$\hat{\mathscr{F}}_* \equiv \langle \Lambda \hat{\zeta}_0, \hat{\zeta}_1, \hat{\zeta}_2, \hat{\zeta}_3 : (\hat{\zeta}_0 \hat{\zeta}_1 (\hat{\mathbb{S}} \hat{\zeta}_2)(\hat{\zeta}_1 \hat{\zeta}_2 \hat{\zeta}_3)) \rangle$$

LEMMA 11.29. Let $\hat{H}$ and $\hat{Y}$ be given objects. Then, for a numeral $\hat{p}$,

$$(\hat{0}\hat{\mathscr{F}}_*\hat{\mathscr{F}}_0\hat{H}\hat{p}\hat{Y}) \Rightarrow \hat{Y}$$
$$(\widehat{m+1}\hat{\mathscr{F}}_*\hat{\mathscr{F}}_0\hat{H}\hat{p}\hat{Y}) \Rightarrow (\hat{m}\hat{\mathscr{F}}_*\hat{\mathscr{F}}_0\hat{H}\widehat{p+1}(\hat{H}\hat{p}\hat{Y})) \qquad (m \geq 0)$$

Proof. By Lemma 11.23, $(\hat{0}\hat{\mathscr{F}}_*\hat{\mathscr{F}}_0\hat{H}\hat{p}\hat{Y}) \Rightarrow (\hat{\mathscr{F}}_0\hat{H}\hat{p}\hat{Y})$. In view of the definition of $\hat{\mathscr{F}}_0$, $(\hat{\mathscr{F}}_0\hat{H}\hat{p}\hat{Y}) \Rightarrow \hat{Y}$. Again by Lemma 11.23, $(\widehat{m+1}\hat{\mathscr{F}}_*\,\hat{}_0\hat{H}\hat{p}\hat{Y}) \Rightarrow (\hat{\mathscr{F}}_*(\hat{m}\hat{\mathscr{F}}_*\hat{\mathscr{F}}_0)\hat{H}\hat{p}\hat{Y})$. In view of the definition of $\hat{\mathscr{F}}_*$, $(\hat{\mathscr{F}}_*(\hat{m}\hat{\mathscr{F}}_{*0}\hat{\mathscr{F}})\hat{H}\hat{p}\hat{Y}) \Rightarrow ((\hat{m}\hat{\mathscr{F}}_*\hat{\mathscr{F}}_0)\hat{H}(\mathbb{S}\hat{p})(\hat{H}\hat{p}\hat{Y}))$. Recognizing from Definition 11.22 that $(\hat{\mathbb{S}}\hat{p}) \equiv \widehat{p+1}$, the proof is complete. ∎

LEMMA 11.30. Let $\hat{H}$ and $\hat{Y}$ be given objects. Then, for a numeral $\hat{p}$, $(\hat{m}\hat{\mathscr{F}}_*\hat{\mathscr{F}}_0\hat{H}\hat{p}\hat{Y}) \Rightarrow (\hat{H}\widehat{m+p-1}(\hat{H}\widehat{m+p-2}(\ldots(\hat{H}\widehat{p+1}(\hat{H}\hat{p}\hat{Y}))\ldots)))$, where, in case $m = 0$, the righthand side is interpreted to mean $\hat{Y}$.

Proof. This is proved by induction on m. Basis, $m = 0$: This is immediate from Lemma 11.29. Induction step: Assume the result holds for $m = q$; we compute as follows:

$$\begin{aligned}(\widehat{q+1}\hat{\mathscr{F}}_*\hat{\mathscr{F}}_0\hat{H}\hat{p}\hat{Y}) &\Rightarrow (\hat{q}\hat{\mathscr{F}}_*\hat{\mathscr{F}}_0\hat{H}\widehat{p+1}(\hat{H}\hat{p}\hat{Y})) && \text{(Lemma 11.29)}\\ &\Rightarrow (\hat{H}\widehat{q+(p+1)-1}(\hat{H}\widehat{q+(p+1)-2} \\ &\qquad (\ldots(\hat{H}\widehat{(p+1)+1}(\hat{H}\widehat{(p+1)}(\hat{H}\hat{p}\hat{Y})))\ldots))) \\ & && \text{(Induction Hypothesis)}\end{aligned}$$

Since $q+(p+1)-1 = (q+1)+p-1$, $q+(p+1)-2 = (q+1)+p-2$, $\ldots,(p+1)+1 = p+2$, and $(p+1) = p+1$, we have established the induction step. ∎

We can now settle III-5 in two parts as follows:

DEFINITION 11.31. Primitive Recursion Scheme ($n = 1$). To model the primitive recursion scheme defined for a given constant g and function h by

$$\varphi(0) = g$$
$$\varphi(m+1) = h(m,\varphi(m))$$

take $\hat{\mathfrak{T}}_1 \equiv \langle \Lambda \hat{\zeta}_1, \hat{\zeta}_2 : \langle \Lambda \hat{\zeta}_3 : (\hat{\zeta}_3 \hat{\mathscr{F}}_* \hat{\mathscr{F}}_0 \hat{\zeta}_2 \hat{0} \hat{\zeta}_1) \rangle \rangle$.

LEMMA 11.32. Let $\hat{G}$ and $\hat{H}$ be given objects. Then,

$$((\hat{\mathfrak{I}}_1 \hat{G}\hat{H})\hat{0}) \Rightarrow \hat{G}$$
$$((\hat{\mathfrak{I}}_1 \hat{G}\hat{H})\widehat{m+1}) \Rightarrow (\hat{H}\hat{m}\ldots(\hat{H}\hat{1}(\hat{H}\hat{0}\hat{G}))\ldots)$$

Proof. By the definition of $\hat{\mathfrak{I}}_1$, $((\hat{\mathfrak{I}}_1 \hat{G}\hat{H})\hat{M}) \Rightarrow (\hat{M}\hat{\mathcal{F}}_* \hat{\mathcal{F}}_0 \hat{H}\hat{0}\hat{G})$, for any object $\hat{M}$. Letting first $\hat{M} \equiv \hat{0}$, then $\hat{M} \equiv \widehat{m+1}$, the results are immediate consequences of Lemma 11.30. ▮

Before settling the second part of III-5, it is convenient to introduce the following special objects:

DEFINITION 11.33.

$$\hat{\mathcal{A}}_n \equiv \langle \Lambda \hat{\zeta}_0' : \langle \Lambda \hat{\zeta}_2, \ldots, \hat{\zeta}_n : \langle \Lambda \hat{\zeta}_1', \hat{\zeta}_2' : (\hat{\zeta}_0' \hat{\zeta}_1' \hat{\zeta}_2' \hat{\zeta}_2 \cdots \hat{\zeta}_n) \rangle\rangle\rangle \qquad n > 1$$
$$\hat{\mathcal{B}}_n \equiv \langle \Lambda \hat{\zeta}_0' : \langle \Lambda \hat{\zeta}_1', \hat{\zeta}_2', \hat{\zeta}_1 : \langle \Lambda \hat{\zeta}_2, \ldots, \hat{\zeta}_n : (\hat{\zeta}_0' (\hat{\zeta}_1' \hat{\zeta}_2 \cdots \hat{\zeta}_n)(\hat{\mathcal{A}}_n \hat{\zeta}_2' \hat{\zeta}_2 \cdots \hat{\zeta}_n)\hat{\zeta}_1) \rangle\rangle\rangle \qquad n > 1$$

DEFINITION 11.34. Primitive Recursion Scheme ($n > 1$). To model the primitive recursion scheme defined for given functions g and h by

$$\varphi(0, x_2, \ldots, x_n) = g(x_2, \ldots, x_n)$$
$$\varphi(m+1, x_2, \ldots, x_n) = h(m, \varphi(m, x_2, \ldots, x_n), x_2, \ldots, x_n)$$

take $\hat{\mathfrak{I}}_n \equiv (\hat{\mathcal{B}}_n \hat{\mathfrak{I}}_1)$.

LEMMA 11.35. Let $\hat{G}$ and $\hat{H}$ be given objects. Then, for objects $\hat{X}_2, \ldots, \hat{X}_n$,

$$((\hat{\mathfrak{I}}_n \hat{G}\hat{H}\hat{0})\hat{X}_2 \cdots \hat{X}_n) \Rightarrow (\hat{G}\hat{X}_2 \cdots \hat{X}_n)$$
$$((\hat{\mathfrak{I}}_n \hat{G}\hat{H})\widehat{m+1}\hat{X}_2 \cdots \hat{X}_n)$$
$$\Rightarrow (\hat{H}\hat{m}(\hat{H}\widehat{m-1}(\ldots(\hat{H}\hat{0}(\hat{G}\hat{X}_2 \cdots \hat{X}_n)\hat{X}_2 \cdots \hat{X}_n)\ldots)\hat{X}_2 \cdots \hat{X}_n)\hat{X}_2 \cdots \hat{X}_n)$$

Proof. By the definitions of $\hat{\mathfrak{I}}_n$ and $\hat{\mathcal{B}}_n$, $((\hat{\mathfrak{I}}_n \hat{G}\hat{H})\hat{M}\hat{X}_2 \cdots \hat{X}_n) \equiv (\hat{\mathcal{B}}_n \hat{\mathfrak{I}}_1 \hat{G}\hat{H}\hat{M}\hat{X}_2 \cdots \hat{X}_n) \Rightarrow (\hat{\mathfrak{I}}_1 (\hat{G}\hat{X}_2 \cdots \hat{X}_n)(\hat{\mathcal{A}}_n \hat{H}\hat{X}_2 \cdots \hat{X}_n)\hat{M})$, for any object $\hat{M}$. Letting $\hat{M} \equiv \hat{0}$, the first result follows at once from Lemma 11.32. Before letting $\hat{M} \equiv \widehat{m+1}$, let us observe that, by the definition of $\hat{\mathcal{A}}_n$, $((\hat{\mathcal{A}}_n \hat{H}\hat{X}_2 \cdots \hat{X}_n)\hat{Y}\hat{Z}) \Rightarrow (\hat{H}\hat{Y}\hat{Z}\hat{X}_2 \cdots \hat{X}_n)$, for any objects $\hat{Y}$ and $\hat{Z}$. Now letting $\hat{M} \equiv \widehat{m+1}$, the second result is seen to follow also from Lemma 11.32. ▮

Finally, to settle III-6, we begin with

DEFINITION 11.36.

$$\hat{\mathfrak{G}} \equiv \langle \Lambda \hat{\zeta}_0 : \langle \Lambda \hat{\zeta}_1 : \langle \Lambda \hat{\zeta}_2 : (\hat{\zeta}_1 \hat{\zeta}_2 (\langle \Lambda \hat{\zeta}_1', \hat{\zeta}_2' : \hat{\zeta}_1' \rangle (\hat{\zeta}_0 \hat{\zeta}_0 \hat{\zeta}_1 (\hat{\mathfrak{S}} \hat{\zeta}_2)))\hat{\zeta}_2)\rangle\rangle\rangle$$

LEMMA 11.37. Let $\hat{F}$ be a given object. Then, for a numeral $\hat{p}$,

$$(\hat{\mathfrak{G}}\hat{\mathfrak{G}}\hat{F}\hat{p}) \Rightarrow \begin{cases} \hat{p} & \text{if } (\hat{F}\hat{p}) \Rightarrow \hat{0} \\ (\hat{\mathfrak{G}}\hat{\mathfrak{G}}\hat{F}\widehat{p+1}) & \text{if } (\hat{F}\hat{p}) \Rightarrow \widehat{t+1},\ t \geq 0 \end{cases}$$

Proof. By the definition of $\hat{\mathfrak{G}}$, $(\hat{\mathfrak{G}}\hat{\mathfrak{G}}\hat{F}\hat{p}) \Rightarrow (\hat{F}\hat{p}(\langle\Lambda\hat{\zeta}_1',\hat{\zeta}_2':\hat{\zeta}_1'\rangle(\hat{\mathfrak{G}}\hat{\mathfrak{G}}\hat{F}(\hat{\mathfrak{S}}\hat{p})))\hat{p})$. Suppose $(\hat{F}\hat{p}) \Rightarrow \hat{0}$. Then, by Lemma 11.23, $(\hat{F}\hat{p}(\langle\Lambda\hat{\zeta}_1',\hat{\zeta}_2':\hat{\zeta}_1'\rangle(\hat{\mathfrak{G}}\hat{\mathfrak{G}}\hat{F}(\hat{\mathfrak{S}}\hat{p})))\hat{p}) \Rightarrow \hat{p}$. On the other hand, suppose $(\hat{F}\hat{p}) \Rightarrow \widehat{t+1}$, $t \geq 0$. Then, again by Lemma 11.23,

$$
\begin{aligned}
&(\hat{F}\hat{p}(\langle\Lambda\hat{\zeta}_1',\hat{\zeta}_2':\hat{\zeta}_1'\rangle(\hat{\mathfrak{G}}\hat{\mathfrak{G}}\hat{F}(\hat{\mathfrak{S}}\hat{p})))\hat{p}) \\
&\quad \Rightarrow (\langle\Lambda\hat{\zeta}_1',\hat{\zeta}_2':\hat{\zeta}_1'\rangle(\hat{\mathfrak{G}}\hat{\mathfrak{G}}\hat{F}(\hat{\mathfrak{S}}\hat{p}))(\hat{t}(\langle\Lambda\hat{\zeta}_1'\hat{\zeta}_2':\hat{\zeta}_1'\rangle(\hat{\mathfrak{G}}\hat{\mathfrak{G}}\hat{F}(\hat{\mathfrak{S}}\hat{p})))\hat{p})) \\
&\quad \Rightarrow (\hat{\mathfrak{G}}\hat{\mathfrak{G}}\hat{F}(\hat{\mathfrak{S}}\hat{p}))
\end{aligned}
$$

by virtue of the definition of $\langle\Lambda\hat{\zeta}_1',\hat{\zeta}_2':\hat{\zeta}_2'\rangle$. Recognizing from Definition 11.22 that $(\hat{\mathfrak{S}}\hat{p}) \equiv \widehat{p+1}$, the proof is complete. ▮

LEMMA 11.38. Let $\hat{F}$ be a given object. If, for $r = p, p+1, \ldots, p+q-1$, $(\hat{F}\hat{r}) \Rightarrow \widehat{t_r+1}$, $t_r \geq 0$, and if $(\hat{F}\widehat{p+q}) \Rightarrow \hat{0}$, then $(\hat{\mathfrak{G}}\hat{\mathfrak{G}}\hat{F}\hat{p}) \Rightarrow \widehat{p+q}$.

Proof. The proof is by induction on q. Basis, $q = 0$: As $\widehat{p+q} = \hat{p}$, so that $(\hat{F}\hat{p}) \Rightarrow \hat{0}$, the result for $q = 0$ follows at once from Lemma 11.37. Induction step: Assume the result holds for $q = s > 0$. Because $s > 0$, $(\hat{F}\hat{p}) \Rightarrow \widehat{t_p+1}$, $t_p \geq 0$, so that, in view of Lemma 11.37, $(\hat{\mathfrak{G}}\hat{\mathfrak{G}}\hat{F}\hat{p}) \Rightarrow (\hat{\mathfrak{G}}\hat{\mathfrak{G}}\hat{F}\widehat{p+1})$. Because $(\hat{F}\hat{r}) \Rightarrow \widehat{t_r+1}$, $t_r \geq 0$, for $r = (p+1), \ldots, (p+1)+s-1$, and $(\hat{F}\widehat{(p+1)+s}) \Rightarrow \hat{0}$, we have by the hypothesis of the induction that $(\hat{\mathfrak{G}}\hat{\mathfrak{G}}\hat{F}\widehat{p+1}) \Rightarrow \widehat{(p+1)+s}$. Since $\widehat{(p+1)+s} \equiv \widehat{p+(s+1)}$, we have $(\hat{\mathfrak{G}}\hat{\mathfrak{G}}\hat{F}\hat{p}) \Rightarrow \widehat{p+(s+1)}$, establishing the induction step. ▮

We can now settle III-6 in two parts as follows:

DEFINITION 11.39. Minimization Scheme ($n = 0$). To model the minimization scheme defined for a given function f by $\varphi = \mu_y[f(y) = 0]$ (that is, φ is a constant), take $\hat{\mathcal{M}}_0 \equiv \langle\Lambda\hat{\zeta}_0':(\hat{\mathfrak{G}}\hat{\mathfrak{G}}\hat{\zeta}_0'\hat{0})\rangle$.

LEMMA 11.40. Let $\hat{F}$ be a given object. If, for $r = 0, 1, 2, \ldots, m-1$, $(\hat{F}\hat{r}) \Rightarrow \widehat{t_r+1}$, $t_r \geq 0$, and if $(\hat{F}\hat{m}) \Rightarrow 0$, then $(\hat{\mathcal{M}}_0\hat{F}) \Rightarrow \hat{m}$.

Proof. As $(\hat{\mathcal{M}}_0\hat{F}) \Rightarrow (\hat{\mathfrak{G}}\hat{\mathfrak{G}}\hat{F}\hat{0})$, by the definition of $\hat{\mathcal{M}}_0$, the result follows at once from Lemma 11.38. ▮

It is convenient to introduce the following special object:

DEFINITION 11.41.

$$
\hat{\mathfrak{D}}_n \equiv \langle\Lambda\hat{\zeta}_0':\langle\Lambda\hat{\zeta}_1,\ldots,\hat{\zeta}_n:\langle\Lambda\hat{\zeta}_0:(\hat{\zeta}_0'\hat{\zeta}_0\hat{\zeta}_1\cdots\hat{\zeta}_n)\rangle\rangle\rangle \qquad n > 0
$$

For then, we may settle the second part of III-6 as follows:

DEFINITION 11.42. Minimization Scheme ($n > 0$). To model the minimization scheme defined for a given function f by

$$
\varphi(x_1,\ldots,x_n) = \mu_y[f(y,x_1,\ldots,x_n)]
$$

take $\hat{\mathcal{M}}_n \equiv (\hat{\mathfrak{C}}_{n+1}^1\,\hat{\mathcal{M}}_0\hat{\mathfrak{D}}_n)$ (for $\hat{\mathfrak{C}}_{n+1}^1$ see Definition 11.26).

LEMMA 11.43. Let $\hat{F}$ be a given object. Then, for any objects $\hat{X}_1, \ldots, \hat{X}_n$, if, for $r = 0, 1, 2, \ldots, m-1$, $(\hat{F}\hat{r}\hat{X}_1 \cdots \hat{X}_n) \Rightarrow \widehat{t_r + 1}$, $t_r \geq 0$, and if $(\hat{F}\hat{m}\hat{X}_1 \cdots \hat{X}_n) \Rightarrow \hat{0}$, then $((\hat{\mathfrak{M}}_n\hat{F})\hat{X}_1 \cdots \hat{X}_n) \Rightarrow \hat{m}$.

Proof. By the definition of $\hat{\mathfrak{M}}_n$, $((\hat{\mathfrak{M}}_n\hat{F})\hat{X}_1 \cdots \hat{X}_n) \Rightarrow (\hat{\mathfrak{M}}_0(\hat{\mathfrak{D}}_n\hat{F}\hat{X}_1 \cdots \hat{X}_n))$. Before calling upon Lemma 11.40, let us observe that, for any object $\hat{M}$, $((\hat{\mathfrak{D}}_n\hat{F}\hat{X}_1 \cdots \hat{X}_n)\hat{M}) \Rightarrow (\hat{F}\hat{M}\hat{X}_1 \cdots \hat{X}_n)$ by virtue of the definition of $\hat{\mathfrak{D}}_n$. Hence, $((\hat{\mathfrak{D}}_n\hat{F}\hat{X}_1 \cdots \hat{X}_n)\hat{r}) \Rightarrow \widehat{t_r + 1}$, for $r = 0, 1, 2, \ldots, m-1$, and $((\hat{\mathfrak{D}}_n\hat{F}\hat{X}_1 \cdots \hat{X}_n)\hat{m}) \Rightarrow \hat{0}$. The result is now seen to follow from Lemma 11.40. ▮

We have thus proved

THEOREM 11.44. The calculi Γ_K and Λ_K are adequate for the classical formulation of partial recursive functions. ▮

In regard to the formulation of partial recursive functions given in Chapter 3, we shall show in the remainder of this section how one may represent the notion of an n-tuple and how one may carry out some of the basic operations thereon. But we shall not proceed to a detailed proof of the adequacy of Γ_K and Λ_K for this formulation because of the rapidly increasing complexity of the objects that must be dealt with, as well as the variety of objects one might employ.

Let us introduce the following objects:

DEFINITION 11.45.

$$\hat{\mathfrak{C}}_0 \equiv \langle \Lambda\hat{\zeta}_0 : \hat{\zeta}_0 \rangle$$

$$\hat{\mathfrak{C}}_n \equiv \langle \Lambda\hat{\zeta}_1, \ldots, \hat{\zeta}_n : \langle \Lambda\hat{\zeta}_0 : (\hat{\zeta}_0\hat{\zeta}_1 \cdots \hat{\zeta}) \rangle \rangle \qquad n \geq 1$$

Then, we propose to take the following objects to represent an n-tuple ($n \geq 0$) of objects $\hat{X}_1, \ldots, \hat{X}_n$:

DEFINITION 11.46.

$$[] \equiv \hat{\mathfrak{C}}_0 \qquad n = 0$$

$$[\hat{X}_1, \ldots, \hat{X}_n] \equiv (\hat{\mathfrak{C}}_n\hat{X}_1 \cdots \hat{X}_n) \qquad n \geq 1$$

That we do indeed have a valid representation of the notion of an n-tuple is the subject of the following lemma and corollary:

LEMMA 11.47. For any object $\hat{F}$:

$$([]\hat{F}) \Rightarrow \hat{F} \qquad n = 0$$

$$([\hat{X}_1, \ldots, \hat{X}_n]\hat{F}) \Rightarrow (\hat{F}\hat{X}_1 \cdots \hat{X}_n) \qquad n \geq 1$$

Proof. The results are immediate from the foregoing definitions. ▮

COROLLARY 11.48.

$$([\hat{X}_1, \ldots, \hat{X}_n]\hat{\mathfrak{U}}_n^m) \Rightarrow \hat{X}_m \qquad 1 \leq m \leq n$$

Proof. From Lemma 11.47, $([\hat{X}_1,\ldots,\hat{X}_n]\hat{\mathfrak{U}}_n^m) \Rightarrow (\hat{\mathfrak{U}}_n^m\hat{X}_1\cdots\hat{X}_n)$. By Lemma 11.25, $(\hat{\mathfrak{U}}_n^m\hat{X}_1\cdots\hat{X}_n) \Rightarrow \hat{X}_m$. ▮

Of the more general results that could be derived from Lemma 11.47, the following is useful:

COROLLARY 11.49.

$$([\hat{\mathfrak{C}}_n^m\hat{\mathfrak{T}}_m\hat{\mathfrak{U}}_n^{i_1}\cdots\hat{\mathfrak{U}}_n^{i_m}][\hat{X}_1,\ldots,\hat{X}_n]) \Rightarrow [\hat{X}_{i_1},\ldots,\hat{X}_{i_m}] \quad 1 \le i_1, \ldots, i_m \le n, 1 \le m \le n$$

Proof. Using Lemma 11.47 twice,

$$\begin{aligned}([\hat{\mathfrak{C}}_n^m\hat{\mathfrak{T}}_m\hat{\mathfrak{U}}_n^{i_1}\cdots\hat{\mathfrak{U}}_n^{i_m}][X_1,\ldots X_n]) &\Rightarrow ([\hat{X}_1,\ldots,\hat{X}_n](\hat{\mathfrak{C}}_n^m\hat{\mathfrak{T}}_m\hat{\mathfrak{U}}_n^{i_1}\cdots\hat{\mathfrak{U}}_n^{i_m}))\\ &\Rightarrow (\hat{\mathfrak{C}}_n^m\hat{\mathfrak{T}}_m\hat{\mathfrak{U}}_n^{i_1}\cdots\hat{\mathfrak{U}}_n^{i_m}\hat{X}_1\cdots\hat{X}_n)\end{aligned}$$

By Lemma 11.27,

$$(\hat{\mathfrak{C}}_n^m\hat{\mathfrak{T}}_m\hat{\mathfrak{U}}_n^{i_1}\cdots\hat{\mathfrak{U}}_n^{i_m}\hat{X}_1\cdots\hat{X}_n) \Rightarrow (\hat{\mathfrak{T}}_m(\hat{\mathfrak{U}}_n^{i_1}\hat{X}_1\cdots\hat{X}_n)\cdots(\hat{\mathfrak{U}}_n^{i_m}\hat{X}_1\cdots\hat{X}_n))$$

By Lemma 11.25, for $j = i_1, \ldots, i_m$, $(\hat{\mathfrak{U}}_n^j\hat{X}_1\cdots\hat{X}_n) \Rightarrow \hat{X}_j$ so that

$$(\hat{\mathfrak{T}}_m(\hat{\mathfrak{U}}_n^{i_1}\hat{X}_1\cdots\hat{X}_n)\cdots(\hat{\mathfrak{U}}_n^{i_m}\hat{X}_1\cdots\hat{X}_n)) \Rightarrow (\hat{\mathfrak{T}}_m\hat{X}_{i_1}\cdots\hat{X}_{i_m})$$

The result is now a consequence of Definition 11.46. ▮

EXERCISES

1. Show that one may also take the object $\langle\Lambda\zeta_1:\langle\Lambda\zeta_2,\zeta_3:((\zeta_1\zeta_2)(\zeta_2\zeta_3))\rangle\rangle$ for the successor function (cf. Definition 11.22).

2. Show that there is an object $\hat{Y}$ (of Γ_K and Λ_K) such that, for any object $\hat{F}$, $(\hat{Y}\hat{F}) \Rightarrow (\hat{F}(\hat{Y}\hat{F}))$, that is, $(\hat{Y}\hat{F})$ is a *fixed point* of $\hat{F}$.

3.$^{\Delta}$ Show that the calculi Γ_I and Λ_I are adequate for partial recursive functions on the positive integers as in I–III but replacing each reference to zero by one. Note that, as neither Γ_I nor Λ_I has a cancellative capability as do Γ_K and Λ_K (see pp. 284–285), there cannot be in either Γ_I or Λ_I an object $\hat{0}$ satisfying Lemma 11.23.

11.4 Equivalence with Partial Recursive Functions

In the previous section, we demonstrated the adequateness of both Γ_K and Λ_K for the classical notion of partial recursive functions and indicated how one might demonstrate their adequateness for the definition of partial recursive functions given in Chapter 3. Taking advantage of the main result of Section 11.6, the equivalence of Γ_K and Λ_K—a result that is in no way dependent on the results here—we shall prove here the converse for the much simpler case Γ_K only.

Throughout, we shall always have in mind the linguistic formalization of Γ_K—the objects of Γ_K (p. 284) are (finite) words over the alphabet of Γ_K, and reduction is a relation between words. But we must ever keep this viewpoint separated from the (finite) words over the set $\Sigma = \{\bar{(},\bar{S},\bar{K},\bar{)},z,1,\$\}$ which shall represent the objects of Γ_K in a way in which reduction may be interpreted as a partial recursive function (in the sense given in Chapter 3) over Σ^*. To simplify the notation we will omit the bars over the members of Σ whenever the meaning is clear from the context. The choice of the symbols (, S, K, and) of Σ is not meant to confuse this issue, but to help make clearer what we are about to do. We shall certainly have it that, for example, corresponding to the object $((SK)((K\zeta_2)\zeta_3))$ of Γ_K will be the word $((SK)((Kz11)z111))$ of Σ^*, which we may abbreviate as $((SK)((Kz_2)z_3))$.

We shall presume it known from the results of preceding chapters that certain elementary functions are primitive recursive. For example, from Section 3.6, the following are known to be primitive recursive:

$$x \cdot y = \text{the concatenation of } x \text{ and } y$$

$$\text{occurrences}(x,\sigma) = \text{the number of occurrences of } \sigma\ (\sigma \in \Sigma) \text{ in } x$$

$$x \preccurlyeq y = 1, \text{ if } x \text{ occurs as a substring of } y, \text{ and } 0 \text{ otherwise}$$

$$\text{part}(x,\sigma,k) = \text{the substring of } x \text{ between the } k\text{th and } (k+1)\text{st occurrences of } \sigma\ (\sigma \in \Sigma) \text{ in } x, \text{ if occurrences}(x,\sigma) > k, \text{ and } 0 \text{ otherwise}$$

$$x \in 1^* = 1 \text{ if } x \in \{0, 1, 11, 111, \ldots\} \text{ and } 0 \text{ otherwise}$$

Also known to be primitive recursive are functions defined by bounded minimization $(\mu y \le b)[f(y,x_1,\ldots,x_n)]$ from a primitive recursive function f and functions defined by bounded quantification $\bigvee_{y=a}^{b} [g(y)]$ and $\bigwedge_{y=a}^{b} [h(y)]$ from primitive recursive functions g and h, respectively.

Our first task is to show that the set of objects of Γ_K (p. 284) is primitive recursive. Consider the following function:

$$\text{ob}(x,0) = (x = S) \vee (x = K) \vee (x \in z1^*)$$
$$\text{ob}(x,k+1) = \text{ob}(x,k) \vee \bigvee_{y,z=0}^{x} [\text{ob}(y,k) \wedge \text{ob}(z,k) \wedge x = (\cdot y \cdot z \cdot)]$$

First, $\text{ob}(x,0) = 1$ iff the word $x \in \Sigma^*$ corresponds (under the intended interpretation) to the primitive constant S or to the primitive constant K or to one of the indeterminates ζ_j $(0 \le j)$ of Γ_K; that is, $\text{ob}(x,0) = 1$ iff $x \in \Sigma^*$ corresponds to a primitive object of Γ_K. Second, $\text{ob}(x,k) = 1$ $(k \ge 1)$ iff $x \in \Sigma^*$ corresponds to a composite object of Γ_K for which the maximum depth of nested pairs of parentheses is less than or equal to k. Clearly, $\text{ob}(x,k)$ is primitive recursive.

Consider next the following function:

$$\mathfrak{D}(x) = (\mu y \le x)[\text{ob}(x,y)]$$

It is clearly primitive recursive. When, for some $0 \leq k$, ob$(x,k) = 1$, $\mathfrak{D}(x)$ gives the maximum depth of nested parentheses of the object of Γ_K corresponding to the word $x \in \Sigma^*$. Consequently,

$$\text{ob}(x) = \text{ob}(x,\mathfrak{D}(x))$$

is a primitive recursive function such that ob$(x) = 1$ iff $x \in \Sigma^*$ corresponds to an object of Γ_K.

In the sequel when ob$(x) = 1$ and $\hat{X}$ is the object of Γ_K corresponding to x, let us write $x = \#\hat{X}$ and $\hat{X} = @x$. Certainly, $\#\hat{X} = \#\hat{Y}$ implies $\hat{X} = \hat{Y}$ (that is, $\hat{X}$ and $\hat{Y}$ are equiform objects), and $@x = @y$ implies $x = y$.

Our next task is to characterize the components of an object. This we do simply by considering

$$x \text{ Comp } y = \text{ob}(x) \wedge \text{ob}(y) \wedge (x \preccurlyeq y)$$

It is not difficult to prove by induction on $\mathfrak{D}(y)$ that x Comp y iff $@x$ is a component of $@y$.

Next, we characterize instances of the rules of Γ_K (p. 284) as follows:

$$x \text{ Rule } K\ y = \bigvee\nolimits_{u,v=0}^{x} [\text{ob}(u) \wedge \text{ob}(v) \wedge [x = (\cdot(\cdot K \cdot u) \cdot v \cdot)] \wedge [y = u]]$$

$$x \text{ Rule } S\ y = \bigvee\nolimits_{u,v,w=0}^{x} [\text{ob}(u) \wedge \text{ob}(v) \wedge \text{ob}(w) \wedge [x = (\cdot(\cdot(\cdot S \cdot u \cdot) \cdot v \cdot) \cdot w \cdot)] \wedge [y = (\cdot(\cdot u \cdot w \cdot) \cdot (\cdot v \cdot w \cdot) \cdot)]]$$

It is clear that both functions are primitive recursive, and that x Rule $K\ y = 1$ (alternatively, x Rule $S\ y = 1$) iff $@x \rightarrow @y$ is an instance of Rule K (Rule S).

With this characterization of Rule K and Rule S, we are able to interpret contraction by means of the following primitive recursive function:

$$x \text{ Contract } y = \text{ob}(x) \wedge \text{ob}(y) \wedge \bigvee\nolimits_{u=0}^{x} \bigvee\nolimits_{v=0}^{y} ((u \text{ Comp } x) \wedge (v \text{ Comp } y) \wedge [(u \text{ Rule } K\ v) \vee (u \text{ Rule } S\ v)] \wedge \bigvee\nolimits_{w_0,w_1,=0}^{x} [(x = w_0 \cdot u \cdot w_1) \wedge (y = w_0 \cdot v \cdot w_1)])$$

At last, recall that $\hat{X} \Rightarrow \hat{Y}$ iff there are objects $\hat{R}_0, \hat{R}_1, \ldots, \hat{R}_n$ $(0 \leq n)$ such that (a) $\hat{R}_0 = \hat{X}$, (b) $\hat{R}_n = \hat{Y}$, and (c), for $1 \leq j \leq n$, $\hat{R}_{j-1} \rightarrow \hat{R}_j$. For $0 \leq j \leq n$, let $r_j = \#\hat{R}_j$. Then, encode the sequence $\hat{R}_0, \hat{R}_1, \ldots, \hat{R}_n$ by the word $r_0 \cdot \$ \cdot r_1 \cdot \$ \cdots r_n \cdot \$$ of Σ^*. Certainly, for $r_0, r_1, \ldots, r_n$ such that, for $0 \leq j \leq n$, ob(r_j), there is a one-to-one correspondence between words $r_0 \cdot \$ \cdot r_1 \cdot \$ \cdots r_n \cdot \$$ of Σ^* and sequences of objects $\hat{R}_0, \hat{R}_1, \ldots, \hat{R}_n$ of Γ_K given by $\hat{R}_j = @r_j$ and $r_j = \#\hat{R}_j$, $0 \leq j \leq n$. Moreover, we see that, if $w = r_0 \cdot \$ \cdot r_1 \cdot \$ \cdots r_n \cdot \$$, then, for $0 \leq j \leq n$, $r_j = \text{part}(w,\$,j)$. Consequently, the following partial recursive function interprets exactly the relation $\Rightarrow$ (reduction):

$$x \text{ Red } y = \bigvee\nolimits_{w}([x = \text{part}(w,\$,0) \wedge (y = \text{part}(w,\$,\text{occurrences}(w,\$) \dot{-} 1)] \bigwedge\nolimits_{j=1}^{\text{occurrences}(w,\$) \dot{-} 1} [\text{part}(w,\$,j \dot{-} 1) \text{ Contract part}(w,\$,j)])$$

This accomplishes our goal: The class of functions definable by means of Γ_K is the class of partial recursive functions.

11.5 Consistency

The following four arithmetic expressions†

$$((4 \times 8) - (2 + 2))$$

$$((4 \times 8) - 4) \qquad\qquad (32 - (2 + 2))$$

$$(32 - 4)$$

have in common a property that the following four do not

$$((3 \times 9) - (2 + 2)) \qquad\qquad (16 - (2 + 2))$$

$$((3 \times 9) - 6) \qquad\qquad (16 - 6)$$

Namely, each of the first four evaluates to one and the same integer, while no two of the last four do. Indeed, the first four are intimately related: Each of those on the second line may be seen to be obtainable from the first arithmetic expression by replacing, on the one hand, the subexpression $(2 + 2)$ by its value 4 and, on the other hand, the subexpression (4×8) by its value 32. The last of the four may be seen to be obtainable from either of those on the second line by replacing the subexpression (4×8), on the one hand, and $(2 + 2)$, on the other hand, by their respective values 32 and 4. It is important to note that either of the two possible evaluation paths leads to the same value 28. Indeed this is a property of fully parenthesized arithmetic expressions, analogous to the Church–Rosser property 11.5 discussed earlier.

It is clear that one may partition the set of all arithmetic expressions by putting all those evaluating to one integer in one subset, all those evaluating to another integer in another subset, all those evaluating to still another integer in a third subset, and so forth. It is clear that there is in each subset of such a partition a uniquely simple arithmetic expression, one that does not possess an operator, namely that which is an integer, *the* integer that characterizes the whole subset!

We are suggesting, of course, that there is an analogy between arithmetic expressions and their evaluation procedures and objects of our calculi and their rules of reduction. The preceding two paragraphs have pointed out two relations: For arithmetic expressions e and f, $e \succ f$ iff f is obtainable from e by replacing a subexpression of e by its value and $e \leftrightarrow f$ iff e and f evaluate to one and the same integer. It is clear that $\leftrightarrow$ is an equivalence relation whose equivalence classes yield the above mentioned partition of the set of all arithmetic expressions. Moreover, letting $\rightarrow$ denote the reflexive transitive

† For the purposes of the discussion, we limit the operators to $+$, $-$, and $\times$ and permit only integers to appear.

closure of $\succ$, it is clear that $\leftrightarrow$ is the equivalence relation generated by $\rightarrow$. Between $\rightarrow$, $\leftrightarrow$, and $\Rightarrow$, $\Leftrightarrow$, the analogy is particularly close.

Taking the situation in regard to arithmetic expressions as clear, let us consider our calculi. From the viewpoint of our intended interpretation of each object of our calculi as an (intuitive) function of one variable, since $\hat{F} \Leftrightarrow \hat{G}$ implies, for every object $\hat{A}$, $(\hat{F}\hat{A}) \Leftrightarrow (\hat{G}\hat{A})$, we may take the equivalence classes of $\Leftrightarrow$ as representing the (intuitive) functions of one variable. But we must here warn the reader that it is possible that two objects may represent an (intuitive) function $y = f(x)$ of one variable as a set of ordered pairs $\{(x_v, y_v)\}_{v \geq 0}$ and still not be interconvertible. For example, see Exercise 1 in Section 11.3. In not one of the calculi we have mentioned in Section 2 is $\langle \Lambda\zeta_1 : \langle \Lambda\zeta_2, \zeta_3 : (\zeta_2((\zeta_1\zeta_2)\zeta_3))\rangle\rangle$ interconvertible with $\langle \Lambda\zeta_1 : \langle \Lambda\zeta_2, \zeta_3 : ((\zeta_1\zeta_2)(\zeta_2\zeta_3))\rangle\rangle$. Indeed, by a result of Böhm [1968], this will be the case in general.

Perhaps the first indication that things are not as simple for combinatory calculi and Λ-calculi as for arithmetic expressions is given by the following remarkable objects:

$$\text{in } \Gamma_I\text{: } (WWW) \qquad \text{in } \Gamma_K\text{: } (S(SKK)(SKK)(S(SKK)(SKK))) \tag{11-3}$$
$$\text{in } \Lambda_I \text{ and } \Lambda_K\text{: } ((\lambda\hat{x}.(\hat{x}\hat{x}))(\lambda\hat{x}.(\hat{x}\hat{x})))$$

Consider (WWW) first: In view of Rule W (p. 281), (WWW) is not irreducible. But it is itself the only object to which it reduces! Similarly for $((\lambda\hat{x}.(\hat{x}\hat{x}))(\lambda\hat{x}.(\hat{x}\hat{x})))$, while Rule β (p. 290) is applicable, the only objects to which $((\lambda\hat{x}.(\hat{x}\hat{x}))(\lambda\hat{x}.(\hat{x}\hat{x})))$ reduces are all α-interconvertible with it! Finally for $\hat{H} \equiv (S(SKK)(SKK)(S(SKK)(SKK)))$, while $\hat{H}$ is not irreducible (cf. Rule S, p. 284), all the objects to which $\hat{H}$ reduces reduce, in turn, to $\hat{H}$! How then may one assign a "value" to these objects?

We need to put the discussion on a more formal basis, so let us introduce the following definitions:

DEFINITION 11.50. Normal Form. An object $\hat{X}$ will be said to be *in normal* form iff:
(combinatory calculus)
No rule is applicable to a component of $\hat{X}$.
(λ-calculus)
There is no object $\hat{Y}$ α-interconvertible with $\hat{X}$ such that $\hat{Y}$ possesses a component to which a rule other than Rule α is applicable.

DEFINITION 11.51. An object $\hat{X}$ will be said to *possess a normal form* $\hat{Z}$ iff $\hat{Z}$ is in normal form and $\hat{X} \Leftrightarrow \hat{Z}$.

We need to concern ourselves with the basic relationship between interconvertibility and reduction:

DEFINITION 11.52. Church–Rosser Property. If $\hat{X} \Leftrightarrow \hat{Y}$, then there exists a $\hat{Z}$ such that both $\hat{X} \Rightarrow \hat{Z}$ and $\hat{Y} \Rightarrow \hat{Z}$.

THEOREM 11.53. The combinatory calculi Γ_I and Γ_K and the λ-calculi Λ_I and Λ_K satisfy the Church–Rosser property. (As elsewhere in this section, a more general result holds. For example, all the calculi indicated in Section 11.2 satisfy the Church–Rosser property. It is no mean task to circumscribe the domain of validity.) ▮

Unfortunately, there is not space enough here for the lengthy proof. For Λ_I and Λ_K, the most readable proof is still Church and Rosser [1936] and although Curry and Feys [1958] criticize this proof, their extensive elaboration of Church and Rosser [1936] painfully purchases the extension of the results of Church and Rosser [1936] to Λ-calculi possessing Rule η (p. 291). We refer the reader to the author's elementary, but lengthy proof to be published. Recently a quite sophisticated proof has been announced by Martin Löf. (See Hindley, Lercher, and Seldin [1972].) But the situation in regard to Γ_I and Γ_K would appear to be too trivial for the literature, notwithstanding the fact that the equivalence of Γ_K and Λ_K (alternatively, Γ_I and Λ_I) to be established in the next section does not permit one to carry over the Church–Rosser property from Λ_K to Γ_K (from Λ_I to Γ_I).

The following are immediate consequences of Theorem 11.53 and Definitions 11.50 and 11.51:

COROLLARY 11.54. If $\hat{X}$ possesses a normal form $\hat{Z}$, then, $\hat{X} \Rightarrow \hat{Z}$. ▮

COROLLARY 11.55. If $\hat{X}$ and $\hat{Y}$ are in normal form, and if $\hat{X} \Leftrightarrow \hat{Y}$ then:
(combinatory calculi Γ_I and Γ_K)
$\hat{X} = \hat{Y}$ ($\hat{X}$ and $\hat{Y}$ are equiform)
(λ-calculi Λ_I and Λ_K)
$\hat{X} \approx \hat{Y}$ ($\hat{X}$ and $\hat{Y}$ are α-interconvertible). ▮

COROLLARY 11.56. If $\hat{X}$ possesses a normal form, then:
(combinatory calculi Γ_I and Γ_K)
That normal form is unique.
(λ-calculi Λ_I and Λ_K)
That normal form is, up to α-interconvertibility, unique. ▮

The following immediate consequence of Theorem 11.53 deserves special consideration:

THEOREM 11.57. The calculi Γ_I, Γ_K, Λ_I, and Λ_K are (simply) consistent in the sense that not every pair of objects are interconvertible. (As noted earlier, here too a much more general result holds.)

Proof. We need only to observe, in the respective cases, that the following pairs of objects cannot be interconvertible:

in Γ_I: B and W in Γ_K: S and K

in Λ_I and Λ_K: $(\lambda\hat{x}.(\lambda\hat{y}.(\hat{x}\hat{y})))$ and $(\lambda\hat{x}.(\lambda\hat{y}.(\hat{x}(\hat{x}\hat{y}))))$

For, each is in normal form (cf. Corollary 11.56). ∎

To be sure, as logicians, we would be far from happy with the results of Sections 11.3 and 11.4, and the result of the next section as well, if the calculi under study were not (simply) consistent in the sense of Theorem 11.57. But all too often, as computer scientists, we quickly throw away just such (simple) consistency for the sake of generality and then turn about and wonder what happens to confuse the "semantics" of programming languages. Observe!

THEOREM 11.58. No (simply) consistent, combinatorially complete combinatory calculus or λ-calculus possesses either of the following objects:

$$\hat{L}\text{: for all } \hat{U} \text{ and } \hat{V},\ (\hat{L}(\hat{U}\hat{V})) \Leftrightarrow \hat{U}$$
$$\hat{R}\text{: for all } \hat{U} \text{ and } \hat{V},\ (\hat{R}(\hat{U}\hat{V})) \Leftrightarrow \hat{V}$$

Proof. In the notation of Section 11.3, let $\hat{B} \equiv \langle \Lambda\zeta_1,\zeta_2,\zeta_3{:}(\zeta_1(\zeta_2\zeta_3))\rangle$ and $\hat{C} \equiv \langle \Lambda\zeta_1,\zeta_2,\zeta_3{:}((\zeta_1\zeta_3)\zeta_2)\rangle$. Let $\hat{X}$ and $\hat{Y}$ be any two objects. Then, for any object $\hat{H}$ whatsoever (say, for definiteness, $\hat{H} = \hat{C}$), consider $(\hat{L}((\hat{C}(\hat{B}\hat{L})\hat{H})\hat{X})\hat{Y})$: On the one hand, we have that

$$\begin{aligned}
(\hat{L}((\hat{C}(\hat{B}\hat{L})\hat{H})\hat{X})\hat{Y}) &\Leftrightarrow (\hat{C}(\hat{B}\hat{L})\hat{H}\hat{Y}) && \text{(Definition of } \hat{L})\\
&\Leftrightarrow (\hat{B}\hat{L}\hat{Y}\hat{H}) && \text{(Definition of } \hat{C})\\
&\Leftrightarrow (\hat{L}(\hat{Y}\hat{H})) && \text{(Definition of } \hat{B})\\
&\Leftrightarrow \hat{Y} && \text{(Definition of } \hat{L})
\end{aligned}$$

while on the other hand, we have that

$$\begin{aligned}
(\hat{L}((\hat{C}(\hat{B}\hat{L})\hat{H})\hat{X})\hat{Y}) &\Leftrightarrow (\hat{L}(\hat{B}\hat{L}\hat{X}\hat{H})\hat{Y}) && \text{(Definition of } \hat{C})\\
&\Leftrightarrow (\hat{B}\hat{L}\hat{X}\hat{Y}) && \text{(Definition of } \hat{L})\\
&\Leftrightarrow (\hat{L}(\hat{X}\hat{Y})) && \text{(Definition of } \hat{B})\\
&\Leftrightarrow \hat{X} && \text{(Definition of } \hat{L})
\end{aligned}$$

That is, $\hat{X} \Leftrightarrow \hat{Y}$, so that $\hat{L}$ cannot exist. Next, consider $(\hat{R}((\hat{C}\hat{H}\hat{X})\hat{Y}))$. On the one hand, we have that

$$(\hat{R}((\hat{C}\hat{H}\hat{X})\hat{Y})) \Leftrightarrow \hat{Y} \qquad \text{(Definition of } \hat{R})$$

while on the other hand, we have that

$$\begin{aligned}
(\hat{R}((\hat{C}\hat{H}\hat{X})\hat{Y})) &\Leftrightarrow (\hat{R}((\hat{H}\hat{Y})\hat{X})) && \text{(Definition of } \hat{C})\\
&\Leftrightarrow \hat{X} && \text{(Definition of } \hat{R})
\end{aligned}$$

That is, $\hat{X} \Leftrightarrow \hat{Y}$, so that $\hat{R}$ cannot exist either. ∎

It is of no small import for those familiar with programming languages like LISP with its primitive functions CAR and CDR (CAR(A B) = A, CDR(A B) = B) to note that there are two ways to circumvent the prohibition of Theorem 11.58 to the breaking apart of objects. First, we could introduce directly (as does LISP with CAR and CDR) two primitive constants L and R with the associated rules $(L(\hat{M}\hat{N})) \to \hat{M}$ and $(R(\hat{M}\hat{N})) \to \hat{N}$ *provided* that we insist that $(\hat{M}\hat{N})$ shall be in normal form (and, for λ-calculi, without a free occurrence of a variable, cf. Rule δ, p. 292). This has the decided disadvantage, as we shall see shortly, that one must then know the normal forms of objects which represent the intermediate results of a computation.† Alternatively, we could prescribe the rules of reduction so that at each step there is but one way to proceed. For example, we could, like LISP, insist that no rule be applied either to a component of an object to the right of and nonoverlapping with another component to which a rule applies or to a component which has a component to which a rule applies. This particular choice is equivalent to insisting that, before any rule is applicable to a component of an object, all the components of that component, but the component itself, must be in normal form. This has the decided disadvantage that one must then know the exact details of reduction, details which, in view of the Church–Rosser property, have been irrelevant in our discussion up to now. But in either case, something more is lost. Our two rules may be viewed as effecting an analysis of the normal forms of objects and then synthesizing from this analysis another object. For the particular rules at hand the resulting object need not represent the same (intuitive) function of one variable as the original object. Indeed there is no direct relationship between these objects as far as the intended interpretation is concerned. Hence, while we have gotten our cake, L and R, and have eaten of it in a way to avoid inconsistency in the calculus itself, we have played havoc with the intended interpretation. In short, we have put off the question of consistency of programming languages to their semantics, complicating the issue to boot!

Returning to our earlier discussion, we see now that each of the objects of (11-3), p. 306, does not possess a normal form. In this they are by no means unique. Moreover, as the following additional examples show, all such are not interconvertible:

$$\text{in } \Gamma_I\text{: } (WW(WW)) \qquad \text{in } \Gamma_K\text{: } (S(SSK)(SKK)(S(SSK)(SKK)))$$
$$\text{in } \Lambda_I \text{ and } \Lambda_K\text{: } ((\lambda\hat{x}.(\hat{x}\hat{x}\hat{x}))(\lambda\hat{x}.(\hat{x}\hat{x}\hat{x})))$$

† Note carefully the difference between Rule δ and the rules for L and R: Rule δ *compares* normal forms of objects; it tests whether these objects are, in the given sense, the same. The rules for L and R analyze an object and synthesize a new object from the analysis. It should be no surprise that the object under analysis must be in normal form to avoid inconsistencies.

Yet, the above facts do not entirely explain why we are reluctant to talk about a "value" for such objects. For, after all, could we not take the equivalence class itself as the "value" of every object therein?

The first surprise is that the equivalence classes of interconvertibility are intrinsically not very nice collections of objects:

THEOREM 11.59. For Γ_I, Γ_K, Λ_I, and Λ_K, there is no decision procedure by which, for any objects $\hat{X}$ and $\hat{Y}$, it can be determined whether or not $\hat{X}$ and $\hat{Y}$ are interconvertible. ∎

THEOREM 11.60. For Γ_I, Γ_K, Λ_I, and Λ_K, there is no decision procedure by which, for any object $\hat{X}$ and any object $\hat{Z}$ in normal form, whether or not $\hat{X}$ possesses $\hat{Z}$ as its normal form. ∎

For direct proofs of these results for the case Λ_I, we refer the reader to Church [1936a].† Proofs for Λ_K are easily obtained from the proofs in Church [1936a] for Λ_I. From the equivalence of Γ_K and Λ_K (Γ_I and Λ_I) to be established in the next section (and the exercises thereto), these results will follow for Γ_K and Γ_I from the corresponding results for Λ_K and Λ_I. Based upon results of preceding chapters, we may give here the following proofs of Theorems 11.59 and 11.60.

Proof of Theorem 11.59. Results of Section 11.3 have shown that every partial recursive function f of one variable can be represented by an object $\hat{F}$ of Γ_K or of Λ_K such that for all numbers m and n, $f(m) = n$ iff $(\hat{F}\hat{m}) \Rightarrow \hat{n}$. But $(\hat{F}\hat{m}) \Leftrightarrow \hat{n}$ iff $(\hat{F}\hat{m}) \Rightarrow \hat{n}$ since $\hat{m}$ and $\hat{n}$ are in normal form in both Γ_K and Λ_K (see Exercise 1). An effective procedure for interconvertibility would immediately provide an effective procedure for deciding whether $f(m) = n$ for arbitrary partial recursive f and numbers m and n. Hence no effective procedure exists for deciding interconvertibility. ∎

Proof of Theorem 11.60. For Γ_K and Λ_K this follows directly from the proof of Theorem 11.59 and the fact that for each number n, $\hat{n}$ is in normal form. ∎

Other surprises in the form of paradoxes have been encountered only when one attempts to operate with objects that do not possess normal forms; no

† Four remarks: (a) Church [1936a] shows, in fact, that Theorem 11.59 and Theorem 11.60 are equivalent; (b) historically, the first published statement of what has become known as "Church's thesis" appears as a footnote in Church [1936a]; (c) Theorem 11.59 is the analogue of Gödel's incompleteness theorem for combinatory logic; because of its syntactic simplicity, it sealed the fate of Hilbert's program; (d) Theorem 11.60 is the analogue to Turing's halting problem—a machine designed to carry out reduction obviously halts on obtaining an object in normal form, and only then.

paradox or inconsistency is known to arise from objects that do possess normal forms. For example, let us present the Curry Paradox, which arose in attempting to model along with a combinatorially complete calculus a deductively complete logic. Thus, let $\supset$ denote a symbol of implication with the property of *modus ponens* (from $\hat{P}$ and $\hat{P} \supset \hat{Q}$, we may infer $\hat{Q}$) and the deduction theorem (if we are able to infer $\hat{Q}$ from $\hat{P}$, then we may infer $\hat{P} \supset \hat{Q}$). Of course, whenever $\hat{X} \Leftrightarrow \hat{Y}$ and $\hat{X}$ (alternatively, $\hat{Y}$) may be inferred, then $\hat{Y}$ (alternatively $\hat{X}$) may also be inferred. Let $\hat{X}$ be any object whatsoever. We proceed to show that we may infer $\hat{X}$.† Consider $\hat{R} \equiv \langle \Lambda\hat{\zeta}:((\hat{\zeta}\hat{\zeta}) \supset \hat{X})\rangle$, where we are again making use of the notation of Section 11.3. (Here, $((\hat{\zeta}\hat{\zeta}) \supset \hat{X})$ is to be understood in the sense that, for any object $\hat{Y}$, $((\hat{Y}\hat{Y}) \supset \hat{X})$ is that object taken to represent the implication $(\hat{Y}\hat{Y}) \supset \hat{X}$.) We have that $(\hat{R}\hat{R}) \Leftrightarrow ((\hat{R}\hat{R}) \supset \hat{X})$.†† Assume we are able to infer $(\hat{R}\hat{R})$. Because of $(\hat{R}\hat{R}) \Leftrightarrow ((\hat{R}\hat{R}) \supset \hat{X})$, we are then able, by the intended interpretation, to infer $((\hat{R}\hat{R}) \supset \hat{X})$. From our assumption $(\hat{R}\hat{R})$ and from $((\hat{R}\hat{R}) \supset \hat{X})$, we may infer $\hat{X}$ by *modus ponens*. That is, from $(\hat{R}\hat{R})$, we have been able to infer $\hat{X}$. Therefore, by the deduction theorem, we have inferred $((\hat{R}\hat{R}) \supset \hat{X})$. Because of $(\hat{R}\hat{R}) \Leftrightarrow ((\hat{R}\hat{R}) \supset \hat{X})$, we have thus inferred $(\hat{R}\hat{R})$. But we have just seen that from $(\hat{R}\hat{R})$, we may infer $\hat{X}$. Having now been able to infer $(\hat{R}\hat{R})$, we have inferred $\hat{X}$! The logic is thus not (simply) consistent; everything can be inferred!

EXERCISES

1. Show that the objects (in Γ_K and Λ_K) of Section 11.3 for the numerals (Definition 11.22) are in normal form. Hence if $\hat{F}$ represents a partial recursive function as specified in Section 11.3, then it cannot be the case that $(\hat{F}\hat{m}) \Rightarrow \hat{p}$ and $(\hat{F}\hat{m}) \Rightarrow \hat{q}$, where $p \neq q$.

2. Further, show that the objects (in Γ_K and Λ_K) of Section 11.3 for

a. the identity functions ($\hat{\mathfrak{U}}_n^m$, Definition 11.24)
b. the composition schemes ($\hat{\mathfrak{C}}_n^m$, Definition 11.26)
c. the primitive recursion schemes ($\hat{\mathfrak{I}}_n$, Definitions 11.31 and 11.34)
d. the minimization schemes ($\hat{\mathfrak{M}}_n$, Definitions 11.39 and 11.42)

all possess normal forms.

3. Show that there is an object in Γ_K possessing a normal form that may be taken as $\hat{Y}$ of Exercise 2, Section 3. Also show that no such object exists in Λ_K, that is, every candidate in Λ_K for $\hat{Y}$ has no normal form.

† While the argument follows Rosser [1955] the paradox was discovered jointly by Kleene and Rosser.

†† In fact, $(\hat{R}\hat{R}) \Rightarrow ((\hat{R}\hat{R}) \supset \hat{X})$, suggesting, what in actuality is the case, that $(\hat{R}\hat{R})$ has no normal form.

11.6 Equivalence of Γ_K and Λ_K

Between the objects of Γ_K (p. 284) and the objects of Λ_K (p. 287), there are the obvious maps λ and γ defined as follows:

$\lambda:\Gamma_K \to \Lambda_K$

$$K \to K_\lambda \equiv (\lambda x_1.(\lambda x_2.x_1))$$
$$S \to S_\lambda \equiv (\lambda x_1.(\lambda x_2.(\lambda x_3.((x_1x_3)(x_2x_3)))))$$
$$\zeta_{2n} \to x_n \qquad 0 \leq n$$
$$\zeta_{2n+1} \to \zeta_n \qquad 0 \leq n$$
$$(\hat{F}\hat{A}) \to (\hat{F}\hat{A})_\lambda \equiv (\hat{F}_\lambda \hat{A}_\lambda)$$

$\gamma:\Lambda_K \to \Gamma_K$

$$x_n \to \zeta_{2n} \qquad 0 \leq n$$
$$\zeta_n \to \zeta_{2n+1} \qquad 0 \leq n$$
$$(\hat{F}\hat{A}) \to (\hat{F}\hat{A})_\gamma \equiv (\hat{F}_\gamma \hat{A}_\gamma)$$
$$(\lambda x_n.\hat{E}) \to (\lambda x_n.\hat{E})_\gamma \equiv \{\Lambda\zeta_{2n}:\hat{E}_\gamma\} \qquad \text{(cf. Definition 11.11)}$$

For example:

$$(SK)_\lambda \equiv (S_\lambda K_\lambda) \equiv ((\lambda x_1.(\lambda x_2.(\lambda x_3.((x_1x_3)(x_2x_3)))))(\lambda x_1.(\lambda x_2.x_1)))$$
$$(\lambda x_1.(\lambda x_2.x_2))_\gamma \equiv \{\Lambda\zeta_2:(\lambda x_2.x_2)_\gamma\} \equiv \{\Lambda\zeta_2:\{\Lambda\zeta_4:\zeta_4\}\}$$
$$\equiv \{\Lambda\zeta_2:(SKK)\} \equiv (K(SKK))$$

Let us agree to write $\hat{X} \overset{\gamma}{\Longrightarrow} \hat{Y}$ (or $\hat{X} \overset{\gamma}{\Longleftrightarrow} \hat{Y}$) iff $\hat{X}$ and $\hat{Y}$ are objects of Γ_K and $\hat{X} \Rightarrow \hat{Y}$ (and $\hat{X} \Leftrightarrow \hat{Y}$) in Γ_K. Likewise, let us agree to write $\hat{X} \overset{\lambda}{\Longrightarrow} \hat{Y}$ (or $\hat{X} \overset{\lambda}{\Longleftrightarrow} \hat{Y}$) iff $\hat{X}$ and $\hat{Y}$ are objects of Λ_K and $\hat{X} \Rightarrow \hat{Y}$ (and $\hat{X} \Leftrightarrow \hat{Y}$) in Λ_K.

THEOREM 11.61. $\hat{X} \overset{\gamma}{\Longrightarrow} \hat{Y}$ implies $\hat{X}_\lambda \overset{\lambda}{\Longrightarrow} \hat{Y}_\lambda$.
Proof. It is sufficient to observe that, for any objects $\hat{X}$, $\hat{Y}$, $\hat{Z}$ of Γ_K, $(K\hat{X}\hat{Y})_\lambda \equiv (K_\lambda \hat{X}_\lambda \hat{Y}_\lambda) \overset{\lambda}{\Longrightarrow} \hat{X}_\lambda$ and $(S\hat{X}\hat{Y}\hat{Z})_\lambda \equiv (S_\lambda \hat{X}_\lambda \hat{Y}_\lambda \hat{Z}_\lambda) \overset{\lambda}{\Longrightarrow} ((\hat{X}_\lambda \hat{Z}_\lambda)(\hat{Y}_\lambda \hat{Z}_\lambda)) \equiv ((\hat{X}\hat{Z})(\hat{Y}\hat{Z}))_\lambda$. ∎

However, the converse of Theorem 11.61 is false. For an example, consider $(SK)_\lambda$, which we worked out above. One easily verifies that $(SK)_\lambda \overset{\lambda}{\Longrightarrow} (\lambda x_1.(\lambda x_2.x_2))$ in Λ_K. Let us calculate $(SK)_{\lambda\gamma}$ as follows:

$$(SK)_{\lambda\gamma} \equiv (\{\Lambda\zeta_2:\{\Lambda\zeta_4:\{\Lambda\zeta_6:((\zeta_2\zeta_6)(\zeta_4\zeta_6))\}\}\}\{\Lambda\zeta_2:\{\Lambda\zeta_4:\zeta_2\}\})$$
$$\equiv (\{\Lambda\zeta_2:\{\Lambda\zeta_4:(S(S(K\zeta_2)(SKK))(S(K\zeta_4)(SKK)))\}\}\{\Lambda\zeta_2:(K\zeta_2)\})$$
$$\equiv (\{\Lambda\zeta_2:(S(K(S(S(K\zeta_2)(SKK))))(S(S(KS)(S(KK)(SKK)))$$
$$(K(SKK))))\}(S(KK)(SKK)))$$

For then, employing Proposition 11.12, we have that

$$(SK)_{\lambda\gamma} \overset{\gamma}{\Longrightarrow} (S(K(S(S(K(S(KK)(SKK)))(SKK))))(S(S(KS)(S(KK)(SKK)))(K(SKK))))$$

This is nothing like $(\lambda x_1.(\lambda x_2.x_2))_\gamma$, which we also worked out above. In view of the results of Section 11.5, it is not the case that $(SK)_{\lambda\gamma} \overset{\gamma}{\Longleftrightarrow} (\lambda x_1.(\lambda x_2.x_2))_\gamma$, let alone that $(SK)_{\lambda\gamma} \overset{\gamma}{\Longrightarrow} (\lambda x_1.(\lambda x_2.x_2))_\gamma$.

Where shall we put the blame? How shall we remedy this negative result?

One might point the incriminating finger at the maps λ and γ between the objects of Γ_K and Λ_K. Except for the exact relationship between the indeterminates of Γ_K and the indeterminates and variables of Λ_K, one will clearly have to deal with maps that differ basically only with respect to the choice of the abstraction algorithm.

One might thus point to the abstraction algorithm. But the situation above, where $(SK)_{\lambda\gamma}$ reduces neither to $\{\Lambda\zeta_4:\{\Lambda\zeta_6:((\{\Lambda\zeta_2:\{\Lambda\zeta_4:\zeta_2\}\}\zeta_6)(\zeta_4\zeta_6))\}\}$ nor to $\{\Lambda\zeta_4:\{\Lambda\zeta_6:\zeta_6\}\} \equiv (K(SKK))$, will almost certainly persist. At least, no one has yet discovered such a fortunate abstraction algorithm.

Well then, perhaps reduction in Γ_K is, compared with reduction in Λ_K, too "weak"; (SK) ought to reduce in Γ_K. The question is to what (SK) ought to reduce. From $(SK)_\lambda \overset{\lambda}{\Longrightarrow} (\lambda x_1.(\lambda x_2.x_2))$ and $(\lambda x_1.(\lambda x_2.x_2))_\gamma \equiv (K(SKK))$, it would not be unreasonable for (SK) to reduce to $(K(SKK))$. Indeed, Curry and Feys [1958] produce an elaboration of $\overset{\gamma}{\Longrightarrow}$ that has just this property. Curry and Feys [1958] show that their "strong reduction" satisfies the Church–Rosser property, and that the calculus based upon this strong reduction is equivalent (in the sense given below) to Λ_K. But there are two unfortunate aspects of (SK) reducing to $(K(SKK))$. First, one easily verifies that, while $(SK)_\lambda \overset{\lambda}{\Longleftrightarrow} (K(SKK))_\lambda$, it is not the case that $(SK)_\lambda \overset{\lambda}{\Longrightarrow} (K(SKK))_\lambda$, so that now Theorem 11.61 fails to hold. And second, of all things to happen, (SK) no longer has a normal form! Quite simply, if (SK) reduces to $(K(SKK))$, then (SK) will reduce to $(K(SKK))$, $(K(K(SKK)))$, $(K(K(K(SKK))))$, and so on. Curry and Feys [1958] avoid this unfortunate happenstance by introducing I into Λ_K, so that (SK) reduces only to (KI). Even so, Theorem 11.61 still fails (see Curry and Feys [1958]).

The question remains: Can we strengthen $\overset{\gamma}{\Longrightarrow}$ so that Theorem 11.61 and its converse both hold? The conjecture is no. It will take us too far afield to argue the conjecture here.

How then are Γ_K and Λ_K equivalent? First, let us recall that an object—be it an object of Γ_K or an object of Λ_K—represents a (intuitive) function of one variable. Next, let us observe that if $\hat{F}$ and $\hat{G}$ are two objects (either both of Γ_K or both of Λ_K) which are interconvertible, then, because $\hat{F} \Leftrightarrow \hat{G}$ implies, for every object $\hat{X}$, $(\hat{F}\hat{X}) \Leftrightarrow (\hat{G}\hat{X})$, both $\hat{F}$ and $\hat{G}$ necessarily represent one and the same (intuitive) function of one variable. Hence, we can expect that there is a correspondence between the equivalence classes of $\overset{\gamma}{\Longleftrightarrow}$ and the equivalence classes of $\overset{\lambda}{\Longleftrightarrow}$. Indeed, we shall, following Rosser [1955], show that the maps between the objects of Γ_K and the objects of Λ_K given earlier do establish a one-to-one correspondence between certain unions of equivalence classes of $\overset{\gamma}{\Longleftrightarrow}$ and equivalence classes of $\overset{\lambda}{\Longleftrightarrow}$, where if an object in an equivalence class of $\overset{\lambda}{\Longleftrightarrow}$ or an object in the corresponding union of classes of $\overset{\gamma}{\Longleftrightarrow}$ represents a (intuitive) function of one variable, then all objects in the equivalence class of $\overset{\lambda}{\Longleftrightarrow}$ and all objects in the corresponding union of equivalence classes of $\overset{\gamma}{\Longleftrightarrow}$ represent the same (intuitive) function of one variable. This will establish the equivalence of Γ_K and Λ_K as calculi for an intuitive theory of functions, and for, in particular, the class of partial recursive functions. Especially so, since both Γ_K and Λ_K satisfy respective Church–Rosser properties (cf. Section 11.5).

We begin the demonstration by producing an axiomatic formulation for the equivalence relation ($\overset{*}{\Longleftrightarrow}$) whose equivalence classes are those unions of the equivalence classes of $\overset{\gamma}{\Longleftrightarrow}$ that will be seen to correspond to the equivalence classes of $\overset{\lambda}{\Longleftrightarrow}$.

DEFINITION 11.62. The relation $\overset{*}{\Longleftrightarrow}$, defined on the set of objects of Γ_K, is determined by the following system of axioms:

A1. if $\hat{X} \overset{*}{\Longleftrightarrow} \hat{Y}$ and $\hat{X} \overset{*}{\Longleftrightarrow} \hat{Z}$, then $\hat{Y} \overset{*}{\Longleftrightarrow} \hat{Z}$

A2. if $\hat{X} \overset{*}{\Longleftrightarrow} \hat{Y}$, then, for every $\hat{Z}$, $(\hat{X}\hat{Z}) \overset{*}{\Longleftrightarrow} (\hat{Y}\hat{Z})$

A3. if $\hat{X} \overset{*}{\Longleftrightarrow} \hat{Y}$, then, for every $\hat{Z}$, $(\hat{Z}\hat{X}) \overset{*}{\Longleftrightarrow} (\hat{Z}\hat{Y})$

A4. for every $\hat{X}$ and $\hat{Y}$, $((K\hat{X})\hat{Y}) \overset{*}{\Longleftrightarrow} \hat{X}$

A5. for every $\hat{X}$, $\hat{Y}$, and $\hat{Z}$, $(((S\hat{X})\hat{Y})\hat{Z}) \overset{*}{\Longleftrightarrow} ((\hat{X}\hat{Z})(\hat{Y}\hat{Z}))$

A6. $\{\Lambda\zeta_2{:}\{\Lambda\zeta_4{:}((K\zeta_2)\zeta_4)\}\} \overset{*}{\Longleftrightarrow} K$

A7. $\{\Lambda\zeta_2{:}\{\Lambda\zeta_4{:}\{\Lambda\zeta_6{:}(((S\zeta_2)\zeta_4)\zeta_6)\}\}\} \overset{*}{\Longleftrightarrow} S$

A8. $\{\Lambda\zeta_2{:}\{\Lambda\zeta_4{:}(K(\zeta_2\zeta_4))\}\} \overset{*}{\Longleftrightarrow} \{\Lambda\zeta_2{:}\{\Lambda\zeta_4{:}((S(K\zeta_2))(K\zeta_4))\}\}$

A9. $\{\Lambda\zeta_2{:}\{\Lambda\zeta_4{:}\{\Lambda\zeta_6{:}((K(\zeta_2\zeta_6))(\zeta_4\zeta_6))\}\}\} \overset{*}{\Longleftrightarrow} \{\Lambda\zeta_2{:}\{\Lambda\zeta_4{:}\{\Lambda\zeta_6{:}(\zeta_2\zeta_6)\}\}\}$

A10. $\{\Lambda\zeta_2{:}\{\Lambda\zeta_4{:}\{\Lambda\zeta_6{:}\{\Lambda\zeta_8{:}(((S(\zeta_2\zeta_8))(\zeta_4\zeta_8))(\zeta_6\zeta_8))\}\}\}\} \overset{*}{\Longleftrightarrow}$
$\{\Lambda\zeta_2{:}\{\Lambda\zeta_4{:}\{\Lambda\zeta_6{:}\{\Lambda\zeta_8{:}(((\zeta_2\zeta_8)(\zeta_6\zeta_8))((\zeta_4\zeta_8)(\zeta_6\zeta_8)))\}\}\}\}$

where $\{\Lambda\zeta{:}\hat{E}\}$ is given by the Rosser abstraction algorithm 11.11.

Note that $\overset{\gamma}{\Longleftrightarrow}$ satisfies A1–A5 only. Note also that A6–A10 are of the form $\hat{P} \overset{*}{\Longleftrightarrow} \hat{Q}$ where neither $\hat{P}$ nor $\hat{Q}$ contains a component equiform to an indeterminate. (Be careful! $\{\Lambda\hat{\zeta}{:}\hat{E}\}$ is an abbreviation for an object of Γ_K which, by Definition 11.11, will not possess a component equiform to $\hat{\zeta}$.)

The first goal is to prove that $\hat{X} \overset{*}{\Longleftrightarrow} \hat{Y}$ iff $\{\Lambda\hat{\zeta}{:}\hat{X}\} \overset{*}{\Longleftrightarrow} \{\Lambda\hat{\zeta}{:}\hat{Y}\}$, for any indeterminate $\hat{\zeta}$ of Γ_K. In the process, of course, a number of useful results will be developed. The following four propositions are basic:

PROPOSITION 11.63. The relation $\overset{*}{\Longleftrightarrow}$ is an equivalence relation.

Proof. In view of A1, we need only show that $\overset{*}{\Longleftrightarrow}$ is reflexive and symmetric. For reflexivity, we have from A4 that $((K\hat{X})\hat{Y}) \overset{*}{\Longleftrightarrow} \hat{X}$. Then, from A1, since $((K\hat{X})\hat{Y}) \overset{*}{\Longleftrightarrow} \hat{X}$ and $((K\hat{X})\hat{Y}) \overset{*}{\Longleftrightarrow} \hat{X}$, $\hat{X} \overset{*}{\Longleftrightarrow} \hat{X}$. For symmetry, suppose $\hat{X} \overset{*}{\Longleftrightarrow} \hat{Y}$. Then, having just established reflexivity, since $\hat{X} \overset{*}{\Longleftrightarrow} \hat{Y}$ and $\hat{X} \overset{*}{\Longleftrightarrow} \hat{X}$, $\hat{X} \overset{*}{\Longleftrightarrow} \hat{Y}$ follows from A1. ▮

PROPOSITION 11.64. Suppose $\hat{Y}$ results from $\hat{X}$ by replacing a component $\hat{P}$ of $\hat{X}$ by $\hat{Q}$. Then, $\hat{P} \overset{*}{\Longleftrightarrow} \hat{Q}$ implies $\hat{X} \overset{*}{\Longleftrightarrow} \hat{Y}$.

Proof. If $\hat{P} \equiv \hat{X}$, then the result is immediate. We proceed with an induction on the number of components of $\hat{X}$. If $\hat{X}$ has but one component, then $\hat{P} \equiv \hat{X}$ and the basis of the induction follows from the preliminary observation. Assume, as the hypothesis of the induction, that the result holds whenever $\hat{X}$ has at most n components. Consider an $\hat{X}$ with $n + 1$ components. Necessarily, for some objects $\hat{M}$ and $\hat{N}$, $\hat{X} \equiv (\hat{M}\hat{N})$. Again, if $\hat{P} \equiv \hat{X}$, then the induction step follows from the preliminary observation. But if $\hat{P} \not\equiv \hat{X}$, then $\hat{P}$ is either a component of $\hat{M}$ or of $\hat{N}$. Suppose first that $\hat{P}$ is a component of $\hat{M}$. Let $\hat{R}$ be the result of replacing the component $\hat{P}$ of $\hat{M}$ by $\hat{Q}$. Since $\hat{M}$ has at most n components, the hypothesis of the induction holds, and $\hat{M} \overset{*}{\Longleftrightarrow} \hat{R}$, The induction step now follows from A2: $\hat{X} \equiv (\hat{M}\hat{N}) \overset{*}{\Longleftrightarrow} (\hat{R}\hat{N}) \equiv \hat{Y}$. Suppose, on the other hand, $\hat{P}$ is a component of $\hat{N}$. Let $\hat{S}$ be the result of replacing the component $\hat{P}$ of $\hat{N}$ by $\hat{Q}$. Since $\hat{N}$ has at most n components, the hypothesis of the induction holds, and $\hat{N} \overset{*}{\Longleftrightarrow} \hat{S}$. The induction step now follows from A3: $\hat{X} \equiv (\hat{M}\hat{N}) \overset{*}{\Longleftrightarrow} (\hat{M}\hat{S}) \equiv \hat{Y}$. ▮

PROPOSITION 11.65. Let $\hat{\zeta}_y$ be an indeterminate different from $\hat{\zeta}_x$. And, let $\hat{F}$ result from $\hat{E}$ by replacing each component of $\hat{E}$ equiform to $\hat{\zeta}_x$ by $\hat{\zeta}_y$. Then, if $\hat{\zeta}_y$ is not equiform to a component of $\hat{E}$, $\{\Lambda\hat{\xi}_x{:}\hat{E}\} = \{\Lambda\hat{\zeta}_y{:}\hat{F}\}$.

Proof. We proceed with an induction on the number of components of $\hat{E}$, dividing our considerations into three cases in parallel with Definition 11.11.

Case 1. $\hat{\zeta}_x$ is not equiform to a component of $\hat{E}$: Here, $\hat{F} = \hat{E}$ and $\{\Lambda\hat{\zeta}_x{:}\hat{E}\} \equiv (K\hat{E}) = (K\hat{F}) \equiv \{\Lambda\hat{\zeta}_y{:}\hat{F}\}$, as $\hat{\zeta}_y$ is not equiform to a component of $\hat{F}$.

Case 2. $\hat{E} \equiv \hat{\zeta}_x$: Here, $\hat{F} = \hat{\zeta}_y$ and $\{\Lambda\hat{\zeta}_x{:}\hat{E}\} \equiv (SKK) \equiv \{\Lambda\hat{\zeta}_y{:}\hat{F}\}$.

These two cases establish the basis of the induction wherein $\hat{E}$ may be S, K, or an indeterminate.

Case 3. $\hat{\zeta}_y$ is equiform to a component of $\hat{E} \equiv (\hat{M}\hat{N})$: Here, $\hat{F} \equiv (\hat{P}\hat{Q})$, where $\hat{P}$ and $\hat{Q}$ are the results of replacing the components of $\hat{M}$ and $\hat{N}$, respectively, equiform to $\hat{\zeta}_x$ by $\hat{\zeta}_y$. Since $\hat{\zeta}_y$ cannot be equiform to a component of either $\hat{M}$ or $\hat{N}$, it follows by the hypothesis of the induction that both $\{\Lambda\hat{\zeta}_x:\hat{M}\} = \{\Lambda\hat{\zeta}_y:\hat{P}\}$ and $\{\Lambda\hat{\zeta}_x:\hat{N}\} = \{\Lambda\hat{\zeta}_y:\hat{Q}\}$. Consequently, $\{\Lambda\hat{\zeta}_x:\hat{E}\} \equiv ((S\{\Lambda\hat{\zeta}_x:\hat{M}\})\{\Lambda\hat{\zeta}_x:\hat{N}\}) = ((S\{\Lambda\hat{\zeta}_y:\hat{P}\})\{\Lambda\hat{\zeta}_y:\hat{Q}\}) \equiv \{\Lambda\hat{\zeta}_y:\hat{F}\}$. In conjunction with Case 1, this establishes the induction step. ▮

PROPOSITION 11.66. Let $\hat{R}$ be the result of replacing each component of $\hat{E}$ equiform to an indeterminate $\hat{\zeta}$ by $\hat{A}$. Then, $(\{\Lambda\hat{\zeta}:\hat{E}\}\hat{A}) \overset{*}{\Longleftrightarrow} \hat{R}$.

Proof. As in the preceding proof, we consider, in parallel with Definition 11.11, three cases.

Case 1. $\hat{\zeta}$ is not equiform to a component of $\hat{E}$: Here, $\{\Lambda\hat{\zeta}:\hat{E}\} \equiv (K\hat{E})$ and $\hat{R} = \hat{E}$. By A4, $(\{\Lambda\hat{\zeta}:\hat{E}\}\hat{A}) \equiv ((K\hat{E})\hat{A}) \overset{*}{\Longleftrightarrow} \hat{E} = \hat{R}$.

Case 2. $\hat{E} \equiv \hat{\zeta}$: Here, $\{\Lambda\hat{\zeta}:\hat{E}\} \equiv (SKK)$ and $\hat{R} = \hat{A}$. By A5, $(\{\Lambda\hat{\zeta}:\hat{E}\}\hat{A}) \equiv ((SKK)\hat{A}) \overset{*}{\Longleftrightarrow} ((K\hat{A})(K\hat{A}))$. By A4, $((K\hat{A})(K\hat{A})) \overset{*}{\Longleftrightarrow} \hat{A}$. Hence, by Proposition 11.63, $(\{\Lambda\hat{\zeta}:\hat{E}\}\hat{A}) \overset{*}{\Longleftrightarrow} \hat{A} = \hat{R}$.

Case 3. $\hat{\zeta}$ is equiform to a component of $\hat{E} \equiv (\hat{M}\hat{N})$: Here, $\hat{R} \equiv (\hat{P}\hat{Q})$, where $\hat{P}$ and $\hat{Q}$ result from $\hat{M}$ and $\hat{N}$, respectively, by replacing the components of $\hat{M}$ and $\hat{N}$ equiform to $\hat{\zeta}$ by $\hat{A}$. Moreover, $(\{\Lambda\hat{\zeta}:\hat{M}\}\hat{A}) \overset{*}{\Longleftrightarrow} \hat{P}$ and $(\{\Lambda\hat{\zeta}:\hat{N}\}\hat{A}) \overset{*}{\Longleftrightarrow} \hat{Q}$. Now, by A5, $(\{\Lambda\hat{\zeta}:\hat{E}\}\hat{A}) \equiv (((S\{\Lambda\hat{\zeta}:\hat{M}\})\{\Lambda\hat{\zeta}:\hat{N}\})\hat{A}) \overset{*}{\Longleftrightarrow} ((\{\Lambda\hat{\zeta}:\hat{M}\}\hat{A})(\{\Lambda\hat{\zeta}:\hat{N}\}\hat{A}))$. Hence, by Propositions 11.63 and 11.64, $(\{\Lambda\hat{\zeta}:\hat{E}\}\hat{A}) \overset{*}{\Longleftrightarrow} (\hat{P}\hat{Q}) \equiv \hat{R}$. ▮

Let us note, before proceeding, that Propositions 11.65 and 11.66 establish for the abstraction operation in Γ_K the analogues of Rules α and β of Λ_K (cf. Λ_K-(Λ_I-) Rules on p. 290). In particular, note that Proposition 11.65 does permit us to change the indeterminate of the abstraction operation as if it were a dummy variable. Also note that Proposition 11.66 is a generalization—from $\overset{\gamma}{\Longleftrightarrow}$ to $\overset{*}{\Longleftrightarrow}$ —of Proposition 11.12.

We are now in a position to establish half of our first goal:

PROPOSITION 11.67. If $\{\Lambda\hat{\zeta}:\hat{E}\} \overset{*}{\Longleftrightarrow} \{\Lambda\hat{\zeta}:\hat{F}\}$, then $\hat{E} \overset{*}{\Longleftrightarrow} \hat{F}$.

Proof. By virtue of Proposition 11.66, on the one hand, $(\{\Lambda\hat{\zeta}:\hat{E}\}\hat{\zeta}) \overset{*}{\Longleftrightarrow} \hat{E}$ and, on the other hand, $(\{\Lambda\hat{\zeta}:\hat{F}\}\hat{\zeta}) \overset{*}{\Longleftrightarrow} \hat{F}$. If $\{\Lambda\hat{\zeta}:\hat{E}\} \overset{*}{\Longleftrightarrow} \{\Lambda\hat{\zeta}:\hat{F}\}$, then by A2, $(\{\Lambda\hat{\zeta}:\hat{E}\}\hat{\zeta}) \overset{*}{\Longleftrightarrow} (\{\Lambda\hat{\zeta}:\hat{F}\}\hat{\zeta})$. By Proposition 11.63, $\hat{E} \overset{*}{\Longleftrightarrow} \hat{F}$. ▮

COROLLARY 11.68. If $\{\Lambda\hat{\zeta}:\hat{E}\} \overset{\gamma}{\Longleftrightarrow} \{\Lambda\hat{\zeta}:\hat{F}\}$, then $\hat{E} \overset{\gamma}{\Longleftrightarrow} \hat{F}$.

Proof. Reviewing the proofs of the Propositions 11.63–11.67, no use has been made of A6–A10. ▮

The next two propositions, as well as the intervening corollary, may be seen to hold for $\overset{\gamma}{\Longleftrightarrow}$ also.

PROPOSITION 11.69. Let $\hat{\zeta}_y$ be an indeterminate different from $\hat{\zeta}_x$. Let $\hat{R}$ be the result of replacing each component of $\hat{E}$ equiform to $\hat{\zeta}_y$ by $\hat{A}$. And, let $\hat{T}$ be the result of replacing each component of $\{\Lambda\hat{\zeta}_x:\hat{E}\}$ equiform to $\hat{\zeta}_y$ by $\hat{A}$. Then, if $\hat{\zeta}_x$ is not equiform to a component of $\hat{A}$, $\hat{T} = \{\Lambda\hat{\zeta}_x:\hat{R}\}$.

Proof. We again concider three cases.

Case 1. $\hat{\zeta}_x$ is not equiform to a component of $\hat{E}$: Here, $\{\Lambda\hat{\zeta}_x:\hat{E}\} \equiv (K\hat{E})$, so that $\hat{T} = (K\hat{R}) \equiv \{\Lambda\hat{\zeta}_x:\hat{R}\}$, as $\hat{\zeta}_x$ cannot be equiform to a component of $\hat{R}$.

Case 2. $\hat{E} \equiv \hat{\zeta}_x$: Here, $\hat{R} = \hat{E}$ and $\{\Lambda\hat{\zeta}_x:\hat{E}\} \equiv (SKK)$, so that $\hat{T} = (SKK) \equiv \{\Lambda\hat{\zeta}_x:\hat{R}\}$.

Case 3. $\hat{\zeta}_x$ is equiform to a component of $\hat{E} \equiv (\hat{M}\hat{N})$: Here, $\{\Lambda\hat{\zeta}_x:\hat{E}\} \equiv ((S\{\Lambda\hat{\zeta}_x:\hat{M}\})\{\Lambda\hat{\zeta}_x:\hat{N}\})$. If $\hat{R}_M$ and $\hat{R}_N$ are the results of replacing each component of $\hat{M}$ and $\hat{N}$, respectively, equiform to $\hat{\zeta}_y$ by $\hat{A}$, and if $\hat{T}_M$ and $\hat{T}_N$ are the result of replacing each component of $\{\Lambda\hat{\zeta}_x:\hat{M}\}$ and $\{\Lambda\hat{\zeta}_x:\hat{N}\}$, respectively, equiform to $\hat{\zeta}_y$ by $\hat{A}$, then, since $\hat{\zeta}_x$ cannot be equiform to a component of either $\hat{M}$ or $\hat{N}$, the induction hypothesis for $\hat{M}$ and $\hat{N}$ implies that $\hat{T} \equiv ((S\hat{T}_M)\hat{T}_N) = ((S\{\Lambda\hat{\zeta}_x:\hat{R}_M\})\{\Lambda\hat{\zeta}_x:\hat{R}_N\}) \equiv \{\Lambda\hat{\zeta}_x:(\hat{R}_M\hat{R}_N)\} \equiv \{\Lambda\hat{\zeta}_x:\hat{R}\}$. ▌

COROLLARY 11.70. Let $\hat{F}$ result from $\hat{E}$ by replacing each component of $\hat{E}$ equiform to distinct indeterminates $\hat{\zeta}_1, \ldots, \hat{\zeta}_n$ by indeterminates $\hat{\zeta}'_1, \ldots, \hat{\zeta}'_n$, respectively. Then, if $\hat{\zeta}'_1, \ldots, \hat{\zeta}'_n$ are different from each other and different from each indeterminate equiform to a component of $\hat{E}$, $\{\Lambda\hat{\zeta}_1:\ldots\{\Lambda\hat{\zeta}_n:\hat{E}\}\ldots\} = \{\Lambda\hat{\zeta}'_1:\ldots\{\Lambda\hat{\zeta}'_n:\hat{F}\}\ldots\}$.

Proof. The proof is by induction on n. The basis ($n = 1$) is Proposition 11.65. For the induction step, we assume

$$\{\Lambda\hat{\zeta}_1:\ldots\{\Lambda\hat{\zeta}_n:\{\Lambda\hat{\zeta}_{n+1}:\hat{E}\}\}\ldots\} = \{\Lambda\hat{\zeta}'_1:\ldots\{\Lambda\hat{\zeta}'_n:\hat{T}\}\ldots\}$$

where $\hat{T}$ results from $\{\Lambda\hat{\zeta}_{n+1}:\hat{E}\}$ by replacing each component of $\{\Lambda\hat{\zeta}_{n+1}:\hat{E}\}$ equiform to $\hat{\zeta}_1, \ldots, \hat{\zeta}_n$ by $\hat{\zeta}'_1, \ldots, \hat{\zeta}'_n$, respectively. By repeated (n-fold) use of Proposition 11.69, $\hat{T} = \{\Lambda\hat{\zeta}_{n+1}:\hat{R}\}$, where $\hat{R}$ results from $\hat{E}$ by replacing each component of $\hat{E}$ equiform to $\hat{\zeta}_1, \ldots, \hat{\zeta}_n$ by $\hat{\zeta}'_1, \ldots, \hat{\zeta}'_n$, respectively. By Proposition 11.65, $\{\Lambda\hat{\zeta}_{n+1}:\hat{R}\} \equiv \{\Lambda\hat{\zeta}'_{n+1}:\hat{H}\}$, where $\hat{H}$ results from $\hat{R}$ by replacing each component of $\hat{R}$ equiform to $\hat{\zeta}_{n+1}$ by $\hat{\zeta}'_{n+1}$. Hence,

$$\{\Lambda\hat{\zeta}_1:\ldots\{\Lambda\hat{\zeta}_n:\{\Lambda\hat{\zeta}_{n+1}:\hat{E}\}\}\ldots\} = \{\Lambda\hat{\zeta}'_1:\ldots\{\Lambda\hat{\zeta}'_n:\{\Lambda\hat{\zeta}'_{n+1}:\hat{H}\}\ldots\}$$

Since $\hat{F} = \hat{H}$, the induction step follows. ▌

PROPOSITION 11.71. Let $\hat{F}$ be the result of replacing a component $\hat{P}$ of $\hat{E}$ by $\hat{Q}$. Then, if $\hat{\zeta}$ is not equiform to a component of $\hat{P}$ or $\hat{Q}$, $\hat{P} \overset{*}{\Longleftrightarrow} \hat{Q}$ implies $\{\Lambda\hat{\zeta}:\hat{E}\} \overset{*}{\Longleftrightarrow} \{\Lambda\hat{\zeta}:\hat{F}\}$.

Proof. Choose $\hat{G}$ such that $\hat{E}$ and $\hat{F}$ would result from replacing a component of $\hat{G}$ equiform to an indeterminate $\hat{\zeta}'$ (different from $\hat{\zeta}$ and different from each indeterminate equiform to a component of $\hat{E}$ or $\hat{F}$) by $\hat{P}$ and $\hat{Q}$, respectively. Let $\hat{M}$ and $\hat{N}$ be the result of replacing each component of $\{\Lambda\hat{\zeta}:\hat{G}\}$ equiform to $\hat{\zeta}'$ by $\hat{P}$ and $\hat{Q}$, respectively. By Proposition 11.69, $\hat{M} = \{\Lambda\hat{\zeta}:\hat{E}\}$ and $\hat{N} = \{\Lambda\hat{\zeta}:\hat{F}\}$. Now, it follows easily that, because there is but one component of $\hat{G}$ equiform to $\hat{\zeta}'$, there is but one component of $\{\Lambda\hat{\zeta}:\hat{G}\}$ equiform to $\hat{\zeta}'$. (A proof by induction on the number of components of $\hat{G}$, paralleling Definition 11.11, is evident at once.) Hence, by Proposition 11.64, $\hat{P} \overset{*}{\Longleftrightarrow} \hat{Q}$ implies $\hat{M} \overset{*}{\Longleftrightarrow} \hat{N}$. ▮

From here on, our results hold only for $\overset{*}{\Longleftrightarrow}$.

PROPOSITION 11.72. $\{\Lambda\hat{\zeta}:(\{\Lambda\hat{\zeta}:\hat{E}\}\hat{\zeta})\} \overset{*}{\Longleftrightarrow} \{\Lambda\hat{\zeta}:\hat{E}\}$
Proof.

Case 1. $\hat{\zeta}$ is not equiform to a component of $\hat{E}$: Here, $\{\Lambda\hat{\zeta}:\hat{E}\} \equiv (K\hat{E})$, so that $\{\Lambda\hat{\zeta}:(\{\Lambda\hat{\zeta}:\hat{E}\}\hat{\zeta})\} \equiv \{\Lambda\hat{\zeta}:((K\hat{E})\hat{\zeta})\}$. Choose $\hat{\zeta}'$ different from $\hat{\zeta}$. Then utilizing Corollary 11.70, $(\{\Lambda\hat{\zeta}':\{\Lambda\hat{\zeta}:((K\hat{\zeta}')\hat{\zeta})\}\}\hat{E}) \overset{*}{\Longleftrightarrow} (K\hat{E})$ follows from A6. By Proposition 11.66, $(\{\Lambda\hat{\zeta}':\{\Lambda\hat{\zeta}:((K\hat{\zeta}')\hat{\zeta})\}\}\hat{E}) \overset{*}{\Longleftrightarrow} \hat{T}$, where $\hat{T}$ is the result of substituting $\hat{E}$ for each component of $\{\Lambda\hat{\zeta}:((K\hat{\zeta}')\hat{\zeta})\}$ equiform to $\hat{\zeta}'$. By Proposition 11.69, $\hat{T} = \{\Lambda\hat{\zeta}:((K\hat{E})\hat{\zeta})\}$, so that $\{\Lambda\hat{\zeta}:\hat{E}\} \overset{*}{\Longleftrightarrow} \{\Lambda\hat{\zeta}:(\{\Lambda\hat{\zeta}:\hat{E}\}\hat{\zeta})\}$ as required. We leave it to the reader to check that all conditions required for the application of Proposition 11.69 are satisfied.

Cases 2 and 3. $\hat{\zeta}$ is equiform to a component of $\hat{E}$: Here, $\{\Lambda\hat{\zeta}:\hat{E}\} \equiv (S\hat{P}\hat{Q})$, where neither $\hat{P}$ nor $\hat{Q}$ has a component equiform to $\hat{\zeta}$, so that $\{\Lambda\hat{\zeta}:(\{\Lambda\hat{\zeta}:\hat{E}\}\hat{\zeta})\} \equiv \{\Lambda\hat{\zeta}:(S\hat{P}\hat{Q}\hat{\zeta})\}$. Utilizing Corollary 11.70, $(\{\Lambda\hat{\zeta}':\{\Lambda\hat{\zeta}'':\{\Lambda\hat{\zeta}:(S\hat{\zeta}'\hat{\zeta}''\hat{\zeta})\}\}\}\hat{P}\hat{Q}) \overset{*}{\Longleftrightarrow} (S\hat{P}\hat{Q})$ follows from A7. Employing first Proposition 11.66 and then Proposition 11.69 twice in regard to $\hat{P}$, and then employing 11.66 and 11.69 in regard to $\hat{Q}$, $(\{\Lambda\hat{\zeta}':\{\Lambda\hat{\zeta}'':\{\Lambda\hat{\zeta}:(S\hat{\zeta}'\hat{\zeta}''\hat{\zeta})\}\}\}\hat{P}\hat{Q}) \overset{*}{\Longleftrightarrow} \{\Lambda\hat{\zeta}:(S\hat{P}\hat{Q}\hat{\zeta})\}$. ▮

PROPOSITION 11.73. Let $\hat{F}$ result from $\hat{E}$ by replacing a component $\hat{G}$ of $\hat{E}$ by $(\{\Lambda\hat{\zeta}:\hat{G}\}\hat{\zeta})$. Then, $\{\Lambda\hat{\zeta}:\hat{E}\} \overset{*}{\Longleftrightarrow} \{\Lambda\hat{\zeta}:\hat{F}\}$.
Proof. Instead of the familiar induction on the number of components of $\hat{E}$, we proceed with an induction on the number of components of $\hat{F}$. Observing that $\hat{F}$ is necessarily a composite object, let $\hat{F} \equiv (\hat{P}\hat{Q})$. Consider first the possibility that $\hat{P} \equiv \{\Lambda\hat{\zeta}:\hat{G}\}$ and $\hat{Q} \equiv \hat{\zeta}$. Then, $\hat{E} \equiv \hat{G}$, and the result follows at once from Proposition 11.72. There remains only the possibility that $\hat{E} \equiv (\hat{M}\hat{N})$, where $\hat{P}$ (or $\hat{Q}$) results from $\hat{M}$ (from $\hat{N}$) by replacing a component $\hat{G}$ of $\hat{M}$ (or $\hat{N}$) by $(\{\Lambda\hat{\zeta}:\hat{G}\}\hat{\zeta})$. If, on the one hand, $\hat{G}$ is a component of $\hat{M}$, then $\{\Lambda\hat{\zeta}:\hat{M}\} \overset{*}{\Longleftrightarrow} \{\Lambda\hat{\zeta}:\hat{P}\}$ follows from the hypothesis of the induction and $\{\Lambda\hat{\zeta}:\hat{N}\} \overset{*}{\Longleftrightarrow} \{\Lambda\hat{\zeta}:\hat{Q}\}$ follows from Proposition 11.63 as $\hat{Q} \equiv \hat{N}$. While, on the other hand, if $\hat{G}$ is a component of $\hat{N}$, then $\{\Lambda\hat{\zeta}:\hat{N}\} \overset{*}{\Longleftrightarrow} \{\Lambda\hat{\zeta}:\hat{Q}\}$ follows from

the hypothesis of the induction and $\{\Lambda\hat{\zeta}:\hat{M}\} \overset{*}{\Longleftrightarrow} \{\Lambda\hat{\zeta}:\hat{P}\}$ follows from Proposition 11.63 as $\hat{P} \equiv \hat{M}$. On either hand, both $\{\Lambda\hat{\zeta}:\hat{M}\} \overset{*}{\Longleftrightarrow} \{\Lambda\hat{\zeta}:\hat{P}\}$ and $\{\Lambda\hat{\zeta}:\hat{N}\} \overset{*}{\Longleftrightarrow} \{\Lambda\hat{\zeta}:\hat{Q}\}$. Suppose first $\hat{\zeta}$ is equiform to a component of $\hat{E}$. Then, $\{\Lambda\hat{\zeta}:\hat{E}\} \equiv ((S\{\Lambda\hat{\zeta}:\hat{M}\})\{\Lambda\hat{\zeta}:\hat{N}\}) \overset{*}{\Longleftrightarrow} ((S\{\Lambda\hat{\zeta}:\hat{P}\})\{\Lambda\hat{\zeta}:\hat{Q}\}) \equiv \{\Lambda\hat{\zeta}:\hat{F}\}$ follows from Propositions 11.63 and 11.64. Suppose, on the other hand, that no component of $\hat{E}$ is equiform to $\hat{\zeta}$. As there is a component of $\hat{F}$ equiform to $\hat{\zeta}$, it is the case that $\{\Lambda\hat{\zeta}:\hat{E}\} \equiv (K(\hat{M}\hat{N}))$ and $\{\Lambda\hat{\zeta}:\hat{F}\} \equiv (S\{\Lambda\hat{\zeta}:\hat{P}\}\{\Lambda\hat{\zeta}:\hat{Q}\}) \overset{*}{\Longleftrightarrow} (S\{\Lambda\hat{\zeta}:\hat{M}\}\{\Lambda\hat{\zeta}:\hat{N}\}) \equiv (S(K\hat{M})(K\hat{N}))$ because $\hat{\zeta}$ does not occur in $\hat{E} \equiv (\hat{M}\hat{N})$. Utilizing Corollary 11.70, Propositions 11.69 and 11.66, $(K(\hat{M}\hat{N})) \overset{*}{\Longleftrightarrow} (\{\Lambda\hat{\zeta}':\{\Lambda\hat{\zeta}'':(K(\hat{\zeta}'\hat{\zeta}''))\}\}\hat{M}\hat{N})$ and $(S(K\hat{M})(K\hat{N})) \overset{*}{\Longleftrightarrow} (\{\Lambda\hat{\zeta}':\{\Lambda\hat{\zeta}'':(S(K\hat{\zeta}')(K\hat{\zeta}''))\}\}\hat{M}\hat{N})$. By virtue of A8, utilizing Corollary 11.70, $(K(\hat{M}\hat{N})) \overset{*}{\Longleftrightarrow} (S(K\hat{M})(K\hat{N}))$. ∎

PROPOSITION 11.74. Let $\hat{F}$ result from $\hat{E}$ by replacing a component $(K\hat{X}\hat{Y})$ of $\hat{E}$ by $\hat{X}$. Then, $\{\Lambda\hat{\zeta}:\hat{E}\} \overset{*}{\Longleftrightarrow} \{\Lambda\hat{\zeta}:\hat{F}\}$.

Proof. Let $\hat{G}$ result from $\hat{E}$ by replacing $(K\hat{X}\hat{Y})$ by $(\{\Lambda\hat{\zeta}:(K\hat{X}\hat{Y})\}\hat{\zeta})$, and let $\hat{H}$ result from $\hat{G}$ by replacing $(\{\Lambda\hat{\zeta}:(K\hat{X}\hat{Y})\}\hat{\zeta})$ by $(\{\Lambda\hat{\zeta}:\hat{X}\}\hat{\zeta})$. Then, $\hat{F}$ will result from $\hat{H}$ by replacing $(\{\Lambda\hat{\zeta}:\hat{X}\}\hat{\zeta})$ by $\hat{X}$. By Proposition 11.73, $\{\Lambda\hat{\zeta}:\hat{E}\} \overset{*}{\Longleftrightarrow} \{\Lambda\hat{\zeta}:\hat{G}\}$ and $\{\Lambda\hat{\zeta}:\hat{H}\} \overset{*}{\Longleftrightarrow} \{\Lambda\hat{\zeta}:\hat{F}\}$. Hence, it remains only to show that $\{\Lambda\hat{\zeta}:\hat{G}\} \overset{*}{\Longleftrightarrow} \{\Lambda\hat{\zeta}:\hat{H}\}$. By virtue of Propositions 11.69 and 11.66,

$$((\{\Lambda\hat{\zeta}':\{\Lambda\hat{\zeta}'':\{\Lambda\hat{\zeta}:(K(\hat{\zeta}'\hat{\zeta})(\hat{\zeta}''\hat{\zeta}))\}\}\}\{\Lambda\hat{\zeta}:\hat{X}\})\{\Lambda\hat{\zeta}:\hat{Y}\}) \overset{*}{\Longleftrightarrow} \{\Lambda\hat{\zeta}:(K(\{\Lambda\hat{\zeta}:\hat{X}\}\hat{\zeta})(\{\Lambda\hat{\zeta}:\hat{Y}\}\hat{\zeta}))\}$$

and

$$((\{\Lambda\hat{\zeta}':\{\Lambda\hat{\zeta}'':\{\Lambda\hat{\zeta}:(\hat{\zeta}'\hat{\zeta})\}\}\}\{\Lambda\hat{\zeta}:\hat{X}\})\{\Lambda\hat{\zeta}:\hat{Y}\}) \overset{*}{\Longleftrightarrow} \{\Lambda\hat{\zeta}:(\{\Lambda\hat{\zeta}:\hat{X}\}\hat{\zeta})\}$$

for a suitable choice of $\hat{\zeta}'$ and $\hat{\zeta}''$. From A9, utilizing Corollary 11.70,

$$((\{\Lambda\hat{\zeta}':\{\Lambda\hat{\zeta}'':\{\Lambda\hat{\zeta}:(K(\hat{\zeta}'\hat{\zeta})(\hat{\zeta}''\hat{\zeta}))\}\}\}\{\Lambda\hat{\zeta}:\hat{X}\})\{\Lambda\hat{\zeta}:\hat{Y}\}) \overset{*}{\Longleftrightarrow} ((\{\Lambda\hat{\zeta}':\{\Lambda\hat{\zeta}'':\{\Lambda\hat{\zeta}:(\hat{\zeta}'\hat{\zeta})\}\}\}\{\Lambda\hat{\zeta}:\hat{X}\})\{\Lambda\hat{\zeta}:\hat{Y}\})$$

Consequently,

$$\{\Lambda\hat{\zeta}:(K(\{\Lambda\hat{\zeta}:\hat{X}\}\hat{\zeta})(\{\Lambda\hat{\zeta}:\hat{Y}\}\hat{\zeta}))\} \overset{*}{\Longleftrightarrow} \{\Lambda\hat{\zeta}:(\{\Lambda\hat{\zeta}:\hat{X}\}\hat{\zeta})\}$$

Therefore, by Proposition 11.73, $\{\Lambda\hat{\zeta}:(K\hat{X}\hat{Y})\} \overset{*}{\Longleftrightarrow} \{\Lambda\hat{\zeta}:\hat{X}\}$. Since $\hat{H}$ is also the result of replacing $\{\Lambda\hat{\zeta}:(K\hat{X}\hat{Y})\}$ in $\hat{G}$ by $\{\Lambda\hat{\zeta}:\hat{X}\}$, and since neither $\{\Lambda\hat{\zeta}:(K\hat{X}\hat{Y})\}$ nor $\{\Lambda\hat{\zeta}:\hat{X}\}$ has a component equiform to $\hat{\zeta}$, $\{\Lambda\hat{\zeta}:\hat{G}\} \overset{*}{\Longleftrightarrow} \{\Lambda\hat{\zeta}:\hat{H}\}$ follows from Proposition 11.71. ∎

PROPOSITION 11.75. Let $\hat{F}$ result from $\hat{E}$ by replacing a component $(S\hat{X}\hat{Y}\hat{Z})$ of $\hat{E}$ by $((\hat{X}\hat{Z})(\hat{Y}\hat{Z}))$. Then, $\{\Lambda\hat{\zeta}:\hat{E}\} \overset{*}{\Longleftrightarrow} \{\Lambda\hat{\zeta}:\hat{F}\}$.

Proof. Analogous to the proof of 11.74, but based upon A10 instead of A9. ▮

We are now able to prove the second half of our first goal.

PROPOSITION 11.76. If $\hat{E} \overset{*}{\Longleftrightarrow} \hat{F}$, then $\{\Lambda\zeta{:}\hat{E}\} \overset{*}{\Longleftrightarrow} \{\Lambda\zeta{:}\hat{F}\}$.

Proof. Consider the demonstration of $\hat{E} \overset{*}{\Longleftrightarrow} \hat{F}$. We construct a demonstration of $\{\Lambda\zeta{:}\hat{E}\} \overset{*}{\Longleftrightarrow} \{\Lambda\zeta{:}\hat{F}\}$ as follows: Each time A1, A2, or A3 is invoked with respect to $\hat{X}$, $\hat{Y}$, and $\hat{Z}$, we invoke A1, A2, or A3, as the case may be, with respect to $\{\Lambda\zeta{:}\hat{X}\}$, $\{\Lambda\zeta{:}\hat{Y}\}$, and $\{\Lambda\zeta{:}\hat{Z}\}$. Each time A4 is invoked, we invoke Proposition 11.74. Each time A5 is invoked, we invoke Proposition 11.75. Finally, each time A6–A10 is invoked, we invoke Proposition 11.71. (Notice that 11.71 cannot be used for A4 and A5 because ζ may be equiform to a component of $\hat{X}$, $\hat{Y}$, or $\hat{Z}$.) ▮

THEOREM 11.77. $\hat{E} \overset{*}{\Longleftrightarrow} \hat{F}$ iff $\{\Lambda\zeta{:}\hat{E}\} \overset{*}{\Longleftrightarrow} \{\Lambda\zeta{:}\hat{F}\}$.

Proof. Propositions 11.67 and 11.76. ▮

We now proceed quickly to our main goal, proving for $\overset{*}{\Longleftrightarrow}$ the analogue of the converse of Theorem 11.61 first and then the analogue of Theorem 11.61 itself. Proving also that $\hat{X} \overset{*}{\Longleftrightarrow} (\hat{X}_\lambda)_\gamma$ and $\hat{Y} \overset{\lambda}{\Longleftrightarrow} (\hat{Y}_\gamma)_\lambda$, our goal will follow easily.

PROPOSITION 11.78. If $\hat{X} \overset{\lambda}{\Longleftrightarrow} \hat{Y}$, then $\hat{X}_\gamma \overset{*}{\Longleftrightarrow} \hat{Y}_\gamma$.

Proof. Consider the demonstration of $\hat{X} \overset{\lambda}{\Longleftrightarrow} \hat{Y}$. We construct a demonstration of $\hat{X}_\gamma \overset{*}{\Longleftrightarrow} \hat{Y}_\gamma$ as follows: Each time Rule α is invoked, we invoke Proposition 11.65. And, each time Rule β is invoked, we invoke Proposition 11.66. In order to carry out the necessary replacement operations to get from these rules to $\overset{\lambda}{\Longleftrightarrow}$, we employ A2, A3, and Theorem 11.77, with the aid of Proposition 11.63. ▮

PROPOSITION 11.79. $\hat{X} \overset{*}{\Longleftrightarrow} (\hat{X}_\lambda)_\gamma$.

Proof. In view of A2, A3, and Theorem 11.77, it will suffice to show that $K \overset{*}{\Longleftrightarrow} (K_\lambda)_\gamma$ and $S \overset{*}{\Longleftrightarrow} (S_\lambda)_\gamma$. Consider first $K \overset{*}{\Longleftrightarrow} (K_\lambda)_\gamma$: Since $K_\lambda \equiv (\lambda x_1.(\lambda x_2.x_1))$, it follows that $(K_\lambda)_\gamma \equiv \{\Lambda\zeta_2{:}\{\Lambda\zeta_4{:}\zeta_2\}\}$. From A4, $((K\zeta_2)\zeta_4) \overset{*}{\Longleftrightarrow} \zeta_2$, so that $\{\Lambda\zeta_2{:}\{\Lambda\zeta_4{:}\zeta_2\}\} \overset{*}{\Longleftrightarrow} \{\Lambda\zeta_2{:}\{\Lambda\zeta_4{:}((K\zeta_2)\zeta_4)\}\}$ follows from Theorem 11.77. By A6, $\{\Lambda\zeta_2{:}\{\Lambda\zeta_4{:}((K\zeta_2)\zeta_4)\}\} \overset{*}{\Longleftrightarrow} K$. Consider next $S \overset{*}{\Longleftrightarrow} (S_\lambda)_\gamma$: Since $S_\lambda \equiv (\lambda x_1.(\lambda x_2.(\lambda x_3.((x_1x_3)(x_2x_3)))))$, it follows that $(S_\lambda)_\gamma \equiv \{\Lambda\zeta_2{:}\{\Lambda\zeta_4{:}\{\Lambda\zeta_6{:}((\zeta_2\zeta_6)(\zeta_4\zeta_6))\}\}\}$. From A5, $(((S\zeta_2)\zeta_4)\zeta_6) \overset{*}{\Longleftrightarrow} ((\zeta_2\zeta_6)(\zeta_4\zeta_6))$, so that

$$\{\Lambda\zeta_2{:}\{\Lambda\zeta_4{:}\{\Lambda\zeta_6{:}((\zeta_2\zeta_6)(\zeta_4\zeta_6))\}\}\} \overset{*}{\Longleftrightarrow} \{\Lambda\zeta_2{:}\{\Lambda\zeta_4{:}\{\Lambda\zeta_6{:}(((S\zeta_2)\zeta_4)\zeta_6)\}\}\}$$

follows from Theorem 11.77. By A7, $\{\Lambda\zeta_2{:}\{\Lambda\zeta_4{:}\{\Lambda\zeta_6{:}(((S\zeta_2)\zeta_4)\zeta_6)\}\}\} \overset{*}{\Longleftrightarrow} S$. ▮

COROLLARY 11.80. If, for objects $\hat{X}$ and $\hat{Y}$ of Γ_K, $\hat{X}_\lambda \overset{\lambda}{\Longleftrightarrow} \hat{Y}_\lambda$, then $\hat{X} \overset{*}{\Longleftrightarrow} \hat{Y}$.

Proof. By Proposition 11.78, $\hat{X}_\lambda \overset{\lambda}{\Longleftrightarrow} \hat{Y}_\lambda$ implies $(\hat{X}_\lambda)_\gamma \overset{*}{\Longleftrightarrow} (\hat{Y}_\lambda)_\gamma$. The result now follows from Proposition 11.79. ▮

To prove the reciprocal results, we require the following lemma:

LEMMA 11.81. $\{\Lambda\zeta_{2n}: \hat{E}\}_\lambda \overset{\lambda}{\Longleftrightarrow} (\lambda x_n.\hat{E}_\lambda)$.

Proof.

Case 1. ζ_{2n} is not equiform to a component of $\hat{E}$: Here, $\{\Lambda\zeta_{2n}: \hat{E}\} \equiv (K\hat{E})$, so that $\{\Lambda\zeta_{2n}: \hat{E}\}_\lambda \equiv (K_\lambda \hat{E}_\lambda)$. It suffices to observe that

$$(K_\lambda \hat{E}_\lambda) \equiv ((\lambda x_1.(\lambda x_2.x_1))\hat{E}_\lambda) \overset{\lambda}{\Longrightarrow} ((\lambda x_{n+1}.(\lambda x_n.x_{n+1}))\hat{E}_\lambda) \overset{\lambda}{\Longrightarrow} (\lambda x_n.\hat{E})_\lambda$$

because ζ_{2n} not equiform to a component of $\hat{E}$ implies x_n is not equiform to a component of $\hat{E}_\lambda$.

Case 2. $\hat{E} \equiv \zeta_{2n}$: Here, $\{\Lambda\zeta_{2n}: \hat{E}\} \equiv (SKK)$, so that $\{\Lambda\zeta_{2n}: \hat{E}\}_\lambda \equiv (S_\lambda K_\lambda K_\lambda)$. It suffices to observe the following:

$$\begin{aligned}(S_\lambda K_\lambda K_\lambda) &\equiv ((\lambda x_1.(\lambda x_2.(\lambda x_3.((x_1x_3)(x_2x_3)))))(\lambda x_1.(\lambda x_2.x_1))(\lambda x_1.(\lambda x_2.x_1)))\\ &\overset{\lambda}{\Longrightarrow} ((\lambda x_2.(\lambda x_3.(((\lambda x_1.(\lambda x_2.x_1))x_3)(x_2x_3))))(\lambda x_1.(\lambda x_2.x_1)))\\ &\overset{\lambda}{\Longrightarrow} ((\lambda x_2.(\lambda x_3.((\lambda x_2.x_3)(x_2x_3))))(\lambda x_1.(\lambda x_2.x_1)))\\ &\overset{\lambda}{\Longrightarrow} ((\lambda x_2.(\lambda x_3.x_3))(\lambda x_1.(\lambda x_2.x_1)))\\ &\overset{\lambda}{\Longrightarrow} (\lambda x_3.x_3) \overset{\lambda}{\Longrightarrow} (\lambda x_n.x_n)\end{aligned}$$

Case 3. ζ_{2n} is equiform to a component of $\hat{E} \equiv (\hat{P}\hat{Q})$: Here, $\{\Lambda\zeta_{2n}: \hat{E}\} \equiv ((S\{\Lambda\zeta_{2n}: \hat{P}\})\{\Lambda\zeta_{2n}: \hat{Q}\})$, so that

$$\{\Lambda\zeta_{2n}: \hat{E}\}_\lambda \equiv ((S_\lambda\{\zeta_{2n}: \hat{P}\}_\lambda)\{\Lambda\zeta_{2n}: \hat{Q}\}_\lambda) \overset{\lambda}{\Longleftrightarrow} ((S_\lambda(\lambda x_n.\hat{P}_\lambda))(\lambda x_n.\hat{Q}_\lambda))$$

by the induction hypothesis. Since $\hat{E}_\lambda \equiv (\hat{P}_\lambda \hat{Q}_\lambda)$, it suffices to observe the following:

$$\begin{aligned}((S_\lambda(\lambda x_n.\hat{P}_\lambda))(\lambda x_n.\hat{Q}_\lambda)) &\equiv (((\lambda x_1.(\lambda x_2.(\lambda x_3.((x_1x_3)(x_2x_3)))))(\lambda x_n.\hat{P}_\lambda))(\lambda x_n.\hat{Q}_\lambda))\\ &\overset{\lambda}{\Longrightarrow} (((\lambda x_1.(\lambda \hat{y}.(\lambda \hat{z}.((x_1\hat{z})(\hat{y}\hat{z})))))(\lambda x_n.\hat{P}_\lambda))(\lambda x_n.\hat{Q}_\lambda))\\ &\overset{\lambda}{\Longrightarrow} (\lambda \hat{z}.(((\lambda x_n.\hat{P}_\lambda)\hat{z})((\lambda x_n.\hat{Q}_\lambda)\hat{z})))\\ &\overset{\lambda}{\Longrightarrow} (\lambda x_n.(((\lambda x_n.\hat{P}_\lambda)x_n)((\lambda x_n.\hat{Q}_\lambda)x_n)))\\ &\overset{\lambda}{\Longrightarrow} (\lambda x_n.(\hat{P}_\lambda \hat{Q}_\lambda))\end{aligned}$$

where $\hat{y}$ and $\hat{z}$ are chosen different from each other and different from the variables occurring free in $\hat{E}_\lambda$. ▮

PROPOSITION 11.82. If $\hat{X} \overset{*}{\Longleftrightarrow} \hat{Y}$ then $\hat{X}_\lambda \overset{\lambda}{\Longleftrightarrow} \hat{Y}_\lambda$.

Proof. Consider the demonstration of $\hat{X} \overset{*}{\Longleftrightarrow} \hat{Y}$. We may construct a demonstration of $\hat{X}_\lambda \overset{\lambda}{\Longleftrightarrow} \hat{Y}_\lambda$ as follows: Each time A1, A2, or A3, is invoked with respect to $\hat{X}$, $\hat{Y}$, and $\hat{Z}$, we invoke the analogous (and evident) result for $\overset{\lambda}{\Longleftrightarrow}$ with respect to $\hat{X}_\lambda$, $\hat{Y}_\lambda$, and $\hat{Z}_\lambda$. Each time A4 or A5 is invoked, we invoke the following results:

$$(K_\lambda \hat{X}_\lambda \hat{Y}_\lambda) \equiv ((\lambda x_1.(\lambda x_2.x_1))\hat{X}_\lambda \hat{Y}_\lambda) \overset{\lambda}{\Longrightarrow} \hat{X}_\lambda$$

$$(S_\lambda \hat{X}_\lambda \hat{Y}_\lambda \hat{Z}_\lambda) \equiv ((\lambda x_1.(\lambda x_2.(\lambda x_3.((x_1x_3)(x_2x_3)))))\hat{X}_\lambda \hat{Y}_\lambda \hat{Z}_\lambda) \overset{\lambda}{\Longrightarrow} ((\hat{X}_\lambda \hat{Z}_\lambda)(\hat{Y}_\lambda \hat{Z}_\lambda))$$

And, each time A6–A10 is invoked, we call upon Lemma 11.81 to give an analogous result to invoke; for example, in the case of A8, we have

$$\begin{aligned}\{\Lambda\zeta_2{:}\{\Lambda\zeta_4{:}(K\zeta_2\zeta_4)\}\}_\lambda &\overset{\lambda}{\Longleftrightarrow} (\lambda x_1.(\lambda x_2.(K_\lambda(x_1x_2))))\\ &\overset{\lambda}{\Longleftrightarrow} (\lambda x_1.(\lambda x_2.(S_\lambda(K_\lambda x_1)(K_\lambda x_2))))\\ &\overset{\lambda}{\Longleftrightarrow} \{\Lambda\zeta_2{:}\{\Lambda\zeta_4{:}(S(K\zeta_2)(K\zeta_4))\}\}_\lambda\end{aligned}$$

as $(S_\lambda(K_\lambda x_1)(K_\lambda x_2)) \overset{\lambda}{\Longleftrightarrow} (K_\lambda(x_1x_2))$. ∎

PROPOSITION 11.83. $\hat{X} \overset{\lambda}{\Longleftrightarrow} (\hat{X}_\gamma)_\lambda$.

Proof. The proof is by induction on the number of components of $\hat{X}$. Basis step: Either $\hat{X} \equiv x_n$ or $\hat{X} \equiv \zeta_n$. If $\hat{X} \equiv x_n$, then $\hat{X}_\gamma \equiv \zeta_{2n}$ and $(\hat{X}_\gamma)_\lambda = x_n \equiv \hat{X}$. If $\hat{X} \equiv \zeta_n$, then $\hat{X}_\gamma \equiv \zeta_{2n+1}$ and $(\hat{X}_\gamma)_\lambda = \zeta_n \equiv \hat{X}$. Induction step: If $\hat{X} \equiv (\hat{P}\hat{Q})$, then $(\hat{X}_\gamma)_\lambda \equiv ((\hat{P}\hat{Q})_\gamma)_\lambda = (\hat{P}_\gamma \hat{Q}_\gamma)_\lambda = ((\hat{P}_\gamma)_\lambda(\hat{Q}_\gamma)_\lambda) \overset{\lambda}{\Longleftrightarrow} (\hat{P}\hat{Q}) \equiv \hat{X}$. If $\hat{X} \equiv (\lambda x_n.\hat{E})$, then $\hat{X}_\gamma \equiv (\lambda x_n.\hat{E})_\gamma = \{\Lambda\zeta_{2n}.\hat{E}_\gamma\}$, so that, with the aid of Lemma 11.81, $(\hat{X}_\gamma)_\lambda = \{\Lambda\zeta_{2n}.\hat{E}_\gamma\}_\lambda \overset{\lambda}{\Longleftrightarrow} (\lambda x_n.(\hat{E}_\gamma)_\lambda) \overset{\lambda}{\Longleftrightarrow} (\lambda x_n.\hat{E}) \equiv \hat{X}$. ∎

COROLLARY 11.84. If, for objects $\hat{X}$ and $\hat{Y}$ of Λ_K, $\hat{X}_\gamma \overset{*}{\Longleftrightarrow} \hat{Y}_\gamma$, then $\hat{X} \overset{\lambda}{\Longleftrightarrow} \hat{Y}$.

Proof. By Proposition 11.82, $\hat{X}_\lambda \overset{*}{\Longleftrightarrow} \hat{Y}_\gamma$ implies $(\hat{X}_\gamma)_\lambda \overset{\lambda}{\Longleftrightarrow} (\hat{Y}_\gamma)_\lambda$. The result now follows from Proposition 11.83. ∎

THEOREM 11.85. Equivalence of Γ_K and Λ_K. There is a 1-1 correspondence between the equivalence classes of $\overset{*}{\Longleftrightarrow}$ and $\overset{\lambda}{\Longleftrightarrow}$ determined by the maps γ and λ.

Proof. Proposition 11.78 shows that γ indeed maps equivalence classes of $\overset{\lambda}{\Longleftrightarrow}$ to equivalence classes of $\overset{*}{\Longleftrightarrow}$. Proposition 11.82 shows that λ indeed maps equivalence classes of $\overset{*}{\Longleftrightarrow}$ to equivalence classes of $\overset{\lambda}{\Longleftrightarrow}$. Corollaries 11.80 and 11.84 ensure that γ and λ, as maps on and to equivalences classes, are 1-1. ∎

We have shown that Γ_K and Λ_K are equivalent with respect to their ability to represent functions. If an object $\hat{X}$ of Λ_K represents a function of one variable and $\hat{X} \overset{\lambda}{\Longleftrightarrow} \hat{Y}$, then for all $\hat{Z}$ in Λ_K we have $(\hat{X}\hat{Z}) \overset{\lambda}{\Longleftrightarrow} (\hat{Y}\hat{Z})$ so $\hat{X}$ and $\hat{Y}$ represent the same function. Hence each member of the equivalence class of $\hat{X}$ with respect to $\overset{\lambda}{\Longleftrightarrow}$ represents the same function as does $\hat{X}$. It is important to note that the converse is not true: $\hat{X}$ and $\hat{Y}$ may represent the same function and not be interconvertible. Moreover, there are objects which do *not* represent meaningful functions.

The same property as above is true for $\overset{\gamma}{\Longleftrightarrow}$. Hence to prove the equivalence of Γ_K and Λ_K, with respect to the class of functions they can represent under a given interpretation, one might try to show that there is a correspondence between equivalence classes of $\overset{\lambda}{\Longleftrightarrow}$ and $\overset{\gamma}{\Longleftrightarrow}$ such that if the objects of a class of $\overset{\lambda}{\Longleftrightarrow}$ represent a function, then the objects of the corresponding class of $\overset{\gamma}{\Longleftrightarrow}$ represent the same function. This may be accomplished by defining functions $\lambda:\Gamma_K \to \Lambda_K$ and $\gamma:\Lambda_K \to \Gamma_K$ which satisfy

$$\hat{X} \overset{\gamma}{\Longleftrightarrow} \hat{Y} \text{ implies } \hat{X}_\lambda \overset{\lambda}{\Longleftrightarrow} \hat{Y}_\lambda \qquad \text{for all } \hat{X},\ \hat{Y} \text{ in } \Gamma_K$$

$$\hat{X} \overset{\lambda}{\Longleftrightarrow} \hat{Y} \text{ implies } \hat{X}_\gamma \overset{\gamma}{\Longleftrightarrow} \hat{Y}_\gamma \qquad \text{for all } \hat{X},\ \hat{Y} \text{ in } \Lambda_K$$

Unfortunately, the natural definition for γ given at the beginning of this section does not satisfy the second of the above conditions. This occurs because, for this definition of γ, equivalence classes of $\overset{\lambda}{\Longleftrightarrow}$ are not mapped into a single class of $\overset{\gamma}{\Longleftrightarrow}$ but into a union of classes. Conversely, objects from different classes of $\overset{\gamma}{\Longleftrightarrow}$ are mapped, by the natural λ defined above, into the same class of $\overset{\lambda}{\Longleftrightarrow}$. To avoid this problem we defined an equivalence relation $\overset{*}{\Longleftrightarrow}$ on Γ_K each class of which is a union of classes of $\overset{\gamma}{\Longleftrightarrow}$. As with $\overset{\lambda}{\Longleftrightarrow}$ and $\overset{\gamma}{\Longleftrightarrow}$, if an object of a class of $\overset{*}{\Longleftrightarrow}$ represents a function, then all objects of the class represent the same function. We then showed that the natural definitions given for λ and γ provide a bijection between the classes of $\overset{*}{\Longleftrightarrow}$ and the classes of $\overset{\lambda}{\Longleftrightarrow}$. This then proved that the same functions can be represented in Γ_K and Λ_K.

In closing, a couple of additional remarks are in order: First we have seen that the interconvertibility of $(\hat{F}\hat{X})$ and $(\hat{G}\hat{X})$ for every $\hat{X}$ need not imply the interconvertibility of $\hat{F}$ and $\hat{G}$ (see Sections 11.1 and 11.2 of this chapter). Second, whether or not the foregoing holds, it need not be the case that all the objects that may be taken to represent a given function of one variable belong to one and the same equivalence class of interconvertibility (see Exercise 1, Section 11.3). Indeed, in view of the discussion in Section 11.5, it is hardly likely that such could ever be the case.

EXERCISE

1. Adjoining

$$\text{A11.} \quad \{\Lambda\zeta_2:\{\Lambda\zeta_4:(\zeta_2\zeta_4)\}\} \overset{*}{\Longleftrightarrow} \{\Lambda\zeta_2:\zeta_2\}$$

to axioms A1–A10 of Definition 11.62, prove, in place of Theorem 11.77, the stronger result: If $\hat{F}$ and $\hat{G}$ do not possess a component equiform to an indeterminate $\hat{\zeta}$, then $(\hat{F}\hat{\zeta}) \overset{*}{\Longleftrightarrow} (\hat{G}\hat{\zeta})$ iff $\hat{F} \overset{*}{\Longleftrightarrow} \hat{G}$.

References

Ackermann, W. 1928. Zum Hilbertschen Aufbau der reelen Zahlen. *Mathematische Annalen* 99:118–133.

Asser, G. 1960. Rekursive Wortfunktionen. *Zeitschrift für Mathematische Logik und Grundlagen der Mathematik* 6:258–278.

Bar-Hillel, Y., M. Perles, and E. Shamir. 1961. On formal properties of simple phrase structure grammars. *Zeitschrift fur Phonetik, Sprachwissenschaft, und Kommunicationsforschung.* 14:143–172.

Blum, M. 1967. A machine-independent theory of the complexity of recursive functions. *Journal of the Association for Computing Machinery* 14: 322–336.

Böhm, C. 1968. Alcune proprietá della forma β-η-normali del λ-κ-calcolo. *Consiglio Nazionale delle Ricerche Publicazioni dell-istitodo per le applicazioni del Calcolo.* 696:1–19. Roma.

Borodin, A. B. 1972. Computational complexity and the existence of complexity gaps. *Journal of the Association for Computing Machinery* 19:158–174.

Büchi, J. R. 1962. Turing machines and the entscheidungsproblem. *Mathematische Annalen* 148:201–213.

Cantor, G. 1874. Uber eine Eigenschaft des Inbegriffes alles reelen algebraischen Zahlen. *Journal für die reine und angeweandte Mathematik* 77:258–262.

Chomsky, N. 1959. On certain formal properties of grammars. *Information and Control* 2:137–167.

Church, A. 1932. A set of postulates for the foundations of logic. *Annals of Mathematics* 33:346–366 and 34, 839–864.

Church, A. 1936a. An unsolvable problem of elementary number theory. *American Journal of Mathematics* 58:345–363. (Also in Davis 1965, 89–107.)

Church, A. 1936b. A note on the entscheidungsproblem. *Journal of Symbolic Logic* 1:40–41, 101–102. (Also in Davis 1965, 110–115.)

Church, A., and J. B. Rosser. 1936. Some properties of conversion. *Transactions of the American Mathematical Society* 39:472–482.

Cleave, J. P. 1963. A hierarchy of primitive recursive functions. *Zeitschrift für Mathematische Logik und Grundlagen der Mathematik* 9:331–345.

Cobham, A. 1964. The intrinsic computational difficulty of functions. *Proceedings of the Congress on Logic, Methodology and Philosophy of Science*, Haifa, Israel, North-Holland, Amsterdam, 24–30.

Constable, R. L. 1968. Extending and refining hierarchies of recursive functions. University of Wisconsin Technical Report Number 25.

Constable, R. L., and A. B. Borodin. 1972. Subrecursive programming languages, part 1: efficiency and program structure. *Journal of the Association for Computing Machinery* 19:526–568.

Curry, H. B., and R. Feys. 1958. *Combinatory Logic*. Amsterdam: North-Holland.

Davis, M. 1958. *Computability and Unsolvability*. New York: McGraw-Hill.

Davis, M., ed. 1965. *The Undecidable*. New York: Raven Press.

Dedekind, R. 1888. Was sind und was sollen die Zahlen. Braunschweig (6th ed. 1930). English translation in W. W. Beman, 1901, *Essays on the Theory of Numbers*, Chicago: Open Court, 31–105.

Dekker, J. C. E., and J. Myhill. 1958. Some theorems on classes of recursively enumerable sets. *Transactions of the American Mathematical Society* 89:25–59.

Eilenberg, S. 1973. *Automata, Language, and Machines*. New York: Academic Press.

Eilenberg, S., and C. C. Elgot. 1970. *Recursiveness*. New York: Academic Press.

Elgot, C. C., and A. Robinson. 1964. Random-access stored-program machines, an approach to programming languages. *Journal of the Association for Computing Machinery* 11:365–399.

Farber, D. J., R. E. Griswold, and I. P. Polonsky. 1964. SNOBOL, a string manipulation language. *Journal of the Association for Computing Machinery* 11:21–30.

Friedberg, R. M. 1957. Two recursively enumerable sets of incomparable degrees of unsolvability. *Proceedings of the National Academy of Sciences* 43:236–238.

Galler, B. A. and A. J. Perlis. 1970. *A View of Programming Languages*. Reading: Addison-Wesley.

Ginsburg, S. 1966. *The Mathematical Theory of Context-free Languages*, New York: McGraw-Hill.

Gödel, K. 1931. Uber formal unentscheidbare Sätze der Principia Mathematica und verwandter Systeme, I. *Monatschefte fur Mathematik und Physik* 38:173–198. (English translation in Davis 1965, 5–38.)

Gödel, K. 1934. On undecidable propositions of formal mathematical systems. Lecture notes, Institute for Advanced Study, Princeton, N.J. (Published for the first time in Davis 1965, 41–71.)

Griswold, R. E., J. F. Poage, and I. P. Polonsky. 1971. *The SNOBOL 4 Programming Language*, 2nd ed. Englewood Cliffs, N.J.: Prentice-Hall.

Grzegorczyk, A. 1953. Some classes of recursive functions. *Rozprawy Mathematyczne* 4. Instytut Mathematyczny Polskey, Akademe Nauk, Warsaw, Poland, 1–45.

Hartmanis, J., and J. E. Hopcroft. 1971. An overview of the theory of computational complexity. *Journal of the Association for Computing Machinery* 18:441–475.

Hartmanis, J. and R. E. Stearns. 1965. On the computational complexity of algorithms. *Transactions of the American Mathematical Society* 117:285–306.

Hermes, H. 1969. *Enumerability, Decidability, Computability*, 2nd Ed. New York: Springer-Verlag.

Hilbert, D. 1901. Mathematical problems. *Bulletin of the American Mathematical Society* 8:437–445, 478–479.

Hilbert, D. 1926. Über das Unendliche. *Mathematische Annalen* 95:161–190. (English translation in Van Heijenoort 1967, 367–392.)

Hindley, J. R., B. Lercher, and P. Seldin. 1972. *Introduction to Combinatory Logic*. London: Cambridge University Press.

Hopcroft, J. E., and J. D. Ullman. 1969. *Formal Languages and their Relation to Automata*. Reading, Ma.: Addison-Wesley.

Kalmar, L. 1943. Egyszerü pelda eldönthetlen aritmetikai problémára (Ein einfaches Beispiel für ein unentscheidbares arithmetisches problem). *Mathematikai és fizika lapok*, 50:1–23. (Hungarian with German abstract).

Kleene, S. C. 1934. Proof by cases in formal logic. *Annals of Mathematics* 35:529–544.

Kleene, S. C. 1935. A theory of positive integers in formal logic, *American Journal of Mathematics* 51:153–173, 219–244.

Kleene, S. C. 1936a. General recursive functions of natural numbers. *Mathematische Annalen* 112:727–742. (Also in Davis 1965, 237–253.)

Kleene, S. C. 1936b. λ-definability and recursiveness. *Duke Mathematics Journal* 2:340–353.

Kleene, S. C. 1938. On notation for ordinal numbers. *Journal of Symbolic Logic* 3:150–155.

Kleene, S. C. 1943. Recursive predicates and quantifiers. *Transactions of the American Mathematical Society* 53:41–74. (Also in Davis 1965, 255–287.)

Kleene, S. C. 1952. *Introduction to Metamathematics*. Princeton, N.J.: Van Nostrand.

Kleene, S. C. 1967. *Mathematical Logic*. New York: Wiley.

Landweber, L. H., and E. L. Robertson. 1972. Recursive properties of abstract complexity classes. *Journal of the Association for Computing Machinery*, 19:296–308. (Also in *Conference Record of the Second Annual ACM Symposium on Theory of Computing* 31–36, 1970.)

Lewis, F. D. 1970. Unsolvability considerations in computational complexity. *Conference Record of the Second Annual ACM Symposium on Theory of Computing*, Northampton, Ma., 2–30.

Margaris, A. 1967. *First Order Mathematical Logic*, Waltham, Ma.: Xerox.

Markov, A. A. 1954. *Theory of Algorithms*. Works of the Steklov Mathematical Institute, Vol. 42. English translation published in 1961 available from the Office of Technical Services, U. S. Department of Commerce.

McCreight E. M. 1969. Classes of computable functions defined by bounds on computation. Doctoral thesis. Pittsburgh Pa.: Carnegie-Mellon University.

McCreight, E. M., and A. R. Meyer. 1969. Classes of computable functions defined by bounds on computation. *Conference Record of the ACM Symposium on Theory of Computing*, Marina del Rey, Ca.: 79–88.

Mendelson, E. 1964. *Introduction to mathematical logic*, Princeton, N.J.: Van Nostrand.

Meyer, A. R. and R. Moll. 1972. Honest bounds for complexity classes of recursive functions. *Proceedings of the 13th Annual Switching and Automata Theory Conference*, College Park, Md., 61–66.

Meyer, A. R., and D. M. Ritchie. 1967a. The complexity of loop programs, *Proceedings of the ACM National Meeting*. 465–469.

Meyer, A. R., and D. M. Ritchie. 1967b. Computational complexity and program structure. IBM research paper RC-1817. Yorktown Heights, N.Y.: IBM Watson Research Center.

Muchnik, A. A. 1956. On the unsolvability of the problem of reducibility in the theory of algorithms (Russian). *Doklady Akademii Nauk SSSR*. 108:194–197.

Naur, P. 1960. Report on the algorithmic language ALGOL 60. *Communications of the Association for Computing Machinery* 3:299–314.

Péter, R. 1936. Uber die mehrfache Rekursion. *Mathematische Annalen* 113:489–527.

Post, E. L. 1936. Finite combinatory processes. *The Journal of Symbolic Logic* 1:103–105. (Also in Davis 1965, 289–291.)

Post, E. L. 1943. Formal reductions of the general combinatorial decision problem. *American Journal of Mathematics* 65:197–215.

Post, E. L. 1944. Recursively enumerable sets of positive integers and their decision problems. *Bulletin of the American Mathematical Society* 50:284–316. (Also in Davis 1965, 305–337.)

Post, E. L. 1946. A variant of a recursively unsolvable problem. *Bulletin of the American Mathematical Society* 52:264–268.

Post, E. L. 1948. Degrees of recursive unsolvability, preliminary report. *Bulletin of the American Mathematical Society* 54:641–642.

Rice, H. G. 1953. Classes of recursively enumerable sets and their decision problems. *Transactions of the American Mathematical Society* 89:25–59.

Rice, H. G. 1956. On completely recursively enumerable classes and their key arrays. *Journal of Symbolic Logic* 21:304–341.

Ritchie, R. W. 1963. Classes of predictably computable functions. *Transactions of the American Mathematical Society* 106:139–173.

Robertson, E. L. 1971. Complexity classes of partial recursive functions. *Proceedings of the Third Annual ACM Symposium on Theory of Computing* Shaker Heights, Oh., 258–265.

Rogers, H. 1967. *Theory of Recursive Functions and Effective Computability*. New York: McGraw-Hill.

Rosenkranz, D. J. 1969. Programmed grammars and classes of formal languages. *Journal of the Association for Computing Machinery* 16:107–131.

Rosser, J. B., 1935. A mathematical logic without variables. *Annals of Mathematics*, 36:127–150 and *Duke Mathematical Journal* 1:328–355.

Rosser, J. B. 1936. Extensions of some theorems of Gödel and Church. *Journal of Symbolic Logic* 1:89–91. (Also in Davis, 1965, 231–235.)

Rosser, J. B. 1942. New sets of postulates for combinatory logics. *Journal of Symbolic Logic* 7:18–27.

Rosser, J. B. 1955. Deux esguisses de logique. *Collection de Logique Mathematique* A,7. Paris: Gauthier-Villars.

Sacks, G. E. 1963. *Degrees of Unsolvability*, *Annals of Mathematical Studies*. 55. Princeton, N.J.: Princeton University Press.

Schönfinkel, M. 1924. Uber die Bausteine der mathematischen Logik, *Mathematische Annalen*, 92:305–316. (English translation in Van Heijenoort 1967.)

Sheperdson, J. C., and H. E. Sturgis. 1963. Computability of recursive functions. *Journal of the Association for Computing Machinery* 10:217–255.

Thue, A. 1914. Probleme uber Veränderungen von Zeichenreichen nach gegebenen Regeln. *Skrifter utgit av Videnskapsselskapet i Kristiana, I.* Matematisk-naturvideskabelig klasse, 10.

Tsichritzis, D. 1970. The equivalence problem of simple programs. *Journal of the Association for Computing Machinery* 17:729–738.

Turing, A. M. 1936. On computable numbers with an application to the entscheidungsproblem. *Proceedings of the London Mathematical Society*, series 2, 42:230–265 and 43:544–546. (Also in Davis 1965, 116–151.)

Turing, A. M. 1937. Computability and λ-definability. *Journal of Symbolic Logic* 2:153–163.

Van Heijenoort, J. 1967. *From Frege to Gödel.* Cambridge: Harvard Univ. Press.

Yngve, V. 1957. A framework for syntactic translation. *Mechanical Translation* 4:59–65.

Author Index

Subject Index